Foreign
Policy
of
the
American
People

Foreign Policy of the American People

CHARLES O. LERCHE JR.

Professor of
International Relations
The American University

SECOND
EDITION

Prentice-Hall, Inc.
ENGLEWOOD CLIFFS, N. J.

Fourth printing . . . . *June, 1965*

LIBRARY OF CONGRESS
CATALOG CARD NO.: 61–11093

PRINTED IN THE UNITED STATES
OF AMERICA
32670—C

Preface

TO THE SECOND EDITION

The first edition of this book, completed as the first Sputnik was settling down into its orbit around the earth, was based on several operating assumptions and one act of faith. The assumptions amounted generally to the conclusion that the foreign policy of the United States was a part of the broader democratic experiment in self-government going on in the nation, and that it could usefully be studied by making "the American people" its primary point of reference. The tenor of the first edition also testified to the author's optimistic faith in the capacity of the United States and its people to solve the foreign-policy problems they were facing and would face.

Now, as a major revision is presented, it is worth emphasizing that in these essentials, this is the same book. The discussion is still centered upon the critical role of the "mass attitudes, responses, values, and demands" of the American people and upon popular responsibility for the quality of the international action taken in the name of the United States. Nor has the author's optimism receded: he is as convinced as ever of the solubility of the foreign-policy conundrums of the 1960's and beyond.

Otherwise, a comparison of this edition with the first will reveal extensive changes and—it is hoped—improvements. Overall, the text is somewhat shorter. Certain topics, notably the discussion of policy-making and the brief review of American diplomatic history, have been rearranged. The recommended readings have been revised and brought as close to being up to date as publication schedules will permit.

The text has been given virtually a line-by-line revision, with a sizeable number of topics having received extensive rewriting. Evidence of this will be found throughout the book, most obviously in the increased attention given to certain subjects whose new importance has become clear only in the past few years: Latin America, Africa, the space and missile races, the Sino-Soviet split, and the changing United Nations.

The final section now consists of two chapters written in their entirety especially for this edition. They represent a somewhat more determined effort than is made elsewhere in the book to peer into what is generally admitted to be a very cloudy future. They are offered to the reader for two reasons: first, they represent one estimate of the direction in which contemporary trends are leading the United States; second, they might serve as a basis from which the reader may differ in making his own evaluations.

One conclusion that the author holds firmly will probably be shared by his readers: the more difficult the international problems with which the United States is confronted, the more important it is that all Americans do their best to grapple with them. The author can hope for no more worthy purpose to which his work might be put than that it be used either as a stimulus or as a guide in this critical effort.

Acknowledgements

In addition to those whose contributions and assistance were acknowledged in the first edition, the author would especially like to express his gratitude to his many academic, military, and civilian friends, in and out of government service, who have given him the benefit of their general and detailed criticism of the first edition. He has been both surprised and flattered that his thoughts and words have provoked such insightful responses. Many of these helpful critics will find their suggestions reflected in the pages that follow.

The students in the several courses in American foreign policy to whom the author has "taught the book" since its original publication are, inevitably, the inspirations of many of the revisions in this edition. Generally, student response has provoked a major effort toward greater clarity in thought and precision in language.

Particular gratitude is due the students, faculty, and staff of the 70th session of the Salzburg Seminar on American Studies, held in Salzburg, Austria, during August and September, 1960. While the author was serving as a faculty member at the Seminar, this group of European and American scholars played a large part in the formulation of the ideas expressed in Part VII of this edition. No suggestion is made, however, that anyone at Salzburg except the author is in any way responsible for the content of the two chapters.

Mr. Kai Olaf Lie, while serving as the author's graduate assistant, was of immeasurable assistance in the revision of a large part of the text.

As previously, the author is eager to accept full responsibility for all errors of fact, omission, and judgment that more discerning scholars than he may discover, and will be grateful for having these called to his attention.

Washington, D.C.

C.O.L., JR.

Preface
TO THE FIRST EDITION

Everyone agrees that Americans should be interested in their foreign policy; more of them are actually concerned with it today than at any time in their nation's history. Foreign affairs is truly everybody's business. Many citizens are realizing that fulfilling the duties of citizenship demands both more attention to and more competence in dealing with the subject matter of the foreign relations of the United States. It is as a contribution to this augmented "attentive public" that this book seeks its justification.

This is an analytical-topical study of American foreign policy. Its objective is not to transform its readers into top-level experts on all phases of American foreign policy, both procedural and substantive; a more modest purpose has governed the selection and presentation of its content. If it suggests some clues to a sounder and more inclusive understanding of a rapidly moving and often bewildering sequence of events, and if it points out a few avenues and techniques for more effective popular decision and choice, its author's goal will have been thoroughly achieved. Throughout the discussion that follows, therefore, more emphasis has been placed on "principles" and long-term problems than on details; a self-conscious attempt has been made to concentrate on the "big picture." Historical, organizational, and administrative data, as well as elaborate region-by-region surveys, have been avoided.

The material has been selected and organized with reference to a set of three assumptions, and perhaps evaluation of the value judgments found throughout the book will be facilitated if they are stated explicitly: (1) American foreign policy can be usefully analyzed in terms of a generalized conceptual pattern of foreign policy. (2) Contemporary American foreign policy has accumulated enough historical antecedents to be analytically conceived of as a whole and discussed in such terms, rather than being described as a series of more or less independent and unrelated enterprises.

(3) The crucial point of reference in discussing the foreign policy of the United States is "the American people"; mass attitudes, responses, values, and demands are of central importance to any analysis. With each of these three propositions there is admittedly room to disagree, and selection of some other assumptions would have resulted in a different book. The author, however, can enter two justifications for his adherence to them: first, they represent his own position; second, they have proved to be useful postulates upon which to ground his exposition.

One final point should be made. If it were possible to develop a scale for the measurement of relative optimism and pessimism, this book would be placed well over toward the optimistic pole. The point of view expressed here is hopeful—even confident—that the problems facing the United States are soluble by the means presently available and that neither catastrophe nor Armageddon are necessary outcomes of American foreign policy. No guarantee is made that the solutions will actually be found; indeed, the book concludes by leaving open a question on that very point. But the author is convinced that the answers can be found; considering the apocalyptic character of so much contemporary comment on America's role in international politics, such a profession as this one automatically moves its maker into the camp of the cheerful.

Acknowledgements

Leading the list of those to whom gratitude is due for assistance in the preparation of this book are the hundreds of students who have passed through the author's graduate and undergraduate courses in American foreign policy at several institutions. Out of classroom interplay and the necessity of organizing and sharpening teachable concepts grew the skeleton of this study. From among this large group, Hoke L. Smith should be singled out; as undergraduate and graduate student he has helped many of the ideas take shape by subjecting them to his own brand of incisive, searching, and fruitful criticism.

The author is also particularly grateful to Professors Arno Mayer of Brandeis University, J. David Singer of Vassar College, and Robert L. Smith of Southern Methodist University, whose insights and suggestions helped immeasurably in giving form to an almost amorphous project. The author's colleagues in the department of political science at Emory University, particularly Professors Lynwood M. Holland, Charles D. Hounshell, and Ronald F. Howell, all read parts of the manuscript and gave generously of suggestions and encouragement.

Professors H. Field Haviland of Haverford College, Charles P. Schleicher of the University of Oregon, and Harold Sprout of Princeton University read all or part of the manuscript. Their severest criticisms were uniformly just; many an egregious error has been spared the reader due to their patience and wisdom.

Mrs. Judith Watkins Smith performed the unenviable task of translating a heavily edited manuscript into coherent form and served as a constant watchdog on idiosyncratic grammar and whimsical spelling.

The foregoing share credit for what is creditable in what follows. For all sins of omission and commission, however, the author bears full responsibility.

Emory University

C.O.L., Jr.

TO

Margaret

AND

Herky

Table

of

Contents

◀▶

3

**THE
NATIONAL
INTEREST:
MYTH
AND
REALITY**

Armed Force in the American Tradition; The American Method in Foreign Policy. Public Opinion and American Foreign Policy: Weaknesses of American Public Opinion; Strengths of American Public Opinion; Preliminary Verdict on Public Opinion.

The Classification of Foreign Policies. The United States and the Status Quo: The United States as a "Have" Power; The American Attitude Toward Change; The Procedural Status Quo. Peace, Order, and Stability: The American Interest in Peace; Order and Stability. Action Principles: The Constant Interests: Self-Defense; Cooperation for Peace; Hostility to Nonpeaceful States.

4

SITUATIONAL FACTORS IN CONTEMPORARY AMERICAN POLICY

The World in 1945. The Redistribution of Power; The Eclipse of Europe; Asian Instability; The United Nations. New Forces in World Politics Since 1945: Economic and Political Instability; The Impact of Communism; The Afro-Asian Revolution; The Impact of Technology; The New Warfare. Political Trends Since 1945: Great-Power Rivalries; The Rise of New Power Centers; The Challenge of the Non-Western World; New Techniques in World Politics.

The Rise of Soviet Revisionism. Soviet Postwar Policy: General Characteristics; Soviet Relations with the United States; The Soviet Union and the United Nations; The Development of Satellitism. Early Soviet Moves: Europe; The Middle East; The Far East. Soviet Foreign-Policy Techniques: The Transformation of Diplomacy; Soviet Non-Negotiating Techniques. The American Perception

of the Threat: The End of "Appeasement"; The Beginnings of a Policy.

Formulating the Problem: The Limits of
Capability Analysis; Assumptions of This
Analysis. Tangible Elements in Amer-
ican Capability: Geographic Factors in
the American Position; Population and
Manpower; Natural Resources; Industrial
and Agricultural Production; Military
Power. Intangible Elements of Capabil-
ity: Political, Economic, and Social Struc-
ture; Educational and Technical Level;
National Morale; International Strategic
Position. Some Tentative Conclusions.

5

AMERICAN
POLICY
IN
ACTION

Why the Cold War?: Non-Reasons for
the Cold War; What the United States
Wants from the Communists; The Free
World and the Cold War. Containment:
Assumptions and Program: Soviet Motivations; The American Decision; Containment: Basic Elements; The Framework
of Accommodation. The Pattern Applied: Successes and Failures of the Pattern; The Pattern and the Public; "Liberation"; The New Cold War.

Containment: The Evolution of Bipolar-
ity, 1947–1950: First Steps in Contain-
ment; Economic and Military Aid; The
Beginnings of Alliance; Issues Outside the
Anti-Soviet Context; The Dynamics of
Bipolarity. Stalemate: Bipolarity Domi-
nant, 1950–1954: The Korean Conflict;
The "Mutual Security" Context; Major
European Trends; Soviet Policy, 1950–
1954; Climax: Indochina. The New
Cold War: Bipolarity in Decline, 1954–
1961: The Renaissance of Flexibility;
"Khrushchevism" in World Politics; New
Components of American Policy.

6

**CONTINUING
ISSUES
IN
AMERICAN
POLICY**

7

**LOOKING
AHEAD**

P
A
R
T

1

◂▸

A

Conceptual

Framework

◂▸

What
is
Foreign
Policy
?

This volume is an essay on the foreign policy of the United States. It is one of the truisms of political science that every state has a foreign policy. Each sovereign political unit, existing as it does in a world that contains approximately 90 other states, cannot escape having some kind of relations with them; common sense would seem to dictate that these relations should, if possible, be ordered and governed by some more or less rational plan. Foreign affairs, always one of the major fields of government action, has grown in importance under the conditions of modern technology so that today it is the principal concern of many states and is of primary significance to all.

Our major interest in this study will be the foreign policy conducted by the government of the United States in the name of the American people. We shall devote the bulk of our attention to a consideration of the ways in which government and people meet and attempt to solve the peculiar problems of international relations that fall to them. We shall be making our examination in terms of an analytical device that we may call our "conceptual scheme." We shall develop a number of general concepts and will then suggest some relationships among them; this device, it is hoped, will permit us to view our subject as more of a whole than it sometimes appears to be, and will also provide a number of insights into both the strength and the weaknesses of American foreign policy. In this opening chapter, therefore, we shall attempt to lay most of these preliminary foundations.

THE CONCEPT OF "FOREIGN POLICY"

In this book, by "foreign policy" we mean the courses of action and the decisions relating to them that a state undertakes in its relations with other states in order to attain national objectives and to advance the national interest.[1] Such a definition contains several terms that themselves require definition, and it obviously stands in need of further analysis and refinement. We shall devote ourselves to this task in this chapter. This definition, as expanded, will incorporate the system by which we shall analyze American policy.

The Nature of Foreign Policy

Foreign policy, as an area of government action, shares many of the characteristics of any public policy; many of the generalizations about the conduct of public affairs developed by political scientists and other students of government are applicable to the study of the foreign relations of any state.[2] We shall not attempt to enumerate these here, nor to isolate the features that make the formulation and execution of foreign policy different from other forms of state action. Instead, in this chapter we shall discuss some of the considerations fundamental to an understanding of our subject without direct concern for their relevance to other problems of government.

----

[1] Compare the following definition advanced by Charles B. Marshall, then a member of the Policy Planning Staff of the Department of State: "... the foreign policy of the United States [is] ... the courses of action undertaken by authority of the United States in pursuit of national objectives beyond the span of jurisdiction of the United States." *Department of State Bulletin* (March 17, 1952), p. 415.

[2] On the governmental process in general, see, for example, David Truman, *The Governmental Process* (New York: Alfred A. Knopf, Inc., 1951); for the most exhaustive recent study of American policy-making machinery, see the report prepared by the Brookings Institution for the Senate Foreign Relations Committee, *The Formulation and Administration of United States Foreign Policy* (Washington: U. S. Government Printing Office, 1960).

Foreign policy, as we analyze it here, has three major components, from the interaction of which various discrete steps develop. In the order of their appearance in the foreign policy process, they are: (1) the state's criteria of measurement, which we usually call national interest; (2) the situational factors impinging on the state; (3) the action taken by the state. Although the possible action patterns states may follow are so numerous that their classification and description fall outside our purpose in this book, an analysis of the first two notions is necessary to our analytical method. In a moment we shall attempt to clarify both the notion of national interest and the typology of situational factors; later in the chapter we shall examine both of them in some greater detail.

Foreign Policy as Process.

Before proceeding, however, we should emphasize that foreign policy is here conceived as a social and political process. It is an on-going affair, not one that may be seized and studied in all its ramifications at a particular moment in time. Dynamism is the keynote of all international relationships, and our analysis should be so oriented as to take account of unceasing evolution and change. Only by devising techniques that encompass the notion of process can we develop a picture of foreign policy that is at all relevant to reality.

Of what does the foreign policy process consist? If we define "process" as action consisting of a series of steps each leading to the next and all aimed at a predetermined end, we may put the matter this way: the foreign policy process consists of the repeated application of a set of relatively constant criteria to an infinitely variable pattern of situational factors, and the subsequent adjustment of state action in response to the conclusions reached from such application. We can list the steps of the process as follows: (1) the establishment of the criteria; (2) the determination of the relevant variables in the situation; (3) the measurement of the variables by the criteria; (4) the selection of a goal; (5) the elaboration of a strategy to reach the goal; (6) the decision to act; (7) the action itself; (8) the evaluation of the results of the action in terms of the original criteria.[3]

We may further postulate that this process, since it goes on within every state and since all states function within a dynamic system, is for

---

[3] Contrast the process here suggested with the simpler formulation found in an earlier Brookings Institution study, *The Administration of Foreign Affairs and Overseas Operations* (Washington: U. S. Government Printing Office, 1951), p. 13.

analytical purposes deemed to be unending. The criteria, as we shall see in a moment, tend to be less constant in practice than in theory; the ends of state action themselves are notoriously prone to revision in response to stimuli both rational and irrational; the system itself usually operates so as to frustrate the ultimate purposes of states. Though we can possibly conceive of an international order in which what we are calling "foreign policy" would no longer be present, the actual world in which we live is one in which the process not only goes on constantly but also shows no sign of diminishing either in importance or in complexity.

The Notion of National Interest.

National interest is the prime criterion (or criteria) in terms of which a state judges situational factors, determines the relative priorities to be given to different goals, and establishes and evaluates courses of action. It is the closest approximation to a fixed factor the policy process affords, but the nature of its components, its lack of absolute specificity, and the variety in the techniques by which it is formulated debar it from postulation as a true constant. Its rate of evolution and change, however, is much slower than is the case of the other raw materials of policy, and its role as the significant criterion gives such consistency as may be present in any foreign policy.

In most states, and certainly in the United States, national interest as a generalized concern arises from two sources. The first (and less specific) is what we call the "myth" of national purpose in international affairs: those mass-shared values in foreign policy whose maximization by government is demanded by a broad consensus. The ego-image a national group has of itself as it views the world cannot help but be basic to the specific foreign-policy steps it takes. The second source of national interest is the group of practitioners of foreign policy (the "decision-makers") themselves. Though forming part of the mass we call the nation and, as such, themselves partakers in the national myth, their insights, experience, and collective responsibility for action—as well as their peculiar bureaucratic point of view—often lead them to conceive the national interest differently than does the mass, and to apply somewhat different criteria to its formulation. Occasionally such varying views of long-range public purpose are the cause of serious internal conflict.[4]

---

[4] There is a steadily growing literature on the subject of national interest, revealing the extent to which scholars are grappling with the problem of its clarification and also the lack of agreement which generally prevails. Among the leading works, we may mention Hans J. Morgenthau, *In Defense of the National Interest* (New York: Alfred A. Knopf, Inc., 1951), Robert Osgood, *Ideals and Self-interest in*

Situational factors that influence policy are infinite in both number and variety, but here we may subsume them under three general heads: (1) the international milieu in which the state is operating; (2) the specific actions taken by other states to which responses of one sort or another are appropriate; (3) the state's own capabilities for action. Elements from each of these categories interact to create the situation to which the criterion of national interest is applied.

Objectives and Courses of Action.

When the national interest is applied to a situation that calls for decision and action, the outcome is the selection of an objective: a reasonably clearly defined state of affairs the accomplishment of which the decision-makers feel would be advantageous, at least under the controlling conditions. An objective is a target of state action: a goal the state wishes to reach. Its justification is the net gain to the state that its achievement would either bring about or make possible. The selection of an objective is followed by the development of a strategy to reach the goal and the subsequent execution of that plan; this last step is the purer (or at least narrower) referent to the term "policy."

The "Chain" of Policy.

We have now reached the point in this highly generalized survey of the concept of foreign policy at which we may suggest some causal relationship among the various steps. We can conveniently put this in the form of what we might almost call a "chain reaction."

Step 1. Popular traditions and official points of view, applied to (relatively long-range and fixed) conditions, interact to produce a formula of national interest.

Step 2. A formulation of national interest, applied to (middle-range and evolving) conditions, results in the selection of precise objectives.

Step 3. An objective, analyzed in terms of (short-range and immediate) conditions, leads to the selection of a course of action (a policy).

The energizing factor that moves the reaction from step to step is, of course, the varying impact of the situational factors impinging on the

---

America's Foreign Relations (Chicago: University of Chicago Press, 1953), Frank Tannenbaum, *The American Tradition in Foreign Policy* (Norman: University of Oklahoma Press, 1955), and Stanley Hoffman, ed., *Contemporary Theory in International Relations* (Englewood Cliffs: Prentice-Hall, Inc., 1960). Several leading articles have also appeared in such journals as the *American Political Science Review, World Politics,* and the *Political Science Quarterly.*

state. Foreign policy does not just happen; the state's decision to act is always the result of some change in the situation—internal or external—with which it is faced. Since we have agreed that the situational elements of international politics are in constant flux, it would be logical for us to conclude, as we suggested above, that the foreign-policy process is constantly operative, each step leading to the next and each new situational change touching off a new chain reaction of adjustment.

FOREIGN POLICY AND THE STATE SYSTEM

Although in our study we shall be interested primarily in the purposes and actions of one state—the United States—we shall be reminded at every turn that its foreign policy must be planned and executed within the confines of the state system. In many ways and at all times the requirements of the system affect the behavior of any of its members, and success most frequently comes to those states that best fit their policy into the peculiar demands of the society of which they are a part.

Although no purpose would be served by reviewing here a detailed theory of international politics, a summary of some fundamentals might throw a little light on our subsequent discussions. We shall briefly examine three notions: (1) the state's freedom of choice; (2) the channels of state action; and (3) the limiting controls on such action.

The State's Freedom of Choice.

The mystique of sovereignty confers one important area of freedom on the members of the state system: the freedom to choose. No external force can rightfully dictate to a state what its national interest should be; each state, in terms of its internal processes and dynamic, reaches and ratifies its own version of what is best for it. Each state is similarly free to make such situational analyses as suit its concerns and to select such objectives as it wishes. And finally, each state may adopt such policies as it sees fit, using such combination of techniques as to it seems expedient and wise. Interest, objectives, and policy are all—from the state's point of view—egocentric; each member of the state system may choose any policy at all and owe responsibility for its decision to no one outside itself. The basic motivations of foreign policy are therefore to be found within the state.[5]

---

[5] One of the early developments of this point among American scholars was by Nicholas J. Spykman, in *America's Strategy in World Politics* (New York: Harcourt, Brace and Co., 1942), Chapter I: "Power Politics and War."

State action in pursuit of an objective may assume any of a great variety of forms. Modern technology has added greatly to the supply of foreign-policy techniques available to the statesman. Despite their increased number, however, they all fall into one of the four traditional categories of tools and techniques, the four channels of state action. These four are: political action, through the mechanisms of diplomatic representation; economic action, through the productive and distributive system of the state; psychological action, through the techniques of mass persuasion; military action, through armed force. From among these four types, a statesman chooses in such combination as seems to him to be best suited to the particular purpose he has in mind.[6]

The Limits on State Action.

There are both formal and informal limits on the possible action any state might take in pursuit of an objective. Their combined effect is largely to inhibit the state's real freedom.

The formal limits may be summed up as international law and international organization. International law incorporates a body of rules prescribing acceptable state conduct in a broad variety of situations. Although the system is incomplete and of uncertain enforcement, all states recognize its existence and admit it to be—to a substantial if imprecise extent —a limiting factor. International organization—most clearly epitomized in its major contemporary manifestation, the United Nations—limits state action both by its statutory competence to sit in judgment on state behavior and by its unique ability to form and express a mass international consensus. Although the formal limits on state action are yet rudimentary, and despite the fact that states occasionally succeed in evading their restraints, their over-all limiting effect is perceptible and sometimes controlling.[7]

The informal limits on state action grow out of the dynamic of the state system itself. Each state, in pursuing its own policies, is confronted by all its fellows doing the same thing. Each therefore is faced with the ominous likelihood that any interstate relationship in which it becomes involved will be a competitive one and may well develop into open con-

---

[6] See E. H. Carr, *The Twenty Years Crisis, 1919–1939.* 2nd ed. (London: The Macmillan Co., 1946), Chapter 8, and Harold and Margaret Sprout, eds., *Foundations of National Power,* 2nd ed. (New York: Van Nostrand, 1951), pp. 40–43.

[7] For a thorough demonstration of this point, see Charles de Visscher, *Theory and Reality in Public International Law,* trans. P. E. Corbett (Princeton: Princeton University Press, 1957).

flict. No state can afford to be engaged in disputes simultaneously with all other states; it must therefore seek to adjust its pattern of relations so as to maintain a satisfactory balance of support, sympathy, noninvolvement, and nonopposition from those states with which actual or potential conflicts are minimal or nonexistent. In this way it conserves its energy and power for use against those states with which it is involved over more important matters.[8]

In any such direct confrontation, another type of limit is operative. The principle of expediency that governs state action in a relativistic world demands that a state not press its cause against another beyond the point of its own capacity. The absence of effective institutional controls over state action tends to make each international dispute a clash of power, with victory going to the state better able to enforce its will. The point here is that prudent statesmanship allows for this condition and accepts as a limit on state action the general rule that a state should not voluntarily become involved in a controversy in which its position would be, on balance, weaker than that of its opponent.

NATIONAL INTEREST

We have identified "national interest" as denoting the relatively constant criteria by which a state judges the evolving situation it faces and in terms of which operating decisions are made and policies undertaken. We have also pointed out that it arises, in somewhat different forms, from two sources: the controlling myth and value system of the nation as it contemplates the international scene, and the somewhat more sophisticated and operationally more precise notions that emanate from specialized official personnel. Each of these aspects merits some further examination.

THE MYTH OF NATIONAL MISSION

Within any nation of more than rudimentary political experience there exists a more or less well-formulated image of its national mission: this, indeed, is one of the characteristics of the modern nation-state. There may be some sovereignties in the world in which the population is so politically inert that such a myth does not exist, but such states would be few in number and of relatively minor importance in world affairs. Politically sig-

---

[8] See this point as developed by George F. Kennan, in *Realities of American Foreign Policy* (Princeton: Princeton University Press, 1955), Chapter II: "The Non-Soviet World."

nificant states all incorporate some such notion, and its role in articulating national interest and in determining the direction and frequently the methods of foreign policy is always large and sometimes dominant.

The Importance of Mass Attitudes.

It is axiomatic today that foreign affairs is no longer the exclusive plaything of a small group of political insiders, but that the mass of citizens—at least in democratic states—is deeply involved in the process. State objectives have become so broad and the effort demanded to attain them involves so many facets of national power that no statesman dare run the risk of alienating the support of any large portion of his people. This makes nationalism, the mass political emotion, a factor always to be taken into account in policy decisions.[9]

What this means for most policy-makers is that the actions they contemplate must be attuned to mass attitudes. If their projected action falls within the area permitted or demanded by the national myth, they can proceed confidently; if it does not comport with what the dominant attitude feels is satisfactory, a preliminary problem in political leadership must first be solved. The mass must either be persuaded to expand or reorient its values by means of educational or propaganda techniques, or the policy must itself be altered or reinterpreted so as to bring it into conformity with the commands of the popular tradition.

Statesmen frequently chafe under the restraints imposed by such a myth, but contemporary political life affords few clues about how they may escape it. The mass may be manipulated, tricked, cajoled, temporarily evaded, or even tyrannized, but it cannot permanently be ignored. To the extent to which the mass tradition of international mission is clearly formulated and based on genuine value consensus, it is an absolutely controlling determinant of national interest. Statesmen must develop their own formulations within such freedom of action as it permits them.[10]

Popular Preferences and Foreign Policy.

In conceptualizing the myth of national mission, we must be wary not to draw over-rigid inferences from our notion. Even in a tightly-knit authoritarian society organized under a system of rigid social controls, voluntary unanimity on ultimate national purposes is usually impossible

---

[9] See Karl Deutsch, *Nationalism and Social Communication* (New York: John Wiley & Sons, Inc., 1953); for specific examples from Britain and France, see Arnold Wolfers, *Britain and France Between Two Wars* (New York: Harcourt, Brace and Co., 1940), Chapters III, XIII.

[10] Gabriel A. Almond, in *The American People and Foreign Policy* (New York: Harcourt, Brace and Co., 1950), deals extensively with this problem.

to achieve in any notable detail; in a fluid social structure, consensus seldom develops spontaneously except on extremely narrow issues and then only for limited periods. Such myth as exists in a democratic society usually finds expression either in broad value generalizations permitting great flexibility in official interpretation and application to specific situations, or else in emotional slogans equally subject to manipulation by skilled leadership.

Popular preferences, therefore, as a source of national interest only rarely tie official hands completely. In a free society there is competition among individuals and groups who seek to express the controlling version of the myth; a variety of voices purport to speak the basic ("true") national interest. This situation often gives officialdom an opportunity to move shrewdly to cultivate the positions of which it approves and to play a constructive part in shaping the myth to dimensions appropriate to the action demanded at the moment.

Even in this looser version of the concept of the national myth, however, we must nonetheless recognize its basic irrationality. Popular attitudes may seize upon an objective, a technique, or a condition and sanctify it as an integral part of basic national interest. Against such a move the statesman is helpless; as long as the myth is speaking, official discourse is powerless to be heard. Governments must cope with such commands as best they can.[11]

We may repeat, however, that ordinarily the "national interest," to the extent that it is imbedded in the culture as a prevailing myth and value system, finds expression only in the most general terms and is subject to most elastic interpretation. As a rule, officials responsible for government action find it a hurdle not impossible of clearance, although only rarely are they able to ignore it completely. An orderly analysis of the national interest of any particular state must recognize the peculiar role of mass value preferences and make its first task an estimate of their dimensions and effect.

NATIONAL INTEREST AS A POLICY DETERMINANT

When we turn from national interest as myth and consider it in its more material role as perhaps the prime determinant of government policy, we find ourselves capable of somewhat more precision, even though the literature of political science is replete with controversy over the exact

---

[11] For critical comment, see Walter Lippmann, *The Public Philosophy* (Boston: Little, Brown and Co., 1955), especially Chapter II: "The Malady of Democratic States."

meaning of the term. Although defining it in a way satisfactory to every-one has so far proved impossible, we can discover sufficient consensus to permit clarification of the concept to a degree sufficient for our pur-poses. Certain notions reappear regularly in the discussions of scholars and the pronouncements of statesmen; the concrete formulations of inter-est made by states resemble one another relatively closely with reference to a handful of broad concerns. From these sources we may draw a few tentative conclusions.

The Idea of National Interest.

As we analyze the role of interest in the foreign policy of actual states, we find that all of them seem to be perennially concerned to some impor-tant degree with the same three considerations. We may phrase these com-mon desires of states as (1) self-preservation, (2) security, and (3) well-being. It is probable that for most states these three are listed here in their normal order of priority.

But these three areas of interest, as stated, are too generalized and abstract to be of much use, either for analysis or for policy-making. They must be given a more specific content. Each government makes such an elaboration with regard to the generalized situational context in which it is operating and to its long-range aspirations within that situa-tion (the latter consideration is the peculiar province of the myth we discussed in the preceding section). This translation of interest into rela-tively precise and long-lived wants and needs results in the working cri-terion by which the government measures the changing milieu. We need scarcely point out that, since no two states face the same situation, no two formulations of national interest are the same. For our purposes, therefore, the "national interest" as a determinant of policy consists of formulations of those (at least) semi-permanent ends, phrased at a high level of generalization, the accomplishment of which the state feels is necessary to its self-preservation, its security, and its well-being.

"Interest" vs. "Interests."

We have come a little way in making the notion of national interest more intelligible and useful, but our term is yet too abstract to be used as an analytical tool. We will recall that our "chain of policy" made situa-tional factors the motivating element in policy; circumstances also play their part in translating the national interest into useable and concrete terms. One attempt to formulate the process put the matter this way:

> The *national interest* may be defined as the general and continu-ing end for which a state acts.... This is, of course, a highly

generalized definition. But any lower level of generalization tends to lose substantive meaning, and the term becomes increasingly ambiguous. The reason for this is that the requirements of security and well-being not only change with circumstances but are, in addition, matters of judgment and calculation and hence open to varying interpretations. . . .[12]

To replace the general notion of "the national interest," the authors of this selection suggest the plural term "interests," because such usage not only reveals that interests "may conflict in any given set of circumstances," but also that a choice must be made among them "in terms of priorities and values" before specific objectives and policies can be selected. "Interests" are defined as "what the decision-making group in a government determines is important to the maintenance of the state." [13]

Such a substitution of "interests" for "the national interest" as an analytical tool has a good deal to recommend it on grounds of clarity and utility; it makes a great deal more sense to say about a particular situation that "the United States has an interest in . . ." than "the national interest of the United States is . . ." The use of "interests" makes it possible for the statesman or analyst to proceed directly to concrete situations and speeds the process of reaching a policy decision. But there seems to be some danger in relegating the more general term to the discard and in concentrating entirely on what "the decision-making group" in a state thinks is important. Conflicts between competing interests within a state are frequent, and the quotation above admitted that they are to be resolved by a choice made "in terms of priorities and values." It does not seem illogical to suggest that such a choice might well be made in terms of a generalized version of interest rooted in mass tradition.[14]

----

12 William A. Reitzel, Morton A. Kaplan, and Constance G. Coblentz, *United States Foreign Policy 1945–1955* (Washington: Brookings Institution, 1956), Appendix A, "Definition of Terms," pp. 471–2. Italics in original. Reprinted by permission.

13 Reitzel, Kaplan, and Coblentz, *op. cit.,* p. 472. Reprinted by permission.

14 Reitzel, Kaplan, and Coblentz use the term "principles" to refer to such a criterion: "*Principles* is used to mean the enduring modes of behavior or the relatively established guides to action that characterize nations. . . . The decision-making group, concretely concerned with *interests,* tends to think of *principles* as more-or-less subjective and to find them in occasional conflict with *interests.* Nevertheless, *principles* are deeply imbedded in the general culture and political philosophy of a society and are powerful, if intangible and subjective, guides to action. . . . they represent the underlying patterns of value that guide national action and to which determinations of *interests, objectives,* and *policies* over the long run tend to conform." *United States Foreign Policy,* pp. 472–3; italics in original. Reprinted by permission. Such a definition seems to fit quite closely what we are calling the "myth" of national mission and may well be used as a definition for it.

Such an architectonic notion of national interest serves a very useful purpose in enabling a policy maker initially to draw—and subsequently to keep in mind—the necessary distinction between "means" and "ends" in foreign policy. "Ends," being generalized goals largely rooted in the prevailing myth of national purpose, are postulated *a priori;* "means" are the rationally selected techniques selected in order to maximize a predetermined end. Ends, in other words, are internalized. There is no such thing as a "good" end except in terms of the unique value system of the society that establishes the end in the first place. No outsider can rationally criticize any ends-decision. Judgments regarding means, however, are amenable to analysis in terms of more or less objective criteria of efficacy and economy of effort.[15]

Ends may, in turn, be either proximate or ultimate. A proximate end is one the achievement of which will provide a springboard for a further advance toward an ultimate end. In this sense, a proximate end acquires some of the characteristics of a means and is open to critical analysis in those terms. But even so, proximate ends inexorably govern the means selected for their accomplishment; each ends-means relationship, whatever its level of generality, is symmetrical with all others. It is only when a means loses contact with its appropriate end that serious problems both of analysis and of statecraft arise.[16] A successful foreign policy keeps ends and means in balance.

National Interest: the Final Criterion.

One final point needs to be made in this connection about national interest. It is more than the standard by which situational factors are given relevance and action inspired; it is also the ultimate criterion by which the state's "success" or "failure" is measured. A "good" foreign policy is one that advances the notion of interest that inspired the action in the first place; a "bad" one fails. Thus we might aphoristically say that the

---

[15] "[I think] of foreign policy as relating to means and ends and to the gap between them.... Ends are concepts. Means are facts. Making foreign policy consists of meshing concepts and facts in the field of action." Charles B. Marshall, *Department of State Bulletin* (March 17, 1952), p. 416. See also the brief but powerful development of the same point in Walter Lippmann, *United States Foreign Policy: Shield of the Republic* (Boston: Little, Brown and Co., 1943), Chapter II: "A Fundamental Principle of Foreign Policy."

[16] See Karl von Vorys, "The Concept of National Interest," in Vernon Van Dyke, ed., *Some Approaches and Concepts Used in the Teaching of International Politics* (Iowa City: State University of Iowa, 1957), pp. 49–54. Professor von Vorys points out that "end-interests" are *postulated* while "means-interests" are *pursued.* Reprinted by permission.

What is Foreign Policy * *15*

concept of interest is both the starting point and the end of the foreign-policy process, and the entire sequence of action acquires a peculiarly circular character.

The permanence of national interest is, of course, only relative. Nothing stands still in international relations, and interest is no exception to this rule. But we must emphasize that a state's devotion to its self-preservation, its security, and its well-being (in other words, to its end-interests) remains constant, however different may be the forms in which problems present themselves. New political, economic, demographic, psychic, or technological facts may work great changes in the means-interests pursued by the state or even in the pattern of postulated end-interests. In this sense, interest unquestionably evolves in its detailed expression. But this mutability that we can see in the concept does not vitiate its key role in the policy process; some formulation of national interest provides the foundation for all subsequent steps in making and executing foreign policy.

SITUATIONAL FACTORS

We indicated earlier that the situational factors in response to which policies are initiated fall into three categories: (1) the international milieu in which the state is operating; (2) the specific actions of other states; (3) the state's own capabilities for action. Later in this book we shall devote a chapter to each of these as they apply to the United States; here we need only clarify their content briefly to see how they fit into our conceptual system. Each, as we shall see, requires care and discretion in its analysis.

THE INTERNATIONAL MILIEU

The milieu of state action—including both the fixed factors confronting the state and the general "climate" of international affairs—is the source of a large share of what some call the "givens" of foreign policy. The setting in which policy is made and conducted itself influences the decisions states make and the actions they take.[17]

---

[17] A systematic survey and critique of the various interpretations of the milieu has been made by Harold and Margaret Sprout, in *Man-Milieu Relationship Hypothesis in the Context of International Politics* (Princeton: Center of International Studies, 1956); see also, by the same authors, "Geography and International Politics in an Era of Revolutionary Change," *Journal of Conflict Resolution,* IV, 1, 145 (March, 1960).

Fixed Factors in the Milieu.

Each state is faced with a number of relatively fixed factors as it charts its course in international affairs. Some of these relate uniquely to itself, such as its size and location; these are generally considered as part of the tangible component of state capability. Others appertain more directly to the state system and its effect on the state concerned, and must be fed into the policy calculations the state makes. Examples of these might include the global distribution of power, the existing international institutions and their effectiveness, the stability or disorganization of international society, and so on.

The Climate of International Politics.

But we have made the point several times already that no fixed scheme of relationships can convey an accurate impression of the international scene. Dynamic forces also form part of the milieu, and tend to influence the interpretation and modify the impact of the fixed factors. The cumulative effect of the dynamic forces at work at any one time is to create the "climate" of international politics: the general atmosphere of state relationships. Some of the dynamisms that might contribute to the climate are the broad trend toward revolution or toward reaction, mass attitudes on war and peace (the "expectation of war"), the state of ideological disputation, and the level of nationalist identification among large groups of people.

THE ACTIONS OF OTHER STATES

What we really mean when we say that other states affect the course of policy-making by any government is that the state system itself forms a situational factor. What is there about this system that obliges a state to take into account the known and predictable responses of its associates when it is planning a policy move? Why is foreign policy such a mixture of action and reaction?

The Dual Impact of Other States.

Each state impinges on any other in two ways. In the first place, as policy is executed, resistance by other states is encountered. Such opposition may be overt and extensive, it may be covert and nominal, it may even be passive. Each form of resistance must be anticipated as accurately as possible and measures devised for dealing with it. Second, each state must devote a large portion of its capability to coping with policy moves made by other states, resisting, cooperating, or accommodating as its own interest dictates. A surprisingly large share of each state's effort is spent in dealing with situations arising from action originating outside its own boundaries.[18]

Competition in the State System.

The fictions of sovereignty—the independence and equality of all states —produce a system that in logic is absolutely competitive. States are free to—and often do—select policies the accomplishment of which would require the attainment of absolute objectives. When all states seek the same absolute goals, their attainment in a world of dispersed power is impossible to any of them.

The state system is thus inherently frustrating; every member of it is doomed to permanent dissatisfaction as it doggedly plods on in search of illusory objectives. This frustration lends a certain peevish quality to interstate relations; it often seems as if states feel that as long as they cannot really accomplish their goals, they are determined to do the next best thing: to deny their accomplishment to others.

The international order is an intensely competitive one. Each state realizes that at bottom every other state is its actual or potential rival; each views the international scene with the assumption that its fellows would be perfecly willing to deny it the fruits of any of its efforts.

This is a strong statement, and one often belied in practice. We must recall, however, that absolute competition is often modified by the working of the principle of national interest. For particular states and in appropriate circumstances, cooperation in the pursuit of a shared objective may be more mutually advantageous. But if (or when) their interests—determined by each state for itself—again diverge competition would immediately replace the earlier harmony.

The Pursuit of Compensation.

The actual working of the competitive principle usually takes the form of the pursuit of "compensation." Especially among states who are admitted rivals (in other words, between which competition has come out into the open), an advantage gained by one state—usually some move that attains an objective or at least brings it nearer realization—touches off a search for compensation by the others. They may attempt to offset the gain by resistance or by retaliatory action; they may readjust their relations with each other so as to reestablish the former relationship; they may seek gains of their own to restore the balance.

---

[18] This and the succeeding points are discussed at greater length in the author's *Principles of International Politics* (New York: Oxford University Press, 1956), Chapter V.

International politics may be viewed as a complex series of such initial moves followed by compensatory reactions. Statesmen contemplating policy moves must assume that any but the most minor steps will precipitate such an attempt at compensation by some states.

The Effect of Other States.

When a statesman makes his judgment about the reactions his move will provoke, he knows that a broad range of action is open to the affected states. Some will agree with him, and perhaps will actively cooperate; others will be affected only slightly, and their moves in either direction will be minimal; still others will be in opposition and will initiate compensatory policies. The task of the policy-maker is to move through these permutations and combinations as deftly as he can and to extract from the situation such freedom of action—usually brought about by balancing favorable reactions off against opposing ones—as will permit him to make some contribution to the notion of interest he is serving.

STATE CAPABILITY

By "capability" we mean the ability of a state to achieve its objectives.[19] This definition, being almost perfectly circular, does not define; perhaps it is more accurate to say that capability is the measure of the capacity of a state to have other states agree with it on matters in which it is interested. Among sovereignties the only way differences can be eventually terminated is by agreement, and it is immaterial whether such agreement is forced or free.

Force and Consent.

There are, as we have suggested, two different ways by which a state may secure agreement from other states. It may either compel agreement by force—the application of coercive or semi-coercive techniques—or it may win agreement from them by free consent. Both force and consent, as devices for obtaining agreement, form parts of capability.[20]

Generally speaking, the more free consent a state can command in support of its policy, the less it needs force to reach its objective. Con-

---

[19] For systematic attempts to give content to the concept of capability (or "power"), see Harold and Margaret Sprout, *Foundations of National Power,* Chapter IV, and Stephen B. Jones, "The Power Inventory and National Strategy," *World Politics* (September, 1954).

[20] This notion is extensively developed by Louis J. Halle, in his *Civilization and Foreign Policy* (New York: Harper & Bros., 1955), and earlier in his "Force and Consent in International Affairs," *Department of State Bulletin* (September 21, 1953).

versely, the less consent available, the greater the amount of force needed. Since under most circumstances agreement by consent is preferable to agreement by force (for reasons both of permanence and of economy of effort), states as a rule endeavor to maximize their area of consent.

There is, however, an inherent limit on this effort. No state would dare to depend entirely on the voluntary consent of other states in estimating its ability to fulfill its mission. Neither, for that matter, can a state trust itself entirely to force for any but the briefest of periods or the narrowest of objectives. "Capability" must, for each state, be a measure of the effective action open to it in the particular context, such effectiveness being composed variously of its coercive power and its command of the free consent of its associates.

The Content of Capability.

A state's ability to achieve its objectives is so much a function of time, place, and situation that we cannot ever attain anything like mathematical precision in its analysis.[21] We can, however, suggest here the broad areas of state life that bear directly on the concept; in Chapter 9 we shall fill in some of the details as they apply to the capability of the United States.

Capability involves both tangible and intangible factors. The former are to a great extent susceptible to measurement by objective criteria; the intangibles defy exact measurement—and often exact formulation as well —by statistical techniques. Students of international affairs—as well as statesmen—realize, however, that both sorts of concerns contribute to the total ability of the state to act constructively.

The tangible factors are usually listed under five heads: (1) geography; (2) population and manpower; (3) natural resources; (4) industrial and agricultural production; (5) military organization and power-in-being. Each of these has been studied in detail; a wealth of information about their status in the majority of states is now available, and a host of revealing comparisons has been and is being made. Insofar as capability analyses can be made by the yardsticks represented by these five categories, we can do the job quite presentably.

Intangibles are nonquantifiable (as are indeed many of the aspects of the tangibles in the list above), but estimates must nevertheless be made of their effect if capability judgments are to have any utility at all. Among the many ways of listing the nonmaterial components of capability, the

---

[21] "Capability analysis proceeds from the tangible and easily measured factors to those which though still very tangible—indeed crucial—involve so many imponderables as to defy measurement." John S. Reshetar, Jr., *Problems of Analyzing and Predicting Soviet Behavior* (Garden City: Doubleday, 1954), p. 33. Reprinted by permission.

one that follows is an attempt at synthesis; other lists might have more or fewer entries, but the general points included would be generally the same. We stipulate four categories: (1) the political, economic, and social structure of the state under consideration; (2) the educational and technological level; (3) the state of national morale; and (4) the international strategic situation of the state—its need for allies, its opponents, its general leader-follower status in international society, and the amount and kind of consent it can command.

The Relativity of Capability.

Capability is a slippery concept, for it acquires meaning only in a relative sense. A state is not "capable" or "incapable" in any absolute way; instead, it is "capable" or "incapable" of doing some particular thing. A capability judgment about a state is intelligible only when a decision is being reached about whether or not it can attain a particular objective. A state may be able to reach a goal when opposed by one state, but may be impotent when confronted by another; one objective may be within its capacity while another is completely out of reach.[22]

Thus each time a policy decision is under consideration, a capability judgment about the attainability of the various alternatives helps influence the choice of one of them. Capability is not a status to which states attain, but rather a device of measurement by means of which policymakers can judge the relative feasibility of different courses of action.[23]

The Dynamism of Capability.

Another controlling characteristic of the concept of capability is its dynamism. The several factors interact so subtly and in such a variety of ways that capability judgments must be made, so to speak, on the run.

We can almost say that it is impossible to reach any conclusion about the relative capabilities of states that is not at least partially obsolete at the time it is made. Many of the factors influencing such a judgment are moving so rapidly that even the latest information is out of date. This makes the detailed measurement and comparison of capabilities really a matter of isolating the significant trends of development within each

---

[22] This warning is even more apposite when the notion of "power" is under discussion in the same sense that "capability" is being used here. It is easier to visualize a "powerful" state than a "capable" one, and even more deceptive to do so. "Power" does not convey as clear an implication of the ability to perform a specific act as does "capability"; this is perhaps one of the more compelling reasons why the latter term has come generally to be regarded as both more accurate and more useful than the older one.

[23] See Feliks Gross, *Foreign Policy Analysis* (New York: Philosophical Library, 1954), p. 124, for an elucidation of this point.

relevant component, and then projecting each of these into the future. In this way, calculations of relative competences of states become the best possible guesses about conditions yet to arise.

The Time Factor.

The relativism and dynamism of capability combine to suggest another qualitative element: the pervasive influence of time. Questions of "now" and "then" enter into every judgment. A state's capability to reach an objective may be inadequate at one moment, but ample a short while later after conditions have changed. In like manner, time may work against a state. The components of capability change at an uneven rate, and the determination of the moment of maximum capacity for a particular course of action requires that the statesman carefully coordinate a number of factors moving at different speeds. The effect of time appears at every turn in international politics, and success in foreign policy rests to a great extent upon the ability of the policy-maker to calculate the optimum moment for action.

OBJECTIVES AND POLICY

We turn now to two more concepts that play an important role in the foreign policy process: objectives as goals of state action, and policy considered as a course of action designed to reach an objective.

OBJECTIVES

The Nature of Objectives.

Foreign policy involves action in the national interest, but such action must be purposive. Each state organizes its purposes into a set of objectives that represent the goals it seeks to reach by deliberate action. We have defined an objective generally as a state of affairs that a state attempts to bring about. It may be positive in nature and demand affirmative action; it may be negative and demand only that a particular position be held against external pressure. Objectives are preferably verbalized in concrete terms that afford some criteria for determining when and if the objective is attained and for devising strategies for their attainment.

From Interest to Objectives.

In the policy process, the development of a situation to the point where it either requires or suggests action by the state calls for the application of the yardstick of national interest. Every government asks itself a question more or less as follows: "Considering the situation as of this moment, what possible state of affairs would be most advantageous in terms of the national interest?" The answers it discovers to the question furnish the objectives it accepts and will seek to attain. Objectives, as we have seen, arise out of the situation as interpreted by a notion of interest.

The Mutability of Objectives.

Realizing that any formulation of interest is subject to modification and that many situational factors themselves are inherently unstable, we are led to conclude that objectives (derived from these two elements) are themselves absolutely liable to change along some minimum-maximum continuum. It is no wonder that states are constantly overhauling their patterns of objectives. Some goals are discarded as either no longer valuable or as beyond attainment; some are modified in the light of situational change; some entirely new ones are adopted. No state can safely assume that the application of its version of interest to a general situation will produce the same result twice in succession; indeed, the contrary assumption is usually safer. Objectives provide targets at which to shoot and combine to indicate a direction in which policy moves, but only rarely does a state reach the exact goal after which it originally set out.

The Pattern of Objectives.

Every state, of course, has a number of objectives. Each of the components of national interest normally gives rise to a more or less numerous family of specific concerns ("interests"), in response to each of which some concrete objective is selected from the situational context. It is only seldom that these objectives fall neatly into a homogenous or harmonious relationship which each other; usually there is some degree of inner contradiction within the larger outline of interest and policy.

When this contradiction involves fundamentals, a real dilemma confronts the policy-maker; sometimes he may advance his state's interest in one area only by doing it serious or irreparable damage in another. Normally at this point major readjustments become necessary. More frequently, however, conflict among objectives is resolved in terms of time priority (Objective A, being urgent, must be achieved as soon as possible; Objective B, contradictory but less immediately critical, may be attacked at a later time) or some other rationalizing device.

If the controlling notion of interest is sufficiently clear, we would expect that all the specific objectives of a state could be comprehended within its terms, even if only at a very high level of generali: Conversely, some approximation of what a state considers its int reached by induction from an analysis of the motivations underlying its choice of objectives. In any case, a rationally conceived foreign policy, maintaining a working relationship with an understood and accepted notion of interest, would normally have more of harmony than of contradiction.

POLICY

Early in this chapter we defined foreign policy and warned that this definition would require further analysis. Between that point and this one we have examined the foreign policy process and several of its components. We now return to the subject of "policy" itself, initially in a much narrower frame of reference than in our original definition, and later in its original broader sense. "Policy," as we are discussing it here, is not necessarily the same thing as "foreign policy."

The Meaning of Policy.

Our concern at this point is with "policy" considered in a strategic and tactical sense. Policy in these terms assumes an objective to have been already selected, and refers to a method for its attainment. The term therefore has two connotations: it means either the actions actually taken to accomplish a purpose, or the principles that govern such action. It may refer either to a series of overt moves made by a state in order to reach an objective, or to the prepared plan under which such steps are taken. Both meanings are useful, and analytically the distinction between them is important; as we use the word in this discussion, however, the particular reference will usually be indicated by the context.

Reaching a Policy Decision.

Making a policy decision to act in accomplishment of an objective is a power monopolized by the official decision-making personnel of a government. Action in international affairs takes place only by government mechanisms, and only those officials authorized in the name of the state to commit the government to act can make real decisions. Considerable study has been made of the process by which decision-makers, particularly in the United States, perform this task, and the nature of the operation is fairly well understood.[24]

---

[24] Three useful, although very different, analyses of the foreign-policy process are Richard C. Snyder, H. W. Bruck, and Burton M. Sapin, *Decision-making as an Approach to the Study of International Politics,* Foreign Policy Analysis Series No. 3 (Princeton: Princeton University, 1954); Kurt London, *How Foreign Policy Is Made* (New York: Van Nostrand, 1949); and Philip W. Buck and Martin Travis, eds., *Control of Foreign Relations in Modern Nations* (New York: W. W. Norton & Co., Inc., 1957). See also the 1960 Brookings Institution study, *supra.*

Without going into the minutiae, however, we may say that as a rule governments follow some version of the generalized process we outlined on page 5. Interests and situations are catalogued and analyzed and the optimum possible state of affairs is determined. Particular emphasis is placed on canvassing all the possible alternatives of action. Each course that has any feasibility at all is spelled out, and each is evaluated rigorously in terms of the prevailing idea of national interest, the impact of the developing situation, and its possible success in attaining the objective. The final selection (at least in theory) is made of the one that seems to promise the greatest success (or, sometimes, the minimum loss) in the fulfillment of the demands of national interest.

Various states formalize this process of developing alternatives to different degrees, and within any state it may vary from one situation to another. But some approximation of the technique is used in every government that takes foreign affairs seriously. No less detailed method would take enough of the variables into account.[25]

The Flexibility of Policy Decisions

Policy decisions, being concerned more with "how" than with "what," are as often as possible taken with an eye to their possible revision as conditions evolve. This is one major reason for the elaborateness with which the open alternatives are frequently analyzed; if the strategy selected should prove unworkable, the state presumably can fall back on the policy line originally judged next best. States normally attempt to preserve the maximum room for maneuver; sometimes an objective will prove beyond reach by any possible policy technique, and then a new objective must be fixed and a new program accepted to reach it. Flexibility is sought in time, in quantity, in kind, and indeed in every dimension by which policy is measured.

The dynamism of the state system swiftly penalizes the state that fails to allow for change. A rigid policy—based on the (explicit or implicit) assumption that conditions will continue unchanged indefinitely—stands in constant danger of becoming irrelevant to new situational elements. If a policy supported by commitments of power faces the loss of effective rapport with its milieu, the state may well be forced into the expensive and hazardous effort of extemporizing to buy time while it adjusts to the new dimension of its problem. Prudent statesmen avoid this danger whenever possible by holding their commitments to the necessary minimum.

---

[25] Examples of this process are provided by the specimen "problem papers" included in each volume of the series prepared by the International Studies Group of the Brookings Institution, *Major Problems of United States Foreign Policy* (Washington: Brookings, 1947–54).

In this discussion we have been emphasizing that "policy" refers to the course of action a state follows in pursuing a single objective. A state thus has many policies—as many as it has objectives—and it follows each of them simultaneously. It is in this connection that we speak of a "policy decision": a decision to commit the government to act in a certain way in order to achieve an objective.

But, despite the built-in ambiguity that results, "policy" has another meaning. As used in the phrase "foreign policy," "policy" refers to the general pattern and direction revealed by the aggregate of a state's specific undertakings and the broad principles that undergird them. Thus we may say that Soviet foreign policy is expansionist, and we may also say that the Soviet pursues the policy of cultivating the friendship of the uncommitted states. There is no easy escape from this confusion of language; we may, however, suggest one possible clue. "Policy" as a generic concept is usually verbalized in general or abstract terms, while a particular policy of a state is (or, at any rate, should be) precise and concrete in its referents. Further than this we must fall back on the context to clarify the sense in which the term is being used.

AMERICAN FOREIGN POLICY: CONTENT AND METHOD OF ANALYSIS

Up to this point, we have been outlining and commenting upon a conceptual scheme for a reasonably rational analysis of foreign policy. With some modifications it could be used to reach some conclusions and evaluations about the foreign policy of any state in the world; generally speaking, the key notions of interest, situational factors, and state action apply to all states with approximately the same force. But our aim in this book is to consider American foreign policy, and the purpose of this chapter is to lay out the method of inquiry we shall be using in our consideration of the foreign relations of the United States. Here in the concluding section of the chapter, we should spell out as precisely as possible just what phenomena we shall be examining.

THE CONTENT OF "AMERICAN FOREIGN POLICY"

In approaching American foreign policy by way of the leads furnished by our over-all system, we can find over a dozen different categories of data into which we should inquire. Each of them has some relevance to the foreign policy the United States is conducting at the present time, and each has a place in our model of the foreign-policy process. Each therefore forms part of the "American foreign policy" with which we are concerned. The list that follows includes 13 separate components of our study.

1. The national interest of the United States as tradition and concept.
2. Specific formulations of the national interest.
3. The historical background of American policy.
4. The mechanisms and procedures for making and executing American policy.
5. The international milieu in which the United States is acting.
6. The policies of other states to which the United States must react.
7. The capabilities of the United States, general and specific.
8. The general international action pattern of the United States.
9. The specific objectives sought by the United States.
10. The courses of action taken by the United States to attain its objectives.
11. The evaluation of the policies of the United States.
12. The unresolved issues remaining in American policy.
13. The probable future course of American policy.

An Analytical Scheme.

The chapters that follow are an attempt to fit these separate areas of inquiry into a reasonably coherent analysis of American foreign policy. The remainder of this book divides the material into sections, each one constituting a segment of our generalized concept of foreign policy or logically deriving from it.

Part I is comprised of this opening chapter. Parts II and III deal respectively with the structures and processes for making and executing American policy and with the historical antecedents of contemporary American action. They are considered at the outset because of their relatively fixed and continuing impact on policy: as part of the "givens" of American foreign affairs they constitute bases on which we build other factors.

Part IV deals with the national interest, including both the national value system that we have called the myth of national mission and the operating formulations that American decision-makers have derived from this broad-gauge image of the national good. Part V devotes a chapter to each of the three major categories of situational factors affecting the United States: the international milieu, the actions of other states (in this case largely the USSR), and American capabilities.

Part VI considers American action in the contemporary era. One chapter discusses the general pattern of American policy; another gives a chronological overview of the cold war organized around the concept of bipolarity.

Part VII examines certain continuing issues of American policy that have continued to be important through all the situational changes that have taken place. Part VIII concludes the study with an attempt at some limited-range forecasting of the future of American policy.

Such an organization not only encompasses the 13 areas we listed as being of interest, but also puts to the test the general conceptual scheme this chapter has outlined. If we have made an accurate list of the important considerations and if our analytical techniques are reliable, we should emerge from our study with a better rounded and more consistent understanding of at least the fundamentals of American foreign policy.

◀▶

Fundamentals

of

the

Policy

Process

◀▶

Foreign Policy in American Democracy

All Americans agree that the United States is a democracy. Whatever that much-abused word may mean in differing value systems, it is pretty well agreed that an essential element in any democratic government is the establishment and use of mechanisms for the registration and implementation of popular attitudes. Government in a democracy is a device by means of which public opinion is translated into public policy, and this proposition holds as true in foreign affairs as in any other area of government action.

And so we come to the central concern of this chapter. A democratic government like that of the United States is ideologically committed to follow, as nearly as it can, the dictates of its constituents. This means that the policy-makers cannot confine their attention to the national interest as they perceive it themselves, but must always heed whatever they feel the voice of the people is saying. Popular influence on the decision-makers, present to some extent even in the most dictatorial of governments, is different in a democracy primarily in that it is thought to be normal, is constantly taken into account, and is accepted as controlling most of the time.

If we admit that responsible policy-makers have the duty and the necessity of shaping policy in response to mass wishes, a dilemma inherent in the democratic idea immediately arises. Does the public have an equivalent obligation? Can (or should) the people exercise their right of ultimate policy determination in happy irresponsibility, or should they confine their function to those areas in which they can operate effectively? Who speaks for the public? Does "the people," considered as a single factor, verbalize something called "the national interest" as well as, better than, or not as well as the official experts who are both better trained and closer to the scene of action?

All we are suggesting here is that the troublesome theoretical and practical issues of democracy are no more easily resolved when the significant problems are those of foreign policy. The interlocking roles of officialdom and the mass public remain difficult either to disentangle or to rationalize. We shall look at this dilemma again at the end of the chapter.

THE DECISION-INFLUENCERS

Those government officials, executive and legislative, that actually make the decisions in foreign policy have the influence of the public brought to bear on them from a variety of sources. These "decision-influencers" speak variously for the entire people or for significant sub-sections of the body politic, and each exerts its effect in a different way.

PUBLIC OPINION

We should begin with a brief and general consideration of that amorphous and slippery shibboleth, public opinion. Although students of democracy have long realized that even though the concept of "public opinion" is in some way relevant to democratic thought, attempts either to define it precisely or to locate it empirically have largely come to grief. This is not to say that the idea, because it is not susceptible to free quantitative manipulation, is useless; our principal concern is to make as clear as possible just what we mean by the term.

What Is Public Opinion?

In the first place, "public opinion" is merely a shorthand way of expressing something basic in democratic ideology, at least in the United States: total opinion is the sum of individual opinions. There are several "publics," and each has its own peculiar type of "opinion." But the fundamental ingredient in all of them is the individual member of the social group who —under whatever influences—makes up his own mind.

"Opinion" in this sense has two components. In the first place, it sums up all the *attitudes* that individuals have toward such questions as make an impression on their consciousness. On each such issue the individual has an attitude that may be the result of a sophisticated rational process or the crudest type of emotional response, that may be the outcome of a lonely private struggle or merely a pumped-in predigested stand originating in an organized group. In any case, the individual reaches his conclusion by his own devices, subject only to the overriding influence of the second component, the prevailing *mood*.[1] Out of these individual attitudes certain common patterns emerge, to be ascertained impressionistically by observers, journalists, or Congressmen, or to be measured statistically by survey and poll techniques.

The Several Publics.

Students of public opinion agree that there are several "publics" that share in what is called public opinion. Gabriel Almond distinguishes three such within the American society:

> One may speak of a "general public" if one keeps in mind that while it is characterized by a sense of identification and reacts to general stimuli, it also contains a variety of interests and groupings which are affected differentially by both general and specific stimuli. Second, there is an "attentive public" which is informed and interested in foreign policy problems, and which constitutes the audience for foreign policy discussions among the elites. Third, one may speak of the policy and opinion elites, the articulate policy-bearing stratum of the population which gives structure to the public, and which provides the effective means of access to the various groupings.[2]

Professor Almond feels that the "elite public" is the only portion of the whole that has policy relevance, since the competition among its various sub-sections (political, administrative, interest, and communications elites) is what really determines "public" opinion. "The 'masses,'" he contends, "participate in policy-making in indirect and primarily passive ways."[3] The attentive public listens to the discussions among the elites and, presumably,

---

[1] Gabriel Almond, in *The American People and Foreign Policy* (New York: Harcourt, Brace and Co., 1950), analyzes the American mood in terms of movement along several axes: withdrawal-intervention, optimism-pessimism, tolerance-intolerance, idealism-cynicism, and superiority-inferiority (pp. 53 ff.). Reprinted by permission.

[2] Almond, *American People and Foreign Policy*, p. 138. Reprinted by permission.

[3] Almond, *American People and Foreign Policy*, p. 139. Reprinted by permission.

plays the most important role in making up the mass mind by telling it what to think.

Whether or not one accepts the whole of Professor Almond's rigorous analysis, it is difficult to question either its thoroughness or its fruitfulness. His catalogue of the various elites is roughly adapted for use in this chapter; succeeding sections will deal with the impact of interest groups, political parties, mass media, and nonpolitical ("prestige") leadership on American foreign policy. His major proposition remains beyond doubt; there are indeed several different publics, each with its peculiar characteristics, of which policy-makers must take account.

Who Speaks for the Public?

"The public" has no voice of its own; someone must speak for it. The policy-maker who, either because of ideological conviction or from sheer prudence, wishes to guide his conduct generally by the commands of the public must decide for himself whose voice is authentically that of the mass.

There are many who wish to speak for the public and who claim to do so; we shall see in a moment how at least some of them function. But there is almost always some confusion of voices; the mass rarely speaks unanimously through one spokesman. The policy-maker therefore knows in advance that whatever decision he makes will please some of those who clamor for his ear, and that it will displease others. The best he can hope for is that his decisions will not violate the implicit consensus that underlies all the Tower of Babel we call public opinion. On details the successful (or lucky) official may fly in the face of mass opinion; on fundamentals, however, and over any significant period of time, he must stay within the bounds the mass public lays down.

INTEREST GROUPS

Many sophisticated students of American government claim that the dominant political characteristic of the American people is their division into interest groups.[4] According to this line of analysis, the individual today lacks significance. He gains importance only to the extent to which he allies himself with an organized group that represents his particular interests. The group, large enough to be important and led by skilled manipulators of pressure, can fight actively for the public policy desired by its members and obtain a much greater degree of success than all its members, acting indi-

---

[4] A leading exposition of this point of view is David Truman, *The Governmental Process* (New York: Alfred A. Knopf, 1951).

vidually, could accomplish by themselves. In this way the role of government is primarily that of referee among the competing groups; out of the warring factions of private and group interest will come some working approximation of the national interest.

This doctrine, as we can easily see, does violence to the democratic myth of individualism. Yet one need not be a confirmed "interest-grouper" to admit that these particular organizations have tremendous significance in the determination of public policy (including—perhaps especially—foreign policy) and that they form one of the major influence elements in policy decisions.

The Organization of Interest.

An interest group scarcely needs elaborate definition. It is a group of individuals organized on the basis of a single common interest or set of interests. The purpose of the group is to use any combination of a long list of techniques—all subsumed under the rubric of "pressure"—to persuade appropriate government officials, legislative or bureaucratic, to decide in its favor. Almost every conceivable interest in American life has been organized today; on major policy issues, both domestic and foreign, there are groups that represent almost every possible opinion.

Individuals join these groups in response to their own interests. Since very few well-adjusted persons have only one interest in their lives, it is normal for any individual to belong to, or at least to accept the program of, several different groups. In this way unperceived contradictions often develop. A college professor, for example, may maintain membership simultaneously in the American Association of University Professors and in the American Legion. The AAUP opposes loyalty oaths for college faculties; the Legion favors them. On which side does the professor stand?

The leaders of each group (who collectively form the "interest elite" Professor Almond discusses) each claim to speak for their total membership—including our hypothetical professor. Obviously at least one of the spokesmen is mistaken. And yet the policy-making official is unable to know definitely to what extent the interest elite is taking unwarranted liberties with its constituency. Frequently he must accept their claims at face value for want of reliable evidence to the contrary.

The Mechanics of Pressure.

Interest groups apply pressure of two kinds on government officials, usually termed "direct" and "indirect." Direct pressure is applied by the group leadership upon the officials personally. Techniques are varied: persuasion, threats of political reprisal (more effective on elected office-holders), technical information (even on foreign policy private groups may be better informed on special issues than are the responsible officials), promises of voting support for the official's party, and so on. The object of direct pressure is to impress the group's wishes forcibly on the decision-making official(s).

Direct pressure has certain limitations. In the first place, it is largely dependent on the ability of the group's leadership to gain access to the decision-makers. It does no good to exhaust one's armory of persuasive techniques on officials who do not have the power to grant the group's wishes. More importantly, even if a group can penetrate directly to the key officials, this advantage is largely vitiated unless it can command a near-monopoly of the bureaucratic ear. This happy situation seldom arises. Even when applying pressure to the appropriate official, the group must realize that other groups, arguing the opposite point of view, can probably do the same thing.

Indirect pressure concentrates on the creation of an active mass opinion that will in turn exert pressure on officials to take the desired steps. This usually involves disseminating propaganda aimed at the least common denominator of the public and stressing a simple action formula. The interest group's victory comes nearest to completion when it is able to stir up the public to the point where policy-makers face an opinion *fait accompli* to which they have no choice but to bow. Quantitatively, it is probable that the significant majority of interest group effort is expended in this kind of indirect pressure.

But again we must note the competition among the groups for the public ear. When major policy questions are at issue, the "average citizen" is bombarded with appeals from every point of the compass. The battle of the propagandists is never-ceasing. The individual chooses from among the various "messages" and takes his place on one side or the other of the question. One unexpected outcome of this group conflict is anathema to propagandists but increasingly evident to observers: there seems to be a growing tendency among members of the mass, when confronted with such a barrage of appeals for action, to express their confusion by a simple withdrawal and a refusal to take any stand at all. To a thoughtful person, this appears to be a perfect parody of democratic procedure.

Categories of Interest Groups.

To call the roll of the interest groups that bear on foreign policy would require a list many pages long. Gabriel Almond provides a convenient scheme of categories.[5] We should remember only that within each classifica-

---

[5] Almond, *American People and Foreign Policy,* Chapter VIII. Reprinted by permission.

tion are many separate subgroups, each considerably different from all the others in its pattern of desires. Almond identifies seven groups: (1) labor groups (AFL-CIO); (2) business organizations (United States Chamber of Commerce, National Association of Manufacturers); (3) agricultural groups (American Farm Bureau Federation, National Grange); (4) veterans' groups (American Legion, Veterans of Foreign Wars, AMVETS); (5) women's groups (League of Women Voters, National Federation of Business and Professional Women's Clubs); (6) religious organizations (Federal Council of Churches of Christ); (7) ethnic groups (Jews, Germans, Italians, Poles).

POLITICAL PARTIES

Another source of influence on American decision-makers is the institution of the political party. American parties operate in a fashion almost diametrically opposed to pressure groups. Where the interest group is tightly identified with a specific program, the party by definition is decentralized and pluralistic. Where the interest group is largely concerned with policy, the party's focus is on government personnel. Where the interest group seeks to sharpen issues, the party attempts to blur them.

The Parties and Foreign Policy.

In the American two-party system, each party approaches foreign policy somewhat ambivalently. Foreign policy is a perfectly valid election issue, and party politicians see no fundamental difference between foreign issues and domestic ones; each type is important to them only to the extent to which it wins or loses votes. Consequently, we find professional politicians manipulating foreign-policy questions as expertly as those of domestic policy; party divisions on international issues run as deep as they do on any others.

Yet, in the past decade or more, the increasing significance of foreign policy to the United States has penetrated even into the high councils of the specialists in winning elections. There seems to be a feeling that decisions about NATO may, in the last analysis, be more important than those concerning agricultural support prices or public power in Tennessee or Idaho. There has, in other words, begun to evolve something like an interparty consensus on foreign policy that has tempered the party battle to some extent. Disagreement between the parties now tends rather to center on the preferred methods of implementing policies rather than on basic approaches to them. So far has this progressed that many serious-minded and independent citizens are concerned because there is often no "respectable" way to dissent from current American policy since the parties have reached such a high level of agreement.[6]

The President and His Party.

This raises an interesting issue. The President is responsible for his administration's foreign policy; he is also his party's leader. His party must stand on the President's record. If the opposition is to defend its own position, it must attack the President; such is the logic of American politics. But, if the interparty consensus has been operative during the previous two or four years, for the opposition to challenge the President's foreign policy would require it to question a program with which it largely agrees. Here the dual role of the President—as national leader and as party chief—serves to confuse the operation of the American political system.[7]

More difficult is the problem of maintaining presidential leadership in foreign policy over all elements of a party. This is particularly applicable to Congress, and especially to Senators. The decentralized structure of American parties makes it impossible for a President to keep his fellow party members completely under control; belligerent independence of executive leadership is often good politics for a Senator. Often the President must act like the leader of an interest group and use indirect pressure on his party, stirring up public opinion to demand action from the recalcitrant legislators.

Party Splits on Foreign Policy.

Since 1945 it has become apparent that both major parties are split into two or more groups on major questions of foreign policy. American par-

---

[6] H. Bradford Westerfield, *Foreign Policy and Party Politics* (New Haven: Yale University Press, 1955), analyzes this trend in terms of Congressional votes on foreign policy issues between 1943 and 1950. Even the chorus of criticism directed at President Eisenhower during the spring and summer of 1960 for the failure of the summit conference and the cancellation of his trip to Japan focused upon "ineptness" and "bungling" rather than raising any questions about the substance of American policy. See the Senate speech of Senator Fulbright on June 28, 1960, as reported in *The New York Times* (June 29, 1960).

[7] For example, the Democratic leadership was caught in a dilemma in May, 1960. The crisis brought on by the U-2 episode, when the Soviets captured an American aviator on a reconnaissance flight well within Soviet territory, gave the opposition the opportunity to castigate the Administration both for the act itself and for its "inept" handling of the episode. Fearful that such open division would hamper American policy on the eve of the summit, however, Adlai Stevenson, Senator Lyndon Johnson, Senator John Kennedy, and other Democrats instead assured President Eisenhower of their support and approval. It was no secret, however, that many Democrats regretted their inability to capitalize on the event. See *New York Times*, May 10–16, 1960, for a running commentary on the issue. Their discomfort was reflected in the noncommittal report issued by the Senate Foreign Relations Committee in June. Also to be noted is the restraint demonstrated by Senator John F. Kennedy in his discussion of the problem during the Presidential campaign of 1960.

ties are not "responsible"; they owe no official allegiance to any central leadership, although the national conventions purport to exercise such authority through their party platforms. Much more revealing of party attitudes toward foreign affairs than any platform is the behavior of the party delegations in both houses of Congress, and here is where the sharp cleavages reveal themselves.

Both parties suffer from what may be called—somewhat inaccurately— an isolationist-internationalist division. There are not really two clear camps in each party, but rather a continuum covering the entire spectrum of foreign policy. But on crucial foreign-affairs votes in Congress, something like definite points of concentration appear on either side of the boundary between these two popular terms.[8]

The Republican split is best known, taking roughly the form of a separation between the Middle West on the one hand and both coasts on the other. Under the leadership of President Eisenhower, the importance of the Midwest group declined both relatively and absolutely, but was never completely eliminated. The Democratic cleavage was less obvious for a time, but came into the open during the first years of the Eisenhower administration. Fundamentally it represents a split along North-South lines, with the South developing something that observers tended to identify with prewar Middle West isolationism.[9]

The upshot of the parallel divisions in both parties—at least in Congress—has been the development of informal foreign-policy coalitions that transcend party lines. Southern Democrats ally themselves with Republicans from the Middle West; northern and western Democrats make common cause on foreign policy with Republicans from the same regions. Like most generalizations about party politics, this conclusion cannot be elevated to the status of a hard and fast rule. It is sufficiently applicable, however, to qualify sharply any serious attempt to delineate party positions or party programs on foreign-policy matters. The illusory specificity of party platforms should not be permitted to obscure the fact of the actual lack of "party" foreign policies.

Bipartisanship.

Were the parties to develop clear lines of distinction on foreign policy, it might be possible to conduct America's international relations on a

---

[8] Westerfield, *Foreign Policy and Party Politics,* pp. 51–52.

[9] On at least one issue, the Mutual Security Program, Southern opposition in Congress came to surpass that of the Middle West. In 1959, 48 per cent of the Southern members of the House voted "nay" on the MSA renewal authorization, while only 41 per cent of the Middle Westerners accompanied them; in 1960, the respective percentages were 50 for the South and 40 for the Middle West. Oddly enough, nearly half of the Middle West's negative votes were cast by Democrats! See, for the figures, the present author's article, "Southern Congressmen and the 'New Isolationism,' " *Political Science Quarterly* (September, 1960).

"partisan" basis: that is, one party would be responsible for all policy and the other would constantly criticize it, always ready to take charge if public support were withdrawn from the incumbents. This is more or less the way British government functions. To do this, however, would require a degree of party unity on foreign policy that does not seem possible under the American federal system, where national parties are loose confederations of "sovereign" state organizations. If pure partisanship is out of the question as a guiding principle, some form of "bipartisanship" becomes necessary.

In a strict sense, bipartisanship is as difficult as pure partisanship, for it really means that the parties in effect remove foreign policy from the area of controversy and that their positions on specific questions are substantially identical. To be effective, this would require that party leadership control the rank and file and that there be distinct party positions that could be harmonized. As we have seen above, this is most unlikely; there is no workable way at present for both parties to share equally in the responsibility of foreign policy.

H. Bradford Westerfield has coined the word "extrapartisanship" to describe what actually happens in the American government and what is probably the best compromise attainable under the present conditions of party politics. The President remains as the most important policy maker and clearly identifies the bulk of his party with his own policy. The support of the opposition is brought about by deliberately including some of its leadership in the policy process by invitation of the President, and then trusting these opposition leaders to swing enough of their party membership behind the joint policy to guarantee a workable consensus. Ordinarily it is most profitable to include the opposition's foreign-policy spokesmen in Congress in the group of consultants, provided only that they be of sufficient prestige to carry real weight. Of the many examples of extrapartisanship, Mr. Truman's close association with Republican Senator Vandenburg of Michigan during 1948–9 and Mr. Eisenhower's working arrangement with Democratic Senator George of Georgia during 1955 are outstanding.

But ever since at least 1940, there has been some kind of two-party support in Congress for the policy of whatever administration has been in power.[10] Straight party-line votes are always rare in Congress, but they are especially so on foreign policy. If a President keeps his policy in

---

10 Westerfield, *Foreign Policy and Party Politics*, Part 3, "The Record of the Parties in Foreign Affairs, 1939–1950"; see also Cecil Vann Crabb, *Bipartisan Foreign Policy: Myth or Reality?* (Evanston: Row, Peterson, & Co., 1959). The votes on the successive renewals of the Mutual Security Act between 1953 and 1960, for example, are summarized in Lerche, "Southern Congressmen and the 'New Isolationism,'" *supra*.

reasonably good tune with the prevailing currents of popular opinion, he can frequently count on constituent pressure (among other techniques) to bring the bulk of both houses of Congress over to his side. The development of extrapartisanship only makes this principle more workable.

MASS MEDIA

The media of mass communication—newspapers, radio, television, motion pictures, magazines, advertising, and—to a lesser extent—books, have become of tremendous importance in American culture as it has become more complex and dehumanized. Face-to-face contacts are of less significance in the transmission of ideas today than at any earlier time in the history of American culture. If mass media are indispensable and if foreign-policy ideas are the most important political concerns of our time, we would expect the media to play a large part in shaping foreign policy.

The Mass Media and Public Attitudes.

A mass medium is a technique of communicating simultaneously (or nearly so) with a large number of people. In every case the audience is one that, by definition, transcends the limits of face-to-face contact. Mass media became possible by the advance of technology—printing, electronics, high-speed transportation, and so on; mass communication has become almost a necessity because of the increasing impersonalization of modern civilization.

Being aimed at people in the mass, the messages brought by mass media are usually phrased in terms that will have a broad appeal: simple, brief, and striking. They must place no insuperable burden on the absorptive capacity or the tolerance of their consumers. Their content must be tailored to the sensed needs and desires of the audience; such changes as they bring about in audience attitudes are gradual, usually enlarging rather than breaching the existing bounds of acceptance.

In some intellectual circles it is currently fashionable to argue that mass media are positively dangerous to American democracy because of their grip on the imaginations and the value systems of the mass public. Horrifying pictures are painted of the ease with which the "architects of consensus" can create public demands for particular programs, and dark prophecies are made of the fate of freedom if the tycoons of mass communication were ever to make full use of the power that is theirs. This picture is somewhat overdrawn, although to the casual observer it might seem as if Americans take all their standards from Hollywood, the television studios, and the picture magazines.

Mass media can, to a considerable extent, play successfully on the pre-existing prejudices of people; they have proved to be able to sell soap, sex, and sensationalism. But there is little persuasive evidence that they are able to change significantly the patterns of mass wants and needs; audiences simply leave them when they seek to work substantive alteration in fundamental systems of preferences. As long as the mass media are kept within these limits, we may regret that they do not elevate the public instead of pandering to it [11] but there seems little reason to fear overmuch that they will destroy freedom.

Mass Media and Foreign Policy.

What generalizations can we make about the impact of mass media and their manipulators on the foreign-policy process? We must first repeat our general conclusion that such effect as they have takes place generally within the pre-existing preference pattern of the mass public. If any attitudinal change takes place among the mass, the media may well be in a position to capitalize on it [12] but they have been so far unable to bring about any such change themselves.

Within these limits, however, we may identify at least three different effects of mass media on foreign-policy decision-making. (1) The media help focus issues during a period of readjustment and reassessment by means of constant and extensive discussion of various alternatives. (2) They do a non-discreditable job of mass education, informing the public of data and points of view that otherwise would not receive wide circulation. That this is done often for reasons other than public service should not detract from its value. (3) On the debit side, it must be admitted that the mass media approach to foreign policy stresses its controversial and sensational aspects and minimizes its continuing, affirmative, and harmonizing functions. We are familiar with the cynical attitude of many newspaper employees that "nobody buys a newspaper to read good news"; this assumption underlies much of what all the mass media do in the foreign-policy area.

Nonpolitical Leadership Elites

The final entry in this brief listing of the decision-influencers is the most difficult to specify, and yet it may well be as important in shaping public attitudes as the more formal groupings we have been considering.

---

[11] David Riesman, Nathan Glazer, and Reuel Denney, in *The Lonely Crowd* (Garden City: Doubleday [Anchor Books ed.], 1953), point out, however, that the mass media have done considerable service in the elevation of mass taste in such fields as furniture and architectural design (p. 339).

[12] The manner in which some more sensational American newspapers and magazines seized on the issue of Communist China after public attitudes crystallized after 1949 is an apt example of this adaptation to a new mood. See also Alfred O. Hero, *Mass Media and World Affairs* (Boston: World Peace Foundation, 1959).

This is the existence, at all social levels, of unofficial but powerful "opinion leaders" whose attitudes—however derived—are influential in shaping the opinions of large numbers of their associates. Their role is central to any study of public opinion in the United States.[13]

An Elite of Influence?

Students of American society all agree on the existence and importance of the opinion leaders, although they disagree widely as to the nature of their role and its impact for good or bad. Whether it is argued that this leadership constitutes a "power elite" that really rules America [14] or that the leadership merely operates on the periphery of important decisions, that there are nonpolitical leaders whose effect is perceptible although difficult to measure seems beyond doubt. It would seem likely that in the aggregate they are more powerful in changing mass attitudes (through mass response to their own shifts) than are the mass media. There is some empirical evidence to support this thesis.[15]

The Characteristics of Opinion Leaders.

Generally speaking, the nonpolitical elite consists either of those individuals in any segment of society who occupy some prestige position, either personal (wealth, beauty, notoriety, social-economic group leadership), or status (the clergy, teachers, attorneys). Americans are famous for their willingness to lend weight to the opinions of prestigeful individuals on any subject, even one on which the particular leader is unqualified to speak. This propensity gives any such leader a ready-made followership prepared to accept many of his opinions as their own.

By and large, opinion leadership tends to come from the upper economic brackets, to be better educated, more widely traveled, and somewhat more catholic in taste and outlook.[16] Their opinions, however, cover the entire possible spectrum, and their influence is exerted in many different ways; there is no necessary implication in what we have been saying that their influence is always—or usually—exerted on the side of enlightenment, of reason, or of tolerance. If it turns out to be, however, it goes far to contribute to a more effective mass opinion within the area of its effect. There are some scholars who attribute much of the growing

---

[13] Floyd Hunter, *Community Power Structure* (Chapel Hill: University of North Carolina Press, 1953), makes an exhaustive analysis of the structure and pattern of community leadership in "Regional City" (reputedly Atlanta, Georgia).

[14] See, for example, C. Wright Mills, *The Power Elite* (New York: Oxford University Press, 1956).

[15] Paul Lazarsfeld, B. Berelson, and H. Gaudet, *The People's Choice* (New York: Duell, Sloan, and Pierce, 1944), Chapter XVI, "The Nature of Personal Influence."

[16] See, for corroboration of this thesis, Alfred O. Hero, *Americans in World Affairs* (Boston: World Peace Foundation, 1959).

popular sophistication about international affairs to the work of this kind of leadership.

The Elites and Pressure Groups.

The key role of opinion leadership has long been recognized by the directors of interest groups. These organizers and manipulators of pressure always seek to enlist the services of leadership elites at every possible level, from the small community to the entire nation. We are all familiar with the imposing letterheads of such groups that feature a long list of "sponsors" with well-known names who—for one reason or another—have lent their prestige to the particular cause involved. If the member of the elite contents himself with the use of his name, his effect will be limited, although real; if he actively busies himself with the promotion of the cause, he will gain converts and play a significant part.

The Elites and Foreign Policy.

It is difficult to generalize about the special impact of the prestige elites on foreign-policy decisions. Gabriel Almond calls them "the articulate policy-bearing stratum" of the public and feels that they have the truly critical role; they "give structure to the public." [17] This is true at the national level, and in concentrated metropolitan communities; there is some difficulty, however, in conceiving of a smalltown clergyman or high school teacher as a member of Professor Almond's elite public. It might be safer to allocate a minority of them to the elite public, the bulk to the attentive public, and another relative handful to the mass public, at least as far as their reaction to international issues is concerned.

If this group—the prestige leadership—comes together on one side of any foreign-policy issue, a solid public opinion on that issue is as good as made. On most issues, however, such unanimity does not develop; the opinion leaders divide among themselves and compete for mass support. The side of the question that gains the consensus of the prestige elite generally carries mass opinion with it; this is the "public opinion" of which government officials usually take account. This fact explains why local opinion leaders are such important targets of organized interest groups. As Almond suggests, "who mobilizes elites, mobilizes the public."

A DEMOCRATIC FOREIGN POLICY?

We now turn to the somewhat more detailed consideration of a question that has been implicit through the entire discussion. Can American foreign policy be truly democratic? American ideology demands that it be;

---

[17] Almond, *American People and Foreign Policy*, p. 138. Reprinted by permission.

American government is alleged to be responsive to the demands of the people. And yet, as we shall see, there are both strong arguments and objective facts that may lead us, and have led many people, to conclude more or less regretfully that the nature of the foreign-policy problem is such that the democratic ethic provides no guides, but only pitfalls. No issue can be imagined that is more fundamental to the outcome of the American experiment in democracy.[18]

THE DEMOCRATIC DILEMMA

The French Revolution democratized foreign policy by taking it out of the hands of absolute monarchs; modern nationalism conferred on the mass of the people of a state the right and the power to "make" foreign policy, at least in its broad outlines. In return, the populace acquired a reciprocal duty, that of executing the policy of which they were at least the partial architects. Compulsory military service was the first new civil responsibility; additional burdens of taxpaying, economic activity, intellectual pursuits, and other fields were added until today it is possible to speak of a "total" foreign policy in almost the same sense as we use the term "total war." Corresponding to the increase of mass responsibility for service in behalf of the national foreign policy came an increase in the degree of control popular attitudes exercise over foreign policy.

The more "democratic" foreign policy became, however, the more difficult became the foreign-policy process itself. The demands mass opinion made on government tended steadily to become less and less concrete, and more and more absolute, and ultimately often verging on the unattainable. Caught between the pressures of emotionally involved and articulate public opinion on one side and the inexorabilities of the state system on the other, statesmen in many countries found themselves involved in an unhappy dilemma. They were obliged either to follow the whims of popular demand and undertake policies they thought unwise, or to flout their people and run the risk of repudiation.

The Undemocratic Nature of Foreign Policy.

It is often said, therefore, that foreign policy, by its history and by its nature, is inherently undemocratic. Of the many reasons advanced to support this generalization, we shall mention four of the most frequently encountered.

---

[18] For a somewhat different attack on this problem, see the symposium, "Can Foreign Policy Be Democratic?" *American Perspective* (September, 1948); also Max Beloff, *Foreign Policy and the Democratic Process* (Baltimore: John Hopkins University Press, 1955).

(1) Foreign affairs is a government monopoly. The relations of states are carried on among governments, and in the exercise of the function officials must be free from close checking by irresponsible laymen.

(2) Foreign policy requires, if it is to have any success, both speed and flexibility. Governments must be able to move quickly to meet unexpected contingencies; they must also be able to adapt their actions to meet whatever conditions prevail. Both these qualities collide with the practice of democratic states generally and the United States particularly. American democracy, except in the most extreme emergency, does not operate with any notable speed. Once committed, the United States finds it difficult to change its policy (domestic or foreign) in response to new conditions.

(3) Foreign affairs necessitates a constant concern with secrecy. Negotiations usually take considerable time to consummate; premature release of information often endangers the whole enterprise. Nothing more fundamentally opposed to American ideology can be imagined. The idea that the government is keeping secrets from the people immediately gives rise to powerful currents of resistance, resentment, and opposition.

(4) A foreign policy must concern itself with what are often called "multiple constituencies." The American government is serving not only the American people, but also the populations of its forty-odd allies; furthermore, the clientele of American foreign-policy personnel also includes all the opponents and enemies of the United States. This means that the requirements of policy often demand that the State Department (for example) accede to the wishes of a foreign state rather than to those of the American people. This is also ideologically repugnant; a democratic government is popularly supposed to serve its people first and always.

We might add a fifth undemocratic requirement of foreign policy: the definition of the national interest. In later chapters we shall consider both the myth of American foreign policy and the working notion of interest that governs contemporary government action. In practice, however, the operating definition and formulation of interest is undertaken by the official elite.[19] This again suggests some conflict with democratic principles.

The Claims of Democratic Ideology.

The democratic myth,[20] on the other hand, has certain strong implications for foreign policy. They may be formulated as a series of propositions.

(1) There is something called a "public interest," composed of the

---

[19] "Hence the national interest becomes defined in practice as what those in power declare it to be." Thomas I. Cook and Malcolm Moos, "The American Idea of International Interest," *American Political Science Review* (March, 1953), pp. 28–44. See p. 30. Reprinted by permission.

[20] This term is used in the sense that it is employed by Gabriel Almond, "The

arithmetic total of individual interests. This is the "national interest" that the government should serve in foreign policy.

(2) The "average citizen" knows and understands his own interests and those of his fellows; in other words, he knows where his private concerns fit into the total public interest.

(3) The average citizen possesses the intellectual and moral resources satisfactorily to comprehend the issues of foreign policy.

(4) The average citizen can—and will—make meaningful decisions on those issues, and the total of individual decisions will constitute a clear directive to his servants in the government hierarchy.

(5) The average citizen is a better (because disinterested) judge of basic alternatives than are special interest groups or even highly specialized experts.

These propositions arise from the application of the individualist faith of traditional democracy to the questions of foreign policy. They incorporate a deep suspicion of special interests, government experts, institutional mechanisms, and indeed of any social structure that stands between "the citizen and his government." In their total impact they collide directly with the essentially undemocratic aspects of foreign policy we noted above. These two alternatives—expertise or popular will—constitute the two horns of what we call the "democratic dilemma."

LEADERSHIP: THE ELITE OF THE COMPETENT

We shall first consider the effect of elite leadership on the ideal of a democratic foreign policy. During the years that foreign affairs have been a major concern—since 1945—much attention has been lavished on the determination and evaluation of the role of leadership. Certain general characteristics of both the leadership itself and its apologists and defenders have become apparent.

Government: The Monopoly of Decision.

Foreign-policy leadership is of course concentrated in the government hierarchy. It is axiomatic that foreign-policy decisions in the technical sense can be made only by responsibile officials,[21] and that only they can con-

---

democratic myth is that the people are inherently wise and just, and that they are the real rulers of the republic," *American People and Foreign Policy*, p. 4. Reprinted by permission.

[21] Richard C. Snyder, H. W. Bruck, and Burton Sapin, *Decision-Making As An Approach to the Study of International Politics* (Princeton University: Foreign Policy Analysis Series No. 3, 1954), is devoted to an elaboration of this thesis and an inquiry into how decision-making may be most profitably analyzed. See also the 1960 Brookings Institution study, *The Formulation and Administration of United States Foreign Policy*, especially Chapters III and VI.

duct relations with other states. Furthermore, only they have access to the steady flow of information upon which to base intelligent decisions. All of these elements contribute to making the "political" leadership the central element in all foreign-policy discussion.

Whenever official personnel feel called on to justify their stewardship, their attitude finds expression in several general lines, whose net effect is a plea for public tolerance and a continued free hand.

First, they stress the difficulty of the task: "...foreign policy is a tapestry of infinite complexity, and even the expert can only hope to achieve familiarity with a part of its intricate designs." [22] Second, they emphasize the inherent limits on their real freedom of action.[23] Third, they imply that the problems are really beyond the understanding of ordinary citizens.[24] Fourth, they elaborate on the importance—indeed, the critical character—of their own function.

There is no intention here to challenge the importance or the ability of the official leadership group; American national interest is best served by having the most efficient and dedicated official personnel obtainable. What does give rise to some concern, however, is the implication that a final dichotomy exists between the general public and the government bureaucracy and that, when all is said and done, the ultimate safety of the United States rests on the skill and insight of its officials rather than on the morale, intelligence, and patience of the people.[25] There would seem to be some grounds for argument that no leadership can be more than a magnified reflection of the people it leads, and that no improvement in the quality of American leadership is possible without also bettering the political performance of the people.

The "Democratic Elites": The Monopoly of Knowledge.

Implicit in the newer studies of the political process in the United States is the more or less specific assumption that only a part of the public is of any policy significance: the "democratic elites," to use Almond's phrase.[26]

---

[22] Almond, *American People and Foreign Policy*, p. 143. Reprinted by permission.

[23] Charles B. Marshall, *The Limits of Foreign Policy* (New York: Henry Holt and Co., 1954). See also his "The Nature of Foreign Policy," *Department of State Bulletin* (March 17, 1952), pp. 415 ff.

[24] A former member of the Policy Planning Staff of the Department of State, Dorothy Fosdick, disagrees with this position, however. See her *Common Sense and World Affairs* (New York: Harcourt, Brace and Co., 1955). So also does Thomas K. Finletter, in *Foreign Policy: The Next Phase, The 1960s* (New York: Harper & Brothers, 1960).

[25] Thus Almond says: "The problem of contemporary American foreign policy is not so much one of mass traditions and resistances as it is one of resolution, courage, and intelligence of the leadership," *American People and Foreign Policy*, p. 88. Reprinted by permission.

[26] See especially Truman, *The Governmental Process*, Part II: "Group Organization and Problems of Leadership."

Our earlier overview of the various publics indicated that there is indeed a division of labor between the so-called attentive public and the mass. The former is distinctive because of its near-monopoly of knowledge over the data of foreign policy, the viable alternatives, and the preferable courses of action. In the sense in which we are using the general term "leadership" in this discussion, we are therefore including these elites in the leadership group in the United States.

The knowledge possessed by this minority is more than sheer information. If they actually possess more data, it is not necessary because they have access to more sources than does the uninformed mass; rather, their advantage arises from their concern that motivated them to take the time and trouble to become better informed. But by the constant exercise of their perceptive and critical faculties the elite groups have acquired a facility in at least the elementary analysis and synthesis of foreign policy issues; they have made a beginning at competence.[27]

The division of "the public" into two unequal groups, the smaller consisting of those who have knowledge, the larger encompassing the unsophisticated, raises a question basic to democratic thought. Is it in any sense "right" to allow the raw, emotional and uninformed opinion of a member of the mass to cancel out the thoughtful and serious judgment of a member of the informed elite? To argue the negative is to condemn democratic policy always to be tied to the level of the lowest stratum of the mass public. But to agree that not all opinions are equally valuable is to open the door to a host of elitist and nonegalitarian doctrines of social and political action. Officials, for example, may well be tempted to deal frankly only with this informed minority and to content themselves with manipulating the masses by the crudest stimuli.[28]

The Professional Attitude.

It is natural—and probably wholesome—for foreign-policy officials to acquire a professional attitude toward their own calling, and to regret the circumstances that force them to bow to the wishes of the uninformed. George F. Kennan put this very forcefully:

> ...I cannot refrain from saying that I firmly believe that we could make much more effective use of the principle of professionalism in the conduct of foreign policy; that we could, if

---

[27] See Hero, *Americans in World Affairs,* Chapter IV: "Personality Sources of World Affairs Behavior."

[28] Almond, *American People and Foreign Policy,* p. 233: "An effective approach to public information on foreign policy questions will therefore be selective and qualitative. It will be directed toward enlarging the attentive public and training the elite cadres." In another connection Almond speaks of the "containment of mass moods." Reprinted by permission.

we wished, develop a corps of professional officers superior to anything that exists or ever has existed in this field; and that, by treating these men with respect and drawing on their insight and experience, we could help ourselves considerably. However, I am quite prepared to recognize that this runs counter to strong prejudices and preconceptions in sections of our public mind, particularly in Congress and the press, and that for this reason we are probably condemned to continue relying almost exclusively on what we might call "diplomacy by dilettantism." [29]

By "professionalism," Mr. Kennan clearly means that attitude among foreign-policy specialists that conceives their mission as a service calling, dedicated to a self-devised code of ethics beyond nonprofessional scrutiny. The analogy that springs readily to mind comes from other professions, such as the law, the clergy, medicine, and university teaching. None of these groups admits the right of the public to interfere with its own professional conduct; each of them formulates its own mission within only the broadest of general limits; each feels it should be responsible ultimately only to itself.

The hope for professionalism undoubtedly has its roots in a sincere concern for the welfare of the United States. It is not surprising that these specialists generally feel that knowing *how* to perform a function qualifies them to determine *whether, when,* and *under what circumstances* it shall be performed. It does little good to contend that the "how" function is a question of administration while the others are matters of policy; many shrewd analyses demonstrate that it is impossible completely to separate policy and administration. The next step, of course, is to argue that policy control by right belongs to the administrators.[30] A cynic might be pardoned for wondering whether or not one of the less explicit reasons for the professional urge is a desire on the part of the officials to escape from the annoyance of popular control.

The Denigration of the Mass.

The argument that official personnel should be free from popular control is often complemented by a denial of the ability of the mass to function in any effective way. The public, it seems, cannot do its job. One critic puts it in this way:

> There are inherent limitations in modern society on the capacity of the public to understand the issues and grasp the

[29] George F. Kennan, *American Diplomacy, 1900–1950* (Chicago: University of Chicago Press, 1951), pp. 93–4. Reprinted by permission.

[30] Dwight Waldo, in *The Administrative State* (New York: The Ronald Press, 1948), has brought together in Chapter VI, entitled "Who Should Rule?", most of the orthodox arguments on the superior right of administrative expertise in the determination of public policy.

significance of the most important problems of public policy. ...The layman ordinarily cannot formulate alternatives so that he can see how and in what way his interests are engaged.[31]

George Kennan echoes this position:

> ...a good deal of our trouble seems to have stemmed from the extent to which the executive has felt itself beholden to short term trends of public opinion in the country and from what we might call the erratic and subjective nature of public reaction to foreign-policy questions.[32]

The picture that is presented by this school of thought is of a mass public that is ordinarily inattentive to public affairs except as it is stirred to emotional excesses by misunderstood events or vote-conscious politicians. The general public is thought to be incapable of judging issues on their merits, of understanding their complexities, or of appreciating the delicacies and subtleties of the problems of dealing with them. The mass public is not to be consulted or followed; it is to be appeased, manipulated, and led by forceful leadership backed by the resources of mass communication and modern public relations.[33]

Granted this *a priori* judgment of the inability of the general public to act in any affirmative way, it is natural for the advocates of government and elite control to argue that the bulk of the populace be kept as far away from foreign policy questions as possible. "Let those who can, make policy; let those who can't, pay their taxes and follow the orders of the competent" seems to be the slogan of the more extreme defenders of this position.[34] They regret the tendency toward popular involvement, and hope for its reversal.

---

[31] Almond, *American People and Foreign Policy,* pp. 5, 8. Reprinted by permission.

[32] *American Diplomacy,* Kennan, p. 93. Reprinted by permission. See also Walter Lippmann, *The Public Philosophy,* for an elaboration of this thesis.

[33] One State Department official once confided his dismay at the American people to the author: "You can't handle these people. If you scare them too much they go crazy; if you don't scare them enough, they go fishing!" See also John D. Millett, *Management in the Public Service* (New York: McGraw-Hill Book Co., Inc., 1954), Chapter 6: "Public Relations."

[34] See, for example, Walter Lippmann's attack on contemporary democracy in *The Public Philosophy* (Boston: Little, Brown and Co., 1955), pp. 24–5: "There is no mystery about why there is such a tendency for popular opinion to be wrong in judging war and peace. Strategic and diplomatic decisions call for a kind of knowledge—not to speak of an experience and a seasoned judgment—which cannot be had by glancing at newspapers, listening to snatches of radio comment, watching politicians perform on television, hearing occasional lectures, and reading a few books. It would not be enough to make a man competent to decide whether to amputate a leg, and it is not enough to qualify him to choose war or peace, to arm or not to arm, to intervene or to withdraw, to fight on or to negotiate." Reprinted by permission.

FOLLOWERSHIP: THE ROLE OF THE GENERAL PUBLIC

What of the public in this equation? Must Americans accept government-elite domination, or is there a sphere in which the citizens have a valid claim to act? In one sense this question answers itself, because democratic values are not going to wither away in the United States. Americans, for a very long time to come, are going to have to live with popular prejudices and mass action on foreign policy. But what we are really interested in is whether the public has an affirmative role in international affairs, or whether it must content itself with being a "crude and passive instrument."

We know that "the public" does not function as a single anthropomorphic entity, but instead brings its influence to bear in several different ways. It operates initially, and perhaps most frequently, by way of interest groups whose impact is usually quite specific in advocating particular points of view. Second, and more broadly, the public functions as the electorate after the political parties have performed their function of polarizing the many possible alternatives into a simple choice (or sometimes, as we have seen, into no real choice at all). Finally, the public affects decisions through the national mood: the broadly-based mental sets that govern the popular threshold of tolerance of government action.

How the Public Functions.

Looking at the way foreign policy issues actually are handled within the American democratic context, we can distinguish three functions of the mass public. These are not only quite defensible in theoretical and ideological terms, but also have proved to be operationally feasible. The three tasks mass opinion performs are: (1) the determination of the outermost limits of permissible government action; (2) the delineation of a general direction in which policy should move and the isolation of certain landmark objectives and techniques; (3) the debate and decision of crucial issues so important in themselves that the governmental elite dare not proceed until public sentiment has come to rest. In the aggregate, they make popular participation a reality. Each requires some further analysis here.

The Public as a Limiting Factor.

Nearly all observers admit, whether regretfully or happily, that popular opinion acts as a limiting factor on government action. Substantively and procedurally, mass opinion fairly clearly indicates how far the government can go in conducting foreign policy. To cite two extreme examples: American opinion would not tolerate a policy aimed at the conquest and annexation of Canada (substantive) nor would it approve immediate American entry into a world federal government (procedural). Policy-makers do their best to have as accurate an idea as possible of the outlines of their area of operating freedom as described by these limits, and accept them more or less as "givens" of the situation in which they have to act. Even the most outspoken critics of American attitudes on foreign affairs grant the effectiveness and the relative permanence of this degree of control.

The Public as Direction-Setter.

But this does not, it would seem, exhaust the positive function of the public. In addition, a picture emerges from the various indices of public-opinion measurement, revealing that the general public sets a general direction in which government must aim its policy. Without concern for detailed situational influences, or operational timetables, the popular image of national destiny, more or less clearly formulated, perforce imposes the broad outlines of policy on the decision-making officials. To put it in other terms, we may say that the general public, by a process admittedly cumbersome, formulates at least the skeleton of the notion of national interest that government must implement.

This process is probably more intimately connected with the general evolution of American society and the consequent changing pattern of socio-political values than it is with any conscious application of rational effort to international issues. It represents the translation into foreign-policy terms of the prevailing complex of wants and needs within the society at any given time. And yet, vague as this may be and difficult to discover, policy-makers (if they are interested in maintaining effective rapport with the public) must seek valiantly to "tune in" on this social wavelength. Failure to do this may well result in their tacit repudiation.

It seems probable, for example, that formulating American national interest as "peace, order, and stability"—as we shall do later—is a reflection of the pattern of social expectations of the bulk of the American people. This is, to put it bluntly, the kind of world most Americans (when they specifically think about it) want to live in; they feel that it is up to their government to get it for them. Nor may policy-makers afford the luxury of consistently disregarding these inchoate and inarticulate urges of the mass in favor of the more insistent clamor of the interest groups. No more dangerous mistake could be made than to assume that popular silence on fundamentals always means apathy; let the government unthinkingly violate an element of the unspoken consensus and the resulting storm might well blow the responsible officials into a keener realization of the importance of public sentiment. The public is always at least a silent partner when directions are being set.

The heading of this paragraph is not to be taken literally; we know already that the public cannot really "make" decisions. Its figurative import, however, illustrates another basic function of mass attitudes. Many occasions arise in the conduct of foreign policy when new conditions, either predicted or unforeseen, create the necessity for new categories of government action. If these are of relatively minor importance, if they fall within the area of pre-existing consensus, no difficulty is presented to the responsible officials. But if they involve far-reaching new consequences or if there is real doubt in Washington about what the reaction of the general public might be, something like a public decision must be made before the government can, or will, act.

Arriving at a mass consensus under such circumstances is preceded by a widespread debate within each of the various publics. It usually begins with discussion within the various elites, with the attentive public being drawn in as the concentric rings of controversy widen. Ultimately, whether in accurate or in over-simplified form, the issue comes to the attention of the mass public. Not until the bulk of the people have become aware of the problem and, on some basis, made up their minds can the top layer of officialdom feel confident in committing themselves to a course of action. The consensus must be clear; until then policy must remain in suspension.[35]

Elitists of one school or another tend to regret the fact that the public retains this key role and take pains to point out the shaky foundations of much individual opinion. But there seems no other convenient way to handle the problem of gaining support for new ventures foreign to the immediate experience and attitudes of the mass. On the other hand, there is some reason at least to hope that recent experience indicates that public attitudes provide not only a necessary base for policy, but also a frequently effective one.

A DEMOCRATIC COMPROMISE

Can these positions of leadership and fellowship on foreign policy be rationalized? Is it possible to resolve the democratic dilemma? Can Americans develop a working partnership between their officials and themselves,

---

[35] From the recent past we may cite a few of the more significant "great debates": on the Truman Doctrine in 1947, on the Marshall Plan in 1948, on the North Atlantic Treaty in 1949, on "troops for Europe" in 1951, on "liberation" in 1952, on entry into the Indochina war in 1954, on "going to the summit" in 1955, on sanctions against Israel in 1957, and on a nuclear test agreement in 1959 and 1960.

in which each set of parties will contribute its best features and in which the shortcomings of each are at least partially neutralized?

It is no function of a textbook to prescribe cures for social ills, and we shall not elaborate any formulation of a perfect situation here. A description of the ideal made some years ago by a State Department official, however, illustrates some of the requirements:

> Our national policies should reflect the will of the people, a will that is not distorted by false propaganda or slogans, that is based upon a solid knowledge of all the facts, that has taken into account all factors and considerations, and has resulted from open and active debate so that all points of view have been thoroughly aired and discussed.[36]

Fortified by the support of a rational and temperate opinion such as this, officials could operate efficiently and to good purpose in making the decisions and executing the policies that come before them.

If Elysium is represented by a sophisticated and alert public opinion cooperating with a democratically-minded, responsible, and dedicated officialdom, it is perfectly clear from our discussion that the United States has not yet arrived there. What can be done to improve effective relationships between public and bureaucracy?

A Two-way Relationship.

One basic consideration seems to have been rather generally overlooked in most of the discussions about the possibility of a democratic foreign policy. Reflection on the leader-follower relationship suggests a conclusion that it is a street that runs two ways. The governmental elite has the responsibility of initiative, but it also has the duty of effective communication with its mass constituency. The executive department must tell the people what, in good conscience, the people ought to know; leaders, however, must also listen to what their followers say. The people have the obligation to use their political power to select the leaders they trust, but then they must trust them; democracy is in no way advanced by a constant ill-tempered squabble between the bureaucracy on the one hand and Congress and the public on the other—for Congress, at least in this particular context, is really a part of the public.

If an effective working relationship is one that calls for the best efforts of both sides, if we are not to accept the somewhat repellent hypothesis (repellent at least to anyone who believes that the democratic idea retains

---

[36] Francis H. Russell, "The Function of Public-Opinion Analysis in the Formulation of Foreign Policy," *Department of State Bulletin* (March 6, 1949). Mr. Russell was at this time Director of the Office of Public Affairs of the Department.

vigor and pertinence in the twentieth century) that only a small minority of co-opted elites can speak for the public, progress toward a more democratic foreign policy will require conscious effort from both the personnel of government and the public, however organized it may be. Some concrete suggestions can be advanced that promise some improvement without smacking of illusory utopianism.

The Duties of Leadership.

Each of the points included in this paragraph could be expanded into a detailed discussion, but we shall content ourselves with a brief listing. Some of the steps that government officials—perhaps in cooperation with the elite publics—might take to improve the democratic character of American foreign policy would include: (1) a real effort to trust the good sense of the general public; (2) an attempt to acquaint the people with the peculiar method of analysis used by government; (3) a policy of formulating issues for public discussion in the actual terms used by government; (4) an end to thinking of the "mass" as something to manipulate for short-run purposes and a new emphasis on long-term education of public opinion; (5) a minimization of the tendency to play politics with foreign policy; (6) a greater reliance on candor, explaining the real reasons for government action to the maximum extent commensurate with real national security. This set of suggestions is by no means thought of as a panacea; it would seem logical to expect, however, that their adoption would represent a not inconsiderable contribution to a healthier public opinion.

The Responsibility of the Public.

But, as we suggested above, this responsibility works both ways. There are few indeed who would argue that the present conduct of Americans constitutes a model worthy of imitation by all democratic peoples. There are a number of things that individual Americans, be they members of the elite, attentive, or mass publics, could themselves do that would contribute to the over-all improvement of public opinion on foreign-policy matters. None of them aim at creating a nation of experts; expertise is best left to the government officials themselves. The aim of this set of suggestions is rather better to fit the general public and its individual component parts for the foreign-policy mission that is rightfully theirs.[37]

Any list like this will probably err either on the side of brevity or of prolixity; the present one probably fits the first description. We may say that the tone of public opinion on foreign policy would be noticeably

---

[37] "Not expertness but improved understanding is the target which the public should be urged to set for itself." Almond, *American People and Foreign Policy*, pp. 6–7. Reprinted by permission.

improved if any substantial portion of the American people would do any or all of the following things: (1) attempt to formulate a clearer picture of the kind of world that Americans would be satisfied with— thus giving the government a more constant pattern of interest within which to work; (2) gain some awareness of the limits on the capability of foreign-policy instruments—thus allowing government to set more realistic objectives for itself; (3) take such strides as are possible toward acquiring patience—thus freeing the government from the maddening insistence on immediate results that plagues officialdom today; (4) make more efficient use of the sources of information presently available— thus making it possible for the government to operate on the basis of a more informed consensus without any necessity to "educate" public opinion all over again each time new decisions are called for. That these four steps would help make American policy more genuinely democratic seems self-evident. Persuading enough people to take them, however, calls for leadership, political and nonpolitical, of the highest order.

Framing
and
Implementing
Decisions

CHAPTER ◄ 3 ►

As we suggested in Chapter 1, foreign policy does not just happen. It is the result of a long, difficult and never-ending process. Although in a democracy such as the United States every effort is made—for reasons both of ideology and of practicality—to take popular opinion into account and to make government action square as much as possible with the wishes of the people, by its very nature the actual formulation and execution of foreign policy is a government monopoly. In considering the specific questions of who makes policy, how it is made, and how it is carried out, we must make our inquiry within the sprawling structure of the government of the United States.

We shall discover early in our discussion that—due to the importance and complexity of the subject—foreign policy machinery has become very elaborate. Many people in government "speak for the United States" in particular contexts and have the power to commit it to action. Responsibility is highly concentrated; authority to act, however, is dispersed throughout the official hierarchy. The sheer size of the policy-making establishment will force us to confine ourselves in this chapter largely to generalization and summary.[1]

Our discussion in this chapter will initially focus on

the organizational arrangements for foreign policy that exist within the national government. The second half of the chapter will consist of some analysis and evaluation of the manner in which this structure functions under the stress of decision and action. In conducting the actual foreign policy of the United States.

THE PRESIDENCY

EXECUTIVE LEADERSHIP

The executive branch of the federal government has a greater responsibility in making foreign policy than have its two fellows, the legislative and judicial branches. Logic, history, law, and necessity unite to confer on the President and his subordinates a peculiarly advantageous position in making the decisions that govern American action. From among the several reasons for such executive pre-eminence, we may select three that are especially pertinent.

In the first place, the executive branch has access to, and possesses a great fund of, information without which action becomes impossible, useless, or dangerous. Second, the executive branch is the medium of official international contact; it deals directly with the other states of the world. This creates the intimate relationship between decision and execution that places the executive in the position of being prepared to act quickly. Third, the executive branch has the expertise, the competent agents, who know the "how" and the "where" of policy and are thus able more effectively to suggest the "what" and the "why."

We must not assume, however, that executive leadership in foreign policy means executive monopoly. There are many important functions of policy-making that are shared with Congress; competition and frequent

---

[1] Detailed studies include: William Yandell Elliott, *et al.*, *United States Foreign Policy, Its Organization and Control* (New York: Columbia University Press, 1952); Brookings Institution, *The Administration of Foreign Affairs and Overseas Operations* (Washington: U. S. Government Printing Office, 1951); H. H. Bundy and J. G. Rogers, *The Organization of the Government for the Conduct of Foreign Affairs,* Task Force Report on Foreign Affairs, Hoover Commission (Washington: U. S. Government Printing Office, 1949); and Arthur Macmahon, *Administration in Foreign Affairs* (University, Ala.: University of Alabama Press, 1953). The most recent study, emphasizing suggestions for improvement in both organization and procedure, is the Brookings Institution's Report to the Senate Foreign Relations Committee, *The Formulation and Administration of United States Foreign Policy* (Washington: U. S. Government Printing Office, 1960).

conflict between legislature and executive are as normal as is cooperation. Whether or not this is desirable cannot be answered in any absolute way, for opinions may legitimately differ; a good case can be made that it is, in any event, inevitable.

If we agree that the executive branch is central to policy formulation, it follows that the President is the heart of the whole policy-making process. It is often said that the presidency is the most powerful political office in the world. Not the least of the factors contributing to this judgment is its great span of control over foreign affairs.

THE PRESIDENT'S ROLE

A combination of factors interact to make the President the key figure in foreign policy-making, although the exact nature of his position in any context is often difficult to define in detail. We know that his unique status as both head of state and head of government contributes largely to the possibilities of power and influence inherent in his office.[2]

The Powers of the President.

We may say that the President's powers come from four separate sources, of unequal importance but each critical in appropriate situations. (1) The Constitution grants the President a limited number of foreign-affairs powers, including such important ones as command over the nation's armed forces and the power to negotiate and (with the consent of two-thirds of the Senate) to ratify treaties. (2) Congress has made literally dozens of grants of foreign policy power to the President; some of the most significant policy moves of recent years have been implemented by the grant of discretionary powers to the President by act of Congress.[3] (3) The Presidency has also what can safely be called "inherent powers," at least in the field of foreign affairs; in the leading case on the subject, the United States Supreme Court admitted that the President has "a degree of discretion and freedom from statutory restriction which would not be admissible were domestic affairs alone involved."[4] (4) The President's unique role as

---

[2] See Edward S. Corwin, *The Presidency: Office and Powers,* 3d ed. (New York: New York University Press, 1948); more introspective studies include Clinton Rossiter, *The American Presidency* (New York: Harcourt, Brace and Co., 1956), and Jack Bell, *The Splendid Misery* (Garden City: Doubleday & Co., 1960).

[3] The entire foreign-aid program of the United States has been handled in this way. See, for example, Title I of the Foreign Assistance Act of 1948, Public Law 472, 80th Congress.

[4] *United States v. Curtiss-Wright Export Company,* 299 U.S. 304 (1936). For a later case limiting the inherent powers of the President, see *Youngstown Sheet and Tube Co. v. Sawyer,* 343 U.S. 579 (1952).

national political leader gives him a special opportunity to grasp and hold the collective imagination of the American people.

This last point merits further elaboration. The President's power to act affirmatively has increased in direct relation to the augmentation of the public's image of the presidential office. If he maintains effective rapport with public attitudes, he has an almost ready-made consensus in support of whatever decisions he reaches. It is difficult for opposition to crystallize against a decision that a reasonably popular President has made and is actively defending before the public. No other executive official enjoys this advantage.[5]

The Functions of the President.

The most important foreign-policy function of the President is that of assuming ultimate responsibility for all executive decision and action. As the only official voice of the United States in foreign relations, only he can make final policy decisions. He may and usually does delegate much of his operational authority to subordinates, but these latter officials can operate only because of their receipt of fiduciary presidential power and subject to his final (perhaps only implicit) ratification. The President cannot escape this responsibility; even in the case of policies virtually forced on him by Congress, his responsibility for execution and implementation cannot be shifted.

Within this general context, the President may make his role as large as his competence and inclinations dictate. He usually finds it congenial to confine himself to establishing a general line of action, formulating objectives, developing verbalizations of the national interest, and suggesting future emphases. These general charges are transmitted to subordinates for elaboration; from this point forward the President's task is largely one of administrative supervision.

Of course, he may make decisions at any level of detail he wishes. Ordinarily, administrative requirements confine him to the broad areas listed above, but he may intervene in the decisional process at any point. Various presidents have exercised this function to different degrees, but it is a power open to any of them.

---

[5] An instructive example of the impact of presidential leadership was furnished by the controversy between Congress and the President during February, 1957, over the prospect of United Nations sanctions against Israel. Although congressional leadership was virtually unanimous against sanctions, the President's position, strengthened by a radio-television speech on February 21, remained substantially unchanged. The final resolution of the issue—Israel's agreement to withdraw from Egyptian territory—was on the terms stipulated by the executive rather than those suggested by Congress. The day-by-day story of the issue is covered in *The New York Times* for February and the first few days of March, 1957. This same factor was obviously at work during the "U-2" crisis of May, 1960.

Because of the President's status as legal head of all executive foreign-affairs activity and his unique policy-making function, an elaborate staff organization has been gathered about the chief executive. Its purpose is to assist the President in performing his mission of initiating, coordinating, and bearing responsibility for action. Most of its members are grouped in an administrative holding company, the Executive Office of the President.[6]

The National Security Council.

The National Security Council, although part of the Executive Office of the President, is a unique body, both in its composition and its function. Created by law in 1947, it is the high strategy board for American security policy—called by one author "the American Politburo." [7] It consists of the President as chairman, the Vice-President, the Secretary of State, the Secretary of Defense, the Director of the Office of Civil and Defense Mobilization, and—in practice—such other high officials as the President may invite. Under President Eisenhower, the Secretary of the Treasury, the Chairman of the Joint Chiefs of Staff, the Director of the Central Intelligence Agency, and certain others regularly attended.

The NSC has a permanent staff headed by an executive secretary, who —despite his anonymity and his lack of command authority—is often thought of as one of the half-dozen most influential men in the government in the field of foreign policy. He has direct access to the President and assists him in planning the agenda of the weekly meetings of the Council.

The Council's function, in practice, is double. In the first place, it makes recommendations to the President on all matters that bear on the security of the United States and that require Presidential decision. Second, it brings together—at the highest level—the most important officials concerned with foreign policy and provides a setting for full and frank discussion among them. In these matters the NSC is of critical importance; evidence is accumulating that its already major significance will become even greater in the future as successive Presidents learn more about its usefulness and its limitations.[8]

---

[6] E. H. Hobbs, *Behind the President* (Washington: Public Affairs Press, 1954), discusses the executive staff in detail.

[7] John Fischer, *Master Plan USA* (New York: Harper & Bros., 1951), Chapter I.

[8] The most complete study of the NSC is Burton M. Sapin, "The Organization and Procedures of the National Security Council Mechanism," Appendix B in the Brookings Institution's study, *The Formulation and Administration of United States Foreign Policy*. Dr. Sapin's study makes use of the earlier writings on the subject.

The President's Personal Staff.

The White House Office contains the President's personal staff. It consists of a relatively small number of administrative and personal assistants, aides, and secretaries. It performs such duties as are set for each of the members by the President himself and, especially under President Eisenhower, has taken over a significant number of more or less routine executive functions. Included in this group, but of special importance, is the Special Assistant to the President, whose mission is entirely in foreign affairs and who, under Presidents Truman and Eisenhower, gained a relatively large degree of freedom in making policy decisions on his own.

Other Special Advisory Bodies.

The Executive Office of the President includes (in addition to the two foregoing bodies) the Bureau of the Budget, the Council of Economic Advisers, the Office of Civil and Defense Mobilization, the National Aeronautics and Space Council, and the President's Advisory Committee on Government Organization. Each of these exists for the purpose of advising the President in the special area of its interest, and collectively include the major problems facing the chief executive. Not included in the Executive Office, but as close to the President as if it were, is his top military advisory body, the Joint Chiefs of Staff.

The Central Intelligence Agency.

The Central Intelligence Agency, established by the National Security Act of 1947, can be most usefully conceived of as an intelligence clearing house, directly subordinate to the National Security Council. The United States has a number of other agencies engaged in gathering information upon which to base policy decisions; the CIA seeks to coordinate all of them, and to serve as a central agency for the distribution of intelligence data, as a correlator of intelligence emanating from other sources, and as a synthesizer of "intelligence estimates." It performs a number of intelligence activities of its own, but (according to law) only those that are most efficiently performed centrally. Its detailed operations are one of the most security-cloaked activities of the government.[9]

---

[9] See Harry Howe Ransom, *Central Intelligence and National Security* (Cambridge: Harvard University Press, 1958). For a general discussion of the importance of strategic intelligence in the formulation of foreign policy, see Sherman Kent, *Strategic Intelligence for American World Policy* (Princeton: Princeton University Press, 1949), and Roger Hilsman, *Strategic Intelligence and National Decisions* (Glencoe, Ill.: The Free Press, 1956).

THE EXECUTIVE ESTABLISHMENT

THE STATE DEPARTMENT

The Department of State, headed by the Secretary of State, constitutes the major single source of foreign policy decisions in the entire governmental structure. Under the pressures of international problems that have forced American policy mechanisms to proliferate, the Department has been obliged to renounce its once-exclusive control over foreign policy, but yet retains a central position. Even when interdepartmental consultation and coordination is necessary, it is most often the Department of State that serves as the principal medium of cooperative action.

The Role of the Secretary of State.

The Secretary himself is perhaps the most important decision-maker. As the President's major adviser on foreign policy, his exact role is largely dependent on his personality and that of his chief, on the problems that arise during his tenure, and on the specific issues that fall to him to decide.

The Secretary's relationship to the President is an elastic one. The law of 1789 that created the office did not give the Secretary any detailed responsibilities in foreign affairs, but directed him instead to assist the President in any way that the latter directed. This legal directive empowers the President to establish almost any kind of relationship he wishes.

He may give the Secretary his head and pointedly refrain from having any policy of his own; although fairly frequent during the nineteenth century, such a relationship would be suicidal today. He may go to the other extreme and become "his own Secretary of State." This practice also may be effective for a short time (President Roosevelt, for example, often simply ignored Secretary Hull during much of World War II), but in the long run the State Department is too important to be left out entirely. In practice, some form of teamwork based on an agreed division of labor seems to be the most effective form of rapport; the blueprint of presidential functions we outlined above would leave the Secretary's role both well-defined and critical. Within the broad limits thus laid down by the chief executive the Secretary of State could move with some freedom in making decisions of his own.[10]

Today perhaps the most important policy-making role carried on by

---

10 A recent evaluation of the changing role of the Secretary of State is Don K. Price, ed., *The Secretary of State* (Englewood Cliffs: Prentice-Hall, Inc., 1960). These readings served as background for the Eighteenth American Assembly.

the Secretary is that of coordination. While the Department's functions and staff have increased, its relative share in foreign policy has diminished. The military establishment, special agencies of all sorts, and Congress itself all play much larger parts than before 1941. As the key individual advising the President, however, and as the "senior" member of all varieties of coordinating bodies (such as the National Security Council), the Secretary is in a strategic position to exert major influence in determining decisions, whether or not he makes them himself.

The Organization of the Department.

Although it is impossible to keep abreast of the Department of State's frequent (one is tempted to say, constant) reorganizations, the chart below is fairly recent and reveals its basic structure. It is doubtful whether any future reorganization will make significant modifications.

The Department, as the chart indicates, is organized at five levels. The highest level is represented by the Office of the Secretary, containing the department head, the Undersecretary, the Undersecretary for Political Affairs, and the Executive Secretariat. The next group is at the Deputy Undersecretary level, and includes deputy undersecretaries for political affairs and administration, as well as the Director of the International Cooperation Administration. The third level, the habitat of the Assistant Secretaries or their equivalent, includes four special-purpose advisers to the Secretary; the fourth—also with Assistant Secretaries at their heads—comprises the "functional" bureaus with specialized operational responsibilities. The fifth group from the top is made up of the "geographic bureaus," in each of which is centered operational responsibility for American policy in a sector of the world. The Assistant Secretaries who head up the geographic bureaus are obviously key people in the flow of policy decisions. The sixth level is made up of the field missions sent out by the Department.

The Geographic Bureaus.

Because of their central role in policy-making, the geographic bureaus are uniquely significant. There are, as the chart indicates, six such subdivisions. Each, in turn, is broken down into "offices," which are divided into "desks." The "desk officer" is usually known as "Officer in Charge of ——— Affairs," and is the specific point of contact the Department maintains with the country of his interest.

The Assistant Secretary in charge of a geographic bureau has a host of duties which vary literally with each turn of events. They may, however, be grouped under four main headings: (1) to communicate in all directions—upwards to the Undersecretary and the Secretary on all matters needing their attention, downward to the subsections of his bureau and the

ORGANIZATION OF THE DEPARTMENT OF STATE

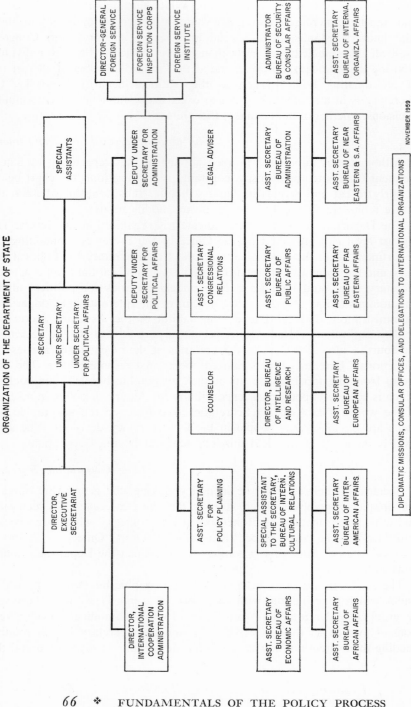

NOVEMBER 1959

"desk officers" within them, and laterally to his fellow Assistant Secretaries and others who may be interested parties; (2) make decisions on questions that fall within his scope, on which he is empowered to decide, and on which he has appropriate general directives for guidance; (3) coordinate the offices within his bureau so that in his particular geographic area United States policy is both consistent within itself and also coordinated with American efforts in other parts of the world; (4) make recommendations on policy to the higher levels of the Department.

The geographic breakdown among the bureaus reflects the changing international environment. Illustrative of the manner in which change affects organization is the recent (1959) creation of the Bureau of African Affairs; elevation of that region to Assistant Secretary status indicates the increasing importance of Africa to the United States. Also revealing is the classification of relations with international organizations as equally important as Europe, the Far East, and Latin America.[11]

We should not be deceived by the illusory clarity with which functions are divided in the Department. Organization charts can do no more than suggest relationships; human beings persist in developing their own channels of communication and operation. The neat distinction between "functional" and "geographic" bureaus—with the former being in principle "non-operational" and the latter charged with exclusive responsibility for operations—does not obtain in practice. Nor does every observer agree that they should remain mutually insulated.[12]

The Problem of Personnel.

The Department of State is vexed by a constant personnel problem. The United States Foreign Service—a career service of professionals—was created by the Rogers Act of 1924 for the purpose of representing the United States abroad. Always small in number and high in quality, the career foreign service performed very creditably until World War II.[13] Under the pressure developed by the vast increase in functions, however, the career officers were joined by large numbers of non-career civil service personnel. A serious cleavage developed within the department between the elite group of FSO's and the much larger group of civilians. The latter,

---

[11] We should note also that reorganization in response to new needs also occurs in the functional bureaus. For example, the Bureau of International Cultural Relations was also created in 1959.

[12] See the discussion in the Brookings Institution, *The Formulation and Administration of United States Foreign Policy*, pp. 57–61.

[13] A valuable sketch of the history and the problems of the American foreign service is contained in J. Rives Childs, *American Foreign Service* (New York: Henry Holt & Co., 1948); an eloquent defense of the career service is made by former Ambassador Hugh Gibson, in *The Road to Foreign Policy* (Garden City: Doubleday, Doran, 1944), Chapters III, IV.

moreover, tended to monopolize lower- and middle-level policy-making positions in the Department, with the predictable effect of further intensifying disagreement.

The obvious solution had long been known. In a permanent large-scale operation such as that in which the Department was engaged, there was no rational reason to continue a bifurcated personnel system. It made no sense to deny the United States the policy-making wisdom accumulated by long overseas service by the career personnel; it was equally nonsensical to require that policy be made by men who usually had no personal experience in the areas for which they were responsible. Amalgamation of the two services would solve both these operating difficulties at once.

Between 1948 and 1953 several attempts had been made to put some such plan into operation, but without success. The Foreign Service wished to keep its exclusive status; many of the civil-service group had no interest in overseas service. It was not until 1954, under the direction of Secretary Dulles, that amalgamation was accomplished. It came about as the result of recommendations by the Secretary's Public Committee on Personnel, known as the "Wriston Committee" after its chairman, Dr. Henry Merritt Wriston, the former president of Brown University.[14]

"Integration"—a word that became common currency in the Department for several years—involved the classification of virtually all the nonclerical posts of the Department, both overseas and home, as "dual": that is, capable of being filled either by career FSO's or civil service personnel. A directive from the Secretary then ordered the gradual integration of the two services, not to be accomplished by the creation of an entirely new hierachy, but by the absorption of the great bulk of the civil service policy personnel into the Foreign Service by "lateral entry." Civil service employees not wishing to become liable for overseas service were to be separated without prejudice. The upshot was to be the creation of a vastly augmented Foreign Service.

There were many administrative difficulties involved in lateral entry, and not a small amount of hard feelings; by and large, however, there was general satisfaction that the Foreign Service under the new scheme was destined to retain a sizeable amount of its old esprit and at the same time to benefit from the large infusion of new blood.[15]

---

14 The Committee's report, *Toward a Stronger Foreign Service* (Washington: U. S. Government Printing Office, 1954), was submitted to the Secretary on May 18, 1954. See also Dr. Wriston's *Diplomacy in a Democracy* (New York: Harper & Bros., 1956).

15 Zara S. Steiner, *The State Department and the Foreign Service; the Wriston Report—Four years Later* (Princeton: Princeton University, Center of International Studies, 1958).

The Wriston Report also dealt with another difficulty of the old Foreign Service. A combination of a peculiar philosophy of selection and restricted personnel budgets had made the FSO's an over-homogenous group. The Committee argued that recruitment policies should be amended to attract candidates from a broader social, economic, educational, and geographical base. Its assumption, though never made explicit, was that the Service should be "democratized." [16]

Beginning in 1955 the recruitment recommendations were put into effect. An entirely new examination procedure was instituted, stressing general education and innate intelligence rather than specialized knowledge. Emphasis was placed on obtaining young men and women whose training encompassed such diverse fields as agriculture, accounting, and law. The first round of appointments under the new system revealed greater diversity than any under the old, and there was some ground for hoping that the Committee's ideal of a "more representative" Foreign Service would be, to some extent, realized.

The Departmental Point of View.

As the result of its own history, traditions, and place in the governmental hierarchy, the Department of State has developed a distinct point of view toward the problems with which it is called upon to deal. Although this attitude has elements of real strength, such as its emphasis on professionalism, its concern with the concrete and the practical, and its insistence on the service of its notion of the national interest, it also has a number of shortcomings that affect its role in modern American society and government.

Some of the deficiencies in the departmental point of view are not peculiar to it, but grow instead out of its status as a major government department. Many of the familiar bureaucratic vices are present in the State Department, some of them in excessive amounts. The Department often seems obsessed with procedure and routine; many of its members are hypersensitive to considerations of career, prestige, and power.

More peculiar to the State Department itself is the sharp sense of cleavage between departmental personnel (domestic or foreign) and the American public at large. This may be explained to some extent by the unique relationship the Department has with the American people; after all, the argument sometimes runs, the Department's clientele is not the American public at all. "State" deals with foreign governments rather than with

---

[16] *Toward a Stronger Foreign Service*, pp. 39–44.

American citizens. In whatever way one may defend or explain it, however, the fact remains that a sense of nonidentification with the American mass public has led to two clear consequences of great importance. On the part of the Department, it has helped foster the growth of elitism: a self-generated impression that only the Department knows fully the real problems confronting the United States and what should be done about them. Large segments of the public have reciprocated by developing disdain, contempt, and distrust for departmental personnel. On both sides this is a disquieting outcome.

Operationally, the Department's point of view stresses caution, a faith in precedents (substantive and procedural) proved by time, and a preference for "making policy on the cables." Despite the lessons learned during the period since 1945 and many reorganizations of structure, and also despite uncounted high-level directives stressing the need for prevision and an adequate operational plan, the Department retains much of its pre-1941 disinclination to plan in advance. The obvious misuse of the Policy Planning Staff as a high-strategy board instead of as a group freed from day-by-day operations underscores this tendency. The usual desk officer refuses to deal with "hypothetical questions" and seems to extract much satisfaction out of making the "brush fire" approach to policy a normal operating procedure. This tends to make the Department swing between routinized administration during periods of calm and frenzied extemporization during crises, neither of which seems to the casual observer as the ideal way to conduct American foreign policy.

The Military

One of the significant changes in American foreign-policy making since 1945 has been the systematic inclusion of the military point of view. This, as we shall see later, is not part of the traditional image of how American foreign policy is made; military and foreign affairs were usually thought to be two separate worlds, to be kept apart at all costs. Today, however, the picture is completely reversed; most of the controversy over the point deals with whether or not the views of the armed forces receive too much consideration rather than too little.[17]

---

[17] The general subject of military influence on foreign policy is discussed critically in Burton M. Sapin and Richard C. Snyder, *The Role of the Military in American Foreign Policy* (Garden City: Doubleday, 1954). See also Samuel P. Huntington, *The Soldier and the State* (Cambridge: Belknap Press of Harvard University Press, 1957), William R. Kintner, *et al., Forging a New Sword* (New York: Harper & Bros., 1958), and Walter Millis, *Arms and the State* (New York: Twentieth Century Fund, 1959).

What sort of military considerations are appropriate to American policy decisions, and why has it become so important since World War II that they be included? The answer lies in certain basic relationships between ends and means in any state's foreign policy.

The ends of policy—the objectives of the state—must be served by such means as are available and appropriate. Military power is one of these possible means open—at least to some limited extent—to every state. Any policy-maker, therefore, should take account of his state's ability to apply military pressure and, conversely, of its ability to withstand any probable similar pressure applied by other states. As long as international politics goes on within the state system as we know it today, such judgments will continue to be necessary.

American policy, therefore, must in part be based on two kinds of military judgments: the calculation of the affirmative employment of military measures and the provision of defensive measures against hostile (or potentially hostile) measures taken by others.

One final statement seems in point. Means-ends analysis is a very tricky subject. In practice means often look disconcertingly like ends, and vice versa. Particularly so is this true in American military policy. Weapons supremacy, such as in strategic bombardment aircraft or in thermonuclear bombs, in theory is significant primarily as a means to some other policy objective, such as superiority over a potential enemy; as actually carried out, however, weapons leadership over all comers (or, as sometimes among air-power enthusiasts, over any combination of comers) becomes a policy end of the first priority. This point has led to more controversy over the military contribution to American foreign policy than perhaps any other.[18]

The Pentagon and Foreign Affairs.

The Department of Defense and the three service departments under its direction share directly in the foreign policy process at all levels. The Secretary of Defense is, of course, a member of the Cabinet where—especially

---

[18] From the many statements made by Alexander P. De Seversky, one of the most outspoken advocates of supreme air power for the United States, one of the most carefully worked-out is *Air Power: Key to Survival* (New York: Simon and Schuster, 1950); see, in a different vein, the arguments of Henry A. Kissinger in *Nuclear Weapons and Foreign Policy* (New York: Harper & Bros., 1957). The various facets of the problem are summarized in Gordon B. Turner and Richard D. Challener, eds., *National Security in the Nuclear Age* (New York: Frederick A. Praeger, 1960).

during the Eisenhower administration—his views have been solicited by the President. He is also a permanent member of the National Security Council where his special concerns are even more directly in point.

The Secretary of Defense and the three service secretaries each have special foreign-policy assistance in the form of an assistant secretary or other high-ranking civilian official who is charged with direct responsibility for making the department's contribution to all interagency or joint decisions. Since so many operational decisions are taken on a multi-departmental basis via the National Security Council or lower-level joint bodies, it can be seen that great care is taken to have the "military point of view" represented in almost every sort of decision-making body of more than routine importance.

The Joint Chiefs of Staff.

The preceding paragraphs considered the Secretary of Defense as the spokesman for the military, even though most of the top leadership of the Defense Department is civilian. It is via the Joint Chiefs of Staff that the viewpoint of the uniformed services is expressed.

The Joint Chiefs are the principal military advisers to the President, the National Security Council, and the Secretary of Defense. Their approach is professional and technical; they personify the "means" role of the military. Their advice in theory does not concern itself with any aspect of policy other than its military feasibility and/or its military consequences. Much of the dispute over the role of the Joint Chiefs (such as the heated battle that developed as the aftermath of the Indochina crisis of 1954) stems from the widely-shared suspicion that they often slip out of their purely instrumental role into an advocacy of substantive policy.[19] To the extent that this charge can be substantiated, there is some basis for arguing that civilian supremacy is being undermined and that the always unclear distinction between substantive policy ends and purely military means is also being eroded.

OTHER EXECUTIVE AGENCIES

Foreign-policy making power is widely shared in the executive branch.[20] To make a catalogue of the exact part played by each of the

---

[19] Admiral Arthur B. Radford, the then Chairman of the Joint Chiefs, presented his notion of the role of the group in an interview in *United States News and World Report* (February 25, 1955), entitled "We Give Military Advice Only."

[20] A famous chart appearing in the Hoover Commission's Task Force Report on Foreign Affairs indicated the "Organization Units of the Executive Branch Participating in the Conduct of U. S. Foreign Affairs." What was striking was the

hundred-odd agencies that participate in one way or another would exhaust both compiler and reader. All we can do is to sketch some of the broader outlines and to indicate one or two bodies of special importance.

The Treasury Department.

The Treasury Department constitutes the third in the foreign-policy "big three" Cabinet departments. In part, this stems from the central proposition that foreign affairs consumes the great bulk of the annual budget of the United States; with so much money involved, the Cabinet's fiscal expert naturally becomes a key figure. The requirements of a budget in balance, or at least in near-balance, in time of peace often could have great controlling and directing effect on American policy.[21]

But the Treasury Department has operating responsibilities as well; a good share of American policy deals with financial and monetary matters and the Treasury makes basic decisions in this area. There is in the department an Office of International Finance concerned entirely with this general problem; perhaps its major concern is with American membership in the International Monetary Fund, the International Finance Corporation and the International Bank for Reconstruction and Development. Tariff administration, direct international loans, and other aspects of economic foreign policy are other areas in which Treasury recommendations carry great weight. Its importance is underscored by President Eisenhower's decision to include the Secretary as a regular member of the National Security Council.

Other Cabinet Departments.

All the other Cabinet departments share in policy-making, athough in unequal amounts. All of their administrative heads participate in Cabinet meetings and thus have access to the President when international issues are being discussed. All of them, in addition, enter the foreign policy field to some extent in performing their statutory duties.

Perhaps the most significant of this group are the Departments of Commerce and Agriculture, for reasons that are largely self-evident. Commerce is responsible for the whole matter of foreign trade; Agricul-

---

small number—less than twenty—of executive agencies that did not in some way share in foreign policy; even some of these were open to debate. Among the few that the Task Force felt did not qualify were the National Archives, the Office of the Housing Expediter, the Indian Claims Commission, the National Labor Relations Board, the National Capitol Park and Planning Commission, the Railroad Retirement Board, and the Commission on Fine Arts. Also in this group was the Selective Service System; many a recent draftee might argue that this agency plays a great—if indirect—part in American foreign policy!

[21] Under President Eisenhower, Treasury Secretaries Humphrey and Anderson were generally supposed to be peculiarly influential in holding down government expenditures on military and international programs.

ture enters such fields as the international movement of food products and the procurement of agricultural experts for American technical assistance programs. The rest of the Cabinet departments—Labor, Post Office, Justice, Interior, and Health-Education-Welfare—have roles that, while equally as direct as those of Agriculture and Commerce, are not as extensive. Labor, for example, functions through the International Labor Organization; the Post Office represents the United States in the Universal Postal Union; the Justice Department controls immigration and resident aliens; Interior administers American overseas possessions.

Non-Cabinet Agencies.

One of the administrative problems of American government—a perennial concern of all attempts at reorganization—is the large number of administrative bodies that lie outside the Cabinet-department structure and are responsible only to the President. This condition applies in foreign affairs as well as in any other area; some of the most significant policy decisions are made and implemented by non-Cabinet bodies.

Perhaps the most important of these, now that foreign aid has once again been taken directly into the Department of State, is the Atomic Energy Commission. It is responsible for dealing with all aspects, domestic and international, of the development of atomic energy—a subject most Americans would admit is of considerable importance today.

Other independent agencies with foreign-affairs functions include the Maritime Commission, the Civil Aeronautics Board, the Federal Communications Commission, the Export-Import Bank, and the United States Tariff Commission. Each of these to some extent makes policy in its own area and influences decisions—often by representation on interdepartmental bodies—on questions in which it is interested.

COORDINATION IN THE EXECUTIVE BRANCH

The Decentralization of Policy.

It has become clear in the foregoing discussion that policy-making is highly decentralized in the executive branch. The power to commit the United States to action has been widely diffused. Foreign policy today is so multiformed, with so many aspects of human action having relevance to the objectives of the United States, that it is difficult to conceive how such decentralization could have been avoided. It is true that total responsibility for all executive action lies on the President, but it would not be humanly possible, or even desirable, to force him to actually make all the decisions for which he is responsible. He must, in some way, delegate authority so as to reduce his own task to manageable proportions.

But administrative theory and the needs of foreign policy agree that delegating decision-making power is not in itself a sufficient answer. Guidance and control must be exercised by the delegating authority; a general policy line must be stipulated and mechanisms developed to guarantee that the action taken by subordinates agrees with the over-all orientation. We might suggest that one index of the efficiency and effectiveness of American foreign policy is the extent to which detailed decisions made by operating personnel are consistent with the broader policy directives issued by higher-ranking officials.

The Need for Coordination.

Since policy-making is so extensively decentralized, some apparatus for coordination becomes necessary. This task has dimensions both horizontal and vertical. Horizontally, there must be agreement at any level among the various agencies making policy so that their cumulative effort is exerted to a common end; this basic harmony must be both intra-departmental and interdepartmental. Vertically, units lower in the hierarchy must coordinate with those higher up (even though in a different department). Only if this be done successfully can excessive confusion, contradiction, and frustration be avoided and something like a single American foreign policy be forged.

The Forms of Coordination.

In the attempt to devise a sufficiently high working level of coordination, four sorts of devices have been developed and are used individually or in conjunction.

(1) The first, dealing mainly with vertical coordination, involves the President himself and the White House Office. The prestige and position of the chief executive make it possible for him to demand—and usually to receive—a considerable amount of effective harmony in making and executing policy. The National Security Council is the archtype of this kind of coordinating body; the Bureau of the Budget, in a different way, performs the same task.[22]

(2) A second coordinating device consists of assigning coordinating authority over a particular policy area to a single department. Such agency is directed to provide general guidance to all other interested agencies and to see to it that their various efforts mesh into a coherent whole. The Department of State has been most frequently given this sort of directive. The Treasury has something of a similar role with regard to a number of multi-agency financial programs.

(3) Most commonly, coordination is attempted by means of the interdepartmental (or interagency) committee. On these bodies—of which there

---

[22] Hobbs, *Behind the President, op. cit.,* Chapter 2, "Bureau of the Budget."

are dozens—all "interested" units are represented and are supposed to achieve a happy harmony, both in reaching decisions and in seeing to their execution. Although hallowed by much use, and despite the very considerable success that some of them have enjoyed, the interagency committee remains a technique of only limited utility. Their numbers have multiplied to the point where membership on any of them is apt to be conferred on such low-ranking members of the department that none may authoritatively speak for their own agencies; so widespread has representation become that it has become quite difficult to arrive at any consensus on most of the committees. If the appropriate committee cannot do its job of providing coordination, this leaves the department that has the inside track on the policy area in question to enjoy virtually a clear field.

(4) Finally, a "super-coordinator" was created in 1955 when the Operations Coordinating Board came into existence by executive order. This body consists of the Undersecretary of State as chairman, the Deputy Secretary of Defense, the Director of CIA, the Director of the United States Information Agency, a representative of the President, and a representative of any other agency the President selects. Its efforts were clouded in controversy, and President Kennedy decided upon its dissolution in February, 1961.

This high-level body is supposed, as one wag put it, to "coordinate the coordinators." Its coordinating function is obviously top-level, and is designed to oversee the implementation of the National Security Council's operational plans, primarily those involving interagency planning and action. Its history is too short to furnish the basis for any general estimate of its effectiveness.

It appears from this analysis that coordination in foreign policy, despite the obvious need, has not yet been achieved. This judgment may be confirmed by any reasonably sophisticated newspaper reader; the evidence is unmistakable that there are dozens of foreign policies in the executive branch rather than a single American policy. Yet the problem is being attacked; this same sophisticated reader cannot fail also to be impressed by the extent to which a unity of purpose and effort actually permeates much of what the United States does. That it is not done better is no reason to discount how well it is being done.

CONGRESS AND FOREIGN POLICY

Although it has become commonplace to point out that the part played by Congress in foreign policy has increased, both relatively and absolutely, during the decade since the end of World War II, we must nevertheless admit that even this augmented role remains secondary to that of the executive. From the very beginning of the Republic, Congress has chafed at the logic that has made the presidency the chief inspiration for foreign policy; the history of legislative-executive relations over international issues is one of recurrent dispute. In recent years the legislative branch has made some progress in defining its own place in the foreign-policy process; today Congress has a role that is of major importance.[23]

But this is not to say that the national legislature has achieved equality in policy-making, or that it is desirable that it should. As we suggested in our discussion of the executive's function in foreign affairs, law and logic agree that the initiative and the lion's share of the decisions naturally reside "at the other end of the [Pennsylvania] avenue." This would lead us to suppose that Congress's role in the process is essentially a reacting one; we would expect its function to be that of modifying, amplifying, and expediting decisions already taken by the President or his assistants. Recognizing the operation of checks and balances in the American system, we would further assume that Congress would be peculiarly prone to exercise some form of negative control on executive decisions, either by refusing to accept them or by changing their substance, direction, or timing. These indeed seem to represent the nature and extent of Congressional power over foreign policy.[24]

We should make one further qualification before briefly examining the ways in which Congress affects the course of policy-making. Although Congressional *power* itself has definite and measurable limits, the same cannot be said for Congressional *influence*. Being generally more sensitive to the tides of electoral politics than is the President (this is especially true of the House, whose members must face the voters every two years), Congress is prone to reflect shifts of public opinion that its members detect (or think they detect). This gives Congressional opinion great weight in the executive branch whenever the responsible bureaucrats believe that the legislators are convinced that they are expressing a popular consensus. This matter of Congressional influence, so difficult to measure, often goes farther to explain the legislative impact on foreign policy than does any detailed consideration of the legal powers of Congress.

CONGRESSIONAL FUNCTIONS

How does Congress enter into the policy-making process? One very interesting answer was made in a study generally favorable to the legislature's aspirations to a major role, and listed six specific functions:

---

[23] The leading study is Robert Dahl, *Congress and Foreign Policy* (New York: Harcourt, Brace and Co., 1950); see also Ernest S. Griffith, *Congress, Its Contemporary Role,* 3d ed. (New York: New York University Press, 1960).
[24] See especially Daniel Cheever and H. Field Haviland, *American Foreign Policy and the Separation of Powers* (Cambridge: Harvard University Press, 1952).

1. It has a responsibility to identify and inquire into problems that may call for legislative action.
2. It shares with the Executive the function of framing broad national objectives.
3. It can help to estimate the relative merits of alternative approaches to dealing with various problems.
4. It may give attention, on a selective basis, to questions of detail related to broader issues.
5. It has the exclusive responsibility for enacting authorization and appropriation legislation.
6. It can help, as part of its investigatory function, to evaluate the performance of the Executive, again on a selective basis.[25]

Without seeming captious, we may point out that these six functions, although phrased generally in favorable terms and aimed at portraying Congress's role at its largest, are all essentially reactive in nature. Congress may question, evaluate, investigate, and often must authorize; it plays an indispensible role in assaying the climate of politics in which decisions must be taken. But important as this role is, even the most sympathetic students of Congress cannot elevate the legislative function to as critical a place as is occupied by the executive.

In carrying out its function, Congress has a significant array of powers. Most of these partake of the general legislative role, and are of special relevance to foreign affairs only because of the expanded place international relations now occupies in the concerns of Congressmen.

The Senate: Treaties and Appointments.

Of the two houses, the Senate enjoys superior power and prestige in foreign affairs.[26] Part of this primacy arises from the popular notion of the Senate as the "upper house"; part from the greater age, average length of service, and freedom of discussion that characterize Senators. But the bulk of Senatorial leadership comes from two specific constitutional provisions: the power to approve treaties and the power to confirm appointments.

The Constitution gives the President the power to make treaties with the "advice and consent" of two-thirds of the Senate. As students well know, the "advice" part of this provision is a dead letter except as the President chooses to consult with individual Senators during the negotiation phase of a treaty. "Consent" involves a two-thirds vote of the Senate

---

[25] Brookings Institution, *The Formulation and Administration of United States Foreign Policy,* p. 24.

[26] However, see Holbert N. Carroll, *The House of Representatives and Foreign Affairs* (Pittsburgh: University of Pittsburgh Press, 1958), for a sympathetic study of the lower house.

in favor of a treaty, the effect of which is to open the document to ratification of the President.

The Senate thus enjoys, as one author puts it, a "treaty veto"; [27] it may simply refuse to approve the treaty. Such action voids the entire enterprise. The Senate, however, may not change the treaty in any way. It may suggest amendments which, if made, would make the document acceptable; what happens to these proposed amendments, however, depends on the President. He may choose to renegotiate the treaty and seek to have the amendments written into the agreement; on the other hand, he may find them unacceptable and simply drop the whole affair. The treaty veto has been a favorite subject for discussion by critics of the American constitutional system ever since the defeat of the Treaty of Versailles in 1919; [28] the historical record indicates, however, that only a small minority of all treaties have been defeated. Nor should we overlook the fact that executive agreements are free from any necessary Congressional control, although some Congressional opinion feels that a legislative veto should be placed on these agreements as well.

Appointments of ambassadors, ministers, and consuls—the entire foreign service—must receive Senatorial approval. Occasionally, as in the struggles over the confirmation of Mr. Charles Bohlen as Ambassador to the Soviet Union in 1953 and Mrs. Claire Booth Luce as Ambassador to Brazil in 1959, this power has great significance for foreign policy. It has been generally felt in the Senate, however, that the President should have a free hand in selecting his foreign-policy personnel and it is seldom that confirmation of a diplomatic appointment becomes an important issue.

Legislation.

It is in the general function of legislation that the whole Congress comes squarely to grips with foreign policy. There are only a few areas of foreign policy in which the President can move freely without the necessity of any legislation; usually some implementing law must be passed before policies can be effectively carried out. This means that most major programs must be submitted to Congress in the form of bills. Here is where the legislature may exercise its amending or negating authority, and it is rare for an executive suggestion to pass through the Congressional mill without being reshaped in some way.

So important is the potential impact of Congress on any project that

---

[27] D. F. Fleming, *The Treaty Veto of the American Senate* (New York: Putnam, 1930).

[28] For a textbook summary of the arguments against Senate approval of treaties, see Robert K. Carr, Donald H. Morrison, Marver H. Bernstein, and Richard C. Snyder, *American Democracy in Theory and Practice* (New York: Rinehart, 1951), pp. 997–999.

the executive tends to consult with Congressional leaders in advance so as to tailor his requests to what Congress will accept; sometimes—as in the case of the Marshall plan—Congress will run away and develop its own program anyway.[29] To the extent that policy declarations come to be formalized into specific programs of action—and this is a great extent indeed today—Congress has great power to alter the executive designs; at the very least, such a constant possibility requires that the President and his advisers always take Congressional opinion into account.

The legislative history of the so-called "Eisenhower doctrine"—the administration's Middle East proposals of early 1957—illustrates this relationship. Before submitting the proposals in his special message of January 5, the President consulted with leaders of both houses; the Congressmen, on their part, were irritated that details had been leaked to the press before they had been informed. Once in the legislative mill, amendments were offered in profusion, and the administration was hard put to keep the proposals in anything like their original form. Their final passage revealed that, although the general framework had remained intact, a number of changes had been made, the effect of which was to place Congressional controls over executive action. A typical example of the way Congress functions in this regard was the requirement that the President should inform Congress of his intention to spend any of the funds involved in the act at least 15 days before obligating them.[30]

Appropriations.

What is true of legislation applies even more sharply to one special manifestation of legislative power: the appropriation of funds. American foreign policy demands money in great amounts, and no funds at all are forthcoming from the United States Treasury except as a result of Congressional appropriation. Congress tends to be more generous in authorizing appropriations than in actually making them; the appropriations committees of Congress (particularly in the House) are more wary of granting funds than are the substantive committees.

Investigations.

We must also recognize the importance of investigations by Congressional committees to foreign policy. This is a case of influence rather than power; the net effect of committee investigations is frequently to create powerful currents of public opinion for or against particular policy emphases. On occasion these have had great impact on the executive branch

29 John C. Campbell, *The United States in World Affairs, 1947–48* (New York: Harper & Bros., 1948), p. 503.
30 *New York Times* (March 6, 1957).

by affecting mass opinion and forcing department heads to conform to the wishes of the particular committee. Obviously the extent to which an investigation succeeds in this regard depends on public reaction; what direction is taken usually depends on the orientation of the committee's efforts.

Resolutions.

Also in the category of functions of influence is the device of the Congressional resolution, either by one house or—more effectively—by both. A resolution, expressing the "sense of the house(s)" but without legal effect, serves notice to all concerned that the Congressional mind has been made up on the particular point. Such resolutions are most effective (1) when they represent accurately the state of public opinion on the questions and (2) when they are passed prior to the making of a firm commitment by the executive. Examples of important resolutions include the so-called "Vandenburg" resolution in 1949 that was in effect an advance acceptance of the North Atlantic Treaty and the several resolutions of the House between 1953 and 1956 opposing Communist China's admission to the United Nations.

CONGRESSIONAL CHARACTERISTICS ON FOREIGN POLICY

Recognizing that generalizations about 537 legislators are hazardous, we may nevertheless suggest a few common characteristics revealed by Congress as it copes with the issues of foreign policy. Perhaps the safest and broadest statement we can make is that the legislative branch is quite well equipped to perform its checking and amending function and does so with reasonable success; when it turns from this, however, and attempts to make policy on its own, the outcome is usually unfortunate.

Negativism.

One reason for this limitation on the effectiveness of Congress is that body's fundamentally negative orientation to foreign policy. Because of the nature of the problem and its place in the scheme of government, Congress is best fitted for saying "no." It usually cannot take the initiative efficiently; its function is commonly confined to reacting to proposals emanating from the executive offices. Only in special and infrequent cases is it possible for Congress to play a positive role. The frequent pleas for Congress "to seize the initiative" in foreign policy have uniformly failed to mark out any clear procedure whereby the legislature could make its will effective in opposition to the President.

Framing and Implementing Decisions ❖ *81*

A second characteristic grows out of the first. Under the checks and balances system of American government, competition and conflict between legislature and executive is to be expected; this is the reason why Congress is made to share in so many executive powers. On purely domestic policy, Congress may and often does take the initiative, and the resulting relationship with the executive is more nearly an equal one. But on foreign policy, certain advantages inhere in the President, and Congress's exercise of its checking role gives rise to much controversy. Many Congressional moves in foreign policy defy rational explanation on any other ground than its simple determination to differ with the executive and to make disagreement effective.

It should be emphasized in this connection, however, that both the amount and the kinds of legislative-executive conflict in foreign policy are in a state of constant evolution. Today there is much more partnership than open disagreement between the branches on fundamentals; Congress (or, more frequently, its committees) cooperates with the executive both in identifying objectives and in exploring basic approaches.[31] In exact relationship to the extent to which agreement has increased on fundamentals, the tendency of Congress to quarrel about details has grown stronger. This situation is made more acute in an election year when, as was the case throughout the second Eisenhower administration, Congress is under the control of the opposition party.

Political Orientation.

We have already alluded to the all-too-obvious fact that Congress in general, and the House of Representatives in particular, tends to be more responsive than the President to short-range voter (or interest-group) pressure. Repeatedly the executive has recommended programs that, although open to question on their merits, at least were devised in all seriousness as an attempt to advance the prevailing idea of national interest. When the Congress seized upon them and attacked the problem of their implementation, far too often for comfort the dominant concern of many members was not whether the programs would be advantageous to the nation. Rather their preoccupation was with the effect of such policy im-

---

[31] An interesting example of this relationship is furnished by the series of 15 studies on particular problem areas of United States policy undertaken during 1958 and 1959 by private and university research organizations under contract for the Senate Foreign Relations Committee. These reports in the aggregate constituted a major mobilization of the nation's intellectual resources on foreign policy issues, and evidence multiplied that the recommendations they contained were being taken seriously by the executive.

plementation on their individual political fortunes. Foreign-aid and military appropriations have been especially obvious political footballs in this respect; an articulate and powerful bloc in Congress has consistently felt that voters in the grip of a cold war would never object to large military expenditures but that they would resent "giveaway" of which foreigners were the beneficiaries.

But although a major indictment can be made of Congress on the grounds of a short-sighted truckling to vociferous and self-serving elements of public opinion, it would not do for us blithely to dismiss the political approach of Congress as being entirely without justification. We must not forget that there is always an "ivory-tower" tendency in any government bureaucracy, and particularly in a foreign-affairs bureaucracy; it is all too easy to dismiss mass opinion as beneath serious consideration. To the extent that the top echelon of decision-makers becomes divorced from the tides of popular attitudes, it is thoroughly salutary for Congress continually to remind them that there is an American public and that its wishes must be taken into account.

Deliberateness and Lack of Information.

Two final characteristics of Congressional activity in foreign policy remain to be noted. Congress tends to operate slowly, and it almost always acts upon incomplete and inaccurate information. The first stems from its function as a deliberative body; it would be violative of the Congressional responsibility in American democracy for it to be expected to reach its decisions with great speed and in total silence. Yet, even after granting this, we may still contend that much of Congress's slowness is unnecessary; it seems evident that it could work more rapidly without sacrificing anything essential to the legislative process.

The poverty of Congressional information is a much more serious problem. In the past ten or fifteen years, Congress has made great efforts, and with some success, to improve the amount and the reliability of the information on which it must base its decisions. Yet the question is still unsolved, and may even prove insoluble. How can Congress play its part in shaping American policy if it simply does not have available enough data to make the right kind of decisions? The information that is necessary is often by definition a secret; to open the executive files to Congressional investigation would make extremely delicate matters subject to heated, partisan, and very public debate. Alongside this we must place the lack of mutual trust and confidence between Congress and the executive department.

If Congress must depend on the executive for all its information, there is a real danger that the data fed it will be—in the delicate bureaucratic word—"selective": that is, deliberately chosen and slanted so as to influence Congress in the direction the bureaucracy desires. The most the legislative branch has been able to do up to this point is to staff its specialized committees on foreign affairs and related subjects with experts of its own, and to try to develop such liaison with the executive as is possible and effective.

LEGISLATIVE-EXECUTIVE COOPERATION

There is little purpose in our reiterating the need for legislativeexecutive cooperation in foreign affairs. Everyone realizes that the United States cannot afford to have its President and its Congress always at swords points over foreign policy. There is likewise no advantage in wishing more or less plaintively (as many scholars have done) [32] that the United States had a parliamentary system such as that of Great Britain, in which the problem would simply never come up. The United States has separation of powers and checks and balances, and there is no possibility of their abandonment in the foreseeable future. Within their context Americans must devise a workable mechanism of foreign policy.[33]

Consultation.

The most frequently relied-upon device for achieving some such sustainable level of agreement is that of formal or informal consultation. The President frequently calls meetings of Congressional leaders (not necessarily limited to foreign-policy experts) and briefs them, sometimes submitting to questioning. Less often, similar sessions are held by department heads. Informally, legislative-executive contacts are extensive and frequently quite productive. There is no doubt that consultation has been at least a qualified success in reducing the chasm between Congress and the executive; how effective it is in any particular case depends on both the political climate and the personalities involved.

Liaison.

Recently executive departments have begun to add to their staffs specialists on Congressional liaison. The State Department has an Assistant Secretary for Congressional Relations whose mission is, as one department official put it privately, "to keep Congress happy." President Eisenhower

---

[32] See, for example, the argument advanced in James MacGregor Burns, *Congress on Trial* (New York: Harper & Bros., 1949).

[33] This problem, and some recommended solutions, are dealt with in Cheever and Haviland, *American Foreign Policy and the Separation of Powers.*

added a liaison specialist (General Wilton B. Persons) to his personal staff; other agencies have done the same. In this way the executive, needing the support of Congress, has sought to establish a favorable relationship. We may perhaps regret that no reciprocal effort may be remarked on the part of Congress.

Commissions.

Less widespread than the first two, and by nature perhaps destined to remain so, are the mixed legislative-executive investigating commissions. Part of their membership is appointed by the President, the remainder consists of members of Congress; the Congressional representation is usually drawn from both parties in both houses. Such a body, once it deals with an issue and makes a recommendation, represents a fusion of opinion that cannot help but be reflected in some way in subsequent policy. Outstanding examples of recent years are the two Hoover Commissions on administrative reorganization and the Randall Commission on foreign economic policy.[34]

The Permanence of the Need.

But none of these devices has solved the problem; legislative-executive relationships on foreign affairs are always uncertain and, as we know, often hostile. It is probable that the issue can never be thoroughly resolved as long as the United States retains its peculiar political system. No one would deny, however, that the importance of maintaining enough cooperation to ensure the adoption and implementation of adequate policies is great enough to justify continuing effort, however much we may despair of final perfection.

THE EXECUTION OF AMERICAN POLICY

While any over-sharp distinction between the formulation and the execution of American foreign policy would give rise to serious misunderstanding (since each impinges upon and affects the other), it is nevertheless true that there is specialization of function between those who make decisions and those who execute them. Generally, this division follows a home office-field service breakdown. As might be expected, most of American foreign policy is executed beyond the boundaries of the United States.

---

[34] The Randall Commission's report: Commission on Foreign Economic Policy, *Report to the President and Congress, January 23, 1954* (Washington: U. S. Government Printing Office, 1954).

DIPLOMACY

The State Department is the instrument of American diplomacy, operating through the mediums of the United States Foreign Service and the overseas missions. Because of the multiplication of overseas programs and the discovery and exploitation of new channels of power, the diplomatic specialists today must share responsibility with other executive agencies. Yet it is true that the diplomatic instrument of policy, personified by the resident American ambassador, still occupies the paramount position in executing American foreign policy.

Multiagency Representation.

The non-State Department representatives abroad can be grouped in three categories: military, foreign-aid, and informational. Between 1947 and 1954 each of the three types of representation grew to the point where in many states it rivalled the American diplomatic mission in prestige and in importance.

Military representation occurred through the various service attaches in the embassies, through the military-aid missions, and through the training groups. Foreign aid representation was at its height under the Economic Cooperation Administration where the various "country chiefs" of ECA had more money to dole out and consequently were in a position to maneuver the resident American ambassador off the stage and into the wings. A few of them, it might be noted, did exactly that. The Mutual Security Administration, since it simplified the administration of American aid, somewhat improved this situation. Informational activities were never the threat to regular diplomats that the first two types were, largely because State carried on so many itself.

In line with the general doctrine now governing the execution of American policy that State is the single agency *primarily* responsible for foreign *policy,* and that coordination is to be brought about under State Department *leadership,* the moves taken in the past five or six years have all been aimed at strengthening the position of the senior foreign-affairs agency. The theory behind the attack on multiagency representation abroad can be summed up in President Eisenhower's language when he sent the foreign affairs reorganizations plans to Congress in 1953: "[It shall be the duty of] each Chief of Diplomatic Mission in each foreign country [to] provide effective coordination of, and foreign policy direction with respect to, all United States Government activities in the country." [35] Unassailable as

---

[35] *Congressional Record* (June, 1953), p. 5849.

this administrative principle is in the abstract, our knowledge of the tenacity of the bureaucratic urge to survive will make it a reasonably safe assumption that the full implementation of the directive will require a formidable amount of time.

The Ambassador.

As the quotation above indicates, the United States Ambassador is responsible for the orderly and coordinated execution of all U. S. policy in the country to which he is assigned. Because of the sheer size of the operation, American ambassadors are to a surprising extent primarily administrators. They operate their own embassies (in some states no small task in itself) and supervise the activities of a congeries of other American operating groups. Administrative talent is an only-recently recognized requirement for a successful ambassador.

The "traditional" diplomatic functions of representation, communication, and negotiation are still performed, but in terms more appropriate to contemporary technological conditions. Communication with the home office is nearly instantaneous, negotiation tends to be back-seat driven from Washington, and representation is much more ceremonial than heretofore. The changed circumstances under which an ambassador operates have given rise to the frequent accusation that the ambassador has become a mere messenger boy for the Secretary of State. This judgment is overdrawn; there remains a great reservoir of power in the ambassadorial role.[36]

One factor underscoring the new significance of the ambassador's function is the evolving concept of what constitutes representation. In the eighteenth century, "Citizen" Genet, French Ambassador to the United States was declared to be *persona non grata* because of his attempt to "go over the heads of the government" and appeal directly to the American people for support of his government's policy. This era has passed. Today the American ambassador to any country is—as much as he is anything else—a specialist in public relations. He is expected to make himself available to the public as the visible embodiment of the United States, and to do whatever he can to create an image favorable to the United States. Difficult to specify, this new form of representation is an important part of the ambassador's task.

The Overseas Mission.

The American diplomatic mission to a foreign country varies in size according to the volume of business and the intrinsic importance of the relationship. The organizational structure is likewise flexible. Generally

---

[36] For a memoir developing the role of the modern ambassador, see (ex-Ambassador) Charles M. Thayer, *Diplomat* (New York: Harper & Bros., 1959).

speaking, the ambassador, as chief of mission, has as his principal assistant a counselor of embassy. The latter usually succeeds to leadership (as chargé d'affaires) when his chief is absent. Below the counselor the mission splits into operating sections according to the nature of the work load; political and economic sections are universal, while consular and administrative sections are increasingly common. Outside the normal hierarchy of the mission, but full parts of it, are the various special attaches. In addition to the familiar military, naval, and air attaches, commercial, agricultural, legal, labor, cultural and several other types of attaches exist. The attaches have a peculiar status. Although they are full-fledged members of the ambassador's staff, they remain employees of other agencies than the State Department. They are nominated by the Departments of Commerce, Agriculture, Army, Navy, Air Force, Justice, and so on; they remain administratively under their home department's control.

MILITARY FOREIGN POLICY

One index of the growing maturity of American foreign policy has been the gradual although yet incomplete meshing of military policy with foreign affairs. There is little disagreement today that foreign policy has a military dimension and that armed might is both an end in itself and a means to the accomplishment of other American objectives. A good deal of what the United States does in international affairs today is oriented to military calculations. The execution of what we call military foreign policy therefore becomes a separate problem.[37]

Generally speaking, operational responsibility for the military aspects of foreign policy—with the principal exception being the negotiation of treaties of alliance, agreements on bases, and so on—rests with the Department of Defense, acting usually through the Secretary or his principal assistant for these matters, the Assistant Secretary for International Security Affairs. The three service departments have roughly similar arrangements in their respective hierarchies for the accomplishment of the same general purposes.

War.

Perhaps the most obvious, but also the most basic, military operation with a foreign-policy implication is the conduct of war. We shall remark in a later chapter on the time-honored American tendency to regard war as an interruption in the orderly course of international affairs, and to con-

---

[37] See Burton M. Sapin and Richard C. Snyder, *The Role of the Military in American Foreign Policy* (Garden City: Doubleday, 1954).

ceive the spheres of diplomacy and warfare as occupying different universes. This idea has virtually disappeared among policy-making officials; there is also some reason to believe that its acceptance is declining among the general public.

There is no more important foreign-policy mission than the prosecution of a war. This is the supreme test of a nation's ability to achieve its objectives; to exert the enormous effort required for modern warfare without having a concrete political objective in mind is today a waste that not even the United States can afford. The Korean conflict—despite General MacArthur's valedictory to the effect that "in war there is no substitute for victory"—is an example of a military struggle that was kept always at the service of a reasonably clear set of political objectives. No more effort was expended than was necessary to reach those goals; once they were attained, it was immaterial to American interest whether or not the military test was settled conclusively.

Today, with hydrogen bombs, intercontinental ballistic missiles, biological warfare, and the other horrors of modern total war, there is considerable doubt about the long-range utility of large-scale warfare as an effective instrument of national policy. The time may come when a military establishment will lose all utility in executing policy and become instead merely an example of national conspicuous consumption; mankind, however, is not yet at that point. As long as total war remains a possibility, the United States must be prepared if necessary to implement at least the bare minimum of its objectives—continued survival—by military means.

Occupation of Defeated States.

Following World War II another example of the execution of foreign policy by military means was provided by the American occupation of the defeated enemy nations.[38] Occupation had a political purpose; to occupy Germany and Japan merely for the sake of revenge would have been childish. The military outcome of the war required physical occupation of the terrain as the only way the Allies could make any beginning on their ambitious plans for postwar reconstruction. The Allied plan called for the reasonably early replacement of military by civilian control over the Axis; the cold war, however, intervened and the whole project was drastically remodeled. It is generally agreed, however, that the military branches performed their share of the mission creditably.

---

[38] For Germany, see E. H. Litchfield *et al., Governing Postwar Germany* (Ithaca: Cornell University Press, 1953); for Japan, see Russell Brines, *MacArthur's Japan* (Philadelphia: J. B. Lippincott Co., 1948), and Robert B. Textor, *Failure in Japan* (New York: John Day, 1951). See also Hajo Holborn, *American Military Government* (Washington: Infantry Journal Press, 1947).

In the contemporary period, one of the major preoccupations of the military establishment of the United States is the administration of the American military aid program. Since the cold war became acute, the military buildup of America's allies has been a major order of business. Starting with the Mutual Defense Assistance Program of 1949 and including the various Mutual Security Acts, furnishing military assistance to growing numbers of foreign states has been a major element of American policy. The execution of these programs has been entrusted to the Department of Defense.

Control over military aid, under the terms of the various statutes, is vested in the Secretary of Defense and exercised by the Assistant Secretary for International Security Affairs. To supervise the general assistance program by coordinating requests from the various states, there was created the Joint American Military Advisory Group (JAMAG) that works in close harmony with the Assistant Secretary. In each foreign state receiving American military aid there is a Military Assistance Advisory Group (MAAG) that cooperates with its host government in developing recommendations for aid. Both JAMAG and MAAG are composed of representatives of the three uniformed services.

Another form of international military assistance, often coupled with the supply of materiel, is a training mission. The Department of Defense and the service departments have sent a sizeable number of training missions to states in Europe, the Middle East, the Far East, and Latin America. Obviously the military establishment of a nonindustrialized nation that receives large shipments of American equipment—Turkey, for example—needs considerable instruction in its employment. Even if formal assistance in "military end-items" is not involved, it is in the interest of the United States to see to it that its allies have as efficient a military force as possible.[39]

Alliances.

One final form of policy executed by the military is the fulfillment of continuing American responsibilities in the various mutual-security pacts to which the United States is a party: NATO, SEATO, ANZUS, OAS, CENTO, and a number of bilateral agreements. Since the primary military mission today is deterrence, it would seem that this elaborate alliance structure plays a major part in discouraging Communist attack.

Of all the alliances, NATO is both the most elaborate and the neatest

---

[39] See Arthur Macmahon, *Administration in Foreign Affairs* (University, Ala.: University of Alabama Press, 1953), pp. 132–137.

example; military planning and military action in the others are not nearly so advanced. NATO is, of course, under civilian control at the highest level, the North Atlantic Council. From there on, however, it is a military matter, organized into a Supreme Headquarters, various subordinate commands, and elaborate logistical arrangements. Throughout all of these American military personnel may be found; the post of SACEUR—Supreme Allied Commander, Europe—has never been filled except by an American.[40] In 1956, however, efforts at discovering a political dimension to NATO were intensified, and the appointment of Paul-Henri Spaak of Belgium as Secretary-General seemed to presage a new era for the alliance.

FOREIGN AID

One of the most dramatic departures in American policy after World War II was the popular acceptance of responsibility to extend large-scale assistance of all sorts—economic, military, and technical—to friendly foreign states. With the details of that program we shall be concerned later; at the moment we are interested only in the organizational pattern for administering this aid as it has developed since 1947.

The State Department and Foreign Aid.

From the very beginning of the aid program there was serious disagreement about the most efficient and expeditious method of its administration and now, after more than a decade, the issue is in no way settled. The central problem has always been the relationship of the Department of State to the over-all aid program. Obviously, if the Department is the principal agency for policy recommendation, and if foreign assistance is to be at or near the center of American policy, there are good reasons for the State Department to exercise some manner of control over the whole operation. On the other hand, the serious diminution of the Department's prestige with Congress and the public, and the formidable arguments against loading the Department down with extensive operating responsibilities, raised doubts about the value of giving it direct responsibility for the program. Various solutions have been attempted, involving virtually every possible form of relationship between the Department and the aid program, but no clear verdict has yet been rendered.[41]

---

[40] Between 1951 and 1960, the several commanders were Generals Eisenhower, Ridgeway, Gruenther, and Norstad.

[41] The various alternatives are discussed in the 1951 Brookings report, *The Administration of Foreign Affairs,* pp. 90–101. See also two later Brookings studies: *Administrative Aspects of U. S. Foreign Assistance Programs* (Washington: U. S. Government Printing Office, 1957), and *The Formulation and Administration of United States Foreign Policy,* pp. 65–71.

The ECA: Vague Equality.

The first organization to administer foreign aid was the Economic Co-operation Administration, set up in 1948. The ECA was a separate agency headed by an Administrator (Mr. Paul Hoffman) of Cabinet status. Congress deliberately made the ECA independent of control by the State Department and, although it is generally agreed that the ECA was well operated and that it accomplished its mission with an enviable degree of success, its exact status vis-à-vis the Secretary of State was never defined.

The MSA: Complete Independence.

By 1951, when ECA was dissolved, the foreign-aid program had acquired a new dimension. ECA had been concerned only with economic assistance to Europe; the Korean conflict had launched large-scale military assistance programs in Europe, Latin America, and the Far East. Some new administrative device seemed appropriate.

The result was the creation of the Mutual Security Administration in 1951. The general tenor of expert opinion during 1950 and 1951 favored the consolidation of all foreign assistance in one agency that would be responsible for all action in the field—that is, it would be entirely independent of the Department of State. This provision Congress wrote into the new law; the MSA was in no sense to be subordinate to the Secretary of State, and had jurisdiction over all phases of assistance except technical cooperation, which retained a semi-autonomous status in the Department of State as the Technical Cooperation Administration (TCA).

Although Mr. Averell Harriman, the Mutual Security Administrator, actually did create mechanisms for coordination with the State Department, the Department of Defense, the Treasury, and other interested agencies, the significant fact is that he did this by preference, not by law. The clear intent of Congress at this time was to debar the Department of State from any direct part in foreign aid administration; the law even deprived the Department of any control over the military aid program, which was divided between MSA and the Department of Defense.

The FOA: Policy Direction.

President Eisenhower, by executive reorganization directive, abolished MSA in 1953 and created in its place the Foreign Operations Administration. This new body's sphere of authority was extended to include not only all the duties of MSA but also those of the Technical Cooperation Administration. FOA brought all aid operations except the supply of military end-items (vested in the Secretary of Defense) under a single operating control; the Administrator (Mr. Harold Stassen) was charged with coordinating the military aid program with the others.

Although FOA had complete action responsibility, it was not in as independent a position as had been MSA. The Secretary of State, according to the reorganization plan, had direct policy control over the FOA Administrator; even "subordinate levels of the Department of State" were given authority to furnish direction to FOA. FOA's organizational structure paralleled the geographic bureaus of the Department, and it was clearly expected that at all levels coordination between FOA and State would take the form of policy direction to the former by the latter. The net effect of the shift from MSA to FOA was a gain in policy authority by the State Department that more than balanced its loss of operating responsibilities.

The ICA: Back to the Department.

The most recent organizational shift took place in 1955 when FOA was abolished and replaced by the International Cooperation Administration, which—so much for a "non-program" State Department—was brought within the administrative structure of the Department.[42] ICA performs all the functions of FOA; the difference is purely hierarchical. ICA is a division of the Department; the Administrator is a subordinate of the Secretary of State and is completely under his authority. The new arrangement had one great advantage, in that it finally gave the Secretary the power directly to coordinate non-military foreign aid activities with other aspects of foreign policy.

INTERNATIONAL INFORMATION

Another policy area of great significance is "international information," a delicate euphemism for the somewhat more blunt words "propaganda" and "public relations." Like military foreign policy and foreign aid, the development of large-scale information programs was an event of the postwar period. Propaganda for political purposes is a pursuit in which Americans do not yet thoroughly feel at home (although why this should be so is somewhat difficult to understand; in the United States advertising is a fine art), and the record compiled by the various information programs is not breath-taking.[43]

---

[42] See the statement by Secretary of State Dulles (January 23, 1956), *Department of State Bulletin* (February 6, 1956).

[43] For an interesting statement of the problems of informational activities and their administration, see the report by Howland H. Sargeant, "Information and Cultural Representation Overseas," in Vincent Barnett, ed., *The Representation of the United States Abroad* (New York: The American Assembly, Columbia University, 1956), pp. 67–119. This volume is the report of the findings of the Ninth American Assembly, on the subject of American representation overseas, held May 3–6, 1956.

The pressures of the cold war forced the United States to develop an elaborate, if somewhat helter-skelter, propaganda program. The State Department was central to the process from the beginning, with its own activities being conducted by the International Information Administration. The two major areas of the Department's work in this field prior to 1953 were the Voice of America, a global network of radio stations beaming propaganda at hostile and neutral nations, and the United States Information Service, under whose auspices hundreds of American "information centers" were set up throughout the world. These last provided outlets for American publications of all sorts, and gave thousands of foreigners their first insights into what the United States was really like.

But the Department of State was not alone in the field. It is a characteristic of American government today that every operating agency in the executive branch is acutely sensitive to the need for good public relations, and nearly every one of the many agencies with responsibilities in foreign policy began to handle the propaganda aspects of its own mission. The State Department's principal competitor in this field was the series of foreign-aid agencies, notably ECA and MSA. Rapid turnover in personnel, persistent attacks from all directions by a variety of opponents, discontinuity in policy, and a failure in its own public relations made the International Information Administration a somewhat less than popular agency. Its critics pointed it out as a glaring example of the inadvisability of conferring program responsibility on the Department of State.

Psychological Warfare.

Further complicating American information policy was the concept, born apparently some time in the early stages of the Korean war, of "psychological warfare." This phrase implied something new in foreign policy, aimed at undercutting the strength of opposing regimes by destroying the bonds of loyalty between the people and their governments. It was argued that, if the United States were to use the resources of modern techniques of persuasion in a coordinated attack on the stability of opposition governments, it might be possible to solve all the problems of the cold war at one blow, with great economy in manpower, resources, and money. It was indeed an attractive prospect.

Interagency committees of various sorts were created to develop an over-all strategy of psychological warfare and to coordinate its execution by the appropriate departments. Between 1951 and 1953 a great deal of effort was expended with little perceptible change in the pattern of propaganda being put forth by the United States overseas.[44] President Eisenhower, shortly after taking office, instituted an entirely new survey of the entire field of psychological warfare by the so-called Jackson Committee. The committee's report, made in mid-1953, exploded the entire concept of psychological warfare as a specialized technique, susceptible of manipulation by specialists in persuasion, and capable of ending the cold war speedily and economically. The committee contended that all policy had its psychological aspects, that they could not be separated from other facets, and that everyone engaged in policy implementation was in effect carrying on psychological warfare.

The United States Information Agency.

The United States Information Agency (USIA) was created in 1953 by executive reorganization directive. This body was the counterpart in its field of the Foreign Operations Administration; it took over all information programs from whatever agencies had been carrying them on. In particular, it absorbed the International Information Administration and the Voice of America. Again like the FOA, its operational monopoly was not matched by equal freedom in policy. Instead it was ordered to follow the policy direction of the Secretary of State; the material it distributed (whether by broadcast or by printing) was subject to censorship by the Department.

Even more illustrative of the status of the Agency was the relation of its overseas representatives, known as Public Affairs Officers (following the delicate nomenclature of the Division of Public Affairs [relations] in the Department of State). These propaganda chiefs were to be part of the American diplomatic mission in the country to which they were assigned and, although under the general administrative direction of the Director of USIA, were also under the operational control of the resident American chief of mission. Both in Washington and in the field, the propaganda arm of American policy is now under the day-by-day control of the State Department.[45] This development is part of the broader plan of clarifying the status of the Department as chief policy-maker for the entire government.

---

[44] An interesting view of the early stages of the American "sykewar" effort is presented by Edward W. Barrett, former Assistant Secretary of State for Public Affairs, in his valedictory, *Truth Is Our Weapon* (New York: Funk and Wagnalls Co., 1953).

[45] Sargeant, in Barnett, *Representation,* thoroughly approves of this status for public affairs officers (p. 79).

The
Heritage
of
the
Past

CHAPTER ◄ *4* ►

For many Americans, "foreign policy" as something about which the citizen should concern himself dates from some point in the period between 1940 and 1946. Prior to the crisis that brought about World War II, American disinterest in international affairs was endemic; popular ignorance and unconcern about international relations was a dominant cultural trait in the United States between 1920 and 1939. Foreigners have often remarked about the non-historical outlook of American culture and its alleged effect of eliminating a sense of continuity between the present and the past. In no area is it more true that Americans are unaware of the record of their own past than it is in foreign affairs.

But American foreign policy has a history, and a long and complicated one at that. Present day Americans are in large measure the heirs of the record, good and bad, made by their ancestors. That the statesmen of an earlier day are today often without honor or even any particular recognition by their descendants in no way minimizes the importance of their work.

This chapter will attempt to characterize the course

of American foreign policy up to the end of World War II. We shall not attempt to detail, or even to summarize, the continuous story in a strict chronological sense; excellent studies of superb scholarship and considerable literary value have already performed this task for us.[1] Our task will rather be to extract from the whole of the history of American foreign policy those particular elements, whether broad trends or uniquely important events, that have special pertinence to contemporary American foreign relations.

THE FORMATIVE CENTURY

The nineteenth century—by which we mean the period of somewhat more than a hundred years between the Treaty of Paris (1783) and the Open Door notes of 1899 and 1900—may be called the "formative era" in American foreign policy. During this time two sorts of things happened that have had consequences far beyond their historical setting. First, a number of relatively fixed policy lines aimed at particular objectives were developed by the American government and came to acquire the semi-sacrosanct character of fixed commitments. The United States is still struggling with the more unfortunate consequences of some of these undertakings. Second, and related to the first by the normal processes of democratic government, a rather clear popular tradition of American participation in foreign affairs became an article of faith with the bulk of the politically articulate and active population.

Continental Expansion: "Manifest Destiny"

Certainly the most obvious foreign-policy trend of the nineteenth century was the process of continental expansion that began almost as soon as the new United States set itself up in business as an independent sovereignty. We should recapitulate briefly the series of moves that brought the United States to its present continental boundaries within a short fifty-year period of active expansion.

---

[1] The leading diplomatic histories are those by Samuel Flagg Bemis, *A Diplomatic History of the United States,* 3rd ed. (New York: Henry Holt, Inc., 1950); Thomas A. Bailey, *Diplomatic History of the American People,* 3rd ed. (New York: Crowell, Inc., 1949); Julius W. Pratt, *A History of United States Foreign Policy* (Englewood Cliffs: Prentice-Hall, Inc., 1955); and Dexter Perkins, *The Evolution of American Foreign Policy* (New York: Oxford University Press, 1948). Among the many shorter collections of documents, one of the most useful is Ruhl J. Bartlett, *The Record of American Diplomacy,* 3rd ed. (New York: Alfred A. Knopf, Inc., 1953).

The first great acquisition—and the largest single one—was the purchase of the Louisiana Territory from France in 1803.

In 1800 Napoleon of France had persuaded Spain to cede him the Louisiana Territory. The United States became uneasy at the thought of having powerful France as its neighbor to the west instead of weak Spain, as well as at the possibility of being forever barred from access to the port of New Orleans. Napoleon, on his part, soon lost his interest in Louisiana in the light of his pressing need for funds to continue his European conquests. Jefferson, supported by Britain, offered to purchase Louisiana for $15,000,000. Napoleon agreed, and in one stroke of a pen the United States had more than doubled its area.

The Floridas.

The next step took the United States southward. "The Floridas," comprising today all of the state of Florida and the Gulf coast of Alabama and Mississippi, were under Spanish sovereignty at the time of the Louisiana purchase. For fifteen years after 1803, American expansionism clashed with weak Spanish rule. Finally, in 1818 Secretary of State John Quincy Adams presented Spain with a virtual ultimatum. The Bourbons surrendered; in 1819 Spain ceded the United States all her lands east of the Mississippi in return for some token concessions from the United States.

Texas.

In 1845 the independent republic of Texas was annexed to the United States by joint resolution of Congress. Texas had seceded from Mexico in 1836 after a successful war of independence and had thereupon sought admission to the Union. Political pressures, generated largely by the slavery issue, made it impossible to secure the necessary two-thirds majority in the Senate in favor of a treaty of annexation. A bare majority could be scraped up in both houses for a joint resolution, and this somewhat questionable device was used to approve the annexation of the first independent sovereignty to become one of the United States.[2]

Oregon.

The Oregon territory, including most of the northwestern corner of the United States and part of present-day British Columbia, had long been claimed by both Great Britain and the United States. President James

---

[2] Pratt, *A History of United States Foreign Policy,* pp. 231–233, discusses the political maneuvering. Hawaii also was an independent republic at the time of its annexation by the United States.

K. Polk took a strong diplomatic line with the British in 1845; by mid-1846 a relatively favorable compromise was reached. The boundary, running along the 49th parallel, added a rich and large territory to the existing United States.

The Mexican Cession.

By the terms of the Treaty of Guadalupe Hidalgo that terminated the war with Mexico, in 1848 the United States gained another enormous bloc of territory. The area ceded included present-day California, Nevada, Utah, and parts of Arizona, Colorado, New Mexico, and Wyoming. Vast as this new acquisition was, it almost failed to satisfy the expansionist elements in the United States. The "all-Mexico" movement gained such momentum that total annexation was seriously discussed in high government circles.[3]

The Gadsden Purchase.

The territory won in the Mexican War filled in the outlines of the continental United States of today with a single exception: the Gila River valley in southern Arizona and New Mexico. In 1853 (a half-century after the Louisiana purchase) the American minister to Mexico, James Gadsden, successfully negotiated the purchase of this area from Mexico for $10,-000,000. Subject to some minor frontier rectification, the limits of the United States on the North American continent had been reached.

HEMISPHERE HEGEMONY: THE MONROE DOCTRINE

To many Americans, the phrase "Monroe Doctrine" has a familiar ring. Depending on their historical knowledge, their political sophistication, and their educational background, they know a variety of things about it. Most people suspect that it has something important to do with Latin America; a smaller number understands that it also has implications for the "Old World" in general and Europe in particular. Its more subtle ramifications tend to be overlooked in its contemporary relevance as a symbol of the "good old days" in American foreign policy.

The Original Declaration (1823).

The "Monroe Doctrine" proper refers to certain paragraphs in President James Monroe's annual message to Congress on December 2, 1823. In

---

[3] Bailey, *Diplomatic History of the American People*, p. 278.

these sections he dealt with the problem of the newly-independent republics of Latin America and the growing possibility that the European powers might intervene to return them to the European colonial powers. On the basis of this specific issue a doctrine was formulated that went far beyond the crisis at hand.

Monroe's message first declared that the "American continents" were "henceforth not to be considered as subjects for future colonization by any European power." Any attempt on the part of the European states "to extend their system to any portion of this Hemisphere" would be considered as "dangerous to our peace and safety." In return for forbidding European penetration in the Americas, Monroe then restated the intention of the United States to refrain from interfering in exclusively European matters.[4] This latter point, often thought of as one of the doctrinal roots of isolationism, we shall discuss later in this chapter.

The Polk Restatement (1845)

The doctrine, so bravely enunciated, lapsed without application until the Oregon crisis in 1845. As a part of the vigorous diplomacy he was conducting with Great Britain, President Polk's message to Congress in December, 1845, averred flatly that "no future European colony or dominion shall with our consent be planted or established on any part of the North American continent."[5] This carried Monroe's original doctrine a step farther. The original doctrine had been intended to inhibit European colonization or armed intervention; Polk's reformulation was expanded to include even diplomatic action as falling within the forbidden area.[6]

The Mexican Crisis.

The first real test of the Monroe Doctrine came during the American Civil War when Napoleon III of France established his puppet, Maximilian of Austria, as Emperor of Mexico. This was an open defiance of the doctrine; once the American decks were cleared by the end of internal conflict, however, American pressure on the increasingly uncomfortable Napoleon induced him to withdraw his troops, and the native Mexican forces destroyed Maximilian's *papier-maché* empire. The Monroe Doctrine had been vindicated; an open European attempt to penetrate an American preserve had been turned back.

---

[4] The relevant portions of Monroe's message are quoted in Bartlett, *The Record of American Diplomacy,* pp. 181–3.

[5] Dexter Perkins, *Hands Off: A History of the Monroe Doctrine* (Boston: Little, Brown, and Co., 1941), p. 62.

[6] Perkins, *Hands Off,* p. 90.

After the Civil War, the United States turned to Central and South America as a matter of right. With American power demonstrated both in internal warfare and in its relations with France, the United States came to interpret the Monroe Doctrine as meaning something more than merely the defense of the hemisphere against European penetration. Little by little, beginning in the Caribbean and working gradually southward, an increasing measure of American control over Latin America became apparent under the cloak of the Monroe Doctrine. So far had this gone by 1885 that Secretary of State Olney could claim that "the United States is practically sovereign on this continent, and its fiat is law upon the subjects to which it confines its interposition." [7] The development of this trend into what was known as "dollar diplomacy" did not occur until after 1900, but the principle was well established long before the turn of the century.

ANGLO-AMERICAN COOPERATION: THE UNADMITTED ALLIANCE

What is remarkable about the long record of Anglo-American relations during the nineteenth century is that neither party would openly admit the fact of cooperation. The burden of responsibility for this condition rests mainly on Americans; the popular image of Britain as the enemy of American independence made open and admitted coordination of effort a political near-impossibility. "The redcoats are coming" had too strong a hold on American ideology for any formalization of what was for many years a real—if tacit—working agreement.

It was not until the crisis of the Spanish-American colonies that cooperation became real. Although the United States rejected Prime Minister Canning's proposal for joint action because of Secretary of State Adams' disinclination "to come in as a cock-boat in the wake of the British man-of-war" [8] the American government's decision for a unilateral declaration was clearly founded on an assumption of Britain's approval.[9] Canning himself gloated that he had "called in the New World to redress the balance of the Old."

---

[7] *Foreign Relations of the United States, 1895,* I, 558 (Washington: U.S. Government Printing Office, 1896).

[8] John Quincy Adams, *Memoirs,* C. F. Adams, ed. (Philadelphia: J. B. Lippincott Co., 1875), Vol. VI, p. 179.

[9] Walter Lippmann, *United States Foreign Policy: Shield of the Republic* (New York: Pocket Books, Inc., 1943), p. 14.

It was British sea power that made the Monroe Doctrine effective; it was British sea power that made American continental expansion possible. Continental Europe could not break through the wall of ships thrown up by Britain to strike at the United States; neither, for that matter, could the United States easily exert much influence on European affairs. This whole situation pleased London immensely. At least until the United States entered into the Pacific and came into direct contact with the states of Europe there, most American dealings with continental states were conducted, either directly or at one remove, via the British Foreign Office. Though Americans would have bitterly resented being told so, the facts are that the United States was, during most of the nineteenth century, the protégé of British sea power.

The Latter Half of the Century.

After the Civil War the nature of the Anglo-American relationship changed, at first subtly and then radically.[10] In the western hemisphere itself, the burgeoning American feeling of competence encouraged the United States to act vigorously on its own, even—as in the Venezuelan boundary dispute of 1895—to the point of defying Britain itself. Britain found that the young American republic was no longer a protégé in Latin America, but a rival.

Meanwhile, both the United States and Britain were expanding into the Pacific. Here the old relationship was untenable; American sea power was, at least in the central and eastern Pacific, superior to the British. By the time of the rise of Japan, Britain found itself obliged to accept the United States as an equal power in many Pacific ventures and in some cases to defer to American leadership.

Even Britain's European position deteriorated so sharply in the face of German dynamism that Canning's idea of the "new world redressing the balance of the old" came to take on a new meaning. Instead of wanting to keep the United States out of Europe, Britain began to think wistfully of the advantages of having it as a full participant in the system.[11] Active American entry into European affairs was to wait until after 1900 and the presidency of Theodore Roosevelt, but long before that time Britain

---

[10] For this general point, see Crane Brinton, *The United States and Britain* (Cambridge: Harvard University Press, 1945), pp. 122–132; for a graphic elucidation of the necessity of Anglo-American cooperation in sea power, see Eugene Staley, "The Myth of the Continents," in H. F. Armstrong, ed., *The Foreign Affairs Reader* (New York: Harper & Bros., 1947), pp. 317–333.

[11] See L. M. Gelber, *The Rise of Anglo-American Friendship* (New York: Oxford University Press, 1938).

was planning to extend Anglo-American cooperation into the area of European great-power relationships.

NONINVOLVEMENT IN EUROPE: "ISOLATIONISM"

We come now to one of the most misunderstood elements in nine-teenth-century American foreign ploicy, as well as being perhaps the most abused term in the entire language of discourse about the external relations of the United States: isolation. No other single idea has had such an influence on the shaping of American attitudes toward the out-side world, nor can we name any that has had a more complicating effect on the American task of coming to terms with the international issues the United States faces in the twentieth century.

Europe and the Young United States.

Americans sometimes forget that the accomplishment of American inde-pendence was only partially due to the valor and the patriotism of the Revolutionary generation in the United States. The war of American inde-pendence was only one part—and a relatively minor part at that—of the long series of great-power struggles that persisted in Europe for nearly two centuries. The Treaty of Paris that ended the American war marked a phase in this Europe-wide conflict; the next era opened with the wars against revolutionary France only a few years later. The birth of the United States was a direct outcome of a convulsion in the society of European states and several of its members naturally looked on the new state as a creature of their system.

The Post-Revolutionary Involvement.

During the thirty-one years between the Treaties of Paris and Ghent, the young United States was buffeted by the tides of great-power politics. American policy was tossed back and forth by the three great powers of the period: Britain, France, and Spain. With Britain the United States fought the War of 1812 and relations with France included an undeclared war and twenty-five years of bickering over navigation, commercial regu-lation, and so on. With Spain was opened the tedious and ill-tempered maneuvering that continued until the cession of the Floridas in 1819.

The early experience of the United States with the states of Europe was an unhappy one. Young, weak, inexperienced, and sensitive, the American government found its abrupt introduction to the ways of great-power politics an event not to be celebrated and if possible to be avoided in the future.

The Monroe Doctrine.

The Congress of Vienna, in 1815, ended the long period of general European war and ushered in the peaceful century of what is sometimes called the *pax Brittanica.* This left the way open for the brave pronouncement of the Monroe Doctrine. We will remember that President Monroe's statement not only denied the western hemisphere to future European colonization, but also foreswore any American interest, present or future, in "the wars of the European powers, in matters relating to themselves. . . ." "The political system of the allied powers [in Europe] is essentially different in this respect from that of America," he went on. This was the genesis of formal American isolation.

Up to 1900.

The principal of noninvolvement, thus promulgated at a moment when the times were most propitious to its success, endured throughout the rest of the nineteenth century as the basis of American attitudes toward Europe.[12] It was because of its operational feasibility, given the political and technological conditions, that isolationism became so firmly imbedded in the American consciousness.

It was never intended that isolation should be complete to the point of noninteroourse. Indeed, the very word "isolation" did more to confuse than to illuminate. Perhaps the more accurate term to characterize American policy toward Europe would be "independency." [13] This word carried a double connotation. In the first place, it suggested that the United States would intervene in European affairs only when, under the circumstances, and to the extent that American national interest demanded. It also implied clearly that such intervention would never create a precedent but would always be a matter of circumstance.

Operational Bases of Noninvolvement.

Why did noninvolvement work so well for so long? What were its working bases? What happened to make it irrelevant after 1900? There are three

---

[12] One of the most famous later expressions of the principle was that of Secretary of State Seward in 1862: "The American people must be content to recommend the cause of human progress by the wisdom with which they should exercise the powers of self-government, forbearing alliances, intervention, and interference." Quoted in John Bassett Moore, *Digest of International Law* (Washington: U. S. Govment Printing Office, 1906), Vol. VI, p. 23.

[13] The word was popularized by the late Charles A. Beard, who developed his ideas in detail in several works including *The Idea of National Interest* (New York: The Macmillan Co., Inc., 1934), *The Open Door at Home* (New York: The Macmillan Co., Inc., 1935), and *The Devil Theory of War* (New York: Vanguard Press, 1936).

explanations for the effectiveness of the policy and its eventual obsolescence.

The first reason is geographic. The United States was separated from Europe by an ocean, and this fact does more to explain isolationism than do many more complex exegeses. The three thousand miles separating Europe from the Altantic coast of the United States might as well have been three million; they made America as remote from European concerns as if it had been on the moon.

The second explanation has a political root. British success in keeping the European states pinned down on the Continent during all but the last quarter of the century left the United States with only one possible enemy: Britain itself. We have seen that the harmony of interest between Britain and the United States prevented any fundamental clash from developing out of this relationship. Thus the United States again had Britain to thank, this time for making the reality of isolationism some approximation of the ideal.

Finally, we must mention technology. In 1823 all the great powers were European and played their major roles on that continent. As long as the technology of warfare and statecraft enabled Europe to maintain its global dominance, the principle of American noninvolvement squared with the facts of international life. When the great British effort collapsed in the face of the new technology, the bases of American policy were washed away. The extension of the European state system to non-European areas, the breakout of Germany into rivalry with Britain, and the rise of Japan all spelled the end of *pax Brittanica* and of American isolation.

BEGINNINGS OF A PACIFIC POLICY

American interests in the Pacific grew bit by bit during the nineteenth century. As we have noted above, the original base of American entry into the affairs of Asia and the Pacific rested on non-political foundations. It was a combination of economic and missionary activities, plus the urge to abolish the humiliating status ceremonies that all Westerners endured before Oriental courts, that brought the United States into the Pacific in the first place. American Far Eastern policy was already a reality before the outcome of the war with Spain made the United States a full-fledged Pacific power.

China.

Although the United States was one of the leaders in the commercial penetration of China, it refused to follow Britain and France into the practice of extracting economic concessions by strong diplomacy and, occasionally, by force. Candor compels us to admit, however, that American insistence on the most-favored-nation clause in dealings with China usually resulted in any new concessions won by Britain and France being extended to the United States in turn. This technique was later formalized as the "Open Door."

Japan.

In 1854 the famous expedition of Commodore Matthew C. Perry succeeded in forcing Japan to open its gates to the outside world. Throughout most of the rest of the century a succession of able American diplomats played a large part in Japan's transformation. So important was their work that one scholar has said that "Japan at the turn of the century was in considerable measure the child of American diplomacy." [14]

Alaska, Samoa, and Hawaii.

In 1867, the United States acquired Alaska by purchase from Russia,[15] thus giving the nation a strategic position overlooking the entire north Pacific and bringing it within a few miles of Asia. Only after 1941 did Americans realize the critical importance of this northern outpost. Much less well known are the circumstances surrounding the acquisition of Samoa during a confused period between the first treaty in 1878 and the German-American agreement of 1899 that divided the archipelago between the two states. In the South Pacific the United States found itself directly involved in European great-power politics.

Then in 1898 the United States annexed Hawaii—an independent republic at the time. This action was the culmination of a half-century of American religious and economic penetration by the United States into the native government of the islands. Pressure from American sugar interests for annexation, the overthrow of the native government, and the expansionist fervor generated by the war with Spain combined to persuade Washington to undertake the annexation, but only after long and partisan debate.

Summary on American Pacific Policy.

This brief recital of American penetration into the Pacific and the Far East suggests one or two conclusions. First, isolation, or noninvolvement,

---

[14] Bailey, *Diplomatic History of the American People,* p. 336.

[15] A brief survey of the negotiations leading to the purchase of Alaska is found in W. A. Williams, *American-Russian Relations, 1781–1947* (New York: Rinehart & Company, Inc., 1952), pp. 21–2; see also Pratt, *A History of United States Foreign Policy,* pp. 324–8.

was never a reality in the Orient. American expansion in that region had a long history, and the United States was perfectly willing to come to grips with the great powers of Europe in an Asiatic setting. Second, there is little evidence that most Americans—or their government—were self-consciously pursuing a crystallized idea of national interest in the Orient. Each step in United States policy in the Far East was either accidental, prompted by a special interest group, or brought on by a vague nationalist expansionist urge. By the time the war with Spain made the United States a major power, Americans already had large Pacific commitments without being overly sure of what they were supposed to do with them.

THE BIRTH OF GREAT-POWER STATUS

Historians often divide their time periods into centuries, with each hundred years characterized in a different way. This device is sometimes artificial; very seldom does human history move from one era to another just as a century ends. In the case of United States foreign policy, however, this method fits the actual facts with more than a casual approximation. During the last two years of the nineteenth century the United States passed through a major change in status; it entered the twentieth century with a new set of problems and a new orientation to them.

THE WAR WITH SPAIN

It was the American victory over the decaying monarchy of Spain that signalled the arrival of the United States at international maturity. Out of this brief and in many ways sordid conflict came the new posture that has so radically altered the foreign policy of the United States.

The Coming of the War.

There is no need for us to analyze the complex and unedifying train of events that led up to the American decision to go to war.[16] Perhaps most important was the Cuban insurrection that was so bloody on both sides and so close to the territory of the United States. But there were other factors at work as well. The expansionist urge, fortified by the Samoa and Hawaii incidents and American truculence in the Venezuelan dispute with

---

[16] See Walter Millis, *The Martial Spirit* (Boston: Houghton Mifflin Co., 1931), for a highly critical study of the preliminaries of the war.

Great Britain, was frankly searching for someone upon whom to test America's newly-realized national strength.

It was also during this era that "yellow journalism" began to have a major influence on mass attitudes on foreign policy. In the Spanish crisis, such newspapers as the New York *Journal* and the New York *World* took credit for forcing the government's hand. Just as it seemed as if diplomacy had succeeded in adjusting all legitimate (or even quasi-legitimate) American claims against Spain, public opinion—whipped up by the yellow press—shook off all restraint. Popular clamor for war and a belligerent Congress forced a reluctant President McKinley to accept battle.

Military Victory.

Although marred by stupidity and ineptitude, the Spanish-American war resulted in an American victory in an *opera bouffe* atmosphere. The Spanish fleet was destroyed at Santiago, Cuba, and Admiral Dewey sank the Spanish naval force in Manila harbor in the Philippines—a long way, we may note, from the Cuba the United States was allegedly fighting to liberate. On land, the fighting in Cuba was fitful and inconclusive, although admittedly sanguinary. The Americans won a few small victories in Cuba, occupied Puerto Rico, and looked around for more worlds to conquer. But Spain had had enough.

Legal war with Spain had begun on April 21, 1898; on August 12, hostilities were ended by a protocol signed (on behalf of Spain) by the French ambassador to the United States. The peace conference convened in October at Paris. Negotiations continued until the peace treaty was signed in December; the treaty was approved by the United States Senate in February, 1899. By the terms of this agreement the United States served notice on the world that a new great power had been born, with augmented interests in both oceans.[17]

THE EXPANDED FRONTIER

The most visible result of the war was the acquisition of a vast (or, at least, far-flung) empire. The American security frontier had been thereby tremendously expanded. In the two areas where American naval power could be expected to exploit the new bases most effectively, the Caribbean and the Pacific, the outcome of the war presented the United States with entirely new situations.

---

[17] For an interesting analysis of the peace negotiations, see A. L. P. Dennis, *Adventures in American Diplomacy, 1896–1906* (New York: E. P. Dutton & Co., Inc., 1928).

By the terms of the treaty of peace, the United States succeeded to what was left of Spain's world position: a colonial empire in the western hemisphere and a position as a major power in the Pacific. There were two major territorial acquisitions and several smaller ones to serve as booty for the "splendid little war."

Cuba, the ostensible pretext for the war, achieved independence—but only of a sort. In a compromise between the "no-annexation" Democrats and the expansionists, Cuba became a protectorate under the terms of the "Platt Amendment" of 1901. The island republic continued in this status until the wholesale revision of the Latin American policy of the United States that took place during the 1930's.

The Philippines, on the other hand, were openly annexed, but only after a bitter debate among Americans. The "anti-imperialists," led by William Jennings Bryan, seemed to be winning the argument in favor of early independence for the Philippines, but they were routed by the Filipino insurrection of 1899. By the time the islands were pacified, annexation was a *fait accompli;* World War II intervened before the Philippines were freed.

Of the rest of the new empire, Puerto Rico was the most important segment. Annexed outright—there being no indigenous independence movement to complicate matters—Puerto Rico rapidly became an essential American base for Caribbean operations. Guam, also won from Spain, was transformed into a naval base; Wake Island became, in its turn, an outpost of American power in the Pacific.

The Caribbean.

We have noted that American hegemony over the Caribbean and northern Latin America had been claimed before the Spanish-American war, most explicitly by Secretary Olney during the Venezuelan boundary dispute. After 1898, with the acquisition and occupation of advanced offshore bases in Cuba and Puerto Rico, American influence in the Caribbean became paramount beyond any doubt. Operating from Cuba and Puerto Rico, President Roosevelt was to find it relatively simple to maneuver the winning of the Panama Canal Zone; the maintenance of a force-in-being made the later evolution of the Monroe Doctrine much easier to formulate and implement.

A natural outgrowth of the new bases was the southward extension of the area of Latin America in which the United States was able to exercise primacy. Before the war, Mexico, the West Indies, and Central America had marked the effective limits of American power; after the war American control extended to substantially all of South America north of the "bulge" of Brazil.

The Pacific.

The principal effect of the war, however, resulted from the changed American status in the Pacific. It is doubtful that Americans realized fully just how deeply they had put themselves into Asia; even after the Japanese attack on Pearl Harbor in 1941 it came as a shock to many Americans to realize that to go from Tokyo to Manila required a compass setting to the southwest. The other Pacific acquisitions of this era—Guam, Wake, Samoa, and Hawaii—formed a series of stepping stones that made it possible for the United States to sustain its advanced base in the Philippines.

The United States arrived in the far Pacific just as the late phase of European imperialism in Asia was reaching its height. The European powers were at work trying to carve up and divide the last rich imperial prize, the apparently prostrate China. Japan had just come on the scene as an imperial power to be reckoned with; the Sino-Japanese War had just ended, and the Russo-Japanese War was just a few years away. The "Open Door" policy of the United States, enunciated almost at the very moment that Washington was settling uneasily into its new seat among the mighty, marked the new departure in American policy. The expanded security frontier of the United States had brought Americans into the thick of what was probably the most important theater of great-power controversy at the turn of the century, the ticklish question of Asiatic imperialism.

THE NEW IMPERIALISM

At various points in the preceding pages we have noted the growing expansionist spirit that seized Americans during the last 15 or 20 years of the nineteenth century. We have suggested that in some ways the war with Spain and its consequences were the logical aftereffects of this new spirit. If being tagged with the opprobrious term "imperialist" was an outcome of achieving the new version of American manifest destiny, most Americans were willing to bear that burden.

Most, but not all. The ratification of the peace treaty with Spain provoked a bitter fight in the Senate and the two-thirds vote that finally passed it was a bare minimum. The Senate battle was only a pale reflection of a deep division among the public, one that was never to heal fully.[18]

---

[18] For the American debate over imperialism, see Julius W. Pratt, *Expansionists of 1898* (Baltimore: Johns Hopkins University Press, 1936).

Anti-imperialism drew its justification from ideological, historical, and logical bases. Ideologically the opponents of empire claimed a fundamental disharmony between the professions of democracy and the possession of an overseas empire of subject peoples. Historically, they raised the issue of isolationism, the negative aspects of the Monroe Doctrine, and the wisdom of the American record of staying out of great-power embroilments. Logically, they pointed to the folly of undertaking a war to free Cuba and then becoming a Pacific power on the opposite side of the globe from the Caribbean.

Underlying anti-imperialist sentiment was a combination of what our era would call guilt feelings and insecurity. Imperialism as a too familiar manifestation of power politics seemed to many people to be something that the American political genius was constitutionally incapable of carrying off successfully. The prospects of imperial rule were admittedly intoxicating, but many well-meaning people wondered if, in gaining the renown of the world, Americans were not running the danger of losing their own souls.

Imperialist Attitudes.

The imperialists, if they felt such scruples, kept them well under cover. We need not recite the catalogue of imperialist arguments in detail; they are all familiar to students of modern history. Economic advantage, strategic gain, the siren call of prestige, the iron law of history, the beckoning finger of destiny, and the requirements of Christianity were all pressed into service in the fight—as indeed they had been used in every state that felt the call to imperial greatness. Perhaps the rationalization that played the largest part in carrying the day for the imperialists—in addition to popular resentment at the Filipino insurrection—was the seductive idea of the "white man's burden." [19] Today a term of derision, in 1898 and 1899

---

[19] Rudyard Kipling's poem, "The White Man's Burden" (1899), helped persuade Americans where their duty lay. The most impressive of the poem's seven stanzas is the fifth:

> "Take up the White Man's Burden —
>   And reap his old reward:
> The blame of those ye better,
>   The hate of those ye guard —
> The cry of hosts ye humour
>   (Ah, slowly!) toward the light: —
> 'Why brought ye us from bondage,
>   'Our loved Egyptian night?' "

Quoted from *McClure's Magazine* (February, 1899).

it provided the ideological escape hatch through which many worried citizens could make their way to the acceptance of imperialism.

THE UNITED STATES AMONG THE GREAT POWERS

The New American Attitude.

The more informed and sophisticated among the Americans of 1900 had a fairly clear understanding that the United States had come to the end of an era. The new overseas territories of the United States meant a good deal more than just a vast augmentation in prestige, however satisfying to nationalist appetites that might be in itself. They required the United States to walk a new path in foreign affairs, to concern itself with new problems and to solve them in new ways.

But even though informed opinion grasped the implications of the new role of the United States, if only imperfectly, not even that much can be said about the general content of public opinion. If we may generalize about a dangerous subject from the vantage point of over half a century, it seems probable that the mass of the American people in 1900 did not realize what had happened to them. There was great pride in the victory over Spain; there was a good deal of self-congratulation at being an imperial people; there was considerable missionary zeal for spreading the message of the American way to backward peoples. But except for a few belligerent and quasi-chauvinist voices, there seems to have been little inclination to recognize the fact that, for good or ill, the United States had left the past behind. The oceans still existed and the British navy still sailed upon them; Europe and the great powers still seemed as far away as they had a hundred years before.

This failure to awaken to the responsibilities of great-power status has sometimes been called one of the greatest errors that Americans have ever committed. This judgment seems, if not overly harsh, at least somewhat beside the point. There was no error involved at all, if by "error" we mean a deliberate choice of what turned out to be a wrong alternative. Instead, most Americans never understood that there was any choice to be made at all; they simply assumed that now that the war with Spain was over and the predictable result had taken place, things would somehow readjust themselves and the United States could again rock along in its pleasant insularity.

The Attitude of the Other Powers.

If the United States was ignorant of what had happened to it, this happy state was not shared by the other great powers. As much earlier as the time of the American Civil War, the European states, contemplating the awful military might that the United States mobilized on both sides, realized that America was ready then to join the circle of the internationally elect. By 1900, as the European state system analyzed the American victory over Spain, each of its major members thought through what the entry of the United States into their councils might mean.

Great Britain, alone among the major powers, welcomed the United States as a potential ally; the others were to some extent disturbed by being obliged to expand their closed system to accommodate a new member. France and Russia were perhaps the least inconvenienced: France was pointedly neutral, while Czarist Russia was solicitous to preserve its long-standing (if not overly impressive) history of friendship with America. Germany was discomfited at this new obstacle to her project of undermining British control of the seas, and anti-German sentiment in the United States was already a reality. Japan, itself a new member of the great-power group, was the most immediately affected of all the states: the United States arrived in the Far East just as Nippon was beginning its own program of expansion there. From this almost accidental historical coincidence was to grow the rivalry that was to culminate in open war in 1941.

THE FIRST WORLD WAR

The first major consequence of American great-power status was the historical process that drew the United States into the first world war. We have seen that the United States owed its birth to a general European war, and until it successfully disentangled itself from the European state system in 1820, the United States was part of the general society of states. Between 1820 and 1900, however, the United States stood outside the mainstream of world affairs and escaped all the wars that occurred within it. When Americans rejoined the family of nations, there was no way for them to avoid being caught up in the next major upheaval. What makes the 1914–1918 period important for us is the extent to which this—the war's major lesson to the United States—was missed by Americans.

The Prewar Era, 1900–1914.

During the period between the war with Spain and the onset of the World War in 1914, the United States made an attempt to capitalize on its new power. In several parts of the world, American action demonstrated an unusual forcefulness and vigor. The United States was following the advice of its favorite contemporary political leader, Theodore Roosevelt, and was undertaking to live "the strenuous life."

In the Caribbean, President Roosevelt obtained the Panama Canal Zone in 1903 by direct and effective—if questionable—action.[20] He laid down the "Roosevelt corollary" to the Monroe Doctrine, thus giving the United States the self-proclaimed right to intervene into the domestic affairs of the Latin American countries.[21] Spurred by the protection thus guaranteed, American investments flowed into the Caribbean; American government action in promotion and support of this effort rapidly gained the unpopular name of "dollar diplomacy" and contributed to the lasting discredit of the United States in Latin America.[22]

China was the second great arena of American action during this period.[23] Involved as the United States was with all the major states in the problem of China, it was imperative that an American position be developed quickly. This took the form of the "Open Door" policy of 1900 —long regarded as a landmark of American diplomacy. Put at its simplest, it called for equality among imperialist states as they went about their economic penetration of China, and for the preservation of "Chinese territorial and administrative entity." Neither high-minded philanthrophy nor realistic power politics, the Open Door had one great merit: it was based solidly on the American interest in a Far Eastern balance of power and the consequent need for the continued existence of a free China. It suffered, as later events were to show, from a lack of follow-up: the United States was unwilling either to support it with power or to bargain realistically with the states that were willing to do so.[24]

The new American posture as the defender of China did not escape the attention of Japan; Tokyo was already eyeing China with anticipation. The United States rapidly drifted into a series of disagreements with Japan over the Russo-Japanese War in 1905, and over Japanese immigration into the United States during 1906. Tension seemed to be rising and, although the disputes were resolved by the Root-Takahira Agreement of 1908, the old relationship was never resumed. The era of American sponsorship of Japan was over; both states had major interests in the

---

20 See H. C. Hill, *Roosevelt and the Caribbean* (Chicago: University of Chicago Press, 1927), Chapter 3.

21 On the corollaries of the Monroe Doctrine, see Perkins, *Hands Off*, Chapter VII: "The Policeman of the West."

22 See the criticism in Scott Nearing and Joseph Freeman, *Dollar Diplomacy* (New York: The Viking Press, 1925).

23 A. Whitney Griswold, *The Far Eastern Policy of the United States* (New York: Harcourt, Brace & Co., 1938), Chapters 2, 3.

24 George F. Kennan has a wryly humorous and heavily critical interpretation of the Open Door in *American Diplomacy, 1900–1950,* Chapter II: "Mr. Hippisley and the Open Door."

Pacific that were irreconcilable. Rivalry had replaced friendship and the United States had acquired an enemy in the Pacific.

The Moroccan crisis of 1905, involving Germany and France directly and the other European powers indirectly, seemed for a time to threaten general war. President Roosevelt offered his good offices to help settle the crisis, and it was largely due to this effort that the Algeciras Conference was called. At this conference the United States had official delegates; there was no pretence of isolation. Americans negotiated, composed differences, and played a large part in the proceedings.

There was some soul searching in the United States over this adventure, for it was in clear violation of the noninvolvement policy of hallowed memory. Nobody was particularly pleased about it, but its apologists justified American intervention on grounds of sheer necessity. The Moroccan intervention foreshadowed the eventual total irrelevance of noninvolvement in Europe to the working interests of the United States.

The Effect of Wilsonianism.

American policy during the era of the first world war was materially affected, if not actually governed, by the fact that its major architect was President Woodrow Wilson. Mr. Wilson brought a distinct philosophy of foreign affairs to the presidency and self-consciously sought to order the behavior of the United States according to its principles. Both his great successes and his ultimate repudiation grew out of this preoccupation.

Wilson adopted a "democratic" theory of international relations entirely in harmony with what Walter Lippmann called the "great illusion" of the nineteenth century.[25] He submitted the behavior of states to the measurement of moral criteria, derived from the democratic ideology of the United States and a strict Puritanical conscience. He accepted a set of morally desirable values: peace, self-determination, the rights of small states, the superiority of public opinion to the calculations of diplomats, and the abolition of self-seeking national interest. He attempted to circumvent the apparatus of traditional power politics and to substitute therefor a new methodology in world affairs stressing the implementation of the democratic dogma. In so doing he was giving forceful and very literate expression to long-standing and basic popular attitudes in the United States.

Wilson was obliged, however, to cope with some hard realities. Up to the time of American involvement in the war, his foreign policy forced him to deal with a series of problems inherited from his predecessors. To do Wilson justice, he attempted—with some success—to alter American

---

[25] In *United States Foreign Policy* (Boston: Little, Brown and Co., 1943), p. 30.

tactics in Latin America and in relations with Great Britain; the record of his prewar policy is not a discreditable one.

NEUTRALITY AND ITS FAILURE

The coming of the European war in August 1914 at first had little impact on Americans. Here, mass attitudes seemed to imply, was another European struggle of the old type, growing out of certain inherent flaws in the political structure of Europe and the states within it. In this kind of conflict the United States had no interest. The proper role of Americans was to remain on the sidelines and to capitalize on their advantage by dealing with problems nearer home. With this popular attitude President Wilson and his advisers, principally Secretary of State William Jennings Bryan, were in general agreement.

Neutrality vs. Unneutralism.

At the onset of the war, therefore, the United States issued proclamations of neutrality almost as a matter of routine.[26] As Americans watched the course of the fighting, however, they discovered that noninvolvement could not and did not mean impartiality. The sympathies of the bulk of the people were unquestionably on the side of the Allies. Certain ethnic groups in the United States were either pro-German or anti-British, but the predominant attitude was pro-Ally. Here again the government, although better informed and somewhat more sophisticated than mass opinion, shared its predilections; Mr. Wilson himself was tortured by the conflict between his pro-British leanings and his insistence on a policy of noninvolvement. Only Secretary Bryan, by now almost a confirmed pacifist, was relatively untroubled by any bias in favor of Britain.

The Violation of American Rights.

The unneutral attitude of Americans was strained by the studied violation of American "neutral rights" by both sides from almost the very beginning of the war. During the first part of the war, Britain seemed to be the more persistent violator of American rights. The United States grew restive under the constant diet of harrassment, and the considerable agitation for forthright action was barely offset by the persistent Anglophilia of the government and the people.

The British, however, enjoyed another natural advantage in the struggle for American sympathy. Germany, without enough of a surface navy to

---

[26] The standard work is Charles Seymour, *American Neutrality, 1914–1917* (New Haven: Yale University Press, 1935).

challenge British supremacy, turned to the submarine as its preferred weapon against seaborne commerce. Submarine warfare, by definition, made mincemeat out of the ordinary rules of neutral shipping, rules that the British had retained in principle however drastically they might have interpreted them in practice. The crowning blow, and the one event that tipped American sympathies irrevocably in favor of the Allies, was the sinking of the *Lusitania* in 1915.

The German Choice Forces War.

The United States responded quickly to the German challenge. Secretary Bryan resigned rather than approve a stronger American policy, and President Wilson took over active direction of American strategy. He sought by vigorous diplomacy to persuade Germany to limit its submarine warfare and, for a time, seemed to have won his point as Germany promised to restrain itself.

By early 1917, however, Berlin made a deliberate calculation of what was involved and elected to resume unrestricted submarine warfare. The imperial government realized that this might bring about American belligerency; it reasoned, however, that it could win the war before American participation could tip the scales. The United States immediately broke off diplomatic relations; in April, after the revelation of German plots in Mexico and the revolution in Russia, the United States declared war.[27]

THE UNITED STATES AND THE WAR

American participation in the war furnished almost a laboratory example of the traditional American attitude toward war in general. The war, as popular opinion saw it, was forced upon the United States by vicious and depraved men. The American government had been patient; it had reasoned with the aggressors; it had sought to stave off battle as long as possible. Finally, given no choice, the United States went to war. America had no sordid objectives of material gain or the satisfaction of national interest; its concern was with principle. After the war was won, Americans were prepared to help straighten out the world before they went back to their own concerns.

American Idealism.

Put as baldly as we have stated them above, these propositions seem almost fatuous and puerile to a more skeptical generation of Americans.

---

[27] For critical studies of American entry into the war, see Walter Millis, *Road to War* (Boston: Houghton Mifflin Co., 1935), and Charles C. Tansill, *America Goes to War* (Boston: Little, Brown and Co., 1938).

Later scholars (and some contemporary ones) have proved that President Wilson was as sensitive to the requirements of the European balance of power as were his associates in Britain, and American entry into the war was a natural decision to attempt to forestall German hegemony on the continent.[28] And yet—and this is a danger peculiar to our time—we must not overlook an historical fact. Most Americans believed that these abstractions were what they were actually fighting for—and so did most foreigners, enemy and Allied alike. We must never forget that Germany surrendered on the basis of the Fourteen Points, Wilson's most ambitious effort to translate his own idealism into practical terms.

Wilson's War Aims.

President Wilson thought himself fighting the war for a single objective: peace—durable, honorable, and satisfying. To him, the only kind of peace settlement that stood any chance of enduring was one that incorporated his own (and his country's) philosophy of international relations and applied it to the settlement of concrete issues.

As Wilson saw it, peace for the world required the simultaneous application of a handful of general principles. These were self-determination, political democracy, untrammeled intercourse between peoples, and international organization (the last of Wilson's Fourteen Points—the crucial one for Americans in dealing with the Treaty of Versailles—dealt with a "general association of nations" to guarantee "political independence and territorial integrity" to all states). He wrapped all of these up into a single operating hypothesis that was in turn dependent on a basic article of faith: that the spontaneous common opinion of mankind, if given the chance to speak freely, would always declare for peace, justice, and freedom. He dedicated the United States to the cause of creating mechanisms for the expression of that mass will.[29]

The United States and the Allies.

The fundamental distinction that Americans drew between their own war and that being fought by the rest of the Allies is shown by the amorphous

---

28 See Edward Buehrig, *Woodrow Wilson and the Balance of Power* (Bloomington: University of Indiana Press, 1956). Compare this recent study, however, with another that takes the opposite position: John M. Blum, *Woodrow Wilson and the Politics of Morality* (Boston: Little, Brown and Co., 1956), especially Chapter VIII.

29 Wilson's war message (April 2, 1917) put this proposition at its simplest:

"Our object ... is to vindicate the principles of peace and justice in the life of the world as against selfish and autocratic power and to set up amongst the really free and self-governed peoples of the world such a concert of purpose and of action as will henceforth insure the observance of those principles. ...

"We are glad ... to fight thus for the ultimate peace of the world and for the liberation of its peoples ... : for the rights of nations great and small and the relations between them. The United States never became an "Ally," but remained only an "Associated Power" to the end. At the Paris Peace Conference itself, Wilson (although the popular idol of the European masses) ran into constant opposition from his opposite numbers around the table, and finally fell between the two stools. He failed to get the kind of peace settlement he wanted at Versailles, but what he did get was too much for the United States Senate. Neither Europe nor the American people were ready for a Wilsonian peace in 1919.

THE RENAISSANCE OF ISOLATIONISM

Looking back to the 1920's, we can suggest several explanations for the renaissance of isolationism that flowered after the end of the war. It was perhaps inevitable that a people whose insight was so limited that they could not grasp the meaning of great-power status, who had fought their greatest war with emotional slogans and crusading zeal and without any rational understanding of how to approach their idealistic goal, and who thought of war as a matter of punishing sinners, would lapse into disillusionment when Heaven proved difficult to locate. Party politics, always a factor in American political decision, played its part as well in bringing back isolationist prejudice; President Wilson's unbending insistence on his own particular way alienated many otherwise sympathetic internationally minded people. But it serves no purpose to analyze the motives of 1920. For good or ill, Americans once again turned their backs on the world. Their action had a perceptible effect on the course of events during the next twenty years, called by E. H. Carr "the twenty years crisis." [30]

The Rejection of the League

The genesis of neo-isolationism is found in the struggle over the ratification of the Treaty of Versailles and American entry into the League of Nations. Once this battle was over and the concept of "normalcy" had captured American political life, the emotional drive for noncommitment had taken charge of American policy. The issues raised during the 1919–1921 period were not to be settled until after V-J Day.

---

privilege of men everywhere to choose their way of life and of obedience." *Congressional Record*, LV, 103, 104 (April 2, 1917).
[30] E. H. Carr, *The Twenty Years Crisis, 1919–1939* (London: The Macmillan Co., 1940).

To a considerable, although immeasurable, extent, the rejection of the League of Nations was the outcome of the political tactics of President Wilson. Never noted as a compromiser, and prone to insist on his way if he felt a moral issue was involved, he laid a political trap for himself in the manner in which he handled the issue of international cooperation.

His first error was made prior to the congressional election of 1918; he urged the election of a Democratic Congress as the surest way to guarantee a successful peace settlement. Such an identification of either party with superior virtue or patriotism is never especially good politics in the United States and, under the circumstances, practically guaranteed the eventual Republican victory. The election meant that Wilson went to Paris after what amounted to a popular repudiation—an outcome he could possibly have avoided. What was worse, the delegation he chose to accompany him included no Senators and only one Republican—and a lukewarm one at that. It would seem that Wilson had omitted doing nothing that might antagonize the majority party in the Senate.

After the treaty was submitted, the President made his lot even more difficult. He rejected the Lodge reservations which, had he accepted them, would have permitted American membership in the League on a slightly different basis (Britain and France were both prepared to accept the Lodge reservations). Instead, he insisted on his own version of the League and expressed his determination to stand or fall on it. Even after all of this (and the President's physical collapse that further complicated an already tangled situation), there was enough Republican support for the Treaty that it fell only eight votes short of the required two-thirds.[31]

The Election of 1920.

The presidential election of 1920, coming after the long and bitter battle over the League, sealed the fate of the United States. Although the victorious Harding was, as a candidate, vaguely in favor of "an association of nations," the Democratic defeat was correctly interpreted as a mandate. The American people were turning away, not only from the League, but from the broader idea of systematized and institutionalized action to preserve peace. During the Republican era of the 1920's—and even during Franklin D. Roosevelt's first term—it was axiomatic in American politics and in American foreign affairs that the United States was not to become involved in any permanent international arrangements requiring political

---

[31] See Denna F. Fleming, *The United States and the League of Nations, 1918–1920* (New York: Putnam, 1932).

commitments. The interwar isolationism was much more a state of mind—popular and official—than it was a matter of practical policy. The people had spoken and, this done, turned to other matters.

DISARMAMENT

Perhaps the most conspicuous and well-meaning effort of the United States toward the establishment of a peaceful order during the interwar period was the long attempt at "disarmament." The word is put in quotation marks here, although in the minds of Americans of the day it was taken literally to mean the ultimate abolition of all weapons of war.

The disarmament movement suited American predilections exactly. By stripping nations of their capacity to fight a war, the desire to fight would be eliminated; by making a commitment for peace, peaceful process would be guaranteed. Foreign policy for the United States would then consist only of trade relations with the outside world and the exploitation of America's natural hegemony, principally in the western hemisphere.

The Washington Conference.

In 1922 the United States led the way in moving toward disarmament. The Washington Conference, called on the initiative of the United States, attempted to arrest the postwar naval race among the United States, Britain, and Japan. Although the United States had a construction program under way that would have made it the world's greatest naval power in a few years, America agreed to suspend the building effort and to the stabilization of the three greatest navies on a capital-ship ratio of 5-5-3. France and Italy were added to the ratio at 1.75 each, and it seemed as if a great stride had been taken for peace.[32]

The Geneva Conference.

The Washington Conference had provided a ratio by which to control capital ships, but left the door open to a new naval race in smaller vessels. President Coolidge therefore called for a new naval disarmament conference in 1927, to meet at Geneva. Here the United States sought to

---

[32] The Conference also dealt with the problems of the Pacific. The Four-Power Treaty abrogated the Anglo-Japanese alliance and engaged the United States, Britain, Japan, and France to respect each other's rights in the Pacific; the Nine-Power Treaty reaffirmed the Open Door, pledging the signatories (the Pacific powers) to respect the "sovereignty, the independence, and the territorial and administrative integrity of China." See Raymond Leslie Buell, *The Washington Conference* (New York: Appleton-Century-Crofts, 1922). A more recent study is John Chalmers Vinson, *The Parchment Peace* (Athens, Ga.: University of Georgia Press, 1955).

extend the 5-5-3 ratio to all classes of warships, but it proved impossible to reach any agreement. The conference ended in a total fiasco.

The Kellogg-Briand Pact.

In this connection we should mention the ill-starred Pact of Paris, the Kellogg-Briand Pact for outlawing war. This document, once thought of as one of the major diplomatic triumphs of the United States, renounced war "as an instrument of national policy" and promised that the settlement of international disputes would not be attempted "except by pacific means." Almost all the states of the world finally ratified it, but many (including the United States) added significant reservations that permitted "defensive" war. Signed in 1928, the Pact became politically irrelevant in 1931, when Japan's invasion of Manchuria ended the myth of achieving a warless world by proclamation.

The London Conference.

The next disarmament effort was made in 1930. After long preliminary negotiations between Britain and the United States, the five major naval powers met at London. Here some concrete results were achieved, although the total reduction in naval strength was negligible. The major result of the conference was to stabilize the relative strength of the three largest navies. The United States and Britain agreed to complete parity in all types of vessels; Japan accepted smaller ratios than the other two in very category except submarines; a ceiling was placed on the construction of all types of ships. The naval race seemed halted, except for the famous "escalator clause." This provided that the ratios were to be null and void in case a nonsignatory power entered into a naval race with any of the parties to the treaty.

The World Disarmament Conference.

In 1932, after over a decade of preparation, the League of Nations "World Disarmament Conference" finally convened. The great goal of this gathering was the creation of some limits for land armaments analogous to those hammered out for naval vessels. The United States participated and tried its admittedly feeble best to promote something concrete; President Hoover even went so far as to propose an immediate one-third cut in all existing armaments. But the politics of security in Europe and Japan's Manchurian adventure cast a pall over the conference, and it broke up without any progress. The next year Hitler came to power in Germany and the entire discussion became irrelevant as the world began its downhill march to World War II.

It is impossible to find fault with American intentions during the whole long and ultimately tragic history of the attempt at disarmament. The difficulty with the American conception was its general irrelevance to the actual problems with which it was designed to deal. It was no use to dismiss French concern with security as frivolous and stubborn; it was pointless to shrug off Japanese insistence on naval parity as presumptuous. The political problems of the interwar period were real and pressing, regardless of the fact that they may have seemed slightly indecent to Americans. The way to peace was not to be found—at least in the 1920's—by voluntary acts of self-abnegation by sovereign states.

THE DEPRESSION

During the period we have been considering, European relations had changed swiftly from crisis in 1924 (marked by French occupation of the Ruhr) to a remarkable degree of reconciliation after 1925 (the year of the signature of the Pact of Locarno). Between 1925 and 1930, the climate of international relations in Europe raised hopes for permanently improved relations. This was the era of the Pact of Paris and the heyday of the League of Nations. This more or less halcyon phase came to a close with the depression of 1929.

Even before the stock-market collapse that touched off the world-wide economic distress, economic relations between the United States and Europe had been complicated by the question of the so-called "war debts." [33] The coming of the depression elevated what had been an annoyance to the level of a major crisis. The economic tensions remained strong until the war began in 1939.

The Debt Question.

About two-thirds of the debt owed the United States by its European allies had orginally been contracted during the war; the remainder had taken the form of a post-Armistice loan. The end of the war found the Allies at first arguing for cancellation of the entire debt; this the United States rejected as being both a matter of bad faith and of bad business. The next European contention was to assert that there was a connection between the interallied debt and the collection of reparations from Germany. This the United States found equally unacceptable, since there was

[33] See Harold Moulton and Leo Pasvolsky, *War Debts and World Prosperity* (New York: Appleton-Century-Crofts, 1932).

already (by 1922) a suspicion that the reparations bill would prove uncollectible. Throughout the 1920's, payments trickled in from the European debtors accompanied by a rising tide of ill will. To millions of Europeans, the United States became "Uncle Shylock," intent on getting his pound of flesh at whatever cost. American attitudes, already sensitive toward European criticism, retaliated by becoming more belligerently nationalistic and isolationist.

The Moratorium and Default.

In 1931, President Hoover attempted to reverse the disastrous trend of international economic relations by proposing a one-year moratorium on the payment of Allied debts. During the year, the European powers substantially cancelled the reparations due from Germany (by the terms of the Lausanne Agreement, 1932) and then looked expectantly to the United States for the cancellation of their own debt. President Hoover refused; his example was followed early in 1933 by Franklin D. Roosevelt. Despairing of obtaining relief from the United States almost all the debtors defaulted by June 1934. The single exception was Finland, whose debt was miniscule and who reaped a harvest in favorable publicity over the years worth far more than its negligible payments.

Economic Isolationism.

By 1933 the European states realized that only an international solution could be found for an international depression. Accordingly, an International Economic Conference convened in London in June to consider some form of joint international action to restore prosperity. After some encouraging progress, the discussion turned to the gold standard and currency stabilization. Here was the rock on which the conference foundered.

The Roosevelt New Deal, it must never be forgotten, was in the grand tradition of American reform movements; as such, it emphasized domestic policy and was profoundly and quaintly isolationist in spirit.[34] Currency manipulation was part of its program for fighting the depression at home; it had no intention of sacrificing any part of its control over the American economy on behalf of any illusory scheme of international cooperation. As a result, President Roosevelt intervened in the Conference, rebuking the membership for considering joint currency stabilization and cutting the ground out from under the American delegates. The United States had joined the major states of Europe in a policy of economic nationalism that was to endure until World War II.

---

[34] Eric F. Goldman, *Rendezvous with Destiny: A History of Modern American Reform* (New York: Alfred A. Knopf, Inc., 1953), pp. 374–9.

One break in the otherwise solid front of economic nationalism was the Reciprocal Trade Agreements Program, originally enacted in 1934. This program authorized the negotiation of bilateral executive agreements covering tariff reductions. By means of the most-favored-nation clause, reductions brought about in American duties under the terms of one of these agreements were given application to many other nations. By 1941 the Reciprocal Trade Agreements Program had brought about an over-all reduction in American tariff barriers that, although encouraging, was never any more than moderate.[35]

The Liquidation of Dollar Diplomacy

One credit mark in the record of American foreign policy prior to World War II was the liquidation of dollar diplomacy in Latin America and the adoption of the Good Neighbor policy. Credit for this movement in the direction of the abandonment of imperialism must be divided between the administrations of Hoover and Roosevelt.

The Reinterpretation of the Monroe Doctrine.

From its beginning, the Hoover administration made clear that it was abandoning the more extreme interpretations of the Monroe Doctrine popular under Theodore Roosevelt, Taft, and Wilson. In 1930 there was published a long and detailed *Memorandum on the Monroe Doctrine,* written in 1928 by Undersecretary of State J. Reuben Clark.[36] This document returned to the original conception of the doctrine as a policy vis-à-vis Europe rather than Latin America. During the Hoover administration the government remained generally faithful to its new principles, recognizing *de facto* governments in the western hemisphere without concerning itself with their legitimacy and withdrawing American forces from Haiti and Nicaragua.

The Good Neighbor.

The New Deal followed up the initial advantage. The Montevideo Inter-American Conference (1933) resulted in a pact, supported by the United States, that denied any right of intervention. Later the President specifically underscored the end of intervention and dollar diplomacy by a studied policy toward recurrent Latin American crises a good deal different from former American tactics. The United States entered World War II with

---

[35] For further discussion of the program and its more recent history, see p. 400.
[36] J. Reuben Clark, *Memorandum on the Monroe Doctrine* (Washington: U. S. Government Printing Office, 1930).

The Heritage of the Past ❖ *125*

the hemisphere more united and less hostile toward the "Colossus of the North" than at any time in sixty years, although provisions for multilateral action in enforcement of the Monroe Doctrine—hemisphere cooperation against outside threats—were not worked out until later.

THE RISE OF THE DICTATORS

The rise of Hitler, Mussolini, and imperial Japan to the point where the United States finally recognized them as menaces marks one of the major turning points in the history of American foreign policy. Before a rational course of action could be decided on, however, the last full measure of noninvolvement was to be tried and found wanting.

THE NEW THREAT OF TOTALITARIANISM

The Totalitarian Menace.

In the policies of Nazi Germany, Fascist Italy, and a newly intransigent Japan the United States found something for which it was unprepared. The initial American reaction to their irrational behavior was simply one of shocked incredulity; the United States could not take seriously the threats uttered by the Axis. When Americans finally realized that these governments meant exactly what they were saying, something like panic replaced the earlier bemusement. The democracies appeared to be almost hypnotized by the speed and precision with which the dictators won victory after victory. After a quasi-hysterical attempt at total withdrawal, the United States came at last to realize that there was only one way to deal with the sort of menace it faced: to meet force with greater force.

First Step: Manchuria.

Japan opened the dictatorial drive for world power by invading Manchuria in 1931. The United States, both because of its interest in the Open Door and its concern with peace, opposed the move and ultimately gave voice to the "Stimson Doctrine": the United States would not recognize any territorial changes brought about in violation of treaty obligations.[37] This was a weak move at best, and when Britain and France refused to follow the American lead the attempt collapsed.

The Japanese invasion of Shanghai in 1932 produced a stronger re-

---

[37] For the "Doctrine" itself, and for a picture of the crisis from the point of view of a major participant, see Henry L. Stimson and McGeorge Bundy, *On Active Service in Peace and War* (New York: Harper & Bros., 1948), pp. 226–39.

action in the United States. Public opinion at last grew seriously concerned and urged strong action against Japan. The government of the United States, however, contented itself with strong protests. Japan finally withdrew, but the damage had been done; Tokyo had broken the peace and had been permitted, not only to escape punishment, but to retain most of the fruits of its aggression.

Ethiopia and Spain.

There then ensued a pause of some three years while Hitler came to power in Germany and Mussolini poised to strike. In 1935 Italy invaded the African kingdom of Ethiopia and succeeded in making good its conquest in the face of an abortive attempt to impose sanctions by the League of Nations. In 1936 civil war broke out in Spain, with the rebels receiving open support from Hitler and Mussolini. Once again the best efforts of the European democracies were weak and futile; the dictators scored another victory.

ISOLATION BY LAW

How was the United States reacting to the rise of totalitarian power? In the first place, there was the depression to combat at home; this absorbed the bulk of official and popular attention. When foreign affairs finally forced themselves on American attention, the reaction was all too familiar. The United States attempted to legislate isolation.

The Neutrality Acts.

The only way war could come to the United States, Americans felt, was by deceit. The United States would fight only if tricked into it by the wiles of European diplomats or by the selfish manipulation of war profiteers —the "merchants of death" who became famous through the activities of investigating committees of Congress. So the United States sought to protect itself from these twin dangers by passing laws: the Neutrality Acts of 1935, 1936, and 1937.

The 1935 act made it illegal to sell or ship munitions to belligerents. In 1936 loans to belligerents were prohibited. In 1937 the law was extended to include such civil wars as were proclaimed by the President. One concession was written into the 1937 law: the "cash-and-carry" rule that raw materials could be sold to belligerents if they paid cash and took them away in their own ships. This provision had only a two-year life; this turned out to be important because World War II was to begin within a few weeks after this provision expired.

The Heritage of the Past ❖ *127*

The Neutrality Acts were misnomers; they represented the complete abandonment of neutrality rather than any protection of it. Their effectiveness, of course, would depend in practice on an intangible: would the United States remain sufficiently impartial in a major war so that both sets of belligerents could be treated alike, particularly if the prospective victor had interests inimical to the United States? This question, to be answered during the 1939–41 period, was not raised while the acts were being passed.

The Naval Race.

But American policy during this era was not all a matter of head-in-the-sand. The 1935 London Naval Disarmament Conference failed because of Japan's withdrawal and Italy's nonadherence to the draft treaty. Recognizing finally that disarmament was a futile effort during the 1930's, President Roosevelt moved to build up the United States Navy to treaty strength. By 1938 the United States was active again in the naval race.

"QUARANTINE" AND MUNICH

By 1937 the Roosevelt administration had at last learned that the dictators were actual dangers rather than mere annoyances, and that the United States could not afford any longer to ignore them without seriously undermining American security. In Europe and in the Far East American policy began to grapple with the threat of totalitarianism, at first hesitantly and then later with more determination (if with but little more effectiveness).[38]

The "Quarantine" Speech.

The first clear sign that a new American policy was in the making was the famous "quarantine the aggressors" speech of President Roosevelt in October 1937. Attacking what he called "international lawlessness," he emphasized the American interest in peace, and suggested that aggressors should be "quarantined." The President declared that 90 per cent of the

---

[38] For American policy beginning with the "Quarantine" speech and leading up to American entry into the war, the literature is already enormous. Worthy of special note are the two volumes by William L. Langer and S. Everett Gleason, *The Challenge to Isolation* (New York: Harper & Bros., 1952) and *The Undeclared War* (New York: Harper & Bros., 1953), and Basil Rauch, *Roosevelt from Munich to Pearl Harbor* (New York: Creative Age, 1950). Bitterly critical of United States policy during this period are the two works of Charles A. Beard, *American Foreign Policy in the Making, 1932–1940* (New Haven: Yale University Press, 1946) and *President Roosevelt and the Coming of the War* (New Haven: Yale University Press, 1948), and Charles C. Tansill, *Back Door to War* (Chicago: Regnery, 1952).

world wanted to live in "peace under law" and according to accepted moral standards, and that the ten per cent who were lawless should be restrained. "There must be," he said, "positive endeavors to preserve peace."

Though forcefully stated, Roosevelt's speech represented only the line of official thinking rather than any clear action program. Public opinion, although probably inclined toward his position, was nevertheless divided; the American people had not gone as far as had their government in awakening to the changed situation.

Troubles with Japan.

Meanwhile, troubles were multiplying in the Pacific where, earlier in 1937, Japan had initiated the "China incident," a euphemism for a general war of aggression against China. It was inevitable that episodes would occur involving Americans; the most serious event was the sinking of the United States gunboat *Panay* in December, 1937.

In the diplomatic dispute that then ensued, Japan announced a "New Order in East Asia," the end of the Open Door and the establishment of Japanese hegemony. This the United States was obviously unprepared to accept and, in mid-1939, the government abrogated its commercial treaty with Japan preparatory to the establishment of a munitions embargo.

Munich and the Threat of Hitler.

Up to this point Japan and Italy had been the most conspicuous dictator-ships; Germany's Hitler was a semi-comic figure with many apologists in the United States. During 1938, however, Hitler moved to the front as the leader of the new Axis of fascist states and became the most ominous threat to American security.

After destroying the Versailles Treaty in 1935 by rearming and by reoccupying the Rhineland, Hitler struck next in 1938. Early in the year he annexed Austria by a superlatively efficient coup; in the autumn came the great crisis over the Sudetenland area of Czechoslovakia. In this critical moment the United States moved quickly and, in contrast to some of its earlier efforts, to some effect. President Roosevelt personally urged Hitler and Mussolini to accept a peaceful solution to the crisis and, when the fateful Munich conference was convened, felt relieved that war had been averted.[39] American policy was by this act deeply involved in the tangled course of European affairs.

But the United States swiftly learned the folly of what was already being called "appeasement." Peace—of a sort—had been sustained at Munich, but only at the price of giving the dictators what they de-

---

[39] Arthur S. Link, *American Epoch* (New York: Alfred A. Knopf, Inc., 1955), p. 473–4.

manded. When, in the spring of 1939, Hitler tore up the Munich agreement and annexed all of Czechoslovakia, to be followed shortly by Mussolini's rape of Albania, the United States placed itself in support of Britain and France in their attempts to prepare for what now seemed to be an inevitable open clash. During the last six months of peace, American policy sought to mobilize world opinion against the dictators and to give what help it could to the democracies who were struggling to get ready for the war they had hoped they would not have to fight.[40]

The Coming of the War

Hitler, who seemed to be timing his moves to coincide with the equinoxes, began his next aggression during the late summer of 1939. His target this time was Poland. Warsaw, backed by the now-spirited allies, Britain and France, resisted Nazi pressure; the western democracies were busy negotiating a pact with the Soviet that, they hoped, would prevent Hitler from going to war. These plans evaporated late in August when the famous Nazi-Soviet nonaggression pact was announced. Hitler had won the diplomatic battle.

War and Neutrality.

President Roosevelt made one more attempt to head off the conflict, personally urging Hitler, the President of Poland, and the King of Italy to submit the dispute to peaceful settlement. Hitler, however, was ready for the battle and saw no reason to defer either to public opinion or to any adjusting agency. On September 1, the Nazi forces invaded Poland. On September 3, Britain and France declared war on Germany after the Nazis had ignored their ultimatums; on September 5, the United States issued its proclamations of neutrality. The Neutrality Acts were invoked, and President Roosevelt said: "As long as it remains within my power to prevent it, there will be no blackout of peace in the United States." [41]

THE WAR YEARS

With the course of battle during World War II, we have little to do; what is important from our point of view is the basic reorientation in American foreign policy that took place during the fighting. During the

---

[40] For Roosevelt's policy in this period, see Link, *American Epoch,* pp. 472–75.
[41] *New York Times* (September 4, 1939), quoted in Bailey, *Diplomatic History of the American People,* p. 754.

second great war Americans finally learned a good deal of what they should have known before the first.

COOPERATION BEFORE PEARL HARBOR

The United States, although sympathetic toward the Allies, was determined to remain out of the war. Up to the fall of France in June, 1940, American policy sought more and more ways of making explicit its policy of noninvolvement. Hitler's sensational victories in the West in 1940 overturned this illusion; once the Allied foothold in Europe had been reduced to the British Isles, American statesmen were forced into a frenzied recalculation of the entire situation. Never before had it been so clear that American success in remaining uninvolved in Europe depended on the British navy; if Britain fell, there would be nothing to protect the United States from the full wrath of the dictators.[42]

The End of Neutrality.

The American government immediately began giving extensive "aid short of war" to the Allies. Arms shipments were made under strained interpretations of the law—or even in defiance of it; British warships were repaired in American shipyards; the United States provided sites and personnel for the training of British flying crews. The most spectacular of these moves, made in September, 1940, was the famous transfer of 50 overage destroyers to Britain in return for a series of sites for American naval bases in a number of British possessions in the western hemisphere. There was no doubt that the United States had scrapped any notion of neutrality; America was becoming a nonbelligerent ally.

Lend-Lease and Convoying.

But more was to come. Early in 1941 the United States adopted the Lend-Lease Act that converted America into the "arsenal of democracy." Under this law, the United States pledged itself to "lend" or "lease" defense commodities of every sort to any government that the President saw fit to support in this way.[43] Since everyone knew that all such aid was to be given to those states fighting the Axis, the distinction between lend-lease and outright war was a very slender one; this, however, was about as far as American opinion cared to go at the time.

During the spring and summer of 1941, German submarine sinkings of Allied convoys reached the point of real danger, capped by open Nazi

---

[42] On this period, see especially Langer and Gleason, *The Undeclared War.*
[43] E. R. Stettinius, *Lend-Lease: Weapon of Victory* (New York: The Macmillan Co., 1944).

attacks on American shipping. By July the United States Navy was convoying merchant vessels and defending them against submarine attacks; in September Roosevelt ordered American ships to "shoot on sight" at submarines; in October the Neutrality Acts were repealed and American merchant ships began to be armed. Most Americans by this time regarded the United States as virtually at war.

The Atlantic Charter.

In the purely political area the most sensational single event of the pre-Pearl Harbor era took place: the "Atlantic Charter" issued by Roosevelt and Churchill in August 1941. This eight-point program was a joint declaration of peace terms (they could not be called "war aims," since the United States was not officially a belligerent) and were widely discussed at the time, during the war, and afterwards. The particulars were not novel; one author calls them a "mixture of the New Deal and the old Fourteen Points." [44] It is significant, however, because it tied the United States to Britain in working for a common peace—an enterprise that could be accomplished only by fighting a common war.

The Japanese Explosion.

World War II came to the United States via the Pacific. Japan had capitalized on the Nazi victory in Europe to launch a strong diplomatic offensive aimed at establishing its "New Order" in Asia, with the wealth of Indochina and the East Indies as the tempting lure that drew it on. American opposition grew in turn more rigid, and throughout the latter half of 1941 the respective positions hardened. Japan insisted on American recognition of Japanese economic and political pre-eminence in Asia; the United States demanded nothing less than the abandonment of Japan's foreign policy line after 1931 and Tokyo's retreat to its pre-Manchuria position. It seems obvious today (and, as a matter of fact, it was obvious at the time) that there was no way to reconcile these two positions.

The Tojo cabinet that took office in Japan in October 1941 was pledged to no retreat, and during the last phases of Japanese-American negotiation, Tokyo was making secret military preparations. President Roosevelt made one last try on December 6, personally appealing to Emperor Hirohito to keep the peace. It was too late; the Japanese task force was already at sea. Early in the morning of December 7, Japan attacked Pearl Harbor and war had come to the United States. [45]

[44] Bailey, *Diplomatic History of the American People,* p. 784.

[45] The most dramatic of the many accounts of the events leading to the attack is that by Walter Millis, *This Is Pearl!* (New York: William Morrow & Co., 1947); more sober and factual is Herbert Feis, *The Road to Pearl Harbor* (Princeton: Princeton University Press, 1950).

THE UNITED NATIONS

Unlike American experience in 1917–18, almost from the very beginning the United States was part of a massive international body for fighting the war. The United Nations Organization—the wartime fighting alliance—was not only the closest and most intimate arrangement ever created among so many states for such a large object, but it also provided within itself the basis for the establishment of permanent cooperation and organization for postwar unity. The United States received its baptism of fire in the troubled arena of joint action during the war; the lessons learned were to be applied later.

The United Nations Declaration.

On January 1, 1942, the formal structure of cooperation was set up by the signature of the Declaration by the United Nations, adhered to originally by twenty-six anti-Axis states and finally by over forty. This document bound all the signatories to the principles of the Atlantic Charter and pledged no separate peace. Thus the specific provisions of the Roosevelt-Churchill agreement acquired a policy significance as official war aims that they had not previously had, and involved the United States—at the very beginning of its part in the conflict—in the accomplishment of a set of specific objectives.

Russian Relations.

One consequence of the war was to throw the United States into intimate contact with the Soviet Union, an experience for which Americans were not emotionally or politically prepared. Once the two nations became allies, each was forced to learn how to deal with the other, a task complicated by the fact that it had to go on in the midst of a frustrating, expensive, and total war.

Moscow had its share of objections to American policy. Many were petty, but some had a good deal of substance. The Russians never felt that they were receiving an adequate share of lend-lease equipment. They objected to some of the more questionable features of American wartime diplomacy. They found fault with the Allied policy toward the governments-in-exile in London, particularly the openly anti-Russian Polish regime. Most specific was their constant cry for a second front in Europe so as to relieve the pressure on the Red Army and to speed the defeat of the Axis.

American criticism of the Soviet proceeded generally from an ideological root of anti-communism. Policy-wise, the United States never understood Russia's refusal to go to war against Japan until victory was already assured; there was also considerable official resentment at Moscow's reserved and suspicious attitude toward its western allies.[46]

Even so, after 1943 American-Russian (or—more accurately—Allied-Russian) cooperation proceeded adequately. By means of top-level conferences and an elaborate hierarchy of coordinating committees, liaison officers, and so on, the governments kept each other passably well informed. There was a considerable degree of consultation on major strategy and a lesser amount of tactical coordination.

The Conferences.

The new dimensions of American foreign policy were demonstrated for all to see by something that, although not entirely new, was completely novel in its scope. This was the policy-making device of the top-level conference permitting the heads of the allied governments to meet face-to-face and informally to reach basic decisions. The "Big Three" of World War II was a familiar group to newspaper readers during the war, as they met in several different parts of the world: Washington, Casablanca, Quebec, Cairo, Teheran, and—best remembered of all—Yalta.

In all of these President Roosevelt participated personally, yet probably the most important single conference of the war years was the Foreign Ministers' Conference at Moscow in October 1943. Here the log jam in Russo-American relations was broken and it was on this occasion that Britain, the USSR, and the United States (joined by China) pledged themselves to the establishment of a new international organization to preserve the peace.

The conferences were large-scale diplomacy with a vengeance. It seemed shocking to many Americans, even in the midst of a global war, that their President should sit in a room with the Prime Minister of Great Britain and the dictator of communist Russia and jointly remake the map of the world. When, at the end of the war, the information about the "secret protocols" of the Yalta agreement leaked out, public opinion was strong. The mass revulsion against strong executive action in foreign affairs, originally set in motion by the wartime conferences, continued into the postwar period in the form of proposals (such as the so-called Bricker Amendment) to inhibit the treaty power and to give Congress and state legislatures a suspensive veto over international engagements entered into by the United States. None of these attempts to inhibit the international role of the United States, however, succeeded in winning acceptance.

_____

[46] See John A. Deane, *The Strange Alliance* (New York: The Viking Press, 1947), and W. A. Williams, *American-Russian Relations, 1781–1947* (New York: Rinehart & Company, Inc., 1952), pp. 258–82.

On one account the United States in World War II clearly improved over its record during the earlier conflict—planning for the peace. In the first place, many Americans recognized that there was going to be a peace and that all American problems were not going to end with the consummation of the magic formula of "unconditional surrender." Indeed, the postwar difficulties into which the United States drifted were not a result of the want of a plan, but rather of having too many plans. Perhaps the most accurate way to put the point is this: the deficiency was not in the plans themselves, but rather in the fact that the plans were drawn to cope with a situation that never arose, while the actual problems that appeared were foreign to the blueprints under which the United States was trying to operate.

The Moscow Declaration.

The Atlantic Charter, in words of studied vagueness, had pledged Britain and the United States to work for the creation of some new kind of world organization. This idea languished, as we have seen, during the early years of the war. It was only with the Moscow Conference of foreign ministers, in October 1943, that the promise was made specific. This, the original germ of the United Nations, merits quotation. In the communique the following statement was made:

> 4. That they [the United States, the United Kingdom, the Soviet Union, and China] recognize the necessity of establishing at the earliest practicable date a general international organization, based on the principle of the sovereign equality of all peace-loving states, and open to membership by all such states, large and small, for the maintenance of international peace and security.[47]

Dumbarton Oaks and Yalta.

The major effort in direct implementation of the Moscow Declaration was the Dumbarton Oaks Conference of August–October, 1944. Here representatives of the four major allied powers worked out a draft of a world organization. Despite general agreement that the new structure was to have "teeth" as contrasted with the powerless League of Nations, the thorny question of the voting formula to be used in controlling the enforcement action of the organization could not be finally decided. Without such a decision, there could be no United Nations.

---

[47] *Department of State Bulletin* (October 16, 1943, p. 254).

This was solved—after a fashion—at the Yalta Conference. It was at this meeting that the much-discussed "veto" provision, requiring the unanimous vote of all permanent members for the Security Council to take any action on a nonprocedural matter, was decided upon by Roosevelt and Stalin. With this out of the way, the call was issued at Yalta for the United Nations Conference to draw up the Charter of the proposed organization.[48]

The San Francisco Conference.

Based on dates of its meeting (April 21–June 25, 1945) the San Francisco Conference belongs in a discussion of the war years, but it may also be thought of as the beginning of the postwar era. Before the Conference adjourned, Germany had surrendered and the final blows were being prepared for the destruction of Japan. Another reason for considering it a postwar development was the appearance at San Francisco of what were to become some of the most ominous lines of cleavage in postwar politics: the East-West split and the great power-small state controversy.

The Charter of the United Nations emerged from the Conference much as it had come from Dumbarton Oaks and Yalta. The smaller states made a few significant amendments, mainly in the direction of increased emphasis in structure and function on "non-political" questions—economic, social, and technical. They also succeeded in reducing slightly the almost complete monopoly over security issues that the Big Five had originally hoped for. But in the main the Charter was close to what its original sponsors had planned.

Unlike the Covenant of the League, the Charter had no difficulty winning ratification. The quick action taken by the United States Senate marked something of the distance the United States had come since 1919. The Foreign Relations Committee held only brief hearings, Senate debate lasted only six days, the final vote was eighty-nine to two, and the United States was the first state to ratify. Americans, having come out of one war into attempted isolation and almost complete frustration, were determined to try a different tack as they emerged from the second.

---

[48] See E. R. Stettinius, *Roosevelt and the Russians* (Garden City: Doubleday, 1949), Chapters 7, 10; also John N. Snell, Forrest C. Pogue, Charles F. Delzell, and George A. Lensen, *The Meaning of Yalta* (Baton Rouge: Louisiana State University Press, 1956).

The

National

Interest:

Myth

and

Reality

◆▶

The Popular Tradition of Foreign Policy

CHAPTER ◄ *5* ►

Each nation has a more or less formalized ego-image: a psychic picture of itself as it performs its mission in the world. Such generalized impressions often largely determine much of its behavior; a people's version of its foreign policy goals goes far to shape the decisions their government make. In this chapter we shall analyze the "tradition" of American policy: those ideas, impressions, and feelings about the external relations of the United States that have their roots deep in history and are widely shared among, deeply felt by, and virtually self-evident to the mass of the American people today.

Being imbedded so firmly in popular political consciousness, this tradition represents a relatively constant and fixed factor that must be taken into account by both American and foreign policymakers. Any tradition changes only slowly and reluctantly; the fast-moving world of today has done violence to many of the most cherished presuppositions and preferences of Americans. Although modified to some extent by the impact of circumstances, the tradition endures to this day, alternately srtengthening and stultifying the government's attacks on international problems.

THE TRADITION OF AMERICAN FOREIGN POLICY

The American people have approached foreign policy in general agreement on certain basic assumptions. These have grown out of native American history and culture and have reflected certain basic characteristics of the whole of American life. This was indeed inevitable; a nation's foreign policy may perhaps be less than its over-all *Weltanschauung,* but it can never be more.[1]

THE SECONDARY NATURE OF FOREIGN AFFAIRS

We may lay down a basic postulate at the outset. Foreign affairs, however exciting they may have become during particular crises, in the long run have been of only secondary importance to Americans. They have felt that their ultimate salvation was to be found within the United States and, while agreeing that they must accept the world, they have argued that they dare not trust themselves entirely to it.

The Importance of Domestic Affairs.

Initially, this notion grew out of a very natural preoccupation with domestic affairs. Americans have tended to be most interested in those things that were either close to them in space or that affected them directly, and for most citizens the rest of the world was far away. Today it is less far away than it used to be, perhaps; yet the immediacy of international problems is seldom as great for most Americans as that of local, municipal, state, or national ones.[2]

Nowhere has this been more clearly indicated than in the dominant popular attitude toward domestic politics. Presidential elections are tradi-

---

[1] For somewhat different approaches to the problem discussed in this section, see, among other works, the following: Dexter Perkins, *The American Approach to Foreign Policy* (Cambridge: Havard University Press, 1952); Robert Osgood, *Ideals and Self-interest in America's Foreign Relations* (Chicago: University of Chicago Press, 1953); Frank Tannenbaum, *The American Tradition in Foreign Policy* (Norman: University of Oklahoma Press, 1955); and Emmet John Hughes, *America the Vincible* (Garden City: Doubleday & Co., 1959).

[2] For an explicit example of this attitude, emphasizing the minor importance and essentially amoral character of foreign affairs, see Felix Morley, *The Foreign Policy of the United States* (New York: Alfred A. Knopf, Inc., 1951).

tionally fought out essentially on national issues, and Americans have had some difficulty in grasping the supranational significance of their political struggles. "Foreign policy" has been an election issue to be dealt with by both parties in such a way as to harvest the greatest number of votes; it has been no different—and of no more importance—than agriculture, labor relations, tax policy, or any of a dozen other perennial problems that help decide elections.

Distrust of the Outside World.

A second explanation for the relatively low place occupied by foreign policy in the American attitude has been a genuine distrust of the outside world. This is by no means to say that Americans have been totally uninterested in what goes on abroad; indeed, American curiosity about alien cultures is famous everywhere in the world. But the political overtones of this curiosity have been suspicion, reserve, and mistrust.

Since Americans have had to make their way in a world peopled by men who, if not actually doing evil, were at least capable of it, their tradition tended to place a low estimate on what they could achieve in dealing with them. The rewards of foreign policy were thought to be by their very nature limited in extent, and of only an inferior order of worth. For what good the United States could achieve in the world Americans felt they must count ultimately only on themselves.[3]

Cultural Isolationism.

A final explanation of the basic popular skepticism about foreign policy grows out of the first two. Culturally Americans have been in the past—and to a considerable extent still are—isolated from many of the main streams of social development. Most adult Americans—and most of their forbears—grew to maturity in a climate relatively unsullied by alien influences and free from direct concern about the size or the complexities of other societies.

Thus unaware of the cultural diversity of men, or—more accurately—aware of the diversity but insensitive to the difference such cultural variation made, Americans have tended to judge the world by their own standards. Their self-identification was epitomized in the famous phrase from Washington's Farewell Address: "Why quit our own to stand on foreign ground?" "Why, indeed?" have echoed generations of Americans;

---

[3] This idea was the foundation of the later foreign-policy thinking of the late Professor Charles A. Beard. See especially his *Open Door at Home* and *The Devil Theory of War*, as well as his polemics on American entry into World War II, *American Foreign Policy in the Making* and *President Roosevelt and the Coming of the War.*

The Popular Tradition of Foreign Policy * *141*

foreign policy thus came inevitably to reflect a dominant cultural particularism.

The Uniqueness of the United States

Despite the secondary place of foreign policy in the American attitude, Americans nonetheless recognized early in their history that they must deal with the rest of the world. Into their contacts with other states they carried the second element of their evolving tradition: a profound conviction that they were a unique people, unlike any other and therefore subject to different standards of behavior and judgment.

The Sense of "Difference."

American history led to the conclusion that Americans are different from any other people. Nobody was quite like Americans, and it was unfair to expect them to behave quite like anyone else. The international role of the United States, therefore, came to be conceived as different from that of any other state.

Americans claimed to be uninterested in the ordinary goals pursued by ordinary governments; they felt that they were engaged in a (regrettably) necessary but ultimately loftier enterprise than the common run of nations. The United States was in the world—this much Americans would admit— but it was emphatically not of it. The nation contended that it would not make any compromises with its principles in order to gain advantages that, at best, could never be more than temporary.[4]

Moral Superiority.

This sense of detachment from the world rapidly led into a manifestation of what anthropologists call "ethnocentrism." The differences between other peoples and Americans came popularly to be regarded as measures of the extent to which outsiders fell short of the high American moral standards. Morality became the index of uniqueness; Americans were simply "better" people than the ordinary run of mortals whose shortcomings Americans would endure but never emulate.

One of the unspoken but ubiquitous premises of American foreign policy has been that the United States was always dealing with its moral in-

---

[4] For example, Washington's Farewell Address pointed out: "Our detached and distant position invites us and enables us to pursue a different course [from that of the states of Europe]." James D. Richardson, ed. and compiler, *A Compilation of the Messages and Papers of the Presidents* (New York: Bureau of National Literature, 1897), I, 214.

feriors. Particular states, of course, varied in the degree to which they fell short of the American standard; generally, the more closely they resembled the United States the greater amount of moral conviction they were admitted to have. Generally, Great Britain was agreed to rank the highest. But since no one could ever be quite like Americans, no one could really come up to their moral level.[5]

An International Double Standard.

Being different, and this difference being epitomized and most clearly demonstrated by moral preeminence, it was only a short step for Americans to argue that they should be judged by a different set of standards than those applied to lesser states. In this way deeds wrong in themselves when done by other peoples became perfectly permissible when done by the United States; other forms of state action, regarded as normal by the international community, were barred to Americans. It was not "imperialistic," for example, for the United States to annex overseas territories, since American purposes were high-minded and philanthropic; the United States was to rule colonial peoples for their own good. According to the converse of the same principle, "power politics" was "un-American" and immoral; Americans would not indulge in it, no matter how widespread the practice might be among other states.

For a long time Americans overlooked the ethical trap they were laying for themselves by the advocacy of this double standard. The constant evocation of uniqueness and moral superiority prepared the way for the dangerous doctrine that the ends always justify the means. It has been only recently that this dilemma has finally forced itself on the popular consciousness.[6] Today many Americans are wrestling with the issue, but without reaching any answer that satisfies both the requirements of effective policy and the insistent promptings of their consciences.

----

[5] For a sharp critique of American moralism in international affairs, see George F. Kennan, *American Diplomacy, 1900–1950*, pp. 95–103; for an indignant demand that Americans return to the historic moral base of their foreign policy, see Morley, *Foreign Policy*, pp. 154–156. See also Hughes, *America the Vincible*, and Kenneth W. Thompson, *Political Realism and the Crisis of World Order* (Princeton: Princeton University Press, 1960).

[6] The most dramatic instance of the dilemma of the double standard was provided by the famous "U-2" spy plane episode of May 1960, that wrecked the 1960 summit conference and provoked the most serious crisis of the Eisenhower era. Caught in the act of violating Soviet air space, the United States openly admitted the offense and justified it on the grounds of Soviet secrecy. The official line that Moscow had no reason for resentment of American espionage activities was not questioned widely by the public. The reaction from the free world, however, was generally unfavorable to the American justification, although inclined to accept the necessity of the act. The whole course of the crisis, including the official American statements, is recounted in the *New York Times*, May 5–16, 1960.

Finally, the American approach to foreign policy has been essentially Utopian. This term has been used variously as an anathema or as an accolade, but its substantive import has been fairly consistent. The Utopian assumption has been one of the more durable and versatile components of the American tradition.

A Sense of Mission.

In the first place, Americans have been called Utopian because they have recognized and have accepted a sense of mission. The popular attitude toward foreign policy, once the United States has actively entered the international arena, has usually been an urge to "set things right." Americans disapproved of purposeless action; they affirmatively have sought a goal of improvement, of rectification, or of organization.

Remembering their unique orientation to the world, we would expect that the missions accepted by the American people would be thought of as being of a higher and more moral nature than would ordinarily be expected of a state. There has been a strong popular preference for objectives expressed as moral absolutes. National missions have only infrequently gained popular expression in either concrete or egocentric terms.[7]

The Goal of Perfection.

Utopianism has been also apparent in the deliberate pursuit of the goal of perfection by Americans. Implicitly Americans have seemed to assume that all international problems have a "right" answer, discoverable by men if only they put all their resources of reason and good will to work on it. The right answer usually was one that forever settled the problem and removed it to the category of the not-to-be-thought-about-again. Not only were single issues attacked in terms of finding the correct solution for each of them, but the long-range target was frequently formulated as a world organized into a single, self-regulating system. Such perfection, Americans thought, would obliterate forever the irrational scourges of war, crisis, and turmoil.

---

[7] Although hackneyed by much quotation, Woodrow Wilson's speech on the Fourteen Points merits one more repetition because of its admirable evocation of the idea of "the American mission": "We entered this war because violations of right had occurred which touched us to the quick and made the life of our own people impossible unless they were corrected and the world secured once for all against their recurrence.... The program of the world's peace, therefore, is our program...." *Congressional Record,* LVI, 691 (January 8, 1918).

Leadership by Example.

But we must not infer that Utopianism led Americans into active commitment to the cause of the perfect order they desired. On the contrary, the dominant popular conception of the role of the United States was that of leadership by example rather than that of direct participation in concrete cooperative projects. The best way to bring about a world of law and justice, Americans felt, was for them to act always as the United States wished everyone else to act, to be prompt to point out the failures of other peoples, and to be willing to give advice as to how they should behave. In this way the sheer force of example would do more to bring about a better day than would self-defeating involvement in the imperfect and frustrating process of day-by-day international politics.

TRADITIONAL FORMULATIONS OF THE NATIONAL INTEREST

Within the developed tradition of foreign policy, the American people developed a number of concrete formulations of interest that reflected the national sense of mission. Many of these traditional interests have been carried virtually untouched into the contemporary era; others have been abandoned in favor of newer formulas. As we saw in Chapter 1, however, whatever forms the myth of national purpose may take, it remains as a major factor influencing the decisions made on concrete issues made by the responsible officials of the American government. In times of stress or sudden crisis the spontaneous reaction of much of public opinion is to revert to traditional concepts of interests; to accept some new formulation usually demands an effort of mass will spurred by self-conscious leaders.

The Myth of Isolationism.

We should first dispose of a pernicious but remarkably tenacious component of the American myth: the notion of isolationism. We have already seen that the word itself was more a tool of political manipulation and a component of the mystique of democratic politics than it was descriptive of the actual content of American foreign policy. There is little concrete evidence that the working notion of American national interest was ever based on any purely isolationist premise.[8] Total nonintercourse with the outside world has never been seriously attempted by the United States, and the term is almost meaningless on any other basis. The record indicates

----

[8] See the elaborate synthesis made by Albert K. Weinberg in "The Historical Meaning of the American Doctrine of Isolation," *American Political Science Review* (June, 1940).

that the American tradition of national interest has been too many-sided to be successfully fitted into any slogan as rigid as "isolationism." It has taken a different turn in each major region of the world, and we must consider it in terms of its principal specific manifestations.

Hemisphere Hegemony.

No element of American foreign policy received such unanimous acceptance by the public nor a more solid place in tradition than the principle that the United States should be absolutely dominant in the western hemisphere. The Monroe Doctrine is, as we have pointed out, a phrase with which almost all Americans are familiar, and the package of emotional reactions that it evokes has had a powerful impact on the actual policy of the United States.[9]

As worked out by the interaction of doctrine and practice, the American interest in the western hemisphere consisted of three related concerns: (1) The United States insisted on the exclusion of non-American power from the hemisphere except for the minor colonial holdings of Britain, France, and the Netherlands. (2) The United States was to brook no real rivals in the region; America was to regard the hemisphere as a United States preserve in which Washington reigned unchallenged. (3) The Americas were to be organized into a single more or less cohesive entity under United States leadership.

European Noninvolvement.

We have already pointed out that the principle of "isolationism" was relevant only to Europe, and then only in a rather special sense. Tradition energetically foreswore any entanglement in intra-European politics, a game which Americans felt themselves unequipped to play; many Americans are still uncomfortable at the thought that they may be caught in a political web in the capitals of Europe from which they can never escape.[10] Such participation in European affairs as the United States could not avoid was reluctant and broken off as soon as possible.

We should also note again, however, that noninvolvement was more a matter of geography than of an antipathy to the European states as such. The traditional interests of the United States have always permitted extensive relations and even binding commitments with the powers of

---

[9] This story is well told in Dexter Perkins, *Hands Off: A History of the Monroe Doctrine;* and Samuel F. Bemis, *The Latin American Policy of the United States* (New York: Harcourt, Brace and Co., 1943).

[10] Typical—although somewhat extreme—examples of this attitude can be found throughout Harry Elmer Barnes, ed., *Perpetual War for Perpetual Peace* (Caldwell, Idaho: Caxton, 1953).

Europe on questions that were non-European in nature. It was only at European problems, narrowly defined, that the United States drew the line; in Latin America and in the Pacific, American tradition approved of intimate dealings with the world of Europe.

Balance of Power in Asia.

"Intervention" is as much a key word to characterize American traditions in Asia—or, more properly, the Far Eastern littoral—as "noninvolvement" is appropriate to the American outlook toward Europe. In the Pacific and on Asia's eastern face, crystallized interests called for the United States to follow an active policy and to enter into the thick of affairs.[11]

Simplifying drastically, traditional American interests in the Far East can be reduced to three interdependent propositions, whose application with varying degrees of skill to changing circumstances can tell the story of American policy in the region since 1900. These three propositions are:

1. The overriding concern of the United States is with the internal and international stability of the Far East.
2. Stability in the region can best be achieved by ensuring a balance of power on the Far Eastern littoral; that is, the area must not be permitted to fall under the domination of any single power.
3. Stability and the balance of power, in turn, depend upon the fate of China; only if China were guaranteed "territorial integrity and political independence" could Asia be structured according to American interests.[12]

Imperialism: American Style.

Most Americans would reject the bald statement that imperialism is any part of their traditional version of national interest. The word and the idea both run counter to what has been expressed as the "different" international role of the United States. Yet Americans, although late starters, did get caught up in the international race for overseas colonial possessions, and a rationale for such a policy became incorporated into the American tradition.

The American empire was not particularly large, though it was admittedly widespread. In its acquisition and exploitation Americans revealed the common characteristics of an imperial people, primarily that of rationalizing their colonizing mission into one of philanthropy.[13] The United

[11] See Griswold, *The Far Eastern Policy of the United States.*

[12] See the Open Door note of 1899 and the circular telegram of 1900, quoted in Bartlett, *The Record of American Diplomacy,* pp. 409–11, 413.

[13] For a general discussion of this point, see J. A. Hobson, *Imperialism: A Study,* 3rd ed. (London: Allen and Unwin, 1938), pp. 196–8.

States purported to be interested primarily in the betterment of the unfortunate peoples for whose destinies the American government made itself responsible.

What made the imperial tradition of the United States unusual, however, was the fact that Americans took their own professions quite seriously. The record reveals a constant—although unevenly effective—attempt to live up to the repeated claims of good will. The more "civilized" colonies—Puerto Rico, Hawaii, and the Philippines—were prepared for self-government; the backward peoples were the objects of a host of programs of betterment. In this effort the United States government was responding to a genuine and deep-seated urge growing naturally from the self-image of the American people.

TRADITIONAL TECHNIQUES OF FOREIGN POLICY

Corresponding to their traditional formulations of the national interest, Americans developed what we might call a traditional methodology of foreign policy. The mass of the American people—particularly the less informed, relatively unsophisticated groups—have accepted this tradition as the way foreign policy *should* be conducted and as the way it *will* be conducted when the world is finally arranged the way it should be. Part of the problem of managing American foreign affairs in the contemporary world arises from the necessity felt by officials to meet concrete problems effectively without at the same time doing irreparable violence to the nation's procedural tradition.

THE DISTRUST OF POWER POLITICS

Traditionally, for reasons both too well known and too complex to develop fully here, Americans have distrusted power politics. The United States has practiced it only under duress, and then with acute embarrassment and no great skill. Power politics, the amoral and opportunistic pursuit of national interest by all expedient means, is historically repugnant to Americans. They have preferred instead to prosecute their policy by other—and morally more defensible—methods.

The Immorality of Power Politics.

As a nation whose history has been called "the vindication of Puritan morality," it was strictly in character for the American people to reject power politics on grounds of immorality. The cynicism of many statesmen about human motives and their crass calculations of expedient alternatives have repelled the American conscience and driven them to search for some "finer" principle upon which to base their international conduct.

It has seemed to Americans that power politics as carried on by the courts and chancelleries of the "Old World"—Europe—was a pastime of men whose intellect had overwhelmed their moral sense. The United States, by playing the game by the same rules, would dirty its own hands with the same pitch. To attempt an American version of power politics would be to sully the national ideals and to cheapen the very truths the United States was seeking to universalize.[14]

American Inadequacies.

To be honest, however, we must also admit that popular disgust with power politics had another root. Not only were Americans outraged by its immorality, but they also entertained shrewd doubts about their ability to hold their own in it.

Americans seem to have had a difficult time escaping some of the aftermaths of their long-ago colonial status. One heritage from this era and the struggle for independence with which it closed was a chronic fear of American political inadequacy. Not so strong as to be called a national inferiority complex, it has taken the more restrained form of a reluctance to put the United States to the test of active entry into open diplomatic competition with other states. As the late Will Rogers put it, "The United States never lost a war or won a peace."

We find very few clear admissions of this concern with America's fear of its own possible ineptitude, either in the pronouncements of statesmen, the fulminations of editors, or—until recently—the writings of scholars. Americans have preferred to rest their case for eschewing power politics on moral grounds and to seek their goals by other means. It would be useless to deny, however, that this same fear of proving unequal to the task of close-quarter diplomacy and the strategy of force and counterforce is still at work in the American people in the middle of the twentieth century; for proof we need look no further than the popular impatience with diplomacy and the constant discussion of a "showdown" with the USSR.

ARMED FORCE IN THE AMERICAN TRADITION

A logical outgrowth of this strong opinion about power politics is the traditional American view of armed force as an element in foreign policy.

---

[14] From among the many criticisms of this position, see Kenneth W. Thompson, *Political Realism and the Crisis of World Politics,* Chapter 4: "The Limits of Principle in International Politics."

Not sharing the prevailing assumptions about the nature of interstate life, the American people developed some indigenous ideas about the role of military power in it.

The Nature and Purposes of War.

According to the traditional American idea, war can be either of two things. It may be the outcome of the diabolical schemes of cynical and depraved aggressors; it may, on the other hand, be merely the result of the diseased outlook of unsound rulers. Whether rational but unprincipled or the end product of sheer insanity, war is considered always as an abnormal event. It is never deliberately selected as a technique by worthy statesmen; organized hostility is a departure from the rational norm of international affairs.[15] Americans based much of their approach to international affairs on the assumption that the ideal of a world without war could some day be achieved.

Once the United States became involved in a military struggle, the tradition also provided a guide to the conduct of the conflict. Americans have felt a strong compulsion to fight only for some "higher" purpose than mere selfish interest. Usually American war aims were phrased as lofty abstractions. Americans tended to see their foes as needing chastisement for their anti-social behavior and for their temerity in disturbing the peace. The object of war was to inflict a military defeat with no regard for the political concessions that might be gained from the victory.[16]

The Armed Forces in Peacetime.

The American conception of armed force has been of a piece with this theory of warfare. Until recently the United States did not see the necessity of having a peace-time armed force of more than token size. Americans clung to the myth of the invincibility of the "embattled farmer" of the Revolution, and trusted in the native fighting ability of the ordinary Ameri-

---

15 Robert E. Osgood, *Limited War: the Challenge to American Strategy* (Chicago: University of Chicago Press, 1957), Chapter II: "The American Approach to War."

16 George F. Kennan puts the point this way in *American Diplomacy, 1900-1950,* pp. 65–66: "Democracy fights in anger—it fights for the reason that it was forced to go to war. It fights to punish the power that was rash enough and hostile enough to provoke it—to teach that power a lesson it will not forget, to prevent the thing from happening again. Such a war must be carried to the bitter end.

"This is true enough, and, if nations could afford to operate in the moral climate of individual ethics, it would be understandable and acceptable. But I sometimes wonder whether in this respect a democracy is not uncomfortably similar to one of those prheistoric monsters with a body as long as this room and a brain the size of a pin. . . ." Reprinted by permission. See also Gordon R. Turner, "Classical and Modern Strategic Concepts," in Turner and Challener, *National Security in the Nuclear Age,* pp. 3–30.

can citizen who, armed with the products of American industrial ingenuity and the reinforcement of a just cause, could withstand any possible combination of enemies.

The American people have been far more willing to support a large navy than a large army; in recent years air power has moved to the top of the list in public acceptance, even ahead of the navy. Two factors might help explain this traditional preference for sea and air power: both are less greedy of manpower than is a land army, and both tend to exert their influence beyond the limits of the United States and are less obvious in the midst of American society.

American Policy and the Military.

Seeing no necessary connection between armed might and an orderly foreign policy, and distrustful of a major military establishment in peacetime, it is no wonder that Americans traditionally have given little thought to overt military calculations in foreign policy. The popular image of foreign policy made it the province of diplomats; only when negotiations failed completely was the matter supposed to be turned over to the military. This has meant that the advice of military men was not sought when policy moves were being considered. The military function was thought to be limited to two tasks: (1) to guard the security of the United States; (2) to fight—and win—a war at the command of the civilian authorities. With the circumstances leading up to that war, they were not to be concerned; neither did they have any interest in its political outcome.

THE AMERICAN METHOD IN FOREIGN POLICY

Since tradition rejected the usual basis of international affairs—power politics—and its necessary motive force—armed strength—Americans had to develop a foreign-policy method of their own. Its dominant characteristic was its great reliance upon persuasive and nonviolent techniques; starting from its assumptions, it could scarcely have done otherwise. We must note, however, that the American version of persuasion did not take the form that it did in other conceptions of foreign policy, that of diplomacy. Diplomatic haggling and adjustment smacked too strongly of the immorality of power politics; Americans tended instead to prefer persuasive procedures more in harmony with their own predispositions.

The Appeal to Reason and Morality.

Perhaps most characteristic of the United States and most consonant with its general position was the technique of appealing to the good sense and the good will of the states with which it was in contact. Democratic ideology taught that men were possessed of reason and morality, and that they would respond to appeals made in those terms. Americans therefore attempted to stake out positions that were justifiable in rational and ethical terms, and to apply these norms in relations with other states.[17]

This approach often had two practical advantages. In the first place, when the United States espoused the cause of abstract reason and morality, it frequently put its opponents in an uncomfortable position. To disagree with truth and right as defined by Americans often meant favoring or apologizing for irrational and immoral conduct. Many instances could be cited in which this device left the United States in an unassailable position. Second, anyone who opposed the United States was—according to Americans—*per se* a "bad" (irrational and/or immoral) person, and Americans were thus in a better frame of mind to prosecute the ensuing struggle.[18]

The Invocation of Public Opinion.

In complete harmony with democratic ideology was a great faith in the wisdom and the omnipotence of "public opinion." The policy of the United States has long been to attempt systematically to influence mass attitudes everywhere and to identify American policy with what were taken to be the commands of popular opinion. American political ideas have always assumed a disharmony between the people of any "autocratic" or "dictatorial" state and their government, and Americans felt that it would not be difficult to win the masses of men to the American side in any dispute. Men, the argument ran, are inherently reasonable and just; American policy is reasonable and just; all rational and moral men will automatically support the United States if only they know the truth; the ultimate vindication of the American position is therefore certain.

---

[17] For a provocative treatment of this point—and the American preference for rational and moral techniques generally—see the article by Hans J. Morgenthau, "The Mainsprings of American Foreign Policy: the National Interest *vs.* Moral Abstractions," *American Political Science Review* (December, 1950), pp. 833–54. See also the "great debate" touched off by this article, especially Frank Tannenbaum, "The Balance of Power *vs.* the Coordinate State," *Political Science Quarterly* (June, 1952), pp. 173–197; and Professor Morgenthau's reply, "Another Great Debate: the National Interest of the United States," *American Political Science Review* (December, 1952), pp. 961–88. See also the critique of this discussion in Hoffmann, *Contemporary Theory in International Relations.*

[18] For instance, American reaction to the failure of the 1960 summit conference centered upon the irrationality of the Soviet's objections to American policy and the immorality of the Soviet behavior that had brought the world to this dismal outcome. See the editorials in the *New York Times* and *Washington Post and Times-Herald,* May 16–20, 1960. The observer is tempted to speculate that in this moment of crisis the United States was unable to function effectively without first—at least, to its own satisfaction—putting the USSR into the moral wrong.

The operational problem of United States policy therefore resolved itself primarily into one of communication. All the United States had to do was to make its own position clear beyond misunderstanding (being sure to orient it on objective truth and moral right), and then to discover mechanisms to bring its message to the world. Public opinion everywhere would recognize the justice of American policy, and all wise and good men would demand that their respective governments immediately accede to the wishes of the United States. No regime, however inimical it might be otherwise, could resist this pressure.

The Development and Use of "Law."

Another traditional nonviolent technique much favored by Americans has been a heavy reliance on law, legal reasoning, and legal rules. In international relations the United States has been sensitive to the existence of legal rules and has usually attempted to shape its policy in accordance with them. Not only has the United States attempted to "have the law on its side," but also it has sought to foster the continual elaboration of international legal rules. To Americans, social relations sanctioned by juristic norms are always preferable to extra-legal ones; a "world of law" would be better on all counts than a "lawless" one. The United States has pioneered in the extension of the international legal frontier so as to encompass more and more of interstate life.

Economics: the Punitive Sanction.

But what if reason, justice, law, and public opinion were to prove inadequate; what was the United States to do if the forces of evil did not yield to these rational techniques? The American tradition, although repudiating armed force except in extremes, nevertheless made allowances for a punitive sanction. Such open coercion as was necessary was to be accomplished by economic means.

This again was only to be expected. In a highly materialistic culture in which major emphasis is placed on the rewards of economic activity, the promise of economic reward or the threat of economic deprivation has come to have a distinctly coercive character. What could be more natural for Americans than to conclude that this weapon would prove as efficacious in international relations as it was in their private lives?

And so the United States came to feel that its productive power made it really unnecessary for it to fight wars or to play the more ordinary forms of power politics. All America really needed to do was to use its immense economic strength coercively and any possible opponent would be, if not stopped, at least handicapped to the point where it would yield to American techniques of persuasion.

The Popular Tradition of Foreign Policy ✻ *153*

PUBLIC OPINION AND AMERICAN FOREIGN POLICY

The first two sections of this chapter have dealt with the popular image of foreign policy as it was formed during earlier periods of history. We have considered the mass attitudes and preferences that are still alive today in the subtle and complex phenomenon we call "public opinion." This concluding section will deal with American public opinion as it bears upon specific issues of foreign policy, using the version of its role that we developed in Chapter 2.

The Characteristics of Public Opinion.

We shall be enumerating certain common characteristics of mass attitudes in the United States. It seems scarcely necessary to remind ourselves that any such list contains certain inherent shortcomings: (1) no single person demonstrates all the following characteristics, either of strength or of weakness, in his own attitudes; (2) the general public seldom exhibits all the characteristics simultaneously; (3) no single characteristic is present in the public all the time.

If these limitations be kept in mind, it is possible to construct two almost parallel lists, one including the major weaknesses of American mass opinion, the other its significant strengths, as both apply to questions of international affairs.

WEAKNESSES OF AMERICAN PUBLIC OPINION

It has been fashionable for a number of years for scholars to find ample fault with the American mass mind as it comes to grips with international problems.[19] Either because of an admiration for the "superior" efficiency of dictatorial or aristocratic governments or because of a deep and sincere faith in the greater wisdom of professional officialdom, many writers have made very detailed and thoughtful criticisms of the way Americans think about foreign affairs. We may find their conclusions unpalatable and their recommendations controversial, but we must admit that they have made a very sizeable indictment of American public opinion.

Lack of Information.

Perhaps the most far-reaching, and the most difficult to contradict, of the asserted weaknesses of American opinion is its uninformed character.

---

[19] A recent example is Walter Lippmann, *The Public Philosophy.*

Americans have access to a greater amount of information than does any other people in the world; newspapers, magazines, radio, television, and every other mass medium pour forth data in a great flood. The stark fact remains, however, that mass audiences do not take advantage of the available data to the extent that one might expect.

No one expects laymen to have complete information about all the problems facing the nation. But the "ordinary citizen" does not seem to have enough information at his command to play even his limited public part with full efficiency. Public-opinion polls reveal a startling lack of knowledge about such important matters as the United Nations NATO, the nature of communism, and so on. Without basic data, it is a near-impossibility for individuals to make intelligent decisions—or even any decisions at all.

Impatience.

Americans are an impatient people. Their culture emphasizes direct social action with speedy results; they tend to prefer immediate solutions to problems, with no excuses accepted for delay. When applied to foreign affairs, in which progress is often tortuous and usually slow, this cultural trait can cause serious conflict.

Impatience makes Americans fretful under the tedious and delicate course of most diplomacy; it frequently leads to the advocacy of "show-down" or "all-out" techniques when less extreme measures might be preferable. It makes continued crisis difficult to endure, eroding national self-control and perspective. It generates tremendous pressures for action that officials find to be very difficult to withstand.

Emotionalism.

Emotion bulks large in American international attitudes. Americans go to greater lengths in indulging their international loves and hates than do the people of any other major state. It is difficult to maintain mass enthusiasm for the controlling constant of national interest; the public most commonly follows the course dictated by current likes and dislikes. This gives American opinion toward major issues a peculiar wavelike quality arising from its tendency to great emotional swings from one extreme to the other.[20]

---

[20] One can recall the shattering descent from a high plateau of euphoria on May 1, 1960 to the depths of a full-fledged war scare three weeks later after the failure of the summit conference. It required months for American equilibrium to be restored after this swift trip from the peak of optimism to the valley of near-despair.

Finally, we must mention the American preference for dichotomies. Americans generally have an all-or-nothing attitude in international affairs; the dominant national assumption is that the only alternative outcomes of a situation are extreme ones. Public attitudes think only of total peace or total war, total love or total hatred, Russian friendship or Russian enmity. This simple black-or-white formulation of problems grows out of the first three points we have made above, and in turn influences each of them.

STRENGTHS OF AMERICAN PUBLIC OPINION

Less frequently discussed, at least in any objective fashion, are the positive strengths of American public opinion. It is somewhat surprising that this is so; in a democracy in which public opinion is given a significant role to play we would expect that considerable effort would be expended in analyzing the positive contributions made by mass attitudes. Yet it is relatively rare to find a systematic study of the sources of strength provided by the public.[21]

We may nevertheless prepare a list suggesting some of the favorable or advantageous characteristics of American public opinion on foreign policy. We must keep these in mind in reaching any over-all judgment on the democratic process as it applies to international affairs. Concentrating only on popular shortcomings prepares the way for the possible acceptance of some doctrine of elitism and might ultimately lead to at least a partial rejection of the entire democratic idea. The strengths of American opinion at least help balance the most glaring of its weaknesses.

The Debating of Major Issues.

One of the chief strengths of American public opinion is a popular insistence on thorough public airing and debate of major international issues. On any important question nearly every possible point of view has at least an organization or two to express its views. As each prosecutes its case, the basic alternatives often receive a thorough airing. Pressure groups and political parties also share in keeping debate and disagreement alive, with the party in control of the White House (and therefore presumably responsible for policy) usually defending its record and the opposition engaged in attacking and criticizing.

---

[21] Emmet John Hughes, in *America the Vincible,* attempts to stake out an effective and affirmative role for American public opinion, but he is convinced that the American people have not yet lived up to their democratic potential.

The next characteristic we mention might at first seem contradictory when set alongside our earlier indictment of American emotionalism. There is in American public opinion a strong strain of common sense that historically has often come to the rescue just as it seemed as if emotional excesses were to sweep the United States away.

Americans seem to need their periodic emotional indulgences; perhaps they provide an outlet for pent-up frustrations and tensions. But after each of these outbursts of love or hate, there comes a reaction. Often it goes too far in the opposite direction, and the new attitude is actually as emotional as the old. But ultimately the pendulum tends to come to rest, and most Americans—emotionally purged—take a stand on the dead center of common sense.

If this model be accurate, and if we may assume that such common-sense judgments are usually satisfactory, we may regret that the American people seemingly must go through their initial emotional sprees. But, at least up to this point in history, the American people have not been able to dispense with their preliminary reliance on pure sentiment, and it would be a brave man indeed who would argue that American public opinion would be always of a higher type if all emotional preferences were abandoned and all judgments made on the basis of cold common-sense calculation. A good case can be made in defense of at least some feeling in American mass attitudes.

Altruism.

American public opinion, finally, is genuinely altruistic. We commented earlier on American Utopianism, and tried to suggest some of its failings. No one, however, can question its sincerity. Americans do generally wish everyone well, and devote an unusually large share of their efforts to trying to improve the lot of man.

It is easy—and, in some circles, fashionable as well—to deride the simple good-heartedness of Americans as reflecting naiveté and immaturity. Yet such sophistication frequently misses an important point: America's genuine concern for other peoples is widely recognized abroad. The reputation for altruism that Americans enjoy is itself a source of great strength; when they depart from it and instead seek to play the role of pure power, they are usually the losers. The American government has been struggling to learn to reconcile the conflicting demands of moral and physical power, and could do worse than to trust to the innate altruism of Americans.

Balancing strengths against weaknesses, what can we say at this point about American public opinion on foreign-policy issues, particularly in the light of America's international ego-image as we developed it in the first part of this chapter? In one sense, to answer this question is the purpose of this book, and an attempt to do so is made in the final chapters. But, even at this early stage of our inquiry, certain points can safely be made.

It would be inaccurate to condemn American attitudes as inherently unsound, but equally as erroneous is the assumption that public opinion is an infallible guide to policy. The weaknesses of American opinion are all dangerous to intelligent planning; no policy-maker could safely trust himself and the national interest to the whims of a rapidly-shifting, stereotype-ridden, impatient, and highly emotional body politic. Coping with this phenomenon raises problems of political leadership of a grave difficulty. On the other hand, the advantages we saw in American attitudes strengthen the hand of American statesmen and gives them a freedom of action (once opinion has come to rest) that makes it possible for the government to act in accordance with the major outlines of a preconceived strategy.

Both the strengths and the weaknesses of American opinion, therefore, have an impact on American policy. The concern of both the statesman and the public would seem to be one of curbing the excesses and capitalizing on the advantages of this situation so as to produce a workable relationship between the demands of mass opinion and the concrete purposes of official leadership.

The Contemporary Version of the National Interest

In this chapter we shall approach the problem of American national interest in a different way. Rather than focusing on popular myth and tradition as we did in Chapter 5, we shall attempt to stipulate the basic ingredients of the actual (or at least the dominant) concept of national interest accepted by the American government. Applying this notion to the prevailing conditions facing the United States, we shall formulate a pattern of generalized goals and objectives.

This is a difficult task for anyone not of the government hierarchy, but by no means an impossible one. The American outlook on the world and the imperatives of international life combine to exert a powerful influence on the substance of the contemporary foreign policy of the United States. Certain lines of action are virtually closed to the American government, others are almost ineluctably demanded of it; between these extreme compulsions we can find a broad complex of choices. Even in this area, however, we may suggest a set of reasonably well-clarified wants and needs—what we can call interests—that largely govern the rational choices made by American policy-makers. An understanding of these preoccupations will throw a good deal of light on what has been done and will be done in the future by the government of the United States.

THE CLASSIFICATION OF FOREIGN POLICIES

We should first undertake a preliminary exercise in political taxonomy. We shall be fitting American policy and the concept of national interest that undergirds it into a rough system of classification. From such a scheme, we may draw certain inferences from the general category into which United States policy falls. Our first task, therefore, should be to delimit our classifications.

The Dichotomy of State Attitude.

Despite the obvious fact that no two states have the same foreign policy, and the equally self-evident conclusion that there are many subtle shades of difference among even very similar ones, in the most general sense some type of either-or proposition underlies everything that any state does. There seems to be a single choice that every government makes, consciously or unconsciously; once made, its subsequent action flows naturally and almost inevitably from it. Major change in its foreign policy is difficult and unlikely unless this original decision is reversed.

This crucial determinant, the major criterion of our system of classification, is the state's attitude toward the world situation in which it finds itself. Any state must somehow determine which of two possible alternatives it will choose: it may either accept—at least in general—the combination of advantages and disadvantages that together give it a status relative to all other states, or it may be dissatisfied with its role and determined to improve its place. Which decision it makes, and how and by what means that decision is reached, is determined by forces within the particular state, although external factors must be taken into account. The choice of a fundamental outlook determines the form and the direction of the greater part of all its later action. The two groups of states, divided by this watershed of attitude, provide the two categories of our system of classification.

Status Quo vs. Revisionism.

Scholars have given names to the two halves of our dichotomy. The first group of states, satisfied with what they have and interested in preserving it, is most commonly called the "status quo" states. The other group, interested in overturning the prevailing distribution of rewards and power, is usually called "revisionist." Oppositions other than "status-quo"-"revisionist" are open to serious question because the classificatory words tend to carry policy implications that are not really necessary to the classification. In our discussion we shall confine ourselves to the simple status-quo-revisionist antinomy.[1] We may draw certain limited but basic conclusions about the general foreign-policy line of the these two types.

A status-quo state normally pursues policies aimed at preserving its status: policies of limited objectives that are in the broadest sense defensive in inspiration. Generally such a state is more concerned with devising responses to problems that arise from external sources than with initiating positive long-range programs of its own. It usually has a major interest in peaceful international intercourse, particularly in the process of peaceful change. Switzerland is perhaps the archtype of the status quo.

A revisionist state, on the contrary, is actually or potentially on the offensive. Revisionist policy assumes the strategic initiative, actively exploring any situation that promises advantage. We cannot generalize that such an outlook must be one that looks forward to or plans war, but we can safely stipulate that the choice between war and peace made by a revisionist state is governed only by considerations of operational expediency and utility rather than by any basic demand of national interest; it is a "means" rather than an "ends" decision. Nazi Germany in its heyday, dedicated as it was to incessant attack, is a classic example of revisionism in action.

The Limits of Classification.

We shall be using the status-quo revisionist dichotomy as an analytical device throughout our discussion of American foreign policy. Its usefulness will perhaps be demonstrated as we progress, but at the outset we must enter a large caveat. The "science of international politics," of which taxonomy is such a large part, is still rudimentary and imprecise. Our system of classification can do no more than to suggest certain rough categories divided by a line often difficult to discover and frequently violated in practice, and the inferences we draw from the status-quo or revisionist status of any state can never be any more than tentative.

One additional warning seems in point. Any objective analysis of foreign policies must proceed on the assumption that the choices that states

[1] See Hans J. Morgenthau, *Politics Among Nations,* 2nd ed. (New York: Alfred A. Knopf, Inc., 1954), Chapters IV, V, and VI, for an extended discussion of the classification of foreign policies. Professor Morgenthau finds three types of policies: status quo, imperialist, and prestige. We include the latter two under the more general rubric of "revisionism."

make are rationally determined. No one would be foolhardy enough today to insist that all states (or, for that matter, any state) will follow a policy dictated only by the calculations of pure reason. We are constantly confronted by examples of status-quo states undertaking moves that would seem logical only within a revisionist context; less frequently, we see the opposite. Here is the province of the inescapable irrational factor,[2] and to the extent that it controls the behavior of states the usefulness of our classification is seriously impaired.

THE UNITED STATES AND THE STATUS QUO

The United States is, by our criteria, assumed to be a status-quo state whose major interest is in the preservation of its present advantageous position. We shall modify this generalization as we examine American interest more closely, but in its essentials it will remain as the fundamental consideration of our analysis of the basic American motivations in foreign policy.

THE UNITED STATES AS A "HAVE" POWER

The Satiation of the United States.

What sort of things make a state a "have" power? Why does a state become a defender of the status quo, at least as it perceives it? By answering this question with particular reference to the United States we may examine the broader issue.

Generally speaking, a state accepts a status-quo position for either of two reasons. In the first place, it may lack the capability to achieve any more of its objectives; it therefore settles for the most it can get from the given situation. Sweden's open renunciation of its ambitions after 1721 resulted in such a posture. On the other hand, the status quo may be accepted simply because the state concerned has reached all the objectives it deems important and such as remain unattained would require more trouble than they would be worth. Although capable of getting more, the state elects to content itself with what it has.

It seems clear that if the United States is a status-quo power, it arrived at this position by the second route. It has only been since 1945 that the status quo as a policy channel became fully rationalized to American policy-makers and has served as a base for calculated strategic and tactical

---

[2] Feliks Gross calls this "factor x," to be allowed for in all policy analyses. *Foreign Policy Analysis* (New York: Philosophical Library, 1954), pp. 124–5.

decisions. At the moment that the more or less deliberate choice was made to defend the status quo, the United States possessed ample capability—both of force and of consent—to reach an entirely new set of goals. American statesmen, acting in harmony with popular attitudes as they understood them, instead chose to concentrate on the defense of the post-war situation of the United States.

In 1945 there was little disagreement among either officials or citizens that the United States had reached virtual satiation. The United States no longer had any obsessive objectives; there were no major international adventures upon which Americans were determined to embark. Left alone, Americans would bother no one, conquer no new territory, overthrow no governments, start no wars. They wished only to be free to enjoy the advantages of their civilization and—within reason—were willing to permit everyone else the same right to enjoy their own.

The Nineteenth Century.

As we have seen, American preoccupation with the status quo is a relatively recent development. During much of the nineteenth century the United States had a dynamic, expanding foreign policy that was an accurate reflection of the dominant American revisionism.[3] Until the United States achieved continental expanse, hemisphere hegemony, and economic maturity, it had long-standing purposes to whose accomplishment successive administrations devoted themselves. During the first century and a quarter of American history as a sovereign state, therefore, the United States became involved in a series of major disputes with most of the great powers and fought three large-scale international wars: with Great Britain in 1812, with Mexico in 1846, and with Spain in 1898. Having finally achieved the American "manifest destiny" by 1900 the approach of the United States changed. During the twentieth century the United States has been concerned mainly with holding on to its winnings rather than in adding to them, although full realization of this role did not come until after 1945.

Self-preservation, Security, and Well-being.

In Chapter 1 we postulated that the basic concerns of every state are self-preservation, security, and well-being. As Americans faced the world in 1945 and attempted to apply these general terms to their own situation, the condition of the United States was revealed as one of high satiation. Although there was room for some improvements, the nation was con-

---

[3] See, for example, Julius Pratt's two studies, *Expansionists of 1812* (New York: The Macmillan Co., 1925), and *Expansionists of 1898* (Baltimore: Johns Hopkins University Press, 1936).

sidered to be so well off on all three counts that most Americans thought that to seek major alterations in an already happy situation might jeopardize the foundations of America's enviable status. Indeed, any extreme policy was felt to be dangerous. The decision was reached and ratified that no adventuresome expansion would be undertaken and that henceforth the major American effort would be in defense of already established positions.

The American Attitude Toward Change

"Status quo" as a policy orientation has a reasonably precise meaning that derives from a state's attitude toward the world situation as it sees it. It is dangerously easy, however, to take the next step and to conceive a status-quo policy as merely involving holding a particular position and of resisting and attempting to prevent any and all change. This conclusion does not necessarily follow from a status-quo assumption; one of the distinguishing marks of the American approach to world affairs is the activist implication that is built into the defensive posture the United States assumes on most substantive questions.

The Avoidance of Stand-pattism.

It is a dangerous misjudgment to assume (and it has been done often, by Americans and foreigners alike) that because the United States considers itself a status-quo state, it is committed to rigidly opposing either evolutionary or revolutionary change. The kind of world in which Americans want to live is one that cannot be achieved by simply holding fast and letting the rest of the world take care of itself. The United States cannot stand pat. This would be impossible under the conditions of modern technology and national self-consciousness; what is more, even if it were feasible it would be unwise and possibly disastrous.

Change in the American Interest.

Let anyone attempt to visualize the kind of international society in which he would feel personally secure, and then let him ask himself if this kind of order can ever be born without first making significant change in the world as it is at present. The answer, at least as given by most rational and well-intentioned people, would in most cases call for action and change on a broad front; the world of today is not one that will permit the United States the luxury of ignoring it.

The basic interests of the United States and the American people demand, not stagnation and immobility, but fundamental change in many parts of the world. It would be fatuous for Americans to prate solemnly of "order" or "stability" in the world while at the same time their government neglected or inhibited efforts to remove the conditions that breed war. The final guarantee of the American concept of the status quo demands action; the United States cannot retain its preeminence by denying improvement to everyone else or by neglecting action to create the conditions conducive to peace. In this sense the United States violates the stereotype of the status-quo state; Americans are instead—on this point—truly revisionist.

The Requirement of Affirmative Action.

Nor does the American identification with the status quo confine the United States indefinitely to a passive, negative policy of doing nothing until some kind of threat arises, and then of confining its action to mere countermeasures. Defense—military, political, ideological, and economic—has a real place in American strategy, but it is by no means the only or even the most important concern of policy. The kind of peaceful order that Americans seek—to speak metaphorically—is not the peace of the cabbage patch, but rather the peace of the beehive.

The notion of interest that we are developing here demands, therefore, that the heart of the foreign policy of the United States consist of vigorous, positive action to create the kind of world that Americans want. This means an international order in which the United States and its citizens will be free to enjoy their advantages in the maximum possible security. This means—and this is as good a formulation of American national interest as any—a world of peace, order, and stability.

THE PROCEDURAL STATUS QUO

Thus far we have argued that the United States is basically a status-quo power with a major concern with the defense of its own situation, but with the additional qualification that to a very real extent the United States is also committed to at least some of the principles of what we have called revisionism. Can we now reconcile these two positions and, in doing so, clarify the content of the American adherence to the status quo?

The Scope of American Revisionism.

We may put the matter in this way: as regards the bulk of the substantive questions of international politics, the American attitude is either actually or potentially revisionist. The United States excepts from its general tolerance of change only a few substantive issues that bear adversely and immediately upon American interests. While insisting on the continued maintenance of those factors that contribute to the security and prosperity of the United States, American policy-makers generally retain an open mind on the prospects of material change elsewhere.

We are not claiming here that the American attitude of substantive revisionism makes the United States always in favor of change. The American government is not committed to a principle of constant dynamism any more than it is to simple stagnation. Some forms of substantive change contribute to the advancement of American interest, and these the United States approves, urges, and seeks to bring about; others are potentially or actually inimical, and these the United States disapproves and seeks to prevent. In between these extremes are many developments and evolutions that do not permit of such ready categorization. American interest demands that each of these be scrutinized, measured against the yardstick of relevance to American concerns, and then favored or opposed in its terms.

The American Concern with Procedure.

Where the American identification with the status quo is complete, however, is the general area of international procedure. The United States insists that the mechanisms of international contact, adjustment, and necessary change must be peaceful and orderly. On this point the United States make no concession. Peaceful process—the mark of an orderly society—is the central ingredient of the status quo Americans seek to preserve in their own interest.[4]

This was the major operational decision involved in the post-World War II policy choice made by the United States. Americans recognized, as we shall see below, that the situation in 1945 demanded extensive long-range planning and action by their government if the full results of victory were to be achieved. There was little of the traditional status quo in that

---

[4] No more graphic demonstration of this premise could be made than American reaction to the Anglo-French-Israeli invasion of the Suez Canal Zone in 1956. The basic ingredient in American policy was the principle that no provocation, however extreme, justified the adoption of force as a technique. See President Eisenhower's speeches on October 31, 1956 (*Department of State Bulletin,* November 12, 1956, p. 743), and February 20, 1957 (*Department of State Bulletin,* March 11, 1957, p. 387–90). In the latter speech, he said: "If we agree that armed attack can properly achieve the purposes of the assailant, then I fear we shall have turned back the clock of international order. We will, in effect, have countenanced the use of force as a means of settling international differences and through this gaining national advantages. . . . We cannot consider that the armed invasion and occupation of another country are 'peaceful means' or proper means to achieve justice and conformity with international laws."

decision, except for the central commitment to the ideal of an orderly world. To this commitment the American government and (to a large extent) the American people have remained generally faithful.[5]

PEACE, ORDER, AND STABILITY

We summarized American national interest above as a continuing concern with permanent peace, order, and stability in the international society as the best way to guarantee American independence, security, and well-being. We turn now to a more detailed analysis of this generalization.

The United States and International Controls.

The United States is seeking a flexible and adaptable international order with only one drastic modification in the traditional patterns of state behavior: the introduction of a set of fixed outer limits on permissible state action. One of the long-run objectives of American policy, therefore, is the development and application of a set of controls on the freedom of action of all states and the creation of self-activating mechanisms of adjustment in the international order.

What we mean by "controls" and "self-activating mechanisms of adjustment" can be simply stated. We are referring to procedures and institutions that will: (1) prevent states from resorting to war at their own decision, and (2) provide satisfactory solutions to problems so as to make war unnecessary. War, therefore, is the focus of the entire enterprise. If state action could be confined to nonviolent procedures, the worst dangers of the state system would be eliminated.

This notion, of course, underlies the idea of collective security, and its applicability to the United Nations explains a large part of American support of that organization. The attempt to place controls on state action by United Nations action squares exactly with American interest, and it is only to be expected that the United States would approve most such moves. But the realization that the United Nations, by itself, is not enough has kept the American government active in other areas, attempting in many ways to bring new forms of control mechanisms into existence.

---

[5] Chester Bowles, in *Ideas, People and Peace* (New York: Harper & Brothers, 1958), and Thomas K. Finletter, in *Foreign Policy: The Next Phase. The 1960s,* are among the most outspoken recent advocates of a recapture of substantive dynamism in American policy.

THE AMERICAN INTEREST IN PEACE

We have already dealt briefly with two matters bearing directly on the American interest in peace. We have suggested that the status-quo identification of the United States necessarily implies peaceful process as the preferred vehicle of international adjustment, and we have also noted American concern with the development of a system of international controls that incorporates peace as a way of life.

Are Americans a Peace-loving People?

We should first recognize an old issue. In Chapter 5 we saw that the American ego-image is one of uniqueness: Americans generally think of themselves not only as inherently peace-loving, but as superior to other peoples in this regard. The national self-image is of a people tolerant to a fault, slow to anger, but mighty in its wrath when aroused. The United States has never gone to war, Americans normally argue, except to administer just punishment to vicious and unprincipled aggressors.

It comes as a blow to many Americans to be told that this picture is not shared by most foreign peoples, either in Europe or Asia. The United States is frequently thought of instead as being impatient, trigger-tempered, and liable to explosion at any moment. American history, foreigners point out, is speckled with big and little wars, many of them (including the War of 1812, the Mexican War, the Spanish-American War, and countless campaigns against the Indians) suspiciously similar to acts of aggression. Today many of the allies of the United States are frequently concerned about American bellicosity and the danger to peace that it represents (although, it must be admitted, they often express equally strong doubts about American steadfastness). Americans are not likely to become a nation of pacifists.

The Disappearing Utility of War.

War, as an instrument of national policy, is neither inevitable nor accidental. Wars do not simply happen; they come about as the result of a deliberate policy decision by some state (though it is true that external conditions play a major part in making such a decision probable). The technology of warfare in the twentieth century has made war less and less useful to the foreign policy of major states. The costs of large-scale conflict today are so prohibitively high that there is only a tiny handful of objectives—most of them intimately connected with self-preservation—whose worth would justify a state coolly electing to initiate a total war. With the possible rewards of war so nearly balanced (or actually outweighed) by its predictable costs, American national interest has embraced wholeheartedly the desirability of permanent peace.[6]

What is applicable to offensive war applies, with some modification, to defensive warfare as well. The United States cannot afford to accept a military challenge thrown out by a potential aggressor unless it first exhausts all alternative methods of coping with the threat. Defensive war is a rational alternative for Americans only if they are convinced that there is literally no other endurable way out of the crisis. Accordingly, since 1945 the United States has ignored numerous provocations and threats that, under other circumstances or at some earlier time, might have resulted in a decision to retaliate with force.[7] The American government will wage defensive war only when forced to do so.[8]

The American Interest in a Peaceful World.

But America's interest in peace is more extensive than the mere urge to stay out of war itself. It involves a constant American effort toward the progressive elimination of war as a practice in the state system and the working objective of a warless world.

War anywhere is a threat, either direct or—occasionally—remote, to the interest of the United States. It is not enough for the American government to meet threats to the peace, from whatever source, as they arise. American interest demands a continuing effort to broaden the area in which peaceful process is the controlling technique of international

---

[6] President Eisenhower, in his speech accepting renomination in 1956, emphasized this point by calling war "not only perilous, but preposterous." *New York Times* (August 24, 1956).

[7] This conviction is apparently shared at least to some degree, behind the Iron Curtain; it is obviously imbedded in Premier Khrushchev's "coexistence or war" theme. An interesting outcome of the mutual inability to meet provocation with force has been a great increase in both the frequency and the severity of the provocative moves made by both sides in the cold war. In an earlier day either a four-year policy of espionage flights over foreign territory (which the United States admitted in May 1960) or an insulting tongue-lashing of the head of a foreign state, delivered in his presence and in public (as Mr. Khrushchev administered to President Eisenhower at the abortive summit the next week) would have brought war very near. Neither side made the slightest move toward military action, however.

[8] There is a school of thought in the United States, however, that professes to be very concerned lest the United States lapse into pacificism. Leaders include Henry A. Kissinger who, in *Nuclear Weapons and Foreign Policy* (New York: Harper & Bros., 1957), regrets the American reluctance to fight "limited wars" and feels that Americans lack a "sense of tragedy." Former Secretary of State Dean Acheson, who feels that "tautness" in Soviet-American relations is highly desirable and American refusal to contemplate war against the Soviet is a contributing factor to the weakness he sees in the American approach to world affairs, is of the same opinion. See Mr. Acheson's *Power and Diplomacy* (Cambridge: Harvard University Press, 1958).

relations, both from the United States and from such other states as can be mobilized in this effort.[9] A peaceful world obviously requires that each state limit its policy objectives to those that can be gained peacefully; part of the American concern with peace is a continuing insistence that other states make this kind of self-denying commitment in response to similar action by the United States.

ORDER AND STABILITY

The remaining two components of broad-gauge American interest are order and stability in international society. As used here, "order" refers to the existence of peaceful and regular *methods* of conducting international affairs, while "stability" is the *condition* that will prevail when these orderly techniques are so widely used that state behavior will be, in great measure, predictable. Together, the two terms fill in the outline of the general concept of "peace" and make it a more comprehensive guide to American policy.

The Role of Law and Legal Rules.

In Chapter 5 we noted the traditional American preference for social relationships that are regulated by legal rules. Here is one of the many instances in which a popular, nonrationalized impression is also very good practical policy for the United States. Despite the many chronic overestimations of the potentialities of legalisms as control factors in international relations, it is undeniable that order and stability, as we have defined them, can be permanently realized in international life only when they rest on a sub-structure of legal principles.[10] Law and its practitioners go far to stabilize any society in which they are operative.

It is therefore quite apparent that American national interest should include some appreciation of and concern with the extension of the scope of international law. This may be implemented in two ways, capable of being undertaken simultaneously. On the one hand, the United States may seek to assist in the development of new legal rules to formalize

---

[9] From the many official statements of this position, we may cite two Presidential speeches, one almost immediately after World War II and the other more recent: Mr. Truman's Navy Day speech, October 27, 1945 (*New York Times,* October 28, 1945), and Mr. Eisenhower's campaign speech of September 27, 1956 (*New York Times,* September 28, 1956).

[10] Ralph Linton, in *A Study of Man* (New York: Appleton-Century-Crofts, Inc., 1936), points out: "The only cases in which new forms of society have been established successfully have been those in which the plan for the new society has included a large body of concrete rules for behavior" (p. 97). Reprinted by permission of Appleton-Century-Crofts, Inc.

evolving international relationships that have reached or are reaching stability; one contemporary example is the question of international civil aviation.[11] The other area in which the United States could take the lead is in the formulation of principles of law incorporating the verb "ought," and the attempt to bring the actual conduct of states into conformity with these humanitarian rules. Perhaps the best known recent example of this is the United Nations Convention on Human Rights, a document in whose drafting the United States played a leading part.

The Necessity of Organization.

But order and stability require more than just a system of legal rules. The effective operation of the kind of world order the United States is seeking necessitates a more elaborate structure of institutions, a more detailed organization.

International society is distinguished by a relative scarcity of agencies of joint action. Although the institutional structure of interstate life is not entirely lacking, we must admit that it is no more than rudimentary. There is a lack both of control mechanisms and of instruments for positive cooperation in times of crisis, both types must be extemporized.[12] Many scholars have noted that this shortcoming of the state system is responsible for the tendency of international problems to fail to reach complete resolution except by violence.[13] The converse of this proposition is self-evident; if an adequate institutional structure were to be created, much of the strain and crisis of international politics would be eliminated. This principle leads the United States to its interest in the progressive elaboration of international institutions and to the maximum possible participation in them.

We are not saying that, as of any particular moment, the more organization the better. No institution can be created until the social setting is prepared; men must be aware both of the social need and the suitability of the proposed organization for satisfying the need before they will permit its creation and participate in it.[14] The most we can say is that the United

---

[11] See the International Air Services Transport Agreement, drawn up at the Chicago Conference on air transport in 1944. *Proceedings of the International Civil Aviation Conference* (Washington: Department of State, 1948–9).

[12] For example, the United Nations Emergency Force recruited to enforce the Middle East cease-fire in 1956 was created in great haste in the midst of an extremely dangerous situation.

[13] Clyde Eagleton, *International Government,* rev. ed. (New York: The Ronald Press, 1948), p. 19; J. L. Brierly, *The Law of Nations,* 4th ed. (Oxford: Clarendon, 1949), pp. 42–6.

[14] Marion Levy, *The Structure of Society* (Princeton: Princeton University Press, 1952), pp. 102 ff; Ralph Linton, *The Tree of Culture* (New York: Alfred A. Knopf, Inc., 1955), p. 31.

States has an interest in seeing to it that the level of international organization—both in terms of extent and of effectiveness—is at its practical maximum. As the acceptance theshold of the society of states lowers, more and more organization can be introduced.

Where will it end? Are we saying that the national interest of the United States demands that ultimately the organization principle should be carried to its logical extreme in the form of a world government? We are not going so far, at least at the present stage of our discussion. We are generalizing only to state that order and stability in international relations demands organization, and that the more that international politics is fitted into an effective organizational scheme, the more orderly and stable it will be. Since 1945 the United States has accepted this idea and has been more or less consistently acting upon it.

Peaceful Change.

One final aspect of order and stability, implicit in the preceding discussion of law and organization, merits some consideration in itself. This is the discovery, acceptance, and utilization of the techniques of peaceful change. It would not be overly far-fetched to argue—as many students have done—that this is the central political problem of our time.[15] Man seems to have tacitly agreed that war can no longer be used for the settlement of disagreements among great states; the question that perplexes everyone is what shall be used as a substitute for violence in international affairs. If men could develop an acceptable method of coping with this issue, most of the other political dilemmas of contemporary life might prove to be less fearsome than they seemed when confronted in the face of the specter of war.

Change, as we have seen, is of the very essence of international relations. Other than violence there is no technique of change of guaranteed efficacy. The abandonment of war will not eliminate the need for allowing for constant evolution. A stable world order must contain procedures that will make change possible, feasible, and acceptable, all the while limiting state action to something short of war.

The national interest of the United States naturally leads to American acceptance of the doctrine and—to a lesser extent—the practice of peaceful change. Despite the degree to which its necessity has been obscured by the exigencies of the cold-war decade, a backward look today will reveal that the United States has made real, if limited, progress in promoting the principle. How this has taken place we shall see in later chapters.

---

15 For a recent survey of the rationale of peaceful change and the pacific settlement of international disputes, see Inis L. Claude, *Swords into Plowshares,* rev. ed. (New York: Random House, 1959), pp. 219–34.

ACTION PRINCIPLES: THE CONSTANT INTERESTS

From the highly generalized concept of American national interest that we have been developing, summarized as a continuing concern with the creation of a world of peace, order, and stability, there flows a small number of what we call "action principles." These are the relatively permanent enterprises that are so fundamental to the accomplishment of any part of the American design that their inclusion in actual American foreign policy is axiomatic. These principles might be thought of as an initial step in translating the idea of interest into the concrete courses of action that we call policy. We shall discuss three such constant interests.

SELF-DEFENSE

It might seem almost redundant to make the detailed point that the United States has a great interest in its own self-defense, but the concept of "defense" and the mythology that surrounds it today requires us to examine the point systematically.

The Status Quo in Practice.

We must always remind ourselves that the new world of peace, order, and stability that the United States is seeking to create does not yet exist. The society of states in which the United States fits is one still dominated by the doctrine of sovereignty and the egoistic promptings of national interest. So long as this condition persists—and for safety's sake we must assume its indefinite existence, no matter how the United States attempts to modify it—American national interest must depend for its satisfaction primarily on the acts of the American people and the government of the United States.[16]

Our starting point in this analysis of American interest was the postulate that the United States is a status-quo state. From our previous review

---

[16] This is an elementary example of what is called the "minimax" theory of strategy, drawn from the mathematical theory of games. It is based on the construction of a plan of action that assumes that the worst possible outcome will be the result of the game; by planning in this way the player's losses are held to a minimum and yet he remains in a position to maximize his gains if events are more favorable than he had assumed. See Martin Shubik, *Readings in Game Theory and Political Behavior* (Garden City: Doubleday, 1954), especially the essay by Karl Deutsch, "International Politics and Game Theory." See also the discussion in Morton Kaplan, *System and Process in International Politics* (New York: John Wiley & Sons, Inc., 1957).

of the American concept of national interest, we can see the fundamental place occupied by the requirement of self-defense. Americans wish to preserve their advantages; in the long run the best way to accomplish this is by helping to develop a world in which all states and all people can feel secure. But, if the long-range plan fails, or at least during the period before it is consummated, the defense of the status quo as it affects Americans must rest on the United States itself.

Multiple Defense.

"Self-defense" has a different connotation in the middle of the twentieth century than it has had in any earlier epoch. Traditionally, "defense" has meant the development of the capacity to resist armed attack; this is the classic idea of "security" as a state objective. But one of the paradoxes of modern world politics is the increasingly clear fact that technology, as applied to warfare, is a sword that cuts two ways.[17] It vastly increases the destructive power of weapons and has made it operationally feasible to destroy an entire civilization. But the events of the cold-war decade suggest that just to the extent to which weapons have grown more fearsome and efficient, the likelihood of their use in all-out conflict has decreased. And so military defense—as we shall see in detail in a later chapter—has assumed a new dimension today; deterrence, rather than battlefield mastery, has become the dominant military concern of the United States.

But the decline in the purely military component of self-defense has been matched by a corresponding increase in its other forms. The military danger to the United States may be less today than heretofore, as many experts believe; other sorts of threats, however, pose problems each as acute in its way as a military one would be. "Political warfare," economic conflict, ideological and propaganda war, and the frequently overemphasized but always real danger of subversion are only a few of the areas in which the United States is called upon to defend itself.[18]

There is very little inclination in the United States today to argue that unilateral self-defense is the route to ultimate salvation for Americans. Most Americans realize that, in seeking some approximation of the late Senator Taft's "fortress America," [19] the United States would be volun-

---

17 W. F. Ogburn, ed., *Technology and International Relations* (Chicago: University of Chicago Press, 1949); Bernard Brodie, ed., *The Absolute Weapon* (New York: Harcourt, Brace and Co., 1946); Henry A. Kissinger, *Nuclear Weapons and Foreign Policy*.

18 For an excellent early summary of the multidimensional problem of American defense, see Hanson W. Baldwin, *The Price of Power* (New York: Harper & Bros., Inc., 1948); see also W. W. Kaufman, ed., *Military Policy and National Security* (Princeton: Princeton University Press, 1956), and Hughes, *America the Vincible.*

19 In *A Foreign Policy for Americans* (Garden City: Doubleday & Co., 1951).

tarily sacrificing many of the happy domestic circumstances that American foreign policy is pledged to preserve. It would be stupid for the United States to seek to build a better world without first paying due attention to its own defense, but it would be catastrophic for it to make self-defense, narrowly defined, its only principle of action.[20]

COOPERATION FOR PEACE

If self-defense alone is not enough, and if positive action toward a world of peace and order is demanded in the American interest, we come next to the major question of how the United States is to proceed in this task. Here we consider a much-debated question: the necessity for, and the most desirable extent of, "international cooperation."

The Limits on Unilateral Action.

We may take it as axiomatic that the United States cannot build the new world alone. The detailed framework of a peaceful order will be so many-sided, so complex, and so extensive that even the tremendous potential capability of the United States would be insufficient to construct it without help from outside. The United States cannot enforce peace by its own unaided efforts; it cannot order all the relationships of men, groups, and states; it cannot alone require that all forms of state action everywhere should be confined within the limits declared to be acceptable. The American interest in a new basis for international society is of such dimensions that assistance from other states is a *sine qua non* of success. The United States must have partners if its long-range plans are to bear fruit.

Harmony of Interest Within the Status Quo.

What makes American national interest, as we are formulating it, a viable basis for policy is the fact that there is a sizeable group of states that share the general idea of the status quo as defined by the United States and that have no major disagreement with its particular American version. There are at least several dozen fundamentally status-quo states; that is, they are not revisionist and are willing indefinitely to sustain the

---

[20] An illustration of such a confusion of emphasis was the long controversy about the form to be taken by the American exploration of outer space. A considerable body of opinion, led by military spokesmen, argued that the significance of the space effort was primarily military, and discussed such possibilities as satellite reconnaissance, space outposts, space-launched missiles, and the like. This group objected to President Eisenhower's 1959 decision to place the space program under the control of the National Aeronautics and Space Administration, a civilian body. It was never made clear in the discussion whether the stakes in the "space race" were scientific leadership or military dominance.

present distribution of rewards as it affects them.[21] Though most of them have some quarrel with the United States on points of detail, none makes its abasement a matter of primary concern. Thus a genuine harmony of interest obtains within this group on the commitment to the principle of a world of order; further, all are generally willing to accept American advantages as part of the world system they are interested in preserving.

The Structure of Cooperation.

Granted a harmony of interest in the maintenance of the procedural status quo and the absence of fundamental disagreement on the minimal substantive status quo that Americans demand, the discovery and application of methods of cooperation become a matter of operational technique. Cooperation between states is always possible—and usually practical— if it is based on a genuine, unforced, harmony of interest.

States, however, do not cooperate just for the sheer joy of cooperating. Joint action, if it is to serve a useful purpose, is purposive: it is aimed at specific goals and involves the exchange of definite commitments to do particular things. American interest demands, therefore, that any cooperative enterprise have a predetermined objective in mind, that the participants be limited to those states that share the particular purpose, that the mutual obligations be precisely stipulated, and that each such venture be evaluated rigorously in terms of its contribution toward the long-range purposes of the United States. Under these assumptions the United States has associated itself with many states in a broad variety of cooperative schemes, each one pinpointing a specific objective and the membership of each determined by the interest the members have in its purpose. Some, like NATO, have had relatively productive histories; others, like the abortive Suez Canal User's Association of 1956, have failed. Such failures have generally been due to the nonapplicability of one of the criteria above to the project.

HOSTILITY TO NONPEACEFUL STATES

If we agree that cooperation with like-minded status-quo states is demanded by the national interest of the United States, is the converse of the proposition true? Does American national interest demand hostility toward all revisionist states? If we remember the American version of the status quo, if we confine revisionism to procedural matters, and if we define revisionism sharply, this proposition can be defended.

---

[21] See, for example, Barbara Ward, *Policy for the West* (New York: W. W. Norton and Co., Inc., 1951).

The Defense of Peaceful Process.

The logic of American national interest leads the United States to oppose any state that seems willing to violate the structure of peaceful process in international relations. This is the procedural status quo, pure and simple. American hostility to procedural revisionism is independent of the specific objectives the state is seeking; it is conceivable that the United States might approve or even support an identical program if it were to be prosecuted peacefully.[22] If it is an order of permanent peace that is the goal of American policy, simple logic and common sense would seem to demand that the United States offer immediate and total opposition to any state openly defiant of this end. This principle, as we shall see, underlies the entire anti-Soviet line that has bulked so large in post-war American policy; the United States is hostile to the USSR because of the Kremlin's demonstrated willingness to advance its interests by means of perpetuated disorder, frequent crisis, and threatened war.

The Indivisibility of Peace.

Peace, as the United States defines the term, is indivisible. It is not sufficient for the United States to oppose only those disturbers of the peace that directly threaten purely American interests; any state anywhere that is willing to rupture peaceful international relationships runs equally afoul of American concerns. We can argue that communist China represents a direct and immediate threat to the United States, and that American hostility to Mao Tse-tung can be explained on that basis; no such claim could be made, however, for American resistance to the ambitions of President Nasser of Egypt, to the Castro regime in Cuba, or even to India's provocative behavior on the issue of the Kashmir, to mention a few cases in addition to the most spectacular demonstration of the principle, the opposition to Britain and France in the Middle East in 1956.

It is worth emphasizing in this connection, however, that American resistance to procedural revisionism applies only to overt acts, and not to empty threats or to ideological hostility. Only when tensions boil over into action does the United States feel its interest to be involved and contemplate open opposition. The recent instance of American policy toward Cuba is a case in point. During 1959 and 1960, the regime of Fidel

---

[22] This point may be made with regard to the American attitude toward Israel following the 1956 Middle East crises. The American position, as developed during the long controversy precipitated by Israel's refusal to evacuate the Gaza strip and the Gulf of Aqaba area, was that the United States opposed Israel's use of force while generally supporting the specific objectives Israel claimed to be seeking. See the speech of President Eisenhower, February 20, 1957, *Department of State Bulletin* (March 13, 1957).

Castro made merry with a varied diet of extreme anti-Americanism that periodically seemed expressly designed to tempt the United States into reckless action. So long as Castro confined himself to accusations and threats of retaliation, however, Washington was able to indulge the luxury of forbearance; the maxim controlling American policy seemed to be "sticks and stones may break my bones, but names will never hurt me." Cuba was on notice, however, that any breach of peaceful process would produce immediate and strong American reactions, and American action swiftly followed Castro's transgression over the line of permissibility in late 1960, culminating in a rupture of diplomatic relations.

It is the principle of peaceful process to which the United States is committed as a matter of national interest. Affirmative action in its behalf is naturally to be expected, but so is the policy of resistance to any state that would go to war. Peace, order, and stability require not only that the United States build a new institutional edifice, but also that it protect its work against those who would destroy it.

Situational Factors in Contemporary American Policy

◆◇

The
World
Arena
of
American
Policy

CHAPTER ◄ 7 ►

The end of the four-year war effort between 1941 and 1945 brought the United States to the threshold of a major departure in its foreign policy. It was a new world in which Americans had to find their way; a world in which many of the calculations and assumptions by which Americans had—for better or worse—guided their policy in the past had become invalidated. There were several factors with which policy-makers in Washington and citizens everywhere had to deal for the first time; their cumulative effect was to create an almost entirely novel foreign-policy problem that called for action on an unprecedented scale.

In this chapter we shall discuss the broader dimensions of this new world. We shall consider many individual factors, but some order may be brought into our analysis by subsuming them under three broad headings. The first section will consider the major features of the postwar international scene. The second will enumerate and characterize the major forces that have conditioned the course of world affairs since 1945. The chapter will conclude with a summary of the broad political trends into which American foreign policy has had to fit itself. This is the first in a series of three chapters which will consider the important situational factors affecting American policy.

THE WORLD IN 1945

All wars of any importance rearrange the political relationships of nations. World War II, however, set a new mark in this respect, even surpassing the overturns that resulted from the first general war of the century. No quarter of the globe escaped major effects, and every state in the world was in some significant manner influenced by the struggle. The arena of international politics after 1945 was only in small measure the same as that of before 1939.

THE REDISTRIBUTION OF POWER

World War II, as perhaps its most widespread effect, produced a wholesale redistribution of power on the grandest scale in history. The pre-1939 classification of states into "great powers," "middle powers," and "small powers" was completely invalidated; in its place the postwar world offered the strange spectacle of the overwhelming bulk of the available power concentrated in two states, while at the other end of the scale huddled all the rest, differing from one another only in the degree of their weakness relative to the two giants.

The Disappearance of the Former Leaders.

Of the seven generally accepted "great powers" of 1939,[1] five were summarily removed from the circles of world leadership. Three—Germany, Japan, and Italy—were defeated, humbled, occupied, and in a fair way to be remade by the victors. Britain and France, although among the "victors," had been so drained by the war that neither could present a valid claim to dominance.[2] International affairs presented a strange appearance with these erstwhile leading participants playing a secondary role.

Opinions differed in 1945 as to the permanence of the reduced role of the former great powers. There was general agreement that Italy would never again be a serious contender for top rank. There was much the

[1] See Frank L. Simonds and Brooks Emeny, *The Great Powers in World Politics,* (New York: American Book Company, 1939), p. 154.

[2] Writing in 1944, William T. R. Fox, in *The Super-Powers* (New York: Harcourt, Brace, and Co., 1944), conceived of Britain (and the Commonwealth-Empire) as one of the three peace-keeping "super-powers" of the postwar world.

same opinion about France, although its case was much less clear. Germany presented a different problem, since the Allies agreed in principle that the world's future would be safer if Germany were kept permanently weakened; there was a good deal of disagreement, however, about how best to proceed to dismantle Germany's power base. Japan also offered a ticklish issue; no one was certain how to keep permanently in secondary status a nation of over 80 million people, occupying a strategic economic and political position, armed with a vigorous pride and tradition, and equipped with an elaborate industrial plant.

Britain's status as well was uncertain. Although badly battered by the war, both British prestige and the remnants of British power argued for a fairly rapid return to leadership. Safely installed as the key ally of the United States and as co-author of many postwar plans, Britain was determined to exploit its remaining advantages. British determination not to retreat to secondary status kept London afloat during the period when it seemed as if its former grandeur might be gone forever.

The Rise of the New Leaders.

Of the old great powers, only two survived the war intact. Not only had the United States and the Soviet Union come through the war without serious debilitation; their power positions had improved both relatively and absolutely. The gap between them and the rest of the world had widened, but not only because the weak had become weaker; the strong had become stronger as well.

The USSR, although injured by having been an active theater of combat, had nevertheless become the second military power of the world; it had held off and beaten back the full weight of the Nazi war machine. The war had also ended what was left of its pariah status;[3] Stalin had been a close collaborator in the planning of high strategy during the war and in the framing of the United Nations.[4] The United States, on its part, had dazzled the world with its incredible productivity and, by the end of the war, with its massive military power as well. Economically and militarily, the United States was the most powerful state in the world and, with the Soviet, controlled all but a small fraction of its total available power.[5]

---

[3] Frederick L. Schuman, *International Politics,* 6th ed. (New York: McGraw-Hill Book Co., Inc., 1958), p. 498–503. See also his *Soviet Politics at Home and Abroad* (New York: Alfred A. Knopf, Inc., 1946).

[4] For an early postwar estimate of the Soviet position, see *Major Problems of United States Foreign Policy, 1948–49* (Washington: Brookings Institution, 1948), pp. 16–17, 22–26.

[5] See Harry S. Truman, *Year of Decisions* (Garden City: Doubleday, 1955), Chapters 30–34, for the former President's version of America's situation at the end of the war.

The Small States.

The end of the war left the small powers of 1939 in a precarious position. All of them to some degree damaged by the war, the familiar pattern of international relationships gone, dependent on outside sources for sheer survival, most of them had little real hope of maintaining significant freedom of action. They were obliged to turn to the leaders for assistance.

THE ECLIPSE OF EUROPE

The modern state system was born in Europe and reached its most elaborate development there; from 1648 to the end of World War II, the European subcontinent was the center of the world's political activity. In 1939 four of the great powers were European and one was at least half-European; it is no accident that the war that began in that year, originating in a squabble over a tiny bit of territory, ultimately spread to engulf all the continents and the bulk of the world's people.

The End of European Dominance.

The end of the war saw the eclipse of Europe; the world was no longer ruled from half a dozen European capitals. What had ended its long period of dominance? Why, after surviving so many wars, did Europe undergo a "political collapse" [6] after this one? What had brought man to "the end of the European era"?

Two reasons suggest themselves. First, the two wars of the twentieth century brought the states of Europe to the point of mutual exhaustion. Ruling the world demanded that the states of western Europe maintain high morale and adequate power-in-being; World War II had sapped their interest in world dominion as well as their ability to maintain it. Second, by 1945 technology had progressed to the point that Europe could be said to be suffering from political obsolescence. The end of the war ushered in the age of the giants: the United States (170 million people, over three million square miles, continental expanse) and the USSR (210 million people, eight and a half million square miles, continental expanse). The states of Europe, much smaller and much less populous, no longer could compete with them on any basis of even near-equality. Furthermore, the seats of power had moved away from Europe; both the United States and the USSR were peripheral, and there was no effective way in 1945 for the European states to exert direct influence on them.

---

[6] Hajo Holborn, *The Political Collapse of Europe* (New York: Alfred A. Knopf, Inc., 1951).

The end of the European era was signalled by a complete reversal of that continent's historic role. Europe was transformed from an area in which power was wielded and out from which power flowed all over the globe, into the principal target of power originating outside itself. Europeans, who had traditionally used non-European peoples as pawns in their own games of power politics, found themselves becoming counters in a competition on an even more massive scale.

The major controversy during the first phase of the cold war was for the mastery of Europe. This was most clearly revealed in the struggle for the political heart of the new Europe, Germany. In such a situation very few expected Germany to remain long impotent; her remarkable revival was at least partially due to the strategic advantage arising from her position as an object of courtship by both sides.

But the rest of Europe was not afforded the same opportunity to play East and West off against each other. As the primary target of the policies of the two super-powers, the bulk of the European states found themselves forced to join one side or the other in the cold war; target Europe was divided down the middle by the Churchill-described "Iron Curtain." It was not for a decade, until the cold war apparently changed character in 1955 and 1956 and the forces of European integration gained the upper hand, that Europeans again won some little freedom of maneuver.

ASIAN INSTABILITY

One of the "war aims" of the United States between 1941 and 1945 was "the restoration of the balance of power in Asia." To the extent that this was verbalized during the period of active combat, it turned out to mean largely that the United States was hoping to restore the Asian status quo of about 1937, with the single exception that Japan was to be deprived of all her gains and forced to retire to her home islands. Otherwise the map of Asia was to remain substantially unchanged.

Insofar as this was a real aim of the United States, the war was a failure. Asia after Japan's surrender refused to return to its prewar configuration. Instead of the (perhaps illusory) stability of Asian politics between 1920 and 1931, the entire enormous land mass seethed with powerful and upsetting new forces after V-J Day. All the way from India to Japan instability was endemic.[7]

---

[7] See Ernest Minor Patterson, ed., "Lessons from Asia," *Annals of the American Academy of Political and Social Science*, vol. 276 (July, 1951). This volume contains articles by specialists that cover the several aspects of Asian instability in the immediate postwar period.

The Disappearance of Historic Power.

Perhaps the principal reason for the new round of instability in Asia was the disappearance of the historic sources of power. The upshot of the war was the obliteration of Dutch, Chinese, and Japanese power from the region and the serious diminution of Britain and France. Russia emerged as the dominant land power in Asia and the United States, operating at the end of a 6000-mile supply line and tied to the sea, was unable and unwilling at the time to bring controlling force to bear. In all of Asia there was no indigenous power center; only the USSR and the United States seemed to be in a position to exert significant influence.

The End of Imperialism.

Another dynamic force in the new Asia was anti-imperialism. The obvious weakening of European authority, Japan's success in puncturing the myth of white supremacy despite its eventual defeat, and the hard experience in self-government gained in the resistance movements, all combined to awake the masses. Asian imperialism, if not yet completely dead, was changing out of all recognition.

There is only one way to dislodge an imperial power from a colonial possession—short of the unlikely possibility of voluntary withdrawal. Such a change can be brought about only by creating a mass movement built on nationalism that welds a people into a single political instrument. At least half a dozen former colonies in Asia contained such movements, and in each an at least partially successful revolution took place. But the situations did not stabilize with victory over European rule. New nationalism is a powerful force, and Asian nationalism persisted, acting as a forceful dynamic making for continued instability.

Economic and Social Discontent.

There were more than political pressures shaking Asia. The war brought the twentieth century to Asia, and the masses had awakened to some of the possibilities of self-improvement. A common demand for economic and social betterment, canalized into a dozen or more distinct nationalist movements and often coupled with a program calling for political independence, began to be voiced throughout the continent. The western world has come to call this the "Asian revolution," and has accepted it as a major force in political life.

Several years were necessary before the western world realized the full significance of the change in Asia. By the time the United States came to understand the dimensions of the problem, the American position in Asia had deteriorated badly and an originally complex problem had been made unnecessarily acute. Other states in the western community were similarly embarrassed; only the Soviet and its allies recognized the true nature of their problem and were in a position to capitalize swiftly upon it.

THE UNITED NATIONS

The final item in this brief list of the new situational elements in the postwar world is the existence of the United Nations. The new international organization appeared on the scene enjoying certain operational advantages over its ill-starred predecessor, the League of Nations. Most important was the fact that no significant major-power controversy marred its birth. The wartime allies agreed that there should be a permanent organization to keep the peace they were winning; during the closing days of hostilities there was a rash of new declarations of war on the Axis from erstwhile neutrals to enable these states to claim charter membership in the United Nations.

The Impact of the Charter.

The Charter, and particularly its preamble, had a profound symbolic effect. The stirring statement of purposes with which the document opened furnished a vision of the world of the future that was deeply appealing. Practical statesmen were aware, however, that the instrument created at San Francisco did not institutionalize perfection, that there were mechanical difficulties standing in the way of effective international cooperation, and that the past was not to be erased merely by a cessation of hostilities. But, even so, the first sessions of the United Nations were greeted by a remarkably spontaneous outburst of enthusiasm from governments and peoples alike. The Charter represented hope; the operational problem of realizing that hope was not felt to be beyond solution.

The Super-Powers and the Charter.

The United States and the USSR, at least at the very opening of the postwar era, conceived of the United Nations as the instrument by means of which they and their major associates could police the world and keep it at peace. The Charter revived the ancient doctrine of the "concert of power": the structure of the Security Council, complete with veto, made clear that the maintenance of peace and security was to be a monopoly of the great powers. The "big five" of the United Nations—the permanent members of the Security Council—thought of the organization primarily as a political tool whose significant functions were to be in the area of guaranteeing the security of its members, and thought of themselves as the principal instruments of such action.

Not so the smaller states who made up the vast majority of the mem-mership. Most of them had been members of the League and recalled the successful effort made there to shackle the major states. The lesser powers, acutely aware of their increased insecurity vis-a-vis the giants, were not particularly reassured by the sight of the Big Five sitting in total command of all the security mechanism of the United Nations.[8]

But there was little they could do about it, at least in 1945 and 1946, before the cold war became universal. The great powers, as long as they chose to cooperate, were in an impregnable position in the Security Council. The small states, therefore, chose to concentrate on the so-called "non-political" functions of the United Nations, under the jurisdiction of the veto-free General Assembly (in which they formed a majority) and centralized in the Economic and Social Council.

The very creation of the Economic and Social Council at San Francisco was a victory for the smaller states, and from the very beginning they argued that the security function of the United Nations was to have no more than equal rank with the long-range atttack on the causes of war. The reduction of economic, social, psychic, and demographic tensions, argued the small nations, would make a more lasting contribution to the elimination of war than the putative use of miliary force to punish aggression. The postwar era opened with this serious division of opinion among the United Nation's most devoted supporters.

NEW FORCES IN WORLD POLITICS SINCE 1945

We have just examined the major modifications in the postwar international scene; we turn now to consider some of the new dynamisms that have been operative since 1945.

These forces have given new directions, new structures, and new emphases to international politics. None of them, of course, is entirely novel; the impact of the war, however, had accentuated their effect and changed their nature so that each has had an influence many times greater than before 1939. In the aggregate they have forced governments to adopt a new set of guiding principles as they sought to accommodate to a drastically changed environment. Individually, each has been a factor with which all states have had to cope.

[8] See H. V. Evatt, *The United Nations* (Cambridge: Harvard University Press, 1948), for an able exegesis of the small-state thesis.

ECONOMIC AND POLITICAL INSTABILITY

The second great war of the twentieth century far surpassed World War I in the costs it charged mankind. The wealth destroyed by the actual fighting and by the upheavals that accommpany total war was enormous, and amounted to a huge setback to the world. Even more disrupting, however, was the heritage of instability it left behind. Almost nowhere outside the United States were there peoples whose economies were normal and healthy and whose political systems were secure. During the years since 1945, the solution of one problem of economic or political instability has tended to give rise to a family of others; Americans are still grappling with the unpalatable fact that, although themselves committed to order and stability, they will be forced to cope with chronic instability and change for an indefinite period.

Economic Consequences of the War.

The war dealt most of the industrial areas of the world a shattering blow. Industrial plants were destroyed or obsolete; manpower pools were dissolved. Financial resources were exhausted, and life for the industrialized masses of Europe and Asia seemed to have deteriorated to a grim struggle against poverty or actual starvation.[9] Transportation and trade were paralyzed as well. Agricultural production was upset by the devastation of the land, the dispersal of labor, the loss of markets, and the dislocation of distribution. Economic life in the immediate postwar period, in a word, verged upon stagnation.

The Revolution of Rising Expectations.

The problem of the industrial areas of the world—especially those open to American assistance—was not insoluble. The various assistance programs of the United States combined to restore healthy and prosperous production in most of the free world by approximately 1950. But no such success can be claimed for the second major factor of economic instability: the awakening of the underdeveloped areas and their demand for economic improvement. Here completely unprecedented plans and procedures were unmistakably called for.

The "revolution of rising expectations" in the entire non-Western world is a product of World War II. We have become familiar with the concept

---

[9] For the problem in Europe and the impact of American policies, see Howard Ellis, *The Economics of Freedom* (New York: Harper & Bros., Inc., 1950), and William A. Brown and Redvers Opie, *American Foreign Assistance* (Washington: Brookings Institution, 1953). For a brilliant statement by a European, see Barbara Ward, *The West at Bay* (New York: W. W. Norton and Co., Inc., 1948).

of "underdeveloped area," and realize that such a region is in need of technical and financial assistance in order to realize its economic potential. What is somewhat less well understood is the fact that non-Western peoples generally (who collectively occupy almost all the world's underdeveloped areas) are determined to receive what it takes to bring up their economic and social levels to a point nearer that of the industrialized West. They are not especially interested in the source of the assistance, but demand only that it be given in sufficient quantity and soon enough to bring about the transformation they wish. This constant pressure from two-thirds of mankind has been a powerful factor of continuing instability, not only in the underdeveloped areas of the world but also in the West itself.

Political Flux.

The economic pressures that contributed to constant shifts in the international climate were matched by equivalent mutability in political forms and relationships. The war had been fought by the United States to establish democratic values once and for all against the threats of totalitarianism, but victory brought no such security.

Political apathy and divisive internal forces left democratic regimes in Europe facing a struggle for survival against long odds except for Britain, the Low Countries, and Scandinavia. Eastern Europe fell to Communist domination, France and Italy were long rent by tension, and the west German revival—based as it was so obviously on one man, Chancellor Konrad Adenauer—left doubts of the longevity of democratic patterns. The dictatorships of Spain and Portugal showed no signs of liberalization. Even though the revival of European prosperity quieted the loudest anti-democratic outbursts, no one could be confident that the danger to free government in Europe was over.

Throughout Asia and Africa, change and crisis marked the new political climate. The historic Afro-Asian political structures—imperialism, feudalism, despotism—were challenged everywhere by a variety of new forces. In some places, old orders were swept away almost without a trace; in others the outer appearances of prewar society were retained despite enormous inner modifications.

Such a massive development could not be expected to proceed smoothly. At the end of the war, Asia erupted. At one extremity was Japan, whose entire semi-feudal structure was shaken by the deliberate American policy of unleashing new social and economic forces; in far southwest Asia the Arab world was being transformed by nationalism, independence, and petroleum. Everywhere in between new elements were added to the political pattern whose combined effect was to transform a once-static situation into a highly dynamic one. Africa's shift, although a little later in developing, was even more spectacular. The first state of "black Africa" to gain independence in the postwar era, Ghana (1957), opened a new era. By 1960 only a handful of European colonies remained in all of Africa. It was not surprising that such a rapid transformation produced the wave of tensions that made many observers feel that Africa was to be the next crucial battleground of world affairs.

It was significant that political forms in the postwar world were widely regarded as being susceptible to rapid and drastic change. It meant that no permanent shape could be given to international relationships, no coherent pattern of interstate alignments could emerge, until domestic political life had first been stabilized. Consistent foreign policy can rest only on consensus, and in dozens of states there was no such broad agreement on fundamentals. The arrangements made in international society could not escape being tentative and exploratory, subject to sudden revision in the light of the rapid pace of political change in most of the world.

THE IMPACT OF COMMUNISM

For many Americans the most important—and the most baleful—of the new forces abroad after 1945 was communism; for some, indeed, it was the only important one. We shall see later how the popular tendency in the United States to blame all America's difficulties on the official Soviet ideology has resulted in serious policy distortion; we can thoroughly understand the impact of communism only in relation to other dynamisms of the postwar period. At this point, however, we shall consider communism only in terms of its general impact on the pattern of world politics.

The Rise of Communism.

Communism, as doctrine, was nothing new to students of ideas. Marx had written the "Communist Manifesto" in 1848, nearly a century before; Marxist and Communist parties had long been part of the European political scene. Since 1917 Russia had been under communist rule, and its agents had been active in every part of the world. The world knew communism, and thought it understood it. Yet, at the end of the war, this dogmatic ideology broke out as one of the controlling forces of world affairs. How did this sudden rise take place? [10]

The major reason is of course the revolution in the status of the Soviet Union. Courted instead of shunned, powerful instead of weak, one of the arbiters of the world, Bolshevik Russia had become a global giant. Nothing

---

[10] From among the many histories of communism, one of the most useful is Hugh Seton-Watson, *From Lenin to Malenkov* (New York: Praeger, 1953).

succeeds like success, and Moscow had undoubtedly succeeded in its greatest test. Communism received much of the credit.

In the resistance movements against the Axis occupations between 1940 and 1945, communists everywhere had set examples of courage, organization, ingenuity, and devotion. In Europe they earned—and received payment on—a great debt of gratitude for their wartime services. In Asia they sought positions of leadership in native nationalist movements and used their new respectability to consolidate themselves against the day of peace. In both Europe and Asia, peace found communists either in or near the seats of power in many states, and in all they had improved their positions.

Communism and the Discontented.

But the success of the Soviet Union and the wartime record of communism only explain part of the new impact of the doctrine. We have seen that political and economic instability were widespread at the end of the war. The prevailing mood throughout much of the world was one of discontent, whether sullen and passive in Europe or active and revolutionary in Asia. This presented the communists with a tempting opportunity.

Communism, as its students can testify, is a very elastic ideology; it can be given almost any turn appropriate to circumstances. This gives its manipulators a tactical advantage, in that they can shape their appeal to attract supporters in a great variety of situations. During the immediate postwar era communism, modified to meet differing situations, was aimed squarely at the discontented masses everywhere. The communists preached only one message with infinite variations: hope for a better world. Whatever the complaints peculiar to the society, communism was the one nostrum guaranteeing a cure.

The communist appeal to the discontented was all the stronger because of the seemingly reactionary character of much of its opposition. Democracy in Europe seemed to look backward to 1939 for its ideal; imperialism and authoritarianism in Asia likewise sought to turn back the clock. It seemed to many as if only communism held promise for the future, as if only the communists were advancing any new ideas.

Communism and Soviet Foreign Policy.

Another explanation of the new importance of communism was its extensive and effective use as an instrument of foreign policy by the government of the Soviet Union. Ideology was put to use in the accomplishment of Russian national interest.

After the war, the party's high command in Moscow attempted to coordinate the programs of local Communist parties everywhere. In a theme modified only by local conditions, communists strove for power, created mass movements of the discontented, and preached the virtues of the Soviet Union. It made no difference that the export-variety doctrine bore only a superficial resemblance to the working ideology of the Russians themselves. The Russian purpose was not really to bring about a world revolution and a classless society, but rather a continuous augmentation in Soviet power and prestige.

Communism and Change.

Perhaps one more comment might further clarify what we are saying. Communists, whose stock in trade (at least outside the Soviet bloc) is the constant advocacy of change, have been quite successful in tuning in on the controlling wavelength of the contemporary world. Since 1945 it has frequently seemed as if only the communists of all men were preaching change in economics, in politics, and in social structure. The unsophisticated American tendency to identify communism with the other revolutionary forces of the age—nationalism, anti-colonialism, and so on—has played into communist hands. Americans were bound to be frustrated so long as any overdue change in relationships was fought as being either communist-inspired or at least in harmony with what communists were demanding.

THE AFRO-ASIAN REVOLUTION

By 1900 Africa and Asia had become the football of European politics. Although the stirrings of national and regional self-consciousness had been felt in Afro-Asia prior to 1939, it was not until after the end of the war that the peoples of these continents asserted themselves firmly. They set in motion the enormous mass movement whose consequences are now shaking the world and that may yet prove to be the most significant outcome of the second world war.

There is of course no such thing as "Afro-Asia," but only a number of separate peoples, cultures, and states coexisting upon the two largest continents of the world. Furthermore, there is no single "Afro-Asian revolution," but rather several dozen individual revolutions scattered through the two continents, each following its own course and each seeking its own fulfillment.

But each of these mass movements resembles all of the others in some common features; there is, in other words, a model of *an* Afro-Asian revolution, if not of *the* Afro-Asian revolution. The forces, groups, and trends are analogous if not similar. It is in these general terms that we now speak.

In the first place, revolution in contemporary Africa and Asia is multi-dimensional. It is neither exclusively political, entirely economic, nor purely psychic, but instead partakes of all three characteristics. Particular groups may emphasize one element or another, but success in no single one would satisfy any revolutionary movement; the goal each of them seeks is nothing less than a new posture toward the outside world. Nor is it feasible for the West (or for the communists either, for that matter) to devise a single formula for satiating all revolts individually or the Afro-Asian revolution in general. Despite their general similarity, each movement is rooted in indigenous factors and the technique for coping with them must be conspicuously flexible and capable of infinite adaption.

Roots of the Revolution.

To analyze fully the roots of revolution in Africa and Asia—if any Occidental could do it successfully—would require an extensive and detailed history of the impact of the West on the East. We may at least suggest, however, a very general cause: Africa and Asia are now determined to receive their just due in their relations with the rest of the world.[11]

That western imperialism—political, economic, and cultural—was a technique for the perpetuation of inferior status was long known to the intellectual and political leaders of Afro-Asia. As long as this insight was confined to a tiny and impotent section of the population, however, effective resistance to the West was impossible. It required the catalyzing action of the war to make the masses aware of this situation and to inspire them to end it. The object lesson of Japan, the resistance propaganda of the allies, the improvement in transportation and communication, and a number of other factors contributed to the awakening of new nationalism. Once political self-consciousness had been born, the leaders in each country were able to capture the mass movements and to provide them with both platforms and programs for action. The Afro-Asian revolution represents a reaction against the past and a hope for the future.

Positive and Negative Aspects.

Not the least of the confusing aspects of the revolution is that it has both a positive and a negative side. Affirmatively, the common demands of the various mass movements stress the necessity of developing an equita-

---

[11] See Arnold J. Toynbee, *The World and the West* (New York: Oxford University Press, 1953), Chapter V: "The Psychology of Encounters," for an interesting development of this theme.

ble basis of relationships with the rest of the world. The most common components of the positive creed are political self-determination, economic independence, and cultural and social equality; none of these, we will note, are unfamiliar to Americans. Afro-Asians are demanding the same deference values as do other peoples. Negatively—and frequently overlooked even by western sympathizers—there is a significant element of revenge involved. At last free from the more humiliating aspects of tutelage by the West, many Afro-Asians are deeply committed to demonstrating their new freedom, often in a most flamboyant way. All the old scores that weigh heavily on the conscience of the West are being settled; they are determined to balance their psychic accounts.

No one can yet foretell the direction that revolutionary Afro-Asia will eventually take. Communism early moved to take advantage of it, and many of the nationalist movements acquired a distinct pro-Soviet tinge. But as long as communist ideology requires subservience to Moscow, there is little prospect of a permanent communist victory in Africa and Asia; these peoples did not liberate themselves from western imperialism in order to offer themselves to Moscovite hegemony. The problem facing both the West and the communists is not how to control the revolution (it is too massive for "control" in any ordinary sense) but rather how to come to terms with it.

THE IMPACT OF TECHNOLOGY

It has long been a subject of somewhat ironic comment that the greatest technological advances tend to be made during a time of war. Only in wartime, when ordinary cost calculations become irrelevant, are new scientific findings likely to receive their maximum utilization. Then, after the war, peacetime pursuits often receive the benefits of the new developments.

World War II fit this pattern. During the fighting, hundreds of technological applications of already-known scientific truths were made; some of them were of major significance in combat. The impact of at least some of them on the postwar world was so significant as to make technology one of the major new forces in international politics.

Transportation and Communication.

The major relevant development in transportation during the war was, of course, in aviation.[12] Air transport matured between 1939 and 1945.

---

[12] See William F. Ogburn, "Aviation and International Relations," in W. F. Ogburn, ed., *Technology and International Relations* (Chicago: University of Chicago Press, 1949), pp. 86–101.

The end of the war found the entire world tied together by a network of airlines; no corner of the world was so remote as to be completely unapproachable by the airplane. It is banal, but unquestionably true, to point out that the net effect of the rapid growth of air transportation was to make the world a much smaller place. This was particularly relevant to the United States; obviously American security problems changed if Europe were only twelve hours away instead of seven days. The same may be said, of course, of Europe's security concerns vis-à-vis the United States.

In communication, both wire and wireless facilities had been extended. Radio, telephones, radio telephone, and telegraph systems proliferated under the stimulus of a world-wide war, and remained largely intact after the fighting. Instantaneous communication across continents and oceans was a technological factor of great importance to future world politics.[13]

Medicine.

It would require a long list compiled by a specialist to include all the wartime medical advances bequeathed to the postwar world. We shall mention only a few: the use of DDT as an insecticide; new drugs such as atabrine (replacing quinine as a treatment for malaria), the sulfas, and penicillin; the near-miracles worked in the transportation, storage, and employment of whole blood and plasma; and the mastery of a whole battery of new surgical techniques.

General gratification over these successes in the war against disease tended to obscure certain potentially troublesome implications. Many of these new techniques had public-health applications. This meant that death rates from disease could be drastically reduced by fairly simple and economical methods. What this might mean for the already overpopulated areas of Asia was generally neglected.

Demographers, ecologists, and agronomists warned of the likelihood of "population explosions," creating serious social stresses, pressures on food supplies, and the danger of new expansionist foreign policies as governments wrestled with the tensions caused by constantly increasing populations.[14] The search for a cheap and effective method of birth control had obvious foreign policy implications.

---

[13] See Hornell Hart, "Technology and the Growth of Political Areas," in Ogburn, ed., *Technology and International Relations.*

[14] Among the more outspoken of these arguments are William Vogt, *Road to Survival* (New York: Sloane, 1948), Fairfield Osborn, *Our Plundered Planet* (Boston: Little, Brown & Co., 1948), and Harrison Brown, *The Challenge of Man's Future* (New York: The Viking Press, 1954). See also Harrison Brown, "The Prospective Environment for Policymaking and Administration," Appendix A, Brookings Institution, *Formulation and Administration of United States Foreign Policy,* pp. 139–161.

Atomic Energy.

Best known of the technological feats of the war was the American success in harnessing nuclear energy. The overpowering implication of nuclear fission was of course military; we shall discuss this aspect below. But scientists and technologists realized that atomic energy had a signficance that far surpassed its use in bombs; it carried profoundly revolutionary overtones for the whole of international society.

Atomic Energy and Industrialization.

Atomic energy, despite its spectacular nature, is merely another kind of energy; atoms produce heat as do other kinds of fuel. As such, it is capable of being put to the uses to which other energy sources are put; this means, most commonly, turning the wheels of industry. The principal industrial energy sources today are coal, petroleum, and, less importantly, hydroelectric power. Atomic fuels produce fantastic amounts of energy in proportion to their weight and volume and thus would seem to be ideal for industrial purposes.

This meant that, if the time were to come when men would be free to use atomic power for industrial purposes, the modernization or extension of a mature industrial structure would be no very complicated matter, and the creation of an entirely new one would be very much simplified. As the long-range aspect of atomic energy was pondered, many discussions began to be heard about a "new industrial revolution." [15]

The Equalization Factor.

But if a new industrial revolution were indeed coming, it was destined to be a very different one. The coal-iron technology of the industrial age that began in the eighteenth century tied industry to its energy base; nations without extensive endowments of coal were seriously handicapped in the race for industrial power. Italy and Japan, for example, suffered chronically in this respect.

The introduction of nuclear fuels, however, would change this picture greatly. Relatively inexpensive and needed only in small volume, their procurement and exploitation is beyond the reach of only the smallest and weakest of states. If a new industrial race were to begin, most states would start approximately even; the advantages enjoyed by the handful of presently dominant economies might disappear quickly. This point was understood by both the industrialized and the nonindustrialized states,

---

[15] Fritz Sternberg, *The Military and Industrial Revolution of Our Time* (New York: Frederick A. Praeger, 1959).

and the ultimate implications of atomic power were one of the unknowns as the world entered the postwar era.

THE NEW WARFARE

One of the most pervasive of the new forces in world politics after 1945 has been the effect of the new warfare. The new techniques and doctrines of the military art, developed during the war and refined in the era of constant tension that followed it, found no real place in the day-by-day course of international affairs. The state system, on the other hand, found itself unable to adjust to the changed patterns imposed by military requirements; obvious frustration was the predictable result.

Total Weapons.

The apex of military ingenuity up to the end of the war was the atomic bomb, but it was by no means the only new development of total techniques of war. Dozens of others, less horrible to contemplate but no less effective, were perfected; weaponry was at its highest point of elaboration in history when peace came. But to the array of frightening weapons then existing, the tensions of the cold-war era have led to the opening of even newer horizons in weapons development.

Most awesome of these was, of course, the hydrogen bomb. There were those after 1954 who argued that with it had been born the true "absolute weapon" [16] capable of wiping man off the planet. Equally great effort has been lavished on perfecting vehicles for the delivery of nuclear bombs to their targets. From the supersonic jet aircraft to the ICBM (intercontinental ballistic missile) was an easy step. By May, 1960, both the United States and the USSR had test fired missiles more than 9000 miles—over one-third of the distance around the earth. Truly no one was any longer out of range of the new weapons.

On top of the missile and H-bomb programs came the assault on space triggered by the Soviet's "Sputnik" in 1957. Obviously, the conquest of space had military significance—for reconnaissance, for manned "space stations," or for bases for space-to-earth missiles. It seemed to many, as they watched the pyramiding of the new weapons, as if warfare had indeed reached the point of mutual saturation.

Total War.

The new weapons required a new theory of war. Classically, the object of warfare was to "destroy the enemy's will to resist" and to have him

---

[16] This term was originally applied to the atomic bomb. See Bernard Brodie, ed., *The Absolute Weapon* (New York: Harcourt, Brace, and Co., 1946).

bend to your will. This concept entailed the prosecution of combat by uniformed armed forces, fighting according to a generally understood code. The new weapons, however, had only limited utility under tactical conditions; their most effective targets were the productive centers of the enemy, where they could exert maximum effectiveness on the concentration of facilities and the congregations of people. Total weapons thus led to a theory of total war.

Total war is total in every respect: total in weapons, total in targets, total in strategy, total in mobilization, and finally total in objectives. Total war is war for annihilation. Its alternative objectives are the abject surrender of the enemy or his total obliteration. Negotiated peace becomes a thing of the past; all peace terms are to be either dictated after surrender or else irrelevant because the enemy no longer exists. If total effort be required for total victory, objectives become absolute as well; nothing less than absolute hegemony over the defeated is a sufficient enticement to make the effort and risks worth while.[17]

The Inexpediency of Military Power.

However consistent the new theory of war may have been with its premises and its techniques, it broke sharply with the traditional theory of international politics. War is usually conceived as an instrument of national policy, as the only ultimately efficacious technique available to a state for the enforcement of its will on others. Total war, however, is an efficient instrument only for the accomplishment of total objectives; if total war is the only kind of war that a state is in a position to fight, its less extreme policies are seriously handicapped. It lacks the means of applying force in amounts graduated according to the objective sought and the resistance encountered, and thus is brought to face a hard choice. Objectives less than total must either be prosecuted without any real reliance on military techniques—a frustrating and often futile enterprise— or expanded so that they become important enough to justify the new warfare.

The Balance of Terror.

By 1960 the world had begun to grasp the meaning of total war. Although the United States and the USSR possessed military striking power unmatched in any earlier peacetime era (and probably in any earlier period of war), neither felt any more secure for it. What was worse, neither had any illusions about its ability to use force against the other to win political

---

[17] See B. H. Liddell Hart, *The Revolution in Warfare* (New Haven: Yale University Press, 1947), and W. W. Kaufmann, ed., *Military Policy and National Security* (Princeton: Princeton University Press, 1956).

victories; retaliatory capability so effectively neutralized striking force that both found themselves caught in a "balance of terror." To complete the cycle of frustration, so frightened were both sides by the prospect of war that they acted in unadmitted concert to prevent any smaller states from using war to reach a political decision. Warfare had largely cancelled itself out [18]—and the state of international relations testified to the vacuum it had left behind.

POLITICAL TRENDS SINCE 1945

It has been within the general context outlined in the preceding pages that the course of international politics has proceeded in the years since the end of the war. Certain trends stand out as being more important, and this brief comment on the international scene as the United States surveys it should include some mention of them.

GREAT-POWER RIVALRIES

Central to the course of world affairs during this period—as they have been in every era—are the rivalries and disagreements among the handful of major states. Our catalogue of trends must begin with at least the more significant of these.

The Cold War.

The history of American foreign policy since 1945 is largely the history of the cold war. It is also true that the Soviet-American conflict has been the largest single factor in world politics. We shall be considering the cold war in detail later, so there is no need to elaborate at this point. In our immediate terms of "rivalries," however, we should point out that there are at least three dimensions of great-power disagreement built into the contemporary structure of the cold war.

First, and best known, is the Soviet-American confrontation itself, modified but not fundamentally changed by the fact that associated with the United States are several other major states.[19] Second, there is the much newer Chinese-American controversy, with the full implications of which Americans are not yet acquainted; this battle, furthermore, is one that the

---

[18] We shall be discussing this question in more detail, particularly with reference to the so-called doctrine of "limited war," in Chapter 13.

[19] Henry L. Roberts, *Russia and America: Dangers and Prospects* (New York: Harper & Bros., 1956).

United States must prosecute largely by itself, since its western allies are not involved to the same extent with the new Communist regime in China. Third, and at present not yet in the open, there is the Chinese-Soviet rivalry both for ideological preeminence and for concrete advantages that each feels it may win from the other.[20]

New Rivalries and Old.

Sometimes within, but more frequently without the cold-war structure, other major-power rivalries have given color and tone to international relations. Some are of ancient vintage, others much newer. Most of them have developed since 1954, after the rigidity of the earlier bipolar era relaxed. We may mention three, each of which will appear in our later discussions: (1) the revolt of Europe against American dominance that took form both in the movement for European integration and in the increasing independence of American wishes shown by Britain and France between 1956 and 1961; (2) the revival of the classic balance of power in Britain's European policy, most clearly expressed in London's counterattack on the rise of de Gaulle in France and the whole movement of European economic integration; (3) the sudden eruption of rivalry between China and India, in which the ultimate stakes were no less than the leadership of the new Asia.

THE RISE OF NEW POWER CENTERS

In 1945 there were only two centers of power in the world, Moscow and Washington. Many Americans in the postwar era succumbed to the easy assumption that this was all there ever would be again, and that all questions would ultimately be decided by the relations between the Soviet and the United States. Both the great powers have had difficulty in adjusting to the fact that several new power centers have risen and now exert a major influence on world affairs.[21]

China.

The communist conquest of China, followed so swiftly by Chinese participation in the Korean war, signalled the end of the era when China could safely be written off as an independent power center. Peiping is now a major world capital, whose opinion on any question is listened to and whose intentions are a matter of major concern.

---

[20] Howard L. Boorman, et al., *Moscow-Peking Axis: Strengths and Strains* (New York: Harper & Bros., 1957).

[21] For an interpretation of these developments, see Chester Bowles, *Ideas, People and Peace* (New York: Harper & Bros., 1958).

India.

Although playing a radically different role than China, India has also become a power center of major relevance to world concerns. Nehru has been skillful in mobilizing a pool of international consensus in support of Indian positions, and the international image projected by New Delhi is one that has made India bulk increasingly large. No more eloquent testimony to her critical role could be adduced than the great attention both the Soviet and the United States have lavished on her.

Europe.

The revival of Europe, spearheaded by the "German miracle," also gave birth to still another center of independent power. Not only did West Germany, France, and Britain undertake larger roles, but the evolution of the European Community on the continent gave promise that soon a new entity known simply as "Europe" would be a member of the group of great powers. Americans generally welcomed this prospect, for most expectations were that an independent and unified Europe would act in a way favorable to American long-range interest.[22]

The Middle East.

It is not yet accurate to call the Middle East a power center, at least in the singular; the remarkable rise in influence of the Middle Eastern states on world affairs has not yet been matched by an equivalent consolidation of its inner potential. But it remains true that there is today a great deal of indigenous power within the region, and that eventually it will coalesce— at least for international purposes. Until that day, however, the present situation will generally obtain: there will be several Middle Eastern states with supraregional capacity, and the tendency toward the settlement of Middle Eastern questions by the direct action of the states of the region themselves will increase. Non-regional powers will for a time, however, continue to affect regional affairs.

Africa.

The same sort of comment may be made about Africa. No real center to political power now exists in Africa south of the Sahara, but when the numerous small and young states there come together on an issue, Africa's voice is heard. The trend toward some form of integration or consolidation in Africa is only beginning, but it seems certain to go much further. Future

---

[22] See F. W. Jandry, "United Europe: a Strong Partner," *Department of State Bulletin* (March 10, 1958), p. 385; see also Arnold J. Zurcher, *The Struggle to Unite Europe, 1940–1958* (New York: New York University Press, 1958).

statescraft will have to reckon on African participation in world affairs as a major factor.

THE CHALLENGE OF THE NON-WESTERN WORLD

We have already alluded to the Afro-Asian revolution and have attempted to suggest that it is a much more complex phenomenon than it might appear to be at first glance. Indeed, the longer the revolt of the non-Western world continues, the more the impression gains currency that it is one of the really significant forces in contemporary world politics. We shall be returning to this problem frequently in later chapters.

The End of Imperialism.

The most obvious immediate result of the birth of political consciousness in the non-West was a fundamental change in the map of the world. By 1961, over thirty new states had been born in the aftermath of the war, almost all by conversion from colonial status. Throughout Asia and Africa there remained only a relative handful of colonial possessions, most of them small and undeveloped. Granted the breakneck speed with which independence movements were being born and the inability of any colonial power to hold them off, it seems likely that imperialism as the world has known it for centuries is dead.

Accompanying political independence was the determined and fairly successful effort of the former colonial states, new and old, to rid themselves of "economic imperialism." Making full use of their new freedom of action, many deliberately sought to break their old economic ties with their former mother country and to create new ones. For several this involved the risky but potentially profitable enterprise of turning to the communist bloc and then enjoying the consternation they caused and the better bargains they then received from both sides.[23] This maneuver, however, called for statesmanship of the highest order.

The Voice of the non-West.

The new states of the non-Western world brought a surprising amount of consensus into world politics. For obvious reasons, by and large the non-Western world (with a few conspicuous exceptions) argued for peace, disarmament, a stronger United Nations, technical and capital assistance

---

[23] See especially Bowles, *Ideas, People and Peace,* and Max Millikan and W. W. Rostow, *A Proposal: Key to an Effective Foreign Policy* (New York: Harper & Bros., 1957). For a convenient collection of readings, see DeVere E. Pentony, *The Underdeveloped Lands* (San Francisco: Howard Chandler, Publisher, 1960).

from the West, and full equality of deference and status from their erstwhile masters.

Their chosen instrument was the General Assembly of the United Nations. Here (as well as in regional "Afro-Asian" conferences) they gave expression to their fears of great-power tensions and their demands for satisfaction in both tangible and intangible ways. Although physically weak, even when united, the military frustration of the great powers gave them surprising effectiveness, especially on the questions they made peculiarly their own: the liquidation of colonialism, technical assistance, and human rights.[24]

New Techniques in World Politics

Earlier in this chapter we pointed to the decreasing utility of military power in solving international problems. Since world affairs do not stand still, the international order has been obliged to develop a battery of new techniques so as to perform at least the indispensible tasks of reaching decisions and normalizing relationships.

Economic Assistance.

Inaugurated by the United States in 1947 with the Greek-Turkish aid program and elaborated by all major participants in international politics since that time, economic assistance has become a standardized technique. Applicable in a great variety of circumstances and available in some measure to almost any state with a productive surplus it wishes to put to a political purpose, it has proved to be a method peculiarly suited to the requirements of contemporary international life.[25]

The major unsolved question about economic assistance as a technique of policy lay in the realm of the conditions to be placed on such aid. The instinctive reaction of the United States Congress to put "strings" on aid, whether in the form of controls over the expenditure of funds or of political commitments, had very uneven success: several recipients refused aid programs entirely or seriously compromised them by developing extreme (if largely unfounded) suspicions of American purposes. On the other hand, the Soviet meticulously avoided apparent political conditions, and contented itself largely with negotiating clearly restrictive trade agreements with the recipients of its aid. It must be admitted, however, that Moscow

---

[24] Vera M. Dean, *The Nature of the Non-Western World* (New York: New American Library, 1957).

[25] Millikan and Rostow, *A Proposal: Key to an Effective Foreign Policy,* Chapters I and II.

had little more success in evoking direct responses to its aid program than did the United States. The whole "foreign aid" technique, while of admitted usefulness, clearly was unsuited to any sort of coercive purpose.

Technical Assistance.

The same general observation can be made with regard to the whole area of technical and development assistance. Although all major powers made some effort in this direction, a decade of experience with it indicated that its usefulness was primarily long-range. There was no effective way to use technical or development aid as a tool of short-run policy. So sensitive were the underdeveloped countries to this sort of danger that they made every effort they could to put as much as possible of the whole program under the aegis of the United Nations, where it could not be used as a tool of national policy by any large state and where the recipients could have some control over general policy.

Consensus as a Tool of Policy.

Woodrow Wilson would have been pleased to see the extent to which his dream of an international consensus was realized in the 1950's. The United States, the USSR, and the Afro-Asian states all at one time or another were able to mobilize and capitalize upon a mass consensus as an efficacious tool of policy. The major instrument for verbalizing such broad-gauge agreement was the General Assembly of the United Nations. Among its most convincing statements were the 73–1 vote in 1957 condemning Israel's continued occupation of the Gaza Strip in Egypt and the 70–0 vote in 1960 in support of Secretary-General Hammarskjöld's Congo policy; almost as impressive was the steady decline in the majority by which the United States annually prevented any discussion of the admission of Communist China. No one state had control of this consensus, no one state could turn it on at will in support of its own policy; when it did crystallize on a particular issue, however, it was clear that no countervailing power existed in the international order.

Science and Culture as Techniques.

A final word should be said about the use of science and culture as tools of policy. The postwar era, and particularly the latter half of the 1950's, was a time when science and culture became truly international again, in reaction to the crude nationalism of the interwar and early postwar period. Cultural and scientific delegations criss-crossed the map in almost every direction: across the Iron Curtain, between West and non-West, to and from the new Africa. There was a major internationalizing of these areas after the decline in the militancy of the cold war.

Candor forces the admission, however, that there was at least a duality in the motivations behind these scientific and cultural explorations. On the one hand, most (perhaps all) had a healthy curiosity about other peoples and wished to know more about them; the newly shrunk world made it imperative to acquire a greater cross-cultural sophistication. But there was a distinct element of "one-upmanship" present in all these exchanges as well. Nations were alert to put their best feet forward and to score such prestige victories as were for the taking in what came unfortunately to be thought of as a cultural competition.

This was of course most painfully obvious in the "science race" between the Soviet and the United States that followed the breakthrough into space in 1957. What started as a cooperative scientific venture in the International Geophysical Year soon deteriorated into a contest to determine which nation could send up the most, the biggest, or the most spectacular satellites.[26] But even so, most observers felt that this was a safer way to compete than in military power or diplomatic *faits accompli*.

---

[26] For example, the Soviet launched a "space probe" toward the planet Venus in February, 1961. This "piggyback" vehicle, launched from a satellite already in orbit, was a headline news item throughout the world. The United States, however, ruefully admitted that it proved the Soviet to be "three years ahead" in the space race. See *New York Times*, February 12–16, 1961.

The Soviet Threat

Were it possible (or worthwhile) to classify all American policy moves since 1945 in terms of their situational motivation, there is little doubt that we would discover that the vast majority would owe their original inspiration to Soviet policy. The behavior of the Soviet Colossus has been the most significant fact confronting Americans in the postwar era, and the design of contemporary American policy is to a great extent grounded on certain assumptions about Soviet behavior.

THE RISE OF SOVIET REVISIONISM

The pivot of our discussion of Soviet policy is the assumption that the USSR is a revisionist power. For whatever reasons, Russian leadership emerged from the war committed to a policy of seeking further advantage, and apparently willing to capitalize upon postwar disorganization and distress by any expedient means. Since the United States accepted the contrary status of being and behaving like a status-quo power, the cold war was from the beginning a massive struggle between attackers and defenders of the general shape of the postwar settlement. Through all the twists and turns of world affairs since 1945, the United States has remained determined to frustrate Soviet revisionism.

The Wartime Policy of the USSR.

Many Americans were unnecessarily shocked at the Soviet Union's determination to follow an active and opportunistic policy after the war. Moscow had given adequate warning of its intentions all through the era of active combat; her postwar policy should not have occasioned such surprise. Beginning in 1939 with the annexation of a large part of Poland, and culminating with the mass looting of Manchuria in 1945, Soviet military operations were always at the immediate service of a set of political objectives. The Soviet was primarily interested in three things: (1) the rectification of Soviet frontiers, particularly with regard to territories that Russia had lost after 1917 (Poland, the Baltic States, Bessarabia); (2) the elimination or abasement of hostile regimes on Soviet frontiers (Finland, Turkey); (3) the reestablishment of traditional spheres of Russian influence (northern Iran, the Balkans). Although Soviet policy was to go far beyond these goals in the postwar era, they remain today as apparently fundamental to Soviet policy.[1]

The Breakup of the Wartime Alliance.

American attitudes during the war, public and official alike, tended frequently to magnify unduly the actual area of agreement between the United States and the Soviet Union. Basic harmony of ends between Moscow and the West was confined to a common interest in the military defeat of the Axis, and included only the most general and vague reassurances about the final shape to be taken by the peace settlement. In the latter days of the fighting, when in 1944 and early 1945 the dimensions of the ultimate victory were becoming apparent, the developing divergence of interest between Moscow and the West came into the open. As the allies turned to the task of postwar planning, serious cleavages developed. Soviet policy remained consistent with its fundamental revisionism; Britain and the United States assumed the posture demanded by their status-quo orientation.

This mutual opposition manifested itself on almost all the specific issues that came under discussion, of which three were most important for the future: (1) the disposition to be made of the Axis states, particularly Germany and the reparations she was to pay; (2) the post-liberation status of eastern Europe, epitomized by the problem of Poland; (3) the nature of the United Nations and the place of the great powers in its structure. On each of these points a distinct Soviet position developed, marked by a single-minded pursuit of its own advantage, an apparent unconcern for

[1] See, for example, Anatole G. Mazour, *Russia Past and Present* (New York: D. Van Nostrand Company, Inc., 1951), Chapters 26, 27.

208 ❖ FACTORS IN CONTEMPORARY AMERICAN POLICY

peace, order, and stability in the abstract, and an unwillingness to accept substantial compromise. So clear had it become that allied unity had dissolved that peace-making became from the outset an admitted conflict between the Soviet and the West. The grand alliance did not survive the crisis that had given it birth.[2]

The Soviet's Search for Advantage.

At this point we may generally characterize the evolving Soviet policy at the close of the war as a search for advantage. It is relatively unimportant to us here whether this decision to take the policy offensive was a wartime development or a long-standing (though often ignored) ideological commitment; in 1945 it was clear that Moscow was determined to win whatever rewards were available for the taking.

It is axiomatic that revisionist policies succeed best in periods of stress, insecurity, and disorganization. Such was the condition of the world in the wake of World War II. Conditions were everywhere tailored to Soviet purposes: Europe was prostrate, Asia in ferment, and the fabric of international relationships badly disrupted by twelve years of Hitler, the last six having been years of war. Moscow had ample opportunity to use its newly rationalized position of power to force rearrangements to its advantage. Russian hegemony broke out of its traditional limits and flowed in all directions as the Kremlin sought to profit by the badly roiled waters of international affairs.

SOVIET POSTWAR POLICY

In the policy the Soviet developed in the immediate aftermath of the war was demonstrated the characteristics that have made Moscow the major threat to the United States. Throughout all the twists and turns of events since 1945, the USSR has never significantly departed from the line it laid down at that time.

GENERAL CHARACTERISTICS

Being fundamentally revisionist, Soviet policy has been dynamic, expansive, and alert to seize such initiatives as offer themselves. The USSR

---

[2] For general discussions of deteriorating relations with the Soviet, see Cordell Hull, *Memoirs* (New York: The Macmillan Co., 1948), Chapters 105, 106; and James F. Byrnes, *Speaking Frankly* (New York: Harper & Bros., Inc., 1947), Chapters 2, 3, 4.

is impatient with long-standing commitments and traditional patterns. To the Kremlin, the international order is infinitely fluid; almost any situation is susceptible of manipulation by sufficiently determined and ingenious policy. The Soviet has consistently sought to transform relationships and to direct the course of events to its liking.

The Exploitation of Great-power Status.

From the very outset, the USSR has been anxious to exploit its status as a great power in the nineteenth century sense. At least three trends of Soviet behavior seem to have flowed from this concern. (1) The persistence of the notion of the "concert" in settling disputes; Moscow tends to think in terms of "summits" or conferences of foreign ministers as dispute-settling techniques. (2) The insistence upon total interest; the Soviet seems to feel that, as a great power, it has the prerogative of being consulted on any issue into which it cares to intervene. (3) The lack of regard for the opinions or rights of small states; smaller powers are not to have rights against Moscow nor to criticize Soviet policy. In each of these, it must be admitted, the Soviet has been following a trail well blazed by western statesmen of an earlier day.

The Assumption of Disharmony of Interest.

A second basic characteristic of Soviet policy has been its assumption that no community of interest exists between the USSR and any state not under its control. Soviet leaders entered the postwar world officially committed to the doctrine that Moscow would have to look only to itself for its salvation, and that the motives of other states ranged from the highly questionable to the openly hostile. As a result, the USSR has seemed to place no trust in pledges of good faith or in collective guarantees; its working hypothesis has stressed rather the impermanence of such arrangements and has concentrated instead on the creation of situations absolutely under Moscow's control.[3]

This outlook has made Moscow a most troublesome negotiator. Assuming that noncommunist states are incapable of any interest not unalterably opposed to the continued existence of the USSR leaves little room for maneuver and none for compromise. Every discussion with the West becomes a no-quarter battle in which the Soviet sets minimum objectives for itself and will accept nothing less; offers of partial settlement by the other states are deemed to be admissions of defeat and have been met by demands for further concessions. So long as Moscow postulates the failure

---

[3] For the doctrinal roots of this assumption, see Nathan Leites, *The Operational Code of the Politburo* (New York: The McGraw-Hill Book Co., 1951), Chapters 9, 10, 11, 14, 20.

of any community of agreement, Soviet policy will remain beyond stabilization.

SOVIET RELATIONS WITH THE UNITED STATES

Naturally enough, the Russian decision to break the pattern of wartime cooperation and to initiate a policy of unilateral revisionism required that it reorient its relations with the United States. During the war Moscow had been officially friendly with Washington, although this was a friendship with definite reservations; by mid-1945, however, this attitude had become an encumbrance on the Soviet's postwar plans. Relationships with American were thereupon deliberately transformed from amicability to hostility.

The Change in Attitude.

The new Soviet position became apparent before the end of the war. Even before the death of President Roosevelt the Soviet propaganda line had begun to minimize American contributions to the war, to discredit American motives before and during the fighting, and to discover ideological justification for the assumption that the United States was bound to plot the destruction of the Soviet system.[4]

After victory, Moscow's "hate America" approach solidified. Official Russian policy pretended to discover the reason for American hostility in the distortion of President Roosevelt's intentions by his successors;[5] unofficially the condemnation of everything American became much more general. By the end of 1945 Russian-American relations had become tense; by mid-1946 the conflict was open.

Open Competition.

The policy of hostility to the United States was amplified by the adoption of an action principle: open competition with America. In every area of the world and on every functional issue, a Soviet policy was swiftly developed as a counterpart to each move of the United States. Moscow rapidly took stands that were admittedly relevant to its original revisionist orientation but the detailed implementation of which was to some extent inspired

---

[4] Robert Sherwood, *Roosevelt and Hopkins* (New York: Bantam Books, 1950), Chapter XXXII, "Beginnings of Dissension."

[5] It is interesting to note, that as late as 1960, the Soviet was still using this line. See the remarks of Premier Khrushchev in Paris, May 16, 1960, at the only session of the 1960 summit meeting. *New York Times* (May 17, 1960). He struck this chord again in his message of congratulation to Senator John F. Kennedy upon his election to the Presidency in 1960. *New York Times* (November 10, 1960).

by its determination to demonstrate disagreement with the United States. Analyzing this period from the perspective granted by time, a good case can be made that the Soviet was often more concerned with differing with the United States than it was with the specifics of the program it was following.

The Escape from Inferiority.

This last point suggests another aspect of Moscow's American policy, difficult to measure exactly but possibly of great significance. The USSR seems to have been determined to force the United States to accept it as an equal in every way: in status, in power, in prestige. The Soviet has intended, however, to insist upon exactly those symbols of equality most likely to annoy American prejudices, and often attempted to win their acceptance by violent and direct propaganda attack on the United States. The almost predictable result has been a stubborn American refusal to give ground to Soviet prestige, even in the face of mounting evidence that Moscow is indeed "catching up" or at least narrowing the gap.

How deeply seated this problem of status had become in both Soviet and American policy was shown by the ups and downs of Premier Khrushchev's attempts to soften the hate-America line after 1957. Buoyed up by Soviet triumphs in such disparate areas as space exploration, weapons development, athletics, and folk dancing, Khrushchev attempted to formulate an "equal-to-equal" approach to political coexistence. Not only did this fail to win acceptance in the United States, but by 1960 it had obviously set in motion powerful opposition forces inside the Soviet Union. The escape from inferiority had apparently become a drive for status superiority with natural countereffects among Americans.

THE SOVIET UNION AND THE UNITED NATIONS

Soviet attitudes toward the United Nations provides further clues to Russian policy. With the popular American conception of the United Nations as an instrument for interstate cooperation directed at the institutionalization of peace, the USSR has no sympathy. Moscow instead has brought to the organization its own great-power preoccupation and its assumption of the absence of any genuine community of interest.

The United Nations as a Tool.

Underlying the Soviet approach to the United Nations has been the basic judgment that the United Nations' sole justification is as a tool of Moscow's foreign policy. Certain Russian objectives can be most efficiently pursued through the United Nations; some foreign-policy techniques are more effective when employed there. For these purposes the USSR is willing—almost eager—to employ the institutions and mechanisms provided. Other United Nations functions are politically dangerous; some procedures violate the Soviet's conception of the organization's appropriate role. These "undesirable" aspects of the United Nations system Moscow has set itself to arrest or at least to minimize. Finally, the Soviet feels that a large area of United Nations activity is simply irrelevant to itself; this portion is simply ignored. There has never been any intention on the Soviet's part to make the organization the substantive or the procedural center of its policy; rather the United Nations is thought of as one of its available techniques of foreign policy, to be used when and to the extent to which it is appropriate.[6]

The Soviet Union and the Security Council.

The Soviet idea of the United Nations has been clearly indicated by its conduct on the Security Council. The great-power veto is the USSR's method of guaranteeing that its status will be inviolate. Any measure carrying a threat—however remote—to any Russian interest, the Soviet is prepared ruthlessly to void by means of a negative vote; at the same time Moscow shrewdly capitalizes on the reluctance of the other permanent members to veto in their turns. Thus the Security Council has been put substantially at Russia's mercy; it can deal only with those questions that the Soviet allows it to, and its solutions must meet Soviet specifications in order to win acceptance. Torn by the cold war, the Security Council has rapidly faded into relative impotence under the threat of the veto.[7]

The Propaganda Weapon.

The principal value Russia has found in the General Assembly is as a platform for propaganda. Soviet theorists have only contempt for the idealistic conception of the General Assembly as the "parliament of man" or the "collective conscience of mankind"; ideologically, only the proletariat has a conscience and most of the members of the United Nations are

---

[6] See Rupert Emerson and Inis L. Claude, "The Soviet Union and the United Nations," *International Organization* (February, 1952), pp. 1 ff. A later evaluation is found in Lincoln Bloomfield, *The United Nations and U. S. Foreign Policy* (Boston: Little, Brown & Co., 1960), chapter 8.

[7] Considering the low opinion the Soviet holds of Security Council techniques, it was very striking that Moscow took the "U-2" incident to the Council in May 1960. This was generally interpreted as a device to calm down the crisis rather than a tension-aggravating move, particularly since the Soviet draft resolution only requested the Council to admonish the United States rather than to take any action against it.

noncommunist states. But the great forum of the General Assembly provides a built-in global audience for Soviet arguments, and from its very first session Russian spokesmen have taken full advantage of it. Out of General Assembly sessions have come the outlines of Soviet anti-Americanism, of its emergent anti-colonialism, and of its series of sensational disarmament proposals. As the Soviet grew more skilled in developing and manipulating consensus among the non-Western states, its ability to win sympathetic hearings for its views improved, and Russian opinion of the Assembly's worth grew much more favorable.

The Rejection of ECOSOC.

In marked contrast to its vigorous exploitation of the opportunities it found in the Security Council and the General Assembly, the Soviet has ignored, for the most part, the economic and social activities of the United Nations. It participates in the work of the Economic and Social Council (ECOSOC) itself and its commissions, but with obvious lack of interest and energy; one interesting exception was its feverish attachment to the work of the commission drafting a world declaration of human rights. Except for the Universal Postal Union, the World Health Organization, the International Telecommunications Union, and the World Meterological Organization, the Soviet Union has largely ignored the specialized agencies; even its membership in WHO was terminated in 1949 for the alleged reason of exorbitant cost. It was not until the cold war changed character in 1954 and 1955 that the Soviet indicated any interest in the other specialized agencies,[8] and even went so far as to join the United Nations Educational, Scientific, and Cultural Organization.

Both ideology and realistic politics help explain the USSR's abstention from the economic and social work of the United Nations. Ideologically, there is no reason for a socialist state to cooperate with capitalist societies in attempting to improve the economic and social lot of men; according to Marxist dogma, such reform can come about only after a proletarian revolution that would rebuild society on a more substantial base. Communists could argue, therefore, that Moscow is lending more real assistance to workers everywhere by intriguing to destroy capitalism than it would by cooperating with bourgeois democracies. Politically, it is apparent that Russia's policy thrives best in a distraught world; to stabilize economic and social conditions might well interfere with the satisfaction of Soviet desires. There is no reason for the USSR to take any pains to speed the arrival of stability; on the contrary, there are many reasons to interfere with it.

---

[8] See Daniel S. Cheever and H. Field Haviland, *Organizing for Peace* (Boston: Houghton Mifflin Co., 1954), pp. 193–4.

What the Soviet conception of its great-power status and its assumption of disharmony of interest means in practice has been shown in its relationships with its smaller European neighbors of Eastern Europe. Permanently friendly relations between Moscow and a smaller state are possible on only one basis: the status relationship the world calls "satellitism."

The Meaning of Satellitism.

What is satellitism? As the relationship developed after 1945, it became clear that the price of Russian friendship for a small state was the complete subordination of its foreign policy to Soviet control. The international mission of a satellite is reduced to contributing its share to the accomplishment of Russian designs. In theory, it is not absolutely necessary for a satellite to become a communist state on the Soviet model; the minimum requirements of satellitism are satisfied with an appropriate international orientation.[9] The complex of historic, ethnic, religious, and economic forces in Slavic Europe, Hungary, and East Germany, however, left Moscow no convenient stopping place short of the complete reconstruction of the states in that region; in no other way can the Kremlin exercise sufficiently close control over their foreign policies.

Once a satellite's status is formalized, it loses its freedom of international action. Its position is that of a member of the Soviet team and of the instrument of a foreign policy that remains peculiarly Russian. Moscow's enemies are its enemies; Moscow's friends are its friends. Its traditional objectives are measured against Soviet policy; to the extent that the USSR is gratified by any satellite's success, such goals are permitted. When any conflict arises, Soviet objectives naturally take precedence.

The Application of Satellitism.

The principle of satellitism was put into practice in those areas of Europe that were liberated from the Nazis by the Red Army. In the wake of Soviet military forces came teams of civilian political specialists, who rapidly made contact with local resistance forces and hastily put together provisional governments under the sponsorship of the Red Army. The new regimes were called "democratic" and were ostensibly broadly-based coalitions of all acceptable political factions. As time went on, it became clear

---

[9] This condition is perhaps represented by Finland's relationship with the Soviet. Although internally a free democracy, and not overtly a satellite of the Soviet, nevertheless it is noteworthy that Finland's foreign relations are carefully conducted so as not to antagonize the USSR.

that the coalition structure was a mere facade; the dominant element was the local communist element that drew its strength from its liaison with the Russian army and the Russian party commissars.[10]

The single exception to this pattern was Yugoslavia, where the indigenous strength of Marshal Tito's partisans and the aid they received from the West made it possible for a communist-style people's government to be established without the appearance of Russian troops. This single difference was to have a profound effect on the later development of Russo-Yugoslav relations.[11]

In all the east and southeast European states entered by Soviet forces except Czechoslovakia and Hungary, the principles of satellitism were applied during 1945 and 1946. Bulgaria, Yugoslavia, Albania, Romania, Poland, and the Soviet zone of Germany were swiftly brought under effective communist control. In Czechoslovakia and Hungary Soviet plans did not succeed so swiftly; genuine coalitions with anti-communist elements were voted into office in reasonably free elections, not to be disbanded until the coups of 1947 and 1948. Even with these two exceptions, however, the Soviet created within less than two years a tightly-knit bloc of supporters whose foreign relations were completely under Moscow's control and that formed a buffer belt from the Baltic to the Adriatic.

The Rationale of Satellitism.

The rationale of satellitism has several components that help explain why the Soviet was compelled to move so strongly in dealing with its immediate neighbors. (1) The Soviet conception of great power-small power relations demands such a pattern, since large and powerful states are supposed to dictate to smaller and weaker ones. (2) The Russian assumption of a lack of any community of interest with noncommunist states dictates the necessity of complete control. (3) Russia has reversed the *cordon sanitaire* of the 1920's, throwing up a buffer zone between itself and the West. The flat plain of Poland had served as a highway for two invasions from the West within a single generation. (4) Ideology urges the expansion of the proletarian revolution by capitalizing on such favorable opportunities. (5) The historic Russian role as "protector of the Slavs" coincides with these other factors in persuading Moscow to make Slavic Europe a Russian province. All together, the combination of considerations of prestige, of security, of ideology, and of nationalism make up a sufficient case to

---

[10] For a deft summary of this technique, see Lennox Mills and Charles M. Mc-Laughlin, *World Politics in Transition* (New York: Henry Holt and Co., 1956), pp. 576–81: "The Technique of the Inside Job."

[11] Hamilton Fish Armstrong, *Tito and Goliath* (New York: The Macmillan Co., 1951); see also Fitzroy Maclean, *The Heretic* (New York: Harper & Bros., 1957).

justify the Soviet doing something it would have had difficulty in avoiding doing anyway.[12]

EARLY SOVIET MOVES

For roughly the first two years following the surrender of Germany, the Soviet gained major advantages from the disorganization of the West and the slowness of the United States to grasp the implications of Russian policy. During this brief period the USSR was able to score a number of significant victories and to establish a position relatively well suited to receive the western counterattack. To trace each of the complex and varied maneuvers of Soviet policy during this period would be tedious and unnecessary. We shall confine ourselves to a rapid survey of the major trends.

EUROPE

Europe was the major theater of the cold war from the beginning. Soviet expansionism began in Europe, and Russian efforts there have been continuous. The development of concerted Russian strategies for the Far East and the Middle East was not to come until later and then only in response to drastic changes in conditions; the Soviet program in Europe was full-grown the moment peace arrived.

Germany.

Early Soviet policy toward the problem of Germany may be divided profitably into three subsections. In each of them the Soviet acted vigorously, apparently unconcerned that its actual policies often tended toward self-contradiction.

(1) The first matter was that of occupation policy. The USSR's version of the quadripartite occupation required that its own zone be treated as a captured province. The "democratization" and "denazification" directives formulated at Potsdam gave Moscow ample justification to proceed swiftly to the creation of a satellite regime for east Germany.

(2) The second issue was reparations. The Soviet stripped its own zone of Germany of almost everything that was both portable and valuable in

---

[12] On satellitism, see Owen Lattimore, "Satellite Politics: the Mongolian Prototype," *Western Political Quarterly* (March, 1956), p. 37 ff; Czeslav Milosz, "Poland: Voices of Illusion," *Problems of Communism* (May-June, 1956), pp. 26 ff; E. D. Stillman and R. H. Bass, "Bulgaria: A Study in Satellite Non-conformity," *Problems of Communism* (November-December, 1955).

the guise of reparations, and then presented an enormous bill that it claimed was due from West Germany. To the other three powers it seemed as if the Soviet demand for reparations was insatiable.

(3) The final broad concern was the negotiation of a peace settlement. Although all four powers were pledged to the principle of German unity, the Soviet refused to consider any reunification formula that did not put Germany virtually at the mercy of Russia.[13]

Western Europe.

Soviet policy in Western Europe was executed primarily through its control over the indigenous communist parties there. Although capable of exerting considerable pressure in Scandinavia and the Low Countries, Russian policy concentrated on the key states of France and Italy. A concerted program of alternating pressure and persuasion was exerted on their tottering democratic governments. The object of this policy was to bring about either the collapse of democracy and its replacement by communist regimes or the modification of French and Italian foreign policy in the direction of a pro-Soviet orientation. Outside France and Italy, communist pressure was a complicating annoyance rather than an open threat, although conditions existed that made possible future communist moves.[14]

Eastern Europe.

Our discussion of satellitism has already outlined the general content of Soviet policy in eastern Europe. We need at this point only to stress the continuing Russian effort to weld its bloc into a monolithic entity. The Soviet attempted to force all the satellites to orient their policies entirely toward Moscow, to cut their relations with the West to the bare minimum, and to recast their economies, social structures, and governments on the Russian model. Under Soviet direction economic, political, and military agreements were made with them that validated Russian control.

THE MIDDLE EAST

The early phase of Soviet policy in the Middle East is explicable more with reference to Russian history and tradition than to either rational policy judgment or the imperatives of ideology. During this period Moscow was involved in three sectors of the Middle East, all of time-honored

---

[13] A convenient summary of the interallied negotiations over Germany is given in James P. Warburg, *Germany: Key to Peace* (Cambridge: Harvard University Press, 1953).

[14] See Mario Einaudi, Jean-Marie Domenach, and Aldo Garosci, *Communism in Western Europe* (Ithaca: Cornell University Press, 1951).

significance to pre-Leninist Russia. Two—the Balkans and Turkey—centered about the question of the Straits; the third—Iran—was a memento of nineteenth-century Russian imperialism.

The Greek Civil War.

At the Yalta conference Stalin had agreed that Greece fell into the British sphere of influence. When civil war broke out between the British-sponsored monarchist government and communist-led guerrillas, however, the Soviet could not restrain itself. Operating through the convenient device of its satellites that bordered on Greece—Albania, Bulgaria, and Yugoslavia—large amounts of aid were given to the rebels. Moscow's Greek policy was the first unmistakable demonstration to the West that the Soviet was willing to break its word. We will recall that it was this same Greek crisis that precipitated America into active opposition to the Soviet and touched off the cold war.

Turkey and the Straits.

Soviet pressure on Turkey had two objects. More important was Moscow's insistence on some revision of the Montreux Convention (1936) to give Russia a privileged position in the Bosporous and the Dardanelles. The Soviet also demanded frontier rectifications along its common frontier with Turkey, mainly in Armenia. The Turks, although their long period of neutrality during the war had prevented their establishing firm contacts with the West up to this time, resisted all Soviet advances and were ultimately rewarded with American aid in 1947.

Iran.

Soviet forces had moved into Northern Iran in 1941 to protect a major supply route for United States lend-lease materials that ran from the head of the Persian Gulf to Soviet Azerbaijan. At the end of the war, the Soviet presented the Iranian government with a series of demands that centered on oil concessions in northern Iran. The presence of Soviet forces served as an eloquent threat; not content, Moscow created a communist-led movement that demanded an "independent" state of Azerbaijan, to be carved out of Iranian territory. Iran made some token concessions but otherwise stood fast, and in early 1946 the first serious crisis of the postwar era seemed to be developing. Iran took a complaint to the United Nations and, although no formal enforcement action was decided upon, Moscow withdrew its troops in return for some (later repudiated) concessions.[15]

---

[15] See the account of this episode in George Lenczowski, *Russia and the West in Iran, 1918–1948* (Ithaca: Cornell University Press, 1949).

Early Soviet policy in the Far East, as in the Middle East, centered on problems and areas that had a long history in Russian policy: Manchuria, China proper, and Japan.[16]

The Rape of Manchuria.

The Soviet Union entered the war against Japan just a few days before V-J Day, but nevertheless moved rapidly to garner massive rewards for its brief military effort. Its major prize was the capture of the rich Chinese province of Manchuria that had been ripped away by Japan in 1931 and set up as the puppet kingdom of Manchukuo. Moscow rapidly stripped this territory of a great deal of its industrial equipment and liquid wealth. After seizing this great prize and occupying the key Manchurian ports of Port Arthur and Dairen, the Soviet loomed as the dominant land power in the Northern Far East.

The Chinese Civil War.

Once established in Manchuria, Moscow began to play a part in the rapidly developing Chinese civil war. In every way possible, short of actual participation in the fighting, Soviet policy gave aid and comfort to the forces of Mao Tse-tung. What made the Russian attitude so disruptive was that it was another indication of the Soviet's willingness to violate its own promises. In early 1945 a Sino-Soviet treaty of friendship had been concluded, by the terms of which Stalin had accepted the Chiang Kai-shek government as the legitimate ruler of all China. Only a few months later the Soviet was obviously supporting the opposite faction in a new struggle for total control over China.[17]

Revenge on Japan.

The Soviet took what revenge it could on Japan for the long record of humiliation that began in 1905. It presented Japan with a reparations bill that, if taken seriously, would have by itself destroyed the Japanese indus-

---

[16] On this region generally, see Max Beloff, *Soviet Policy in the Far East* (New York: Oxford University Press, 1953), and David Dallin, *The Rise of Russia in Asia* (New Haven: Yale University Press, 1949).

[17] Among the many recent studies of Sino-Soviet relations, three of the most reliable and useful are Henry Wei, *China and Soviet Russia* (New York: Van Nostrand, 1956); Robert C. North, *Moscow and Chinese Communists* (Stanford: Stanford University Press, 1953); and Howard L. Boorman, Alexander Eckstein, Philip E. Mosely, and Benjamin Schwartz, *Moscow-Peking Axis: Strengths and Strains* (New York: Harper & Bros., Inc., 1957).

trial potential. By the terms of the Yalta agreement Moscow had been promised the Kurile Islands and southern Sakhalin, and Stalin moved quickly to occupy these strategic territories. The final and, as events turned out, the most important of Moscow's anti-Japanese moves was the occupation of that part of Korea that lay north of the 38th parallel.

The net impact of the Soviet's series of moves in the Far East was to make Russian power dominant in the entire area except for Japan. Western governments, remote from the scene and unprepared for the speed of Russian exploitation of Japan's sudden collapse, were caught off guard; Moscow's central position in Far Eastern affairs was not fully realized until the communist victory in the Chinese civil war in 1949.

SOVIET FOREIGN-POLICY TECHNIQUES

What has made Soviet policy particularly baffling for western statesmen, and especially annoying to Americans, is the radically different technique developed by Stalin and his successors. The postwar USSR brought a unique methodology to the problem of advancing its national interest, and its opponents have found themselves confronted by a phenomenon with which they had no experience. A major but immeasurable proportion of Soviet success is due to the inability of American policy-makers to cope with the unexpected combination of techniques used by Moscow.

We may consider Soviet techniques under two heads. The first is the transformation of diplomacy at Russian hands; the second includes the non-negotiatory devices the Soviet has adopted to supplement its unusual concept of diplomacy.

THE TRANSFORMATION OF DIPLOMACY

As the Soviets have used diplomacy on a large scale as an affirmative instrument for the achievement of national objectives, they have made substantial modifications in it. In theory, in scope, and in method the historic idea of the diplomatic instrument now has been discarded and something much broader and more powerful substituted. Western negotiators have been first amazed, then frustrated, and finally angered by what the Russians do, but none deny the effectiveness of the new technique.[18]

---

[18] Philip E. Mosely, "Some Soviet Techniques of Negotiation," Chapter 10 in Raymond Dennett and Joseph E. Johnson, eds., *Negotiating with the Russians* (Boston: World Peace Foundation, 1951). The entire volume is very instructive on the manner in which the Soviet conduct diplomatic encounters.

The Diplomacy of Attack.

The classic conception of diplomacy viewed negotiation as a means of adjusting differences between states as a harmonizing and accommodating instrument, and as a substitute for armed conflict. According to this notion, a "successful" negotiation is one that culminates in the resolution of a dispute and that furnishes each party a proportionate share of the object in controversy. To this idea the Soviet gives no service.

The Russians conceive of diplomacy as a technique of attack. Whether or not agreement is reached is secondary to the really important consideration: whether or not the negotiation, in any strategic or tactical sense, improves the Soviet position. There is no virtue in agreement as an end in itself; accepting a settlement incorporating less than what the position promises is equivalent to total defeat. Thus in certain situations the Soviet interest is served by accepting a settlement, and in such cases Russian diplomats have proved easy to deal with. In other instances, however, Soviet policy demands that the question be kept unsettled, and diplomacy is thus turned to the unfamiliar task of keeping a dispute alive rather than of resolving it.[19]

This procedure was most effective before the West, particularly the United States, began to understand its rationale. During this early period, American negotiators were bent on ending the East-West controversy on almost any terms and were eager to dispose of issues by some form of honorable compromise. As soon as the United States perceived the real motivation behind Soviet dilatory tactics in bargaining, the diplomacy of attack began to lose its power. Obstinacy was met by obstinacy, and attack by counterattack.

Vituperation as a Technique.

The philosophy of attack implicit in Soviet diplomacy is emphasized and materially implemented by the astonishing tone in which relations are conducted. Soviet diplomats have raised vituperation to the level of an art— or perhaps it would be more accurate to call it a science—for it is done with deliberate purpose and for calculated effect. Negotiations with the Russians are often conducted amid a barrage of violent language, open threats, accusations of bad faith, and uninhibited mockery.[20] Western representatives have come to expect but never have become accustomed to having their most sincere and innocuous proposals greeted by a chorus of

---

[19] Ideological justification of this position was easy to discover; examples can be found in Leites, *Operational Code,* Chapters 15–20.

[20] The harsh and extreme language used by Khrushchev in May 1960 at the Paris summit was unusual only in its unexpectedness. The vocabulary was familiar; only the target (President Eisenhower) was different.

invective and abuse. In more ordinary days such tactics would have led to major crisis and possible war, but to the Soviet it is all in the day's work; this is the way diplomacy is to be conducted.

The unrestrained violence of Soviet language has at least two distinct purposes. In the first place, it might anger the opposition and provoke replies in kind. Soviet theory holds that this would give the Russian diplomats an advantage, since they themselves are perfectly cool-headed in their tirades while their opponents are likely to lose judgment in their rage.[21] Second, extreme language frequently serves a valuable propaganda purpose and also is an excellent delaying tactic. It was discovered early that Moscow's signal that it is ready to begin serious bargaining often takes the form of a significant relaxation in the tone of its language. When real understandings are to be reached, vituperation has no place.

This last point merits further comment. Diplomacy by insult is not diplomacy at all, but really a means of escaping its necessity. The chief target of intemperate language is usually not the diplomats on the other side of the table, but the vast outside audience. When the Soviets are ready to come down to cases and to reach decisions, they request private sessions free of publicity, where old-fashioned give-and-take is possible.

The Refusal to Compromise.

Soviet diplomacy has never contemplated reaching a solution by significant compromise. The classic technique of the alternation of proposal with counter-proposal, gradually narrowing the area of disagreement between the parties, is unthinkable to the Kremlin. Instead, Russians negotiate by stating a position upon which they absolutely insist, and monotonously repeating their proposals over and over in increasingly violent language until either the opposition gives in or negotiations are broken off.

Starting as they do from an assumption of absolute conflict of interest with all noncommunist states, there is no ideological justification for genuine compromise with the West. Settlements are reached by diplomatic means only when the Soviets have achieved complete victory or when the Kremlin is satisfied that all the possible advantage has been wrung from the situation. Under the latter circumstances accepting a settlement, even if only a temporary one, might often be expedient. A stalemated situation is often better left unresolved if there is any possibility of its eventual reopening. In such a case a completed negotiation might embarrass later Russian decisions by leaving them open to the accusation of bad faith— a technique they prefer to use on their opponents.

---

[21] The failure of the Soviets to provoke an angry American response to their "U-2" crisis undoubtedly helped persuade Moscow to tone down its accusations.

The Bombshell Technique.

Another device chosen more for its psychological effect than for its contribution to effective negotiations is the "bombshell." Soviet diplomats make most effective use of surprise. By suddenly introducing a new agenda item, by announcing a complete reversal of position, by repudiating an implicit (sometimes explicit) understanding, or by any of a dozen other methods, Russian negotiators create an atmosphere of consternation and mystery. Usually the Soviet is uninterested in seriously pursuing the new lines it opened up by the bombshell device; its purpose is served when it has had its effect on the other negotiators (and perhaps on public opinion abroad as well).[22]

The Manipulation of Procedure.

One final diplomatic technique, closely allied to the bombshell, remains to be mentioned. This is the Soviet skill at manipulating matters of procedure to Moscow's eventual substantive advantage. Questions that Americans are likely to dismiss as mere mechanics, such as seating arrangements, the order of presiding, and so on, are often seized on by the Russians as pretexts for long (and often angry) argument.

Western diplomats are often caught in a dilemma by this device. If they fight the issue out, tempers are exacerbated and valuable time lost that could more profitably be spent on the substantive items of the agenda. On the other hand, if they accept Soviet proposals on procedure, they find themselves in a double danger. Apparently innocent procedural details (such as the preparation of the agenda) often turn into formidable substantive questions in the hands of the Soviet; in addition the USSR vigorously exploits the minor prestige victories it wins on procedural matters by alleging them to be symptoms of western weakness.

Soviet Non-negotiating Techniques

Soviet diplomacy is closely articulated with a variety of direct methods of foreign policy. This is not in itself remarkable; all statesmen seek to mesh diplomatic pressures with economic, psychological, and military methods. But the Soviet contribution is distinctive in the new dimensions that have been added to the whole idea of direct action, converting it into another vehicle of attack to match its diplomacy.

---

[22] Secretary of State Byrnes had extensive experience with the bombshell. See his *Speaking Frankly,* especially Chapter 7: "London Again and Paris Twice." Mr. Khrushchev's outlandish behavior at the 1960 General Assembly of the United Nations was a frank employment of the bombshell.

Perhaps the most distinctively Soviet direct technique is that of subversion. Under the direction of the Kremlin, the systematic undermining of foreign governments has been elevated to the level of a standardized procedure of foreign policy. The worldwide apparatus of communist parties provides the vehicle for this device; its application is closely coordinated with other policy techniques, diplomatic and direct.

In this connection, by "subversion" we mean the deliberate attack on a government and the loyalty pattern of its people by a group of its own nationals acting on behalf of and under the direction of the Soviet Union. It is only rarely that the subversive method has been employed with the intention of going the whole way and bringing the government down in ruins; indeed, only in the Czech and Hungarian coups can clear instances be found of this extreme. Normally, subversion has more limited objectives.

Initially its purpose is to weaken the government against which it is aimed by the creation of internal cleavages, the intensification of domestic crisis, the diversion of official and public attention, or the creation of distrust between people and rulers. Such weakening as these tactics are able to produce is of some value for its own sake, but is sought primarily for its effect in reducing the ability of such a government to resist Soviet pressure applied through other—and often more orthodox—channels. This calls for careful control of the subversive elements lest they move too suddenly and too far.[23]

Propaganda.

Soviet propaganda is another non-negotiatory technique that Moscow employs in a new way. It is remarkable on three counts: its violence, its volume, and its flexibility.

The vituperative language of Soviet diplomacy pales into near-insignificance alongside the vocabulary of invective that forms the vehicle of Moscow's propaganda line. Epithets not normally used in civilized society, let alone in the more dignified circles of international intercourse, have become the stock in trade of Soviet propagandists. Both for domestic consumption and for export, Moscow's message is couched in highly inflammatory language, with the choicest insults being reserved for the opposition to whatever line the Soviet is pursuing at the moment.

The Soviet has expended great effort and considerable money in devising perhaps the most elaborate propaganda network the world has ever seen.

---

[23] Philip E. Mosely, "Soviet Exploitation of National Conflicts in Eastern Europe," and Stephen Kertesz, "Methods of Soviet Penetration in Eastern Europe," in Waldemar Gurian, ed., *The Soviet Union: Background, Ideology, Reality* (Notre Dame, Ind: University of Notre Dame Press, 1951).

The Soviet Threat ✦ *225*

Local communist parties are transmission belts, and party newspapers and other periodicals are filled with the orthodox Moscow doctrine; operating deficits of these publications are made up by the Soviet government. Every Soviet diplomatic mission is a disseminating and coordinating center for propaganda. Major efforts are made to enlist fellow travelers in all states who, although not identified formally with the party, will serve Moscow's purpose as apologists.

Finally, Soviet propaganda is remarkably flexible, considering the rigid ideology it is ostensibly expounding. Despite the Marxist imperatives, Russian appeals can reach widely different groups of people, of a great variety of social, cultural, and economic backgrounds. By shrewd manipulation of all forms of social maladjustment, communist propaganda has been able to move such dissimilar groups as French peasants, Italian factory workers, Chinese coolies, Indian intellectuals, and Guatamalan stevedores.[24]

The Fait Accompli.

Soviet policy also makes effective use of the *fait accompli*. This, the operational counterpart of the diplomatic bombshell, involves a sudden and usually dramatic move taken without warning. Its rationale stresses that such a step will present other states with a radically altered situation with the aftermath of which they can do nothing. The essence of the *fait accompli,* at least as used by the USSR, is to scrupulously confine its use to situations in which other states are embarrassed in taking retaliatory action. Sudden action that provokes a riposte more often than not produces an undesirable outcome, as the Soviet learned to its sorrow during the Hungarian and Suez affairs in 1956.

The Military in Soviet Policy.

The Soviet leadership has been quite effective in gearing military factors to its foreign policy. Initially, it was the Red Army that won eastern Europe for the Soviet and maintained its position there. As the cold war wore on, the Kremlin was able to challenge the United States to an arms race and to carry it off to a stalemate. Premier Khrushchev proved adept at what some commentators called "atomic blackmail": the indiscriminate use of military threats (also called "rocket-rattling") aimed at the weaker members of the western coalition. By 1959, the Soviet was able to open a "missile gap" over the United States, and in certain categories of weapons un-

---

24 See Ernest B. Haas and Allen S. Whiting, *Dynamics of International Relations* (New York: The McGraw-Hill Book Co., Inc., 1956), Chapter 9, "Propaganda and Subversion," for a discussion of these topics in behavioral-science terms, with some reference to the USSR. See also 'Ferreus,' "The Menace of Communist Psychological Warfare," *Orbis* (April 1957).

questionably enjoyed some margin of superiority. Soviet policy was not slow to exploit both the increments of prestige that came with military power and the improved bargaining position it provided in relations with the West.

Some of the questions we raised in Chapter 7 about the efficacy of military force in contemporary international relations seem to have occurred to the Soviet leadership, if we are to judge by the increased emphasis the Soviet has placed on "peace," "disarmament," and a "relaxation of tensions," since it achieved nuclear parity. Small states on the Soviet periphery are less immediately perturbed by the prospects of Soviet invasion than they once were, and the military impact of Soviet policy has been correspondingly decreased. The observer finds it difficult to escape the conclusion that too much is made in the West of the Soviet military menace, and too little of certain other more immediately effective techniques at the disposal of the masters of the Kremlin.

THE AMERICAN PERCEPTION OF THE THREAT

The United States was not caught completely off guard in 1945 by the rapidly developing Soviet menace, despite the many attempts to "prove" this point that have been made by both special pleaders and serious scholars. There was enough of a heritage of misunderstanding and tension left over from the war to make American policy-makers cautious and quizzical, if not openly suspicious, as they faced the Soviet after the surrender of Germany and Japan. It is well known, for example, that President Roosevelt's last state paper before his death was a message to Prime Minister Churchill expressing concern about Stalin's latest moves.

The difficulty faced by the United States, rather than being one brought on by naivete and self-deception, grew essentially out of a well-intentioned belief that Soviet obduracy, despite its frustrating quality, could eventually be dissolved by patience and the development of mutual understanding. It was not until some practical experience with the radical implications of Russian plans had been gained by President Truman and his aides that a consistent American policy could develop.

THE END OF "APPEASEMENT"

A number of politicians, journalists, and historians of an iconoclastic turn of mind have characterized American policy toward the USSR during 1945 and 1946 as one of "appeasement." This highly elastic term, of

The Soviet Threat ❖ 227

imprecise content but clear import, carries the implication that American policy-makers and negotiators during these critical two years were concerned only with "handing over central Europe and China to the communists." In point of fact, of course, these two years were for the United States a period of evolving purpose and growing understanding. The Soviet began with certain advantages; until American policy could develop effective countermeasures it was only to be expected that Moscow would continue largely to have its way.

The First Year: American Concessions.

There is ample ground for contending that the period from mid-1945 to mid-1946 was one in which the United States made substantial concessions and the USSR made off with most of the booty.[25] During this year the great powers were primarily engaged in attempting to work out a peace settlement, and negotiations, covering many subjects, went on almost continuously. On at least three major issues Moscow was able to win important victories.

First, the Soviet was permitted to develop a distinct occupation policy of its own in its areas of Germany and Austria. Not only were the Russians enabled to make over east Germany and to strip their area of Austria, but the operation of the veto on the Allied Control Authority made it possible for them to obstruct the creation of any coherent policy by the West. Second, and connected with the first, the United States made a long series of concessions on the troublesome issue of reparations, making large deliveries of both capital equipment and finished goods from the western zone of Germany. Finally, in the negotiations that led to the peace treaties with the Axis satellites in 1947, Moscow was able to make good its claim for sizeable indemnities from Italy and a variety of territorial concessions from the minor states.

Why did the United States acquiesce in all these—and many other—Soviet demands? We have already hinted at part of the reason. Probably the most important factor explaining American lack of resistance was a practical one: the United States had very little with which to resist. Neither military nor economic nor psychological power nor—be it admitted—a strong diplomacy was available to American policy-makers as they sought to stem the wave of Soviet aggrandizement.

Second, and almost as important, there was an element of almost philosophical detachment in the American view of the postwar settle-

---

[25] The most valuable sources for ascertaining the thinking of high-level American personnel during this period are their various memoirs, particularly James F. Byrnes, *Speaking Frankly,* and former President Harry S. Truman's two volumes, *Year of Decisions* and *Years of Trial and Hope* (Garden City: Doubleday, 1956).

ment. The aftermath of the war was thought of as a part of the war era, and not as an integral part of the postwar period. Peacemaking was attacked as the last phase of the war itself, to be disposed of as quickly as possible so as to free the American people for the important long-range tasks of the future. The American attitude therefore stressed making peace on almost any terms that would ensure Soviet cooperation in building the permanent world order. The preservation of a satisfactory working relationship with Moscow was conceived of as an objective that was worth a very high price.[26]

American Doubts.

The United States was willing to coexist with Soviet intransigence in peacemaking. The true cause of the final American break with the USSR was not the interminable squabble over the peace treaties, but the growing American realization that Soviet ambitions went far beyond merely appropriating whatever was available in the wake of a general war. It became clear that Moscow was not prepared to agree on any base for permanent cooperation with the West; instead of attempting to bring stability the Soviet was interested in perpetuating instability.

In Chapter 10 we shall analyze the motives for American policy in the cold war. We may anticipate, however, by stressing that the American decision to oppose the Soviet on a broad front was not due entirely, or even principally, to Moscow's provocative behavior during 1945 and 1946, nor was it prompted by any desire to deprive the Soviet of the fruits of its victory over the Nazis. The American rupture with the Soviet grew out of the American policy judgment that, in at least the foreseeable future, the USSR was going to persist in seeking to upset the existing distribution of rewards in international society. This was the doubt that ended the period of concessions.

THE BEGINNINGS OF A POLICY

"Get Tough with Russia."

When American mass opinion and the calculations of American officials agreed that a major modification was needed in the attitude of the United States toward Soviet dynamism, the first move was actually a negative one. The new American approach was summed up in the popular phrase "get tough with Russia." In every possible way the United States sought to

---

[26] A very articulate statement of this position was made by Sumner Welles in 1946. See his *Where Are We Heading?* (New York: Harper & Bros., Inc., 1946), pp. 369–383.

demonstrate new resistance to Soviet demands, a new willingness to brave and endure Foreign Minister Molotov's ire, a new determination to present positive counter proposals to match those emanating from Moscow. In the early stages, of course, there was little the United States could do except in a negative way; most American action amounted to being as unyielding and obstinate as the Soviets were themselves.

"Patience and Firmness."

But at its best "getting tough with Russia" was an almost spontaneous reaction without a solid policy base. As 1946 drew to a close, a new phrase replaced the earlier one: "patience and firmness" was the watchword of the more solidly conceived approach that the United States was developing.

The implications of the new tag were more than verbal. "Getting tough with Russia" was a last echo of the traditional American penchant for basing policy decisions on emotional attractions or repulsions. Its effectiveness was confined to the ultimately irrelevant demonstration that Americans were capable of being as "tough" as Russians and that they were no longer subject to being manipulated freely by the Soviet leadership. This point was worth making in itself, but its utility for the long-range purpose of the United States was sharply limited. Something of longer purview was necessary if American efforts were not to be dissipated in a futile effort to defeat the Soviet in a game of muscle-flexing.

"Patience and firmness" carried definite connotations that helped prepare the American public for the broad-gauge policy that was being devised. Patience was necessary because the developing contest with the Soviet was obviously destined to endure for a long time; it was not the sort of crisis that could be settled and forgotten within a few months or years. Americans needed to gird themselves for an indefinite, but certainly protracted, period of tension and recurrent crisis. Firmness also foreshadowed the design that was in the making. For a long time to come American-Soviet relations, at least as the United States viewed them, were to be based on a continuing assumption of mutual conflict and hostility. The United States was bent on carrying on foreign policy in a novel climate—novel at least for what purported to be a period of peace. Pressure was going to be applied upon the Soviet, and defenses were to be built to resist Soviet power. The American people were to learn during the next decade more of the implications of "patience and firmness" as the cold war developed and matured.

American policy, as it developed into a pattern of action, rested on a judgment about Soviet intentions, purposes, and motivations. We shall examine the analysis to which the United States subjected Soviet policy, together with the responses selected, in Chapter 10.

American
Capabilities

CHAPTER ◀ *9* ▶

In Chapter 1 we noted that the concept of state capability refers to the tools and techniques that a state has available to use in accomplishing its objectives and advancing its interests. Now that we have laid some of the groundwork for our consideration of American foreign policy and have examined both the operating concept of interest and the major external factors affecting American policy since 1945, the next step in our analysis is a somewhat more detailed study of the capabilities of the United States.

FORMULATING THE PROBLEM

The techniques of capability analysis, as we pointed out earlier, do not yield results of mathematical precision. We can discuss American capability intelligibly only after carefully recognizing the limits on what we are attempting and stating the assumptions upon which we are proceeding. We cannot manipulate the concept in a vacuum; on the other hand, an elaborate catalogue of "factors" would be of only minor usefulness to us. We shall attempt to formulate our problem in terms that will permit us enough leeway to reach helpful (if only tentative) conclusions and at the same time will prevent us from attempting overmuch.

THE LIMITS OF CAPABILITY ANALYSIS

Relativity, Dynamism, and Time.

At the outset we should restate the three most important qualitative factors in the notion of capability. (1) State capability is highly relative, as to other states, as to objectives, and as to time; no state is "capable" in a vacuum. (2) Capability is a dynamic condition whose contributory elements are always changing. A state's capability to accomplish an objective is always either rising or falling; it cannot remain static. (3) Finally, time has a major impact on capability. Comparative analyses may be made either on the basis of existing information (and by that token are always obsolete) or on the basis of the projection of trends, and thus must involve a large element of guesswork.

The Concrete Context.

One other limit on capability analysis seems to be even more fundamental. No study of a state's capability can be made without some reference to what it is that the state is capable of doing. In other words, a concrete context is a prerequisite to an intelligible capability study; the more detailed the context, the more valid the analysis.[1] It is also true that capability analysis is always undertaken with reference to a set of (implicit or explicit) assumptions regarding objectives and strategy, both of the state itself and of the other states involved. Comparative capabilities, therefore, are most usefully analyzed with regard to a particular problem situation.

This problem will be with us throughout this chapter. The context of our analysis must be total, and the objectives of the United States must be postulated in the broadest possible terms. We shall, therefore, remain at a high level of generalization; there will be all too obvious limits on the precision with which we can draw conclusions from the raw data we discover. Our later estimates of American capability in narrower situations will attempt to build upon the less specific conclusions we shall reach in this chapter.

---

[1] Harold Sprout, a pioneer in the development and refinement of the concept of state capability, emphasizes the contextual element in his treatment of the term, particularly with reference to the role of the estimator: "... capability analysis, by which the military, diplomatic, industrial, or other capacities [sic] of states are described, evaluated, and compared, consists mainly of estimating the opportunities and limitations which the estimator judges to be significant with reference to various hypothetical contingencies." Harold and Margaret Sprout, *Man-Milieu Relationship Hypotheses in the Context of International Politics* (Princeton: Center of International Studies, 1956), p. 47; reprinted by permission. The present author is indebted to Professor Sprout for much of the theoretical structure upon which the analysis in this chapter rests.

In this chapter we shall be assuming the analytical role of the "non-participating observer"; that is, we shall make our judgments independently of the strategic requirements of contemporary and continuing American policy. This will give us great breadth in analysis, but at the same time will deprive us of the special point of view of the official decision-maker. We suggested earlier some of the substantive assumptions of our approach; we may list them here serially:

1. American capability will be considered in relation to the over-all foreign-policy problem of the United States rather than to any particular issues within it.

2. The objectives of American policy to the attainment of which the capability of the United States is put are those stemming naturally from the concept of American national interest discussed in Chapter 6.

3. The situational context in which American capability will be analyzed is the broadest possible one: the world as it emerged from World War II and as it has evolved since that time.

4. The major operational problem of American policy calling the nation's capability into question has been the Soviet threat; the most frequent comparison with another state has been with the Soviet Union.

Operating under this set of assumptions, our study of the capabilities of the United States, although largely independent of specific issues, is nevertheless geared intimately to the course of American foreign policy since 1945. From a catalogue of sources of strength and evidences of weakness, we should be able to reach certain conclusions about the pattern of American policy and its possible future modifications.

TANGIBLE ELEMENTS IN AMERICAN CAPABILITY

We listed the tangible elements of state capability in Chapter 1; there we found they include geography, population and manpower, natural resources, industrial and agricultural production, and military organization and power-in-being. On each of these we may comment briefly as they appertain to the situation of the United States as it confronts its present and future problems.

GEOGRAPHIC FACTORS IN THE AMERICAN POSITION

We shall assume that the fundamentals of American geography are common knowledge and do not require reiteration. What we shall consider here are some of the specific ways in which American geography confers strength or weakness (actual or potential) on the United States.[2]

Geographic Advantages of the United States.

In the light of the conditions of world politics in the twentieth century, we may conclude that the United States has been fortunate in the geographic material with which it has been obliged to work. In terms of the more common criteria by which states are measured geographically, the United States ranks consistently high.

In area, the continental United States incorporates just over three million square miles, the fifth largest state in the world. Its topography, although varied, is nevertheless generally favorable, permitting (under modern conditions of transport) easy movement into and across its area. The climate is generally temperate, although great variations are found; with certain exceptions rainfall is adequate and in some areas abundant. The soil is generally fertile.

No strong neighbors menace American security. The eastern, the western, and a large part of the southern frontiers of the United States are formed by the open sea; its common boundaries with Canada and Mexico do not constitute security problems. The coastlines furnish many excellent ports; the United States has easy access to the high seas and to the rest of the world. In general we may say that, except for a few points noted below, the effect of geography is to make a near-maximum contribution to American capability.

Shortcomings of American Geography.

The major geographic handicaps of the United States are functions of distance. In the first place, for Americans both internal and external distances are usually great. The longest east-west dimension in the United States is 2,807 miles; from north to south it is 1,598 miles. Airline distances to points abroad are similarly great: New York-Paris is 3,630 miles; Seattle-Tokyo, 4,700; New York-Rio de Janiero, 4,840.

We should emphasize, however, that sheer distance is not automatically a shortcoming, but might well actually be a source of advantage. To the extent that American policy emphasizes defense, distance from hostile centers is still an advantage, even under conditions of modern aircraft and missiles. But if—as is the case—the major preoccupation of the United

---

[2] Among the more useful summaries of the American geographic position are Harold and Margaret Sprout, eds., *Foundations of National Power,* 2nd ed., Chapter VIII, "The American Realm in World Politics"; and W. Gordon East and A. E. Moodie, eds., *The Changing World* (Yonkers, N. Y.: World Book Co., 1956), Chapters X, XI.

States is to extend its influence outward from its own shores, the greater the distance to be traversed the greater the difficulties of doing so.[3] This should, however, be calculated against the corresponding difficulties faced by other states who may also be operating at great distances from their own bases. Internally, distance also has a complicating effect, stemming primarily from the pattern of population distribution. The clusters of people along east and west coasts are separated by the vast underpopulated area of the Great Plains, the Rockies, and the intermountain basin.

Internal distance becomes even more significant when another geographic handicap is considered: the concentration of population and industry in a relatively few areas. One of the often-alleged advantages of size to a state is the facility of dispersal. The fact remains, however, that important portions of American activity cluster within certain confined geographical areas, particularly in Southern California and in the so-called "Boston-Chicago-Washington" triangle. Such uneven human and economic spacing raises questions both of vulnerability to modern weapons and of the efficient distribution of goods through the entire area of the United States.

POPULATION AND MANPOWER

The human base of American capability is a population of approximately 180,000,000. The more sophisticated analysis of population figures requires us to consider additional factors to sheer numbers; these demographic ponderables throw more light on the present and future importance of American manpower.

Demographic Pattern of the American People.

There are approximately one and one-half million more females in the United States than there are males. In recent years the median age has risen to its highest point in history: 30.6 years. This rise in the median age occurred as the result of a great increase in the number of people over 65 years of age; late estimates put the total as over 15 millions. These were balanced, however, by the nearly 40 millions under 18 years of age. The bulk of the American people clustered between 18 and 65, the age bracket of maximum effectiveness. The total manpower pool (male and female) for military and industrial service was nearly 90 millions.

Population density varies widely in the United States. In 1960 the national average was 50.4 persons per square mile; the state that most closely

---

[3] This idea is developed by Kenneth Boulding, in "Economic Issues in International Conflict," *Kyklos*, VI (1952), 97ff.

approximated this figure was Iowa (48.8), followed by Mississippi (45.8). In contrast to these averages, however, were such concentrations as were found in New Jersey (800.2), Rhode Island (798.7), and Massachusetts (650.1), as well as such underpopulated states as Alaska (0.4), Nevada (2.6), and Wyoming (3.4).

Two additional distributional factors are of some significance. In 1959, over 64 per cent of the American people lived in urban areas. The northeast, with 79.5 per cent, was the most urbanized region; the west and north-central regions ranked next with urban percentages of 69.8 and 64.1 respectively; the south trailed with only 48.6 per cent of its people urbanized. The other important datum is that of racial distribution. In 1950 there were 134.9 million white persons in the United States and 17.4 million non-whites; of the latter, just over 15 million were Negroes.

Population Trends.

The basic population trend in the United States is one of numerical growth, at a higher rate than was the case earlier in the century. Vital statistics bear out this conclusion. The birth rate has stabilized at something over 24 per thousand per year; the death rate has steadily declined to its present rate of slightly over 9.6 per thousand. As long as these trends continue, the American population will grow steadily at a slowly increasing rate. One result of the decline in the death rate is the slow rise in the median age, now for the first time over 30 years.

Demographic Conclusions.

From the point of view of sheer statistics, the American manpower situation is absolutely favorable except in comparison with China, India, and the Soviet Union. Americans constitute a numerous people whose steady increase to the neighborhood of 200 millions is—barring unexpected catastrophe—probable.[4] There is no reason for us to assume that any likely American policy would fail because of a shortage of raw manpower.

In addition, the United States has certain intangible manpower advantages that do not show up in a mere population tally. We shall consider them at greater length in a later section of this chapter, but we may say at this point that they rise generally from the demographic "quality" of the American people. The high levels of literacy, tool skill, technological

---

4 Some demographers of repute, however, are not convinced that the birth-death rate patterns of the last fifteen or twenty years are anything more than a statistical aberration. They do not share the opinion expressed in this paragraph, and we should note that such a dissent exists. For a strong statement in support of the stated position, however, see Harrison Brown, "The Prospective Environment for Policymaking and Administration." *The Formulation and Administration of United States Foreign Policy,* (Brookings Institution), pp. 140–143.

orientation, formal education, and cultural homogeneity require that the verdict of pure numbers be revised upward. In productive efficiency, in aptitude for modern warfare, and in other categories of manpower utilization, 50 million Americans (for example) have more impact than do two or three hundred million other people without this relative head start. Except for certain situations involving sheer weight of numbers (such as a large-scale ground war), the manpower of the United States is thought to be adequate for any probable purpose.

NATURAL RESOURCES

The American Resource Endowment.

The United States is among the more fortunate states of the world in its natural resource endowment. Many of the materials most critical to the capacity to execute foreign policy are present within the United States or immediately available outside its borders. Crucial shortages exist, and are increasing in number; other reserves are nearing depletion. The general picture is not so serious, however, as to require deep anxiety. Most of the resource problems that exist promise to be soluble by the normal devices of foreign policy and do not present major dilemmas.[5]

The most basic category of materials includes coal and iron—the foundation of modern industry. American known coal reserves are conservatively estimated to be adequate—at present rates of consumption—for a thousand years. Domestic iron ore reserves of high quality are dropping rapidly—production from Minnesota's Mesabi Range fell 65 per cent between 1953 and 1954—but recent discoveries of rich deposits in Labrador and Venezuela open the prospect of ample supplies for certainly the next forty or fifty years, and perhaps for a century.

Energy sources—in addition to coal—are also substantial. The United States leads the world in the production of hydroelectric power and has vast untapped resources for further exploitation. Exact American petroleum reserves cannot be formulated because the rate at which new reserves are "proved" exceeds that of actual production by approximately one billion barrels a year; proved reserves in 1956 surpassed 30 billion barrels. Other rich petroleum pools exist in Venezuela and Canada, while American industry has made extensive investments in the incredibly rich oil fields of the Middle East.

The United States is in a less favorable position with regard to other

---

[5] Extensive data on resources may be found in the Report of the President's Materials Policy Commission, *Resources for Freedom* (Washington, D. C.: U. S. Government Printing Office, 1952. See also Percy W. Bidwell, *Raw Materials: A Study of American Policy* (New York: Harper & Bros., 1958).

industrial raw materials. The common ferroalloy metals—manganese, chromium, nickel, vanadium, cobalt, and so on—must be largely imported and stockpiled. So must large percentages of the critical nonferrous metals, including tungsten, copper, tin, and lead. Food, fiber, and timber resources, on the other hand, are generally adequate, although certain commodities within this class—such as coffee, hemp, and wool—must be procured abroad.

The Dependence on Foreign Supplies.

Thus we can see that the United States, for all its enviable position with reference to the basic raw materials, is nevertheless dependent on foreign sources for what are yet small—though critical—amounts of those resources vital to the maximum realization of its potential. What does this mean for American policy?

Nature distributed the important resources very unequally throughout the world. Whereas the early industrial centers grew up where coal and iron appeared in reasonably close proximity, today the major deposits of the newly important minerals are frequently in Africa, Central and South America, and Asia. American policy has concerned itself with the problem of guaranteeing adequate supplies of these items.

However much the United States might wish to preserve its freedom of maneuver in a region—Central Africa, for example—steps to gain access to such critical raw materials as there may be there must take precedence. The protection of sources of supply is a fixed dimension of American policy, and it is fortunate that at the present time enough of each material needed can be found within the portions of the world outside the Soviet sphere to which the United States can gain access. Any increase in the territory controlled by Moscow might have serious repercussions for America's resource position.

Industrial and Agricultural Production

Of the tangible elements of capability, the one most directly pertinent to the contemporary role of the United States is that of industrial and agricultural production. The three we have so far discussed are relatively fixed; there is little a state can do about its geography, its population, or its resource endowment—at least in the short run. But what a people does on its own land to transform raw materials (which are, after all, only a potential source of power) depends to a great extent upon human will. Industrial and agricultural production is an index of the results derived from purposive activity by individuals and by government.

The Measure of American Industrial Strength.

Industrial production is at the same time the predominant economic activity in the United States and the major contributor to American power in international affairs.[6] Americans are generally sensitive to the major role played in their own lives by industry, and many have some appreciation of its place in foreign policy, but the exact configuration of American industrial strength is difficult to visualize.

The United States includes less than 6 per cent of the land area of the world and slightly more than 8 per cent of its people, yet since 1945 the United States has consistently outproduced all the other states of the world combined, at least as far as strategic commodities are concerned. Americans produce three-fifths of the world's telephones, four-fifths of the automobiles, 70 per cent of the crude petroleum, three-fifths of the pig iron, and over half the cotton and lumber. The American industrial machine has a nice balance between capital and consumer production; war and postwar experience have indicated that it is technically a relatively simple matter to shift emphasis from one to the other. The flexibility and versatility of American industry is an important element in national strength.[7]

Few economists today would venture to predict a production ceiling for American industry. During World War II industrial production expanded to two and a half times its 1935–39 level in the face of the loss of a substantial portion of the labor force to the armed forces.[8] Since 1950 industry has proved capable of handling $30–40 billion annually of government orders for military goods while at the same time increasing its output of consumer items. The expansion of industry in peacetime is aided by extensive applied research conducted both by industry itself and by private and government agencies.

Not the least significant aspect of American industrial strength is the fantastically elaborate network of transportation and communication facilities that tie the United States together and connect it intimately with the rest of the world. The steady expansion of air transportation facilities and, beginning in 1956, the development of an entirely new Federal superhigh-

---

[6] For analyses centered around this point, see John K. Galbraith, *The Affluent Society* (Boston: Houghton Mifflin Co., 1958), and Massimo Salvadori, *The Economics of Freedom* (Garden City: Doubleday & Co., 1959).

[7] Klaus Knorr, in *The War Potential of Nations* (Princeton: Princeton University Press, 1956), qualifies this judgment sharply but concludes that it retains a good deal of its validity, even under conditions of nuclear weapons.

[8] See Geoffrey H. Moore, *Production of Industrial Materials in World Wars I and II* (New York: National Bureau of Economic Research, 1944).

way system have gone far to improve an already efficient transportation pattern; communications networks have likewise been extended.

Weaknesses and Vulnerabilities.

The over-all picture of American industry is one that makes it a central element in American strength. This optimistic generalization must be tempered by the recognition of certain shortcomings that may be classified as inherent weaknesses or as vulnerabilities to external pressures.

By "weaknesses" we mean only those built-in difficulties that bear on industry's contribution to American capability; no judgment is intended here on the social, economic, political, or psychic values that may attach to any of the conditions we shall mention.

In these terms we may briefly stipulate five such weaknesses in the American industrial machine. (1) Being a private enterprise system posited on competition, maximum efficiency through unified and coordinated effort is often difficult to achieve. (2) The industrial plant is so closely knit that maladjustment in one small segment may be rapidly transmitted to all parts of the economy. (3) There is a growing shortage of certain categories of key personnel, particularly middle- and high-level executives. (4) Long-range prospects are clouded by a relative overemphasis on applied research at the expense of more fundamental—although less obviously profitable—basic research. Dramatic demonstration of the inadequacy of American basic research was afforded by the entire nation's embarrassment at Moscow's technological leap forward after the launching of "Sputnik" in the autumn of 1957. (5) Certain key sectors of the economy, such as the machine-tool industry, are inadequately developed; strains and delays follow any unusual demand on these sensitive areas.

The vulnerabilities of the American industrial plant are somewhat better known; we shall list what are perhaps the three most significant. (1) The heavy concentration in the northeastern quarter of the nation and along the New York-Chicago axis; this has been only partly alleviated by planned and unplanned dispersal.[9] (2) The critical role played by labor relations; the growing sense of responsibility of organized labor has not yet obviated the danger inherent in work stoppages of various sorts. (3) The dependence of so much of American industry on stockpiles of key raw materials that must be imported. Any interruption in the flow of ferroalloys, other critical metals or certain chemicals would disrupt great areas of American industrial production.[10]

---

[9] "Planned dispersal" is a problem complicated by the reluctance of interests adversely affected to cooperate. An apt example is provided by real estate and labor groups in such areas as New England.

[10] See Jules Backman, *War and Defense Economics* (New York: Rinehart &

Agricultural production in the United States is remarkable for the enormous output derived from the efforts of only a small portion of the national labor force. In 1954 there were less than eight and a half million persons employed on the nation's 5.4 million farms; of the 1.1 billion acres in farms, only 337 million acres were planted to crops. The remainder was largely pasture or grazing land, with a smaller portion in timber. Farm income in 1954 was just under 30 billion dollars. The total number of American farms has been slowly decreasing since 1920, while the mean acreage has shown a corresponding slow increase. Farm tenancy is also on a slight rise.

From American farms pours a steadily increasing flow of agricultural products that far surpasses American capacity to consume, making possible both the export of farm goods and the accumulation of embarrassingly large surpluses. The United States leads the world, usually by a large margin, in the production of corn, raw cotton, wheat, and oats. The beef cattle, dairy cattle, and hog population of the United States is the largest in the world; America leads in the production of meat, milk, and dairy products.[11] The only agricultural products that Americans cannot grow themselves are those requiring tropical or other special weather conditions. The United States is unquestionably the leading agricultural nation in the world today.

The only food products imported into the United States in significant quantities are coffee, sugar, and cocoa; imported fibers include sisal and wool. Although there is considerable importation of other goods, such supplies are either unessential luxuries or are in direct competition with domestic sources. The enviable agricultural situation of the United States not only gives it the capacity to resist pressure on its food supplies to which other states might be vulnerable, but also—in an era of widespread food shortage—gives it a weapon of great versatility and sometimes controlling effect. The availability of food has several times been of real value to American policy-makers.

Company, Inc., 1952); George A. Lincoln and associates, *The Economics of National Security* (New York: The Macmillan Co., 1954); Seymour E. Harris, *The Economics of Mobilization and Inflation* (New York: W. W. Norton and Co., Inc., 1951); Albert G. Hart, *Defense Without Inflation* (New York: Twentieth Century Fund, 1951). All these works deal with the impact of defense, war, mobilization, and foreign policy on the American industrial plant. See also Knorr, *War Potential of Nations.*

[11] It was notable that Soviet leaders boasted frequently after 1957 that Russia would catch up with the United States in meat and milk production in the "near future." Apparently this was part of the new emphasis on the production and distribution in consumer goods in the USSR. Premier Khrushchev made major changes in the administration of Soviet agriculture after this date.

Military power is at the same time the most obvious element in a state's capability and the most difficult to assess accurately except in the most short-run of situations. Power-in-being is never more than a (possibly large) fraction of a state's potential; the men and materials available to a state in any context are susceptible of being employed according to different strategic and tactical theories. The mission to which armed force is put influences the techniques of its employment; the new technology of warfare has increased the relative importance of power-in-being. The most that we can do is to sketch the outlines of the problem and to suggest one or two of the operational decisions that must be made before serious calculation of American military capability can be undertaken.

American Military Power.

Unless the United States should be put to the ultimate test of survival, it is impossible to set a maximum figure for American military power. In mid-1945, during the mobilization peak of World War II, there were 12,-300,000 Americans in the armed forces; during 1945 the armed forces spent 78.7 billion dollars. At the same time, there yet remained a surplus—both of manpower and of resources—that had been untapped during the war.

The military establishment maintained by the United States in a combat-ready condition during the cold-war era represented the best guess of what was necessary, and varied with the rise and fall of the level of international tension. There was always some time lag, however, caused by the time necessary (usually about two years) before appropriations could be translated into troops, ships, and missiles. In 1958, for example, military manpower totalled some 2,600,000; the Army and Air Force each had roughly 900,000, and the Navy and Marines divided the remainder on a 3–1 basis. While manpower totals were tending downward, budgets were edging upward, although a plateau seemed to be reached between 1958 and 1960 at around 40 billion dollars.

The radical advances in missiles and rockets that accompanied the space race after 1957, plus the Soviet policy of cutting its military man-power and emphasizing weapons of strategic deterrence, brought on a continuing debate in the United States about both force levels and budgets. In an era when evaluating the real contribution of men and weapons to national security was the most difficult in history, the dispute (which we shall examine in Chapter 13) was inevitably inconclusive (or perhaps we should say interminable). Neither the "budgeteers" nor the "security" group had enough concrete data to give their arguments the strength needed to win a consensus.

The Importance of Strategic and Tactical Theory.

The present military posture of the United States emphasizes the so-called "new look" dating from 1953 and 1954.[12] Under this concept the major American effort is to be made in strategic air power with a concentration on nuclear weapons; the military mission of the Air Force is both that of a deterrent and of a decision-forcing instrument in the event of actual combat. The Army and the Navy have roles in support of the Air Force in case of all-out war; in a limited war context they are expected to hold their own with the corresponding forces of any possible enemy.

Although the tactical doctrine of the armed services has been worked out in great detail in terms peculiar to each branch, we may nevertheless suggest some principles common to all three. We might call these the "American tactical theory." Stripped to their essentials, they can be stated as follows: (1) American armed forces stress mobility, speed, and flexibility in performing their missions. (2) Aggressiveness is emphasized as being most parsimonious of both manpower and material. (3) Machine power—in the broadest sense—is both more efficient and more expendable than manpower; in tactical situations emphasis is placed on weapons and machines rather than on the commitment of large bodies of men. (4) The tactical goal of all branches is firepower, whether from the ground, from the sea, or from the air; the object of maneuver is to subject the enemy to overwhelming fire.

How Much Mobilization?

One of the ubiquitous problems facing any responsible statesman, and one that endlessly complicates judgments on absolute or relative state capability, is the sliding relationship between actual military power-in-being and theoretical potential. For the United States it has proved difficult in the postwar era to decide on a mobilization level that satisfies all the categories of requirements.

American military theory, relying on citizen-armies and heavy indus-

---

12 See W. W. Kaufmann, ed., *Military Policy and National Security* (Princeton: Princeton University Press, 1956); for a semi-official "retreat" from this position, see John Foster Dulles, "Challenge and Response in United States Policy," *Foreign Affairs* (October, 1957). Of later vintage, see the newest in the attacks on the "new look" by a retired Army General, Maxwell D. Taylor, *The Uncertain Trumpet* (New York: Harper & Bros., 1960). Previous expositions of the Army positions had been written by Generals Ridgeway and Gavin. A convenient summary of the anti-"New look" arguments is also found in Bernard Brodie, *Strategy in the Missile Age* (Princeton: Princeton University Press, 1958). Turner and Challener, in *National Security in the Nuclear Age,* make much the same points.

trial production as the preferred ways of winning wars, has always insisted that the peacetime military establishment has only one real mission: to buy time against the enemy until war-level mobilization is attained. This system served the United States well throughout the nineteenth century and brought victory in World Wars I and II. The technology of modern war, however, has reduced the value of mobilization and production planned to occur after the outbreak of hostilities. The advantages of surprise are so great that a three-week war (or, for that matter, a three-hour war) is a real possibility. Thus it follows that the United States might well have to fight and win a total war with only the personnel and equipment it had available at the moment the first bomb fell.[13]

But to remain constantly prepared to retaliate overwhelmingly to any possible attack is beyond American capacity—or that of any people. Americans, for reasons at the same time economic, political, ideological, and psychic, refuse to live forever on a total-war footing. Some bearable compromise between all-out readiness and underpreparedness has had to be devised. Any solution must take account of the changing nature of the threat confronting the United States, of its relative imminence, of the tolerance of Americans toward taxation and conscription, and of the general climate of world politics.[14] The result has been that since 1945 a persistent struggle, no less fierce because confined within a reasonably narrow range of alternatives, has raged over the amount and the kinds of the American mobilization potential that should be kept in readiness.[15]

The solution accepted to date, as we have briefly considered it above, is only the latest in what has become a long series. Newer ones may take their turn as part of the process of attempting to adjust American military power-in-being to the requirements of American policy.

INTANGIBLE ELEMENTS OF CAPABILITY

We now turn to the intangible factors that affect the way in which the tangibles are employed and often set outer limits to their usefulness.

---

[13] On this point, see Knorr, *War Potential of Nations,* and Rockefeller Brothers Fund, *International Security, the Military Aspect* (Garden City: Doubleday & Co., 1958).

[14] In his report to the people following the failure of the 1960 summit. President Eisenhower, in listing his policies at a moment of tension, called for a military establishment neither "... neglected in complacency nor overbuilt in hysteria," *New York Times* (May 26, 1960).

[15] See, as major contributions to this debate, Henry A. Kissinger, *Nuclear Weapons and Foreign Policy* (New York: Harper & Bros., Inc., 1957); see also Robert E. Osgood, *Limited War: Challenge to American Strategy* (Chicago: University of Chicago Press, 1957).

We must first, however, make one final remark about the catalogue in the preceding section: even the most concrete element of capability has intangible implications that modify its significance in practice. Geography, population, and resources seem to be fixed entities that can be manipulated objectively, yet each of them gains its final relevance and value only in terms of human assumptions about them. Production and military power are even more obviously functions of human perception and will, and no automatic answers about state capability can be derived from any generalizations about these two. Even the tangible elements of capability, therefore, have indefinite dimensions of choice; at the level of all-out effort, this is often thought of as the "will to fight." [16]

This is even more the case, of course, when we take up the group of considerations that we are calling the intangibles. Here there are by definition very few concrete data on which to found generalizations; here each element is measured on a sliding scale and any conclusion we reach is subject to immediate revision. The most that we can attempt in this section is to raise the kind of questions that offer some relevance to our general inquiry, and to suggest certain broad conclusions that arise from measuring the United States with our set of yardsticks.

POLITICAL, ECONOMIC, AND SOCIAL STRUCTURE

This broad heading refers to the way in which the American people are organized for the accomplishment of political, economic, and social purposes. Each area deserves extended treatment, but our consideration of the American social order will be confined only to the most direct implications of the political, economic, and social system of the United States for the accomplishment of American foreign policy.

The Nature of American Society.

The American political, economic, and social system remains, despite the massive strains to which it has been subjected during the past half century, one of the most impressive monuments to human freedom the world has ever known. Founded and operated on the principle of encouraging the maximum of meaningful individual choice commensurate with the accomplishment of common goals, the United States has preserved its essential doctrine in the face of pressures both internal and external.[17]

---

[16] See Knorr, *War Potential of Nations*, Part II: "The Will to Fight."
[17] Many scholarly and statistical analyses of American society provide extensive raw data for this generalization. Very suggestive, however, are three recent books by non-social scientists that are remarkable for their insights: Louis Kronenburger, *Company Manners* (Indianapolis: The Bobbs-Merrill Co., 1954), Jacques Barzun,

Politically, the United States is organized into a federal democracy that institutionalizes private rights, limits government, and determines policy by the mass will. Economically, the partially free enterprise system retains its vigor although subject to extensive and increasing public control. The American social system is one of the least stratified in the world, permitting broad mobility both upward and downward as well as laterally.

The energizing principle of freedom in the major areas of life, however, has become subject to broad limitations largely stemming from the rising concept of bigness. Big government menaces much of the democratic myth as people stand outside the political process rather than participate in it; the major function of the mass is often conceived as that of serving as audience for the deliberations of the ruling elite. Big business and big labor together control much of economic life and their struggles work great inconvenience and frequent hardship on the unorganized public.[18] Socially, the cult of conformity and the rise of "middle-class America" have given much of American life undertones of drabness, uniformity, and rigidity that do violence to the dream of a free society.[19] These trends, rather than proving the total collapse of the American system, are instead a measure of the extent to which American professions fall short of actuality. Their influence on the vigor of the foreign-policy effort of the United States is not yet great, although some observers are confident that it will increase.

Strains in the Body Politic.

In addition to the generalized threat of bigness in American life, there are specific maladjustments within the political, the economic, and the social sphere that create internal stresses. Each of them has direct influence on the broad questions of foreign policy and on the way in which it is executed.

In government, two issues defy final solution today and both are engaging the attention both of scholars and of practitioners. The first is the problem of discovering the working basis of federalism in the twentieth century. There are extremists on both sides; the states rights advocates who insist on the denigration of national authority and the transfer of broad grants of power to state and local governments, and the supernation-

---

God's Country and Mine (New York: Harper & Bros., Inc., 1954), and Joseph Wood Krutch, Human Nature and the Human Condition (New York: Random House, 1959).

[18] This theme is elaborately developed in John K. Galbraith, American Capitalism: the Concept of Countervailing Power (Boston: Houghton-Mifflin Co., 1952).

[19] David Riesman, Nathan Glazer, and Reuel Denney, The Lonely Crowd (New Haven: Yale University Press, 1950); William A. Whyte, The Organization Man (New York: Simon and Schuster, 1956); and Thomas Griffith, The Waist-High Culture (New York: Harper & Bros., 1959).

alists who argue for increased federal power and the abasement of the states to the status of administrative districts. Somewhere between these two positions a more satisfactory balance must ultimately be found.[20] The second problem concerns the accurate determination of the majority will. When apathy limits voting in presidential elections of 60 per cent of the eligibles, and if "engineers of consent" can mobilize public opinion on call by the use of techniques of advertising and mass communication, there is obviously something out of tune in American democratic processes.

In economic life, problems abound. Perhaps the two most important are the trend toward larger and larger units of production, symbolized by the rash of corporate mergers that broke out during the 1950's. How to continue to enjoy the advantages of large-scale production while avoiding monopolistic trends is a many-sided problem. The other issue, as much social as economic, has to do with the future of agriculture. The family farm, as a way of life as well as an economic unit, seems to be heading toward extinction. The consequences of any such outcome would be of deeper signficance than to the limited number of persons directly involved.

In social relations, the two leading issues (or at any rate, two leading issues from among several) are the troublesome questions of inter-racial adjustment and the changing nature of the family in American society. Both racial conflict and family disorganization have results that extend into many other areas of social life, and both have a stubbornness that defies simple solutions. Some observers fear that either or both of them threaten to work basic changes in America that would radically alter the fundamentals of the entire American system. Whether or not their eventual importance will be this great, there is no doubt of their constantly eroding effect and the need for their resolution.[21]

Is Major Change Necessary?

We frequently hear arguments to the effect that American society, American government, and the American economy are unsuited to the problems of foreign policy, and that great change in the American social order will be necessary before the United States can cope successfully with the world. It is often said, for example, that the American government should remake itself on the British model, that public opinion should

---

[20] See Arthur Macmahon, ed., *Federalism: Mature and Emergent* (New York: Columbia University Press, 1955), and K. C. Wheare, *Federal Government* (New York: Oxford University Press, 1947).

[21] On race relations, see Gunnar Myrdal, *An American Dilemma* (New York: Harper & Bros., Inc., 1944); on family problems, see Earnest Burgess and Harvey Locke, *The Family: from Institution to Companionship* (New York: American Book Co., 1953) and Ruth S. Cavan, *The American Family* (New York: Crowell, 1953).

leave foreign-policy decision-making to experts, that the economy should be overhauled in the direction of government planning and control, and that egalitarian social doctrine has no place in the essentially aristocratic business of international affairs.

Even if these propositions have some theoretical validity, they have only slight practical relevance. For better or worse, the United States will be obliged to live with the social order it has inherited from the past; rapid and thorough remodeling is simply out of the question. The most that planning and direction can do is to exert a moderate directing influence on the course of evolution, and to shape—within limits—the America of the future. Radical reconstruction of American society, to be accomplished within a relatively short time span, is beyond the capacity of anyone.

EDUCATIONAL AND TECHNICAL LEVEL

Modern political power is inseparably wedded to modern technology, and the capacity of a state to exert pressure to accomplish its objectives depends in large measure on the extent to which its people have mastered contemporary techniques. An examination of the educational level and technical competence of Americans throws some light on American capability in this respect.

American Education and "Know-how."

The American people are the beneficiaries of the most elaborate program of mass education in the world. Free public education is available to everyone through high school, and low-cost higher education at public expense is almost universal. Just what results has the United States had from its extensive educational effort?

By 1958 more than 97 per cent of the population over 14 years of age was at least minimally literate. The school population, fed by the increased birthrates since 1945, passed 42 million in 1958 and showed no signs of ceasing its growth. In 1950 the median level of educational accomplishment was 9.3 years of schooling; by 1960 it had risen to 10.8 years and projections called for stabilization at around 12 years by 1970. In 1958, nearly 366,000 bachelor's degrees were granted by American colleges and universities, 65,000 received some form of master's degree, and 8,942 doctorates were awarded. On the score of formal education, Americans seem to be making extensive use of the opportunities open to them.

We should also recognize a factor more difficult to measure. Americans live in a technological culture and they have shown remarkable aptitudes for coping with it. The facility with which Americans use the tools and techniques of technology—what is often called "know-how"—has become a byword in much of the world. Americans think of themselves as well-educated, and to a considerable extent the assumption is justified—at least on the scores of literacy and tool skill.

Potential Shortages: Engineers and Scientists.

The American educational and scientific picture is not so attractive, however, when certain categories of highly trained specialists are studied. In 1958, 35,332 engineers were graduated from American colleges, while 5,788 master's degrees and 647 doctorates were awarded in engineering. These totals fell far short of actual and anticipated needs for these specialists; the estimates of what could profitably be absorbed per year ranged from 40 to 60 thousand engineers per year, and 15 to 20 thousand scientists, including three times as many Ph.D.'s and Sc.D.'s as are now being produced.

These current shortages promise to become even more acute in the future as trends in higher education reveal a growing disinclination among students to submit to the rigorous discipline necessary for scientific education. Some commentators laid the blame for this condition on teaching that emphasizes "adjustment to life" as a "democratic" base for education and dismisses intellectual training as "sterile" and "aristocratic." Democratic education, according to this thesis, stresses conformity and mediocrity; both the poor students and the brilliant ones are classified as "problems," while the "average" student becomes the "normal" one.

A whole new argument over education was touched off in the wake of the nation's sudden embarrassment over the revelation of Soviet scientific and technical prowess between 1957 and 1960. From the first "Sputnik" in 1957 to the successful Soviet moon shot in 1959, the space race revealed for the world to see that the vaunted American educational system was not producing the scientists, technicians, and "know-how" specialists the United States needed to claim the first rank Americans had confidently assumed was automatically theirs. Charges and rebuttals flew for several years over where the fault lay, but without any clear result. Out of the discussion, however, came a few concrete results. The national government began a limited program of assistance to students of science; educational systems all over the nation established programs designed to challenge the gifted student; and the assumptions of several generations of educational philosophy were re-examined. There was no real interest, in spite of the emotional reaction of some spokesmen, in a sudden importation of Soviet educational techniques; dictatorial education, in spite of its apparent success, was not thought to be suitable for a free society.

There is a more general and pervasive problem in American education. In 1954 the National Manpower Council's report revealed a chronic shortage of trained "brainpower." [22] Although the elementary schools are crowded and college enrollments are booming, there is an inadequate supply of thoroughly trained personnel in almost every area of scholarship, pure and applied.

As American foreign policy involves more and more areas of American life, the need for genuine experts becomes more pressing. Economic pressures, the declining standards in public secondary education, the urge to conform and to avoid distinction (what David Riesman calls "other-directedness"), and a hyperconcentration on economic security have been suggested as explanations for the lack of interest among Americans for thorough intellectual training. Whatever the explanation, it is obvious that the inadequacy in the supply of educated men and women represents a substantial limitation on the capacity of the United States to accomplish the goals of its foreign policy.

NATIONAL MORALE

Morale is defined by Webster as "condition as affected by, or dependent on, such moral or mental factors as zeal, spirit, hope, confidence, etc." The importance of such a concept to any consideration of state capability can scarcely be overestimated. From the point of view of the operating statesman, morale is a measure of the extent to which his people are united behind their government and its mission and of the extent to which they will actively cooperate in accomplishing the ends of national policy.

American Morale: Characteristics and Problems.

There is a constant "morale problem" in the United States, and policy-makers must be always alert to its requirements.

The state of American morale at any given time is materially affected by three factors. (1) There is a tendency for wide, relatively sudden, and frequently rapid shifts in the prevailing mood of the public. (2) American morale is notoriously sensitive to short-run or temporary influ-

---

[22] National Manpower Council, *A Policy for Skilled Manpower* (New York: Columbia University Press, 1954). It is noteworthy that the number of doctorates earned during the latter part of the 1950's did not increase in the same ratio as did the other degree totals. In 1954, 8,896 doctorates were awarded; in 1955, 8,840. In 1958, there were 8,942—only a tiny increase. In the physical sciences, the number of doctorates actually decreased from 1,661 in 1955 to 1,589 in 1958.

ences, such as a sudden crisis or unexpected good news. (3) It is easier to maintain high morale on negative issues than on positive ones; that is, Americans traditionally are more at home when they are opposing some state than when they are pursuing an objective of their own.

Government morale policy, dealing with a public opinion and mass attitudes that are subject to extensive and frequent modifications, cannot be rigid. The constant concern of American statesmen is to keep morale relatively constant in its acceptance of the objectives and procedures of the government. This requires effort to anticipate the swings of popular sentiment and to meet them with appeals designed to restrain both excessive optimism and extreme depression.

Not only is there a question about how much information to make public, but related issues of how to treat the information that is released are also pertinent. If relations with the public are wrapped in crisis, sudden and extensive popular reaction is to be expected; a more relaxed or unconcerned presentation will calm down some of whatever popular tensions exist. Both dictatorial and popular governments must be aware of the state of national morale, but a democracy like the United States must develop more elaborate strategies for dealing with it.[23]

Morale and Discipline.

From the point of capability analysis, of course, national morale is an index of the degree to which a people will follow its leaders through the vicissitudes of foreign policy and, while doing so, exert maximum effort in the accomplishment of public tasks. We might say that by "morale" we really mean "endurability": the capacity to perform efficiently under prolonged stress. If this is what we mean by morale, then obviously another factor enters into its makeup besides "zeal, spirit, and hope"; this is the matter of mass discipline. It seems probable that some societies (Germany and Japan during World War II, for example) have been able to maintain a satisfactory level of performance by the sheer force of discipline even after hope and spirit had fled. There is a good deal of doubt, however, whether such would be the case in the United States; American behavior does not place so high a premium on discipline as does that of some of the other national groups.

Morale: the Central Issue?

A very good case can be made that the morale of the American people —their "zeal, spirit, hope, confidence, etc."—is the central problem of

---

[23] For some further discussion of morale strategies, see the present author's *Principles of International Politics* (New York: Oxford University Press, Inc., 1956), pp. 87–9.

American capability. Whether the American effort in world affairs is well planned and energetically executed, whether American policy will "succeed" or "fail," will in the last analysis depend on whether or not the mass of Americans play their various parts effectively. Statesmen may plan and negotiate forever, but their efforts will be sheer futility without the active cooperation and allegiance of the people. It is not overoptimistic to conclude that the broad-gauge pattern of American policy is one that does not overtax the maximum capability of the United States; the major unanswered question is whether or not the American people will become sufficiently convinced of the worth and the desirability of their policy to make the necessary effort. On these grounds national morale becomes a matter of highest importance for American foreign policy.

INTERNATIONAL STRATEGIC POSITION

Perhaps the most relative of the elements of state capability is the factor of strength or weakness that arises from the general strategic position of the state in the world. The situation of a state with regard to strategic advantage or disadvantage depends on the mission that the state sets for itself. If its goals are limited to what it can gain by its own resources, it is in a better position than if it needs help from other states to accomplish its objectives. If it must devote a large portion of its resources to the defense of its homeland against powerful and aggressive neighbors, it is deprived of part of its ability to prosecute its own purposes at greater distances. Here is the case of a state's ability to achieve its objectives being at least partially determined by the very objectives it selects.

America's Need for Allies.

It is beyond doubt that the United States for the indefinite future is going to be required to work in close harmony and cooperation with other states. The objectives of American foriegn policy—summed up in an earlier chapter as the achievement of a world of peace, order, and stability—by their very nature require that the United States forge a series of close and long-lasting agreements with all like-minded states. The prosecution of the cold war also has necessitated that Americans ally themselves with over forty states and fit their policy into a common framework.[24]

To the considerable extent to which the United States is closely tied to its many allies, American freedom of action (and, consequently, Ameri-

---

[24] For a succinct official statement of the United States' need for allies, see President Truman's *First Report to Congress on the Mutual Security Program* (Washington: U. S. Government Printing Official, 1952), pp. 2–7.

can capabilities) are reduced. The kind of alliance the United States prefers to enter into (because of its greater usefulness and flexibility) is one that is genuinely voluntary and that springs from a sensed identity of interest. In dealing with its allies, Washington must therefore preserve the free and voluntary character of the alliance by minimizing the force component of capability and by seeking the maximum return from the exploitation of consent. Intra-alliance relationships are therefore sharply conditioned by America's need for allies.

The same is generally true with regard to all joint free-world programs, whether directed against the USSR in the cold war or—less frequently—in situations not directly stemming from the East-West conflict. The United States must temper the intensity of its policy moves and confine its actions to measures that are acceptable to the other states with which it is acting in concert.

An apt illustration of the inhibiting effect of alliances upon American freedom of action was provided by the Suez crisis of 1956 that grew out of Egypt's seizure and nationalization of the Suez Canal Company. Throughout the entire complex negotiations, including special international conferences, direct diplomatic negotiations, discussion before the Security Council of the United Nations, and extensive propaganda campaigns, American policy was at least partially governed by the necessity of maintaining a common front with France and Britain.[25] In the process, the United States was obliged to take a much less forthright stand than might have been the case had it been free to act completely according to its own desires. It was no longer under such compulsion after Britain and France took military action on their own initiative, and American policy then developed with unwonted speed.

Allies: Strength or Weakness?

The vexations inherent in intimate and long-lasting cooperation among sovereign states have caused periodic resentments among segments of the American people. The whole idea of alliances is recurrently called into question; each crisis in the free world produces renewed pleas for the United States to "go it alone."

This position, however rationally it may occasionally be argued, is ineluctably based on a frankly emotional premise. It seems to grow out of two disparate sources: an evocation of a happier past and an urge to vent the inevitable frustrations attendant upon a multi-dimensional foreign

---

[25] On several occasions, when Secretary of State Dulles intimated that the United States was following an "independent" course on some issues, strong British and French protests were immediately voiced. See *New York Times* (October 3, and October 10, 1956).

policy. For the United States seriously to seek to dismantle the alliances it has so painfully put together would involve far more than merely abandoning one foreign-policy technique and substituting another in its place.

To take on a purely lone hand would require—if collapse were not to be swift and ignominious—a drastic truncation of the objectives of American policy and the abandonment of most of the world to its own fate (or to the clutches of the Soviet camp). It would further the transformation of American society into the true "garrison state," heavily mobilized, constantly on the alert, and eroding all remaining private rights in the name of national security. Put in terms of practical alternatives, the opponents of alliance find themselves defending a position whose costs would far outweigh the advantages alleged to accrue from a more extensive area of American "freedom."

A less extreme view of the pros and cons of the alliance structure of the United States would argue, even after admitting the embarrassments that have appeared and will continue to appear, that the United States cannot afford to do without them. So long as the current concept of national interest retains its applicability, the American government must fit its policy within the framework of an alliance system. That valuable freedom of maneuver is sometimes sacrificed thereby no one will deny; that frequently the United States is forced to do things it really does not want to do seems obvious; that many of the alliances seem to be more advantageous to the other parties than to the United States is a suspicion that will not down.

Even after admitting all these—and many other—unpleasant side effects of the free-world pattern, it seems demonstrable that, save for two or three possible exceptions, the United States gains more than it loses from its arrangements with other states. For each diminution in capability vis-a-vis an ally, a greater gain is won in some other policy area. Under the policy pattern America is now following, some such calculation must lie behind each commitment undertaken.

SOME TENTATIVE CONCLUSIONS

Finally we now come to answer the question implicit in this entire chapter: do American capabilities square with American objectives? Is the United States going to be able to meet the requirements of its own policy, at least under such conditions as we can foresee? At the end of our discussion, we may no more advance a categorical answer than we could at its beginning. The best we can do is to divide it into two parts, about one of which we have some certainty, but about the other of which we can do no more than conjecture.

First, there is little ground to quarrel with the general proposition that the pattern of American objectives is within the theoretical capacity of the United States, at least within any probable set of circumstances. Were Americans to mobilize all their potential and commit it to the accomplishment of their present foreign-policy goals, there would be adequate means at hand to achieve the end. To put it briefly, we may say that the United States *can* eventually reach its objectives, at least as they are phrased today.

The other, equally blunt, question comes at the matter from another direction: *will* the United States have available, at the appropriate place and at the right time, enough of its capability to surmount each of the obstacles it will be called on to meet? The potential is there, at least as far as rational calculation can suggest, but whether the skill of American policy makers and the understanding of the American people will prove equal to the operational mission of mobilizing, committing, and employing it is a question to which no one yet knows the answer.

The Adequacy in Tangibles.

Taking into account the mission, the situation, the nature of the visible threat, and the operating principles of the United States, the tangible raw materials of capability would seem to be adequate for the purpose as presently formulated. The American geographic situation is advantageous; the manpower balance—when modified by qualitative considerations—is satisfactory and promises to improve relatively and absolutely; the resource endowment is sufficient if prudently managed. Industrial and agricultural production have no inherent imbalances sufficient to threaten the continuation of their present and possible high levels; American military capacity, backed by technology and an elastic industrial plant, can be raised to almost any point that seems today to be possibly necessary. In each of the five tangible classifications are certain shortcomings; we have attempted to indicate at least some of the more important of them. None, however, seems beyond control or to be of such importance as to inhibit seriously future American efforts. On the score of the visible and tangible factors of capability the United States receives a satisfactory rating.

The Area of Uncertainty.

It is, of course, the intangibles that provide the grounds for such doubts as may exist about the future. Questions bristle at every point. Will the American social order survive the strains of the coming decades, or is a quasi-totalitarian garrison state the only way to organize Americans for long-term coordinated effort? Will Americans match the Russian educational effort in training enough scientists, engineers, and technicians to meet national needs; alternatively, if American education should become science-oriented, will it mean the end of the humanistic, liberal education that has contributed so largely to the American version of the "open society"? Will American morale be equal to the task it faces; can rational calculation replace emotional fervor as the guide to mass attitudes toward foreign policy? Can the United States live indefinitely in close relationship with 40 or 50 other nations, each bent on its own purposes and most of them aggravatingly different in culture, tradition, and social structure?

These questions, and the hundreds more like them that could be raised, constitute the area of uncertainty about American capabilities. No one has any capsule solution to the problem they raise, but their relevance to our concern seems unquestionable. It is not the part of a textbook to exhort its readers, but it does not seem inappropriate at this juncture to suggest that in the ability of the American people to cope with the intangible factors determining the success or failure of the United States in its international mission will be found one of the most important tests of the applicability of the democratic idea to the conditions of the twentieth century.

PART

5

◆

American

Policy

in

Action

◆

The
Pattern
of
American
Policy

CHAPTER ◂ *10* ▸

In Chapter 6 we developed an outline of the concept of national interest that the United States seems to be using as its guide as it goes into the latter half of the twentieth century. In Chapters 7, 8, and 9 we elaborated the major situational factors affecting American action since 1945: Chapter 7 characterized the state of the international scene, Chapter 8 considered the Soviet threat, and Chapter 9 examined American capabilities for action.

These two sets of considerations—a dominant idea of interest and a set of situational elements confronting the United States—provide the raw material out of which American foreign policy is fashioned. In this chapter we shall describe the outcome of the interaction of the American concept of interest and the prevailing situational factors since 1945. Our approach will be one of attempting to delineate the "pattern" of American policy: the set of assumptions upon which decisions have been based and the action formulas that have grown from these decisions.

WHY THE COLD WAR?

The end of World War II found the United States in a uniquely favorable position. All its visible enemies had been defeated and were under occupation; all its powerful associates were bound together in an international mechanism for postwar cooperation, the United Nations. As Americans seemed to see it, the future policy of their government was to be largely one of binding up the wounds of the war and of initiating programs to eliminate the maladjustments and tensions that yet remained in the world. The era of peace, order, and stability seemed within grasp, if not actually at hand. Americans, it must be admitted, grasped only a few of the complexities and difficulties of the task they faced, but even so their lack of dismay and their bouyant hope seem remarkable to us today.

It was into this apparently idyllic picture that the Soviet intruded itself. Americans were generally quite slow to grasp the Soviet threat for what it was; as late as 1948 they had only begun to comprehend the implications of the status to which the United States had fallen heir. When, as we have already seen, the United States realized that peace had yet to be won, the action principles of its national interest asserted themselves. The cold war was on.

The American response to the Soviet threat was at first purely emotional; the first phase of American cold war policy consisted largely of replying to each Russian *"nyet"* with a thunderous "no." However satisfying it might have momentarily been to bruised egos, in the long run this approach was merely to compound futility. Gradually, as the American people grew more accustomed to coping with permanent crisis, a more coherent picture of why the United States was involved in the cold war took shape. The nature of the controversy became more clear; Americans began to learn what they wanted from Russia.

NON-REASONS FOR THE COLD WAR

We ought first to examine briefly some of the invalid explanations for American cold-war policy that have (or have had in the past) considerable vogue. So much mass emotion has been involved in the development of American strategy that an entire mythology has been created to "explain" and "justify" a phenomenon whose rationale is not especially complex. It seems almost as if each American has his own reasons why he fights the cold war.

Communism.

Americans are not mainly concerned with fighting communism, nor with fighting the USSR because it is officially a communist state. Communism as an ideology and the Soviet Union as a communist state both existed long before 1945, yet Americans did not feel themselves particularly menaced prior to the end of the war in that year. No principle of the American political tradition and foreign policy is more firmly grounded than that of noninterference in the internal affairs of other states—particularly large and powerful ones. It would violate both democratic ideology and American national interest to base a long-range policy on popular hostility to any belief system in the abstract, however repugnant it might be on moral grounds.[1]

Dictatorship.

Neither does the United States oppose the Soviet simply because of the existence of the dictatorial form of Russian government. Americans have no necessary political quarrel with any form of government, no matter how reprehensible it may be in theory. The United States has often proved (and, indeed, is proving today) that it can do business with a dictatorship that is—from the American point of view—well-behaved.

Power.

Some "super-realists" attempt to explain American antipathy to the Kremlin in terms of a simple power rivalry.[2] Moscow is the only capital in the world in a position to challenge Washington, they say; only the Soviet stands between the United States and world dominion. From this premise they conclude that Americans must therefore destroy Russia and then assume their rightful place as rulers of the world. *Pax Americana* would be the dominant principle in world affairs.

This frightening idea never had very many adherents in the United States (and virtually none at all outside American frontiers). It reached its peak of popularity during the early days of the cold war, and has declined steadily ever since. It would be difficult to reconcile such an objective with America's basic interest in peace, order, and stability; it would

---

[1] A position directly opposed to that taken in this paragraph has been often advanced with great sincerity; one of the most able advocates of the doctrine that communism is the real enemy of the United States is Anthony Bouscaren, in *America Faces World Communism* (New York: Vantage, 1953). See also Robert Strausz-Hupe, *et al., Protracted Conflict* (New York: Harper & Bros., 1959); and Walter F. Hahn and John C. Neff, eds., *American Strategy for the Nuclear Age* (Garden City: Anchor Books, Doubleday & Company, 1960).

[2] An influential exposition of this doctrine is James Burnham, *The Struggle for the World* (New York: John Day Company, Inc., 1947).

conflict as well with almost all the ingredients of the national tradition. The United States has no absolute objection in principle to a strong Russia; on the contrary, if Soviet friendliness were guaranteed, American interest would demand the maximization of Russian strength.

Expansionism.

Finally, the United States is not involved in the cold war simply because of Moscow's interest in expansion. To the extent that Russian interests can be classified as "legitimate" (admittedly a difficult distinction to pinpoint in practice), there is no reason for the United States always to oppose increases in Soviet power, prestige, or well-being. We may grant that there are inherent limits on what America would conceive of as permissible Soviet aggrandizement, and perhaps these boundaries might prove in fact to be unacceptable to the Kremlin; with reference to the basic principle, however, we may safely say that the United States has no eternal interest in keeping the Soviet forever inferior to America.

WHAT THE UNITED STATES WANTS FROM THE COMMUNISTS

The Procedural Base of American Policy.

The reason why the United States fights the cold war is much simpler than any explanation based on ideology, or governmental forms, or power, or expansionism. American opposition to the Soviet, as we suggested in Chapter 6, is based on procedural grounds. The postwar policy of the Kremlin has been based primarily upon the perpetuation of crisis and the use of disorder, violence, and revolution as operating techniques. This alone would be sufficient to keep the United States hostile to the Soviet as long as Moscow plays the foreign-policy game by such rules. Americans went into opposition as soon as they realized fully that Stalin did not share their concept of a world of peace, order, and stability marked by a general acceptance of the status quo and the cooperative solution of problems. At the moment the Soviet accepts procedural rules as well as their substantive implications, the cold war will end. It will not, of course, be replaced by total agreement and friendliness; Soviet-American controversy in a non-cold war era, however, would be much easier of adjustment and less likely to break out of control.

The Limits of American Demands.

What, then, do Americans want from the communists? The United States does not demand the obliteration of communism, but only that it no longer be used as a technique of international disorder. It does not demand that the Kremlin dictatorship be dissolved, but only that such form of government not be forcibly exported to smaller states. It does not demand that Russian power be destroyed, or even drastically reduced, but only that it be put to serve a socially useful purpose. It does not demand that the Soviet abandon its traditional concern for Russian security, prosperity, and prestige, but only that its leaders interpret these objectives more realistically and pursue them in an orderly fashion. In short, the United States does not demand surrender; an American victory in the cold war could be brought about by a mere procedural change by the communist leadership. The United States will be satisfied when the Soviet agrees to conduct its foreign policy on the same basis as do most civilized states.[3]

This is the major objective of the United States vis-a-vis the Soviet. We must distinguish it carefully from what Americans often say their objectives are; the United States often overstates its case for reasons of diplomatic bargaining, international propaganda, or domestic politics. In times of crisis, official and unofficial spokesmen (particularly U.S. Senators) are prone to say a great deal more than they mean.

But anything more than the limited goal we have stipulated would do a good deal of violence to the basic requirements of the American situation. To demand the destruction or the abasement of the USSR would be extremely dangerous. It would either produce total war with its attendant horrors, or prove unattainable and doom the United States to deep frustration. What is more, what sort of world might follow the utter elimination of Soviet power? Some analysts, as we have seen, would be quick to point out that this would mean unchallenged American mastery of the world. We may inquire, however, how many Americans really hunger for that lofty but shaky eminence? And who could guarantee that the United States would actually be in a position to dominate the globe after a destructive total war with the Soviet?

The Goals of American Policy.

We may put American goals in simple and homely language by saying that the United States wants to "housebreak" the Soviet. The entire pattern

---

[3] See for example the formulation of the issues made by then Secretary of State Dean Acheson in 1950, in a speech, "Tensions Between the United States and the Soviet Union" (Department of State Publication 3810): "The United States is ready ... to cooperate.... But it takes more than one to cooperate. If the Soviet Union could join in ... we could all face the future with greater security. We could look forward to more than the eventual reduction of some of the present tensions. We could anticipate a return to a more normal and relaxed diplomatic atmosphere and to progress in the transaction of some of the international business which needs so urgently to be done." See also Council on Foreign Relations, *Basic Aims of United States Foreign Policy* (Washington: U. S. Government Printing Office, 1959), pp. 16–21.

of American policy is aimed at convincing the Kremlin of two points, one positive and one negative. Negatively, the United States is attempting to persuade the Soviet dictators that the way they have chosen, the way of disorder, violence, and crisis, will not produce victory; frustration and failure will instead be their reward. Positively, the United States is prepared to prove that the Kremlin's reasonable interests and objectives—or at least those that are compatible with world political stability—can be successfully and satisfactorily attained only by cooperative effort in a climate of peace and order. This, stripped to its essentials, is the basic American view of the cold war.

The Free World and the Cold War

Where does the noncommunist world fit into this picture? American policy toward the free states flows naturally from American interests and assumptions. In practice the United States tends to deal with the free world at two different levels.

Long-term Harmony of Interests.

There is a fairly large group of states, including especially most of those within the orbit of western culture, whose circumstances and level of development lead them to share largely in the basic American interest in peace and order. It was only natural for such states, including (among others) the Commonwealth of Nations, France, and the Low Countries, to find a good deal of common ground with the United States. They have as great a concern as has the United States with finding effective programs that might lead to the creation of a more stable world society. Although the United States is also allied with most of this group against Soviet expansionism, the close cooperation that exists is to a large extent independent of the cold war. The United States would be virtually as intimate with them even if there were no Soviet threat.[4] With these states American relations assume an almost predictable shape.

Arrangements of Convenience.

Another group of noncommunist states, however (and also at least one communist one), for a variety of reasons each peculiar to the state involved, is not as interested as is the United States in institutionalizing stability, but have instead revisionist ambitions of their own. Some of them, nevertheless,

---

[4] This idea permeated the original conception of American economic assistance to Europe. See the text of Secretary of State Marshall's speech at Harvard University on June 5, 1947, in which he outlined the proposed program. *New York Times* (June 6, 1947).

feel themselves menaced by Soviet policy. With such governments, including such otherwise dissimilar cases as Yugoslavia and Spain, the United States has made alliances of convenience against a common danger. In these agreements no commitments are exchanged or expected concerning the day that Russian policy no longer furnishes a possible cement of alliance. In the meantime these sometime associates serve a necessary purpose from the American point of view and gain concrete advantages for themselves.

Ambiguities in American Free-world Policy.

The bifurcated nature of America's attitude toward the free world is perhaps the most subtle and certainly one of the most frequently misunderstood aspects of American policy. It is easy for Americans to think of the "free world" as a unit, as a weapon to be used against communist power. They find it difficult to recognize valid grounds for disagreement among its members. They classify noncommunist states that do not actively join the western alliance as "neutralist" and drift into thinking of them as at least potentially pro-communist. They cannot understand how India, although outspoken in criticism of many anti-communist moves by the West, nevertheless receives favors and deference from the United States, while Spain, "the most anti-communist state in Europe," has only a tenuous connection with the free world and is dealt with gingerly and at arm's length.

The Cold War and the Long View.

This, and most analogous paradoxes, can be largely resolved in terms of American long-run interest. The cold war, despite its contemporary significance, is actually only a phase in a larger program. The United States cannot afford to concentrate entirely upon the Soviet; it must be prepared for the day when the cold war has been liquidated and the way is again open for positive action in behalf of the kind of world Americans want. The United States, even in the present circumstances, must make such moves in this direction as it can. The problem of world order will outlive the Soviet threat, and requires a much broader set of tactics if it is to be successfully attacked.

At the same time, the frustration of the Kremlin's immediate plan is the first order of business. In order to resist the Soviet, the United States must mobilize as powerful a force as possible, and aid from any source is welcome. It would be too much to expect that the entire group of 40-odd states with which the United States is allied would agree in their long-range plans. Americans realize that they are putting aside many future quarrels in return for promises of immediate support against Moscow. The end of the cold war would probably be the signal for an outburst of new disputes between the United States and many of its allies;

indeed, even the relaxations in Soviet-American tensions between 1955 and 1960 produced exactly such intra-alliance disputes.

CONTAINMENT: ASSUMPTIONS AND PROGRAM

American policy since 1945 has not been merely a haphazard business of putting out "brush fires" as they have flared up. Brush fires there have been plenty; underlying all of Washington's calculated moves, however, and giving point to many emergency measures as well, has been a reasonably well-rationalized plan. The American strategy and tactics have been grounded upon a detailed analysis of the nature of the Soviet threat and the selection of a general line to meet the varying forms in which Russian expansionism developed. Known by several names, none has proved as durable as the policy's original informal title. In this chapter we shall call the American plan and policy by its popular name of "containment." [5]

The present era is almost the first time in American history that the United States government has acted upon a theory of foreign policy; never before have Americans attempted to apply a consistent body of doctrine to an evolving international situation. Despite the persistence with which certain generalizations were invoked during the nineteenth century, the United States since 1945 has surpassed its earlier record in setting its course in harmony with a set of basic premises.

SOVIET MOTIVATIONS

The fundamental assumption upon which the American government has proceeded is easily stated: Soviet policy is inherently expansionist. Left alone, the Kremlin would continue indefinitely to bring more and more of the world under its domination. Why did Americans conclude that Russia would always expand? What, in George F. Kennan's words, did the government believe were "the sources of Soviet conduct"?

---

[5] Any discussion of "containment" must rely heavily on the writings of George F. Kennan who, as chief of the Policy Planning Staff of the State Department in 1947, made a major contribution to its conception and also helped make it public property by means of a justly famous magazine article ("X," "The Sources of Soviet Conduct," *Foreign Affairs* [July, 1947]; reprinted in H. F. Armstrong, ed., *The Foreign Affairs Reader* [New York: Harper & Bros., Inc., 1948], and in George F. Kennan, *American Diplomacy 1900–1950* [Chicago: University of Chicago Press, 1951]). Although what we shall be discussing here is more the actual practice of American policy rather than its theoretical formulation by Mr. Kennan, any systematic analysis of recent American policy must be greatly in his debt. The catalogue of Soviet motivations included here is drawn largely from his writings.

Attempts to demonstrate conclusively that Russian behavior since 1945 has been the result of a single overriding motivation have not been particularly successful. The safest judgment emerging from more than fifteen years of analysis seems to be that Soviet policy arises from a mixture of motives. Several individual factors may be isolated, but their interaction, the extent to which each modifies the others in practice, and which one is primarily responsible for any single policy move, all are yet impossible to show accurately.

This much, however, we may accept confidently: any single-factor theory of Soviet behavior explains either too much or too little for the purposes of American foreign policy. The United States, as a matter of sheer self-defense, has been obliged to adopt the thesis of multiple motivation of Soviet action.

The Roots of Soviet Action.

Soviet leadership, in making policy decisions, seems to be subject to three different pressures. The first arises from communist ideology, the second from Russian history and tradition, and the third from the peculiar dynamics of dictatorship in a police state.[6]

Thus Marxism-Leninism—and its later variants—impels them toward conflict with the capitalist world, assures them of inevitable victory, and teaches them that time is forever on their side. Russian historical tradition gives them a grip on their people and sets them in pursuit of objectives sanctified by time; the Kremlin has driven toward the Straits, has demanded Balkan hegemony, and has established spheres of influence in central Asia and the Far East.

The compulsions of dictatorship create certain imperatives for the ruling clique in Russia. The continued survival of the regime requires—as was the case in Imperial Rome—"bread or circuses." The expectations of a higher standard of living for the masses have not materialized in any significant way. The apparatus of the police state therefore becomes essential as the only way to guarantee the security of the regime if the better life for all remains out of reach. If no bread be forthcoming, circuses become vital; if the circuses fail, then the bread must be made available.

---

[6] In contrast to these three as listed by Kennan, see Waldemar Gurian, "Permanent Features of Soviet Foreign Policy," *Yearbook of World Affairs, 1947* (London: Stevens, 1947); reprinted in Hans J. Morgenthau and Kenneth Thompson, *Principles and Problems of International Politics* (New York: Alfred A. Knopf, 1951). Professor Gurian finds the "two mainsprings" of Soviet policy to be "utopianism" and "cynical realism."

Soviet policy therefore has attempted to provide a scapegoat for the unsatisfactory conditions at home; it is all the fault of the imperialist West that is encircling the worker's Paradise and is ever plotting a war of destruction. And so the myth of self-defense is polished up and made to serve as a rationalization of domestic oppression. Its outcome is what has been called "defensive aggression" or "aggressive self-defense"; according to this doctrine, the Soviet expands only to forestall the West.

The Nature of Soviet Action.

Thus ideology, history, and the greed for power all affect the minds of the top layer of the Soviet hierarchy. Which is the fundamental level of being? Which would be, in the final analysis, the controlling factor if the teachings of the three were to contradict each other?

During the early postwar period, this was a purely academic question; as long as Stalin lived, all three made the same point: expansion. Russian policy called for a constant outward pressure in all directions, probing along the perimeter until a weak spot was discovered through which Soviet power could flow. Indeed, this has sometimes been called the "strategy of the amoeba." Its result was a steady expansion of the Soviet sphere between 1945 and 1950 that gratified all three Soviet motivations.

The Need for a Choice.

In order to fashion a policy, however, the United States had to determine for itself the most deeply rooted of the three influences. What it felt to be basic to Soviet behavior made a great deal of difference to America's future policy. If ideology were fundamental, the United States would have to prepare to deal with fanatics who were immune to reason and who might well stop at nothing to achieve their goal of world communism. If "Russianism" were the inspiration for Moscow's policy, there were ample historical guides provided for the United States by the two centuries of British struggle with Czarist imperialism. If the Soviet leaders were first of all political adventurers who were most concerned with retaining their power, American statesmen again would be able to draw upon the rich store of experience that Western man had accumulated in coping with this type of political force. The direction of American policy depended on this initial decision.

THE AMERICAN DECISION

After a good deal of painful study, complicated by lack of experience with the Soviet and the shortage of Americans equipped with the necessary data and insights, American policy-makers reached a decision.

The Rejection of Ideology.

It was apparent that Marxist-Leninist ideology was important to the Soviet as a tool of policy, as a guide in new and unfamiliar situations, and as an orienting and idea-shaping influence. The framers of American policy could not, however, bring themselves to believe that it was the ultimate answer to Moscow's behavior. The doctrine itself was simply too flexible.

Communist dogma had been interpreted and reinterpreted so many times by Soviet leaders that it could be used to provide a theoretical justification for any policy at all, or even for several mutually contradictory ones. Even hardened communists grew dizzy from keeping up with all the twists in the party line. It was undeniable that ideological versatility aided Russian policy; it could be applied to support and justify anything the high command decided to do. This very strength, however, made it unreliable as a guide to Moscow's future conduct.[7]

The Limits of Historicism.

In the same way, the influence of Russian history and tradition, although great, was finally not thought to be basic. Much of Moscow's policy was in the historic Russian pattern, but more of it was not. Lithuania, for example, was traditionally a Russian sphere, but East Prussia never was. Tradition might serve a purpose in winning mass support for the regime, and undoubtedly played its part in suggesting possible channels for expansion.[8] It failed, however, to explain enough of Soviet policy for the United States to safely accept it as controlling.

The Compulsions of Dictatorship.

The conclusion was reached that the Soviet leadership, when finally judged, was composed of men who were first of all dictators with all the strengths and weaknesses of the breed. They were dictators under peculiar Russian and Marxist influences. But beneath the veneer of ideology and patriotism, the men in the Kremlin were driven by the same compulsions that have obsessed political adventurers in many other places: a lust for power and an urge to preserve and expand it.[9]

---

[7] See, however, Barrington Moore, Jr., *Soviet Politics: The Dilemma of Power* (Cambridge: Harvard University Press, 1950). Moore argues the opposite position, especially on pp. 404–12. For an opposing view, see Edward Crankshaw, *Khrushchev's Russia* (Baltimore: Penguin Books, 1959).

[8] See Julian Towster, "Russia: Persistent Strategic Demands," *Current History* (July, 1951).

[9] The general American impression that Khrushchev's behavior over the "U-2" episode was prompted primarily by an internal Kremlin crisis in the spring of 1960 tended to strengthen this thesis. See the remarks of Secretary of State Herter, *New York Times* (May 26, 1960).

This judgment, if accurate, had profound importance for the United States. It meant that, if driven into a tight corner, the leaders of Russia would probably react primarily from a desire to save their own power and to preserve their regime. It meant that the Soviet system was subject to the stresses and strains of any dictatorship, most conspicuously a conspiratorial psychology permeating the bureaucratic structure and an incessant competition for power. It meant that Soviet policy was, rather than a carefully worked-out timetable and battle plan, a highly experimental and pragmatic program subject to frequent revision in the light of changing circumstances. It meant that the dictators would be likely to stake their survival on a policy only after carefully calculating its probable effect on their own security. It meant, finally, that the leaders, although vicious and unprincipled men, were basically rational and could be dealt with by a rationally conceived policy.[10]

CONTAINMENT: BASIC ELEMENTS

Upon this assumption—that the USSR's policy is that of a dictatorship modified but not controlled by ideological and traditional influences —the United States has built its anti-Soviet policy. The program was designed to take advantage of the enemy's weaknesses and to minimize his strengths. It called for action upon an unprecedentedly broad front, and of a variety of forms at first undreamed of and still bewildering to many Americans. Its development has involved the United States in complex relationships everywhere in the world.

The First Phase.

Containment visualized several phases of American action against the Soviet, although only the first ever became a matter of general comprehension by the public. This initial line required the United States to take a position all along the perimeter of the Soviet world and to resist any further advance by Moscow. America committed itself to meet each threat as it presented itself, by such action as was appropriate to the particular time, place, and conditions. The United States adopted no single pattern of re-

---

[10] Thus Kennan says: "...it will be clearly seen that the Soviet pressure against the free institutions of the western world is something that can be contained by the adroit and vigilant application of counter-force at a series of constantly shifting geographical and political points, corresponding to the shifts and manœuvres [sic] of Soviet policy, but which cannot be charmed or talked out of existence." "Sources of Soviet Conduct," by X. *Foreign Affairs* (July, 1947). Copyright by Council on Foreign Relations, Inc. Reprinted by permission.

sistance, but instead reserved its freedom to choose techniques demanded by the form of Russian expansionism it was meeting, whether political, psychological, economic, or military.

This decision pledged the United States to hold an enormous arc extending from the North Cape in Norway down through central Europe, the Middle East, and South Asia, and then turning northeastward and running up through Southeast Asia, China, Korea, and Japan. This was the geopolitical "shatter zone" abutting on the Soviet Heartland. If Moscow was to be stopped short of total domination of Eurasia, America must draw a line and hold it before Russian power broke out to the open sea. Despite the loss of China and half of Indochina to communist control since 1947, however, the United States has held the line tolerably well.

The Second Phase.

For many Americans this is all there ever was to it; the United States was to "stop communism," and that was what containment was all about. Unfortunately, the problem of American policy was never this simple. Stopping the Soviet threat would not eliminate it, and for the United States to fight the cold war forever would be a poor way to fulfill American goals of a better world—a strange version of the peace, order, and stability that is the announced American objective. The theorists of containment had anticipated stalemate as the most probable outcome of the first phase of American action, and had devised a strategy to follow up any success the United States might enjoy in holding the line.

Their formula was based on the pattern of American policy and its assumptions about the kind of people the Russians were. The second phase of American policy called for the United States to exploit its own advantages, to capitalize on the difficulties inherent in the Soviet position, and ultimately to confront the Kremlin with such an unfavorable situation that peaceful accommodation with the free world would be the only convenient way for the leadership to escape with the regime intact. Put baldly, the doctrine might sound over-simple. It had, however, sound reasoning and considerable historical evidence to lend it credence.

The Rationale of the Second Phase.

Soviet policy was expansionist, Americans reasoned, but it was also opportunistic. This meant that it would continue to expand only as long as it met weakness. Confronted by equal strength, Moscow would stop; met by superior power, it would recoil. Ultimately, it would lose its dynamism and become amenable to restraint. This has been the key to the entire American approach.

The first objective of the United States was the stabilization of the line of containment by plugging up the soft spots through which the Soviet threatened to move. The American government planned then to create "situations of strength": particular areas at various places along the line of containment where the United States enjoyed superiority over Soviet power and could apply controlling pressure on its own part. The advantages that could produce such local preponderance, we should note, were not necessarily military; any relationship could suffice if its net effect was to give the United States a policy leverage. If the Soviet found itself in a clearly inferior position, the reasoning ran, it would withdraw rather than risk open defeat.

Why did the United States feel it necessary to win local victories at all? The answer to this question lies in the controlling American theory of Soviet motivations. The Russian leaders, unable or unwilling to fulfill their promises of domestic plenty made to their people, needed a dynamic foreign policy as an outlet for the powerful energies they had liberated in their people. If, by containment, the United States could deny them release, enormous frustrations would result. Internal pressures, pent up, would multiply their effect; the ubiquitous stresses within the Soviet structure would worsen.

This, we should remember, might result from a mere negative program of containment. The United States, the argument ran further, could heighten the effect and speed up the process of reversing Soviet dynamics by scoring significant if limited victories within the compass of its own situations of strength.

Since power and its distribution (and enjoyment) are the primary concerns of any dictatorship, the intramural struggle within the Soviet hierarchy would probably intensify if foreign policy were not to produce a constant flow of victories. The luckless bureaucrats officially tagged with responsibility for failure would be ousted and humiliated; [11] new plans, put forward by other members of the high command, would replace those that had failed. The demoted leaders would seek to obstruct and inhibit their successors as they pursued their own vindication; competition for rank and status, never far submerged in the Soviet system, would come out into the open. This, added to the embarrassing necessity of explaining away defeats to the mass of the Russian people, would compound an already difficult situation. The Soviet leadership, beset by internal struggles, would then have to lessen its external pressure.

---

[11] The Kremlin revolt against Premier Khruschchev that produced the change in Soviet policy at the 1960 summit was generally felt to be due to his failure to win concessions from the United States on the question of Berlin. See the opinions of Secretary of State Herter, New York Times (May 26, 1960).

So the second phase of American policy—the attempt to roll back Soviet power at points where the United States enjoyed local superiority—had as its object the intensification of stress within the Soviet government. Such a development, it was contended, would hasten the moment at which the leadership would cry quits and undertake to prosecute Russian policy by a different and—from the American point of view—more satisfactory method. This was a more delicate matter, however, than might appear at first glance.

The United States had always to plan its victories carefully, allowing the Kremlin the opportunity to withdraw gracefully with its prestige intact. If America were over-militant, if it forced the Soviet so tightly into a corner that the stability of its regime were directly menaced, the Russians in their desperation might choose war rather than accommodation. This would be fatal; total war with Moscow was just what the United States was seeking to avoid.[12]

American local victories had to be just convincing enough that the Soviet would retreat, yet not so obvious that the leaders could not rationalize them to their people. It has proven difficult for Americans generally to grasp this point. Why not, if the United States has the communists in a real vise, put the pressure on and force either Moscow's surrender or its destruction?

In the first place, there is very little reason to believe that anything short of military defeat would force the USSR to capitulate. Second, trying to force surrender runs a grave risk of provoking total war. Third, if American pressure were to prove unexpectedly successful, and if it should undermine the Soviet regime without causing war, the most probable consequence would be a new—and certainly a bloodier—Russian revolution. This last might sound like an ideal solution on first hearing, but it would defy good sense to argue that a new upheaval in Russia, complete with probable international intervention and certain widespead unrest, would serve the long-range American interest in peace, order, and stability.

We must also remember that the hoped-for change in Soviet tactics is within the power of decision of the Soviet policy-makers themselves. They alone began the cold war, and only they can end it short of blood-

---

12 Kennan says: "...it is a *sine qua non* of successful dealing with the Soviet that the foreign government in question should remain at all times cool and collected and that its demands on Russian policy should be put forward in such a manner as to leave the way open for a compliance not too detrimental to Russian prestige." "Sources of Soviet Conduct." Reprinted by permission.

The Pattern of American Policy ✻ *273*

shed. The most the United States can safely attempt to do is to speed up the process by increasing the pressures on the leadership and by being always ready to act promptly when (and if) signs of change should appear. What is the United States prepared to do if and when the contradictions in the Kremlin's position force Russia into an "agonizing reappraisal" of its own policy?

The Framework of Accommodation

Up to the present time Americans have been mainly concerned with the theory and practice of containment, whose objective it is to convince Moscow that its policy of unilateral revision of the status quo by tactics of subversion, intrigue, and violence simply does not pay. We have seen, however, that the American approach has a further objective, positive where the first is negative. The United States hopes to persuade the Soviet to accept its offers of peaceful cooperation and the orderly satisfaction of justifiable Russian desires. It is the carrot and the stick of the fable; containment is the stick, driving Moscow away from its goal; accommodation is the carrot, tempting the Soviet into abandoning its unattainable objectives by means of satisfactory compromises.

The Failure of the Second Phase.

The cold war, as it progressed after 1947, eroded American political consciousness to the point where many Americans lost sight of this long-run goal. Washington tended to take the easy way; faced with the necessity of obtaining popular agreement to sudden and far-reaching action, high officialdom all too frequently floated programs on a wave of crisis. The crisis was often real, and there was little desire deliberately to deceive the public; one result of the crisis approach, however, was to fix in the public mind the image of the Soviet as an inscrutable and implacable enemy, whose intentions were transparently evil and whose persistence was inhuman.[13]

The public—guided by some less responsible elements of the press—adopted a set of clichés by means of which the problem of Soviet expansionism was fitted into a simple stereotype: "You can't trust the Russians," "the only thing they understand is force," "no appeasement," "their tactics may change but never their objectives," and so on. As Americans became accustomed to constant Soviet hostility, most of them forgot—if

---

[13] In this connection, Winston Churchill's characterization of Russia as "a riddle wrapped in a mystery inside an enigma" became almost a cliché. See a criticism of this attitude by George Fisher, in his review of John L. Stipp, *Soviet Russia Today* (New York: Harper & Bros., Inc., 1956), *Saturday Review* (March 16, 1957, p. 16).

they ever realized—that American policy had actually looked to the day when the Kremlin (although not necessarily any more friendly) was willing to act cooperatively.[14]

The Need for Realism.

Any proposal the United States advances must be attractive enough to the Soviet leaders that they will want to accept it. Americans, if they wish a peace of accommodation, must take the USSR as it is; its attainment remains impossible as long as so many segments of the public claim to oppose peace with Moscow until the Kremlin sincerely repents and apologizes for obstructing American policy.

If repentance and apology are what the United States is working for, then truly the cold war will go on forever. On the other hand, a rational image of American national interest can be constructed that does not require that the USSR should love the United States or that it should agree on everything. All America really insists upon is that Russia behave itself.[15]

Minimum Basis of Accommodation.

There has been relatively little inclination in the United States to consider the minimum bases of a practical settlement with the Soviet Union. Many Americans insist that peace will come only when the Soviet abandons eastern Europe, retreats to its 1939 boundaries, dismantles its worldwide apparatus of Communist parties, disarms drastically, and ends its "interference" in the Middle East, south and southeast Asia, and the Far East.

If these are actually the minimum American requirements, peace is far off. They would require the Soviet to liquidate its policy, renounce its objectives, and leave itself virtually defenseless and at the mercy of the United States. We may find it difficult to imagine a situation in which the Soviet leadership would accept such a proposal as an alternative to war; military defeat itself could scarcely exact a higher price. No dictatorship (nor any other government, for that matter) would dare lightly to risk accepting a settlement so obviously humiliating.

But it is not at all clear that these requirements are actually the least the United States can safely insist upon. Must America deny Moscow any protection against such a threat as a resurgent Germany? Can any-

---

[14] See S. Grover Rich, "Negotiation from Strength: the Psychological Problem," *Antioch Review* (September, 1952). Professor Rich stresses this point.

[15] See George Kennan's article, "America and the Russian Future," *Foreign Affairs* (April, 1951), for his estimate of what changes in the Soviet system the United States may reasonably expect to come about. For the Soviet image of satisfactory relations, see Nikita Khrushchev, "On Peaceful Coexistence," *Foreign Affairs* (October, 1959).

one categorically deny that the Russians have no reason to fear another invasion from the West, the fourth since 1815? Does the Soviet indeed have to be militarily impotent for the United States to feel secure? Would peace be worth conceding the USSR a clear right of continued existence as a great power? Granting an American concern with permanent world order, these questions and others like them would seem to be obviously rhetorical. Peace—real peace, the goal of American policy—would be worth its price.

Principles of Accommodation.

It would be frivolous for us to suggest any detailed terms on which Soviet-American accommodation could be based; they would have to depend on the particular conditions prevailing at the moment any such agreement was reached. We can, however, lay down what might be the guiding principle of any American negotiator working out such details: the United States is willing to make any grants to Soviet interest that would ensure Russian cooperation in a peaceful world but that would not compromise the fundamental American position.

The United States cannot ever "trust" the USSR the way individuals trust each other. This generalization, however, does not invalidate the prospect for lasting accommodation; nations cannot ever safely "trust" each other in that way. Trust and good faith, however, have never proved to be a solid base for viable international agreement.

The real stuff of lasting accomodation between states is a harmony of interest. We may assume that the Soviet leadership—never abandoning for a moment their conspiratorial outlook—will keep only those agreements that individual and mutual interest demands be kept. It is immaterial to the United States whether the Kremlin abides by its promises because of the positive advantage accruing therefrom or because of its fear of the consequences of breaking faith.[16] Both motivations have a

---

[16] In this connection, Walter Lippmann, in criticizing the Kennan hypothesis in *The Cold War* (New York: Harper & Bros., Inc., 1947), p. 60, made this point about accommodation: "At the root of Mr. X's philosophy about Russian-American relations and underlying all the ideas of the Truman Doctrine there is a disbelief in the possibility of a settlement of the issues raised by this war. Having observed, I believe quite correctly, that we cannot expect 'to enjoy political intimacy with the Soviet regime,' and that we must 'regard the Soviet Union as a rival, not a partner in the political arena,' and that 'there can be no appeal to common purposes,' Mr. X has reached the conclusion that all we can do is to 'contain' Russia until Russia changes, ceases to be our rival, and becomes our partner.

"The conclusion is, it seems to me, quite unwarranted. The history of diplomacy is the history of relations among rival powers, which did not enjoy political intimacy, and did not respond to appeals to common purposes. Nevertheless, there have been settlements. Some of them did not last very long. Some of them did. For a diplomat to think that rival and unfriendly powers cannot be brought to a settlement is to forget what diplomacy is all about." (Reprinted by permission.)

place in American thinking. The American problem, therefore, is one of devising a settlement that will make the joint effect of the carrot and the stick sufficient to commit Moscow firmly and—perhaps—irrevocably to cooperation.

THE PATTERN APPLIED

SUCCESSES AND FAILURES OF THE PATTERN

Europe: Holding the West.

As the United States looked over the long line it had pledged itself to defend in 1946–7, several weak spots seemed to demand immediate attention. The gravest danger of a Soviet break-through was in western Europe. The democracies of the continent needed protection against the twin dangers of communist subversion and Russian military aggression. The United States moved quickly, broadly, and—to some extent—over-enthusiastically to meet the threat. Economic aid was poured in via ECA and its successors; military agreements and political commitments were reached in a series of steps culminating in an expanded NATO; a steady— if not devastatingly effective—drumfire of propaganda was launched.

Europe was doubly important to the United States.[17] Not only was it the richest prize within the Soviet's grasp, but the democracies figured largely in American plans. It was not enough for the United States to prop up western Europe so the region would not fall victim to the Kremlin; Europe was to become a "situation of strength" and was to play its cooperative part in future struggle with the USSR. By 1960, balancing unquestioned progress against some equally obvious failures, it was clear that at least a significant beginning had been made on this task.

First Defeat: China.

If Europe represented the first relative American success, Asia was the scene of the first, and so far the greatest, defeat for the United States. By 1947 the situation in China had deteriorated so badly that the Kuomintang government was doomed; the only way for the United States to "save" China was by major war and—rightly or wrongly—Americans were un-

---

[17] See Edward Mead Earle, "A Half-Century of American Foreign Policy: Our Stake in Europe, 1898–1948," *Political Science Quarterly* (June, 1949). See also Foreign Policy Research Institute, University of Pennsylvania, *United States Foreign Policy: Western Europe* (Washington: U. S. Government Printing Office, 1959), pp. 11–16.

willing to go so far.[18] The communist victory upset the line of containment even before it was clearly drawn; communist power had reached the open sea. A rapid recalculation of the situation, however, pointed out a way to escape the worst effects of this setback.

A New Position in the Far East.

Communist sea power was too weak to capitalize fully on the new advantage it had gained by the capture of China. The United States accordingly drew a new line of containment along the chain of island groups that fringe the Asiatic mainland. The Philippines, Formosa, Okinawa, and Japan became fixed points upon which was based a mobile screen of sea and air power to contain communism at the water's edge. This was admittedly a makeshift, but it served the purpose surprisingly well. American reorientation in the Pacific was emphasized by a favorable security treaty with Japan in 1960 that was aimed at making that country into an anti-communist outpost, an offshore anchor (like Great Britain) of the ring of containment.

The Pattern and the Korean War.

From the point of view of this global pattern, North Korea's aggression in 1950 was another communist attempt to break through the ring, this time by the technique of military force. To remain consistent with its announced policy, the United States was required to resist this move as it had all earlier ones. South Korea itself was not actually indispensable to the American perimeter—as Secretary of State Acheson had intimated in an often-quoted but as often deliberately misunderstood statement early in 1950. Blocked from further expansion by revolution, by propaganda, or by diplomacy, the communists attempted open war in Korea. The American purpose was to halt communism militarily as was already being attempted economically and politically.

The Southern Arc.

It was along the southern segment of the Eurasian arc that some of the most complicated problems arose. In the Middle East the United States made a little progress: it kept the Arab-Israeli quarrel from flaming into open war until late in 1956, it shored up the "northern tier"—Turkey, Iran, and Pakistan—by affiliating with the Central Treaty Organization

---

[18] See Secretary of State Acheson's letter of transmittal of the "China White Paper" in 1949: "The unfortunate but inescapable fact was that the ominous result of the civil war in China was beyond the control of the government of the United States." *United States Relations with China* (Washington: U. S. Government Printing Office, 1949), p. xvi.

(CENTO) after the 1958 failure of the Baghdad Pact, and formulated the "Eisenhower Doctrine" in 1957 that threw American protection over the states of the Middle East. It was under the terms of the latter policy that American forces landed in Lebanon in 1958 and stabilized a potentially dangerous situation. It had no luck with India, whose refusal to commit itself kept Russia at bay but also frustrated American efforts to mobilize south Asia. In southeast Asia, the United States was more unsuccessful than otherwise. Thailand and the Philippines were at least partially won for the West, but Burma and Indonesia followed India's neutralist lead, while Indochina was divided with communism and Malaya was barely saved from it.

A Ten-Year Trial Balance.

How did the United States fare in the first ten years of the cold war? The original line had been modified, both favorably and unfavorably; American losses in Asia were to some extent offset by Yugoslavia's at least partial defection from the Soviet camp and by the appearance of obvious cracks in the Soviet's belt of satellites. Europe was comparatively stable, although not yet completely organized. The Far East, although uneasy and potentially explosive, was at least temporarily tenable. South and southeast Asia were worrisome; political and economic instability, communist-led civil war, and Indian-style "neutralism" all seemed to make this region a likely target for Muscovite pressure. The Middle East seethed with internal pressures and Soviet probing. All in all, however, we can say that the policy had paid off; Soviet expansionism had been largely stopped. By 1956, it seemed as if world politics approached balance—or stalemate.

THE PATTERN AND THE PUBLIC

Any foreign policy must be grounded in consensus, regardless of how this mass approval is brought into being. This is especially true in a democracy. How did containment fare with the American public during these ten years, and to what extent did popular attitudes influence its execution?

The Popularity of Containment.

There is no doubt that containment, at least during its heyday, was genuinely popular with the American people. It served the controlling version of the national interest, and at the same time provided a necessary outlet for some of the powerful emotions engendered by the stresses of the postwar period. The world after 1945 was a confusing and frustrating arena for a relatively uninformed and unsophisticated people. Coping with indigestible problems, truculent enemies, fractious allies, and the inscrutable processes of history made many Americans irritable, hostile, and impatient. Containment gave Americans the opportunity to say "no" as often as they pleased and yet glow in the certainty that such behavior was actually serving a real purpose. It took a number of years for this attitude to begin to wear off.

American Negativism.

The most conspicuous characteristic of American attitudes during the cold war has been their essential negativism. The United States has accepted a policy line whose ultimate goal is international agreement, but the American people have often acted as if they feared agreeing with anybody. The practice of containment has made much of the nation behave as if America had a vested interest in the cold war, as if it were afraid of peace.

This negativism has concentrated on the largely hypothetical danger of appeasing Russia. "Appeasement," in this context, has meant making any concessions at all to Russian interest. So obsessed have Americans been with the possibility of being seduced into an unfortunate capitulation that they have lost much of their sense of purpose and their confidence in their ability to hold their own. Mass fixation upon the evil of communism has proved an unstable base for constructive policy. It has instead made the "crisis" approach of Washington almost the only certain way to win popular approval of policy moves. Far too many programs have been accepted by the public for no other reason than that they were certain to be resented and objected to by the Soviet Union. Even so morally ambivalent an issue as the "U-2" espionage flights over the Soviet Union was for many Americans resolved as being perfecly acceptable on no more solid basis than that Khrushchev and his associates became angry about them.

The Over-emphasis on the Soviet.

Perhaps the greatest failure of American public opinion has been its fixation on the problem of Russia. Although in principle the cold war is only an interruption in the orderly development of a rational American policy, in practice the menace of the USSR has largely dominated the public mind. Analytically Americans see Moscow at the root of most of their difficulties—even though, as sometimes has happened, other factors are responsible.[19] Operationally the United States tends to make the Soviet

---

[19] A classic instance occurred shortly after Premier Khrushchev's visit to the United States in September, 1959. Secretary of State Herter announced that the U. S. would hold the Soviet "responsible" for any actions of Communist China. *New York Times* (October 7, 1959).

the immediate target of almost every policy move, regardless of the extent to which the issue may be involved in the cold war.

This has led to two different embarrassments. First, it has proved to be difficult to keep Soviet policy in any kind of perspective; Americans have often overestimated Soviet power as grossly as they once underestimated it. The second unfortunate result of American Russophobia has been a tendency to misjudge specific problems. Since Russia was the only concern, Americans have felt little need to familiarize themselves with the situational details of problems. Local forces and local issues have often been either ignored as insignificant or arbitrarily distorted to fit a cold-war mold. America's policy toward its allies had only one object, and a short-range one at that: to force the states along the Soviet frontier to become vocally anti-communist and to join actively in a political and military alliance against Moscow. By 1956 considerable evidence had accumulated that this had been one of the least successful enterprises of the United States.

The Confusion of Ends and Means.

Another shortcoming of American policy brought about by public attitudes has been a frequent confusion of ends and means. Containment, as we have suggested, was in the largest sense a tactical policy in support of the general strategic goal of bringing the Soviet to the point of settlement on a mutually acceptable basis.

Under a steady diet of tension, crisis, and frustration, Americans have made the cold war a way of life. Moves originally conceived of as maneuvers to an end have become converted into fixed stars in the American policy firmament; no more glaring example could be cited than the stubborn insistence that all American security pacts are forever beyond amendment or even discussion. Each encounter with the Soviet is viewed as a near-cosmic struggle for total stakes, with the first casualty in practice being the issue's place in any general plan. All proportion is in constant danger of being lost; each controversy with the USSR is just as important as any other. "Victory" in the particular context—regardless of any other considerations—is what outraged public sensibilities demand.

American Inflexibility.

What the confusion of ends and means has meant in practice has been great inflexibility in approach. The wooden and mechanical quality of much of American policy has been a far cry from its original intention.[20]

---

[20] See Hughes, *America the Vincible*, and Rockefeller Brothers Fund, *The Mid-Century Challenge to U. S. Foreign Policy* (Garden City: Doubleday & Co., 1959), for suggestions of how to restore American flexibility.

The pattern demanded steadfastness and tenacity in purpose, it is true; in operation, however, it called for great flexibility. The United States was supposed to meet the Soviet threat in the form in which it presented itself, allowing always for great variety in Russian techniques. Rather than to pursue a single line, America was supposed to employ methods varying according to time, place, and circumstances.

Instead, the United States staked out a series of fixed positions and held to them grimly; it developed a limited battery of techniques and insisted that each problem in the endless series could be dealt with by dollars, guns, or "information." The more pressure Moscow applied, the more insistent the United States became upon clinging to methods tried and true. There seems to have been little desire to overhaul the American approach or to frame possible bases for realistic compromise.

Something like a Maginot-line complex came to be grafted onto what had been originally a concept of flexible defense. For several years after 1947 Soviet policy-makers kept battering themselves in frontal attacks on the line of containment, while ignoring tempting opportunities to hit the United States where its ideological flanks or its political rear were exposed. It was not until the Kremlin initiated (what we call later in this chapter) the "new" cold war that the fuller implications of American rigidity became apparent.

The Imitation of the Soviet.

The longer the negative and inflexible aspect of containment remained dominant, the more the United States (at least superficially) came to resemble the Soviet. Unconsciously, as Washington searched for new techniques of resistance, the United States came to adopt many of the very practices it was opposing. Many Americans learned to think of foreign policy in terms verging upon the totalitarian; they developed an emotional preference for military methods, subversion, and other avenues of "direct action"; [21] the American government fell into the trap of attempting to dictate to its allies, just as Moscow was doing to the satellites. The distinction between Moscow's policy and Washington's dwindled; to some uncommitted peoples, the apparent goal of the United States was to be just like the Russians but to be better at it than the Russians were. So far had the United States wandered from its original path.

---

[21] In this connection it is interesting to note that the American defense on the "U-2" issue before the UN Security Council made much of Soviet espionage as justifying the American action. See remarks of Ambassador Henry Cabot Lodge, reported in *New York Times* (May 24, 1960).

"LIBERATION"

The presidential election of 1952 provided the occasion for a fairly systematic attempt to reshape the pattern of American policy as it had developed up to that time. This reappraisal grew out of widespread popular dissatisfaction with the frustrations of containment, and was fed by the partisan fires of a heated electoral campaign. Its brief heyday is important to us because of the new light it threw on the fundamentals of the pattern of American policy.

The Indictment of Containment.

By the time of the 1952 campaign, the cold war had stabilized into a more or less equal stalemate. Both sides had made their basic commitments and neither had discovered any expedient means to break the impasse into which they drifted. The American people, grown familiar with the requirements of the role they were playing, began to find fault with it.

The first charge in the popular indictment of containment boiled down to the claim that it never seemed to get anywhere. It did not spell out any clear objectives. It called for constant effort, directed to no visible purpose except an adamant anti-Soviet line and the neutralization of each of an interminable series of crises.

Containment also failed, Americans said, because it produced no victories. It furnished neither a sense of accomplishment nor any standards by which to measure progress. Its greatest successes were "silent": American action had prevented many unfortunate things from happening. But these were negative, and a steady diet of stalemate had not proved nourishing. Americans were hungry for real, positive success over which they could feel proud and from which they could draw courage for future struggles.

It seemed also as if the United States was always on the defensive and that containment robbed it of any initiative. The United States was obliged to stand fast under an infuriating barrage of communist insult and provocation. Even when a crisis permitted psychic release in national action, mass frustrations were never fully satisfied. American moves were scrupulously limited to exactly what would neutralize communist pressure or, at best, to what would restabilize the original situation on the basis of the status quo ante.

A final objection to American policy in 1952 was a traditional one: it cost too much. The military budget and the international commitments made under its terms seemed to many Americans to be out of all proportion to what the United States was receiving in return. Some political leaders detected a demand by the public either for more results from the foreign-policy investment or else a reduction in its cost.[22]

The "Liberation" Formula.

The formula of "liberation," advertised as a substitute for and an improvement upon containment, was originally the creation of the "radical right" wing of the Republican party. As the electoral campaign of 1952 developed, the doctrine was adopted as party policy by the Republican leadership, and the Eisenhower victory was thought by many to be a mandate to put it into practice.

"Liberation" was tailored to meet each of the major objections to containment.[23] It had a concrete and realizable objective: the rollback of communist power from the places into which it had expanded, and the liberation of the captive and satellite areas of eastern Europe and Asia. It promised clear-cut victories over the Soviet: short-run triumphs accompanying each phase of the rollback, and finally Moscow's surrender as communism became caught in a steadily worsening position. It proclaimed the end of the defensive in American policy: the United States was finally to assume the initiative, mount offensives against the Soviet, and gain the satisfaction that containment had denied it. And—for many the best of all—it was to cost a great deal less in money, manpower, and anxiety. Victory, said the Republicans, could be won without economic strain or the danger of war.

The Rationale of "Liberation."

At any rate, "liberation" purported to call for a new grand strategy. The United States was to abandon the defensive and to seek out the Soviet where Moscow was weak and America was strong. The frontier of communist expansion would be driven back; Americans would no longer wait for Russian moves before taking action themselves. The United States would assume the tactical initiative.

Preventive war—or any form of military aggression—was of course ruled out, but every form of nonviolent attack was to be pressed to the maximum. The United States was to apply economic pressures ruthlessly, subvert communist regimes, encourage and subsidize resistance movements

---

[22] A serious attempt to invalidate containment and to substitute a much more limited policy was made by Senator Robert A. Taft in his *A Foreign Policy for Americans* (Garden City: Doubleday & Company, 1951).

[23] The most ambitious attempt to provide a theoretical rationale for liberation was made by James Burnham, in his polemic, *Containment or Liberation?* (New York: John Day, 1953).

behind the Iron Curtain, step up the propaganda offensive, and give no ground before communist counterattacks.

Eastern Europe was an obvious first target. Satellite resistance to Soviet domination was apparent; why else did Moscow feel compelled to purge, to reprimand, and constantly to re-indoctrinate the "friendly" regimes there? If the United States could step up its pressure sufficiently, it might well touch off a chain reaction that would drive the Kremlin to cover. Breaking open satellite resistance would either destroy Russian control in eastern Europe or would make Moscow tighten its grip so as to hold on—thus weakening Russia vis-a-vis the rest of the world. Either outcome would be a net gain for the United States.

What worked in Eastern Europe might work in Russia itself. A policy of liberating the Ukrainians, the White Russians, the Baltic peoples, and the several submerged populations of Soviet Asia had unlimited prospects. There was no logical stopping place to the rollback short of the Kremlin walls themselves; at the very least, if the Soviets were kept busy trying to put down rebellions in their own domains they would have neither time, interest, nor capability to undertake further expansion.

Military policy was also to be different. The United States would fight no more little wars, no more Koreas. American armed might was not to be dissipated in stopping aggressions chosen by Moscow for their nuisance value or for their debilitating effect on the United States. America was no longer to foil aggression in one place only to let the communists escape to plot more moves in other parts of the world.

American military power was to have a role primarily political. It was initially to serve as a deterrent, threatening total war on the Kremlin in "massive retaliation" [24] for any outbreak, even a minor one. Ultimately, American superiority—especially in nuclear weapons and in air power— would be a major element in forcing a final peace although it would probably not be necessary ever to resort to open war with the Soviet. This general notion was elaborated into the famous "new look" in defense, discussed in detail in Chapter 13.

The Failure of "Liberation."

If the doctrine of "liberation" had any real value, it lay in the debate it provoked. The underlying assumptions of American policy were brought again into public awareness during the recurrent controversies over foreign policy that filled the Eisenhower administrations. The action program called

---

[24] The phrase was apparently first used by Secretary of State John Foster Dulles in January, 1954, in an address before the Council on Foreign Relations (*New York Times,* January 13, 1954), but the principle itself is an integral part of the broader theory of liberation.

for by "liberation" was questionable at best, and it was rapidly rendered obsolescent by the rapid development of the cold war between 1953 and 1958. Today most of the debate has primarily historical value, and only a significant modification in American defense policy remains as a monument to the hypothesis of the rollback.[25]

THE NEW COLD WAR

What invalidated the premises and the conclusions alike of the doctrine of "liberation" was the major change in Soviet tactics in the cold war that became apparent during 1954 and 1955. The new line had been in the making ever since Stalin's death, but came out into the open after the "summit" conference of 1955. The Soviet offensive changed character and American replies, although still conceived within the original pattern, had to be framed in new terms. A new cold war was being fought.

The Shift in Soviet Tactics.

The Soviet line in the new cold war was different in many ways from the Stalin formula; perhaps the simplest way to characterize it is to call its approach to the West "soft," in contrast to the "hard" line identified with Stalin. It apparently called for the abandonment of military aggression or its threat; even the vituperation that the world had grown to accept as a normal concomitant of Moscow's policy was minimized from time to time. Ideological weapons were downgraded as well. Primary trust was placed in economic techniques such as trade agreements, technical cooperation, purchase credits, and so on. Russia was seeking to win consent to its policy rather than coercing acquiescence; Soviet moves were undertaken in harmony with protestations of sweet reasonableness and mutual good will, although with a shrewd admixture of military threats.

Soviet policy also acquired a new set of targets. The Kremlin ceased trying to break through the ring of containment; the network of alliances had proved adequate to hold back direct Russian pressure. Instead Moscow concentrated on the "neutrals," the uncommitted peoples of Asia and Africa. It wooed these states with soft and nonideological words and with tempting offers of economic and political assistance. By emphasizing nonpolitical action, by employing a "strategic" (what one author

---

[25] The failure to find any way to intervene into the Hungarian rebellion in 1956 chilled the enthusiasm of the "liberators." It is noteworthy that after that date American relations with East Europe were scrupulously correct. See, for a semi-formal recantation by a prominent "liberator," James Burnham, "Liberation: What Next?," *National Review* (January 19, 1957).

defines as an "indirect" [26]) approach, the Kremlin was able to breach the line of containment by simply leaping over it. Early maneuvers in the new cold war won the Russians significant victories in Southeast Asia, the Middle East, and Africa.

The Modification in the American Pattern.

American understanding of and reaction to the new Soviet approach was slow—perhaps unnecessarily so—in developing. It seemed to many Americans as if something dazzlingly new had been unveiled by Soviet strategists, and for many months the United States found itself unable either to grasp the significance of the new attack or to devise effective countermeasures.

This did not have to be such a problem. If Americans had recalled the original foundations of their policy and had sloughed off the Russophobe and militarist deviants of the containment hypothesis, the general line of American policy would have been clearer. The purely military phase of American policy had largely achieved its purpose by 1955; the Soviet leaders gave evidence of being convinced of the folly of armed adventure outside the Iron Curtain. Now that Moscow had developed new measures of expansion, these same fundamentals could be called on to point the way to new American counterstrokes appropriate to the nature of the threat.

During the second Eisenhower Administration, no major progress was made toward such a reappraisal of the American response to the new Soviet challenge; we shall examine what was done in the chapters that follow this one. President John F. Kennedy, on taking office in January, 1961, seemed to call for wholesale rethinking of United States policy and in his inaugural address urged a fresh look at the problem and a new beginning. The world watched and wondered what the United States would do next.

---

[26] B. H. Liddell Hart, *Strategy* (New York: Praeger, 1954).

The
Cold
War:
Ebb
and
Flow

CHAPTER ◀ *11* ▶

The major ingredient in the history of American foreign policy since 1947 has been the ebb and flow of the cold war. Despite the pressing dilemmas confronting the United States in every part of the world and the difficult decisions they have forced, the attempt to meet the continuing menace of Soviet expansion has provided the continuing thread of American action and decision.

This chapter is an attempt at an overview of the cold war. Many items of detail are mentioned whose discussion will be deferred until later chapters. Its purpose is to furnish a generalized historical perspective of the phases into which the cold-war era can be divided that might provide a background for our later evaluation of current problems.

We shall give conceptual unity and sequence to this period by using the analytical notion of "bipolarity." By this term we mean a fundamental assumption implicit in the cold war, embodying two basic characteristics: (1) the principal antagonists, the United

States and the USSR, oppose and repel each other at all points, just as do opposite poles on a magnet; (2) all the other states in the world are drawn —again by analogy with a magnet—toward one pole or the other. Thus, a bipolar world is one neatly divided into two totally opposing camps, with no states remaining permanently aloof from such arrangement.

Bipolarity as the governing assumption of the cold war has passed through three different stages. The first phase, from early 1947 to the onset of the Korean war in 1950, was a period during which the idea of bipolarity was evolving and winning acceptance as the dominant rule of world affairs. The second, the era of total stalemate in great-power relations, extended from 1950 to the end of the 1954 Geneva Conference; this was the era of bipolarity dominant. Since then a "new cold war" has been in process, marked by the gradual dissolution of the bipolar construct. The turning point was the Geneva summit conference (1955) when both great powers recognized the nuclear stalemate and decided they would not resort to war to settle their disagreements. So pronounced did the change become that even the ugly crises stirred up by the "U-2" affair and the Congo imbroglio did not cause more than a temporary disturbance. By 1961 the operating assumptions of bipolarity had lost much of their validity.

CONTAINMENT: THE EVOLUTION OF BIPOLARITY, 1947–1950

The American assumptions about Soviet behavior and the policy necessary to cope with it found the United States largely unprepared for the mission it had assumed. The first period of American action was therefore devoted to two related if dissimilar tasks: coping with short-run crisis and developing capabilities and procedures for the long-range program that lay ahead. By 1950 the methods of American bipolar policy had largely stabilized; this precision in technique, however, was not matched by an equally clear understanding of the specific goals and objectives the United States was pursuing.

First Steps in Containment

The Problem.

The problem of the United States in 1947 can be simply stated. Soviet influence, operating from a secure base inside Russia, was pressing outward in all directions. Eastern Europe had already fallen to Moscow; the Middle East lay almost defenseless; in the Far East the new power situation left the Soviet as the major factor in China and a controlling participant in East Asian politics. Of the areas immediately contiguous to the Soviet heartland, only south Asia—protected by the Himalayan barrier—seemed relatively safe, at least for the moment.

The line the United States had drawn to defend varied in its suitability. In some areas it was natural and more or less defensible (the northern frontiers of Turkey, Iran, and Afghanistan); in others it was artificial, difficult, and complex (such as the interzonal boundary in Germany, the 38th parallel in Korea, and the northern frontier of Greece).

Crucial Area: Europe.

It was obvious that the United States could not defend the entire ring simultaneously; some system of priorities was needed. The situation, however, permitted of little discussion. Western Europe—especially France and Italy—was, if not the weakest link in the chain, at least the most endangered. The Middle East, torn by the Greek "civil war," represented at the moment a more localized threat; Asia seemed sufficiently quiet that action—although probably ultimately necessary—might safely be postponed.

Europe's central role in the cold war was not alone due to its vulnerability. It was an immensely valuable prize, either to the USSR or the United States. It contained over 200 million people, highly industrialized and technically proficient, and was of major military and political significance. The common defense against Nazi authoritarianism underscored the determination of the United States to make Europe the scene of its first organized stand against Soviet expansion.[1]

Retooling at Home.

But the decision to act against the Soviet and to defend Europe meant little in itself. Between 1945 and 1947 the United States had tried its best to leave behind both the war and wartime ways of thought. Although the utter unconcern of the immediate postwar period had given way by 1947 to a deep disquiet over the burgeoning Soviet threat, there was relatively little public awareness of the future requirements of American policy.

The government, therefore, was obliged to move slowly. With the Greek crisis as a pretext, Selective Service was enacted early in 1947, but was not put to immediate use in the rebuilding of American military power. Beginnings were made at preparing for economic mobilization. New organ-

---

[1] For a sympathetic study of Europe on the eve of the cold war, see Barbara Ward, *The West at Bay* (New York: W. W. Norton & Co., Inc., 1948).

izational measures, such as the unification of the armed services and the reorganization of the Department of State, were put into effect; new agencies (the National Security Council, the Central Intelligence Agency) were established. But this retooling was more preparatory than operational. Almost by default, the "brush fire" technique of moving breathlessly from crisis to crisis became the accustomed way of doing business.

ECONOMIC AND MILITARY AID

With Europe the area of primary concern, and with the immediate danger being that of economic and political collapse preceding a series of communist revolutions, emergency moves were obviously required. American cold-war policy began as a result with programs of economic and military aid.

The Truman Doctrine.

The first overt step was the "Truman doctrine," formulated and expressed in March, 1947. The inability of Britain to sustain its commitments to the pro-western government in Greece transferred the burden of holding back communist expansion to the United States.[2] President Truman, on March 12, proposed to Congress that extensive military and economic aid be extended to Greece (and Turkey) so as to hold back the Soviet: "... it must be the foreign policy of the United States to support free peoples who are resisting attempted subjugation by armed minorities or by outside pressure...."[3] After over two months of heated debate, the Greek-Turkish Aid Bill of 1947 was approved, but only after specific assurances had been given that the broader doctrinal implications of the measure did not represent any fixed commitment. No one doubted, however, that a precedent had been set.

The Marshall Plan.

The Truman Doctrine had been an avowedly emergency measure aimed at a particular crisis point. Unless the United States was prepared to dis-

---

[2] See Joseph M. Jones, *The Fifteen Weeks* (New York: The Viking Press, 1955), for a thorough account of this period.

[3] John C. Campbell and staff, *The United States in World Affairs, 1947–48* (New York: Harper & Bros., Inc., 1948), p. 33. Data through 1954 have largely been drawn from this valuable series of annual volumes written by the staff of the Council on Foreign Relations. The Truman message is in the *Department of State Bulletin* (March 23, 1947), p. 536. Other recent interpretations of American cold-war policies include W. W. Rostow, *The United States in the World Arena* (New York: Harper & Brothers, 1960), and John W. Spanier, *American Foreign Policy Since World War II* (New York: Frederich A. Praeger, 1960).

sipate its substance in an endless series of such moves, a broader program was needed. This realization prompted the more ambitious "Marshall Plan" and the later ECA.

The popular name of the American aid program came from its first specific expression in a speech by Secretary of State Marshall at Harvard University in June 1947.[4] He offered the prospect of large-scale American aid to the battered European economy. This was, however, no invitation for a mass raid on the American treasury; he attached certain important qualifications to the suggestion.

The initiative, he declared, must come first from the European states themselves. Furthermore, European participation in any program must be based on the maximum of self-help and mutual aid by the participating states, thus demanding extensive intra-European cooperation as a prior condition to grants from the United States. The United States would not extend aid in a mutually contradictory and competitive system of single-nation programs.

The European states moved quickly. After first forcing Moscow to oppose the plan openly, sixteen western European states met in Paris in July. Out of this conference grew the Organization for European Economic Cooperation (OEEC) that was to do yeoman service in coordinating the American aid program in Europe. The conference estimated a need of eight billion dollars to cover the "dollar gap" for 1948 and a four-year program of $22.4 billion.

Once the Marshall Plan came before Congress, one subtle but important change occurred that was to become increasingly important in future American policy. Originally ERP was conceived as a positive program aimed at moving the United States closer to its own long-term goal by helping to create an area of peace, order, and stability; under the pressure of political controversy, it developed into an admitted anti-Soviet move. This changed its context to a considerable extent and, with it, the direction of a good deal of later American thinking.

Eventually, after long debate, Congress passed the bill as the Foreign Assistance Act of 1948 and authorized $5.3 billion for the European program. Smaller amounts were added for Greece, Turkey, and China. The United States had taken the first step toward bipolarity.[5]

Military Aid: MDAP.

The Marshall Plan was limited to economic assistance; the United States, however, had already broadened its plan to encompass military aid.

---

[4] Text of speech in *New York Times* (June 6, 1947).

[5] See Henry Bayard Price, *The Marshall Plan and Its Meaning* (Ithaca: Cornell University Press, 1955).

The Greek-Turkish aid bill had called for the supply of military equipment, particularly to Turkey. It was not until the Military Defense Assistance Program (MDAP) was launched in 1949, however, that military aid became a key aspect of American policy. In the first year of MDAP, one billion dollars was authorized for military assistance to the signatories of the North Atlantic Treaty, and over 300 million for specified nonsignatories (Greece, Turkey, Korea, the Philippines, and Kuomintang China).

THE BEGINNINGS OF ALLIANCE

If containment were to hold Moscow in check, the free world had great need of unity. So long as each non-communist state depended only upon itself for its continued existence, Moscow would enjoy a great advantage over most of the adversaries it confronted. The next move for the free world, therefore, was toward coordination of policy and defense.

If the United States was to expect that the democratic states of the world would agree to stand fast against Soviet pressure, an equivalent pledge would have to be made by Americans. The old bugaboos of "entangling alliances" and "fixed commitments" would have to be set aside; even the most unregenerate isolationists agreed that Washington's "Farewell Address" no longer provided a complete blueprint for American action. The resistance to Soviet aggression would rest instead on a foundation of exchanged pledges of joint action incorporated in hard-and-fast alliances.

The Rio Pact (1947).

The history of American alliances since 1947 demonstrates one of the truisms of international affairs: an alliance can be built only upon a predetermined area of shared interest. As might have been expected, the first mutual-security pact the United States consummated was in an area in which this harmony was already elaborately developed: Latin America.

During the summer of 1947 an Inter-American Conference for the maintenance of hemisphere peace and security, meeting at Brazil's summer capital of Petropolis, drafted the Rio Pact, known officially as the Inter-American Treaty of Reciprocal Assistance. This instrument made mutual defense the rule within the Americas.[6] All the signatories pledged joint action in case of an act of aggression against any of them, whether arising within or without the hemisphere. Action could also be taken on "any fact or situation" which might endanger the peace, even if not distinguishable

---

[6] See Edgar S. Furniss, Jr., "The U. S., the U. N., and the Inter-American System," *Political Science Quarterly* (September, 1950).

as an "aggression." Joint action was to follow consultation; a decision to act taken by two-thirds of the signatories bound all of them. No state, however, was pledged to use armed force without its consent.[7]

The North Atlantic Treaty (1949).

By 1949 it had become clear that another American step was due in Europe. The economic aid program, by revitalizing Europe's economy, had intensified Moscow's opposition. Just as the likelihood of communist revolt faded due to domestic stability, the prospect of Russian military attack in Europe increased.

The North Atlantic Treaty, finally negotiated in April, 1949, was the instrument by which this step was taken. By this document the 12 signatories (the United States, Canada, Britain, France, Italy, Belgium, the Netherlands, Luxembourg, Portugal, Iceland, Denmark, and Norway) entered into an engagement to keep the peace among themselves and to resist aggression jointly. An attack on one would be an attack on all; consultation and collective action were to take place according to automatic procedures.

Always with an eye on the United States Senate, American negotiators pointedly refrained from including any promise of the automatic commitment of armed force without a declaration of war, but this was virtually a technicality. Both the MDAP and the strategic planning that followed the ratification of the treaty put the United States in a position that left little room for American equivocation if the guarantee were ever to be put into effect.[8]

Thus by 1950 the United States had succeeded in tying two highly sensitive areas, Latin America and western Europe, into a mutual security system that seemed destined to grow. There remained great segments of the ring of containment whose stabilization had not yet been attacked systematically, especially the Middle East, south Asia, and southeast Asia. But during the first phase of the cold war—what we might call the European period—American alliances bulked large in the developing bipolar structure.

---

[7] For specific provisions, see pp. 361–62 below.

[8] A useful survey of the rationale of the treaty and of the circumstances surrounding its ratification is Halford L. Hoskins, *The Atlantic Pact* (Washington: Public Affairs Press, 1949); see also Blair Bolles, *The Armed Road to Peace* (New York: Foreign Policy Association, 1952). For more recent appraisals, see Massimo Salvadori, *NATO: A Twentieth-Century Community of Nations* (Princeton: D. Van Nostrand Company, Inc., 1957), Gardner Patterson and Edgar S. Furniss, Jr., *NATO: A Critical Appraisal* (Princeton: Princeton University Conference on NATO, 1957), and Klaus Knorr, ed., *NATO and American Security* (Princeton: Princeton University Press, 1959).

We have already suggested that the American fixation on the Soviet gave rise to some distortion in American policy. Even more serious than the misinterpretation of specific relationships and problems was the tendency in the United States to overlook or to minimize events that did not fit a narrow cold-war pattern. Prior to 1950 at least three crises occurred whose eventual significance was largely missed in Washington and that were destined to return later to plague the United States. Among these were the Palestine problem, the birth of India, and the Indonesian revolution.

Palestine.

American policy toward the creation and development of the Republic of Israel is an issue of great complexity. Here we are interested primarily in the impact of cold-war thinking on the United States during the crisis arising from the partition of Palestine and the Arab-Israeli war.

During these events, the cold war impinged on American policy in two ways. First, the United States was keenly aware of the actual and potential significance of Middle East petroleum. "Oil politics" involved a two-pronged effort to keep the petroleum reserves of Iraq, Iran, Saudi Arabia, and the minor sheikhdoms from falling into Soviet hands and, as part of the same policy, to guarantee their permanent exploitation by the West.[9]

The second influence of cold-war thinking was more broadly oriented. Stability in each region was an objective of containment; crisis in any area along the Soviet periphery might offer tempting opportunities for Muscovite exploitation. America therefore sought a swift and peaceful end to the dispute on almost any mutually tolerable ground, arguing that even an imperfect solution would be in American interest if only it were reached peacefully.

There were, of course, other factors influencing American opinion during this period: humanitarianism, partisan politics, British pressure, and several others. But it would be difficult to prove that cold-war psychology played a lesser part than any of these; certainly the tenseness of Soviet-American relations precluded the possibility of many otherwise valid alternatives.

---

[9] See Benjamin Schwadran, *The Middle East, Oil, and the Great Powers* (New York: Praeger, 1956).

The Partition of India.

The 1947 crisis over the partition of India was likewise seriously misinterpreted by American statesmen. With the actual course of events the United States had of course little do do; the major American miscalculation was in assaying the results.

As Washington saw it, India and Pakistan—once freed from British rule—would automatically side with the West, and especially with the United States. It seemed axiomatic that democratically-inclined peoples, newly independent, would find common cause with Americans, who so long ago set the pattern of liberation. The Indian and Pakistani ruling classes were western-trained and anti-communist; Britain's withdrawal from India was generally regarded as guaranteeing two recruits for the free world.

The easy assumption that India would follow the broad path to the western alliance proved false. Indian "neutralism," so puzzling to Americans in later years, could have been more easily foreseen in 1948 had not Americans been so prone to equate noncommunism with anti-communism. It was not for nearly a decade that the United States was to learn how vast the gap actually is between these two ideas.[10]

The Indonesian Revolution.

Cold-war thinking nearly led the United States seriously astray during the Indonesian revolution. Americans did not become really aware of the revolt in the former Netherlands Indies until 1948, and by that late date certain habits of thought had already developed. Revolution against an ally of the United States was perilously easy to classify as a communist enterprise, and Washington was reluctant to take a firm stand in favor of independence. Not until the Dutch had forfeited much American good will by repeated violations of their word did the United States exert any considerable pressure for a peaceful settlement and to support United Nations moves toward Indonesian independence. This hesitation sowed an unhappy harvest of Indonesian suspicion and distrust in later years.

THE DYNAMICS OF BIPOLARITY

As the American reaction to the Soviet threat crystallized, a dynamic of bipolarity was developed. Certain operational assumptions came to

---

[10] See F. S. C. Northrop, "Asian Mentality and United States Foreign Policy," in *Lessons from Asia*, ed. E. M. Patterson, *The Annals* (July, 1951); also Eleanor Roosevelt, *Indian and the Awakening East* (New York: Harper & Bros., Inc., 1953), p. 115.

underlie the planned moves of both sides; within broad limits the cold-war cycle became stabilized.

The Focus of American Policy.

By 1947, the United States had abandoned hopes for positive results from any direct negotiation with the Soviet. Relations with Moscow were therefore reduced to the minimum while American policy concentrated upon the organization of the free world. No great-power discussion would have any hope of profit until the power balance in the world had been stablized or—better still—until the West had some "situations of strength" of its own with which to bargain. The United States did its best, therefore, to ignore the Soviet and to capitalize on its freedom of action in the non-communist world.

The Agreement to Disagree.

To the extent to which contact with the Soviet was impossible to avoid the policy of the United States was based on an implicit "agreement to disagree" with the USSR. Regardless of the question, it became axiomatic that the American and Soviet positions would be diametrically opposed. Such opposition did not incorporate any real hope by either party that it might persuade the other or win any victories; the agreement to disagree was rather the most obvious indication of the totality of the cold war. When, by quirk of history, the United States and the USSR found themselves on the same side of a question (as on the Palestine issue), their mutual embarrassment was obvious.

The Elimination of Power Vacuums.

Both the United States and the Soviet, once the cold war had been "declared," sought to perfect the bipolar idea. This required the progressive elimination of the so-called "power vacuums": those states and regions that were as yet undeclared in the cold war.

When the cold war began in 1947, the leading power vacuum was China, where the Communist-Kuomintang civil war was about to reach full fury. In Europe the best-known example was, of course, Germany. Less important uncommitted areas included almost all of the Middle East, much of southeast Asia, Japan, and Korea. Indian independence added the Indian subcontinent to the list of future battlegrounds of the cold war.

Both Moscow and Washington enlisted partisans in each of the battleground states and fought the battle through them. Some of these areas were won by the communists, most notably China; others, like Greece and Iran, were saved for the West. The only overt loss of an ally suffered by either side during this period was Yugoslavia's defection from the communist camp; China's status as an ally of the West never became sufficiently formalized after 1945 to count the communist victory as a real minus for the United States in spite of its plus value to Moscow.

Direct Clash: Berlin.

The most open confrontation between East and West before 1950 was the Berlin crisis of 1948 and 1949. Its details are complex; [11] certain of its aspects, however, are relevant to the broader trends of the cold war.

Berlin was the first open test the Soviet made of American determination and American strength. It was important for Moscow to know that the United States was both willing and able to meet coercion with counterpressure. Berlin also stiffened the United States; the Soviet's stubborn and uncompromising attitude hardened American determination to carry containment through to completion.

Most significant of the implications of Berlin was that the issue was finally brought to the point of a time-buying compromise. Moscow, faced with a stabilized power situation, was willing to call a halt to its dynamism. The Soviet, confronted with equal pressure, had shown it would stop; it seemed reasonably safe to conclude that the Kremlin would recoil if faced by superior power. American assumptions had been vindicated.

STALEMATE: BIPOLARITY DOMINANT, 1950-1954

We cannot specify the precise date at which the United States and the USSR lost their freedom of maneuver and became caught by the inexorabilities of the logic of the two-power system. The closest we can come is to place it somewhere in the period beginning with the final victory of the communists in China and ending with the outbreak of the Korean war, although the atomic explosion in the USSR in September, 1949, was undoubtedly the major single event signalling the culmination of bipolarity. By the beginning of 1954 other forces had asserted themselves to the point that the maintenance of bipolarity became impossible.

THE KOREAN CONFLICT

The Korean conflict was at once the most important single element of the rigid cold-war era and its most meaningful symbol. The bloody and

---

[11] See Lucius Clay, *Decision in Germany* (Garden City: Doubleday, 1950) and Walter B. Smith, *My Three Years in Moscow* (Philadelphia: J. B. Lippincott Co., 1949). The diplomatic sequence is related in John C. Campbell, *The United States in World Affairs, 1948–49* (New York: Harper & Bros., Inc., 1949).

inconclusive battle that lasted from 1950 to 1953 was the high point both in the Soviet expansionist policy and in the containment effort of the United States. In its prosecution the bipolar principle received its most severe tests and eventually developed cracks under the pressure. In its indecisive resolution, the Korean struggle epitomized the impact of the cold war on the issues of world affairs.

Cold War in the Far East.

Between 1947 and 1950 the policy of the United States had concentrated on Europe. By 1950, however, a series of events in Asia had alerted the United States to the portentous fact that new arenas were being found for the East-West struggle.

First, and most importantly, the fall of Chiang Kai-shek and the triumph of Mao Tse-tung in China sounded a warning to Washington. Other indices of the broadening of the cold war were the Hukbalahap crisis in the Philippines, the worsening situation in Indochina, and the constant rumblings out of divided Korea. When open war came to the latter country in 1950, it was a strident indication that Communism—at least temporarily balked in Europe—was seeking compensation in Asia.[12]

The Cold-war Significance of Korea.

American leadership thought of the Korean war as a part of a larger policy whole. Korea was an example of a different technique—military force—put to serve the standard communist goal of expansion. The United States reasoned that its real enemy in Korea was neither Korea nor China, but rather the Soviet itself. American policy was therefore derived from an application of the basic principle of containment to the peculiar conditions prevailing in Korea. General MacArthur's more extreme views confused the issue but did not alter the outcome.[13]

One consequence of Korea was the identification of Red China with the Soviet. The active entry of Chinese troops in the Korean fighting and the participation of China in the truce negotiations removed whatever doubt remained about the direction the new regime would take. Henceforth Peking was assumed to be Moscow's most faithful ally.

Korea and Collective Security.

Although military action in Korea was carried on in the name of the United Nations, we must admit that the United States did not fight there in

---

[12] See Robert Payne, *Red Storm over Asia* (New York: The Macmillan Co., 1951), and O. O. Trullinger, *Red Banners over Asia* (Boston: Beacon, 1951).

[13] General MacArthur's views were dramatically presented in his address to a joint session of Congress after his recall from the Far East. See *New York Times* (April 20, 1951).

The Cold War: Ebb and Flow ✢ *299*

support of any abstraction called "collective security." National interest governed American action as it did the 15 other states that joined. The operating concept of the war can best be termed "collective defense" and the real significance of the struggle was the extent to which American alliances proved effective. The only other United Nations members who entered the fighting were those whose concern about Soviet expansionism approximated that of the United States or whose interest demanded the closest possible relations with Washington.

The Korean Crisis and the Free World.

On the other hand, the polarizing effect of the cold war created stresses within the ranks of the non-communist states. Americans had fallen into the habit of using the term "free world" to include loosely all states outside the Soviet orbit and to assume that all of them agreed generally with United States policy. This generalization, always an oversimplification, broke down badly as a result of the intensity of the Korean struggle and the growing militancy of the United States. Serious rifts were caused in what had seemed in 1950 to be an unbroken front against the USSR.

India was the principal defector. Nehru had approved the 1950 finding of aggression against North Korea; as the war wore on, however, he found elements of aggression and provocation in American leadership. By 1953, thoroughly disenchanted, India had carved out a self-styled position of noncommitment in the cold war and had brought along with itself a number of Asian states into what came to be called the "Arab-Asian" bloc.[14]

Even the closest allies of the United States, Britain and France, found much to complain of during the war. Britain protested the rigidly anti-Chinese tone of American policy; France felt that American concentration on victory in Korea obscured understanding of the serious issue in Indochina. The lesser associates of the United Nations forces had similar objections whose general import was that the United States was imposing purely American aims on a collective enterprise.

It cannot be said that the Korean war materially improved American relationships with the free world, while some uncommitted states were lost by American attitudes. By the time of the truce in 1953, bipolarity was losing much of its appeal for the smaller states.

The Korean Truce.

The end of the Korean war brought no settlement. The major point had been made by the West that communist expansion by force would be re-

---

[14] For a summary of the circumstances surrounding India's decision for neutrality, see *Major Problems of U. S. Foreign Policy, 1952–53* (Washington: Brookings Institution, 1953), "The Problem of India," pp. 251–55.

sisted as vigorously as would any other form. This, after all, was really all that could be proved by containment, and in these terms the Korean effort was successful.

But in a larger sense the issue of Korea epitomized the dilemma of the cold war. The USSR was seeking to extend the frontier of the communist world; the United States was dedicated to the frustration of this goal. Once both sides had committed their power, an inconclusive quarrel broken off by mutual consent was inevitable, at least if neither side was interested in precipitating total war. Neither dared go further without risking undesirable consequences; by the same token, neither could conveniently retreat. Diplomacy could discover a point of rough equilibrium at which to stop, but could not dispose of the issues.[15]

THE "MUTUAL SECURITY" CONTEXT

Once past the "crash" program of shoring up weak spots in the line of containment that occupied most of the American government's time between 1947 and 1950, the United States set about rationalizing its approach to the non-communist world by means of the concept of "mutual security." American policy after this date sought hard-and-fast military and political commitments from the free world instead of the more flexible (and more dynamic) formulas of the earlier period. All the programs with which the United States had already become identified—technical assistance, economic aid, information and propaganda, and even diplomatic maneuvers —were modified to fit the notion of mutual security.

The Shift to Military Planning.

The mutual-security context involved a military buildup of the free world, the conceptualization of the cold war as a quasi-military operation, an emphasis on military foreign aid, and the extension of the American security frontier to the Far East, the Middle East, and North Africa. Because this emphasis coincided in time with the Korean War, much of the public saw a connection between this effort and the achievement of military victory in Korea. Although the United States never really intended to "win" the war in the MacArthurian sense, Washington allowed the public to make the connection between Korea and mutual security; it made the military turn American policy had taken much more palatable. The new intellectual content given American policy at this time—as well as the public-relations guise it assumed—have both proved to be remarkably

---

[15] For a thorough discussion of American policy on the Korean episode, see Leland M. Goodrich, *Korea: A Study of United States Policy in the United Nations* (New York: Council on Foreign Relations, 1956).

resistant to changes in the external environment. The decisions made in 1950 are still largely controlling American policy today.

New Dimensions of American Aid.

"Mutual security" was most apparent in the new version of American aid. "Economic aid" on the model of ECA was submerged and made only a minor part of the program as "defense support"; military aid of the MDAP type became the core. The Mutual Security Act of 1951 made it a prerequisite of American assistance that the recipient country unequivocally place itself in support of the United States in the cold war and subscribe to the general foreign policy of the free world. The "technical assistance" program, originally nonpolitical, nonmilitary, and noncoercive, was absorbed into the mutual security concept and put to serve the same paramilitary purpose. The entire foreign-assistance program was geared to the necessity of creating a modernized, coordinated, and efficient military force in the free world capable of resisting any new communist military adventure.[16]

The Impact on the Free World.

The new mutual-security orientation of American policy further split the non-communist world. The approach had its most conspicuous success in Europe; in 1952 the North Atlantic Treaty Organization (NATO) was formed, Greece and Turkey adhered to the pact, and a beginning was made at developing common strategic plans and a harmonized level of military readiness. Buoyed by generous American military aid, the European members of NATO were prepared to support the American policy of the military defense of Europe along the line of the Iron Curtain.

A number of non-European states, however, found the new price of American aid too high. Assistance now required the acceptance of American political leadership (that frequently looked like domination) and the assumption of an overtly anti-Soviet orientation. Some smaller states argued that Washington was leaving them no real choice; to accept American aid was to forswear their independence and to make them more anti-Soviet than they cared to be, while to reject assistance was to leave themselves helpless before any Soviet pressure, whether open or covert.

The smaller states in Asia divided sharply over this issue. India, Indonesia, and Burma led in the formation of the "neutral" bloc; Pakistan, Thailand, the Philippines, Korea, and nationalist China accepted American

---

16 See *Major Problems of U. S. Foreign Policy, 1952–53,* pp. 123–6, "Recovery and Rearmament."

terms.[17] Despite the advantages accruing from the adherence of the latter group, the policy of forcing the smaller Asian nations to "stand up and be counted" resulted in the opening of serious gaps in the wall the United States was attempting to build against communist expansion.

Even in Europe, where American leadership was strongest, "mutual security" produced both resentment and resistance. Many Europeans felt that the United States was pushing them too rapidly and too far in hostility to Moscow. Americans often overlooked the impact of rearmament and militarization on the shaky economies and governments of Europe. Another common plaint was that the United States—so firmly committed to military resistance to the Soviet—was neglecting both the dangers of nonmilitary expansion and the opportunities for constructive negotiation with the Soviet.

MAJOR EUROPEAN TRENDS

While the more spectacular events of the cold war were taking place in Asia between 1950 and 1953, the struggle continued in Europe. Here, with less room for maneuver, the period was marked generally by a continuation and intensification of trends set in motion as early as 1947.

Toward European Integration.

American policy ever since the ECA had emphasized intra-European cooperation, and after 1950 the United States lent what aid it could to the evolving trend toward European integration. The "Schuman Plan" for the consolidation of the steel industries of France, West Germany, Italy, and Benelux countries received both warm encouragement and concrete support; so did the abortive project for a "European army," the European Defense Community (EDC). By 1954 it had become apparent that complete European integration was yet a long time off, but it was also evident that intra-European cooperation had reached a new peak and would probably continue to evolve.[18] This development was generally thought of as being definitely in the American interest.

West Germany and the Cold War.

The United States easily fitted West Germany into its mutual-security context. It moved in 1949 to propose German rearmament under Allied

---

[17] This was the era of the Far Eastern security pacts. New treaty arrangements in Asia dating from this era include a security pact with Japan (1953), one with the Philippines (1951), the ANZUS treaty with Australia and New Zealand (1951), the Korean treaty (1953), and the Nationalist China treaty (1954).

[18] For a compelling argument by a leading European, see Paul Raymond, *Unite or Perish* (New York: Simon and Schuster, 1951); see also F. S. C. Northrop, *European Union and United States Foreign Policy* (New York: The Macmillan Co., 1954).

control, in 1950 to include Germany within the aid program and to sponsor the creation of the Bonn government, and in 1952 to end the state of war by a treaty with Bonn. But the policy problems presented by Germany did not yield easily to American formulas.

The first major issue—how to incorporate Germany into the western defense system without frightening France or precipitating a total crisis with Moscow—was finally resolved in 1955. After the EDC project failed, the United States settled for German membership in NATO and also in the intra-European alliance, Western European Union (WEU). This opened the door to German rearmament, a project that was to bulk increasingly larger as the years went by.

The second problem was German reunification. Constantly concerned lest Bonn negotiate directly with the Soviet for the end of partition, the United States spared no effort to keep the Federal Republic happy with the bargain it had made with the West. Chancellor Konrad Adenauer earned a major debt of gratitude (and reaped a harvest of concessions as well) for his success in keeping the reunification problem from becoming acute.[19]

The Consolidation of Bipolarity: Yugoslavia and Spain.

As the cold war matured in Europe, the United States extended its ranks to include all states whose anti-Soviet orientation was strong enough to lead them into open opposition to Moscow. As a result there were added to the "free world" such oddly assorted (and "free" in only a highly technical sense) states as Yugoslavia and Spain. Yugoslavia's status as an outcast by Moscow made it willing to accept American aid and to fit itself— albeit reluctantly and with many backward looks—into the defense system of the West. Spain accepted a 1953 agreement with the United States whereby Madrid provided facilities for American bases in return for American aid. These moves left Switzerland, Sweden, and Finland the only European states outside the direct Soviet orbit that were not linked with the American security system.

SOVIET POLICY, 1950–1954

What was the Soviet doing during the period that American policy was at its most rigid? Granted the bipolar assumption, it was natural that Moscow's attitude should be the reciprocal of Washington's. The Soviet sought steadily to implement bipolarity on its side of the Iron Curtain.

---

[19] See James F. Warburg, *Germany: Key to Peace* (Cambridge: Harvard University Press, 1953).

Total Hostility.

Direct Soviet-American relationships continued as arid and unproductive as they had been ever since 1947. Moscow loudly protested an utter lack of confidence in American intentions. All possible differences with American policy were discovered and vigorously exploited. During the Korean war, the Soviet gave extensive aid to the communists; economic, military, and technical assistance were extended to Moscow's ideological brethren. The 1954 Geneva Conference saw the Soviet participate as spokesman and defender of the communist cause in opposition to the United Nations.

The Consolidation of the Soviet Sphere.

The Kremlin moved speedily to unify its own sphere. Eastern Europe was knit together in a complex of economic, political, and military pacts that perfected the pattern of satellitism. "Nationalist deviationism" in any form was ruthlessly suppressed. Satellite military forces were modernized with Soviet equipment; joint defense plans were worked out that reduced the armies of eastern Europe to the status of shock troops for the defense of the Soviet itself.

Communist China, with western doubts about its orientation removed after 1950, was brought squarely into Moscow's camp. The adherence of China was a great gain for the Soviet, even though in the future— particularly after Stalin's death—Peiping was to prove to be a troublesome and fractious ally, unwilling to accept the permanently subordinate place demanded of all close associates of the Soviet.[20]

The Attempt to Split the West.

As the power vacuums disappeared one by one and as the two camps sought to consolidate themselves, the major ingredient of Moscow's policy came to be a continuous attempt to split the free world. The American-led coalition was strong enough to hold Soviet ambitions in check; any new Russian successes had as a prerequisite the disruption of the western team.

In playing upon the open conflicts of interest within the West, the Soviet had two effective gambits. German reunification was usually good for an inter-allied crisis whenever Moscow brought it up; it became even more disruptive after the American plan for German rearmament began to be realized. The second device involved suggestions that a settlement of major East-West problems was possible if only the western coalition would dissolve; this was appealing to the weaker or less determined allies.

---

[20] See Boorman, *et al., Moscow-Peking Axis.*

Although these tactics were constantly annoying, they never seriously threatened allied unity; Moscow failed to split the West.

CLIMAX: INDOCHINA

The frustrating inconclusiveness of the Korean settlement presaged the end of the naked bipolar principle in international relations, but it was not until late 1954 that its final consequences were openly recognized. The Indochina crisis of that year and its stalemated settlement were the climax and the finale of the attempt to create the pure two-power world.

The Indochina Struggle.

The Indochina affair is relevant to the broader cold-war picture in two different ways. First, it was almost entirely a battle by proxies. Indochina was thus the cold war in microcosm: Moscow and Washington fought for Indochina by supporting partisan groups native to the country rather than by participating themselves. The second important fact about the Indochina crisis was that both sides, when faced with the likelihood of direct involvement in the war, drew back and accepted a time-buying compromise rather than to risk a repetition of Korea. Cold-war issues in an era of stalemate were as insoluble by hot war as they were by diplomacy.[21]

The Consequences of Stalemate.

The Geneva Conference of 1954 ended hostilities in Indochina without disposing of any of its problems. This was the familiar pattern of stalemate to which the world had grown accustomed—if not inured—since 1947. But the Geneva Conference brought some hard reflection in its wake that contributed largely to the change in the character of the cold war.[22]

Geneva proved beyond doubt that nothing was ever settled finally under the conditions of bipolarity. Communists knew (and, after the death of Stalin, could admit at least to themselves) that the 1947-style techniques of expansion had outlived their usefulness. Western techniques of resistance had proved capable of holding back Soviet expansion. Nuclear weapons had progressed to the point that any policy that might require total war had become obsolete. Some new dimensions of policy had to be discovered or the whole Soviet effort would grind to a standstill.

For the United States, Geneva provided the final vindication of con-

---

[21] For background material on Indochina, see Ellen Hammer, *The Struggle for Indochina* (Stanford: Stanford University Press, 1954).

[22] The work of the Conference is summarized in Claude Buss, *The Far East* (New York: The Macmillan Co., 1955), pp. 647–50.

tainment but also proved its inherent limitations. "Meeting force with force" would hold the communists back, but it was not especially useful in advancing toward the world of peace, order, and stability. New tactics seemed also to be called for by the West.

THE NEW COLD WAR: BIPOLARITY IN DECLINE, 1954–1961

The third and most recent phase of the cold war began immediately after the 1954 Geneva Conference. Bipolarity lost its grip and new international order began to appear. Why did the two-power world break up?

In the first place, many governments not directly involved in the great-power struggle found perpetual stalemate intolerable. Unable to accomplish any of their own major objectives because of the pervasiveness of the cold war, and facing the inability of the major antagonists to settle their own quarrel, more and more states overtly or covertly began to ignore the great powers in the prosecution of their own foreign policies.

The super-powers themselves recognized the extent to which they had lost their once-exclusive ability to control world politics. Partly because of the increasing determination of other states to make their own way, and partly because of the serious inhibitions military stalemate imposed on national policies, the Soviet and the United States toned down both the intensity and the dimensions of the cold war. Their relative positions did not appreciably change, and the issues between them remained as numerous and as difficult as ever; both realized, however, that uncomplicated total opposition has no outcome but futility, and both became aware that other issues demanding solution could no longer be ignored.

As of this writing, it is hard to escape the conclusion that the turn taken by world affairs since 1954 is a fundamental change rather than a mere tactical exercise or accidental aberration. There seems to be no technological or psychological way for the great powers to reimpose bipolarity on the world, short of a total war. Rightly or wrongly, this possibility has been ruled out by states everywhere except as a remote and catastrophic contingency. Bipolarity no longer has any real relevance to the concerns of American foreign policy.

The Renaissance of Flexibility

Perhaps the principal consequence of the abandonment of bipolarity was the rebirth of flexibility in international affairs. After the Geneva Conference, world politics lost most of their former monotonous predictability. New problems arose, old ones acquired a new guise, old alignments weakened, and almost every government found itself facing new opportunities for meaningful choice. For many, this was a much more congenial atmosphere; for others, who were less certain either of their objectives or of their ability to choose effectively, the new flexibility proved to be a mixed blessing. For much of the time since 1954, the United States has unfortunately found itself in the latter camp.

The Summit of 1955.

Although no formal agreements were reached, the "summit" meeting of July 1955 set the tone for the entire era. When President Eisenhower, Premier Bulganin and party leader Khrushchev of the Soviet, and the prime ministers of Britain and France met in Geneva, the whole world was watching. Although no formal treaty emerged from the meeting, the informal pledge exchanged by the United States and the Soviet never to go to war on one another immediately became one of the controlling rules of world affairs. The "spirit of Geneva"—an unfortunate journalistic invention —rapidly became tarnished by later crises, but the no-war pledge has never been seriously endangered. Freed from the dread prospect of deliberately-provoked nuclear holocaust, statesmen were able from 1955 onward to plan and act with fewer inhibitions and more confidence.[23]

The Rise of Neutralism.

The principal beneficiaries of the post-Geneva atmosphere were the states outside the cold war or those who managed to escape from it. Increasingly, states in the Afro-Asian world—most of them new, relatively weak, and underdeveloped—saw in their freedom of action new opportunities.[24] By shrewd diplomacy they played Moscow and Washington off against each other, securing more advantageous treatment from both than they could have ever hoped for from either. Nehru's India set the pattern, but several dozen states in Asia, the Middle East, and Africa followed India's example. Deliberate withdrawal from the cold war spread widely between 1954 and 1961. The "protection" of either great power—once a boon to be avidly sought—became instead an expensive hindrance for many states. And the more neutralism spread, the more helpless the United States and the Soviet became before it, and the more both were obliged to play the game the neutrals desired.

Neutralism contributed to the new flexibility in at least three ways. First, the increase in the number of effective participants in world politics

---

[23] See Pitman B. Potter, "The End of the Cold War," *American Journal of International Law* (October, 1955).

[24] See Hamilton F. Armstrong, "Neutrality: Varying Forms," *Foreign Affairs* (October, 1956).

restored something of the classic mechanism of the multistate system. Second, the General Assembly of the United Nations, where neutrals had their greatest effect, came to be a powerful voice in international relations. Third, neutralism vindicated the small state as a factor in world affairs; the day when the giants held the destiny of mankind in their exclusive keeping was over. The over-all impact of neutralism was to make the international order much more complex and difficult to manipulate, but at the same time it offered large and small states alike opportunities for action they had not had for decades.

The New States.

Related to neutralism is another factor of flexibility: the birth of a large number of new states. The twenty-odd states who first appeared between 1954 and 1961 contributed something distinctive to world politics. Almost all ex-colonies with no great love for the ways of great-power politics, such states as Ghana, Guinea, Malaya, and the Malagasy Republic brought a different orientation into the international arena. It became automatic to assume that any new state would be neutralist, that it would join and vigorously use the United Nations, and that it would champion the interests of small states against large ones. Under the collective impact of so many new states, the world found itself talking about different issues after 1954 than it had been occupied with in the bipolar era.

Tension in the Western Alliance.

The relaxation of bipolar rigidity had its effect on the American coalition. Freed from the need for constant coordination of policy under American leadership in the face of the Soviet threat, every state in the West found it possible to pursue other policy lines. The result was a series of intra-alliance tensions that sometimes unnecessarily vexed the United States but made little difference to the broader East-West confrontation.

The break from American leadership was sharpest in Europe, where each of the NATO allies to some extent defied the United States. Probably France was the most conspicuous. Beginning with the Suez crisis in 1956, she struck for full stature and independence of action in the western camp. After the return to power of General deGaulle in 1958, she moved quickly to assert herself as an atomic power, as the master of her own fate in Algeria, and as a partner in a united Europe seeking to break free of dependence on the United States. Britain did not go so far, but her reaction to American policies ranging from the Middle East to Berlin was clearly one of seeking to relax American militancy and to restore the supremacy of British diplomacy. So confident did London become that Britain allowed herself the luxury of reactivating the classic balance of power policy in

Europe, and actively sought to disrupt the progress of economic integration on the Continent.[25] West Germany likewise showed a degree of independence and stubbornness in both political and economic terms that troubled American planners.

New Issues in World Politics.

Once bipolarity receded, a whole family of new international issues arose to confound the world's statesmen. The old cold-war concerns of security, prestige, armaments, and war did not die, but they were forced to share attention with (and frequently to take second place to) such newer problems as anticolonialism, technical assistance, the financing of development, and small-state nationalism. To these the cold-war formulas offered no answers, and part of the reason for the battery of new techniques developed by the United States (and the USSR) was the necessity of coming to terms with such different issues. American-Soviet disagreements received a new treatment under the impact of the "plague on both your houses" attitude taken by all but a relative handful of states.

"Khrushchevism" in World Politics

Soviet foreign policy during the most recent phase of world politics has been identified with the enigmatic figure of Nikita Khrushchev. After coming to power in 1954 as party leader, he gradually eliminated his rivals and became premier in 1958. No Stalin, either in his view of the outside world or in the absoluteness of his rule, he is largely responsible both for the new flexibility in Soviet policy and for its frequently baffling twists and turns.[26]

Khrushchev and the Soft Approach.

Khrushchev's Russia has developed a new approach to the world, emphasizing a soft, conciliatory, and reasonable manner, an enthusiastic (and noisy) espousal of the "good" issues of peace, disengagement, disarmament, and coexistence, and a relaxed and confident pride instead of the total suspicion and fear of international contacts that marked the era of Stalin. This is the favorable interpretation; in contrast, it is also accurate to point out that Khrushchev and his policy approach have proved to be addicted to braggadocio, bluster and blackmail, and a strange unpredictability in pressure situations.

---

[25] Prime Minister Macmillan stated quite frankly early in 1960 that Britain was duty bound to obstruct and to seek to destroy any European coalition, even as harmless a one as the Common Market. See his remarks in *New York Times* (March 30, 1960).
[26] See Edward Crankshaw, *Khrushchev's Russia.*

It is useless for us to argue the threadbare question of whether the Soviet under Khrushchev has actually "changed" or whether the whole new approach is merely a tactical maneuver. We have already pointed out that in the contemporary context of world politics, there is little the USSR can do to reactivate any version of Stalinist foreign policy. Caught like the United States in a situation no longer possible to control, the Soviet must concentrate its efforts on adjusting to and capitalizing on events rather than causing them. Even the most ambitious Soviet effort to modify the direction of affairs, the *crises des nerfs* touched off in 1960 over the "U-2" crisis and the disputes in Laos and the Congo, failed to evoke any consequent modification in the content of Soviet policy.

Marring the smooth surface of the Khrushchev soft line has been a series of recurrent crises in which Soviet reaction elicited unhappy memories of the pre-1954 era. The Hungarian massacre of 1956, Soviet threats in the Suez affair, Soviet threats to Norway, Pakistan and other small states during the 1960 crisis, and the long-drawn-out tensions over the Congo, Laos, and Berlin are only the most notorious examples of the Soviet's recent contradictions of its often-proclaimed policy of good will. Opinions in explanation of this eccentricity in Russian behavior tended to concentrate on two theories: either Khrushchev himself is not in complete control, and is periodically forced to act in response to the dictates of the "hard" (Stalinist-military-Chinese) group in the communist hierarchy, or he is himself an erratic and unstable personality. Analysts tended to split rather evenly between the two points of view.

Competitive Coexistence.

For the United States the Khrushchev position, if genuine, has major significance. On many occasions he explicitly rejected the Stalinist concept of inevitable conflict with the capitalist West and instead preached that "competitive coexistence" with the United States was not only acceptable but highly desirable as well.[27] He deleted the qualifying adjective "temporary" from his version of coexistence, and forecast permanent stable relations with the West if only the "monopolists, imperialists, and warmongers" would cease their nefarious activities. If he meant what he said, the United States would have won the cold war; the major objective of American policy would have been achieved.

There would certainly be competition in Khrushchev's world. The Soviet openly set out to catch up with the United States in agricultural and

---

[27] See his remarks at the meeting of Communist leaders in Bucharest in June, 1960, as reported in the *New York Times* (June 23, 1960). He seemed to cling to this position in the face of Chinese disagreement during the Moscow "communist summit" in November. *New York Times* (November 15–30, 1960).

industrial production, both for domestic consumption and for export.[28] In science and technology—vignetted most sharply in the space race—the Soviet took an early lead and held it in spite of American efforts.[29] In military development, Soviet concentration on long-range missiles (ICBM's) produced in 1961 a definite superiority in spite of its inability to break the strategic stalemate.

The competitive feature was carried out in foreign policy as well. Both in the employment of abstractions like "peace" and "disarmament" and in the implementation of concrete programs of foreign aid and technical assistance, the Soviet Union set itself up as an open competitor of the United States. What baffled the United States was that Moscow was using techniques identified with America and in the execution of which Americans had felt they enjoyed a natural advantage. Soviet success (although limited by the occasional outbursts of brutality) was sufficient to make the Kremlin quite confident by the end of 1960 that it was able to compete effectively with the United States in a war-free world.

New Targets and Tactics.

The Soviet's new line did not make it willing to disgorge any of the gains won by its hard policy; satellite liberation, for example, remained an illusion after the 1956 Hungarian rebellion. But its new techniques won the Kremlin victories formerly barred to it by American containment.

The major targets were two: the uncommitted world of Asia, the Middle East and Africa, and the tension-weary masses of the Western camp. To the neutrals the Soviet appeared as a good Samaritan, interested only in helping them; to the West, Moscow posed as a reasonable adversary interested in adjusting differences and getting on with the business of living together. After 1954, Soviet policy stressed four continuing lines: (1) a constant agitation for peace and disarmament on its own terms; (2) an identification with the cause of small states and colonial peoples in dispute with their erstwhile masters; (3) an extensive program of military and economic foreign aid accompanied by loud and constant advertising; (4) an all-out cultural offensive that went far to melt the Iron Curtain. This adaptation of tactics to objectives proved very effective; the Soviet was proving it knew how to conduct a soft policy as well as a hard one. Perhaps it would be more accurate to say Khrushchev was able to mix hard and soft components effectively.

---

[28] During his 1959 tour of the United States, Khrushchev repeatedly stressed this theme. See his Los Angeles speech, September 19, 1959, reported in *The New York Times* (September 20, 1959).

[29] Khrushchev's visit to the United States followed the successful Soviet moon-rocket shot (September 13, 1959).

New Components of American Policy

The new cold war placed strains on the United States. Containment, with all its faults, had nevertheless developed a powerful mystique, and the American people were reluctant to jettison techniques developed at such great cost. This hesitation left the Soviet free to exploit the new international environment and the United States at a loss to explain such formidable victories.

The desired new components of American policy were not impossible to discover; they were there for the taking within the general framework of American assumptions and action. What was needed, and never fully realized, was a general overhaul of programs in the light of new conditions, the most important of which was that world affairs had (despite periodic Soviet and communist Chinese rumblings) largely left the quasi-military phase behind. Progress toward such a renovation of American policy was halting and irregular throughout the latter half of the 1950's, and the next decade opened with the ultimate direction of American policy still in doubt.[30]

Finishing Touches on Mutual Security.

The United States felt a continuing need to elaborate further its structure of mutual-security pacts. In 1954 the Southeast Asia Treaty Organization (SEATO) uniting the United States with Britain, France, Australia, New Zealand, the Philippines, Thailand, and Pakistan in defense of Southeast Asia was signed. In the same year, the agreement between Nationalist China and the United States was effectuated. In 1955 the United States —without actually becoming a member—lent its support to the Baghdad Pact that included Britain, Turkey, Pakistan, Iraq, and Iran; in 1959, when the pact was compromised by Iraq's withdrawal after a successful revolution, the organization was renamed the Central Treaty Organization (CENTO) and the United States formalized its relationship by signing bilateral defense agreements with Turkey, Iran, and Pakistan. The United States, while technically still not a member, now includes CENTO among its operative security agreements. The most recent security arrangement was the 1960 security treaty with Japan that touched off powerful resistance within the Japanese public capped by the cancellation of President Eisenhower's projected visit to Japan.

---

[30] The most ambitious attempt at such a review was the series of studies of various aspects of American foreign policy—15 in all—undertaken during 1959 by private research organizations and universities under the auspices of the Senate Foreign Relations Committee. These are all of high quality and very valuable to any student of the subject, although they were mutually contradictory on many points.

The Cold War: Ebb and Flow ✳ *313*

With the western alliance no longer even putatively monolithic, the United States cast about for some more effective basis for its free-world policy. Its success throughout the entire period was far from exceptional; except for the narrow issue of defense against the Soviet military danger, the free world was less unified in 1960 than it had been a decade earlier.

Events forced the United States into several unfamiliar roles in dealing with the free world. The first was that of referee. Several unpleasant intra-alliance disputes provoked American intervention and peacemaking.[31] A second was that of suitor. In order to keep certain of its allies from what seemed to be dangerous shifts, Washington was forced to use all of its persuasive talents, including making substantial concessions. A third was that of competitor for primacy. Both Britain and France openly declared the end of their subservience to the United States and claimed an equal right to speak for the alliance. Out of all the welter of cross-currents one clear impression emerged: in an era of greater relaxation the free world could no longer be counted on as an automatic increment of support to American policy, but would instead have to be dealt with as carefully and painstakingly as the Soviet bloc and the uncommitted nations.[32]

Coping with the Neutrals.

At first inclined to fight the growth of neutralism, by 1955 the United States came to two conclusions. First, any attempt to use coercion of the neutrals would be both useless and dangerous. They had made good their escape from the cold war. American pressure might drive them closer to the Soviet. Second, the necessary minimum objective of American policy should be the preservation of "friendly" neutrality. If the most the United States could accomplish was to guarantee the neutrals' noncommitment to Moscow, than at least that much should be done. It was in this spirit that the mutual-security context of foreign aid was relaxed to the point that in 1959 such states as Burma (who had never budged from its inflexible neutrality) and the United Arab Republic (once thought of as almost a Soviet satellite) both signed aid agreements with the United States.

New Approaches to the Soviet.

Although bemused by Soviet unpredictability and confounded by the refusal of the Soviet to conform to the baleful public image long cherished

---

31 One of the most difficult of these was the British-Greek quarrel over Cyprus, finally settled in 1959.

32 See *Basic Aims of United States Foreign Policy*, by the Council on Foreign Relations (one of the Foreign Relations Committee studies), pp. 9–14.

by Americans, the Eisenhower administration sought between 1954 and 1961 to develop a satisfactory new approach to the Soviet. Caught between the worsening missile race on the one hand and the Soviet insistence (backed by Britain, France, and most of the smaller European states) that the time was ripe for a settlement of outstanding issues, the United States spent most of these years in a fairly rapid oscillation between hopefulness and despair.

By approximately 1958, consensus in Washington was that the new Soviet tactics were worth taking seriously, and cautious explorations of issue revealed that some form of agreement on nuclear test cessation might be possible. Although the Soviet set no example of cooperation and constructivness, American pursuit of an agreement with Moscow was an impressive example of dilatory procedures. More than once the Soviet had much world opinion on its side as it complained about the tortuous course of discussions and the apparent reluctance of the United States to contribute to any relaxation of tension.

In the summer of 1959, both the revived Berlin crisis and the need for greater speed in disarmament negotiations spurred President Eisenhower to take a bold step: he invited Premier Khrushchev to visit the United States and was in turn invited to visit the USSR.[33] Khrushchev came in September, toured the United States, addressed the United Nations, and had several days of private conversations with the President. The "spirit of Camp David" replaced the "spirit of Geneva" as a catchword, and the long-awaited second summit conference (delayed several months at the behest of President deGaulle of France) was set for May, 1960. Disarmament negotiations speeded up, cultural exchanges expanded, and in spite of the Cassandra chorus of pessimism, it seemed as if again the great powers would have a chance to make a real breakthrough for peace. American policy was at last moving to regularize its relations with Moscow.

The Summit Failure.

All of this collapsed in one breathless month of crisis in May. The "U-2" incident provoked a violent Soviet reaction and a series of unacceptable demands on the United States; the summit conference broke up in a cloud of mutual recriminations. Khrushchev cancelled his invitation to the President to visit the Soviet Union and went far out of his way to destroy the favorable image of Mr. Eisenhower that he had formerly industriously projected to the Russian peoples. Relations seemed to take a sudden turn for the worse.

---

[33] Vice-President Nixon visited the USSR during July and received credit for publicly debating with Khrushchev.

And yet in the wreckage of the summit it could be discerned that all the Soviet invective had not modified any substantive policy. The cultural exchanges continued, the disarmament negotiations went on, and Mr. Eisenhower in his report to the nation after his return, stressed the willingness of the United States to continue to deal realistically with Moscow.[34] The impression continued to gain strength in the United States that competitive coexistence—in spite of its Soviet origin—was a term that was going to continue accurately to describe the state of Soviet-American relations. What remained to be done was to discover the terms of both coexistence and competition for the long range. To this task both the USSR and the United States were setting themselves as the world entered the 1960's.

A New Leadership.

The summer and autumn of 1960, filled with the sound and fury of a close and hard-fought presidential campaign, contributed nothing to the clarification of Soviet-American relations. The USSR held aloof, and the Eisenhower Administration would not tie the hands of its successor. It was obvious after the election, however, that at least Khrushchev was gratified by Senator Kennedy's victory; his congratulatory telegram harked back to the days of Franklin Roosevelt and close wartime cooperation. In response, President Kennedy's inaugural address urged a "beginning" in discovering areas of agreement with the Soviet and the administration launched a wholesale "review" of Soviet-American relations. Many observers at home and abroad felt a major change lay in the fairly near future.

[34] The President's speech is reported in *New York Times* (May 26, 1960).

PART

6

◆

Continuing

Issues

in

American

Policy

◆

Continuing
Political
Issues
in
American
Policy

CHAPTER ‹ *12* ›

Within American foreign policy there are a number of "continuing issues." These are problems stemming from the general policy line the United States has been pursuing that are peculiar in that they do not permit of any final resolution. Each has been met within the context of a given set of circumstances, but each change in the situational milieu has required that new answers be given to the old questions. Because they promise to be of long duration, we would profit by discussing at least the most important of these continuing issues.

As we take them up in this section of our study, we will break them down into four functional areas, corresponding roughly to the four channels by way of which states usually execute their policies: the political (or diplomatic) area, the military area, the economic area, and the psychological area. This chapter deals exclusively with issues of a political import; there follows one devoted to each of the other three. These classifications are valid primarily as convenient foci of

319

discussion. In practice the political, military, economic, and psychological dimensions of foreign policy blend into one another and form component parts of a single operational entity.

In this chapter we shall examine four diplomatic-political areas of continuing and fundamental concern to the over-all structure of American policy. Each represents a significant complex of issues; each has great relevance to American action in other areas, both geographic and functional; each has had a variety of answers recommended and, in some cases, attempted. The four we have selected are the issues (1) of American relations with the great powers, (2) of American relations with the free-world alliance, (3) of American relations with international organization, and (4) of American policy toward the smaller states generally and toward the issue of anti-colonialism specifically.

THE UNITED STATES AND THE GREAT POWERS

By the "great powers" in the contemporary world we mean (in addition to the United States) the USSR, Great Britain, China, and India. This listing reflects the new dynamics of world politics and differs markedly from any made at any earlier period of history. With this group of states collectively and with each of them individually American relations are destined to continue to be important, perhaps central. With regard to each of them certain complicating factors exist that make the establishment of a firm orientation difficult.

We cannot lay down any generalizations about American policy toward the entire group. The course of world affairs since 1945 has been characterized by deep and bitter divisions among the major states and we have no reason to believe that this condition will soon be changed. Our discussion, therefore, will deal individually with the Soviet and with Britain, and (because of certain fundamental similarities) jointly with India and China.

The Future of American-Soviet Relations

No one can envisage any possible situation—barring the total eclipse of civilization in the wake of a general war—in which the United States and the Soviet Union would not be the two most powerful states in the world. If this be so, it follows that Soviet-American relations will continue to be the bedrock of American policy, as they have been since 1945. There has been surprisingly little inclination in the United States to consider the long-term future of Soviet-American relations; as American experience accumulates, however, a greater sensitivity toward the necessity of such speculation seems to be dawning.[1]

Granted the intolerability of perpetual stalemate, Soviet-American relations must either deteriorate or improve over time. What is the relative likelihood of either outcome, and what meaning does it have for the United States?

The Possibility of Deterioration.

Any further deterioration in the present tense character of Soviet-American relations would simply bring back the worst days of the cold war, followed by an equally swift breakdown into some form of armed conflict. While this is an ever-present possibility, the prospect is relatively remote. Both sides have perfected their techniques for avoiding war with each other; both have a real interest in preserving the present plateau of less-than-minimal relations—even in spite of recurrent crisis. The dangers of any such worsening of relationships is all too obvious to both sides.[2] We may accord the prospect of deterioration a low priority of probability, at least as far as deliberate policy decisions are concerned.

The Possibility of Improvement.

From the American point of view improvement in Russo-American relations could come about in any of three ways. First, Moscow might undergo a change of heart and surrender totally, adjusting Russian policy to American requirements on all issues. Second, the cold war might be called off by mutual consent and be replaced by an (implicit or explicit) agreement by both sides to ignore each other as much as possible. Third, a set of compromises on outstanding issues adding up to a *modus vivendi* could be worked out, thus providing a firm if limited basis for coexistence.

The various ways in which American relations with Moscow might improve are of differing degrees of probability. The possibility that the Soviet might be willing to ignore the United States, and that America would reciprocate, is perhaps the least likely of all the alternatives we are considering. The requirements of national existence in an interdependent world make continued Soviet-American relations inevitable.

Almost as remote a possibility is the prospect of a Soviet surrender. We may safely disregard it as long as the present Russian regime retains its identity and its mission. Only a major upheaval inside Russia, one of a size sufficient to force a reconstitution of the government, could

---

[1] An outstanding recent example is Henry L. Roberts, *Russia and America: Dangers and Prospects* (New York: Harper & Bros., Inc., 1956).

[2] Khrushchev went so far on January 26, 1959, as to admit that he "is more frightened of war than anybody else." *New York Times* (January 27, 1959).

bring to power a group of rulers willing to accept the renunciation of what the Soviet had been attempting since 1945. Such an outcome, as we have suggested earlier, is unlikely but not impossible; it is of a low enough order of probability, however, that the United States dare not base its policy on its coming about spontaneously.

For the United States deliberately to seek to bring about such revolution would be a policy of some hope for success but with considerable attendant danger. The communist dictators, faced with the erosion of their power, might risk everything in an all-out attempt to destroy the United States; alternatively, even an anti-communist regime in Moscow might not be willing to abandon enough of the foreign policy of its predecessor to please the United States. The latter outcome would leave the United States virtually where it started.[3]

The final possibility of improvement in Soviet-American relations is that of a gradual relaxation brought about by a progressive mutual accommodation of policy. We have indicated the reasons for American confidence that the eventual outcome of the cold war will be the stabilization of Russo-American relations on a mutually tolerable level. It is this conviction that a climate of cold war can and will be changed to one of toleration and a modicum of cooperative action that has inspired the architects of American policy to proceed in the direction the United States has gone since 1947.

Yet we must conclude this rapid survey of alternatives and probabilities with an obvious but necessary reminder. Accommodation is the most probable outcome of Soviet-American tensions, but it is by no means the inevitable or the only one. Its consummation requires good will and effort on both sides, and we need not be pessimists to point out that these prerequisites are not yet visible in Soviet behavior nor—to be candid —in any great measure in American conduct. Much remains to be done before such a happier day arrives including a greater American emphasis on the generation of possible solutions to existing problems.

Possible Areas of Agreement.

We cannot predict the final form of Soviet-American accommodation nor when such an agreement could be reached. We can discover, however, certain issues in the general cold-war context that seem more susceptible to relatively early successful attack than do most of the others. In no particular order of priority, we may suggest four bones of contention between East and West the later history of which gives some grounds for

---

[3] The writings of James Burnham, however, urge such a policy on the United States, especially his *The Coming Defeat of Communism* (New York: John Day, 1950).

optimism about their final resolution: (1) the reunification of Germany; (2) a security agreement and system for Europe; (3) reduction in armaments (discussed in Chapter 13); (4) the expansion of East-West trade and economic life generally.

Each of these questions seems to have received considerable reanalysis by both states since 1955. There is some reason to believe that both sets of leaders are more willing today to accept a viable compromise on them than at any point previously, and that negotiations on each of them are destined to increase in seriousness. Success in any (or all) of them would not, of course, end the cold war, but it would contribute largely to what might become an evolving pattern of accommodation.

The Policy Implications.

Some of the implications for American policy of such an estimate of the future have been suggested in earlier chapters. At this point we need only to stress one or two general considerations. Probably the most important point is that the United States should seek to maintain a larger consistency in the face of circumstances that are often mutually contradictory. In Chapter 11 we saw evidence of failure in this regard. There is real need for a general policy line that concentrates on moving the United States as steadily as possible toward its long-term goal and also provides a rationale for short-range policies. Its continued lack would tend to make American action a series of limited undertakings, consistent neither with each other, with past commitments, nor with future plans.

To illustrate this unfortunate trait of American policy, we may cite American reaction to the two most deeply felt emotional shocks the United States has suffered since 1955: the Soviet breakthrough in space exploration touched off by "Sputnik" in 1957, and the summit crisis of May 1960. In both instances, the spontaneous reaction of much influential opinion in Congress, the executive, and the public was to hit back at Moscow. The urge to "get even" took the form of advocating a return to bipolarity, an end to negotiation with the Soviet, and a reconstitution of American action on a primarily military base. In both instances also, it was the voice of President Eisenhower, exuding calmness and restraint, that stilled the excited clamor by fitting these crises into a larger policy mold. The sense of frustration, however, lingered on in the public.

It would seem logical for us also to suggest that the general frame of American policy should be more directly oriented toward its expected outcomes. At the present time, any particular American action seems to be posited on some one of four mutually contradictory assumptions about Soviet-American relations. Segments of policy assume the inevitability of total war; others presuppose eventual Soviet surrender, the indefinite continuation of the cold war, or the achievement of accommodation. While admitting that a sound policy seeks to take account of all possibilities, greater emphasis could profitably be placed on the alternative that America feels most likely and that the others be given appropriately subordinate places.

BRITAIN AND THE UNITED STATES

Anglo-American relations have been the core of affirmative American policy since the end of World War II. Despite some inescapable controversy and considerable misunderstanding, the problems of American policy toward Britain have been matters more of detail than of fundamental orientation. Agreement on basic premises is as great as can ever be the case between two major states, and prospects for any different basis of relationships are remote.[4]

Britain: the Key Ally.

From the moment that the United States began to implement its postwar policy decisions, Britain has been its key ally. A high degree of coincidence of interest, both in general terms and on a remarkably large number of specifics, has resulted in a long series of joint policy moves and a group of more elaborate collaborative enterprises. In the network of American alliances, Britain has bulked large. The United States has resisted all Soviet invitations to negotiate directly with Moscow on most questions of interest to Britain. In the United Nations close Anglo-American cooperation has been the normal practice, whether in the Security Council, the General Assembly, or any other organs. In the fields of technical assistance, of military and economic aid, and of propaganda, British cooperation has given American policy an extra impact. Recent diplomatic history provides few such impressive examples of close and mutually satisfactory relations between allies in time of peace, considering that both states play the role of "great power" to the hilt.

Anglo-American Disputes.

The closeness of Anglo-American relations has been affected to some significant—although minor—extent by a series of annoying disagreements. These have been most apparent when open breaks between the allies have taken place (the most serious was American opposition to Britain's inva-

---

[4] From among the many studies of Anglo-American relations, we may suggest Henry L. Roberts and Paul Wilson, *Britain and the United States* (New York: Harper & Bros., Inc., 1953) and Leon Epstein, *Britain: Uneasy Ally* (Chicago: University of Chicago Press, 1954).

sion of the Suez Canal Zone in 1956), but there has been a constant undercurrent of tension that has colored relations when it has not directly controlled them.

These conflicts between Britain and the United States grow out of causes both general and specific. Perhaps most fundamental is the inevitable stress caused by the great disparity in power between the two states. For Britons, long accustomed to considering themselves as citizens of the world's leading power, to take second place to a young and inexperienced America has been difficult.[5] Anti-Americanism has complicated the partnership from its very outset. We must also admit that American attitudes have often not been calculated to soothe outraged British sensibilities, and frequently Anglo-American controversy has been a matter of embattled nationalisms nagging at each other.,

On a number of concrete issues, Britain and the United States have disagreed openly. In Europe, the United States has favored European economic integration, while Britain stubbornly fought it as long as it had any hopes of halting the trend. In Asia, London and Washington were steadily at loggerheads over how to handle resistance to communist Chinese expansion. In the Middle East, Anglo-American disagreement reached the point of an open break in the Suez affair of 1956, and has never fully subsided since that time. The more world tension relaxed during the 1950's, the greater the frequency of policy breaks between the two allies.

Maintaining the Tie.

Anglo-American controversy is always fuel for headlines on both sides of the Atlantic; the question is deeply involved in domestic politics in both nations, and each frequently finds in the other a convenient scapegoat for its own frustrations. Yet there is little possibility that the working agreement or the harmony of interest between the two states might dissolve. Both are status-quo powers; both recognize the need for substantive change in many world relationships if stability is ever to be attained; both insist that the necessary change be peaceful. Real disagreement arises only from the differing specifications each has for what would be an optimum solution to its own problems. The identity of purpose, however, is sufficiently great that each has ample room in which to adjust its differences in behalf of maintaining the tie that is so profitable and so necessary for both. Anglo-American relations will never be idyllic, but they will probably continue to be largely harmonious and cooperative. "Anti-Americanism" and Anglophobia alike cannot affect a real coincidence of interest.

---

[5] British reaction to the American handling of the "U-2" incident was unusually acid. See issues of the London *Times*, May 9–14, 1960, especially the "letters to the editor."

THE NEW POWERS: INDIA AND CHINA

India and China are the two new great powers in the arena of world politics. The United States, itself a relative newcomer to this small circle, has had difficulty in orientating itself to deal with them. Its perplexity has been shared by the other major states and, be it noted, India and China as well have found it troublesome to devise effective policies vis-a-vis each other. The world has not yet become accustomed to having so much of its power located in these inexperienced hands.

The United States has a special problem in confronting these two states, both in their own right and as representatives and spokesmen for a newly-militant Asia. Americans, as we have seen, have escaped most of the effects of what we might call the "post-imperialist psychosis" that complicates so much of European policy toward Asia. The United States, never a major imperialist power in Asia, has had little direct concern with the decay of empire there. Its problem has grown instead out of the heavily missionary background of American attitudes toward the Orient. Public opinion in America, although generally favorable toward the aspirations of Asians, nevertheless cannot seem to escape a patronizing attitude toward them. Asians frequently are thought of primarily as subjects for industrialization, westernization, or—in some cases—civilization. Americans want to save Asia from itself; that many Asians do not particularly want to be saved from themselves by Americans is either ignored or brushed off as irrelevant.

This unconsciously invidious approach has produced a reaction often puzzling to Americans: it has frequently infuriated Asians more than does the openly imperialist policy of European states. It irritates Americans to see that Britain has had generally greater success with both India and China than has the United States, despite the British record of imperialist conquest and exploitation. American "do-goodism" has had only limited effect, possibly because its psychic motivation has been apparent to its subjects.[6]

The Problem of India.

It is difficult to characterize American relations with India within any brief compass. They are many-sided, confused, and rapidly changing. In some areas reasonably good understanding prevails, while in others dis-

---

[6] This point is made generally by William O. Douglas, in *Strange Lands and Friendly People* (New York: Harper & Bros., Inc., 1951), and Chester Bowles, in *Ambassador's Report* (New York: Harper & Bros., Inc., 1954) and *The New Dimensions of Peace* (New York: Harper & Bros., Inc., 1955).

agreement is nearly total. The basic tenor of the relationship is made complex by the fact that both states must largely improvise in dealing with each other; neither has any long history or controlling tradition to give shape to the relationship. Indian affairs remain one of the more unclear aspects of American policy.

As we indicated in Chapter 11, the United States originally assumed that an independent India would be pro-western and would find ample ground on which to agree with the United States. Washington's failure to communicate meaningfully with New Delhi and India's conception of its international role as not calling for immediate commitment in the cold war brought about a speedy worsening of Indian-American relations. The policy estrangement that endured from 1950 to 1957 had its roots in massive misunderstandings on both sides. Both governments—particularly the American—struggled to break through the fog of emotion that complicated the development of a base for a stable relationship.

American analyses frequently found five mutually contradictory lines of Indian policy. (1) India considered itself a great power and insisted on being dealt with as such. (2) India also wished to lead and to speak for the small states and newly-independent regimes everywhere. (3) India had ambitions of Asian leadership. (4) India was determined on a literal version of neutralism: to remain entirely outside the scope of the cold war. (5) India was deeply determined to mediate the cold war and to bring peace to the world. Nehru's inability to reconcile these divergent objectives made India's policy subject to misinterpretation by all shades of American opinion.[7]

Especially annoying to the United States was India's approach to Soviet-American relations. Nehru and his advisers apparently felt that the mediator's role required that India maintain good relations with the communist world; there was some evidence also that India was greatly impressed by the Soviet's material achievements.[8] The upshot of this concern was that India felt itself compelled to show sympathy and cordiality toward the USSR and communist China, while feeling free to indulge its official disagreements toward the United States by chilly formality and anti-American propaganda. Americans reasoned that Nehru felt that it was safer to insult the United States than the Soviet; annoying as this attitude might be, Washington was forced to admit that it had some basis in fact.

Beginning with the Hungarian and Suez crises of 1956, however, Indian-American relations took a turn for the better. Part of the reason was a

---

[7] See Werner Levi, *Free India in Asia* (Minneapolis: University of Minnesota Press, 1952), for an analysis of Nehru's Asian policy.

[8] This point is made by William O. Douglas, in *A Russian Journey* (New York: Harper & Bros., Inc., 1956).

growing American sophistication in dealing with India; the 1960 agreement for Indian purchase of American wheat was handled with dignity and restraint instead of the clumsiness of earlier years. Another factor was Nehru's growing disillusionment with the Soviet and its expansionist policies. Perhaps the most important explanation, however, was India's increasing difficulties with China, centering in the Tibetan revolt and the Sino-Indian border dispute in 1959. The new state of relations was epitomized by President Eisenhower's triumphal visit to India in December, 1959, on which occasion Nehru took occasion to stress the community of purpose and interest that exists between the two largest democracies in the world.

The Problem of China.

Chinese affairs, long a concern of the United States, acquired a new dimension after 1949. The problem of China has had three novel features since that date. First, China is now free from (at least Western) tutelage and, partly under Soviet sponsorship, is aggressively prosecuting its own foreign policy. Second, China is a communist state and constitutes the most populous unit in the camp hostile to the United States. Third, China is openly revisionist, seeking in a variety of ways to improve its international position. American policy has been slow to devise a strategy adequate to cope with this new manifestation of Chinese political dynamism.[9]

The base of a good deal of American policy toward China after 1949 was an apparent determination not to accept the fact of communist domination of the mainland. The United States withheld recognition of the Peiping regime, blocked communist representation of China in the United Nations, and openly supported Chiang Kai-shek's regime on Formosa. In general American action toward the Peiping government seemed built on the premise that Mao's victory was only a temporary interruption in the rightful occupation of power by the Kuomintang. Open American combat against Chinese "volunteers" in Korea and Peiping's provocative and belligerent behavior subsequently hardened American determination not to yield an inch to the communists either in principle or in practice.

Throughout the latter half of the 1950's, the United States remained stalled on dead center in its relations with China. Despite a widespread American realization that some regularization of relationships would be

---

[9] See *Asia,* prepared by Conlon Associates Ltd., one of the Senate Foreign Relations Committee Studies (Washington: U. S. Government Printing Office, 1959). This volume, especially pp. 119–55, contains suggestions for a new American policy. Earlier attempts at sketching out new lines of American action vis-a-vis China include W. W. Rostow, with Richard W. Hatch, *An American Policy in Asia* (New York: John Wiley, 1955), and Edwin O. Rieschauer, *Wanted: An Asian Policy* (New York: Alfred A. Knopf, 1955).

desirable, no satisfactory terms could be arrived at and no favorable opportunities for action appeared. Negotiations with Peiping, carried on intermittently throughout the period, were fruitless; Mao Tse-tung and his associates appeared determined to maintain relations at the maximum bearable tension. Aggravating the situation was the recurrent danger of open war with China if Peiping set out to seize the American-protected island territories of the Kuomintang regime.

The heart of the matter was the exact state of Sino-Soviet relationships. Many Americans had expected China to develop some variety of "Titoism" and break from Moscow's domination. It was clear by 1960 that the two communist giants were no longer in total harmony, and that ideological love feasts could not conceal policy disagreement. But the development of Sino-Soviet disagreement did not produce greater opportunities for the United States; instead evidence multiplied that Peiping's position in the communist bloc was so strong that it could influence Soviet behavior. Granted the militant ideological position and inherent dynamism of the communist Chinese regime, this could not but be disquieting to American policy makers. The 1960's opened with the problem of China probably the largest question mark in all of American policy.

AMERICAN-ALLIED RELATIONS

Having to maintain relationships with more than 40 allies in time of peace is a completely novel experience for the United States. "Allies" traditionally are a by-product of war; when the United States has been at peace American tradition has insisted on the working minimum of fixed commitments. The cold war, however, forced the United States to accept the leadership of a massive coalition for the prosecution of free world policy. This new posture has required that Americans accustom themselves to the peculiar requirements of policies framed and executed within a multi-state context. Problems both of theory and of practice have grown out of this situation, and the subject of American-allied relations is one which the United States has yet to resolve satisfactorily.

AMERICAN THEORIES OF ALLIANCE

The Myth of the "Free World."

The basic bipolar assumption of American policy after 1947 contributed to the development of what we might call the "myth of the free world." Americans tended to assume that the world consisted of two groups of states, the communist and the noncommunist blocs, the one led by Moscow and the other by Washington. If every state in the world were on one side or the other, and if the dividing line between them was the choice between freedom and communism, it was then only a short step to reason that all anti-communist states shared the same value system and the same general foreign-policy pattern.

This is the notion of the "free world." Americans seem to feel that the alliance of which their government is the leader is (or ought to be) a monolithic entity that opposes Moscow's pretensions with a single purpose and a single effort. United States policy often purports to speak for all its allies on a great variety of questions, and the revelation of intra-alliance disagreement often throws much of American public opinion and leadership into a strange catalepsy. Americans are fond of the shibboleth of "the unity of the free world," a notion often more pervasive than relevant. The "free world" is a concept of great importance, but in practice it has demonstrated significant limitations as an analytical focus for policy.

Students of international affairs know that the western alliance, like all alliances, is founded on coincidence of interest among its members, and that it cannot be interpreted as covering any substantive or procedural points by sheer implication. Cooperation among the allies is ensured only in those areas of action covering which ironclad agreements, embodying predetermined degrees of harmony, have been worked out. To assume that agreement on any single point implies agreement on any other point is not only to prepare the way for later disillusionment and disappointment, but frequently also to weaken the working effectiveness of such alliances as exist.[10]

The United States: Leader or Partner?

Equally important to the issue of American-allied relationships is the question of the role of the United States within the alliance pattern it has worked out. There is considerable disagreement among Americans and foreigners alike about the nature of American responsibility to its associates and the degree of authority the United States is to be permitted in committing other members to courses of action they may not wish to follow.

During the first two phases of the cold war, the United States followed the self-imposed path of leadership.[11] Both in the development of intra-alliance relationships and in the common front presented to the Soviet world, American wishes were paramount. The weakened condition of many noncommunist states made it difficult and often impossible for them

---

[10] This point is elaborately developed by George F. Kennan, in *Realities of American Foreign Policy,* in Chapter II: "The Non-Soviet World."

[11] Reitzel, Kaplan, and Coblentz, *United States Foreign Policy, 1945–1955,* p. 492.

to resist American pressure, and a number of European, Asian, and Latin American countries were (as they saw it) coerced into accepting a purely American formula for the solution of a joint problem. This tendency reached its height during the Korean war, when American militancy caused serious rifts in the western alliance and forced India and its associates to break with the free world and to adopt a self-styled neutrality.

What caused considerable disquiet, even among the states most in agreement with the United States, was what American "leadership" of the alliance often meant in practice. Western Europe particularly harbored serious doubts of the wisdom and the skill of American policymakers and its leaders questioned the implicit (and sometimes explicit) claim that only the United States knew the right answers to the questions facing the free world.[12] The inclination among many Americans to regard any deviation from the American line as evidence either of a lack of moral fiber or of a half-concealed admiration for Communism often irritated Europeans who considered themselves guilty of no more reprehensible offense than of differing with Washington over how to accomplish a particular objective. American leadership also showed a disconcerting tendency to interpret "western" objectives in purely American terms, and to assume (in a paraphrase of a statement attributed to then Secretary of Defense Charles E. Wilson) that "what is good for the United States is good for the free world." Some plaintive voices were even heard to inquire what in practice was the difference between Soviet satellitism and American leadership of its allies.

In the post-1955 era, the United States has changed to a "partnership" concept of alliance and has placed greater emphasis on persuasion and adjustment as a means of securing allied unity. This "softer" approach, however, rapidly developed its own pattern of difficulties. Its implementation required the United States to accept often extensive modifications of its own demands on the alliance, and also to accept open disagreement and occasional defiance from its associates. Both of these results had unfortunate repercussions among the American people. Partnership to a critical observer often looked perilously like a lack of decision, a failure of will, or an unworthy search after popularity abroad. The American government, once it relaxed its efforts to enforce conformity from the other states of the free-world complex, was attacked by its own constituents for being too weak and by its allies for being yet too dominating.

The growth of neutralism, a predictable outcome of the partnership concept, brought down new torrents of criticism among Americans. As

---

[12] Raymond Aron, *The Century of Total War* (Boston: Beacon Press, 1954), pp. 322–24. Mr. Aron, a distinguished French publicist, argues that the real cause of Europe's resentment at American leadership is Europe's realization of its own weakness.

long as the United States was committed to avoid coercion in its relations with the noncommunist states, it was obliged to accept the possibility that some of them would use their newly guaranteed freedom of action to develop independent courses. When this actually happened, objections were heard both from those who condemned the government for weakness in permitting the neutrals to stray and from those who argued that a more sympathetic American policy would have prevented any such deviation.

In the period since 1955, America's approach to the free world has swung between the poles of leadership and partnership without finding a satisfactory resting place. The result is that the United States is attacked alternately (and sometimes simultaneously) for being too strong or too weak in dealing with its allies. In the 1956 Suez crisis, for example, the United States was accused of attempted dictatorship over its associates; during the post-1957 space race, on the other hand, it was criticized for not offering the leadership the free world demanded. Before the event British Prime Minister Macmillan took credit for bringing Premier Khrushchev and President Eisenhower to the summit in 1960; after it failed, he was perfectly willing to allow the United States to accept the responsibility for its failure. Whenever the United States conspicuously accedes to its allies' wishes, it is attacked at home and frequently abroad as well for lack of will and purpose; when it pushes its side of an intra-allied conflict with vigor, the same critics accuse it of insensitivity and bungling. No simple formula for happy interallied relationships exists. All the long quarrel over it really proves is that the major power's lot in a large coalition is seldom a satisfying one.[13]

Problems of Alliance

The issue of leadership or partnership is important in the American theory of alliance because of certain problems that have arisen within the structure of the free world. There are several fundamental grounds for tension whose consequences must be expected and to which adjustment must be made by all participants. Some of these problems grow out of the nature of alliances in general and are in no sense peculiar to the free world in the cold war, while others are functions of the special circumstances and times that confront the noncommunist states in coping with the Soviet menace.

---

[13] For one set of interpretations of American-allied relationships, stressing military implications and the primacy of Europe among the various groups of allies, see Arnold Wolfers, ed., *Alliance Policy in the Cold War* (Baltimore: The Johns Hopkins University Press, 1959).

Perhaps most relevant to the crises of the free world is the fact that there is such a great disparity of strength between the United States and all of its allies. America's 40-odd associates include states of all sizes and degrees of strength, from such miniscule entities as El Salvador, Luxembourg, and Haiti to such extensive, populous, and relatively powerful states as Britain, Pakistan, and Brazil. None of them, however, is capable of matching American strength except in an occasional category. Much as the United States may wish to rationalize the partnership theory of alliance, the stubborn fact remains that American power towers over that of any of America's allies.

It is not so clear, however, whether American strength is greater than that of all its allies combined; it might be possible to balance the capabilities involved so as to create a situation in which American power was overshadowed by the combined weight of the allies. The American alliance pattern, however, is not a single entity, but rather a group of multi- and bi-lateral pacts. United States membership is the only point common to all of them. Mobilizing all these otherwise largely competitive states in support of the single objective of overbalancing American power would involve an almost total revolution in world political relationships. Whether or not the United States outweighs all its allies is a consideration of only remote significance to the actual workings of the free-world system.

It is undeniable, however, that the disparity of strength among the allies creates problems, of which the central one is that of the role of the United States. The major goal of the free world's political effort is the development of a unified policy not dominated by the United States but to which America will lend adequate support. This would be difficult to work out even if all the partners were of approximately equal stature; in a situation in which one member is overwhelmingly powerful it becomes extremely complex.

Intra-alliance Conflicts of Interest.

One troublesome dilemma of the free world is how to dispose of the conflicts of interest among its members. These, as we know, are inescapable as long as the American bloc is not structured into a simple spokesman-satellite pattern. To what extent are allied interests to be subordinated to American concerns; how far will the United States go in adjusting its wishes to those of its allies; how much independence of action should allies be permitted in following their own purposes; what, in practice, is to constitute a "rupture" of the alliance; how should conflict between two or more of its allies be dealt with by the United States: these are only a

few of the recurrent questions stemming from the central fact that membership in the free world does not entail the abandonment of national objectives.

Certain rough principles have been developed by the United States
to guide it in some of these problems. Under the partnership principle
after 1954, American leadership made a real attempt to work for the
development of a joint policy on major issues. On the central problem of
Russo-western relations, Washington steadfastly refused to deal with the
Soviet except in company with its major allies (we should note, however,
that in principle some American freedom of action was expressly reserved
on certain questions, although never exercised).

The Suez crisis of 1956 demonstrated what the Eisenhower administration felt to be the permissible limits of independent action by its allies.
No free world state could count on either American support or American
approval if it pursued its own interest to the point of violating the basic
American interest in peaceful process and the procedural status quo.
American opposition to Britain and France in that dispute was a natural
application of the action principles of American policy.

After 1955, the United States had also initiated a policy of attempting
to develop new common interests among the members of its alliance to
minimize the prospect of a rupture of the free world. A negative interest
holds a grouping together only as long as the common threat endures; a
more positive purpose would provide for a longer-lasting bond. The new
emphasis in American policy given to such issues as peaceful atomic development, an economic and social dimension to NATO, and issues of international trade are all aimed at minimizing the prospect that internal dis-
harmonies of interest would fray the alliance as the direct Soviet military
threat lessens.

One of the few comforts the United States was able to extract from
the summit failure of 1960 was the fact that, in a moment of what seemed
to be real crisis, its principal allies remained steadfast in preserving
a common front. Both Britain and France resisted Soviet blandishments
to divest themselves of what was—at least for the moment—a disappoint-
ing and embarrassing relationship with the United States, and instead once
again demonstrated the solidity of the West. Washington felt with some
justice that the alliance system had passed one of its severest tests.

Nationalist Resentments.

Emphasis on the common purposes of the western alliance should not
obscure the fact that many of the states with which the United States is
associated harbored fundamental nationalist resentments toward America.
Latin America was prepared to revive the bogey of Yankee imperialism;

Europe tended to remember American isolationism of the 1920's, distrusted American inexperience, impetuosity, and naivete, and rebelled against its own overtly subordinate status; Japan remembered its half-century of hostility; Asia and the Middle East objected to America's missionary orientation and feared American political and cultural hegemony.[14]

Americans proved slow to grasp these nationalist biases and to adequately allow for them. Either they were overlooked entirely in the bland confidence that American generosity, strength, and good intentions were obvious to all, or else they were put down to the machinations of pro-communist propaganda and hence unworthy. It was not until Americans realized they were in danger of becoming "unpopular"—a fate regarded by many Americans in their personal lives as being worse than death—that many of the implications of nationalist hostility became apparent.

Faced with "anti-Americanism," Americans tended to react with reciprocal hostility; instead of believing any more that "everybody loves us," they fell into the equally fatuous trap of assuming that "everybody hates, envies, and fears us." Such a wave of hurt feelings was just as unrealistic as the foreign animosities that had given rise to it; in the world of the 1950's and 1960's, no free-world state of any size or level of power can afford to build its policy upon an assumption of either love or hate. It would seem that the full efficiency of the western alliance must wait upon the willingness both of Americans and of the other peoples of the free world to modify or suspend the worst of their nationalist hosilities in the interest of a common purpose they all agree is of primary importance.

THE UNITED STATES AND INTERNATIONAL ORGANIZATION

American attitudes and behavior toward international organization provide one of the most impressive and instructive contrasts with the period of the 1920's and 1930's. The rebirth of isolationism that followed World War I took its characteristic form from the spontaneous and consistent effort to avoid "entanglement" in the League of Nations system; for millions of Americans the League epitomized the devious world of diplomacy they were seeking to shut out. Throughout the entire period since 1945, on the other hand, American commitment to the principle of international organization, though not total, remained consistently high, and the maintenance, strengthening, and employment of the United Nations endures as a cardinal procedural principle of American policy.

---

14 Reitzel, Kaplan, and Coblentz, *United States Foreign Policy,* pp. 355–56.

THE UNITED STATES AND THE UNITED NATIONS

The United Nations Idea in American Policy.

The framers of the Charter knew better than any one else that they were not drafting a constitution for a world government, and that the United Nations could never be any more than a mechanism for the more efficient implementation of such will to cooperate as existed among the membership. The "United Nations idea" that made the organization such a hopeful portent was the hope that states generally would accept the principle that United Nations procedure was the type of action most conducive to permanent improvement of world relations; the goal was to funnel the great majority of all national policy moves through United Nations channels. The organs of the Charter were thought of as instruments for the harmonization of national interests rather than for the creation of entirely new policies.[15]

How has the United States reacted to the challenge of the "United Nations idea"? On balance, we may say that America has made a reasonably good record in acting through United Nations channels, but by no means an exceptional one. The major elements of postwar American policy have been executed both within the United Nations and outside it; the most important cold-war moves, such as the alliance system, Point 4, economic assistance, and so on, have generally been independently executed. Washington has taken great care, however, to make all its actions square more or less directly with its obligations and privileges under the Charter.[16]

The most spectacular example of American reliance on United Nations procedures was, of course, the series of General Assembly resolutions in 1956 condemning Soviet behavior in Hungary and the Anglo-French-Israeli invasion of Egypt. Here, at a crucial moment in American policy, President Eisenhower placed American trust almost entirely in the mechanisms of international organization and—to the surprise of considerable segments of American public opinion—discovered that in at least this case the essentials of American policy were adequately achieved. American

---

[15] See Daniel S. Cheever and H. Field Haviland, *Organizing for Peace* (Boston: Houghton Mifflin Co., 1954), Chapter 28: "The New Diplomacy and World Order."

[16] The mutual-security pacts of the United States, for example, make specific reference to the obligations of the parties under the Charter. See *Disarmament and Security: A Collection of Documents, 1919–1955* (Washington, D. C.: U. S. Government Printing Office, 1956) pp. 531, NATO; 599, Philippines treaty; 600–601, ANZUS; 607, Japanese treaty; 608–9, Formosa treaty; 612–13, SEATO; 650, Rio Pact. See also Bloomfield, *The United Nations and U. S. Foreign Policy.*

popular reaction to this move reflected a major upsurge in public support of the United Nations.[17]

The United Nations as a Tool.

In general the attitude of the United States toward the United Nations has been the same as that shared by the other great powers. To a major state with global interests, extensive commitments, and a sensitive nationalism, the notion that all policy is to be executed in the chambers of the United Nations cannot help but be considered somewhat naive. The characteristics of United Nations action—publicity, majority vote, the preponderance of small-state opinion, leisureliness, and the disavowal of other than collective force—often are felt to be overly constraining to great powers.

The normal view among the permanent members of the Security Council (who, with India, constitute the group of "major powers" in the organization) is to consider the United Nations as a tool of national policy. Like any policy technique, on appropriate occasions its use is mandatory, at other times either expedient, immaterial, undesirable, or inimical. The decision by such a government whether or not to "go to the United Nations" is not based on any preference for such action in the abstract, but rather upon the circumstances of the case and the nature of the objective sought.

These generalizations roughly characterize the American approach to the United Nations. As a status-quo state interested in stabilizing world relationships, it has been appropriate for the United States to find working through the United Nations expedient a larger share of the time than would such revisionist states as the Soviet Union or Yugoslavia. But despite the relatively favorable record America has made compared to the USSR, many of the smaller states complain that American policy has often bypassed international action in behalf of unilateral procedures, in spite of such conspicuous instances as Suez, the Congo, and Laos.

---

[17] A Gallup Poll of December 9, 1956, made this clear. On the question "How important do you think it is that the United States try to make the United Nations a success—very important, fairly important, or not so imporant?" the comparative percentages for 1952 and late 1956 were as follows:

	1952	1956
Very important	77	85
Fairly important	10	8
Not so important	6	3
No opinion	7	4

The same poll pointed out that the percentage of people who felt that the United Nations was doing a "poor job" had steadily declined from 36 per cent in 1951 to 11 per cent in late 1956. Reprinted by permission of the Atlanta (Ga.) *Journal-Constitution.*

In defense of American policy, it might be pointed out that the first fifteen years of the world's experience with the United Nations has demonstrated that the organization has definite limits beyond which it has no usefulness. Constructed on the principle of great-power cooperation for peace, it has proved itself powerless to cope with the cold war in any but the most indirect ways. The United States was obliged to take direct action in prosecuting the anti-communist struggle simply because no effective means existed to act through the United Nations.

A good case could be made to the effect that significant portions of longer-range American planning (looking beyond the cold war) did take the United Nations into account, and that the "tool" view of the organization in no way embodied a negative judgment about its usefulness in appropriate situations. According to this argument, direct American cold-war policy was in preparation for the day that the United Nations would be able to function effectively in affirmative action for a more stable world.

The United States, the United Nations, and World Public Opinion.

The Middle East crisis of 1956 provided a dramatic demonstration of this thesis. World public opinion (particularly in the uncommitted states) turned sharply against Britain, France, and Israel following their invasion of Egypt. Acting through the United Nations, the United States was able to mobilize this opinion into an overwhelming majority demand that the three states evacuate their conquered territory at once. The weight of American and United Nations disapproval was too heavy for the three capitals to bear and all eventually submitted to the decisions of the General Assembly. In like manner, the leading role taken by United Nations personnel in the strife-ridden Congo in 1960 clearly was supported by American policy as well as by the bulk of world opinion as expressed in the General Assembly.

The broader lesson contained in these events was not lost in Washington. In escaping from the illusions of the interwar period, Americans had lost much of their former faith in international public opinion as a tool of policy. Although moral force was admittedly not the only ponderable in international affairs, American policy-makers had almost fallen into the error of thinking that it had no effort whatsoever. The surprising power demonstrated by the United Nations had implications for the future of American policy. If the United States could keep its policy generally in harmony with the demands of mass opinion throughout the noncommunist world, a powerful new weapon would have been added to the American armory. The problem of the United Nations in American foreign policy thus acquired a new dimension; how to keep the formidable majorities amassed during these two crises together in support of American aims.

During the four years after Suez, locked in a struggle with the Soviet Union for the support of this consensus, the United States was able to gain no better than a draw. It was not until the Soviet overplayed its hand in the "U-2" crisis of 1960 that Americans could again hope that world public opinion expressed in the United Nations might again crystallize in support of American policy.[18] During the 1960 General Assembly, although American moves did not sweep everything before them, it was comforting for Americans to note that Soviet success was even more meager.

THE UNITED STATES AND SUPRANATIONAL ORGANIZATION

The drastic redistribution of power brought about by the war caused a renewed interest in the question of supranational political organization. The concentration of strength in the two new giants made most of the states of the world acutely aware of their own insecurity and set them thinking about ways to escape this unhappy situation. One of the frequently discussed techniques of doing so—particularly in the early postwar period—was the creation of political entities on a basis greater than the national state.

The extensive discussion and the tentative beginnings at the implementation of the idea raised an issue of some pertinence to the United States. It did not become a central question during the first dozen years after the war, but no one dares say unequivocally that the problem will never become critical to Americans. In its details it had relevance at two levels, that of regional federation and of world government.

The United States and Regionalism.

As far as the noncommunist world was concerned, American policy toward regionalism was favorable.[19] The more tightly organized the free world became, the better for the United States. We must point out, however, that this sympathy with regional supranational groupings did not go so far as to suggest that the United States itself might join in such an undertaking. The creation of new vehicles of government was up to smaller and weaker states; the United States was determined to preserve its own freedom of action.

---

[18] The short shrift given in the Security Council to the Soviet's complaint against the United States for violating Soviet air space testified to the extent to which Khrushchev had forfeited the sympathy he had won in the days immediately following the American confession of aerial espionage. See *New York Times,* May 25–30, 1960, *passim,* for the course of the debate.

[19] An interesting analysis of the problem in a context of "sociological jurisprudence" was made by F. S. C. Northrop, in *European Union and United States Foreign Policy.*

Thus Washington spurred the creation of the European Coal and Steel Community, the European Defense Community, the European Economic Community, and the Europe-wide atomic pool known as "Euratom," but turned a deaf ear to the proposals from private sources on both sides of the Atlantic suggesting the creation of some federal superstructure incorporating the "Atlantic Community." Even such a natural grouping as the states of the North Atlantic region was kept at the intergovernmental level of NATO rather than carried forward in any more elaborate framework. Only when western Europe threatened in 1959 to split into rival trading blocs did the United States feel itself intimately involved, and even then the American suggestion for the creation of an Organization for Economic Cooperation and Development (OECD) was officially labelled a "bridge" rather than a full entry into a regional community.

The United States and World Government.

The same general theme ran through the less-than-cursory attention paid to the question of world government after 1945. Official policy, backed by the bulk of public opinion, usually dismissed the entire idea as the crackpot scheme of a group of visionary idealists; some patriotic organizations hinted darkly that the movement was at least quasi-communist.[20] It is true that under the cold-war conditions between 1947 and 1960 there was little immediate relevance to a discussion of whether or not the United States should forthwith merge its sovereignty with that of the Soviet, its western allies, and all the neutrals in a single mechanism of world government. The problem of the United States was phrased more in terms of a formula for survival rather than for the transformation of all political relationships.

And yet the ultimate implications of American national interest in the postwar era could not be dismissed indefinitely. If peace, order, and stability on a worldwide basis were actually the interests that the United States was pursuing and was determined to pursue in the future, at some point the question of supranational organization would have to be faced. The history of societies everywhere demonstrates that social stability is feasible only within an elaborate pattern of institutions; the more complex the working institutional structure, the greater is the stability and predictability of human behavior. If peace, order, and stability were to mean anything in terms of final purposes, the issue of whether or not the United States would be willing to carry its interests to the point of promoting world government would have to be resolved some day.

---

[20] As a representative sample of this latter attitude, see Joseph P. Kamp, *We Must Abolish the United States: the Hidden Facts Behind the Crusade for World Government* (New York: Constitutional Education League, 1950). The Appendix, entitled "Communist Frontiers and Subversive Socialists," is particularly interesting.

SMALL STATES AND ANTI-COLONIALISM

An issue that was relatively late in making its appearance in American policy and that could only with difficulty be fitted into an exclusively cold-war mold is the bifurcated question of American policy toward the small states of the world generally and toward the related burning problem of anti-colonialism. After 1954 some analysts insisted that this question, rather than the more widely-discussed one of direct Soviet-American relations, would hold the key to the success or failure of American policy over the long term.[21]

The two issues are distinct but so closely connected that they can conveniently be discussed together. Not all small states are anti-colonial, nor are all ex-colonial states small. Enough states fit both categories, however, and the questions grow from such similar roots that their combined impact on American policy is exerted in the same general direction.

THE SMALL STATES AND THE COLD WAR

The "small states" of the world include the fifty or so smallest members of the international society, although drawing a definite line between small, medium, and medium-large states is difficult.[22] Their general approach to the cold war has been governed essentially by the fact of their absolute and relative weakness and their groping attempts to find some common cause in restraining the super-powers.

Small-state Groupings.

As of early 1961, there were seven more or less distinct small-state groups active in world politics. These were: (1) the Latin-American bloc; (2) the Commonwealth nations except for Britain; (3) the small states of western Europe led by Scandinavia and the Benelux countries; (4) the Soviet satellites; (5) the minor Asian powers, usually led by India; (6) the Arab states; and (7) the evolving bloc centered in Africa south of the Sahara. The latter three formerly made up the older "Afro-Asian" bloc; the increase in membership and growing divergencies of interest led to fission into the three distinct groups. The effect of these clusters was

---

[21] See, for example, Chester Bowles, *Africa's Challenge to Americans* (Berkeley: University of California Press, 1956).

[22] One interesting attempt to establish criteria of size (both in area and in population) is made in Samuel Van Valkenburg and Carl L. Stotz, *Elements of Political Geography,* 2nd ed. (Englewood Cliffs: Prentice-Hall, Inc., 1954), pp. 54–55.

most obvious in the United Nations, where the requirements of public voting and overt alignments made them apparent; in the patterns of diplomatic maneuvering, increasing intra-group solidarity was shown by all of them after 1954.

Small States and Neutralism.

We have already noted the tendency of smaller states toward neutralism and abstention from the cold war. Increasingly interpreting it as a great-power struggle in the direct issues of which most of them had only peripheral interest, the small states found that the cold war offered them both responsibilities and opportunities. They assumed the duty of keeping the cold war within the limits of safety and urged its eventual accommodation, but as long as it continued they were perfectly willing to fish in troubled waters and to gain what profit they could from the great-power dispute.

The increasing initiative of the small states foreshadowed a possible revolutionary reorientation of world relationships. The cold war era of the 1950's saw three more or less formalized vertical groupings in the world: the United States and its coalition, the communist bloc, and the neutrals. Each of these included major powers, middle powers, and small states. As long as the military danger was acute, smaller states were forced to cling to the coattails of a massive leader. But with nuclear stalemate removing the imminence of the threat, the small states of all blocs are showing a stiffer resistance to any and all great powers. If this development continues into the 1960's, the world may be moving in an era of horizontal cleavages rather than vertical: the small states will form the most numerous group in opposition to the group of giants, with the middle powers holding the balance. Any such outcome would pose major problems of policy reorganization not only for the United States, but for the Soviet Union, China, Britain, France, and the other members of the nuclear club.

American Policy.

American attitudes and policy toward the small states between 1947 and 1960 passed through three perceptible stages, corresponding roughly to the three phases into which we divided the cold war in Chapter 11.

Up to about 1950, the bipolar assumptions of the United States considered all small states as actual or potential allies of one of the two great leaders, and a neutral small state was unthinkable. American policy was therefore aimed at winning as many as possible of these states to the camp of the United States.

Between 1950 and 1954, the United States became officially aware of the distinct groups into which the small states were dividing themselves, with the first obvious ones being Latin America, the Commonwealth, and the Afro-Asians. The strength of the new group orientation of these states was first shown in the General Assembly and later in various regional conferences (such as Commonwealth Conferences, the Bandung Afro-Asian Conference in April, 1955, and various inter-American meetings).

The third stage of American comprehension of the small-state problem came with the recognition of the basic identity of interest of all minor powers when they have a free opportunity to express it, demonstrated most dramatically in the United Nations votes on the Middle-East crisis of 1956. In the most important vote, every member of the small-state group except Australia and New Zealand agreed to demanding a cease-fire and the withdrawal of the forces invading Egypt.[23]

With United Nations membership standing at 100, obviously the small states have become a major factor in world opinion. American policy during the second Eisenhower administration, although clearly unsure of the extent to which it was appropriate and profitable to do so, set itself to pay increasing attention to the demands and expectations of the smaller powers. It had beome clear, although nothing America could do would ever make small states completely happy with such a large one, that the United States could and would go much farther in shaping its responses to suit the wishes of the most numerous group of members of the world political system. Spurring such a judgment was the realization that the Soviet Union apparently had reached the same conclusion.

THE UNITED STATES AND ANTI-COLONIALISM

"Anti-colonialism," a word symbolizing a potent force in world affairs today, is a product of the contemporary era. Since 1945 the great colonial empires of the nineteenth century have been rapidly melting away; coincident with this development (and to some extent its cause), there has appeared a vast current of opinion that condemns as immoral and illegal the very principle of imperial rule. The source of this attitude is found in the nationalist aftermath of the successful colonial revolutions in Asia and Africa after 1945, but it is by no means confined to ex-colonial peoples. There has always been something of a guilty conscience in the western world about the subjugation of alien peoples, and this has come to the surface since the end of the war. The ex-colonial states and the mass support they command in the West (to say nothing of the encouragement they receive from the USSR) have combined to make the word a rallying

---

[23] For a summary of American policy toward the uncommitted states up to early 1956, see Reitzel, Kaplan, and Coblentz, *United States Foreign Policy*, pp. 314–18, 453–57.

point for some of the most potentially explosive forces in the modern world.[24]

The Meaning of Anti-colonialism.

Anti-colonialism has meaning in a variety of contexts. At its simplest, it stands for the rapid and total dismantling of all forms of imperialism. To borrow the language of the Charter (Article 73), anti-colonialism insists that the category of "non-self-governing peoples" be eliminated from the world's political vocabulary. It is the right of one people to rule over another —regardless of any extenuating circumstances—that the missionaries of anti-colonialism are busy denying.

But anti-colonialism in practice goes much further. It does not stop with attacking the legal relationships of ruler-colony, but challenges what some of its practitioners call the "colonial mentality." This means that the task of anti-colonialism is not ended by a declaration of independence, but that it goes further to a variety of social, economic, and (especially) psychic goals. Anti-colonialism will not be content until ex-colonial states are accepted as full and equal partners in the world political process, until equality of deference is accorded them, and until their purposes and objectives are judged to be as important and as inherently worthy as those of older nations. This has meant inevitably that anti-colonialism has come to carry unmistakable overtones of racial equality, of the relative merits of different civilizations and cultures, and of a demand for industrial and technological parity.

The Impact on the United States.

The United States was totally unprepared for the violent effect of anti-colonialism on the pattern of international politics. At a time when Washington was laboring to construct a framework of unity for the free world, and when some of its major partners were the world's leading colonial powers, it seemed a regrettable and almost irrelevant digression when the new states of Asia began to raise the issue of anti-colonialism.

The slowness of American response to the new forces led many Asian and African leaders to conclude that the United States had proved false to its own revolutionary and anti-imperialist tradition. They feared that Americans had been seduced by Britain and France into becoming apologists for an "outworn" imperialist outlook, and that American policy had acquired a racist character that classified the new states as "lesser

---

[24] See Kenneth Robinson, "World Opinion and Colonial Status," *International Organization* (November, 1954); for a critical appraisal of the impact of anti-colonialism on the United Nations, see Vernon Aspaturian, "The Metamorphosis of the United Nations," *The Yale Review* (Summer, 1957).

breeds without the law." With some reluctance and regret, many anti-colonialists turned to the Soviet as being more sympathetic toward the aspirations of freedom and equality that they harbored.

This development again caught the United States off guard. The new turn in the anti-colonial attitude caused sharply divided opinions among Americans. Some argued that this proved the essentially communist nature of the revolt against imperialist authority, and urged that the United States join vigorously in suppressing independence movements aimed at destroying the bonds of empire. Others contended that the liquidation of empire and the appearance of new states was inevitable and that several hundred millions of newly independent people were soon to be added to the world political community. These new states and peoples would constitute a powerful factor, one that the United States would ignore only at its own peril.

A New American Policy?

From 1947 to 1956, American policy on this issue was never clarified. Washington, reluctant to weaken its European allies, did little overtly and very little more covertly to speed the withdrawal of imperial authority, but neither did it ever unequivocally oppose the forces of independence. The upshot was that neither the European states nor the anti-colonial peoples were satisfied.

American policy, however, took what appeared to be a dramatic turn in 1956. The split with Britain and France over the invasion of Egypt won Washington expressions of support and loyalty from the entire ex-colonial world. Since that crisis the United States has been much more sympathetic toward anti-colonialism, a task made much easier by the great victories the forces of nationalism and independence in the colonial world have won over imperialism in recent years. With Britain and France no longer fighting the trend, the United States has felt much less of a division ol loyalties and interests.

The problem, however, is not dead; for example, France's long-drawn-out struggle in Algeria leaves the United States in a congenitally unhappy dilemma. Even more subtle and complex has been the impact of anti-colonial attitudes upon the West's technical assistance and development programs. As long as the United States refuses to channel the bulk of its aid to the underdeveloped world through the United Nations and instead makes it appear to sensitive peoples as white man's largesse, anti-colonial bias will continue to inhibit the whole program's effectiveness. The United States will be obliged to struggle with the aftermaths of imperialism for a long time; during the 1960 Congo crisis, even United Nations assistance ran afoul of anti-colonialism when tempers were sufficiently high.

Continuing
Military
Issues
in
American
Policy

CHAPTER ◄ *13* ►

At various points in the preceding chapters we noted
that one of the characteristics of the post-1945 era
is the closer interrelation of military, political, and
economic factors in the foreign relations of the United
States. Americans, to whom military affairs were a
matter to be traditionally dealt with in a crisis atmosphere of war or near-war, have been obliged to devise a
consistent military policy for times that, if not truly
peaceful, were at least not marked by all-out warfare.
With little of consistent tradition to guide the United
States, and with the stakes in national and international
power and prestige so high, it is no wonder that the postwar era has produced no entirely satisfactory resolution
of the military issues in American policy.

In this chapter we shall examine three of the broader
and more persistent questions that have arisen since
1945. We shall first deal with American military policy
in general, considering the military mission of the United
States and examining the controversy between the
advocates of a "balanced force" and those of the "new

look." Next we shall take up American overseas defense obligations, both in extent and in nature. Finally we shall summarize the problem of arms limitation, reduction, and control, often stereotyped in the popular term "disarmament."

UNITED STATES MILITARY POLICY

THE AMERICAN MILITARY MISSION

The military establishment of any state is an instrument of the state, to be used for the implementation of appropriate policies. As such, it is a part of the arsenal of techniques any government has at its disposal. The military mission of the United States, therefore, is inseparable from the totality of American policy objectives and is comprehensible finally in terms of the contribution it makes to their accomplishment.[1]

Granted the nature of American foreign policy and the concept of national interest which it serves, we may say generally that the American military mission is to put the armed might of the United States at the service of international peace, order, and stability. In this way, American armed forces exist for the purpose of deterring a potential revisionist state (an "aggressor") from seeking to advance its policy by armed attack on the United States security sphere and of warding off such an attack by active combat if one should occur.[2]

The Deterrent Mission.

The story is told that General Curtis LeMay, then Commander of the Strategic Air Command of the United States Air Force, once said: "If war comes, SAC will have failed in its primary mission." Whether or not this is an accurate quotation, the idea it expresses is central to much American military thinking. American military power has the primary mission of preventing wars from happening, for to a status-quo nation such as the United States, the most successful wars are the ones that never have to be fought.

Under conditions of modern technology, deterring a potential aggressor is only partially a matter of defensive ability. Although the race to develop

---

[1] See W. D. Puleston, *The Influence of Force in Foreign Relations* (New York: Van Nostrand, 1955), especially chapters 2, "Land, Sea, and Air Forces as Factors of Peace," and 7, "Averting War by Means of Force"; also Council on Foreign Relations, *Basic Aims of United States Foreign Policy,* pp. 14–16.

[2] See Edgar W. Furniss, Jr., *American Military Policy* (New York: Rinehart & Company, Inc., 1957).

effective neutralizing techniques to nuclear bombs, supersonic aircraft, guided missiles, rockets, and so on is neverending, the offense in warfare yet enjoys the advantage over the defense that it gained at the beginning of World War II. Today, the most elaborate and expensive defenses can afford only partial protection against modern weapons. Military security, therefore, tends to be largely a function of a nation's ability to retaliate to attack. No sane leader will attack another state if he is certain he will be overwhelmed in return; only a foolhardy one will launch a modern total war if he is convinced that his enemy can and will reply with an equal amount of force. Modern warfare, to be a good bargain, requires an enormous margin of superiority. Deterrence, therefore, in theory does not require absolute superiority over any possible enemy or even equality with him; adequate reprisal power to discourage attack is sufficient to accomplish the mission, even if the total available is less than that of the enemy.

The Combat Mission.

But the American military machine must be prepared to deal with the situation arising from an overt resort to arms by an enemy; it must be prepared to fight and win any probable war. This is a more familiar problem to Americans; it has seemed to many as if this is the true and natural mission of the United States Army, Navy, and Air Force.

But here again the impact of modern weapons has complicated what was once a reasonably clear and simple problem. Modern war, in practice, can assume either of two forms: total war for total objectives, or limited war for limited goals (what is sometimes called today the "brush-fire" war). Each presents its own technical problems, and each—and this has been the source of much difficulty—requires its own strategy and its own level of "preparedness."

Total war will probably be won by the side that achieves absolute surprise and buries its enemy in a rain of nuclear bombs. It is conceived of as a quick and sudden assault of a size sufficient to destroy or to impair fatally the enemy's capacity to strike back. Limited war, however, refers to a struggle prosecuted without recourse to total weapons and for objectives that are by that fact themselves limited.

The major question surrounding limited war since 1945 has been one of utility. It is possible, even under modern conditions, to prevent a limited war from growing into an all-out struggle; Korea, Indochina, and Palestine all proved this point. But since the era of total weapons was born, no limited war directly involving major states has been able to produce a final solution to the political problems that were responsible for the conflict in the first place. This is an inhibition that affects the United

States perhaps less than it does the revisionist states, for a stalemated war for America can never be anything less than a qualified victory; for all states, however, it throws much doubt on the efficacy of any form of war other than the total.[3]

American combat missions, therefore, must take two forms. The United States must be prepared to accept the challenge of total war if any aggressor presents it. Americans must also face the necessity of coping with limited wars of all types; "brush fires" may break out at any moment and the United States must have the ability to extinguish them if it be thought desirable. America must recognize, however, that the probability of winning any meaningful affirmative victory by limited war is at best a very low one, and that stalemate will often be the most that can be achieved by any such effort. Short of winning a war of survival, it can be argued that the most important American military mission is preventing big wars rather than winning small ones. This is true not because the small conflicts are unimportant in themselves, but because of the difficulty of "winning" them while keeping them small.

BALANCED FORCE VS. NEW LOOK

This formulation of the American military mission has been controlling within American government circles since the onset of the cold war, but it is by no means the only one that has been advanced. We alluded earlier to the controversy over the optimum form of the American military establishment. Although fought out before the public largely in terms of the conflicting responsibilities of the three armed services, it actually was (and is) an outgrowth of a fundamental disagreement over the nature of the military problem facing the United States and the theory to be adopted in solving it.

Little Wars or Big Wars?

We will recall that the original containment hypothesis of American foreign policy called for the United States to resist further communist expansion at whatever time and in whatever form it appeared. In military terms, this meant that American armed forces would repel any Soviet-inspired attempt to break through the ring by war, and that adequate American military power would be committed to hold the line. The Korean war provided the first clear test of this principle.

---

[3] See, in this connection, Robert E. Osgood, *Limited War: the Challenge to American Strategy* (Chicago: University of Chicago Press, 1957), and Henry A. Kissinger, *Nuclear Weapons and Foreign Policy* (New York: Harper & Bros., 1957); see also Hanson W. Baldwin, "Limited War," *The Atlantic Monthly* (May, 1959), pp. 35 ff.

Korea proved to be an extremely frustrating experience for Americans; no enterprise could be imagined more calculated to fray American nerves and to destroy American perspectives than a war fought under such conditions. There were technical military reasons for questioning American policy in Korea. It defied the historic American theory of war to fight a holding action indefinitely and to refuse to force a battlefield decision.[4] There was also some doubt about the worth of a policy that left it up to the enemy to decide when, where, with what weapons, and for what objectives to fight. It became popular to warn of the "bleeding" effect of such a policy: Moscow, according to this argument, could use its initiative to force a series of profitless little wars on the United States and thus to bleed America to death.

In discussing "liberation," we pointed out earlier that this dogma called for a new military policy, one that came to be known popularly as "massive retaliation." According to this doctrine, the United States—although not totally abandoning the "little war" field to the communists—came to concentrate instead on the big-war problem. Instead of meeting each "brush fire" directly, the United States emphasized the true source of the difficulty, the Soviet itself. The United States reserved the right to meet any new war not by equivalent resistance at the point of outbreak but instead by "massive retaliation" at "places and times" of America's own choosing. Thus deterrence became the preferred method of dealing with the danger of limited war as well as that of total war.

The New Look in Defense.

Beginning in 1953, the Eisenhower administration began reshaping the structure of the American military establishment in conformity with the new doctrine. The "new look" [5] had two major components: (1) a reduction both in expenditure and in manpower—headlined on occasion as "more bang for a buck"; (2) a new strategic theory based frankly on American industrial and technological superiority.

Defense budgets were scaled down to approximately $33 billion in fiscal 1955. After that year the total moved slowly upward again as the cost of new weapons programs continued to mount, reaching over $40 billion

---

[4] This was the major point in General MacArthur's attack on administration and United Nations policy in Korea. See Charles A. Willoughby and John Chamberlain, *MacArthur, 1941–1951* (New York: The McGraw-Hill Book Co., Inc., 1954), pp. 421–22.

[5] The term apparently was first used by Defense Secretary Charles E. Wilson in June, 1953, while testifying before the Senate Committee on Appropriations on the 1954 defense budget. Wilson promised "a new look at the entire defense picture." *Hearings on the Department of Defense Appropriations for 1954,* Senate Committee on Appropriations, 83rd Congress, 1st Session (Washington: U. S. Government Printing Office, 1953), p. 6.

in fiscal 1961. Manpower was likewise reduced, dropping from three and a half million in 1953 to less than two and a half million in 1959.

These new directions were possible, according to official doctrine, because of the new strategic theory. Essentially this new dogma involved a concentration upon air power as the central vehicle of applying force and upon nuclear weapons as being most appropriate to the mission the United States was adopting. Underlying both of these foci of concentration was the basic assumption that the American military problem was one "no longer calling for rearmament by a specific date of peak danger, but as requiring a gradual build up and steady maintenance over an indeterminate period." [6] For the long pull America was to put its trust in science and technology as a means of offsetting Soviet preponderance in manpower and in conventional weapons. Despite the strenuous objections of some military personnel who felt themselves slighted in the redefinition of missions and of other observers who found partisan politics at least partially at the root of the new principles, the United States government moved steadily to make the "new look" a reality.

The Assumptions of "Massive Retaliation."

The doctrine of "massive retaliation," if it were to be taken seriously as the operating principle of American defense policy, rested on a number of assumptions that were independent of the technical issues of budgets and the conduct of warfare. Five of them were of primary importance. (1) All three services would agree on the principle of the "new look." (2) American superiority (qualitative and quantitative) in nuclear weapons would be maintained. (3) The only threats to United States military security would come from the communist world. (4) The decision to employ the weapons of totality would be a unilateral one by the United States. (5) Public opinion, inside the United States and the free world, and among the uncommitted nations, could be safely ignored.

One need not be a partisan in the triangular Army-Navy-Air Force dispute to be convinced that these assumptions have never been simultaneously realized in practice. None of them has been constantly operative, and it has been rare since 1953 to find as many as three of them applying at one time. Each is open to serious question.

The argument against the first simply denies that interservice agreement and consensus, let alone unanimity, has ever existed. The second is challenged on the ground of the history of the development of Soviet nuclear weapons; in the spring of 1956 General LeMay could assert the possibility

---

[6] Reitzel, Kaplan, and Coblentz, *United States Foreign Policy, 1945–1955,* p. 347. Reprinted by permission.

of early Russian leadership both in aircraft and weapons.[7] The General's point was dramatically confirmed in 1957, when in rapid succession the Soviet fired a hydrogen bomb, announced a successful inter-continental missile, and launched several space satellites. During the next four years, as the USSR maintained its lead in both long-range rocketry and the penetration of space, Americans became aware of a "missile gap" opening against them, at least in ICBM's. Despite the over-all success the United States continued to enjoy in preventing the appearance of a corresponding "deterrent gap" in broader capabilities, serious problems resulted from the invalidation of the easy assumption of American strategic dominance.[8]

The third assumption is the least open to question, although many security threats to the United States can be suggested that might arise from other than Soviet sources. The fourth runs counter to the entire alliance system of the United States, and was invalidated by the success of Great Britain and France in independently acquiring a nuclear capability. The fifth was never more than conjectural and, by 1960, had obviously become totally invalid; public opinion, far from remaining quiescent, was instead forcing all the nuclear powers to discuss both test cessation and control of nuclear weapons.

The "new look" was not inseparable from the doctrine of "massive retaliation." It was possible to justify a smaller and more efficient armed force geared into a retaliatory strategy on some basis other than that of meeting every danger with the threat of nuclear assault. The increasing inexpediency of the doctrine stimulated a series of bitter arguments among service personnel, the public, policy-making officials, and within the free-world alliance. By 1956 there were indications that the rigor of the massive retaliation thesis had been somewhat relaxed;[9] by 1961, even its one-time violent partisans were reluctant to use the term itself or to defend its concepts.

Inter-service Disputes.

Complicating the objective evaluation of the "new look" in defense and of "massive retaliation" as the theory for its implementation was the continuing squabble among the three uniformed services. Basic strategic development was obscured by well-publicized barrages of claims and counterclaims by the Army, Navy, and Air Force for privileged positions in the

---

[7] See General LeMay's testimony before the Symington subcommittee of the Senate on April 27 and 30, 1956. *New York Times* (April 28 and May 1, 1956).

[8] A recent attempt at the solution of these problems was made in a report to the Senate Committee on Foreign Relations by the Washington Center of Foreign Policy Research of the Johns Hopkins University, *Developments in Military Technology and their Impact on United States Strategy and Foreign Policy* (Washington: U. S. Government Printing Office, 1959).

[9] Reitzel, Kaplan, and Coblentz, *United States Foreign Policy,* pp. 444–45.

new military machine. In the course of the running battle by the three, however, the various alternatives were thoroughly aired.

Underlying the controversy, and dating back to its initial flareup at the time the armed services were "unified" by the National Security Act in 1947, was the widespread notion among professional military men of all branches that the future belonged to air power. The older services hoped to redefine their own missions so as to give them authority over such air weapons as were appropriate to themselves; the Air Force, itself newly independent of Army control, sought to acquire and to perpetuate a monopoly.

A large, if undiscoverable, share of the devoted care with which each service prosecuted its own case was due to the sincere conviction each held that its own strategic principles, tactical doctrine, and dedicated personnel were best fitted to provide for the security of the United States. We must also recognize, however, that all three services were not unaware of the career implications of the new nature of defense. The service that was granted central responsibility would receive the lion's share of prestige, high rank, and appropriations. Each service felt impelled, therefore, not only to press its own claims but also to deprecate and often to deride the assertions of the other two.

The Army Offensive.

Despite the share of responsibility that the Air Force and the Navy have for keeping the inter-service struggle alive, the Army has been in recent years the most outspoken. The Navy had its day during the Truman era; the "revolt of the admirals" in 1949 [10] and the contemporaneous campaign against the Air Force's B-36 bomber program were the major pre-Korean war struggles. The Navy found itself in the midst of a dispute again in 1960 over the Air Force's demand for operational command of the newly-perfected nuclear submarines armed with the "Polaris" missile. Under the "new look," the Army has felt its position endangered and has gone both to Congress and to the court of public opinion to press its case.

The opening salvo was fired in 1955 by General Matthew B. Ridgeway on the occasion of his retirement as Army Chief of Staff. In an open letter to Secretary of Defense Wilson, he criticized the dismantling of Army strength in favor of the questionable doctrine of "massive retaliation." His views were elaborated in his later autobiography.[11] In May, 1956,

---

[10] On the "revolt of the admirals," see Timothy W. Stanley, *American Defense and National Security* (Washington: Public Affairs Press, 1956), pp. 94–5.

[11] General Ridgeway's letter was printed in full in *United States News and World Report* (July 29, 1955); his autobiography, *Soldier* was published by Harper & Bros. in 1956.

shaken by the Air Force's doctrine that the other two services had roles clearly auxiliary to its own, the Army launched a powerful and coordinated offensive. A series of news "leaks" occurred that added up to a frontal attack on the entire airpower concept.[12] The Air Force retaliated, and the bitterness of the interservice rivalry was laid bare for all to see.

Secretary of Defense Wilson, in an uprecedented press conference, called the three service chiefs together and publicly obtained their renunciation of what their subordinates had been saying.[13] A few months later Mr. Wilson decided the specific points that had precipitated the explosion (missile responsibility and army aviation) in favor of Air Force contentions, and the Army sank into deep gloom.

Since the 1956 flareups and their result, the Army has continued to wage its battle. Supported by the development and elaboration of the "limited war" doctrine and by the growing rigidity of the nuclear stalemate, the Army has fought stubbornly for a revision of basic strategic doctrine and greater appropriations. Books and articles by leading military figures and by sympathetic civilians [14] have appeared in all media; political pressure (exerted primarily through Democratic party channels) has been applied judiciously. In spite of the vigor of the Army's effort, however, it never succeeded (at least up to 1961) in bringing about any significant change in its relative status or role. Its manpower and appropriations kept shrinking and its strategic doctrine received only minor acceptance.

The "Balanced Force" Argument.

What is the Army's argument? Put at its simplest, Army doctrine rejects any single-weapon concept of defense and instead urges a "balanced force."

Its central thesis is, of course, that atomic strategy was feasible only as long as the United States enjoyed great superiority in that category of weapons. Once atomic stalemate was achieved, the utility of total war *for either side* was reduced to the vanishing point. From that moment, the only sort of warfare at all likely to occur was limited war in peripheral areas.[15] Total weapons of whatever type were held to be useless in any such local struggle; the United States would be forced to rely on conven-

---

[12] See the *New York Times* (May 19–22, 1956), especially the dispatches of Anthony Liviero.

[13] *New York Times* (May 22, 1956).

[14] See especially two recent books by retired (and angry) Army generals: James M. Gavin, *War and Peace in the Space Age* (New York: Harper & Bros., 1958), and Maxwell M. Taylor, *The Uncertain Trumpet* (New York: Harper & Bros., 1960).

[15] This point has been made many times by Henry A. Kissinger in his series of articles in *Foreign Affairs*. See, among others, "Military Power and the Defense of the 'Grey Areas'" (April, 1955), "Force and Diplomacy in the Nuclear Age" (April, 1956), "Strategy and Organization" (April, 1957). See also, for a somewhat different

tional weapons and tactical nuclear ones, used in conformity with time-tested strategic concepts. The basic problem was the familiar one of applying force appropriate to the objective sought. If total weapons were all that were available, a small objective would either have to be abandoned or achieved by methods out of all proportion to the goal.

Considerable intellectual effort has been expended in hammering out a doctrinal justification for the "balanced force." [16] It achieved some results. After the 1957 Soviet breakthrough in rocketry, all three services officially adopted some version of "flexible response" as their guiding principle. The Army, however, found itself irrevocably dedicated to less-than-total combat with its maximum contribution to all-out war being through "dual-purpose" forces; the Air Force remained generally loyal to the SAC concept, and attempted to prove that strategic air power had limited-war significance.

Perhaps the most "balanced" of the three services was the Navy, with its conventional forces on the one hand and its air-nuclear capability on the other. Navy stock rose sharply with the public and the Eisenhower administration after 1958 when its nuclear-powered submarines success-fully undertook sensational submerged cruises, including trips under the North Pole and around the world. As its "Polaris" 1500-mile ballistic mis-sile neared operational completion and its missile-launching submarines became operational, the Navy felt in early 1961 that it had developed the ideal deterrent weapons system.[17]

THE ALLOCATION OF RESPONSIBILITY

The inter-service controversy has been, among other characteristics, a disagreement about respective roles and missions. Not the least cause of

---

analysis, James E. King, Jr., "Nuclear Plenty and Limited War," *Foreign Affairs* (January, 1957). Turner and Challener, *National Security in the Nuclear Age*, is frankly an apology for a "peripheral strategy."

[16] As major examples, see Henry A. Kissinger, *Nuclear Weapons and Foreign Policy*, and W. W. Kaufmann, ed., *Military Policy and National Security* (Princeton: Princeton University Press, 1956). About the latter volume Lieutenant General James M. Gavin is reported to have said, "This is the Army's story." *Army* (May, 1956). For an example of a purely professional approach, see Raymond L. Garthoff, "The Only Wars We Can Afford," *Army* (November, 1957).

[17] The Air Force felt that the "Polaris" submarine system menaced its monopoly over strategic air power, and undertook late in 1959 a campaign to win command over the entire "Polaris" capability. It contended that a strategic strike demanded a unified effort and demanded control over all "Polaris" submarines. The Navy resisted, arguing that violation of the integrity of naval forces was contrary both to Navy doctrine and to the allocation of responsibilities among the several services. See the summary of the positions in mid-1960 in an article by John G. Norris, in the *Washington Post and Times-Herald* (June 12, 1960). Later in the summer the Air Force won a large share of the command for which it had been contending.

the conflict is the difference in the way each service presents its claim. From this fundamental divergence in point of view has grown much of the subsequent confusion of purpose.

The Navy adopts a "task force" theory of organization and contends that there should be within the Navy itself everything necessary for the accomplishment of its mission. The Army, on the other hand, is more concerned with command; under Army command (for the Army, committed to the conquest and occupation of the enemy's territory, considers itself the only possible winner of real victory) there should be everything —regardless of service identification—necessary for victory. The Air Force has a simpler theory: anything that flies belongs to the Air Force. These three theories of mission were obviously destined to clash.

The Key West Agreement.

The basic understanding reached on the roles of the services is the so-called Key West Agreement of 1948, revised and expanded slightly by subsequent directives. Under this agreement, the services are given missions based on their respective "primary functions" in land, sea, and air operations. Each has collateral functions that blend into the primary function of one or both of the other two branches. The Army was given primary responsibility for Army anti-aircraft artillery units, thus giving it access to the guided missile field; the Air Force was, among other points, given authority over "strategic air warfare" and for providing "close combat and logistical air support to the Army." Naval air power (including, presumably, naval employment of atomic bombs) was guaranteed.[18]

The original agreement and its later amendments resolved some points:

> Primary interest in the development of *amphibious* techniques was granted to the Marines, while primary concern with *airborne* operations was given to the Army. *Anti-submarine warfare* was made a primary function of the Navy and a collateral function of the Air Force. *Air transport* was assigned to the Air Force. But there were many areas of ambiguity. *Air Defense* was made a primary function of all three services. *Army aviation* was not discussed at all. Nor was any mention made of *guided missiles*. Strategic bombing was made a primary function of the Air Force....[19]

Direct inter-service agreements and directives from the Secretary of Defense served to eliminate or to minimize some of the failures of under-

---

[18] The Key West agreement is reproduced in Stanley, *Defense and Security,* pp. 176–88.

[19] Stanley, *Defense and Security,* p. 89. Italics in original. Reprinted by permission.

standing left after the Key West Agreement and its amendments of 1949 and 1953. By 1956 the principal points of controversy remaining involved authority over guided missiles and rockets on the one hand and the Army's possession and employment of its own aviation on the other.

The Missiles Decision.

During the 1956 dispute all three services had brought up the issue of missiles, praising their own and deriding the others. For all three it was a central problem. If the warfare of the future was to become increasingly robotinized and if ground-to-ground, air-to-ground, ground-to-air, and air-to-air missiles, carrying nuclear warheads, were to become the decision-forcing weapons, the share of authority of each service over the general missile field was a vital concern. The public became familiar with the names of "Nike," "Talos," "Redstone," and other missiles, and the initials "ICBM" (the intercontinental ballistic missile with a projected range of 3,000–5,000 miles) also acquired the status of a household word.

The November, 1956, directive of Secretary Wilson attempted to cut the Gordian Knot.[20] The Army was limited to missiles with a *200-mile range* for use against *tactical targets* within its *zone of operations* (defined as 100 miles beyond the front line and 100 miles to the rear). The Air Force was given jurisdiction over all *land-based missiles* with a range of over 200 miles. Thus existing missiles were divided (the Air Force won control over the Army's "Jupiter," an intermediate-range ballistic missile), and the development of the ICBM was centralized finally in the Air Force.

Since 1956, the Army has struggled against what it regards as the 200-mile straitjacket, but without success. Its progress in the space-satellite field encouraged its supporters for a time, but late in 1959 its highly successful Redstone Arsenal space team, headed by Dr. Werner von Braun, was transferred to the civilian National Aeronautics and Space Agency and the Army was barred from the space field. It vigorously exploited its grant of air-defense capability, developing an anti-missile missile system, the Nike-Zeus, that contrasted favorably with the Air Force's Bomarc. In its "Pershing" guided missile it had a tactical weapon of great value, but its effective range rose rapidly to over 200 miles, raising the specter of an Air Force takeover. All in all, the Army's experience with missiles was unhappy, and its future in this field no more certain in 1961 than ever.

Army Aviation.

The Air Force's victory was as complete on the issue of Army aviation. The Army, envious of the Navy's integral air arm and the fact that each Marine division has its own tactical air wing, has long agitated in favor

---

[20] The directive is summarized in *New York Times* (December 2, 1956), IV, 1.

of some such arrangement for itself. It stresses the difficulties of dealing with Air Force commanders who are not under Army control, and of the danger and inefficiency of having to negotiate tactical air support, troop transport, and airlift operation under combat conditions.

In the same directive as that incorporating the missile decision, the Army was forbidden to provide its own close-combat air support. Its aircraft, furthermore, were limited to those required for battle-zone operations (as defined above) and their functions were confined to essentially Army purposes, such as observation, reconnaissance, and the airlift of Army personnel and materiel. This decision seemingly certified the position of the Air Force as the key service in the American defense scheme. Recurrent Army protests about the inadequacy of the strategic and tactical airlift available to it have had no effect.

AMERICAN OVERSEAS DEFENSE COMMITMENTS

A major feature of American policy during the cold war has been the development and elaboration of a series of overseas defense commitments. For the first time in its history, the United States had found it necessary both to enter into firm alliances with foreign states and to deploy its military forces on the territory of its allies. A logical consequence of this development has been the adoption of the policy of supplying the associates of the United States with materiel for their own defense and for the security of the alliance.[21]

As of 1961 the United States was allied with 44 different states. These ties included four multilateral treaties and a number of bilateral arrangements. The obligations covered the major areas of the world. Western Europe was protected by NATO. Southeast Asia was covered by SEATO, the southwest Pacific by ANZUS, the western hemisphere by OAS, and the Middle East by the series of bilateral pacts that linked the United States to CENTO. The Far East was tied together by a network of bilateral agreements with the Philippines, Nationalist China, the Republic of Korea, and Japan. These pacts together created the greatest peacetime "Grand Alliance" in history.

THE PATTERNS OF ALLIANCE

Although all the 44 states with which the United States had military agreements were, in one sense or another, "allies," the nature of the obliga-

---

[21] An elaboration of this point is undertaken by Herbert Agar in *The Price of Power: America since 1945* (Chicago: University of Chicago Press, 1957).

tion incurred by the American government differed from one pact to another. Each merits mention in order to clarify just what Americans have obligated themselves to do.

The NATO Commitment.

Both the most binding commitment accepted by the United States and the most elaborate institutional implementation are found in American action under the terms of the North Atlantic Treaty of 1949. NATO is, as American leadership delights in pointing out, the keystone of all contemporary American policy, and our consideration of American alliances should begin with it.

The principal obligation under the Treaty is contained in Article 5. Its language is important enough to merit quotation:

> The Parties agree that an armed attack against one or more of them in Europe or North America shall be considered an attack against them all; and consequently they agree that, if such an armed attack occurs, each of them, in exercise of the right of individual or collective self-defense recognized by Article 51 of the Charter of the United Nations, will assist the Party or Parties so attacked by taking forthwith, individually, and in concert with the other Parties, such action as it deems necessary, including the use of armed force, to restore and maintain the security of the North Atlantic Area.[22]

Later provisions define the geographic area included by the pact and the relationships of the treaty to the Charter of the United Nations, and provide for the creation of a North Atlantic Council for implementing the execution of the treaty. It was thrown open to adherence by any other European state "in a position to further the principles of this Treaty" upon unanimous invitation of the members. Under these terms, the original 12 signatories have accepted the later membership of Greece, Turkey, and West Germany.

The SEATO Obligation.

The Southeast Asia Collective Defense Treaty of 1954 is not as precise as the North Atlantic Treaty in specifying either the action to be taken by the parties or the danger which the treaty is designed to meet. Article 4 contains the general pledge of collective defense, resistance to aggression, and joint action:

---

[22] *Disarmament and Security: A Collection of Documents, 1919–1955,* Committee Print, Subcommittee on Disarmament, Committee on Foreign Relations, United States Senate, 84th Congress, 2d Session (Washington: U.S. Government Printing Office, 1956), pp. 530–31.

1. Each Party recognizes that aggression by means of armed attack in the treaty area against any of the Parties or against any State or territory which the Parties by unanimous agreement may hereafter designate, would endanger its own peace and safety, and agrees that it will in that event act to meet the common danger in accordance with its constitutional processes.[23]

Section 2 of the same Article deals with a slightly different contingency. If the "inviolability or the integrity" of any party or of any protected territory "is threatened in any way other than by armed attack or is affected or threatened by any fact or situation which might endanger the peace of the area," the parties will consult together immediately to agree on measures to be taken for the common defense. We will note that Section 1 does not provide for consultation in the case of armed attack, but that Section 2, covering other dangers, requires consultation and the formulation of common measures.[24] Later provisions of the treaty, in much the same way as had the North Atlantic Treaty, define the area covered, establish a Council, and relate the treaty to the Charter.

The ANZUS Obligation.

The Australia-New Zealand-United States security treaty, negotiated in 1951 and put into effect in 1952, involves a commitment less comprehensive than the North Atlantic Treaty and more akin to the SEATO obligations. Articles III and IV are the pertinent provisions concerning consultation and common defense:

> ARTICLE III. The Parties will consult together whenever in the opinion of any of them the territorial integrity, political independence or security of any of the Parties is threatened in the Pacific.
> ARTICLE IV. Each Party recognizes that an armed attack in the Pacific Area on any of the Parties would be dangerous to its own peace and safety and declares that it would act to meet the common danger in accordance with its constitutional processes.[25]

It is noteworthy that nowhere in the treaty is the term "Pacific Area" defined, although what would constitute an armed attack on a Party is declared to include "an armed attack on the metropolitan territory, ... on the island territories under its jurisdiction in the Pacific, or on its

---

[23] *Disarmament and Security*, p. 612. The "State or territory which the Parties may hereafter designate" referred to the Associated States of Indochina (Laos, Cambodia, and Vietnam), barred from entry into any such pact.

[24] This distinction is generally thought to be a gesture in the direction of the Asian neutrals, who—led by Nehru—distrusted the narrowly anti-communist orientation of NATO and were interested in provisions offering protection against any renewed Asian colonialism.

[25] *Disarmament and Security*, p. 600.

armed forces, public vessels, or aircraft in the Pacific." [26] Other provisions are not exceptional, except that Article VIII authorizes the ANZUS Council to maintain a consultative relationship with "States, Regional Organizations, Associations of States, or other authorities" in the Pacific area in a position to contribute to the security of the region.

The OAS Obligation.

The Inter-American Treaty of Reciprocal Assistance of 1947, the first of the mutual-security pacts brought about by the United States and to some extent the model for all subsequent ones, is both more detailed in its provisions and more complex in its structure than are the others we have considered.

Article 3 contains the general guarantee and authorizes individual action on behalf of the group:

> ARTICLE 3. 1. The High Contracting Parties agree that an armed attack by any State against an American State shall be considered as an attack against all the American States and, consequently, each one of the said Contracting Parties undertakes to assist in meeting the attack in the exercise of the inherent right of individual and collective self-defense....
>
> 2. On the request of the State or States directly attacked and until the decision of the Organ of Consultation of the Inter-American System has been reached, each one of the Contracting Parties may determine the immediate measures which it may individually take in fulfillment of the obligation contained in the preceding paragraph and in accordance with the principle of continental solidarity.[27]

Article 6 defined the kinds of situations that would make the treaty applicable:

> ARTICLE 6. If the inviolability or the integrity of the territory or the sovereign or political independence of any American State should be affected by an aggression which is not an armed attack or by an extra-continental or intra-continental conflict, or by any other fact or situation that might endanger the peace of America, the Organ of Consultation shall meet immediately in order to agree on the measures which must be taken in case of aggression to assist the victim of the aggression or, in any case, the measures which should be taken for the common defense and for the maintenance of the peace and security of the Continent.[28]

---

[26] *Ibid.*, p. 601.
[27] *Ibid.*, p. 650.
[28] *Ibid.*, p. 651.

Article 7 authorized the parties to terminate a conflict between two or more American states on the basis of the *"status quo ante bellum,"* and to take action to maintain inter-American peace. Article 9, without attempting a definition of "aggression," listed as examples "unprovoked armed attack by a State against ... another State" and "invasion, by the armed forces of a State, of the territory of another State" by trespassing "boundaries demarcated in accordance with a treaty, judicial decision, or arbitral award" or "territory under the effective jurisdiction of another State." Article 17 provided that the Organ of Consultation should take its decisions by a two-thirds vote of the signatories. Thus the treaty made a major attempt to minimize inter-American conflict.

The United States and CENTO.

American security relations in the Middle East are somewhat less explicit. The principal vehicle is the Central Treaty Organization (CENTO), an association of Great Britain, Iran, Pakistan, and Turkey, of which the United States is not a member. Losing its name of "Baghdad Pact" after Iraq's withdrawal in 1958, CENTO itself is a very generalized cooperative agreement among the signatories. In 1956, the United States established permanent liaison with the pact; in 1957 it joined its economic and military committees. In 1958 the United States associated itself with a declaration by the members that emphasized the pact's defensive nature. On March 5, 1959, the United States virtually closed the circle by concluding bilateral defense agreements with Iran, Pakistan, and Turkey, whereby in case of aggression the United States "in accordance with the Constitution, will take such appropriate action, including the use of armed forces, as may be mutually agreed upon and is envisaged in the Joint Resolution to Promote Peace and Stability in the Middle East [the "Eisenhower Doctrine" of 1957]." [29] With these agreements, the question whether or not the United States should become a "member" of CENTO became purely academic.

Bilateral Obligations.

The United States has entered into bilateral security arrangements with five states: the Philippines, Japan, Korea, and China in the Far East, and Spain in Europe. Each of these has its own pecularities.

The earliest was with the Philippines, negotiated virtually simultaneously with the ANZUS agreement in 1951. Its language is in some parts exactly the same. Article IV, for example, makes identically the same pledge as Article IV of the ANZUS treaty, and Article III, providing for consultation,

---

[29] *New York Times* (March 6, 1959).

differs from the ANZUS provision only in specifying that the vehicle of consultation shall be the Foreign Ministers (or their deputies) of the two states.[30]

The treaty with Japan was first negotiated in 1951 and was completely one-sided because of the limitations on Japanese military strength imposed by the 1946 Constitution. Under the pressure of the evolving Asian cold war and the revival of Japanese nationalism, a new pact was negotiated in 1959. Its ratification touched off a major crisis in Japan and caused the cancellation of a projected good-will visit by President Eisenhower in June, 1960. The treaty itself pledges both parties to "maintain and develop their capacities to resist armed attack," to consult regularly on carrying out the treaty, and to recognize that an attack on either "on the territory of Japan" is a threat to itself. Japan further renewed the authorization given the United States in the 1951 treaty to maintain land, sea, and air bases on the territory of Japan.[31]

The pact with the Republic of Korea, negotiated after the truce in the Korean war in 1953, included most of the concepts that this brief catalogue has made familiar. Article II provides for consultation if either party is "threatened by external armed attack." Article III states that an armed attack on the territory of either party would be dangerous to the peace and safety of the other. Article IV confers the right to "dispose United States land, air, and sea forces in and about the territory of the Republic of Korea." [32]

The 1954 treaty with Nationalist China followed what was by this time the standard pattern for Far Eastern pacts: it provided for consultation, action according to "constitutional processes" to meet the danger of armed attack, and the disposition of American forces on Formosa and the Pescadores. Because of the somewhat anomalous status of the Chinese government, the territorial limits of the treaty were restricted for China to "Taiwan and the Pescadores" and for the United States to "the island territories in the West Pacific under its jurisdiction." [33] This provision was widely interpreted as constituting official American recognition of the Taipei regime's claim to de jure sovereignty over Formosa.

The agreement with Spain, entered into late in 1953, was much less specific and much more restricted in scope than any other of the bilateral

---

[30] *Disarmament and Security,* pp. 598–99.

[31] Text of 1951 treaty, *ibid.,* p. 606. The crisis in Japanese-American relations of 1960 surrounding the ratification of the treaty is portrayed in daily dispatches in *The New York Times* between May 15 and June 30, 1960.

[32] *Disarmament and Security,* pp. 607–608.

[33] *Ibid.,* pp. 608–610. It is interesting that the treaty is silent on the question—so fruitful of later controversy in the United States—of whether the American guarantee also extended to the "offshore islands": Quemoy and Matsu.

pacts. The United States agreed to extend military aid to Spain "during a period of several years to contribute to the effective air defense of Spain and to improve the equipment of its military and naval forces. . . ." Spain, on its part, agreed to permit the United States to construct bases in Spain and engaged itself to acquire the land necessary for that purpose; such areas, however, were to remain "under Spanish flag and command," and Spain was to "retain the ownership of the ground and of the permanent structures which may be constructed thereon." Despite the limited nature of the obligation assumed by both sides, the agreement was generally regarded as bringing Spain within the alliance framework of the United States.[34]

MILITARY AID PROGRAMS

Beginning with the first Mutual Defense Assistance Act in 1949, the United States has consistently supported its political and military commitments to its allies with programs of military aid. The various major phases of the effort to equip the military establishments of friendly nations we have considered in earlier chapters. At this point we need only consider the policy in its present more or less stabilized form.

What Is "Military Aid"?

We ought first to clarify what we (and the United States government) mean when we say "military aid." The term has figured in political and journalistic discussion to such an extent and with such a variety of meanings that a great deal of confusion has resulted. In our discussion we shall be using the term as officially defined by the United States government.

The President's "Tenth Semiannual Report on the Mutual Security Program" classified mutual-security assistance as follows:

> Direct military assistance under the mutual security program is extended by providing weapons and other military supply items, by carrying out training programs, and by sharing in the financing of joint military facilities.
> Nonmilitary assistance is extended in one of three ways, depending on how the needs and circumstances of the participating country relate to the policy objectives of the United States: (1) defense support and technical cooperation; (2) development assistance and technical cooperation; or (3) technical cooperation alone.[35]

---

[34] *Ibid.*, pp. 537–39.
[35] *Report to Congress on the Mutual Security Program*, September 20, 1956 (Washington: U. S. Government Printing Office, 1956), p. 14.

"Defense support" is defined in the same document as being

> designed to help certain countries which are receiving military assistance to support appropriate levels of military strength while also maintaining and promoting political and economic stability. Such support involves furnishing economic resources to enable the recipient country to undertake defense activities that otherwise would not be possible or to increase the recipient's capacity to do so in the future.[36]

"Military aid," therefore, includes direct military assistance and defense support. Although it is possible (and the International Cooperation Administration finds it convenient to do so) to subsume development assistance and technical cooperation under the general notion of aid with a mutual-security purpose, their relationship to military concerns is admittedly peripheral. The brief discussion that follows is confined to the first two categories, direct military aid and defense support.

How Much Military Aid?

The trend of military assistance expenditures is shown by the black portion of the bars on the chart (on page 366).[37] From a high point of 4 billion in fiscal 1953, there has been a steady drop in the face of a rising general price level. In the executive budget requests for 1961, for example, the over-all total shrank to 1.75 billion; included was some 803 million for defense support and the remainder for direct military assistance.[38]

Who Receives Military Aid?

In fiscal 1960, the military assistance appropriation of 1.3 billion was broken up as follows: Europe, 477 million; Africa, 7.3 million; Near and Middle East, 567 million; Far East, 96 million. Defense support went to 12 nations, all underdeveloped and most subject to communist pressure. Of the total of 765 million, the great bulk went to the Far East, especially to Korea, Taiwan, and Vietnam. Increases for these three countries were planned for fiscal 1961.[39]

Thus in Europe the emphasis in military aid was on direct end-item supply and cooperative defense, while in Asia it tended heavily toward defense support. These trends were relatively long term; of much more recent

---

[36] *Ibid.*, p. 14.

[37] Chart from *Report* of the Committee of Foreign Affairs, House of Representatives, 86th Congress, 2nd Session "Mutual Security Act of 1960," p. 10.

[38] *The Budget of the United States Government for the Fiscal Year Ending June 30, 1961* (Washington: U.S. Government Printing Office, 1960), pp. M16, 89.

[39] *Report* on the "Mutual Security Act of 1960," House Committee on Foreign Relations, *op. cit.*, p. 21.

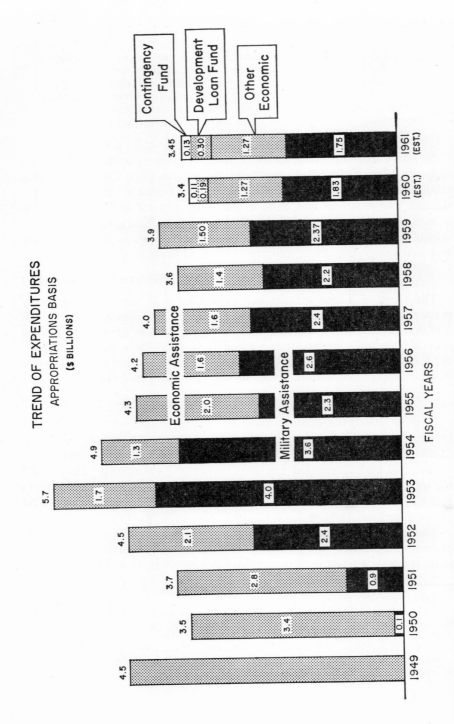

TREND OF EXPENDITURES
APPROPRIATIONS BASIS
($ BILLIONS)

Contingency Fund
Development Loan Fund
Other Economic

Economic Assistance

Military Assistance

FISCAL YEARS

	1949	1950	1951	1952	1953	1954	1955	1956	1957	1958	1959	1960 (EST.)	1961 (EST.)
Total	4.5	3.5	3.7	4.5	5.7	4.9	4.3	4.2	4.0	3.6	3.9	3.4	3.45
Economic	4.5	3.4	2.8	2.1	1.7	1.3	2.0	1.6	1.6	1.4	1.50	1.27	1.27
Military		0.1	0.9	2.4	4.0	3.6	2.3	2.6	2.4	2.2	2.37	1.83	1.75
Development Loan Fund												0.19	0.30
Contingency Fund												0.11	0.13

vintage was the significant increase in the relative share of direct military assistance being extended to the Middle East. The rise of the Middle East to first place among the recipients of military aid dates only from the Soviet penetration into the area that began in 1956.

ARMS LIMITATION IN UNITED STATES POLICY

Our final military issue—which is only partly military in nature, since its conveys heavy overtones of political, economic, and psychological relevance—is the troublesome question of the international regulation and limitation of armaments. In some respects the history of the attempt to devise a workable scheme of armament control since 1945 is a continuation of the story of the interwar period. Certain factors peculiar to the contemporary era, however, have made the issue of arms limitation both more frustrating and more important than ever before in American history.

At the beginning of this brief examination of the issues and problems involved in the international limitation of armaments, we should again point out that what we are discussing here is not the emotion-packed concept of "disarmament." No one in responsible office has ever *seriously* proposed that all nations should lay down their arms and, in the words of the spiritual, "study war no more." [40] The more cumbersome but more exact phrase "arms limitation" describes what we are to consider here: the attempt to discover some basis for a multilateral reduction in the level of national armaments and for guaranteeing that interstate contracts will remain confined within the limits prescribed by these more modest military establishments.

The Arms Race with the Soviet Union

What has changed the issue of arms limitation from a nonspecific concern for a better world to a matter of practical urgency for the United States is the ominous dimensions assumed by the massive arms race with the Soviet Union. In international affairs (as in other areas of social life) there operates a concept known as the "expectation of violence." When social conditions habituate individuals to the probability of a recourse to violence, the prospect of its employment in settling disputes increases. In the relations of rival states, there seems to be positive correlation between the respective levels of armament and the expectation of war. This

---

[40] But Premier Khrushchev, addressing the General Assembly of the United Nations on September 18, 1959, made just such a proposal. Although the United States dismissed it as propaganda, the proposal stirred widespread discussion.

suggests, but by no means proves, that an arms race between the USSR and the United States tends to make war between them more likely.

In any case, since 1956 the intensity of the arms competition between the two giants has become a cause of much concern, both within the United States and among America's allies. Public pressure has multiplied on both governments to make some new efforts to break through the obstacles and to release the world both from the economic burden of armaments and from the menace of nuclear holocaust. It has seemed probable that both major powers would take advantage of any period of relaxation in tension to make some new explorations. The issue of arms limitation has acquired a new significance.

The Arms Race and the Cold War.

How the arms race had begun was well known. As soon as the cold war began in earnest, the United States began to rearm. Never planning to match Soviet preponderance in manpower generally and in ground armies in particular, America's effort centered on the development of mobile and highly effective air and naval defense units; the principal weapons in which the United States placed its trust were atomic. Moscow's reaction to the failure of atomic-control discussions was to intensify its own "crash" program for the development of nuclear weapons; its success in 1949 prompted the United States in turn to strengthen its own ground defenses and to construct the extensive alliance system to contain Soviet expansionism. Since 1950 the cold war has had a clear arms-competition dimension.

Categories of Competition.

Any discussion of armaments since 1945 must take account of the fact that the military equipment of both major states falls today into two categories: "conventional" and nuclear. One of the most vital—but yet unsettled—questions is the relationship of these two to each other. In totting up a nation's armed power, how many infantry divisions equal one hydrogen bomb? No easy formula has yet been devised to answer this obviously pertinent question, and without one it is extremely difficult to make intelligent estimates of military parity.[41]

The United States has recognized that it would be politically inexpedient for the free world to attempt to match Soviet ground power. The United States has sought to keep its own and its allied armies superior to the Soviet on a man-for-man basis, and to maintain a sufficiently large

---

[41] This problem is discussed in Knorr, *The War Potential of Nations,* Chapter 14: "The Present State of War Potential."

ground force to serve as a deterrent in time of peace and as a delaying factor in the event of combat. The major American effort has been in maintaining a controlling lead over Russia in strategic air power, in nuclear bombs, and in missiles of all types. As this lead first began to narrow after 1957 and then disappeared after 1959, the United States found itself trying to catch up (at least in ICBMs) rather than exploiting a safe advantage. It was generally agreed that the missile gap—which everyone admitted existed—would not lead to any "deterrent gap" in the future if the United States followed a rational arms policy,[42] but the arms race was a much more complex thing for Americans after 1959 than it had been previously.

The Kremlin, however, has followed a peculiarly ambivalent line. It would seem obvious that if Moscow could develop its nuclear capacity to the point where it effectively neutralized American strategic power, its advantage in conventional forces would confer a great military preponderance upon the Soviet. The actual course of recent Russian policy, however, has been to match each nuclear-missile breakthrough with a corresponding reduction in Soviet conventional forces. If this policy be carried through, Moscow's arms pattern will correspond to Washington's, with both committed to strategic deterrence and a defensive posture.

In the tense climate of East-West relations, however, clear policies were difficult to discover. The unprejudiced observer might feel justified in feeling that the arms race was nearing totality as both sides made every effort to gain some sort of leverage over the other.

THE UNITED NATIONS AND DISARMAMENT

The United Nations has been the focus of all post war attempts to limit and control armaments. The history of the negotiations in that body over this question is a complex, confusing, and only intermittently interesting one. From it, however, certain important lessons have been learned about the future possibilities of armaments control.

The Charter and Arms Limitation.

It is worth noting at the outset that the Charter does not call either for "disarmament" or the "reduction of armaments"; it speaks instead of the "regulation of armaments." [43] It was expected at San Francisco that armed force would exist in a United-Nations dominated world, but that it would be put only to the purpose of guaranteeing international peace and security.

---

[42] See *Developments in Military Technology . . . ,* by the Washington Center of Foreign Policy Research, The Johns Hopkins University, Part C, Chapter 5: "Stability and Instability in the Equation of Strategic Power."

[43] Article 26.

Charter provisions calling for the creation of a United Nations armed force and for the temporary earmarking of certain national contingents for United Nations use further underscored the point. Military power and armaments were to have a place—limited, controlled, and subordinate, but a place nonetheless—in the world of the United Nations.

"The Diplomacy of Embarrassment."

The long and tortuous course of negotiations in the various organs of the United Nations looking toward the creation of a system of regulated armaments is of little interest to us here. As soon as the issue got caught up in the cold war, any real prospect of arms control was dissipated. The inability of the United Nations mechanisms to check the course of the great-power conflict was nowhere more dramatically demonstrated than in the failure of disarmament.[44]

What was remarkable about these unproductive discussions, however, was the tack taken by both the USSR and the United States. Each was interested in and advocated an arms-control formula that would give it a policy advantage; Washington advanced proposals that would have forever denied Moscow nuclear parity while the Soviet plainly wished to pull America's atomic teeth while maintaining its own primacy in conventional weapons. Each saw the impossibility of achieving its major goal and settled down instead to what we might call the "diplomacy of embarrassment." Each was hoping to extract the maximum policy and public-relations value from an obviously foredoomed negotiation. By early 1948 disarmament discussions were hopelessly deadlocked; no more serious attempts were made until 1955.

DISARMAMENT SINCE 1955

Ever since President Eisenhower opened new horizons for disarmament discussions with his "open sky" proposal for aerial inspection to prevent surprise attack (made at the Geneva summit conference of 1955), the whole subject has been pursued by both cold-war camps with greater vigor. In spite of frustrations, neither side has been willing to break off negotiations. Practical politics and public pressure have impelled both sides to make greater efforts to achieve at least a partial agreement. There is a considerable body of opinion today that argues that the first breakthrough in Soviet-American tension will come in the area of arms control.

---

[44] This point is made clear in Leland M. Goodrich and Anne P. Simons, *The United Nations and the Maintenance of International Peace and Security* (Washington: Brookings Institution, 1955), Chapters 21, 22.

There have been so many twists and turns in the negotiations during the past several years, and the technical data under discussion are so numerous and complex, that to attempt to tell a chronological story would be more confusing than instructive. Instead this section will mention some of the more important topics and attempt to fit them into the general question.[45]

New Channels of Negotiation.

Baffled by the continued impotence of the United Nations Disarmament Commission after its enlargement in 1957 and 1958, the major powers have been equally unable to use traditional diplomatic channels to move constructively on disarmament. In an apparent attempt to focus attention and effort on the question, they have moved to create special agencies exclusively for the discussion of disarmament matters. Late in 1959, the United States, Britain, France, and the USSR announced the creation of a special 10-member group (five from each bloc) to negotiate independently of the United Nations, but to report to the Disarmament Commission.[46] This body set to work early in 1960, but marked time in anticipation of some directives from the 1960 summit conference. When that meeting failed to produce anything but a burst of bad temper by Premier Khrushchev, the group rapidly fell into the familiar total frustration. The lesson seemed clear: even a special negotiating body was helpless in the absence of great-power political understandings about the principles to be built into any arms control system.

The negotiations on nuclear test cessation, a separate and distinct problem, were likewise carried on by special emissaries: initially a commission of scientists from the nuclear powers, and subsequently official political spokesmen. Since nuclear test cessation was generally regarded as the most hopeful area of negotiation with the fewest obstacles to agreement, both the scientists and the political figures were able to make considerable progress in their discussions. In this case, the special-body technique proved workable, because enough of the prerequisites to success were available.

East-West Positions.

During the era of intensive negotiations, the positions of the two camps have come much closer together, but major differences yet keep them apart.

---

[45] A convenient summary is found in Carol L. Thompson, "A History of Disarmament Proposals," *Current History* (January, 1959).

[46] Secretary-General Dag Hammarskjöld, while welcoming the new body, made it clear that the United Nations "retains the ultimate responsibility" for disarmament negotiations, and insisted that the 10-nation group could only "prepare the ground" for later United Nations decisions. *The New York Times* (August 14, 1959).

At the risk of drastic oversimplification, we may say that the Soviet has been most interested in substantive reduction of arms levels on the basis of a declaration of principle and intent by both sides, while the United States has focused primarily upon the control system that would police any agreement. It is hard to escape the conclusion that each side has chosen its emphasis because of its known unacceptability to the other. The USSR is pathologically frightened of the espionage possibilities of any inspection system on Soviet soil; the United States is equally obsessed by the danger of Soviet cheating on any unpoliced (or imperfectly policed) agreement. Both sides, but especially the Soviet, have also tended to inject political issues into disarmament talks as a means of warding off an agreement. Perhaps the most effective has been Moscow's idea of "geographic disarmament": some tactic of disengagement in central Europe that would effectively wreck the American alliance and defense system based on NATO.

Nuclear Test Cessation.

One minor point, originally broached by the Soviet in 1956 as a counter to the American "open sky" gambit, has grown into probably the most active aspect of the whole question: the cessation of nuclear testing. In March, 1958, the USSR scored a propaganda coup by announcing a unilateral test suspension. The United States, after completing a test series of its own, followed suit on a one-year basis in October, 1958. Negotiations looking toward making the test ban permanent were initiated, and figured largely in the Eisenhower-Khrushchev discussions of September, 1959. Although the United States formally announced its freedom of action to resume testing upon the expiration of the one-year time limit, it did not resume the tests since the negotiations were proceeding smoothly during the winter of 1959–60. It was generally felt that the Soviet was genuinely interested in an agreement, since it made by far the larger share of the concessions that were bringing the two sides closer and closer. By the time of the summit, in May, 1960 most of the world felt that an agreement was virtually at hand.

The explosion at Paris, while it did not break up either the negotiations or the high hopes for an agreement, did produce some stiffening in the Soviet stand. There was a new disquiet lest this small sector of the over-all problem, once so promising, would lapse into the frustrating deadlock that had become so characteristic of the problem. The issue of nuclear test cessation became generally regarded as the key to the issue of whether there would ever be any arms control agreement and a relaxation of the high level of international tension. If agreement could not be reached on this point, it could never be reached on larger ones.

When Premier Khrushchev, speaking before the General Assembly of the United Nations in September, 1959, proposed "total disarmament" within a four-year period, the West was startled but not impressed. It was, the United States felt, transparently dishonest and did not merit being taken seriously. As the months passed, however, it became obvious that—whether or not Khrushchev was serious—his notion had captured the imagination of much of the uncommitted world. The Soviet-projected image of a world without arms and therefore without war proved so popular that Khrushchev—at least up to his performance at Paris in May—became identified as a "man of peace."

Whatever his intention, he succeeded in intensifying the pressure on the American government to escape from the fifteen-year deadlock. Part of the difficulties American representatives have faced in trying to negotiate realistically is the knowledge that they speak for a divided government. Part of the policy-making apparatus is opposed to disarmament of any type and on any terms; part has long called for a more bold and imaginative approach.[47] Now that the USSR seems to have discovered a way to make political capital out of disarmament, the need for some effective counter by the United States has grown greater. As 1961 opened and a new Administration took over the reins, no final decision had been reached. Events would not wait much longer for the United States to make up its mind.

THE PROSPECTS FOR ARMS LIMITATION

Where did the arms-limitation issue stand after more than fifteen years of more or less serious attempts to solve it? What can we say about the prospects for regulation and control of national armaments? Is there any ground for hope?

The Implications of "Disarmament."

Among the American people, even the searing experiences of the cold-war era had not entirely eliminated their historic antipathy to things military and warlike. "Disarmament"—stigmatizing the tools of war as illegal and immoral and adopting some "higher" standard for international politics—retained much of its original grip on the emotions of broad sectors

---

[47] During this era Senator Hubert H. Humphrey of Minnesota has been among the leaders in calling for breaking new ground. See his article, "First Step Toward Disarmament," *The Nation* (May 24, 1958).

of the American body politic. Although the obviously sinister intentions and behavior of the Soviet served consistently to inhibit the mass urge to divest the nation of the burden and the threat of a high level of military expenditures and of mobilized power, there seemed to be a general feeling that the perils of national existence would be eliminated or drastically reduced if only weapons could be put away.

Of course, the American government had no such uncomplicated objective in mind as it dealt with the Soviet. Washington, consistent with the Charter's injunction to "regulate" rather than to eliminate armaments, never aimed at anything approximating the popular image of disarmament. The realistic objectives of the United States were two: (1) the development of a system of control over national military establishments sufficient to make impossible the achievement of strategic surprise by an aggressor; (2) the reduction of armament levels to a point sufficient to relax tension and allow relations to go forward on a more nearly normal basis.

A serious hiatus in communication developed between the public and the government; neither a common policy ground nor mutual understanding existed between policy-makers and most of their constituents. The mass public was and remained largely unaware of what was involved in the complicated series of disarmament negotiations, while American leadership failed to realize the extent to which the fear of nuclear war paralyzed the judgment of the public. The development of a coherent American policy could not progress until a greater cohesion developed on the implications of disarmament.

Disarmament and Security.

The postwar arms-reduction issue teaches much the same lesson as that taught by the experience of the interwar years. Disarmament, by itself, is not a cause of peace, but rather a reflection of it. Since 1945 it has proved impossible, just as it was between 1922 and 1932, to separate the issues of disarmament and security. As long as armed force remains the only ultimately efficacious method of guaranteeing national security, states are going to retain their military machines. They will agree to a reduction in arms levels only to the extent that they become convinced that their security problems will be solved by other methods.

Within the circles of academic speculation there is a real cleavage on the point of the relative importance of disarmament and security. There is a sizeable body of opinion that finds certain "positive" values in disarmament. This argument contends that even—or especially—at a moment of crisis, measures to reduce arms levels and to call off an arms race result in affirmative gains in security for everyone involved. On this basis, the time to disarm is just at the moment when affairs seem at their most tense; the beneficent effects of a reduction in armaments will extend to other policy areas, and the creation of an atmosphere of mutual confidence will be expedited.

On the other hand, an equally strong argument is frequently made that disarmament cannot ever precede the establishment of binding security agreements. This was the theory behind Premier Bulganin's suggestion in the summer of 1956 that the first step in arms reduction be the negotiation of a nonaggression pact between the United States and the Soviet Union. It has also been the apparent basis of American action; implicit in United States policy has been the assumption that disarmament could be implemented only if and when Moscow fundamentally changed its foreign policy and minimized its threats to the peace and security of the world.[48]

It seems unnecessary for us to attempt a solution to this "chicken-or-egg" dilemma as to which condition leads to the other. We can be just as informative and on much safer ground if we merely stipulate that disarmament and security are inextricably intertwined and that no formula for one can permanently exclude the consideration of the other. As long as a reduction in arms cannot be imposed by fiat on a major state, if it is to come at all it must come voluntarily. No state will consent to a reduction in its military capacity unless it is convinced that the arms it is giving up are genuinely surplus and not needed. The problem of arms control must be attacked within a total context if it is to yield a solution.

Arms Reduction and Accommodation.

What is this total context? Of what larger whole is the issue of arms limitation a part? In attempting to answer this question we come back very nearly to our original starting place.

The arms race is not the cause of the cold war, but is rather one of its symptoms. The original root of the disarmament issue lies in the fundamental divergence in national interest between the United States and the Soviet. So long as this conflict continues, and so long as there remains the remotest possibility that the disagreements might be prosecuted to the point of open warfare, each side will insist on retaining the practical maximum of armed strength. The arms race is thus one facet of the total policy controversy between the two contemporary giants, and can be dealt with only in connection with the other points at issue.

The road to large-scale arms limitation and reduction will really open

---

[48] See, for a summary of the issues and some suggestions, J. David Singer, "Threat-perception and the Armament-Tension Dilemma," *Journal of Conflict Resolution* (March, 1958).

only at some time in the future of Soviet-American relations when the trend toward mutual accommodation has accumulated sufficient impetus. Only when the resolution of outstanding issues on a basis of substantial compromise is a dominant concern, and when "coexistence" is not a propaganda phrase but rather a formula for problem-solving, can large-scale plans for arms control be discussed realistically.

This might be thought a pessimistic view. Yet, if our analysis in the earlier part of this book has any validity, it would seem to be the most probable one. Weapons are tools of policy; when new policies no longer call for execution by military means, the weapons can be discarded. Any proposal for disarmament advanced before substantial political agreement has been reached (or at least before some sort of "agreement to agree" has been ratified by both parties) is at best irrelevant and at worst possibly dangerous. It may be that the first fruit of any such joint decision to reduce the level of conflict might be an understanding on arms control. There is, however, no way for this to happen before an appropriate broader decision is made at the highest policy level.

Continuing Economic Issues in American Policy

"**E**conomic issues in American policy" is a phrase with two possible meanings; which of them we select will affect the nature of our discussion in this chapter. On the one hand, it may refer to the general range of concerns that are included in the notions of "economic foreign policy" or "international economic relations," primarily involving the pattern formed by the economic objectives and interests of the American people and the techniques used to serve them. The phrase may equally accurately connote, however, the purely economic dimension of total American policy, including both the economic components of American national interest and the economic techniques the United States government employs to advance it.

What makes this dual meaning important to us is that there is a considerable degree of contradiction in the implications of the two meanings. An "economic foreign policy," with objectives drawn from the free-enterprise doctrine accepted at least in principle by most Americans, cannot be thoroughly reconciled with the course of American foreign policy since 1945. The larger questions of national security and the prosecution of the cold war have imposed a number of policies on the United States that cannot be squared with any traditional or rational image of "economic foreign policy" that would call for the maximization of private profit and the free flow of goods, services, credit, and persons.[1]

Our discussion will, as it must, select one of the two meanings upon which to concentrate and will consider the other only to the extent that it is relevant to the first. We shall deal in this analysis, as we have attempted to do throughout this study, with the broader aspects of American foreign policy: the "economic issues" we shall consider are those that bear upon the over-all mission that the United States has set itself and problems that it encounters. We shall discuss initially the basic issue of the impact of American foreign policy upon the national economy. We shall then take up two of the more significant problems of American policy with a uniquely economic pertinence: American economic assistance to foreign states and American trade policy.

FOREIGN POLICY AND THE AMERICAN ECONOMY

It is obvious that the major weapon upon which the United States has relied in its struggle against the Soviet Union has been its economic power. Unable to match Russia in manpower, military mobilization, "political warfare," or subversion, America has counted on balancing the scales by its unique ability to produce and distribute goods and its possession of a highly organized and effecive economic machine.[2] The key role of economic capability has given rise to certain fundamental questions about the relationship of foreign policy to the American economy.

THE COSTS OF FOREIGN POLICY

Foreign policy, involving as it does such a large share of the expenditures of the government, is admitted to cost a great deal of money.

---

[1] "In short, although economic and military developments tend to be shaped by the same forces, a considerable gap separates our strategic and economic interests. How to bridge this strategic gap—rather than any dollar gap—is the central problem our foreign economic policy must overcome." Samuel Lubell, *The Revolution in World Trade and American Economic Policy* (New York: Harper & Bros., Inc., 1955), p. 40. Reprinted by permission.

[2] James P. Warburg, in *The United States in a Changing World* (New York: Putnam, 1954), pp. 425–31, gives a dramatic account of how this decision was originally reached in 1947–8.

So much, indeed, that sectors of the general public, egged on by ideological, political, or opportunistic opponents of the trend of American policy, have come to entertain a genuine fear that the expenditure forced by international affairs will "bankrupt" the United States. Generally speaking, this attitude tends to go hand in hand with a relative unawareness of the exact costs of foreign policy and their relation to the national wealth or the gross national product. It would be salutary, therefore, to begin our discussion with some consideration of just how much foreign policy costs.

The Dollar Cost of Foreign Policy: 1961.

Expenditures for foreign policy fall into two major categories: national security and international affairs and finance. The dollar cost for a single year is instructive: we have selected fiscal 1961 and used the budget estimates as a basis. Expenditures in this period were typical of recent trends.

ESTIMATED FOREIGN-POLICY EXPENDITURES, FISCAL 1961 [3]
(In millions)

National security:

Department of Defense (military)	40,995	
Atomic energy control and development	2,689	
Stockpiling and defense production expansion	134	
Military assistance	1,750	
Total National Security		45,568
International affairs and finance:		
Economic and technical assistance	1,700	
Emergency relief abroad	131	
Foreign information and exchange activities	168	
Conduct of foreign affairs	249	
Total International Affairs and Finance		2,248
Total Expenditures		47,816
Less receipts		7
Net Cost of Foreign Policy		47,809

Thus, out of a total estimated government expenditure for fiscal 1961 of $79.8 billion, nearly $48 billion was earmarked for purposes directly connected with foreign affairs. Within the remaining $31 billion, another large amount—perhaps as much as $6 billion—financed programs with almost as direct an impact on foreign policy. The costs of foreign policy are not only large in themselves, but constitute the most important single charge on the government's budget.

---

[3] Data extracted from *The Budget of the United States for 1961,* pp. M16, M29.

Foreign Policy and the Gross National Product.

But billions of dollars printed in a table are difficult to visualize; the sheer size of the amounts involved serves to obscure both the meaning and the relationships of the totals. More relevant for our purposes is the portion of the gross national product (GNP) that is devoted to foreign policy purposes. The following table shows this relationship over a ten-year period, 1948–1958: [4]

GROSS NATIONAL PRODUCT AND ITS DISTRIBUTION BETWEEN FOREIGN
POLICY AND OTHER PURPOSES, IN 1947–9 PRICES, 1948–1958

Year	GNP (Billions)	Foreign Policy (Billions)	Other Uses (Billions)
1948	248.8	15.6	233.2
1950	275.1	18.3	256.8
1951	285.0	22.7	262.3
1952	310.9	41.8	269.1
1953	313.6	47.7	265.9
1954	321.0	44.0	277.0
1955	359.9	38.6	321.3
1956	368.2	36.2	332.0
1957	374.4	38.3	336.1
1958	367.1	38.8	328.3

From these figures a few conclusions can be quickly drawn. In the first place, the increase in total production of goods and services has been much more rapid than that in foreign-policy expenditures, thus (except for two years) making more available for general consumption each year. Other figures indicate that the steady increase in the "other uses" category has been more rapid than population growth, thus increasing the amount available per capita over the period by approximately 18 per cent. In 1960, America's GNP passed $500 billion, while foreign-policy expenditures were less than $48 billion; that year, the per capita share of goods and services was the highest in history.

The data contained in this table would suggest that the costs of foreign policy have not represented any great strain on the American economy. Americans have been able to bear the burden of maintaining a sizeable military establishment and of conducting a foreign policy heavily loaded with economic programs without impoverishing themselves. On the contrary, with the share of the GNP available for maintenance of the standard of living increasing both relatively and absolutely, large foreign-

---

[4] Data for this table extracted from *Statistical Abstract of the United States: 1959* (Washington: U. S. Government Printing Office, 1959), and *The Budget of the United States for 1961.*

policy expenditures have had no measurable inhibiting effect on the much-lauded American standard of living.

Trends in Foreign Policy Costs.

The costs of foreign policy, viewed historically, demonstrate certain clear trends; data in the following table are in billions of dollars.[5]

YEARLY TOTALS FOR MAJOR FOREIGN POLICY EXPENDITURES

Expenditure	1950	1951	1952	1953	1954	1955	1956	1957	1958	1959	1960§	1961§
+Major nat'l security	13.0	22.4	43.9	50.3	46.9	40.6	40.6	43.2	44.1	46.4	45.6	45.5
=Int'l affairs and finance	4.6	3.7	2.8	2.2	1.7	2.1	1.8	1.9	2.2	3.7	2.0	2.2

§ Estimated.
+ Includes military assistance and direct forces support.
= Includes economic and technical development.

It appears, on the basis of these figures, that American foreign-policy spending has reached something of a plateau at upwards of $40 billion (modified by a rising price level) for major national security, and something slightly over $2 billion for nonmilitary programs. Since the end of the Korean War the figures have remained relatively constant; whether they remain so depends on the accuracy of the Eisenhower administration's judgment that the best course for the United States calls for the stabilization of its programs in pursuit of objectives firmly in view. Any sudden change in world relationships would throw these trends out of line and would create entirely new requirements.

CAN THE UNITED STATES AFFORD ITS FOREIGN POLICY?

In one sense, the question at the head of this section is unnecessary; there is no doubt that the United States can afford the foreign policy it is presently carrying on. It has been doing so for a decade and a half and —despite some danger signals in the economy—there seems to be no real danger that the demands of foreign policy will place any insuperable burden on the economic capacity of the United States.

But there is another sense in which the question has great relevance. We may refer momentarily back to our discussion of American capabilities. We concluded that American capacities are in general adequate to the mission the United States has set for itself. The United States *can,* we suggested, meet all the foreseeable tests; what was much less certain, however,

---

[5] *The Budget of the United States for 1961,* p. 938.

is whether the United States *will* do so. So long as there remains an area of relatively free choice, no one dare state unequivocally that Americans will decide that they can afford their foreign policy.

The "Layer of Fat" in the Economy.

Economists point out that despite the great expenditures the United States has been making in the foreign policy field and the constantly rising GNP and standard of living, the national economy has not been operating at peak efficiency. There remain segments of plant, manpower, and finance capital that are not being used at full effectiveness; there is, in other words, a residue of productivity that has not yet been fully called on. Speaking theoretically, therefore, it seems reasonable to assume that the United States could if it wished increase its foreign-policy expenditure by an indefinite but certainly considerable amount without having any significant effect at all on the standard of living. A simple expansion of productivity to take up the slack would make available great amounts of goods and services for public purposes without reducing the total available for other purposes.[6]

This "layer of fat" in the national economy—the unused (or inefficiently used) productive capacity—may well be the secret economic weapon of the United States. As long as it exists it provides something of an answer to the question we asked above: the United States can afford its foreign policy as long as it retains in uncommitted reserve considerable increments of economic power. Until international requirements force the United States to go beyond this point—that is, until the demands of foreign policy require that serious inroads be made in the goods and services available for civilians—the United States will live within its means.

The Impact of Popular Preferences.

Webster defines "afford" in the sense in which we are using it as "to incur, stand, or bear without serious detriment (as to financial condition

---

[6] In his provocative study, *The Revolution in World Trade,* Samuel Lubell has a typically suggestive statement on this point (p. 40):

"Currently the tendency is to think of our surpluses as costly liabilities. But two world wars and the whole course of the postwar period have shown that the free world's strongest *single* asset is the ability of the American economy to generate sizable surpluses of every kind, from food and machinery, to medicine and clothing. . . .

"Although the heads of many foreign governments do not seem to realize it, our productive reserves are the cushion which permits them to sleep in political stability and freedom. For some time ahead most of the world is likely to continue to be living on the thin edge strategically and, in many cases, economically as well. By far the greatest contribution the United States can make to the well-being and security of the rest of the world is to remain economically strong, a reservoir of productive resources capable of meeting any emergency." (Italics in original; reprinted by permission.)

...etc.).'' Whether or not the United States can afford its foreign policy, therefore, depends in the final analysis on whether the American people, acting through their political channels, decide that the cost of international relations is causing "serious detriment" to their standard of living. A popular decision at any time that foreign affairs are costing too much would be immediately reflected in a cut in government outlays to a level felt to be tolerable.

There is no doubt that Americans are willing to support great deprivations in private economic life if they are convinced that the external peril is real enough to justify them. This fact is at least a partial explanation for the "crisis technique" that surrounded so much of American programming between 1947 and 1953. The policy of the Eisenhower administration, however, has made much of eschewing this approach and of concentrating instead on commitments of a long-term nature and planning for coordinated policies extending over a period of several years. This method, although minimizing the risks of going "too far, too fast," involves dangers of its own.

In view of the mercurial swings of American public sentiment in response to stimuli frequently slight or even irrelevant, a long-range plateau-type policy may at times be thought too expensive and at others too niggardly. Particularly in moments of relative relaxation may the public pressure for a lower rate of expenditure become politically impossible to resist. At these times the danger of unwise retrenchment is the greatest.[7]

The Problem of "Growth."

In the wake of the Soviet's economic and technological advances after 1957, one school of American economists became exercised about the slow rate of "growth" in the American economy. They estimated the Soviet economy as growing between 6 and 9 per cent per year, in contrast to the 3.5 to 4 per cent long-term rate in the United States. They called for heavy American "sacrifice" and the transfer of large increments of production from the "private" to the "public" sector of the economy to increase the American growth rate to 5 or 6 per cent.

It is difficult to evaluate this concern. "Growth rates" expressed in percentages are notoriously deceptive, since they are functions of their bases. A Soviet growth rate of 8 per cent may in fact represent a smaller absolute increase than 4 per cent in the United States (in 1957, the Soviet

---

[7] The Appropriations Committee of the House of Representatives, following the example of Congressman Otto Passman, repeatedly has sought to make large cuts in foreign-policy expenditures, usually in mutual security. In 1960, the Committee cut the program by nearly 25 per cent in the face of a direct appeal by the President. See the *Washington Post and Times-Herald* (June 14, 1960).

GNP was 40 per cent of the American). Furthermore, the factors that go to make up both GNP and "growth" are still far from agreed on by economists or politicians.[8] The most cautious studies agree on only one point: the productive gap between the Soviet and the United States is narrowing. What, if anything, to do about it is yet unclear.[9]

CAN THE UNITED STATES AFFORD PEACE?

A question of a significance only remote in contemporary affairs but of potentially major importance is whether or not the United States can afford peace. We have seen that the cold war, at least at its present level, is bearable; we know also that the United States has fought a major war and avoided a postwar depression. But what if the economic stimulus provided by foreign-policy spending of all sorts (consuming, as we have seen, roughly 10 per cent of the GNP), should suddenly come to an end? Would there be, as some political figures contend, an immediate depression? Does the United States need the cold war to maintain its prosperity?

The Economic Effect of Peace.

These are questions which no one can answer in vacuo; the proof of the American economic pudding must be in the eating. Certain points, however, permit some generalization.

We must initially distinguish between two different ways in which peace could "break out." If the whole pattern of American postwar policy were to be made suddenly obsolete by a dramatic collapse of the Soviet regime, the economic questions that would then be posed would indeed be formidable and would call for rapid—perhaps emergency—action. On the other hand, if the cold war were to relax gradually, the American government would have time to shift its policy emphasis little by little from a quasi-war basis to some other areas of expenditure.

To be more specific, major savings in the cost of foreign policy—of a size sufficient to present a problem to the adjustment capacity of the American economy—can be achieved in only one major category: arma-

---

[8] See, as one statistical comparison, Rush V. Greenslade and Phyllis A. Wallace, "Industrial Materials as a Measure of Industrial Production, Soviet Union Versus United States," *American Economic Review* (September, 1959).

[9] One set of recommendations is made in a report to the Senate Foreign Relations Committee by the Corporation for Economic and Industrial Research, Inc., *Worldwide and Domestic Economic Problems and their Impact on the Foreign Policy of the United States* (Washington: U. S. Government Printing Office, 1959). Their recommendations are on the "liberating" side: instead of demanding sacrifice and higher taxes, they feel growth will be more rapid and certain if investment incentives are provided and production and profits liberated.

ments spending. Other areas of government outlay for foreign policy represent only relatively negligible totals. The economic problem of peace would most probably be presented in the form of a great reduction of government appropriations for military purposes, and it is in this area that the clearest difference between a rapid shutoff and a gradual slowdown is demonstrated.

Were there to take place wholesale demobilization, speedy contract cancellation, renegotiation of purchases, and the other apparatus of rapid transition with which Americans became familiar during 1945 and 1946, this would mean that roughly 10 per cent of the GNP would suddenly become surplus. If no corrective action were taken, massive unemployment, price drops, and deflation would bring on an economic crisis potentially rivalling the depression of 1929. On the other hand, if the cutback in military expenditures were more gradual, its impact could be spread out over a longer period and—even in the absence of palliative government action— the pressure at any one time would not be so great.

Government Policy.

In the event that the cold war relaxes gradually, the United States stands committed to maintain a high level of international spending for an indefinite time. As long ago as 1953, President Eisenhower pledged that the United States would devote substantial portions of any savings brought about by disarmament to a fund for "world development and reconstruction." [10] From the domestic point of view, maintaining prosperity while readjustment takes place is primary; it is a happy coincidence that one technique for accomplishing this purpose also directly advances the foreign policy of the United States. If world stability and order are to follow peace, American financial assistance will be needed. The fact that such a policy will also play a part in maintaining domestic economic health only makes more probable the fulfillment of the pledge.

In the event of a sudden shutoff in the cold war, however, the major problem would be that of emergency action. The American economy contains a number of built-in stabilizers and anti-depression mechanisms that would cushion the shock,[11] including the Social Security System, the Full Employment Act, and the Federal Deposit Insurance Corporation. But emergency action to "prime the pump" (in the phrase of depression days) would be needed to get the economic wheels turning again at full speed. One author lists the following emergency devices to infuse a sudden new

---

[10] In his speech to the American Society of Newspaper Editors, April 16, 1953. See *New York Times* (April 17, 1953).

[11] See David Cushman Coyle, "Leaning on the Kremlin," *Virginia Quarterly Review* (Spring, 1954), p. 192ff.

supply of money into the economy so as to buy time until longer-purview policies became effective:

> Reduce excise taxes for one year only, with notice that at the end of the year they are to be restored.
> Cut lower bracket income taxes and make the cut show at once in the rate of withholding. . . .
> Reduce letter postage to one cent for one year and other rates enough to please the business men. . . .
> Offer generous grants-in-aid to states and municipalities if they will act within a month to make a corresponding reduction in sales and real estate taxes for the current year.
> Pay a 100 per cent bonus on social security benefits.
> Give away large quantities of government-held agricultural surpluses to countries where goods are scarce.
> Stockpile steel, rubber, and other storable materials, with special consideration for foreign suppliers who may be especially fearful of a slump.
> Announce that military aid promised to allies will not be cut, but will be available to help with their relief costs, stiffen their foreign exchange position, and generally bolster their strength and confidence.[12]

Once these emergency measures (or any of the dozens of others that might be mentioned) had been taken, more gradual policies aimed at a smoother readjustment could be initiated. Without the breathing spell gained by quick stopgap devices, however, a serious slide would be a real danger.

FOREIGN ECONOMIC ASSISTANCE

We have discussed some of the aspects of military aid and defense support extended by the United States to friendly nations in another chapter. In the present connection we are primarily interested in the over-all economic implications of foreign aid, not only that portion oriented toward defense, but also including development assistance, technical assistance, and private overseas investment.

FOREIGN AID: AMOUNT AND IMPACT

The Economic Dimensions of Foreign Aid.

How large have American aid programs been, and of what size are they today? The summary figures indicate both amounts and trends: [13]

---

12 Coyle, "Leaning on the Kremlin," pp. 202–203. Reprinted by permission.
13 *The Budget of the United States for 1961*, p. 445.

(In millions)

Year	Military Assistance	Economic and Technical Development	Total, Foreign Aid	Total Expenditure, U. S.
1949	415	5,880	6,295	39,507
1950	130	4,442	4,572	39,606
1951	991	3,506	4,497	44,058
1952	2,442	2,584	5,026	65,408
1953	3,954	1,960	5,914	74,274
1954	3,629	1,511	5,140	67,772
1955	2,292	1,960	4,252	64,570
1956	2,611	1,616	4,227	66,540
1957	2,352	1,683	4,035	69,437
1958	2,187	1,910	4,097	71,936
1959	2,340	3,403	5,743	80,697
1960 §	1,800	1,714	3,514	78,383
1961 §	1,750	1,824	3,574	79,816

§ 1960 and 1961 figures estimated.

The decreasing share of the GNP taken by foreign aid appears clearly from these figures, the cumulative effect of which is heightened by the well-known steady increase in the price index. Dollar costs of foreign aid of various categories are trending downward in contrast to increasing total expenditures by the government.

Our earlier discussions of the over-all impact of foreign policy on the American economy made the point that to the extent that international obligations constitute a net drain on the available goods and services, the primary stress occurs at the point of military expenditures rather than in foreign-assistance programs. This generalization appears to be borne out by the statistics we have quoted. At particular pressure points in the economy, however, there could be some cause for complaint that foreign assistance might actually work a hardship on Americans. This contention is offset, however, by the considerable, if immeasurable, extent to which foreign assistance programs have stimulated other, more normal trade activities and thus brought about a net economic gain to the United States.

The Global Scope of American Aid.

Despite its relatively small dollar volume as compared to the total expenditures of the United States government, the American aid program has brought the United States into direct contact with the economies of virtually all the countries of the free world. Whether American economic assistance is by means of direct supply of military end-items, defense support, development aid, or technical cooperation, the United States and its policy exert a significant effect on economic affairs in the entire noncommunist world.

Military aid administered by the Department of Defense involves some 55 countries. Detailed figures on the amounts involved were made available to the public for the first time in February, 1960. In the decade fiscal 1950–1960, the United States delivered almost $25.4 billion in military assistance. The regional breakdown was as follows: Europe, $13.5 billion; Africa, $47 million; Near East and South Asia, $3.7 billion; Far East, $6.1 billion; and Latin America, $416 million. The eight countries that received the largest individual totals were France, $4.4 billion; Formosa, $2 billion; Italy, $1.98 billion; Turkey, $1.7 billion; Korea, $1.3 billion; Belgium, $1.2 billion; the Netherlands, $1.15 billion; and the United Kingdom, $1.1 billion.[14]

The economic aid program involves both larger dollar amounts and more countries. In a somewhat longer period, fiscal 1945–1958, the United States expended $71 billion in economic aid to 80 countries, the United Nations, and several other international organizations. On a regional basis, Europe received $31.5 billion; Africa, $260 million; Near East and South Asia, $4.9 billion; Far East, $11.2 billion; Latin America, $2.8 billion. The eight major recipients of this type of aid were the United Kingdom, $8.9 billion; France, $6.9 billion; West Germany, $5.2 billion; Japan, $3.5 billion; Italy, $3.2 billion; Formosa, $2.6 billion; Korea, $2.1 billion; and Greece, $1.9 billion.[15]

Putting the two sets of figures together, we see that France has been the major beneficiary of all forms of American aid, followed closely by Great Britain. West Germany is third, Italy fourth; the four leading recipients are thus all in western Europe. Formosa, Japan, and Korea occupy the next three places, followed by Greece, the Netherlands, and Turkey. As one might suspect, the United States has given aid most generously to three categories of states: its major allies in Europe, its key outposts in the Far East, and two sensitive states located between the Soviet colossus and the explosive Middle East. Membership in this group might well change in response to new developments in Africa, south and southeast Asia, and Latin America. Indeed, it seemed certain early in 1961 that both Africa and Latin America were destined for large increases.

---

[14] Data from table: "The Military Assistance Program," prepared by the Office of the Assistant Secretary of Defense, International Security Affairs, found in Hearings before the Committee on Foreign Affairs, House of Representatives, 86th Congress, Second Session: *Mutual Security Act of 1960* (Washington: U. S. Government Printing Office, 1960), pp. 193–197.

[15] These data drawn from Herman L. Ficker, "Some Statistics on Foreign-aid Expenditures," *Congressional Record,* 86th Congress, 1st Session (1959), pp. A828–A836.

No issue has caused more bitter debate among Americans than the question of foreign aid and its future. To some it is simply a "giveaway," inspired by quasi-socialists who want to dissipate the American substance in a mad burst of vapid philanthropy; to others it is a foredoomed attempt to "buy friends" who cannot be bought; to still others it is stupid to arm, modernize, and develop potential rivals, adversaries, and competitors. On the other hand, its defenders claim it is—in one form or another—not only the most efficient weapon of American policy, but indeed an absolutely essential method of holding back communism without war.[16] The ups and downs of the aid budgets over the years not only reflect the changes in the international scene but also roughly indicate the currents of public opinion and legislative interest in the question.

Considering the trends of contemporary world politics, there seems to be no prospect of an end to American foreign aid. Programs may change in response to new conditions and indeed should so do. Administration and planning undoubtedly can be improved. But to some form of aid the United States is indefinitely committed; there is too much in the American interest that can be accomplished only by such measures for anyone seriously to indulge himself in the illusory hope of their early termination. The appropriate argument with existing philosophy and implementation is in favor of a greater emphasis upon tailoring programs to meet actual needs rather than allowing them to develop out of American domestic politics or to take form via an unimaginative perpetuation of time-sanctioned practices. Foreign aid has a future; Americans should be bending every effort to make sure that this future is a good one.

DEVELOPMENT ASSISTANCE

A special form of foreign aid with its own set of problems has been assistance to underdeveloped countries. First broached in 1949 in President Truman's inaugural address, the "bold new program" grew in complexity throughout the 1950's. It still remains a constant concern to policy makers and a perplexity to Americans, with both its goals and its techniques in constant dispute.

---

[16] The literature, both expository and polemic, on foreign aid is already enormous. Of the criticisms, one typical example is Eugene W. Castle, *Billions, Blunders, and Baloney* (New York: Devin-Adair, 1955). A realistic defense is made by James R. Schlesinger, "Foreign Aid: A Plea for Realism," *Virginia Quarterly Review* (Spring, 1959). A critical analysis of the entire rationale of the program is George Liska, *The New Statecraft: Foreign Aid in American Foreign Policy* (Chicago: University of Chicago Press, 1960).

As originally conceived, Point IV was to be an American program of technical assistance to countries desiring the importation of American skills for modernization, development, and industrialization. Thought of as outside the cold-war context, it was a move designed to further peace, order, and stability in those parts of the world where they were menaced by underdevelopment. Its rationale involved relatively little government spending, a heavy element of "people-to-people" contact, and a basically non-political orientation.[17] Between 1950 and 1960 over 50 country programs were initiated, but the program never has achieved the hoped-for results.

Perhaps the controlling consideration affecting the development of technical cooperation has been its inclusion, ever since 1951, within the mutual-security concept. Such technical assistance as has been extended since that date has been geared to generally the same political-military purposes as the other forms of American aid. There has been little official inclination to rely on technical assistance, by definition slow-acting and of long-range scope, for the accomplishment of relatively speedy political purposes. Congress has been particularly prone to view Point IV as a policy of only limited relevance to the cold war, and to be reluctant to move very energetically in its implementation.[18]

But technical cooperation, considered on its own merits, has proved vulnerable to criticism on other grounds. Many of its advocates are easy to portray as zealots with little practical sense; the "quart of milk for every Hottentot" charge is often used to refute the more extreme proponents of the virtues of the exportation of American "know-how." "Boondoggling" is bad enough; even more directly in point is the charge made that the development of industrial capacity in the underdeveloped areas of the world would merely create new competitors for American industry and thus would be—to use another hackneyed phrase—a case of the American "cuckoo fouling its own nest."[19] Protectionist groups as well tended to oppose the program.

---

[17] See Porter Hardy, Jr., "A Congressman's View of Technical Co-operation," *The Annals* (May, 1959), for a sympathetic development of this point of view.

[18] We will recall that mutual-security assistance, as officially defined, sets technical cooperation as an appendage either to defense support or to development assistance before admitting it to be a technique of aid in its own right. See pp. 364–365.

[19] For example, Congressmen from cotton-producing states generally opposed the original American offer to help finance Egypt's Aswan Dam, made in early 1956. Their reasoning was simple; any increase in available water would increase Egypt's cotton production, thus strengthening a potential competitor for world cotton markets. See remarks of Senator Walter George of Georgia, *The New York Times* (April 28, 1956).

But the policy objections to the program have not been the major reasons why Point IV has never really gotten off the ground. The major failure of the enterprise has been its inability to attract enough finance capital to make possible the many projects suggested. In the beginning it was expected that American government participation in technical cooperation would be confined to making available technically competent personnel; financing would come either from the indigenous sources of the host country (rarely) or (more commonly) from American private investors. This goal has never been reached; American private capital has been reluctant to go into the underdeveloped areas. The fiscal policy of the World Bank (the International Bank for Reconstruction and Development) has also been extremely cautious, restricting loans primarily to self-liquidating projects. Very few development programs can qualify on these grounds.

The United States government, following the recognition that development capital would be slow in forming, has undertaken three lines of action. First, it has never ceased to make efforts to stimulate the flow of private capital overseas, making intensive studies of the impediments to foreign investment,[20] and has made what improvements it could in the "investment climate." In this connection it has used the extensive consultative facilities provided by the General Agreement on Tariffs and Trade (GATT; 1947) frequently to urge other states to remove at least the more irksome of these impediments.

The second approach has been through American membership in the International Finance Corporation. Created in 1956, the IFC in 1959 had 57 member states, both developed and underdeveloped. Its purpose is to make investments in private development enterprises (usually industrial) into which private capital is not flowing. Once an investment has stabilized sufficiently to be attractive, IFC will sell its holdings to private investors and reinvest the return. It also serves as a "clearing house" for development capital, bringing together opportunities and potential investors. As of late 1959, the International Finance Corporation had made 13 investments, totalling nearly $24 million.

The third effort has been undertaken unilaterally: the Development Loan Fund, created by the Mutual Security Act of 1958 as a separate corporate entity. Operating under the general policy guidance of the Secretary of

---

[20] See, as an elaborate example, *Factors Limiting U.S. Investment Abroad,* a report prepared by the Office of International Trade, Bureau of Foreign and Domestic Commerce, U. S. Department of Commerce (Washington: U.S. Government Printing Office, 1954). Part I was subtitled: "Survey of Factors in Foreign Countries"; Part II, "Business Views on the U.S. Government's Role."

of State, DLF makes loans both to private enterprises and to governments to finance development projects. In fiscal 1960 DLF was limited to $700 million, but was allowed $1.8 billion in fiscal 1961. DLF is generally thought to have been rather effective, although its luster was dimmed in October, 1959, by the "buy-American" ruling. This rule required that development loans be used primarily to purchase American goods, and was subsequently extended to include all ICA assistance as well.

But the fight to finance development was by no means over. As long as the Soviet was an active competitor for the allegiance of the underdeveloped and uncommitted nations, it was impossible for development to have other than a political connotation. Reconciling the political and the economic aspects of such massive financing operations, to say nothing of the humanitarian considerations that bulked large in the question, promised to be a problem of unique complexity. No clear formula had appeared by the end of the Eisenhower era.

UNITED STATES TRADE POLICY

An economic issue of immediate pertinence to the total of American foreign policy is the question of the status of international trade. Perhaps in no area has it proved more difficult to bring together the competing requirements of a cold-war orientation to immediate issues and a long-term interest in the economic implications of peace, order, and stability.

America's strategic economic position has made it possible for the United States to use international trade as a weapon against the Soviet. Denying exports to hostile nations or extending trade and exchange concessions to friendly ones, and the employment of promises or threats to do either while bargaining, have proved generally useful to American negotiators. What the use of trade control as a tool of policy has meant, however, has been a systematic denial of the pledges of "normal" trade relations made by the United States on other occasions. Freely-operating "multilateralism" in international economic relations has been a casualty of the cold war. The United States has been unable thoroughly to rationalize this confusion of purpose.

Domestic developments have also complicated the problem. The free-enterprise economy of the United States has resisted both forms of government pressure, either toward greater control of trade in the national interest or toward a genuine attempt at the liberalization of international trade. Instead the American economy has been greatly affected by the world-wide urge toward economic nationalism, and considerable pressure-group agitation toward protectionism, boycotts, government-subsidized trading, and other manifestations of "unilateralism" have been a constant factor in government decisions. All of these matters enter into United States trade policy and affect the broader pattern of American policy.[21]

THE PROBLEMS OF TRADE

International trade, for the United States, has presented a series of problems since 1945 that have made the development of a coherent trade policy very difficult. As we shall discuss them here, they break down into three broad categories: the announced pledge of multilateralism and what has happened to it, the "dollar gap" and its eventual conversion into a balance-of-payments deficit, and the political significance of trade, both with the communist bloc and the noncommunist states.

The Pledge of Multilateralism.

The United States entered the postwar era committed in principle to multilateralism in international economic relations, the increase of international trade, and the maximum possible freedom for all forms of interstate economic contacts.[22] The American position in 1945 was flatfootedly in favor of immediate and extensive action to reduce the barriers to trade and to stimulate the flow of goods and services in all directions across national frontiers. The concrete measures the United States (in association with Britain) proposed included tariff reduction and cooperative action by all trading states to create a climate more favorable to trade; particularly important in American (and British) thinking was the early negotiation of the General Agreements on Tariffs and Trade (GATT) and the creation of the International Trade Organization (ITO).

Unfortunately, neither economics nor politics permitted the pledge of multilateralism to be effectively translated from the realm of principle to the area of practice. The first postwar decade saw the United States government clinging to its pledge of ultimately freer trade, but unable to make any major progress toward that goal in the face of constant political

---

21 Samuel Lubell, in *The Revolution in World Trade*, says (p. 26): "To attempt to reassert the doctrine of free trade or free competition in its old laissez-faire sense is unworkable in view of the prevailing pressures for government intervention, from both domestic and foreign sources. Yet expanded government intervention, in itself, offers no solution either, if only because the pressures for government action that arise from domestic sources, are so often in such violent conflict with the needs of international stability." Reprinted by permission.

22 See, as the most forthright statement of this position, *Proposals for Expansion of World Trade and Employment,* Department of State publication 2411 (Washington: U.S. Government Printing Office, 1945).

crisis provoked by the Soviet and recurrent economic trouble at various points in the free world.

The Dollar Gap.

From the point of view of pure economics (assuming for the moment that in this context "economics" can be separated from "politics") official American policy asserted that the reopening of trade channels after 1945 was obstructed by four factors: (1) restrictions imposed by governments; (2) restrictions imposed by private combines and cartels; (3) fear of disorder in the markets for certain primary commodities; (4) irregularity, and the fear of irregularity, in production and employment.[23] In practice, however, all of these proved less important than one that American economists and policy-makers foresaw only dimly in 1945: the dollar gap.[24]

In essence the dollar gap after 1945 meant that the free-world nations wanted and needed American goods, but lacked the means to pay for them. In international trade, payment for American goods in the first instance may be made in dollar credits, but ultimately the payments must balance; if Europe (for example) were to continue purchasing American commodities over any protracted period, it would be obliged to sell an equivalent amount of goods in dollar markets. In 1945 the free world could neither produce saleable goods nor gain access to dollar markets. This was the dollar gap: the margin between a nation's import requirements from the dollar area and its available dollars or dollar-earning capacity.

So great was the dollar gap for all except a very few states that to talk about "normal trade" was preposterous. The United States was forced (both for economic and for political reasons) to undertake large-scale programs of aid to the free world ("unilateral transfers," to use the delicate phrase) so as to keep some trade flowing and to accomplish the minimum objectives of foreign policy. This program was concentrated in Europe, where (in an industrialized society) the problem was more acute; the elimination of the dollar gap in unindustrialized nations (primarily raw-material producers) was to be accomplished by longer-range programs, primarily Point IV development assistance. We have seen some figures earlier indicating the magnitude of the American effort in this regard.

So effectively did American action reduce the dollar gap that by 1952 a real (although invisible) balance-of-payments deficit had opened up for the United States—exactly the purpose of the program, especially as regards Europe. It was not until the recession of 1958, however, that Ameri-

---

[23] *Proposals for Expansion of World Trade and Employment,* pp. 12–18.

[24] See, for a theoretical discussion, J. E. Meade, *The Balance of Payments* (London: Oxford University Press, 1951).

cans generally awoke to the existence of the deficit, and then only after it had impinged directly on the important-export rates with Europe. Despite the fact that the bulk of the $3.4 billion deficit arose as the result of military and other overseas expenditures of a noneconomic sort, protectionists began their attack on the American trade position. Americans by 1960 no longer were worried about a dollar shortage in Europe; instead, there was talk of a "dollar glut." [25] The deficit affected primarily American economic relations with Europe. It was of much less relevance to the underdeveloped nations unless it brought on a totally unexpected loss of confidence in the dollar. But it unquestionably vexed Americans, who could not agree on what should be done about it. One of the last major moves of the Eisenhower Administration was an unsuccessful effort late in 1960 to win assistance from West Germany in bearing the burden of European defense; a move the Kennedy Administration converted into a moderate success early in 1961.

The Political Implications of Trade.

But there were additional reasons why multilateralism was ignored. When the nature of the Soviet threat was made clear and the outlines of an American policy were inked in, America's strategic economic position dictated the use of trade as a political weapon. Since 1945, the use of trade as a tool of foreign policy has taken two forms: (1) the Soviet bloc has been generally excluded from the American trading area; (2) trade concessions have been used to weld the free world into a more cohesive entity. Bipolarity as a policy demanded that the Soviet sphere be boycotted by the entire free world, and American policy has worked to this end. The Battle Act, passed by Congress in 1951, was designed to deny American economic aid to any nation that traded with communists, and much effort was expended by American negotiators to persuade allies and neutrals alike that they should have no dealings with Moscow.

The policy, however bravely it might be stated, was never fully implemented. Too many noncommunist states were faced with economic problems that the United States could not (or would not) solve, and the communist bloc offered too many tempting bargains. From the point of view of allied nations, American tariff policy left a great deal to be desired. There was always a certain amount of trading across the Iron Curtain, even at the height of bipolarity; the rise of neutralism after 1954 and the coincident decline of the two-power concept made it out of the question to restrict free-world trade with the communist empire. After 1957, although the United States was careful not to undertake any full-

---

[25] Corporation for Economic and Industrial Research, *Worldwide and Domestic Economic Problems,* Chapter 4: "Trade, Aid, and the Balance of Payments."

fledged reconsideration of its policy, the volume of East-West trade was at a postwar high and promised to increase steadily.[26]

Just as the effectiveness of bipolar control of East-West trade diminished, so did the utility of using intra-free world trade as a means of unifying the American bloc. This is not to say that the economic interdependence of the western world diminished; what declined was the ability of the United States to hold its allies in line by economic means. In the first place, the economic revival of western Europe and its consolidation by means of the European Economic Community gave those states great economic leverage against the United States. Smaller states as well exploited their freedom of economic maneuver. The 1958 recession taught Americans the hard lesson that economic power was no longer their monopoly, to be put to political purposes at will. Instead the United States was forced to think once more in terms of competition, a concept once generic to the American genius but almost forgotten in the highly political atmosphere of the post-1945 world.

ITO and GATT

In the postwar world multilateral international trade has been subordinated to the twin pressures of domestic planning and economic nationalism on the one hand and of the demands of foreign policy on the other. A clear demonstration of this generalization is the history of the attempts to formalize multilateralism into international institutions. The International Trade Organization, the Charter of which was hailed as a great forward step, has never come into existence; the General Agreement on Tariffs and Trade, although provocative of much negotiation and some reduction in tariffs, has had only a negligible effect on trade patterns.

The Failure of ITO.

The ITO Charter was drawn up at the United Nations Conference on Trade and Employment, held at Havana in 1947–8.[27] It was the culmination of the 1945 American *Proposals* and, in general, provided for an organization charged with the duty of bringing about an increase in the flow of international trade. Even though the Charter contained many exceptions to the general principles of free trade (made on behalf of nations that

---

[26] Premier Khrushchev, on the occasion of his visit to the United States in 1959, talked "trade" at every opportunity. He remained vague, however, on the specific items and terms of trade he had in mind.

[27] United Nations, *Charter for an International Trade Organization,* United Nations Conference on Trade and Employment, Havana, Cuba, 1947–8 (New York: United Nations, 1948).

were in difficulties and that demanded the right to take unilateral remedial action), the theory of the document was clearly in the tradition of multilateralism.

The ITO was stillborn; the Charter remains as a monument to the hopes of the early postwar era, but the organization never came into existence. Failure of the United States to ratify the instrument doomed the entire undertaking, and after 1950 the executive branch ceased even to attempt to win congressional approval. In 1955 President Eisenhower attempted to gain consent for American entry into the Organization of Trade Cooperation, a less elaborate offshoot of ITO. This too proved too much for newly-protectionist Senators to accept, and there was little hope after that date that the United States would—at least in the contemporary climate of domestic and foreign policies—take this step in implementation of its promise of freer trade.

Negotiations under GATT.

The General Agreement on Tariffs and Trade was entered into in 1947.[28] It is actually an understanding providing for multilateral tariff bargaining among the signatories. Under its terms periodic meetings of the Contracting Parties are held. Discussions go on, either for reciprocal tariff reductions or for ironing out particular trade difficulties.

The GATT negotiations, in addition to bilateral and multilateral tariff discussions, have concentrated upon certain semipermanent problems obstructing free trade. Among these have been the issue of import quotas [29] (imposed usually by nations in serious balance-of-payments difficulties), currency convertibility, and price stabilization on primary commodities (usually agricultural). Despite the fairly general good-will with which these problems were attacked, most of the participating states felt sincerely that their own problems were important and unique enough that exceptions to general rules should be made in their case. Understandable as this was, and justifiable as many of the claims were, this emphasis on discovering loop-

---

[28] U.S. Department of State, *The General Agreement on Tariffs and Trade and Texts of Related Documents* (Washington, D.C.: U.S. Government Printing Office, 1950).

[29] The State Department press release discussing the 11th session of the Contracting Parties made the following comment about American action on import restrictions at this 1956 meeting: "... the U.S. delegation held bilateral consultations with the delegations of 13 countries.... These discussions covered import restrictions maintained by these countries on specific commodities which created a hardship to U.S. producers or were unduly discriminatory toward U.S. goods. In each case the U.S. delegation suggested that the other country consider whether a relaxation of the restriction could be made without disrupting that country's balance of payments position. Industrial products were discussed with eight countries, agricultural products with five, and fisheries products with four." Quoted in *Department of State Bulletin* (December 3, 1956), p. 895.

holes in GATT rather than attempting to make forward progress could not but be a disappointment to those who hoped for an increase in trade as a contribution to stability in the world.

The United States and the European Trading Blocs.

One of the most troublesome trading problems facing the United States in the 1960's was that of coming to terms with an increasingly united Europe. In 1957 six states of continental Europe—France, Italy, West Germany, and the three Benelux states—formed the European Economic Community. This body was for the purpose of creating a customs union among its members within a ten-year period,[30] and during 1958 and 1959 began to make changes in the tariff schedules of its members, looking toward the day of internal free trade and a common external tariff. Great Britain, meanwhile, had not been idle. Opposed to the economic consolidation of the Continent on political grounds, and unwilling to join EEC because of a reluctance to compromise its position in the Commonwealth, London first suggested an 18-member free-trade area to comprise all the OEEC states. This failed to win any support from France, and Britain then succeeded in 1959 in negotiating a rival trading bloc, the European Free Trade Association. This 7-nation group included Britain, Portugal, Austria, Switzerland, and the Scandinavian states. EFTA was purely a free-trade area with no common external tariff contemplated.

With Europe threatening to split into rival blocs, the United States became involved. It intervened in the dispute and proposed early in 1960 the conversion of OEEC into the Organization for Economic Cooperation and Development, in which the United States would hold membership.[31] In this way the United States might act as a "bridge" between the groups, and at the same time act to protect its own interests from being adversely affected. Although OECD did not move rapidly toward realization, later developments indicated that Britain was actively seeking closer relationships with EEC and perhaps eventual membership; if this were to come about, the other EFTA members would inevitably join the Community as well—where several of them belonged anyway because of their normal trade-flow patterns. Probably the greatest obstacle to a wider Economic Community was the prospect of eventual political union among its members.

Although thoroughly sympathizing in principle with European integration, the United States saw several potential difficulties in the prospect of a

---

[30] Both a customs union and a free-trade area involve the elimination of tariff barriers among the countries composing the area. A customs union, however, establishes a common tariff applicable to all imports from outside the area, while in a free-trade area each nation retains its own tariff schedules except vis-à-vis each other.

[31] See remarks of Undersecretary of State C. Douglas Dillon, *New York Times* (February 24, 1960).

unified trading Europe. One was the possibility that for certain countries and certain commodities, the new common tariff would be higher than the old single-nation one as it applied to American goods. A second was the worsened competitive position of United States goods in the European market once the equalizing factor of tariffs on intra-European trade was removed.[32] A third was the possibility that the European bloc (or blocs) would not move toward multilateralism but instead toward a larger-scale bilateralism.[33] A fourth centered on Britain. If London proved unable to reach satisfactory arrangements with EEC, there was a possibility that she might "turn to the East" and enter much more extensive trading with the Soviet bloc.

None of these was beyond American competence to solve adequately, but all posed new questions both for American policy-makers and for American businessmen. Trade was obviously destined to be a more important object of controversy in the future than it had been in the immediate past.

The Rebirth of American Protectionism

The title given this section may be unintentionally misleading. It is at best debatable whether or not American protectionism ever reached such desuetude that we may speak of its present importance as a "rebirth." In any case, the sense of our discussion here is clear; the bulk of American opinion and policy, despite powerful economic evidence to the contrary, is still wedded to the principle of the protective tariff. Arguments based on history, economic doctrine, the requirements of foreign policy, or simple humanity all fail to move the high-tariff advocates. They deny the necessity to compete with foreign production in the American market and apply the historically familiar techniques of pressure politics to keep the United States a high-tariff country. The balance-of-payments deficit of recent years only confirmed their worst fears.

American Tariff Policy.

The basic American tariff law is still the Smoot-Hawley Tariff of 1930, the highest tariff in American history and a major contributing factor to

---

[32] One estimate is that 32 per cent of American exports to the EEC countries will be adversely affected, and another 27 per cent may be. Howard Piquet in *Commercial and Financial Chronicle* (January 15, 1959).

[33] It is for this reason that GATT specifies that any free-trade or customs union should not result in tariffs or other protections higher under the new arrangement than they were before, and that tariff preferences for particular outside countries should not be increased. GATT also requires that any trading-area agreement be submitted to the contracting parties for review.

the depression of the early 1930's. The Roosevelt New Deal never repealed this law; such reduction in its prohibitive rates as was accomplished prior to 1941 was by means of the Reciprocal Trade Agreements program (1934). By this device the President negotiated executive agreements for tariff reduction with one nation at a time. He was authorized to lower existing rates by up to 50 per cent in exchange for corresponding concessions. Under the widely used most-favored-nation clause, such reductions in American duties were extended to most other countries as well.

The Trade Agreements program is often thought of as a landmark of New Deal foreign policy, and yet in retrospect we can see that it failed to bring about really important reductions in American tariffs. Congressional pressure has been constant ever since the enactment of the original law in 1934 against any such thorough-going overhaul of American imposts, and each legislative renewal of the Act has brought more limitations on the freedom of executive action. Most revelatory was the so-called "peril point" legislation, originally added to the Act in 1947. Under its terms, the Federal Tariff Commission must fix the point at which foreign goods can compete with any American industry. If tariffs are below this point, Congress must be informed. This carries the implicit threat of legislative increase of rates if the President were to persist in cutting tariffs beyond what Congress felt to be tolerable.

The Pressures of the Tariff.

Actually, of course, the American people are not (and never have been) of a single mind on tariff policy. An industry in an inferior competitive position—cotton textiles or precision watches, for example—is insistent on high tariffs to protect its domestic market. An industry concentrating on domestic sales and without significant foreign competition is largely indifferent to tariff considerations. An industry whose export sales are large and important and whose leaders realize the balance-of-payments implications of international economic relations tends to demand reductions in duties. The first and last groups participate most heavily in tariff pressure politics.

Historically (up to 1914), American industry was generally protectionist and American agriculture (producing raw materials for export and purchasing industrial products) argued for freer trade. The nineteenth-century Republican party, dominated by industrial leaders, was the high-tariff party; the Democrats, led by Southern agriculture, were identified with low rates. Thus tariffs had a regional as well as a partisan basis. The tariff long was considered one of the issues on which party positions were genuinely distinguishable.

Under contemporary conditions, however, the party positions have become strangely confused as the international trade requirements of industry and agriculture have become nearly reversed. Much of American industry depends on exports for its profit margin, while agriculture— many of its overseas markets gone—today demands insulation from the price-depressing mechanisms of the world market. So far has this gone that the 1956 Democratic platform contained a somewhat equivocal pledge to restudy the reciprocal trade agreements program so as to offer a more adequate protection to American producers.

Examples of Protectionism.

It would be impossible for us to catalogue the specific victories won by advocates of protection for particular commodities. Mention of a few of the more recent ones, however, will illustrate the variety of the pressures. In recent years the American watch industry won a major tariff concession against the importation of Swiss watches, and the Midwest dairy farmers won a temporary restriction against the import of cheese and other dairy products. Bicycle manufacturers have agitated against the rapidly developing preference for European bicycles among American consumers, and cotton textile producers engaged in a well-coordinated and well-financed effort to impose quotas on Japanese imports of textiles. Import quotas were imposed after 1958 on lead, zinc, and petroleum.[34]

The Advocacy of Economic Internationalism.

The anti-protection position was officially adopted by the executive branch in 1945. Presidents Truman and Eisenhower have both accepted the commitment that the cause of economic multilateralism is so much in the American interest that it requires wholesale revision of American trade policies. From the Gray Report [35] in 1950 to the Randall Commission's report [36] in 1954, administration leaders have opposed the protectionist trend. Their failure to head it off, however, reveals the extent to which economic internationalism has failed to take hold among the American people. Difficult as the shift to political multilateralism was to Americans, it proved even more taxing in modifying economic views.

Although certain leading industrialists, such as Clarence Randall himself and Henry Ford II, have advocated an entirely new approach to tariff policy, and despite the fact that they have been to some extent supported by trade associations (notably the United States Chamber of Commerce), a low-tariff position is still relatively uncommon among the general public.

---

[34] The Corporation for Economic and Industrial Research found in 1959 that "protectionist sentiment mounts with the competitive pressures from abroad." *Worldwide and Domestic Economic Problems,* p. 89.

[35] Gordon Gray and others, *Report to the President on Foreign Economic Policies* (Washington: U.S. Government Printing Office, 1950).

[36] Commission on Foreign Economic Policy, *Report to the President and the Congress* (Washington: U.S. Government Printing Office, 1954).

Interest in tariff revision is frequently thought of as vague "do-goodism" and simple-minded internationalism, and the most earnest arguments of such groups as the League of Women Voters are shrugged off by "practical" politicians.[37]

Protectionism and American Foreign Policy.

There seems to be considerable reluctance among leaders of the public to face squarely the economic implications of the long-range policy of the United States. If and how peace, order, and stability can be ensured without gearing the American economy into an international system is a question never thoroughly debated by the public.[38] It may well be that such a thorough airing of the problem will have to precede the development of an American policy adequate to the demands of the controlling concept of American interest.[39]

---

[37] As an example of protectionist appeals, see the full-page advertisement inserted by the Trade Relations Council of the U.S. attacking U.S. policy under GATT and citing increased import figures. *Washington Post and Times-Herald* (June 20, 1959).

[38] See Gunnar Myrdal, *An International Economy* (New York: Harper & Bros., Inc., 1956), for an argument on this point.

[39] See H. Piquet, *Aid, Trade, and the Tariff* (New York: Crowell, 1953).

Continuing
Psychological
Issues
in
American
Policy

CHAPTER ‹ *15* ›

The only permanent victories that the United States can win in its search for a world of peace, order, and stability are to be found in the realm of human preferences and desires. This necessarily means that mass states of mind everywhere have a central relevance to the accomplishment of American objectives and the advancement of American interest. The "psychological" area of policy is as replete with continuing issues as are the others we have been discussing.

Of course, every move made by the United States has its psychic overtones, and Washington no longer uses the concept of "psychological warfare" as denoting a distinct dimension of action. We shall not, therefore, discuss narrowly psychological concepts in this chapter. Instead, adopting the same general posture used in the two preceding chapters, we shall consider a number of issues of broader import, each involving a specific psychological implication.

We shall first comment on the question of whether or not the cold war is a "battle of ideas"; that is, we shall attempt to discover the extent to which the Russian-American controversy is an "ideological conflict" and what place ideological considerations have within it. We shall next attempt to analyze American propaganda as to content and as to purpose. A final section, on the maintenance of American morale, will include a discussion of American popular reaction to the propaganda of foreign states and the various "morale policies" used by the government to achieve and maintain the desired level of public morale.

THE COLD WAR AS A BATTLE OF IDEAS

Among the more hotly disputed points stemming from the general line of American policy since 1947 has been a basic disagreement among analysts and the general public about whether or not (and if so, the extent to which) the cold war is actually a struggle between ideologies. That there has been an ideological quarrel between East and West seems beyond question. The controversy, at least among Americans, grows out of the conclusions that can safely be drawn from this admitted divergence in ideological outlook.

Some of the more frequently argued points are the following: (1) Is America's real enemy communist ideology or Soviet expansionism? (2) Is ideological conflict inevitable between communism and democracy? (3) Must ideological disagreement result in overt policy clashes? (4) Is ideological war inevitable? (5) Can the cold war ever be adjusted amicably? (6) Must the cold war go to the point at which one ideology exterminates the other? (7) Can the behavior of the USSR (or, for that matter, the behavior of the United States) be predicted on the basis of ideological imperatives? We should note, however, that the discussion in this section of the chapter will not attempt to answer these questions in detail; its purpose will be rather to suggest a few factors that might influence the responses that any citizen would make to them.

THE IDEOLOGICAL FRONT

What has been the ideological front of the cold war? In what forms have ideological differences been prosecuted?

Ideological Disagreements.

There is no need for us to examine the many detailed points of disagreement and differences between the Soviet and the American belief systems. To do so would require an elaborate analysis of both societies and the roots of their beliefs.[1] We may perhaps make the central point, however, that both ideologies are "total" in the sense that from either may be derived an ideological position on almost any foreign-policy issue. Taking opposing positions on a number of basic philosophic dichotomies—such as free will (democracy)-determinism (communism), or individualism (democracy)-collectivism (communism)—the ideological confrontation of the two systems is as nearly absolute as we can imagine.

We should also note here that it is important to keep clear which level of ideological disagreement we are discussing. Although each belief system exists in a "pure" form to which people and government alike render homage (Marxism for communists; the "natural-rights" dogma of the Declaration of Independence for Americans), the officially-sanctioned credo of each government today represents a significant departure from such original formulation. The ideological controversy most pertinent to our analysis is that between the presently controlling belief systems within the respective societies and governments, and not between the relatively rigid philosophical formulations of Karl Marx and Thomas Jefferson.

Ideological Conflict.

The ideological issues between American-style democracy and Russian-style communism are infinite, but we may conveniently group them under three main headings: [2] (1) the world role to be played by the two states and their relations vis-à-vis each other; (2) the preferred political system for all states—western parliamentary democracy vs. communist "people's democracy"; (3) the preferred economic system on which ultimately to organize the entire world—capitalism vs. socialism. In each of these three broad areas, absolute disagreements exist; in each, ideological controversy is prosecuted vigorously.

IDEOLOGY AS OBJECTIVE

Any ideology has as one of its essentials a vision of the world as it ought to be and as it will be when truth finally triumphs. This means that an ideology incorporates a set of ideological objectives: goals derived from the summary absolutes of the dogma. If the ideology is accepted by the bulk of the people of a state, the attainment of those objectives

---

[1] See, among studies on this point, William Ebenstein, *Today's Isms,* 3rd ed. (Englewood Cliffs: Prentice-Hall, Inc., 1961), and H. B. Mayo, *Democracy and Marxism* (New York: Oxford University Press, 1955).

[2] This formulation is found, in somewhat more detail, in the present author's *Principles of International Politics* (New York: Oxford University Press, 1956), pp. 379–80.

in the real world becomes the putative responsibility of that state's government.

It is clear that both the Soviet and the American ideologies as officially enunciated today lay down such policy objectives. Such ideological concerns can be classified as positive and negative; that is, some call for the destruction of conditions inimical to the doctrine, while others demand the affirmative accomplishment of states of affairs deemed desirable.

Soviet Ideological Objectives.

Soviet ideological objectives can be grouped in three categories, called for convenience economic, social, and political.

(1) Economic objectives. Negatively, Soviet ideology calls for the destruction of private property as an institution and capitalism as a system of production. Positively, capitalism is to be followed by "socialism" that will provide a cure for each of the evils for which private property is responsible.

(2) Social objectives. Negatively, the social classes whose existence depends on private property—the aristocracy, the capitalists, and the bourgeoisie—are to be liquidated, either by conversion and "re-education" or by violence. Positively, the class structure is to be replaced by a reconstituted classless community of "workers, peasants, and intellectuals."

(3) Political objectives. Negatively, all regimes dominated by socio-economic groups hostile to Soviet beliefs (the capitalists and the bourgeoisie) are to be either destroyed or transformed, and all foreign policies opposing Soviet aims are to be defeated. Positively, anti-communist democracies and autocracies alike are to be remade into "people's democracies" on the Soviet model and an era of total ideological peace is to be ushered in.[3]

These objectives as we have stated them are drawn fairly directly from orthodox Marxist-Leninist-Stalinist sources. Since Stalin's death in 1953, however (and to some extent previously), successive official reinterpretations of communist doctrine have blurred the sharper edges of the ideological blueprint. It is no longer necessary, at least according to some formulations of the official line, for the Soviet to act incessantly to destroy the capitalist democracies; coexistence is ideologically respectable.[4] "Socialism" itself, as defined today, permits private property, savings banks, and

---

[3] Many detailed analyses of Soviet ideological goals have been made. We shall cite only two: R. N. Carew Hunt, *Theory and Practice of Bolshevism* (London: Bles, 1950); and Hans Kelsen, *The Political Theory of Bolshevism* (Berkeley and Los Angeles: University of California Press, 1948), especially pp. 26–39.

[4] This was the position taken by Premier Khrushchev during his visit to the United States in 1959. See his speech in Pittsburgh, September 23, 1959, reported in *New York Times* (September 24, 1959).

some free-market economic activity. The newer exegeses of Soviet holy writ so inhibit the impact of the older ones that it is extremely difficult for us to be precise about just what contemporary Soviet ideology demands as objectives.[5]

American Ideological Objectives.

The United States—fortunately or unfortunately—has no such rigid belief system that purports to impose a set of controlling foreign-policy objectives. Americans, proud of being a pragmatic people—and so ill-equipped historically for foreign policy—have no detailed and consistent set of traditional ideological objectives.[6] We may, however, extrapolate certain foreign-policy concerns from the general pattern of American beliefs.

Generally speaking, America's ideological objectives in foreign policy tend to be more negative than positive, to concentrate more on enemies to be defeated and obstacles to be overcome than on concrete aspirations. Ideologically the United States opposes any form of authoritarian regime, although the extent to which this opposition becomes active depends largely on the extent to which the particular autocracy impinges directly on the American consciousness. Violations of individual freedom contradict American predispositions, whether in the economic or political realms. Once involved, American ideological hostilities tend to become extreme and to harden in stereotyped—almost absolute—terms.

Positively, American mass beliefs hold that all people everywhere will eventually accept the essentials of the American system.[7] The victory of American ways over all competitors is foreordained; ultimately the world will consist entirely of democratic political systems, fluid societies, and capitalist economies. This ideological objective is deemed certain of eventual achievement; many people seem to think that ideological vindication will come to Americans as the result of no more taxing effort than that of setting a good example and remaining faithful to their own beliefs.

With the destruction of ideological enemies bulking so much larger than the accomplishment of positive ideological ends, it is natural that official and semi-official analyses of the American ideological position

---

[5] See W. W. Rostow and others, *The Dynamics of Soviet Society* (New York: W. W. Norton and Co., Inc., 1953), pp. 92–97, for an analysis of the evolving role of ideology in contemporary Soviet society.

[6] We will recall that in our earlier discussion of the "American tradition" in foreign policy, we pointed out that long-standing American *objectives* grew out of history and experience, while such ideological tradition as Americans had was concentrated on *methods* of foreign policy rather than on substantive objectives.

[7] For an expression of this position, see Robert Strausz-Hupé, "The Balance of Tomorrow," *Orbis* (April, 1957).

should stress the inherent conflict between the Soviet and the United States. There is a minor tendency to emphasize the positive solidarity of the United States with the free world, but such efforts are usually aimed at the practical end of buttressing the working alliance against the USSR. So little ideological concern has been given to the shape of any post-cold war world that a cynical observer might be pardoned for wondering if American ideology today teaches that the destruction of the Soviet empire and the elimination of the Russian threat would usher in Utopia.

Ideological Objectives vs. Operating Policy.

How important have the rival ideologies proved to be as controlling elements in the foreign policies of the two adversaries? In hazarding an answer to this important question, we must again seek to generalize as the only way to avoid a long and detailed comparison of preachments with practices.

The history of the cold war reveals that both states have used ideology as the dominant guide to policy only when no more trustworthy criteria have been available. When either Moscow or Washington was faced with a decision for which history, experience, logic, or a clearly understood concept of interest failed to prepare it, ideological considerations were most likely to be called upon.[8] In other situations, in which the demands of time and place and the compulsions of history and interest were more clearly grasped, policy was at least to some extent liberated from ideology.

Most of the policy decisions originally rooted in ideology have been eventually modified by both sides. Some, proving to be good and workable programs in their particular contexts, were retained; the Soviet approach to the Asian revolution, for example, was thoroughly feasible as a working policy (at least up to the Hungarian massacres of 1956) although it grew initially out of an ideological base.

We may conclude, however, that the actual conduct of both the United States and the Soviet Union—as apart from what both sets of leaders have said—indicates that ideological considerations are not primary in their respective foreign policies. Objectives, the motivations of which are purely belief-centered, have been accepted only in default of better ones. To the extent that any may be clearly identified in operative policy decision, we may safely conclude that they remain distinctly subordinate to other, more immediate concerns.[9]

---

[8] Early American policy toward the Indochina war and early Soviet attempts to penetrate the Middle East (in both cases prior to 1954) are examples of policies grounded more on ideology than on more concrete bases.

[9] A number of well-qualified analysts, however, differ sharply with this conclusion. Some argue that the Soviet's orientation is totally ideological and that communist theory is the enemy the United States must defeat; others see the cold war simply as a titanic struggle between truth and falsehood and call for unremit-

If we accept the generalization that ideological objectives are of relatively little importance to the participants in the cold war, how then can we explain the great extent to which ideological issues figure in its conduct? It seems probable that ideology, although of limited value as a goal-setting mechanism for either the Soviet or the United States, is of great service as an instrument for executing policy and for achieving ends determined by other criteria. Ideology's major pertinence to the cold war would then seem to be its use as a technique of policy implementation.

"Psychological instruments of policy" or the "psychological channel of power" are concepts long familiar to students of international affairs.[10] The nature of the cold war and the perhaps controlling importance of winning the allegiance of uncommitted millions of men has raised this vehicle of policy to an unprecedented strategic significance. If the only permanent victories are those won in the minds of men, it would seem to make good sense to argue that the most significant weapons of foreign policy are those that have their effect on the human psyche.

Soviet Ideological Techniques.

We have previously alluded to many specific examples of Soviet ideological technique. We may summarize it here as a continuing attempt to identify communism everywhere with the dissatisfactions, aspirations, animosities, and fears of whatever group in any state Moscow feels is most useful for its purposes.[11] In some states this may be the submerged mass just beginning to stir, as in much of Asia and Africa; on the other hand, the Kremlin has no aversion to sustaining or supporting an oligarchy of power even against the wishes of the bulk of the local population.

---

ting effort by the United States, not only to vanquish communism but to make good the final victory of American beliefs. The best-known advocate of the latter position is James Burnham. See especially Chapter III, "The End of Traditional Diplomacy," in his *The Coming Defeat of Communism* (New York: John Day, 1950). A somewhat different development of the same theme is found in Robert Strausz-Hupé, *Protracted Conflict* (New York: Frederick A. Praeger, 1959). A more restrained evaluation of Soviet ideological motivations, is found in the report to the Senate Foreign Relations Committee by the Center for International Affairs of Harvard University, *Ideology and Foreign Affairs* (Washington: U.S. Government Printing Office, 1960), pp. 13–18.

10 See, as an early example, the sophisticated discussion in Frank L. Simonds and Brooks Emeny, *The Great Powers in World Politics,* new ed. (New York: American Book Co., 1939), pp. 149–52.

11 A provocative analysis of Soviet ideological methods, interpreted in the light of the doctrines of modern psychology, is " 'Ferreus,' The Menace of Communist Psychological Warfare," *Orbis* (April, 1957).

Moscow's negative ideological emphasis is on portraying the United States as the enemy of the downtrodden everywhere. America is identified with monopoly, capitalist exploitation, imperialism, and war.[12] By discrediting the United States in ideological terms, the Soviet hopes to accomplish two purposes: first, to weaken American influence and the effectiveness of American policy; second, to procure a more favorable hearing for its own claims. The Soviet's primary goal is to alienate people from the United States and then, on the old principle (made much of by Moscow's propaganda) that "the enemy of my enemy is my friend," to win them to the acceptance of its own position.

Moscow's major victory on the ideological front, of course, has been its success in establishing a communist party in virtually every noncommunist state. These parties, serving under the Kremlin's orders, provide a ready-made pipeline into the social structure of every host state, and the message is more effective when propagated by natives. Soviet emissaries maintain close contact with local communists and coordinate their activities.

American Ideological Techniques.

American ideological techniques are generally the reciprocal of the Soviet's. Like the Russians, Americans insist that they are interested in the welfare of all men everywhere and that American beliefs promise the most for the future. American ideology stresses human freedom, national self-determination, and individual economic well-being.

This last point has been hotly debated. Some observers argue that emphasizing economic betterment under American-style capitalism is a total refutation of the materialistic philosophy of communism, while others insist that the incessant reiteration of the material comforts resulting from adherence to American ideas makes the United States an advocate of a "bathtub and television" culture that entirely neglects the spiritual side of man.[13] Whatever its impact on foreigners, however, there is no doubt that most Americans feel that their high standard of living is in some way an outgrowth of their belief system, and it is only natural for an export

---

[12] Moscow's line on the riots against the Kishi government of Japan that caused the cancellation of President Eisenhower's planned visit in June, 1960, emphasized that it was America's provocative policy that had annoyed the Japanese to the point where they broke out in a "spontaneous" protest. See *The New York Times* (June 17, 1960).

[13] See Chester Bowles, *Ideas, People, and Peace* (New York: Harper & Bros., Inc., 1958), for a discussion on this last point. See also, for a theoretical analysis of the issue in a cultural framework, F. S. C. Northrop, *The Meeting of East and West* (New York: The Macmillan Co., 1947), pp. 454–8. Barbara Ward, in *The Interplay of East and West* (New York: W. W. Norton and Co., Inc., 1957), directs herself to this point as well. The Harvard Center report, *Ideology and Foreign Affairs,* also has a good deal to say on this subject; see pp. 61–73.

ideology to make much of what so many Americans feel is important.

The major use to which American ideological weapons have been put has been the forging of the free-world complex. In this endeavor the ideological concept of the "free world" has been put to extensive use in developing a common ground on which all noncommunist nations could stand. The operative ideology seems to presuppose a simple dichotomy between communism and freedom, and to count as ideological brethren all nations on the non-Soviet side of the dividing line. Some difficulty has arisen, however, because of the natural but unfortunate popular tendency to make "freedom" (in the sense of opposition to communist expansionism) a working synonym for "democracy," peaceful intent, or a shared interest in the American version of the status quo.

The major complaint we can level at the use of ideological techniques by the United States has been the glaring disparity between American professions and the actual policy of the United States. If self-determination, individual freedom, and economic well-being are the cornerstones of America's ideological position, the extent to which American action fails to exemplify these abstractions is one measure of the inadequacy of American policy. Either because ideology has been neglected in shaping decisions or because the American position has been inadequately presented to the world, a considerable gap exists between principles and practice and this opening in American defenses has been exploited by the Soviet.[14]

VERDICT ON FIFTEEN YEARS

To the extent that the cold war is actually a battle of ideas, how has the tide run during the first decade and a half? Can we reach any general conclusions about the relative success of the United States and the USSR in the struggle for the minds of men? Although recognizing that these are treacherous waters indeed, we may suggest some general conclusions.

Russian Balance Sheet.

Before venturing any estimate of Soviet success in winning converts, we should establish some rough criteria of measurement. The Kremlin has had several operational goals in mind, and has made different degrees of progress toward each of them.

The Soviet's announced primary goal—its major "ideological objective" —has been to win converts to the total official ideology of the USSR, the

---

[14] A restrained argument of this position was made by T. V. Smith, "The Ideological Strength and Weakness of the American Position," *Annals* (November, 1951). See also Part III of the Harvard study, *Ideology and Foreign Affairs,* "Implications For U.S. Foreign Policy."

entire communist apparatus of dialectical materialism, the dictatorship of the proletariat, the classless society, and so on. In this area its success has been minimal and, considering the entire period from 1945 to 1961, perhaps negative. Even before the dissension in the communist ranks became obvious after 1956, it had become obvious that throughout the world communists were tending to organize into tiny, almost clandestine revolutionary groups instead of becoming major political forces in their own nations. In only a few states—France, Italy, and China, for example —did communism ever become anything like a mass movement organized under a rigid ideological roof.

In their second ideological purpose—winning foreign support for the foreign-policy objectives of the USSR—the Soviet leadership had some greater success. Once the overtly "hard" line generally identified with Stalin was suppressed in favor of an advocacy of peace, disarmament, and reconciliation, the Soviet discovered large segments of opinion, both in the neutral world and within the ranks of the West itself, that were becoming more disposed to listen to Moscow. Soviet espousal of the cause of underdeveloped and colonial peoples also gained considerable popular approval and some overt diplomatic cooperation from the Asian bloc. To these must also be added the augmentation in prestige that followed the Sputnik breakthrough, weapons development, the successful moon shot of 1959, and other technological achievements.

Moscow's greatest ideological success, however, came in its effort to discredit the United States. Here both American failures and the inability of the United States to present its position convincingly made it possible for the Soviet to claim that events were corroborating its denunciation of everything American. Much of the noncommunist world, distressed by its own weakness, by the heavy-handed manner in which much of American policy was executed, and by its dependence on American largesse, found comfort in accepting Soviet attempts to explain United States action in the most sinister terms. This approach, although it led to only limited pro-Sovietism, served Russian purposes nevertheless by impeding American efforts and can be counted as a major ideological victory.

The American Record.

The American record on the ideological front is (for Americans) one of the less encouraging aspects of the cold war. If we apply the same general criteria as we used on the Soviet record, we find little to justify American self-congratulation.

On the count of winning converts to the total American ideology, there is no indication of any but miniscule success. A lack of agreement at

home about what the American ideology actually is and a general preference for emphasizing those aspects of American belief most likely to offend exotic cultures (material comfort, mechanization, and armed might) have resulted in only a relatively short list of converts. Americans today realize that they are much less "popular" throughout the world than they were two decades ago, and their perplexity at this development is matched by their resentment.[15]

The record of winning ideological support for American foreign policy is an uneven one; broad swings can be detected from acceptance to rejection of the American ideological defense of particular policy moves. The enactment of ECA was one high point at which American arguments were listened to sympathetically; United States opposition to Britain and France at the time of the Suez invasion of 1956 was another, although before a different audience. Other moves, such as America's insistence upon European rearmament after 1950 even though such a policy endangered economic stability, have caused widespread cynicism about American sincerity. The equivocal American position on both anti-colonialism and disarmament also created considerable disaffection with United States leadership.

American ideological obstruction of communist designs was more successful. The constant exposure of the contradictions between Soviet beliefs and Soviet practice impeded Russian policy in many areas. American success was greatest in those regions, such as western Europe, where considerable ideological harmony already existed with the United States; in Asia, the American anti-communist message was so confused with other purposes that its edges were often blunted. Just as unfortunate American actions and statements helped the Soviet discredit the United States, occasional senseless Russian moves played into America's hand. The most impressive of these gaffes was of course Russia's unabashed brutality in dealing with the Hungarian rebellion in 1956. Khrushchev's grotesque distortion of the "U-2" incident of 1960 was so extreme as to retrieve much of the ground that inept American statements had lost, and his blatant obstructionism in the 1960 General Assembly alienated many of the very nonwestern states he was obviously wooing.

---

[15] Edward W. Barrett, in the concluding paragraph of his study of the American information program, *Truth Is Our Weapon* (New York: Funk & Wagnalls, 1953), makes this comment: "When we Americans consistently put our case before the people of the world in a way which shows we respect their intelligence, we will be well on our way. In the world of today there is an enormous stock of good will toward us. . . . America can mobilize this force of good will effectively when it determines to pursue vigorously and *consistently* the aim reflected in the Declaration of Independence—to behave and to speak out of a decent respect to the opinions of mankind." (P. 300; italics in original. Reprinted by permission.)

Ideological conflict within the cold-war context has been, on the basis of the record, inconclusive. Neither side has scored any great or convincing victory; the major effect of the ideological battle has been negative. Each side has had some profit from its attempt to demolish the other's position. One conclusion, however, emerged from the record of ideological disputation: the effectiveness of ideological argument as a technique of foreign policy seemed to depend, in the long run, upon the extent to which actual policy could be reconciled with purported beliefs. The mere advocacy of absolute principles of social, economic, or political organization had only a limited effectiveness by itself; when coupled with demonstrable implementing action, however, ideology not only heightened the effect of other tactics of policy implementation but acquired a significant impact on its own right.[16]

UNITED STATES PROPAGANDA: PURPOSE AND CONTENT

The United States is deeply involved in a propaganda war, most obviously with the USSR but also to some extent with the great majority of the states with which it has relations. It is a relatively new, and for most Americans a somewhat distasteful, outgrowth of the new stature of their nation; Americans do not yet feel thoroughly at home in a systematic attempt to influence other peoples by overtly persuasive techniques. But to forego propaganda would be to concede the psychological battleground to the enemy and the American situation is by no means so advantageous that the United States can allow other states to enjoy a field day in propaganda unimpeded by American countermeasures.

THE PURPOSES OF AMERICAN PROPAGANDA

What are the purposes of American propaganda? What does the United States hope to accomplish by its efforts? In judging the propaganda program of the American government we must keep in mind the objectives it is designed to attain.

What Can Propaganda Accomplish?

The many definitions of "propaganda" agree that it is generally a technique of persuasion, and that its general objective is action taken by the

---

[16] See Arthur Krock, "Why We Are Losing the Psychological War," *New York Times Magazine* (December 8, 1957).

recipient(s) of the sort desired by the propagandist. Appropriate action will not follow a propagandist's appeal unless the recipient's own attitudes were favorable to the receipt of the message. Attempting to persuade tribal groups of native Africans to purchase electric refrigerators would be pointless unless the Africans themselves were aware of what they were missing by not having these appliances. In the jargon of American advertising, this is known as "creating a demand." In the same way, urging a foreign population to rise against its oppressors is of no use unless the people themselves realize that they are oppressed, nor is there any value in begging such a people to support American policy unless they feel that the United States is actually trying to help them.[17]

We may thus subdivide the propagandist's purpose into two different tasks, one precedent to the other. Government propaganda may in the first place concentrate on the creation of a climate in which the propagandist's appeals are favorably received. Advertising men are familiar with this process as "building good will" or "institutional advertising." After the image of the propagandizing nation as a friendly, likeable, and well-wishing people has been constructed on a lasting basis, the second phase of propaganda can be undertaken. At this point open appeals for action may be made, drawing their effectiveness from the base of goodwill created by earlier programs.

This two-phase operation, as we describe it, is obviously schematic. In the case of the United States, there already exists a "reservoir of goodwill" in many parts of the world on which Washington can draw to float its appeals for direct action. In such cases the United States need devote only a small amount of time and effort to the creation of a "set to action," and can move directly to its specific programmatic message. But in dealing with peoples whose attitude toward the United States is either indifferent or hostile, an indispensable first step is the discovery of some channel into the foreign society that will procure a favorable hearing for whatever America has to say. Only such a route, properly exploited, can serve to transmit propaganda with a political purpose.

The Targets of American Propaganda.

We must also distinguish the various groups that form the targets of American government propaganda. Each of them presents a separate problem; for each of them a separate program has been devised.

---

[17] See D. Lincoln Harter and John Sullivan, *Propaganda Handbook* (Philadelphia: 20th Century Publishing Co., 1953), Chapter 7, "The Aims of the Propagandist"; and Daniel Lerner, "Effective Propaganda: Conditions and Evaluation," in Daniel Lerner, ed., *Propaganda in War and Crisis* (New York: George Stewart, 1951), pp 344ff.

The first target of propaganda is, of course, the American people. Public support of the policies undertaken by the leadership is vital; full attention must be paid to the maintenance of public confidence. The second target group consists of America's allies; the object here is to maintain the solidarity of the alliance and to win continuing diplomatic agreement with American moves. The third consists of the states of the "neutral" world; the United States attempts to gain their friendship and support and, if that proves impossible, at least to strengthen their anti-Soviet orientation. Finally, and most obviously, the fourth propaganda target is the communist empire in the Soviet orbit. In this area the United States seeks fundamentally to impair or destroy the loyalty patterns of the peoples of the Soviet world and to set them against their governments.[18]

THE VEHICLES OF AMERICAN PROPAGANDA

The direction of the American propaganda effort is under the administrative control of the United States Information Agency (USIA), operating from a headquarters in Washington through field offices abroad. Its functions are under the policy direction of the Department of State.

The Propaganda Media.

USIA uses all available communications media to carry its message. (1) It has an extensive television program operation, aimed at the 47 free-world countries where about 27 million television receivers were in use at the end of 1959.[19] (2) The Voice of America broadcast in 37 languages during 1959, averaging over 80 hours daily. (3) Magazines and newspapers abroad with a combined circulation of over a billion use USIA material through the Agency's Press and Publication Service; in addition, the agency publishes 70 magazines and newspapers itself. (4) USIA distributes motion pictures, both feature films and short subjects. Five such motion pictures won official awards from international groups during 1959. (5) The agency also maintains over 150 information centers abroad, which include libraries of American books and are also centers for English teaching, lectures, concerts, films, and cultural exhibits. There are also nearly 80 "bi-national" centers in 25 countries, to which USIA provides support.[20]

---

[18] This listing is similar to the one suggested by Barrett, in *Truth is Our Weapon*, p. 290n.

[19] United States Information Agency, *13th Review of Operations, July 1–December 31, 1959* (Washington: U.S. Government Printing Office, 1960), p. 5.

[20] See United States Information Agency, *The U.S. Overseas Information Program*, rev. ed. (Washington: U.S. Goverment Printing Office, 1958).

Field Organization.

USIA is organized for field operations into five regional groupings: Europe, Far East, Latin America, Near East and South Asia, and Africa. In each host country, the operation is known as the United States Information Service (USIS); the principal officer of each USIS is known as the Public Affairs Officer, who serves as a member of the American Ambassador's staff. Under him is a cultural affairs section headed by a Cultural Affairs Officer (sometimes known as a "cultural attaché"), and a press-public relations section. In many countries USIS maintains branch posts (usually information centers). There are 17 branch posts in Germany, 13 in Japan, 9 in India, and 5 in Brazil.[21]

THE MESSAGE OF THE UNITED STATES

What is the content of American propaganda? What message does the United States distribute abroad through the elaborate mechanisms that we have outlined? On what stimuli does the American government count to provide the action abroad that it hopes for?

"Truth Is Our Weapon."

In his authoritative study of the early stages of the American propaganda effort, former Assistant Secretary of State Edward W. Barrett laid down what is still the controlling principle of American information policy:

> *In the contest for men's minds, truth can be peculiarly the American weapon. It cannot be an isolated weapon, because the propaganda of truth is powerful only when linked with concrete actions and policies. . . . Yet, because truth is generally on our side, it can be our decisive weapon if we will only profit from past lessons and employ it with wisdom, consistency, and responsibility.*[22]

Truth can indeed be the decisive American propaganda weapon, if only it remains accurate to say that "truth is generally on our side." Less committed to the "big lie" as a policy technique than is the Soviet, and free by its own decisions to implement its commitment to tell the truth, the United States enjoys a massive advantage in the battle of persuasion.

The development of modern methods of communication and the mass media by means of which simultaneous and instantaneous communication

---

[21] United States Information Agency, *11th Report to Congress, July 1–December 31, 1958* (Washington: U.S. Government Printing Office, 1959), pp. 20–22.
[22] Barrett, *Truth Is Our Weapon*, p. ix. Reprinted by permission.

is possible with hundreds of thousands of people have placed a premium on the propaganda of truth. Maintaining the efficiency of lying propaganda is fantastically difficult when only a modicum of effort will enable almost any target people to check one nation's claims against another's. Any propagandist caught in a barefaced untruth thereby creates a barrier against all his subsequent efforts to penetrate; each exposed lie makes the lot of the persuader that much more difficult. Theodore C. Streibert, then Director of USIA, put the point this way in 1956:

> If the "world's people" are to understand the issue in this contest, we must effectively counter the hostile propaganda of world communism and, at the same time, vigorously project abroad the truth of what we stand for.[23]

We must not suppose, however, that the "truth" that is the American weapon is (or even should be) always the whole truth. What goes into propaganda should be truthful—for reasons both of conviction and of expediency—but this does not imply that American messages must tell everything there is to be told. Propaganda, after all, is persuasive; it would call its very purpose into question to include—out of a single-minded devotion to the ideal of truth—information that might vitiate the persuasive message.[24]

Understanding the United States.

A most important aspect of the American message is that devoted to broadening foreign understanding of the United States and the American people. We must never forget that American ignorance of foreign cultures, particularly of the exotic ones of Asia and Africa, is matched by an almost equal lack of comprehension of the United States abroad. American policy is more likely to receive a favorable response abroad if sympathy for and sophistication about the United States are widespread.[25]

The heart of the continuing USIA mission, therefore, is the "cultural" program: a steady projection of the best in American life, presented in terms that even relatively untutored foreigners can grasp. During the last six months of 1959, for example, the agency expanded its library program,

---

[23] USIA, *Sixth Review of Operations, January 1–June 30, 1956,* p. 1.

[24] No more dramatic demonstration of the danger of "telling the whole truth" could be suggested than the dilemma the United States created in 1960 by confessing to the espionage activities of the famous "U-2" airplane. Something less than full confession would have served the purposes just as well and yet not complicated the mission of American propagandists so extensively.

[25] "The job of U.S.I.A. is to try, in every appropriate and overt manner, to inform the *people* of foreign countries about the United States." George V. Allen, Director of USIA, in USIA, *13th Review of Operations,* p. I. Italics in original.

especially the translation of American books into foreign languages (in 1959 the 5,000th title was brought out). English language instruction was expanded again. This has proved to be one of the Agency's most successful ventures. A "Miniature Science Library" of 30 paperback books was circulated to almost all information centers. A major production was made of the Lincoln Sesquicentennial in every USIS post. A number of foreign universities were assisted in introducing American studies into their curricula. Many other examples of the constant cultural effort could be cited.[26]

Specific Propaganda Lines Relevant to Policy.

American propaganda, however, does not confine itself to background material and audience conditioning. The USIA also stresses particular lines that have immediate relevance to American policy, either by offsetting Soviet propaganda or by advancing an ongoing project of the United States. Great care is taken to keep the number of such emphases being made at any one time as small as possible so as to minimize the danger that each message might be obscured by the others. During the last six months of 1959, for example, USIA concentrated on the breakthrough in Soviet-American relations; its programs stressed the Khrushchev visit to the United States, the American exhibition in Moscow, Vice-President Nixon's trip to the USSR and Poland, and (outside the Soviet-American context) President Eisenhower's 11-nation trip to India and the Middle East.[27] During the preceding six months, the Agency had emphasized the Berlin crisis, the Geneva Foreign Ministers' Meeting, and Communist Chinese actions in Tibet.[28]

THE SHORTCOMINGS OF AMERICAN PROPAGANDA

We suggested earlier in this chapter that the cold war was marked either by a stalemate or by a relative Soviet victory in the ideological struggle. Unless we are willing to admit that there is an inherent superiority in communist dogma, it would seem that America's lack of success can be attributed to a failure in communicating American ideas to the world— in other words, in propaganda techniques. We cannot, however, explain away this difficulty on the ground of a lack of knowledge of the technical problems of persuasion since, after all, it is in America that advertising (the "engineering of consensus") has become both an art and a science.

---

[26] USIA, *13th Review of Operations*, pp. 14–23.
[27] USIA, *13th Review of Operations*, pp. 7–9.
[28] USIA, *12th Review of Operations, January 1–June 30, 1959* (Washington: U.S. Government Printing Office, 1959), pp. 7–10.

The shortcomings of the American propaganda effort must lie somewhere else than in the inadequacy of the message itself or in a lack of technical skill in its transmission.

The deepest-rooted cause of the ineffectiveness of American propaganda would seem to be found in the rather common lack of understanding, both in government and among the general public, of the nature, limitations, and effectiveness of the propaganda instrument. Far too often, the implications of propaganda have been either overestimated or underestimated, and the execution of the persuasive task has been either overenthusiastic or half-hearted. With such a record, the remarkable point is not that American propaganda has not been as effective as that of the Soviet, but rather that the disparity between the two is not greater than it is.

We may list the major shortcomings of American propaganda under four heads, each varying in degree of importance but all of major pertinence to the future program of the United States.

The Expectations About Propaganda.

Americans have swung between extremes in their expectations of what could be accomplished by propaganda. One extreme may be represented by the abortive "political warfare" movement in 1953, when official Washington seemed to think that a magic formula of persuasion could be discovered that would demolish the Soviet threat quickly and cheaply. At the other end we may put the niggardly attitude of Congress toward the entire propaganda effort in the backwash of Senator McCarthy's investigation of the Voice of America; during 1953 responsible lawmakers were arguing that the entire propaganda machine should be dismantled and the money put into bigger and better bombs and aircraft.[29]

Even as of the moment of this writing, we cannot say that the United States has a clear understanding of what its propaganda can do, what it is expected to do, and what will follow the achievement of any of its objectives.[30] There was something almost shocking, for example, in the insistence of the State Department that its "liberation" propaganda of 1952 and 1953 had had nothing to do with precipitating the Hungarian rebellion in 1956.

The Relationship Between Propaganda and Policy.

Edward L. Barrett's warning that "truth is powerful only when linked with concrete actions and policies" is particularly apposite. The American record of promises—both explicit and implicit—not fulfilled by action is

---

[29] See Victor Lasky, "Can Propaganda Make Friends?" *Saturday Review* (September 17, 1955), for an example of this argument.

[30] Compare Barrett, *Truth Is Our Weapon*, Chapter 15: "Home-front Foes."

too long for any partisan of the United States to feel comfortable. Americans are often perturbed when foreigners do not take the unsupported word of the United States, either about its good intentions or about its willingness to act under certain circumstances. It goes against the American grain to admit it, but history (at least as viewed by foreigners) teaches that many American commitments have been repudiated, often in response to changing domestic political currents. To the extent to which American propaganda is not consonant with or implemented by policy, the propaganda itself becomes almost valueless and may on occasion actually prove harmful.

Unintentional Propaganda.

Americans are also largely unaware of the broader dimensions of propaganda. Not all the persuasive messages from the United States are disseminated by USIA; Americans do not realize the extent to which every facet of their lives is under constant scrutiny throughout the world. The bitter language of politics, including accusations of treason; the isolated cases of racial violence and the much more common patterns of racial discrimination; the towering corporate structure of mergers, combines, and cartels; the vulgarity and ostentation of much of American life; these too are part of the American propaganda message. Their effect often is to vitiate much of the overt informational activity of the government. How, USIA representatives abroad are often asked, can the United States be sincere about individual liberty, human dignity, and economic well-being when at home racial, religious, economic, and cultural discrimination is common, political rights are denied, monopoly capitalism is rampant, and cultural life is being reduced to a dead mediocrity? Such questions, of course, reveal inaccurate information and distorted inferences: the fact remains, however, that to the extent to which these propaganda devices are operative (and others we might mention, such as the ubiquitous Hollywood film), the task of the official propagandist becomes more complicated and difficult of achievement.[31]

Translating Abstractions into Specifics.

At the operating level, the major inadequacy in American propaganda shows up in translating the abstractions of American ideological predis-

---

[31] See C. D. Jackson, "Private Media and Public Policy," in Lerner, *Propaganda in War and Crisis,* pp. 328ff. In this connection, in recent years a great concern for the effect of "the overseas American" has resulted in a widespread program of training Americans who live and work abroad to be better "ambassadors." Several universities (among them Syracuse University and the School of International Service of American University) have undertaken training programs for business executives on their way to overseas posts. See Harlan Cleveland *et al., The Overseas Americans* (New York: McGraw-Hill Book Company, Inc., 1960).

positions into specific appeals. Making American propaganda intelligible to its targets has not been simple, nor has the record of performance improved notably during the latter period of the cold war.

What we are saying is that American propaganda, in making such concepts as individual liberty or economic well-being the bases of specific appeals, has failed to clothe these notions with referents intelligible to the actual wants or needs of the target people. The American criterion has instead tended often to be what the "average" American means by these terms, and the net impact of the American message has been to exhort the Greek, the Indonesian, the Sudanese, or the Bolivian to become just like the middle-class citizen of Peoria, Illinois.[32]

Painting rosy pictures of life in America, complete with skyscrapers, television, and indoor plumbing, makes few converts among peasants whose major concerns are with shaking free of the local moneylender and learning to read. Instead of inspiring a desire to emulate the United States, such appeals usually leave the observer unmoved; frequently, indeed, they stir up actual resentment and soften up resistance to Soviet persuasion. American self-praise, particularly when American policy can be interpreted as contradicting ideological professions, often helps no one except the Soviet.

To the extent to which American propaganda is pitched at a level to which its audience is responsive—whatever the audience and whatever that appropriate audience level might be—there is a greater likelihood that a sympathetic hearing can be obtained. As long as the specifics of propaganda fail to reach mass audiences because of their unintelligibility, mass responses are impossible. How to increase the audience for the American message is a problem of growing significance.

THE MAINTENANCE OF AMERICAN MORALE

Perhaps the most crucial psychological issue of all has nothing whatever to do with United States propaganda abroad. It is, of course, the mental state of the American people; can it be maintained at a level adequate to provide the necessary support for American policy?

We discussed American morale as a capability factor in Chapter 9. At this point we shall discuss only one problem bearing on the state of national morale, that of American reaction to foreign propaganda, and then we shall canvass briefly the various approaches to public opinion that we call the "morale policies" of the United States government.

---

[32] Barrett makes this point in a number of places, especially in Chapter 21: "The Quest for a Formula."

"Propaganda" and the American People.

Americans, we have pointed out, are a suspicious people in international relationships, and they have also a deep-rooted cultural antipathy to being taken in by any sort of over-smooth and glib sales-talk. From these two sources has grown a prevailing popular attitude: "propaganda" in international politics (and in many other areas as well) is a dirty word. In the mass mind, propaganda is put to an ulterior purpose, and almost always that purpose is against the better interests of whoever is being propagandized. Furthermore, propaganda carries distinct overtones of deceit: it is almost by definition thought to be compounded of untruths, half-truths, suppressed facts, and deliberate misinterpretations.

This attitude toward anything overtly labeled "propaganda" has made the lot of the foreign specialist in persuading Americans a particularly unhappy one. He must disguise his message so that it does not seem like propaganda at all; he must, in the jargon of the television commercials, do a "soft sell" rather than a "hard" one. Even so, the remarkable aspect of the total foreign propaganda effort in the United States is the relatively minor impact it has had—with certain important exceptions.

Foreign Propagandists in the United States.

With perhaps one or two exceptions, each foreign diplomatic mission in the United States maintains some organization for the dissemination of propaganda and information. The name most commonly given them is that of "information service," and their clientele is divided between the American press (and other mass media) and the general public. Each foreign propaganda agency or individual is required to register with the United States Department of Justice, and their activities are subject to some government control. Perhaps most typically American is the requirement that each piece of literature must bear a notice that its source is a registered foreign propaganda agency and that "registration does not imply" that the information contained is vouched for by the United States government. The Justice Department thus seems to be interested in giving the potential consumer fair warning of "foreign propaganda." [33]

Registration and labeling serve to inhibit the effectiveness of many "infor-

---

[33] The statement used on British material reads: "This material is filed with the Department of Justice, where the required registration statement under 56 Stat. 248–258 as an agency of the British Government is available for inspection. Registration does not imply approval or disapproval of this material by the United States government."

mation services," although all of them have a large area of action, producing press releases, answering questions and requests for information, and in general attempting to gain as large an audience as possible for their material. Some of them, however, are further handicapped by small staffs and inadequate and inefficient facilities; in contrast we may point to the model propaganda service in the United States, the British Information Services. The B.I.S. has a network of regional offices throughout the United States and offers an almost unending variety of materials.

Often much more valuable to a foreign state than its own information service, however, are the voluntary groups of Americans that, each for its own reasons, spring up to advance the "friendship" between the United States and the nation it is interested in supporting. Among the most important are the English-Speaking Union (Great Britain) and the Zionist Organization of America, which is affiliated with the World Zionist Organization and works in a variety of ways to advance the interests of Israel. These private organizations, led by prominent Americans and usually elaborately organized down to the local community level, can prosecute the cause of the foreign state in an effective way totally barred to official propagandists.

The Rejection of Soviet Propaganda.

The USSR has failed almost completely to gain any sympathetic audience among Americans. Its propaganda seems crude and banal, and its ability to affect American attitudes turns out often to be the exact reverse of its intent. For this the Soviets can blame both their own ineptitude—their appeals aimed at Americans betray an appalling ignorance of what Americans are like and of what mass wants, fears, and concerns actually are—and the vigorous counterpropaganda carried on by the American government. Washington attempts to bar Soviet propaganda from American distribution except on a strict *quid pro quo* basis and exerts considerable effort to warn the American people of the deceitfulness and evil intent of Soviet appeals.

Americans generally are aware that the Soviet is attempting to propagandize them—perhaps overly so.[34] Although the militancy of American resistance has relaxed perceptibly since 1952 and 1953, there is no doubt that most people today are highly sensitized to the danger of being

---

[34] Premier Khrushchev's visit to the United States in 1959 filled the nation's editorialists with concern lest the sight of the Communist leader seduce innocent and trusting Americans. See, for example, editorials in the *Washington Post and Times-Herald* (September 12–15, 1959). It was not until Khrushchev had been in the United States for several days and had reached San Francisco that American crowds permitted themselves to show any enthusiasm. See *The New York Times* (September 21, 1959).

trapped by the wiles of communist arguments. Such a normal and ordinarily commendable concern was distorted out of all reason during the red scare of the early 1950's in which the late Senator Joseph McCarthy of Wisconsin figured so largely. During this period anyone who deviated from the Senator's version of orthodox Americanism ran the risk of being accused of "following the communist line"—an offense that, though never made specific, was made to seem treasonable. Since the 1955 summit conference the controlling American attitude seemed to be one that no longer fears communist propaganda as a virus against which there is no defense but a closed mind, although it retained a near-total skepticism about the content of Russian arguments.

After 1957, as the Soviet coupled its technological successes with vigorous prosecution of the "soft" line of peace, coexistence, and disarmament, the old warnings were heard again. Americans seemed to prefer to write off Soviet initiatives as (dishonest) propaganda rather than to consider them seriously. It was almost with relief that the United States accepted the return of tension in the wake of the summit collapse in 1960; this was a much more familiar and normal way for Moscow to talk, with no danger of America being taken in by friendly overtures.

Successful Foreign Propaganda.

A few states have been able to make their propaganda widely effective in the United States, both through direct contact with the public and via domestic informational media. Each of this small group of states has certain advantages—ethnic, cultural, or historic—that create affinities with a mass American audience and guarantee a sympathetic hearing. Each of them also—for perhaps the same reasons—has had the assistance of extensive private organizations in the United States that have worked in close cooperation with official representatives.

Certainly the most successful has been Great Britain. Based upon the superlatively efficient B.I.S., and aided by virtually every Briton temporarily or permanently resident in the United States, Britain has had an extensive network of transmission centers. Amicable relations with news media, friendships with national and local leadership elites, a delicate restraint in capitalizing on the fact of linguistic, cultural, and economic ties, and a uniformly helpful and courteous attitude have made British propagandists the envy of American informational personnel.

During the confused days of the Suez crisis of November, 1956, for example, the British position received extensive and friendly discussion in all media, to the point where serious doubts were raised among Americans of the wisdom and effectiveness of the policy their government had adopted. The crisis receded, however, before anyone could tell whether the British wedge had driven home to the point where American public opinion might force the United States government to modify its policy. The success of the British campaign, however, eloquently testified to the efficiency of British propaganda, and the later evolution on American policy on the Middle East suggested that many of London's shafts had struck home.

Another state with a good record of influencing American attitudes is Israel. Here again something of a ready-made consensus has aided Israel's propagandists, and here also a voluntary apparatus has done yeoman service. But the Israeli government has also shown much imagination in its campaign (particularly in emphasizing the social-service aspect of Israeli domestic policy and in stressing the "western"—pro-American —nature of its experiment in government) and the number and variety of pro-Israeli groups in American society are one indication of its success.

Vivid proof of the effectiveness of Israeli efforts to influence American attitudes was provided during February and early March of 1957. During the crisis caused by Israel's refusal to evacuate the Gaza strip and the Gulf of Aqaba, the American government seemed inclined to accept the possibility of a General Assembly resolution to impose sanctions on Israel. Israeli propagandists, professional and volunteer, succeeded in creating a mass opposition to this move to the point that for Washington to have gone ahead with the project would have touched off a major internal dispute. Fortunately, the crisis was compromised and the full strength of the pro-Israel sentiment was never put to the test.

Nationalist China has also shown great ability to gain a hearing for its cause. Chiang Kai-shek's official governmental mechanisms for propaganda in the United States is only a skeleton, but he has been aided by many volunteers. Whether or not there is a "China Lobby" of Nationalist officials and influential Americans—as has been charged [35]—it is a fact that Formosa's propaganda has won a large and highly sympathetic audience, both within government circles and in the public at large. Its major purpose has been to keep the United States committed to the defense of Formosa and to oppose American recognition of communist China; in both it has had a great degree of success.

The Lack of a Mass Audience.

Except for the states mentioned and perhaps one or two others, however, the story of foreign propaganda in the United States is briefly told: it has had no great and continuing effect because of its failure to achieve a steady

---

[35] See the series of articles by Charles Wertenbaker and Philip Horton, "The China Lobby," in *The Reporter* (April 15 and 29, 1952).

mass audience. The information services of such states as Spain, Laos, Paraguay, or Iceland—to cite a few more examples—never reach large segments of the American public except in very special circumstances. If they penetrate news media, they have a somewhat greater impact, but in this effort there is such fierce competition that many states receive little other than routine coverage.

AMERICAN GOVERNMENT "MORALE POLICIES"

We know that government action in foreign policy must be backed by active mass support by the public. On any but the most minor, short-run matters, mere passive acceptance of what is decreed in Washington is insufficient; what is needed over the long term is an informed, alert, and insightful public opinion that understands the reasons why the government acts the way it does, that has confidence in official leadership, and that cooperates with officialdom in executing the decisions out of which foreign policy is made.

One need not be a pessimist to point out that—if this be an accurate representation of what high "national morale" involves—American mass attitudes leave much to be desired. Mass apathy toward international issues is a problem of growing dimensions; mass emotional clichés all too often are substituted for rational attempts to perceive the national interest. Interest groups and political parties are ever at work to impair public confidence in the leadership of opposition groups, and the level of public understanding and discussion of international questions is often discouragingly low.

The present state of national morale constitutes a continuing operating problem for the American government. Judicious care must be taken that the level of active committed support be retained sufficiently high to guarantee a workable consensus, and that opposition forces be restrained at a safe pitch. A variety of different techniques have been developed for this purpose; which one is used in any particular circumstance depends upon the situational factors and the objective in view.

The "Crisis" Approach.

The "crisis" approach was most useful during the earlier stages of the cold war, when public comprehension of the nature and requirements of American policy was rudimentary. With its general outline all adult Americans are familiar; a particular policy move was identified with an international crisis calling for immediate American action, and speedy and unquestioning acceptance of the government's proposal was asserted to be the only way to stave off the danger. Disagreement, delay, or alternative proposals alike were dismissed as perilous; the official cry for "unity" attempted to drown out dissent.[36]

The methodology of crisis, as long as the crisis is real and the measure under consideration is suited to the problem, has a real utility. Granting popular lack of information and reluctance to act, undoubtedly it has frequently made steps possible that would never have been taken otherwise. Perhaps the most significant example is the fairly rapid passage of the ECA legislation. This complex enterprise might very well have been sunk in a morass of partisan debate and the quarrels of competing interest groups had it not been wrapped in a cloak of anti-Soviet crisis.

But the "crisis approach," as it matured, began to reveal certain inherent shortcomings; perhaps the gravest was the danger of constantly crying "wolf" when the wolf never came. As popular sophistication grew and as the domestic opponents of the trend of American policy found leadership and slogans, it became more and more difficult to convince mass opinion that the crisis was real or that such a crisis as existed was not due to the bungling of American policy-makers. To secure consensus on a crisis basis in those circumstances required that the level of tension be driven higher and higher to the point where a real possibility arose that the public might be oversold on the danger and that public opinion might force unwanted extremes of action. As American policy progressed, less and less reliance was placed after 1950 on crisis as a means of maintaining morale.

Crisis techniques were revived, however, after 1957. Faced with what was generally thought to be an overpowering necessity to launch a "crash" program to overtake the Soviet both in the exploration of space and in the development of long-range missiles, much of American officialdom dusted off the well-worn mechanism of crisis. Military leaders, Congressmen and Senators, and bureaucrats vied with each other in portraying the desperate peril into which the United States had drifted and in demanding far-reaching action and major "sacrifice" to regain "security." President Eisenhower, however, refused to follow this line.

The "Calm-and-Firm" Approach.

Largely replacing crisis psychology was what we might call the "calm-and-firm" approach. Here governmental leaders sought to maintain an

---

[36] As an illustration, see the story of the unveiling of the Truman Doctrine and its public reception in J. C. Campbell, *The United States in World Affairs, 1947–48* (New York: Harper & Bros., Inc., 1948), pp. 34–38. The same technique was used in the aftermath of the explosion of the 1960 summit; political leaders vied with one another in calling for unity "in this hour of crisis."

atmosphere of calmness, of circumspection, and of rationality as they faced problems, and to communicate these characteristics to the public. As long as the leadership refused to get excited, the argument ran, the public would not; if the President coolly suggested that American interest demanded that some particular policy be followed, his detachment might well prove contagious.

This method proved to be especially well suited to President Eisenhower, comporting as it did with his own personality and with his theory of the Presidency. His popularity with the people and the confidence shared throughout the population in his judgment and good intentions made his approach to morale building quite successful.[37] Opinions among students differed as to whether the administration's addiction to the "calm and firm" technique tended toward popular complacency and apathy, but there was no doubt the national temper was calmer after 1953 than it had been previously.

Perhaps the basic question, although an empirically unanswerable one, about the worth of this method was whether or not it was being practiced on a population whose level of information, insight, and understanding had been significantly raised by its experience since 1945. If such were the case, there was no need for a more frenzied program to maintain morale; if not, the "calm and firm" technique was actually concealing serious gaps in the working relationship between government and people.

Senator John F. Kennedy's campaign for the presidency in 1960 was keyed to an attack on American "complacency" and a promise to "get America moving" again, while Vice-President Nixon generally defended the Eisenhower record. The close result—obviously inconclusive about the state of American morale—left the ultimate worth of the Eisenhower "calm and firm" approach still undecided. President Kennedy made the reawakening of a sense of crisis a matter of high priority during his early days in the White House, but public reaction was slow in developing. Later events resulted in a somewhat calmer appeal to mass attitudes.

The Encouragement of Public Debate.

Among Americans, the admitted necessity of effective leadership does not go so far as to permit the mass public to be excluded from the policy-making process. Permitting and encouraging a debate of issues before any

---

[37] An apt example of the Eisenhower technique was the President's radio-TV report to the nation on May 25, 1960, after the collapse of the summit. In this speech he refused to take the more extreme positions some of the Democratic leaders had urged, and instead voiced his confidence that a more congenial climate of Soviet-American relations would again come about. His manner, as well as his words, emphasized calmness and restraint. Text of speech in *New York Times* (May 26, 1960).

official decision is made is a morale technique of relatively infrequent application, but of great importance under appropriate circumstances.

The usual signal for a public "great debate" is the launching of a trial balloon by some (usually nonresponsible) government spokesman.[38] It is seldom that it is labeled as such, but news comment and the ubiquitous interest groups can be counted on to identify it. If the issue is important and controversial enough, the debate begins. In its course a consensus is either reached or identified, and at its end the policy-makers are equipped to act—although not possibly in the way they had originally hoped.

From our point of view here, the significant aspect of such great debates is their effect on morale. Once everyone interested has had the opportunity to express himself and to pay his respects to his opponents, and once a more or less firm verdict has been rendered on the subject of the debate itself, a great clearing of the air can usually be discerned. The issue itself tends to pass from the area of the controversial; it is very rare for any such debate to be reopened, and rarer still for a decision to be reversed.

The principal danger in the technique is the fact that, as long as the debate is on, there is no firm policy on the issue under discussion and it might transpire that unexpected events would work to the significant disadvantage of the United States during such a hiatus. Government officials permit such debates to gain momentum only when a reasonably protracted delay in reaching a decision will not work any undue hardship on American interest—or else when it is simply impossible to head off the debate.

The Education of the Public.

Perhaps the ideal type of morale policy, but one that we must admit has been of limited application, is the education of the public. We discussed the major dimensions of the problem in our analysis of a democratic foreign policy, and there is little that we need add here. To the extent that national morale is based on fundamental agreement on what the public wants, on how generally to obtain it, and on the major obstacles standing in the way, other morale policies are made unnecessary.

The rapid pace of foreign-policy decisions since 1945, the interminable succession of crises, the inescapably political implication of foreign affairs, and the limiting effect of the bureaucratic psyche all have combined to

---

[38] Such a trial balloon was sent up on April 16, 1954, by an "anonymous high administration source" (Vice President Nixon). His speech implied that the administration was preparing to commit ground forces to the Indochina war. The resulting public debate convinced the administration that public sentiment was opposed and the project was abandoned. Speech reported in *The New York Times* (April 17, 1954).

reduce formal public education by government to the status of a pious hope rather than that of a serious objective. This is not to say that government officials do not do a major job of education in obtaining a working consensus, but merely that such an outcome is a by-product rather than an end in itself. There has been relatively little attention paid to the enrichment of public understanding in situations independent of specific policy proposals.[39]

We must admit that such a proposal smacks—at least to Congress and to broad segments of mass opinion—rather much of the "public enlightenment" technique identified with totalitarian propaganda. It will require more maturity on the part of both the bureaucrats and the legislators before a workable system of public education can be devised. In the meantime popular sophistication on international issues must grow primarily from the efforts of interested private agencies and from the outcomes of other morale policies of the American government.

---

[39] The series of reports on various aspects of American foreign policy brought out by the Senate Foreign Relations Committee in late 1959 and early 1960 are one major attempt in this field.

Looking

Ahead

◆▶

The
New
Environment
for
American
Foreign
Policy

CHAPTER ‹ *16* ›

A s the 1950's faded into history and Americans—
faced with no early end to the problems that had
been besetting them ever since 1945—sought to chart
a course for the next decade or more, one salient fact
emerged. The world in which the United States had been
forced to move into international maturity—often with
breakneck speed—was rapidly disappearing. A new
climate of international relations had arrived, new
criteria of choice were gaining acceptance throughout
the world, and new problems were demanding solution. Even the cast of characters of the international
drama had changed almost beyond recognition in the
fifteen years between 1945 and 1960.

The new environment for American foreign policy
imposed different requirements on the United States.
The routinized responses which had made up such a
large part of American action for fifteen years could no
longer be considered adequate; the often-promised but

435

never-realized "agonizing reappraisal" of American policy could no longer be delayed indefinitely. American foreign policy needed revamping to bring it more into harmony with the actual demands international affairs was making of the United States.

Our study, therefore, will conclude with something in the nature of a preliminary forecast of the outlines of such an overhauling. In this chapter, we attempt a projection of the controlling trends in the foreseeable future of international relations, using as our point of departure the accumulated experience of the entire era since 1945. The last chapter seeks to build upon the generalizations we make in this one and to sketch at least the essentials of the sort of foreign policy the United States must conduct if it is to cope successfully with the challenges raised by a new world.

We undertake this most taxing and yet fascinating task with a full awareness of the hazards of our enterprise. Prediction is always dangerous. Yet the purpose of our entire effort has been to prepare us better for this type of exercise, and the possibility that an unperceived factor or a misinterpreted trend might throw our calculations badly out of balance should not deter us. Our analytical problem as students is no more difficult than is that of the policy-maker himself, considering the difference in the level of generalization at which we shall work; our burden of responsibility, furthermore, is much smaller. If the ideal of a popular foreign policy is to retain its vigor in the face of the many criticisms of democracy, each of us must develop his own analytical techniques to the maximum and thus contribute to the formation of an enlightened and articulate consensus. Only in this way can the democratic leader-follower interrelationship of which we have spoken so often in earlier chapters approach the necessary level of effectiveness.

THE RETURN OF FLEXIBILITY

A moment's reflection on the recent past as it impinges on the immediate future brings us quickly to our first conclusion. The pattern of international relationships, badly distorted by the strains of the era of World War II and rigidly formalized by the operative dynamic of bipolarity, is again moving toward its traditional (and normal) state of flexibility. Many of the classic theories of international relations were suspended by new factors dating from the rise of the dictators in the 1930's and the revolution in world affairs brought on by that catastrophic series of events. New doctrines were advanced to take the place of those that had apparently become outmoded, drawing their inspiration from the modified conditions under which the state system was operating. Much of American policy since 1945 has been built of this group of new principles. As the international scene began to change character after 1955, many of the postulates of American action were progressively invalidated. It is with the new flexibility of international affairs that we must begin our canvass of the changing international environment.

THE DECLINE OF THE COLD WAR

We have already had occasion to remark upon the decline of the cold war. We have seen that the rise of new forces in the latter half of the 1950's resulted in the decline in absolute and relative importance of the Soviet-American conflict within the state system. One of the safest judgments we can make is that this trend will continue, and that less and less of the story of international affairs will be told in terms of the power struggle of the two giants of the postwar world. Two comments on this phenomenon merit emphasis here.

The Future of Soviet-American Conflict

In the first place, to argue that the cold war will have a diminishing effect on world politics is by no means to predict any improvement in Soviet-American relations. Such an amelioration of disagreement may in fact come about, and the entire world would be grateful if this were to occur. But no matter how much Moscow and Washington may succeed in prosecuting their own disagreements, they have lost very nearly all of their former capacity to embroil the whole world in their quarrels. So long as the two giants refrain from plunging the world into nuclear war (and, as we have suggested before, this is an increasingly safe assumption), their long-standing controversy will have less and less influence on the day-by-day course of world affairs. It is tempting to speculate that the narrower the scope of the cold war becomes, the easier and the more likely becomes its resolution on some basis of mutual toleration or competitive coexistence; no such prediction, however, is necessary or wise at this early stage of our analysis.

The Great Powers and International Crisis.

A second aspect of the decline of the cold war relates to the common Soviet-American response to crisis. At the high point of bipolarity, only the USSR and the United States had any freedom of maneuver in world affairs; all other states were caught in the vise of the two-power world. International issues tended to be resolved only on terms laid down by the giants. If they failed to agree, problems were simply left unsolved. Smaller powers were forced to conduct their policies in conformity with the leaders of the two blocs.

This effect was most obvious during each of the long series of crises that erupted between 1945 and 1955. The great powers exercised near-complete control over the level of tension, the terms of dispute, and the patterns of maneuver. Only rarely could any smaller state exert any but a peripheral influence on events.

In the past six years, it has become obvious that the two bloc leaders have lost their control over crisis. No longer can they alone decide whether a point of dispute can become a crisis or not. No longer can they control the level of tension. Most important, no longer can they quiet a disturbance merely by passing along a few well-chosen words to their associates. Instead, both the USSR and the United States confront a world gone largely out of control that presents a host of conflicts and dangers not of their own making.

The most the great powers can do today is to adapt their responses to external crises in hopes of reaping advantage out of circumstance. To a major extent both Moscow and Washington are as much the prisoners of an almost inscrutable international order as are the youngest and newest members of the society of states. Such recent crises as the Castro revolution in Cuba, the long-drawn-out confusion in the Republic of the Congo, and the overthrow of the Syngman Rhee government in South Korea illustrated the incapacity of the Soviet Union and the United States alike to control crisis to their own ends. Each contented itself with responding to indigenous forces as best it could; Moscow could not manipulate Premier Lumumba of the Congo to any greater effect than Washington could Fidel Castro.

The Decreasing Danger of War

A large share of the explanation of the new flexibility and the decline in significance of the cold war is found in the fact that the world has largely written off the danger of total war. The frantic search for some protection against nuclear holocaust contributed largely to the creation of the bipolar world, and its dissolution reflects the growing conviction that hard-and-fast military alliances cost more in freedom of action than they were worth. Barring some presently unforeseeable contingency, such an assumption will increasingly govern the decisions states will take in the future.

The Balance of Terror.

The "balance of terror" in nuclear weapons contributes largely to this argument. Granted the awful destructive potentiality of contemporary armaments and the near-parity enjoyed by both East and West in their capability to use them, neither side is able to create a situation in which military power can be a significant determinant. For practical purposes, in other words, the cold war has been fought for a number of years—and will continue indefinitely to be waged—without a military dimension. Only some sort of technological breakthrough of major proportions could alter this situation, and then only for such time as was required to restore the balance.

The Tyranny of the Weak.

The inability of the great camps to enforce their will by arms (except under special and infrequent circumstances, and then only for extremely limited objectives) has given contemporary international politics a peculiarly upside-down character. Instead of the familiar situation of power politics in which great powers work their will upon smaller ones, it seems today that the smaller and weaker a state is, the greater its real freedom of action in prosecuting its policy. Both military technology and the prevailing climate of world affairs make it highly improbable that a large state can successfully use force against a smaller one; paradoxically enough, small states can often act irresponsibly and recklessly against larger ones with little danger of retaliation. A generation ago, no one could have imagined Cuba's government goading the United States with impunity, or a fledgling state like the Congo imperiously dictating terms to all comers. This "tyranny of the weak" may modify its impact as maturity comes to the many new states of the world, but for years to come international politics will continue to be marked by this inversion of what we had come to think of as a normal and natural relationship between large and small states.

New Roles for the United Nations.

The relative impotence of the major states and the growing self-assertiveness of the smaller ones have combined to move the United Nations into a key role in the avoidance of war. Where traditional military force has proved inadequate to restore order, extemporized United Nations military power has proved useful. First employed as a peace-keeping device in the Suez Canal Zone after 1956, the "Emergency Force" technique was broadened in the Congo in 1960 into a real international military posture.

Dominated as it is by non-western, small, and pacific states, the United Nations is obviously destined to expand its activity in this area. Indeed, a persuasive case can be made that the only way in which military power can be used safely in the future will be under United Nations control. Multi-national use of force, it would seem, escapes most of the dangers that complicate single-state military adventures. If history should verify this judgment, a deep-seated revolution in international folkways will have been brought about, and real doubt about the future of the state system will be inevitable.

The Fraying of Alliances

We have seen that the broader areas of maneuver now open to all states have made the cold war already less important. We should not be surprised, therefore, to discover that the contemporary era is one of fraying alliances and the development of new theories of alignment.

Strains on the Blocs.

We know that the serious weakening of the bonds of alliance on both sides of the Iron Curtain began in 1956 and have continued unabated to the present day. The cleavages within the American camp are the most obvious —since most disagreements among the western powers are prosecuted publicly—but perhaps the most revealing intrabloc split of recent years was the Sino-Soviet ideological and policy disagreement that came into the open during 1960. Moscow, obviously shaken by Peiping's insistence upon going its own way, sought to mobilize support among its Communist brethren in the rest of the world, but without any enthusiastic response.

Equally interesting were the quarrels that broke out among the members of the one-time "Arab-Asian" bloc. As soon as "neutralism," their only common ground, lost relevance with the decline of the cold war, the non-western states discovered disagreements of their own and voiced them vociferously. Here the principal sufferer was probably India, thrown on its own international resources and no longer able consistently to speak for a large (if often undifferentiated) group of states.

In spite of the almost nostalgic insistence of the erstwhile leaders that nothing has changed and that the alliance structures remain as solid as ever, the future holds only the prospect of further loosening of the bloc pattern. The less likely war seems, the less attractive will be active membership in either major camp; although open and formal withdrawal will probably not become common, the internal cohesiveness of the various camps will decline sharply.

The New Alignments.

As most states continue to explore the new policy lines that are opening to them, they will discover new harmonies and new conflicts, new friends and new enemies. Each such new relationship will give rise to many possible understandings, agreements, and alignments. These new arrangements will be much different in kind from the ones the world grew familiar with after 1945.

The cooperative undertakings that will emerge from the new conditions will all be more circumstantial, more tentative, and more limited in scope and duration than were their predecessors of the bipolar era. Sheltered by the umbrella of the United Nations, states will abandon the pretense of total commitment that was usually demanded by the older blocs. Associates will be chosen with an eye to particular objectives, and an ally well suited to one project may be totally inappropriate to another. Alliances of this sort will probably be relatively short-lived; limited-purpose understandings negotiated in a changing context tend not to outlast either the achievement of the common goal or its abandonment as beyond reach.

What we are projecting here, of course, is the restoration of something like the nineteenth-century practice of choosing new partners for virtually each dance. In a newly-flexible international system, combinations are assumed to be infinitely fluid; diplomacy will consist primarily in picking one's way through a system incorporating very few fixed points.

The New Diplomacy.

In such a world, diplomacy will regain its historic role as an instrument of adjustment. In the cold-war atmosphere, diplomatic maneuver was severely handicapped; under the twin pressures of public intractability and military stalemate the techniques of compromise and *quid pro quo* atrophied with disuse. Flexibility, however, means unpredictability and fluidity, and bargaining will again become central to world politics.

Of course, the days of Metternich and Palmerston are gone. The consequences of diplomatic failure in a technological age are so awesome that any negotiator will feel inhibited as he acts to adjust differences and seek viable compromises. With easily-inflamed mass opinion on one side and an incalculably destructive warfare on the other, even the most skillful and courageous diplomats dare not move as freely as they might wish to. But if flexibility is not to lead either to breakdown or explosion, the international order must have adequate controls. These restraints can be applied only by high-level (and high-type as well) diplomacy in a world in which retrieving diplomatic ineptitude by war will be a suicidal gamble.

THE NEW POWER CENTERS

Although the process of breaking up the two-power world began almost as soon as the cold war was well under way, it has been only during the most recent phase that the appearance of several independent and rival power centers has become generally recognized. The devolution of power into a complex of self-conscious agents instead of its concentration in only two headquarters is obviously a major contributing factor in the new flexibility we have been discussing. A two-power world cannot be flexible; a multi-power world cannot help being so.

The world's new power centers in early 1961 were: Europe, vital and dynamic again after a postwar renaissance; Asia, highly nationalistic and containing two future giants of world politics; the Middle East, troubled and unstable yet rich and determined; Latin America, gripped by revolution and bursting out of its somnolence; and finally Africa, with a new-born militancy that led it into a central place in world affairs only a few months after independence came to the continent. Each of them, in its own way, set about playing a critical role in the new world order.

THE REVIVAL OF EUROPE

By 1960 the "revival of Europe" was an accomplished fact. From chaos and devastation, coupled with a near-total loss of political balance and energy, the states of western Europe (led by Germany) had made an amazing recovery. Although "target Europe" remained as the most critical area of East-West conflict, Europeans no longer were playing a passive role as the struggle for their continent went on around them. Instead, Europe had become a source of influence on international affairs in many parts of the world. Although few observers would prophesy Europe's return to the center of the world's political stage on any basis reminiscent of the palmy days of the nineteenth century, there was no longer any doubt that Europe and the Europeans were again playing a major role, or that that part was destined to grow steadily in the future.

European Integration.

Of greatest moment to the new Europe was the trend toward integration. Although rooted in "functionalism" and studiously avoiding over-hasty attempts at political consolidation, the European Community carries built-in implications of great political import. Already far beyond dismissal as Utopian speculation or reckless experiment, integrated Europe brings something distinctive and new to the world political scene. When the USSR and the United States are finally joined by a new entity known simply as "Europe" (whether unified, federated, or confederated) which is large and powerful enough to enter their councils as an equal, great-power relations will undergo a significant change. In political, economic, military, and ideological terms, the arrival of western Europe at a high enough level of integration to permit its functioning as an international unit will be one of the true landmark events of the next phase of world politics.

The Morale of Europe.

The impact of the integration movement is multiplied by the way Europeans themselves feel about it. Europeans generally have recaptured their vitality, their verve, and their self-confidence. The oldest center of political power has in many ways become the most forward-looking. When this new spirit, at present dispersed among a dozen separate national units, finally consolidates into a single political force, the entire world will feel the impact. Nationalism is not dead in Europe, nor will it die quickly; it is, however, suffering from technological obsolescence. Only a broader basis of organization can satisfy the new forces at work.

In a peculiar way, Europe has anti-colonialism to thank for much of its new energy. The loss of their overseas empires as well as the aftermath of the war forced many European leaders to look closer to home for avenues of escape from their dilemmas. This, in turn, led to the early discovery of common problems and the formulation of proposals for their common solution. From here it was only a step to the active prosecution of schemes for integration.

ASIA AND THE FAR EAST

There is little reason for us to expand here upon what we have said earlier about the new power centers along the periphery of Asia, from China around to the Middle East. By the end of the 1950's everyone realized that independent seats of power had been erected in Asia. The only real questions involved judgments about the eventual relationships among these new centers and the possible bases of their integration with the rest of the world.

East and South Asia.

The arrival of China and India as major powers is an accomplished fact; almost as clear is the return of Japan to major stature. Less certain is the future of Indonesia and Pakistan, the other two large states of the region, although such large concentrations of population and potentialities of power argue for important roles for them. Even more doubtful is the stature of the several smaller states of Southeast Asia; in a world containing so many very large states, the maintenance of independence of action by Burma, Thailand, or Malaya is a very difficult matter. Also impossible to predict is when—and in what way—the new Asian states large and small will rationalize their relations with each other and the extent to which a regional consciousness will affect their posture toward the rest of the world.

The Middle East.

Without any large concentrations of population within existing state boundaries to serve as a base for political power, Middle Eastern politics show less symmetry than can be found in East Asia. Rivalries among North African and Southwest Asian states, the baffling complexities of Arab-Israeli relations, and the recurrent intrusions of great-power struggles promise to delay Middle Eastern stability for many years. But the region's great natural and human resources, as well as the logic of its strategic position, assure us that a real power center in the Middle East is a near-certainty as soon as its more pressing problems are resolved.

THE RISE OF AFRICA

The dramatically sudden appearance of Africa as an independent factor in world affairs rather than as a mere arena of great-power conflict caught much of the world by surprise. Very few observers, either inside or outside Africa, expected the elaborate structure of colonial rule to collapse as quickly or as completely as it actually did. Millions of people emerged into national existence and political independence before either they or the international community were psychically prepared. The turmoil that marks African affairs today comes largely from the difficulty of the two tasks facing the dozen and a half new states: first, to develop stable and viable governmental and economic units within boundaries drawn originally to suit imperialist compromises; and second, to develop workable concepts of national interest and to formulate foreign policies for their implementation.

Africa in World Politics.

The new states of Africa are striking examples of what we have called the "tyranny of the weak." Although some of them have behaved with commendable restraint as they have begun to make their way in the unfamiliar territory of international politics, others have openly attempted to capitalize upon their nuisance value as weak and unstable regimes. They have indulged their internal feuds and tribal disagreements at the very moment when a high level of internal unity was critical; they have been extreme in their demands on both the major powers and the United Nations; they have played a reckless version of the neutralist game, openly beckoning the Soviet Union and then demanding even greater deference from the West; they have frankly attempted to invoke the explosive emotions of racism and anticolonialism in order to accomplish short-run (and often irresponsible) political purposes. Even the most sincere supporter of national self-determination can be pardoned for entertaining some doubts about the maturity and wisdom of such conduct.

Considering the temptations and provocations offered by these African states, the restraint shown by the major cold-war camps has been commendable. Although Moscow has been more willing than Washington to intervene actively (while the United States has cast about for ways of declaring Africa out of bounds in the cold war, the USSR has moved in Guinea, in Ghana, and especially in the Congo), neither has been willing to risk very much. Both realize that intra-African politics contain so many unpredictable variables that over-extension there might quickly lead to disaster. Both have played their parts within an implicit but well-understood set of limits, both have found the United Nations a convenient vehicle for their purposes, and both will greet the arrival of real stability in Africa with relief.

Also significant is the fact that the brand of African demagoguery we are considering has failed to elicit mass support in the non-western world as a whole. Although sensitive both to anticolonialism and to racial appeals, most non-western leadership has felt it has too much at stake in the future to risk very much in an ultimately profitless and obviously unsatisfying baiting of the major industrialized nations. Each of the several African leaders who has attempted in recent years to mobilize non-western sentiment in his behalf has discovered that such sympathy as he could command had definite limits.

Taking such considerations into account, we can project Africa's future only broadly. African consolidation into one or even several power centers capable of operating independently on the world political scene is fairly far in the future. Too many immediate problems require solution before cool and calculated foreign-policy decisions can be realistically made.

Aware as we are of the rapid pace of change and development in world affairs, we dare not consign African maturity into the category of the really long-range; although no one can cite a possible date, we would be safe in assuming that it will happen more rapidly than anyone now believes possible. The Africans themselves are pressing for quick action: President Nkrumah of Ghana signalled the admission of fourteen new African states into the United Nations in 1960 by demanding a permanent seat on the Security Council for Africa.

Racism in Africa.

Africa's new role has alerted Americans to something of which they were previously only tangentially aware: the impact of racism on contemporary world affairs. Impossible to quantify and difficult to analyze objectively, racial issues and biases play a major part in both the behavior of African states and in the responses made by the outside world; a flagrant example was the recurrent demand by Congolese authorities (later echoed by Khrushchev before the 1960 General Assembly) that all non-African units of the United Nations force be withdrawn from the Congo.

Two consequences of Africa's preoccupation with race will demand attention in the future. In the first place, for many years any overtures by predominantly white peoples to Africa will need to take account of the racist bias of these young states and be particularly solicitous to avoid the mistakes (often well-intentioned) that open the door to racial judgments and consequent exasperating (and frequently irrelevant) political complications. Second, western nations, particularly the United States, will need to have an eye to their own record on racial matters since this will inevitably affect the political judgments many Africans will make.

All of this is by no means to suggest that racial questions are the only ones with which Africa is concerned or that an acceptable record on race relations is all that is needed for a state to qualify as a friend to Africa. We have already noted, however, that at bottom and at least in its early stages, the revolt of the non-western world has been a search for equality of status symbols. For black Africans, race is perhaps the most oppressive symbol of the status from which they are determined to escape. Once this urge is satisfied and once the West learns how to cope better with the troublesome issue, somewhat more realistic and concrete subjects of political discourse will replace the current emphasis.

We should conclude by noting, however, that some African states have already brought the issue of race under control in their foreign policies; perhaps the most successful has been Ghana. For these governments, issues of development, political alignment, and national defense are more pressing. As long, however, as excitable leaders can whip up support by the manipulation of racial issues, and as long as such issues as the *apartheid* policy of the Union of South Africa provide fuel for extremist racist doctrines, the world will have to live with racism in African politics.

African Confederation.

It is obvious that up to this point we have been using "Africa" as a synonym for the new states that have sprung up south of the Sahara. There is a good deal more to Africa than this; we have lumped North Africa in with the Middle East, and little has been said about the future of those parts of the continent in which white culture has obtained a foothold—most especially the Union of South Africa, the Central African Federation, and the Kenya-Uganda region. We should consider briefly the eventual pattern of relationships that might develop among these several sub-regions.

We may begin with a judgment that confederation among the new states of Black Africa would seem to be inevitable. Indeed, discussion of some such project began among the African states as soon as they achieved independence. None of them is large enough, or has a sufficiently diverse resource endowment, to constitute a viable political unit. United, either in one large federation or in two or three smaller ones, their chances of survival and development will be greatly increased. Once the troublesome but really irrelevant question of their cold-war orientation (or lack of it) is satisfactorily resolved and their intra-regional disputes settled, early confederation seems relatively simple to accomplish.

Not so clear is the destiny of the North African states. There has been little inclination to discuss federation (or even economic integration) among such diverse units as Tunisia, Morocco, Libya, the United Arab Republic (which itself is today both African and Asian), and the Sudan. All of them have been troubled by the long-protracted struggle over the future of Algeria. Each of them is still involved in a pursuit of a clear national identity. Whether they will retain a perilous independence, merge into a larger Arab nation, or gravitate toward the new Africa to the South, is yet unpredictable.

Even more cloudy is the future of the white man in Africa. Nowhere a majority, and everywhere beset by the troublesome aftermath of colonialism and a rising tide of native discontent, whether the heavily British white population of Africa will be able to retain a foothold on the continent no one can tell at this point in history. Undoubtedly it will depend upon the turn events take, especially the outcome of the long tension in the Union of South Africa.

THE NEW LATIN AMERICA

The world has realized only recently that, as far as its point of view and its problems are concerned, Latin America is really part of the under-developed world. For many years both the United States and Europe wrote off the other American republics as part of the "western hemisphere," and paid them the minimal attention their familiarity and low problem level seemed to demand. In the past few years, however, Latin America has exploded. The Castro phenomenon in Cuba has probably been the most spectacular event of this upheaval, but a number of analogous troubles in many parts of the hemisphere has finally convinced observers that Latin America, like the Far East, the Middle East, and Africa, is going through mass revolution.

There has been little agreement either within the United States or among the members of the western alliance about what to do with this suddenly difficult region. Much American opinion has seen communism's evil hand at the bottom of all the trouble; other analysts have claimed that the problem has no cold-war roots at all but instead grows out of the same conditions that have produced revolution in the rest of the non-western world: a new mass political consciousness, wholesale economic and social inequities, and a vigorous and articulate leadership willing to use powerful rallying cries like anticolonialism and racism.

Latin American Revolution.

Revolution in Latin America today is no longer the "palace coup" type with which the United States has long been familiar. Instead it fits the contemporary pattern of the "revolution of rising expectations" that we have seen in many other parts of the world.

Using mass protest as a new and powerful vehicle, revolutionary leaders hit at a common group of targets: land distribution to the rural proletariat, expropriation of foreign-owned industry, and a greater measure of independence in foreign policy in the direction of cold-war neutralism. Orderly governmental processes are usually set aside in favor of various types of direct action. Ideological identification with the USSR is not a necessary or common feature; Moscow indicated in Guatamala and Cuba, however, that the Soviet is perfectly willing to capitalize on Latin American revolution wherever and however it can.

In a few Latin American states blessed with adequate resources and less extreme leadership, revolutionary energies have been successfully harnessed to more orderly change. Brazil's development program, marked by a shrewd use of foreign development capital, is in many ways a model for the continent. Generally, however, the new crop of Latin American leaders seem to prefer Africa's kind of revolution to India's, and mass spectacles complete with domestic and foreign scapegoats are an all-too-common feature of the revolutionary process.

For the United States, comprehension of Latin America's troubles has been complicated because of its perhaps inevitable overtones of anti-Americanism. Much of the foreign investment in the region is American, and the political and military dominance of the United States is patent. It is natural enough for *Yanqui* imperialism to serve as a convenient target for all varieties of agitation. The Soviet's eagerness to pose as the friend of any revolutionary movement (provided only that it be sufficiently vocal in its criticism of the United States) has added the final proof in many American minds that revolution to the South—as in many parts of the world—is inspired and controlled by the Kremlin. This tendency to interpret the issue in cold-war terms has stultified many recent American efforts to cope with a problem grown large and unsettling.

Latin America and the United States.

By the 1960's most states had accepted the fact of revolution in the non-western world as a key facet of contemporary international affairs. Even among Americans who had accepted the unhappy fact that revolution had come to Latin America, however, there was considerable reluctance to face the consequences of what this probably would mean to American foreign policy.

The United States was in no hurry to accept the overpowering probability that the consummation of revolution throughout Latin America would mean the end of "hemisphere solidarity," at least on the old scale. Mass-supported regimes in South and Central America—freed from economic dependence on the United States and no longer concerned about the danger of military intervention—will almost certainly develop new freedom of international action. Whether they become "neutralist," as some observers fear, is really a meaningless question. The suppression of the cold war, in any case, would permit them to pick and choose their associates much as any other states in the world.

How American policy will adjust to this new situation in a region in which the United States has been accustomed to having its way without hindrance is difficult to predict. There is some justification for fearing a last-ditch holding action in which Washington would play as strong a hand as it could manage to keep the Latin American states in line. That this would be both dangerous and useless seems clear, considering the aggregate power small states have and the general resentment against any large-state move smacking of dominance.

Probably the most hopeful American approach would be to take the initiative in freeing Latin America from its commitments to the United States, to urge freedom of action on all, and to try to build regional consensus on free consent rather than by means of rigid commitments. Judging by the American reaction to the early stages of the problem, how-ever, probably the most serious danger is that the United States will not move especially quickly in either direction, but will instead vacillate while the situation drifts out of control. In many ways this would be the worst possible outcome; the United States would lose its allies in the hemisphere but would be unable to salvage very much by way of friendship.

Latin American Centers of Power.

If Latin America does indeed follow the path blazed by the other parts of the non-western world, what will be its destiny as a fully independent power? Where will its centers of power be?

Here we cannot take refuge in any easy generalizations about the likelihood of confederation into large and presumably more workable political units. National independence is an old and established fact in Latin America; it would be a far more difficult thing to confederate on a basis of pooled sovereignty than in other regions where nationalism is less solidified. For better or worse, Latin America will probably have to work within its existing national framework in its adjustment to its new status.

In these terms, Brazil and Argentina in South America and Mexico in Central America seem the obvious candidates for full-scale participation in world affairs. The remainder, most of them smaller and less developed, have a harder road to travel with dimmer prospects of success. One possibility might be the development of three groups of Latin American states, each accepting one of the three mentioned as its leader in foreign affairs. Such a three-bloc arrangement would serve the same international purpose as confederation while preserving the structure of national independence, and might win considerable support in Latin American itself. Many local rivalries and animosities, however, such as the eventual orientation of Cuba (with or without Castro), would complicate its achievement, and no one could guarantee that the three blocs could coexist harmoniously after they were formed.

We may be sure, however, that Latin America will follow the general non-Western pattern and will insist on making its weight felt in international politics. If there are too many Latin American states for any of them to be effective, we may expect some arrangement, formal or informal, to consolidate their impact and make it meaningful. Whether it is some multi-bloc pattern such as we have suggested, a loose understanding under a single regional leadership, or outright confederation, Latin America will find its own answer once its series of revolutions is completed. We can only hope that it is one that contributes to stability and orderly relationships in the world at large.

CHARACTERISTICS OF THE NEW ENVIRONMENT

If we accept the points made in the first two sections of this chapter that the new international system in which the United States will operate will be marked by great flexibility and by a major dispersal of power into new hands, what sort of international order will this be? What will the new environment of American action be like? Only by sketching out what kind of a world the United States will be living in can we begin to project a new American foreign policy. Here we enter a realm of even greater conjecture, for our estimates must correlate a number of dynamisms and establish some sort of relationships among them. Yet this is the purpose of our entire analysis in this chapter; we dare not avoid the attempt.

THE DECLINE OF POLITICS

Our first judgment must be that the next phase of world affairs will be much less "political" than has been the era of the cold war. Of course, this is not to argue that the political process will diminish in vigor, but rather that it will be put to the service of values much less related to the traditional goals of national power, national prestige, and the welfare of the national political unit as distinct from that of its human components.

The decline of politics is already well advanced. The major crises of the last half-dozen years have demonstrated a clear tendency to grow out of issues of a non-political character and to defy solution by standard political techniques. In other words, political criteria are of less importance today for two reasons: first, more and more issues of mass concern are appearing in world affairs that have little to do with the traditional motivations of the state and for which national governments are inappropriate instruments of solution; second, governments, under contemporary technological conditions, have an ever-decreasing ability to perform even their more familiar functions. In this section we shall analyze the second of these reasons, while much of the remainder of the chapter is devoted to a consideration of the more important non-political issues that will engage the world's attention in the years that lie before us.

Supranational Problems.

Although we are to some extent anticipating our later discussion, we should emphasize first that the most pressing problems of the present and future will be supranational in character. We know already, for example, that the impact of technology and scientific advance—epitomized in the space race—is global and that no single state can insulate itself from it or devise a satisfactory policy on its own account. We know too that matters of economic, technical, and cultural development cannot be encompassed within a single state's foreign policy, even by as great a power as the United States; the attempts to rationalize development programs within a cold-war context have uniformly come to grief. The even more fundamental question of accepting a host of new non-western members into the international order is obviously beyond solution by any one state, but calls instead for the development of both procedures and structures alien to the settled international habits of states.

We could prolong this list of problems to great length, but much of our discussion in earlier chapters has made the same point. The day of unilateral evaluation of and response to major problems has passed; to calculate national interest in egoistic terms in the face of contemporary conditions is to guarantee failure. As governments increasingly face problems that cannot be measured by the hallowed nationalist yardsticks and that cannot yield satisfactory solutions by ordinary means, the relative importance of the standard national units cannot help but decline.

The Limitations on State Action.

In the face of such new problems, states—at least as long as they stay within the bounds of normal political action—are almost helpless. Even more frustrating is the fact that on the more familiar ground of purely political maneuver their freedom of action has been gravely circumscribed as well.

Most apparent is the effect of military technology, which for most states operates to deny them the opportunities to use force as a device of international adjustment, at least at a bearable cost. On a system which was long ago rationalized on the basis of military power as the *ultima ratio regii,* such a development has had an immeasurable impact. States, particularly the older, better established ones with well-developed political traditions, have not yet learned how to live in a world in which war has become unthinkable. Denied their normal outlet for either powerful interest or frustrated ambition, they find themselves helplessly confronting evolving situations without any capacity to affect them.

Other sorts of limitations on state action multiply this effect. Mass consensus is the indispensable foundation of foreign policy, and mass emotions everywhere are heavily committed to a set of nationalist stereotypes and deeply cherished images of national freedom of action. In an atmosphere as heavily charged with tension as has been that of the cold-war era, all governments have drawn heavily on their stock of popular consensus and paid the price in a higher level of mass commitment to nationalist symbols. Today governments everywhere are tightly caught in a trap largely of their own making. They have populations demanding highly nationalist courses of action and potentially prepared to repudiate any leader who compromises away any item of the mass creed; yet, the avenues of action actually open to them narrow with almost every passing day.

One final limiting factor should be pointed out. For at least a large group of the older states, the cold-war era required extensive commitments to action programs of rather long purview. Most major states today have less of *policy* than they do of *programs.* They implement and carry forward enterprises of various sorts in which they have made heavy investments of money, energy, and prestige; most of them are committed to what they feel to be their practical limit. As a consequence, they have little surplus with which to meet new situations and face crushing administrative and political difficulties in modifying regularized programs in the face of contravening circumstances. The easiest short-run course for many of them is to carry on in the accustomed way, without reckoning too closely upon the eventual consequences of their inability to adapt their policy and programs alike to evolving conditions.

New Organizational Forms.

It is as a response to the obvious inadequacy of the state form and the state system to solve the kinds of problems that arise today that the search for new organizational forms was undertaken. Today we can see several patterns of organization already well established; these, and others at which we can do no more than hint, will grow in importance in the future. At least four new organizational forms may be distinguished, each an attempt to meet particular requirements: (1) general international organization, that is, the United Nations; (2) regional federation, strongest in ex-colonial areas such as the Caribbean and central Africa; (3) functional integration, of which western Europe is today the leading example; (4) tight bloc organization, of which the Soviet satellite group is the most elaborate type.

Each of these four forms functions as a unit for international purposes, performing a task that is beyond the capacity of the members as individuals. The United Nations, in addition to its manifold problem-solving capacities, showed in the Suez and Congo episodes its unique capacity to involve mass consensus in a peace-keeping mission—something no single national state can do in today's world. The West Indian Federation, an example of the second type, was created in order to provide a viable (because adequately broad) base for national independence. We are already familiar with the tasks performed by both the European Community and the Soviet bloc; both perform missions the members feel they cannot do for themselves.

As the obsolescence of the national state becomes even more widely appreciated, we may expect many more types of new action structures to appear. All will engage in *politics,* and all will to some extent involve *political* values, but their focus will be on the newer problems that will demand a freedom of international action that the national state does not possess today.

TECHNOLOGY

One large family of issues that will give point to the new non-political era we are forecasting grows out of technology. Science is apolitical; no state can control the direction in which new discoveries or new applications will carry man. Nuclear energy epitomizes the dilemma inherent in much technological advance: it may be the engine either of the destruction of civilization or of its breakthrough to new heights. The fact that our age is a technological one helps explain many of the trends we are foreseeing.

Increase in Population.

Without any reprise of the by-now-hackneyed danger of a "population explosion," it is obvious that the world's population will increase sharply as modern public health techniques are applied to the mass populations of the underdeveloped world. With more infants surviving to adulthood and the life span lengthening, rapid growth in many parts of the world is a certainty. Whatever the consequences (and many possible ones are foreseen by observers), our major point seems self-evident. The problems that will arise are beyond the competence of individual national states, and will require some new and broader basis of attack.

Food Supply.

Although neo-Malthusians argue in favor of a finite limitation on the world's food and predict famine, war, and disaster as a consequence of human pressure on a limited food supply, most agronomists project an adequate food level for even the much larger world population of the future, but only if new techniques are applied in some cooperative fashion. We know that much more food could be produced today if all resources were utilized in optimum ways; the same technology that produced the problem in the first place may indeed proffer the solution. But its success demands a different pattern of international action than appears to be prevalent today, and it seems unarguable that before man will voluntarily return to barbarism under the whiplash of hunger he will modify his political personality.

Resource Utilization.

The conclusion we reach if we examine the matter of resource endowments is of the same character. Technology eats up resources at a rapid rate; some crucial categories are already running dangerously low on a world-wide basis. If the waste of resources in pointless international competition and conflict were abandoned, if resources were husbanded cooperatively, and if decisions as to their utilization were made within a larger frame of reference than the national state, the prospects of serious shortages would be drastically reduced. Continuation of competition for limited resources, however, will lead to the impoverishment of all states.

To leap quickly from fairly specific consequences of technology to a much more general one, perhaps the most pervasive result of technological advance has been a great increase in the speed of political, economic, and psychic change. Technology has telescoped time; trends appear, develop, and have their impact in a time span shorter than could have been imagined only a decade or two ago.

The classic diplomatic technique of "watchful waiting" has been one of the major casualties of this development. States can no longer allow themselves the luxury of long study and leisurely action in meeting new situations. To do so is to run the serious risk of being left hopelessly behind events and of having no effect at all upon their outcome. Today almost all political judgments are probably out of date at the moment they are made; state reactions to events must be both quick and unceasing.

ECONOMIC ISSUES

Without opening again the hoary arguments about "economic determinism" and attempting to assess the relative importance of economic considerations in international politics, we can safely postulate both the central place that economics has occupied in recent years and a magnification of that role in the years ahead. We should note particularly, however, that the economic considerations of the future will be much more frequently phrased in terms of individual economic welfare rather than that of any abstract collectivity such as the *state,* the *nation,* or the *people;* in other words, economic objectives of states will lose many of the familiar political overtones.

Higher Standards of Living.

Ever since 1957, by decision of the Kremlin hierarchy, the cold war has had a novel dimension: a competition in raising the standard of living for all peoples. This decision to fight such an issue to a decision was a clear acceptance by Moscow of a fundamental of contemporary international life: men everywhere are now demanding—always more insistently—that their share of the good things of life be increased, both absolutely and relatively. This simple uncomplicated pursuit of the individual rewards of modern industrial civilization has become a major condition of international politics.

By a "standard of living" we mean here the consumption level of personal commodities of all sorts by individuals. It must be pointed out, however, that essential to a comprehension of the concept is the element of expectation: the prevailing notion within a society of how high a consumption level ordinary people may expect and rightfully demand. It is obvious that all over the world the demands of private citizens for more goods and services for their personal enjoyment is on the rise. The levels vary, of course; the middle-class American may purchase a motor boat to go alongside his two automobiles, the middle-class Russian is delighted with an electric refrigerator and a sewing machine, while the middle-class Burmese might be very excited over having the street in front of his house paved. But the critical aspect of these different levels of demand is that they are all rising.

Against this notion of a rising standard of living must be placed the demands of the state: what the "growth economists" now call the "public sector" of the economy. For most societies, public expenditures mean a reduction in private consumption, and political considerations of one sort or another must be employed to persuade ordinary citizens of the justice of the appropriate level of taxation. Increasingly, public resistance to the pretensions of government to first claim on private resources is forcing state attention away from purely society-centered purposes and into more policies aimed at contributing to the rising standard of living. Economists, political analysts, and bureaucrats alike may regret the trend, but there seems to be no way to arrest it; it has gone so far already that its contribution to the depoliticalization of international affairs is substantial. With the trend in the non-western world already dubbed the "revolution of rising expectations," we may expect much more of the same in the future.

Development.

It is this urge for consumer goods in the underdeveloped world that has made the problem of non-Western societies so acute. As we have seen earlier, the non-Western world is determined to catch up with the West in its standard of living, and they have lost any inclination to be patient. The frequent clash in outlook between the West—which often feels that an underdeveloped country needs highways, water supply, and elementary schools before it can usefully absorb automobiles and radios— and the underdeveloped societies themselves—who want immediate provision of all sorts of consumer goods—is a function of this impatience. The rationalization of the problem of development will require a long period of adjustment of these two points of view. The West will bear the heavier burden, for it must make enough consumer-goods concessions to these demands to keep public opinion in the underdeveloped world committed to the general plan of broad-gauge development, while carefully avoiding going too far in the other direction.

We need say less about trade as a future issue. The basic requirements of a healthy international environment call for a broad and extensive trade system. With nationalist concerns declining in importance, the discovery of mutually satisfactory ways to solve trade problems will be less difficult. The interests of individual consumers in more goods will force governments everywhere to make the necessary compromises.

THE PSYCHIC DIMENSION

The very stuff of politics, as many students have remarked, is the competitive pursuit of conflicting values. If, as the analysis in this chapter is contending, the nature of international politics has already changed and will continue to do so, we would expect such a change to have its roots in (or at least to be reflected in) a modification in the value system of the participants. A quick look at the recent and contemporary pattern of world affairs reveals indeed that, at least in certain important respects, the assumptions of international politics are shifting. We have explored the causes of this evolution at many points in the latter half of this book. We are interested here only in isolating several of the leading examples of this trend that promise materially to affect the course of international relations in the future.

The Residue of Politics.

We should begin by making a concession that will help us remain on the right track throughout our later discussion: as far as we can see now, the values that men carry into international relations will continue to be heavily political. We have postulated the "decline of politics," and we are by no means retracting that generalization; we must also admit, however, that "decline" is by no means synonymous with "disappearance." The mythology of the national state, the pressures of nationalism, and the accumulated impact of three centuries of state life will combine to preserve political values and political judgments in the life of states. All we need argue at this point is that the political side of human affairs will lose its absolute primacy over international relations; it will be forced to share its place as the motivator of state behavior with other values. In other words, men will continue to be political part of the time, but on other occasions they will respond to various economic, social, or psychic considerations.

The vehicle of international action, furthermore, will continue to be the state, at least in the vast majority of cases. Despite the new purposes and new criteria of judgment that men will bring to them, international affairs will be largely conducted by and through the political instruments we now have. Thus the new values we are projecting will still require, if they are to have any impact on events, a political context and a political orientation.

We are less concerned, however, with continuity of values than we are with their modification in the future. In what ways will the frame of reference of international affairs be different in the future from what it is today and has been in the past?

The Minimization of Differences.

Probably the most fundamental characteristic of the evolving value system of the future will be the emphasis placed on the similarities among human beings rather than—as in the historic state system—upon their differences. Politics among national states has always been postulated upon differences: differences in language, in race, in religion, in ideology, and in culture have all served as pretexts for political action. The assumptions of nationalism picked out for emphasis the characteristics that bound the national group together, we must admit. Nationalism also, however, always stressed the differences between the members of the in-group and all outsiders. The use of nationalist symbols for political purposes has always required the manipulation of this dimension of difference; it is from this notion that statesmen drew the systematized concepts of national interest that have undergirded national policies.

What has distinguished the recent past has been the minimization of the factor of difference among national groups and at least its partial replacement by an evolving sense of likeness among all men. This is not by any means the soft-headed Utopianism of the advocate of some imprecise "brotherhood of man"; its origin lies rather in a dawning awareness of the identity of interest of everyone in the difficult problem of guaranteeing survival in an explosive world. As long as the political process, emphasizing human differences, offers only the unpalatable choice between frustration on one hand and destruction on the other, it is to be expected that at least some men will cast about for some new ordering principle for international affairs. Such a substitution could not leave the world any the worse off.

Thanks to the technology that knits the world together so tightly, many of the familiar ideas of difference are melting rapidly. We have seen traditional nationalist animosities evaporate in Europe at an astonishing rate; we have made a beginning at bridging the cultural gap between *the Orient* and *the West*. We have found unsuspected areas of agreement among populations on both sides of the Iron Curtain. We have discovered remarkable unanimity in codes of decent international behavior as expressed in the universal forum of the United Nations. It is a characteristic of this kind of psychic change that it moves most slowly at the beginning; once set in motion, the tides of change move ever more rapidly. We cannot forecast how far this evolution will go, but we must prepare ourselves for at least material modification in the emphasis which we give to differences among the members of the common body of humanity.

A Broader Community?

If the national state is grounded in differences, and if the unchallenged reign of the state is now threatened by an increased emphasis on human likenesses, what sort of organization will arise to reflect this new awareness? Here we can do no more than indicate a few trend lines; too many possibilities exist for us to attempt anything like prediction.

We have already seen that the movement away from the state has two aspects. Men are first becoming less political in their increasing preoccupation with their individual welfare; they are more and more producers and consumers and less and less citizens—at least in an international sense. At the same time, they have discovered that most individuals share the same desires and are slowly accepting their common humanity (although few would be able to put the proposition in any such abstract terms). We may ask ourselves legitimately what sort of socio-political structure could best reflect this dualism.

The most logical suggestion would be a broader supranational community that included the common interest of its individual members and yet preserved such national and regional autonomy as was desirable. Whether this would or would not be *world government* is really irrelevant; what would be important is whether it justified its existence with instrumentalities adequate to meet the sensed mutual needs of its members. Such a structure would not involve the thorny issues of sovereignty or delegation of powers; rather than abolishing the state system, it would at least to some extent merely supersede it. Any such community organization would thus be free of much of the legalistic overlay that complicates political discussion today.

We have long known that supranational government can come only on the basis of a preexisting moral consensus. We have been arguing in this section that this moral consensus is well on its way toward realization, despite the contemporary furor that surrounds the cold war and other political crises of the day. It may be that generations now alive will be called upon to work the major changes that we are foreseeing; on the other hand, major social and political overhaul may lie much farther in the future. In any case, the political system as we know it today is under irresistible pressure to adapt to the new value judgments of increasing numbers of men, and international politics is already showing the effects.

THE DANGERS OF TRANSITION

We conclude this chapter on a warning note. Our discussion up to this point has been concentrated on fairly long-range projection, attempting to see what sort of international order will evolve from the trends as we see them now. We have postulated flexibility, dynamism, and the liberation of new forces in world politics; we have argued that the chances are reasonably good that a new and less tense climate of international relations is on its way.

We must, however, lower our sights somewhat and consider the very next phase of world affairs, and here we find much to give rise to anxiety. The new trends carry within themselves their own dangers. Bipolarity had one great advantage during the era of its dominance: it dammed up the explosive forces of world affairs and fairly well obviated the probability of an outbreak of uncontrolled violence. By denying the viability of all alternatives except one—or at best a very few—the two-power world minimized the prospect of explosion. It extracted a high price for its success by largely preventing the compromise resolution of conflicts of interest, but this should not obscure the value of what it did accomplish. A flexible world order such as we are projecting removes this safeguard by increasing the number of alernatives open at any one time.

Perils of Transition.

The world is well into a transitional era, and is already suffering the frustrations and indecisions that are inevitable when a generation is caught "between two worlds, one dead and the other unable to be born." The old landmarks of international politics are melting away, and the new ones have not yet been pinpointed. Such a period has its peculiar dangers, and especially so to Americans.

Perhaps the most compelling peril is that of impatience. Americans are by tradition doers. When a situation is moving rapidly, there arises a powerfull mass urge to jump into the middle of things and to come to grips with the active forces. Americans demand a "showdown" most insistently at times of actual or potential change, and the temptation to act boldly becomes almost irresistible. And yet it is just at the moment of transition that bold, forthright action might prove the most destructive of long-range objectives; making a strong move without understanding and isolation of the relevant factors might be much worse than taking no action at all. Action taken only to relieve frustration is always pointless, but in delicate situations it may be dangerous as well.

Almost as great a danger is that of miscalculation. The United States has accumulated considerable experience in dealing with a situation of great peril, the cold war. We must keep in mind, however, that most of the effort was confined to dealing with a single force. No such familiarity exists with a highly dynamic context in which many forces are operative simultaneously. In such an environment there is a greater possibility that misjudgment of a single crisis situation might bring in its train unsuspected consequences. This situation makes the need for patience all the more pressing; when failure awaits he who miscalculates, the danger of doing "too little, too late" may well be less than that of attempting too much, too soon.

This raises the question of timing, always important in statecraft but supremely so in a fluid situation. With the pace of international affairs vastly increased, time factors will bulk much larger than they have in the relatively stabilized cold-war era. With a flexible system demanding more care than ever in searching for *le moment juste,* it will be peculiarly exasperating for statesmen to have to move at a higher speed of analysis and reaction than ever. Yet all states will be affected by this condition, and relatively greater success awaits those who best meet it.

Frustrated Dynamisms.

A transitional era increases the possibility of explosion in another sense. We have indicated that the cold war served to canalize most of the powerful forces of world politics into the relatively narrow channel of Russian-American conflict. As long as the United States and the Soviet Union were able to control these major trends of world politics, they were kept under fairly close control and the danger of extreme action was reduced. The transitional era of flexibility, marked as it is by a reduction in great-power control, makes it more likely that the contemporary dynamisms of world affairs that we have examined in this chapter will break loose and provoke entirely novel crises.

The United States must prepare itself to cope increasingly with the impact of these freshly liberated forces. They are beyond American capacity to dominate, and the problem of the United States has acquired a new form. America must now discover mechanisms to restrain the excesses of the new factors and also capitalize on the opportunities they offer for constructive action. Our final chapter will include some suggestions on this point.

What About World War III?

Considering the possibilities of explosion brings us naturally to the prospect of World War III. Throughout this book we have deliberately avoided any extended discussion of the probability of and the possible results of a third total war. This has been due to other reasons than a mere wish to avoid a subject both unpleasant in itself and not susceptible to rational analysis; from the analytical point of view, ours has been a "probabilist" study stressing the more likely outcomes, and the deliberate selection of total war as a technique of policy is a relatively remote one.

We can say this in terms of our assumptions. We have posited a relatively high level of rationality among American policy-makers and in the leadership groups of other states as well. As long as we can safely assume that the world's decision-makers will apply the normal criteria of prudence and prevision to their actions, we can be safe in relegating total war to the category of the logically unthinkable and the empirically improbable. Our analysis of American policy up to this point has sought to demonstrate how the objectives of American interest can be achieved without recourse to all-out military action.

But the rationality of statesmen is only an analytical assumption. We cannot safely predict that all decisions will be reached as the result of a relatively detached weighing of all the probable outcomes of each of several alternatives; indeed, we cannot even predict that any particular decision will be made in that fashion. Too many irrational factors enter into human choice for the assumption of rational decision to receive more than partial statistical verification. As long as the possibility exists that any political leader possesses the power to opt for total war, we must allow for conflict.

The peculiar and poignant feature of the next phase of international politics, if it develops, as we expect, as one in which maneuver is maximized and alternatives are more numerous, is that the danger of all-out war is materially increased. As long as the explosive forces could blow in only one direction, the problem of their containment could be simply stated, even if fantastically difficult of solution. The American theory has been that restraining Moscow would mean restraining all the potentially disruptive factors in the world. But today World War III may begin in dozens of places, by any of over 90 states, and for any of thousands of possible reasons. The problem of maintaining peace in the future will have many more facets; the difficulties involved in the effort may be individually less taxing, but their increased number will add new complexities and strains to the burdens political man is now carrying.

The
Requirements
of
Future
American
Policy

CHAPTER ◄ *17* ►

If the world of the future should turn out to be much as we have foreseen it, the nature of the foreign-policy problem facing the United States will change materially. From a single-purposed—if many-sided—effort to contain the threat of Soviet aggression, American foreign policy will be obliged to metamorphose into a set of flexible responses to a situation grown dynamic, relativistic, and multi-dimensional. Americans will be forced to discover new intellectual and emotional resources to meet the new faces to be assumed by the old challenges; they will require broader perspectives and more certain courses to steer by in a new and more hopeful, yet more perplexing and potentially dangerous, environment.

This chapter incorporates our attempt to make clear the elements of one answer to the ubiquitous demands of foreign policy in a drastically changed world. We shall build here upon the observations we have made about the contemporary and future patterns of international politics. As we have already stated, it is a basic assumption of this analysis that the world (and the United States with it) is passing through an age of transition from one dominant pattern of international relationships to another. Our frame of reference, therefore, will be the world as we see it now and as we expect it to develop in response to the fulfillment of contemporary trends.

One fundamental point should be emphasized before we take up the detailed matters that will occupy us in this chapter. In spite of the massive changes that have taken place and which will continue to occur in the international environment in which the United States will be operating, we shall be using as our yardstick of preference the same concept of American national interest that we have been expounding throughout this book. A world of peace, order, and stability will continue to be the long-range purpose of American policy, despite the major modifications we see in the circumstances in which it must be advanced and the new techniques for its implementation that must be developed. Indeed, as our analysis will make clear, the stabilizing and rationalizing effect of a clearly understood concept of national interest will be more vital than ever in the new international environment if United States policy is to result in any measure of success and satisfaction.

THE NEW REQUIREMENTS

Valuable as the experience of the cold-war era has been to the American people in deepening their understanding of what foreign policy involves, it will not be adequate to the requirements that the world will place on the United States in the future. The first (and more fundamental) group of changes in American foreign policy must be made in an area usually identified with domestic matters. Americans must, in other words, adapt themselves and their government to the conditions that actually will prevail; what the United States learned in the years of bitter head-to-head struggle with the Soviet will have to be expanded into a much more sophisticated *Weltanschauung* that will help equip American policy-makers for their tasks. Before examining the modifications in emphasis, content, and direction which American policy must submit to, we should first look into the new requirements to be imposed on the United States.

CLARIFICATION OF PURPOSES

The first obvious need is for a clarification of purpose in American foreign policy. Before any improvement in American prestige or power is possible in the new world, the United States must come to quite specific terms with its environment; it must be quite clear in its own mind what it seeks to accomplish and the terms of settlement it will demand and accept.

"Purpose" in foreign policy has not been a popular subject of discussion in recent years. It has been obscured by the steady diet of crisis upon which Americans have fed during the entire cold-war era and rejected as irrelevant by large segments of "realist" opinion. Such statements of long-range goals and interests as were formulated by official spokesmen tended to be phrased in little more than clichés chosen for their oratorical effect rather than for their effectiveness in communication. Thanks to the explicit and (perhaps deceptively) simple way in which the challenges to American capacity were phrased, the United States did not sense any deficiency in its policy as a result; purpose was either assumed to be self-evident in "the American way of life" or ruthlessly imposed from without by the action of evil enemies. Public concern over just what the United States was really attempting to do was slow in developing.

As the new world bore down on the United States, however, apathy toward issues of national purpose began to lift, and the tone of public discussion began to reflect some anxiety about the lack of direction in foreign policy (and in all of American life as well). From the resulting clamor came little consensus, but the various facets of the problem began to receive an airing. There is general agreement today that in the kind of world the United States will be living in very soon, neither aimless drift nor instinctual response will suffice as a guide to international action. If the fate of the shuttlecock is to be avoided, the United States must develop and articulate a clear purpose that will guide it through a succession of complex and ambiguous problem areas.

The End of Negativism.

An early casualty of the search for a national purpose will be the easy negativism of much American policy. No longer will America content itself with opposing those men, those nations, and those forces with which it finds grounds for disagreement; instead Americans will be called upon to formulate their policies in affirmative terms. Difficult problems will no longer be attacked by waiting for the Communists to choose sides and then supporting the anti-communist position. Importunate leaders and governments will no longer be measured on a single cold-war yardstick, and "No!" will no longer be considered a satisfactory answer to any and all proposals emanating from states of which Americans may disapprove. The image of the United States as a nation with a peculiar genius for disapproving, rejecting, and reacting will be replaced by that of a state that knows its own mind, seeks its own goals, and reaches its own decisions.

The Abandonment of Abstractions.

Equally critical to the clarification of national purpose will be the abandonment of the set of empty abstractions that have served as the substitute for real purposes for so many years. "Security," "peace," "good faith," "trust," and all their countless elaborations have—despite their intrinsic desirability—in fact been used as pretexts for a refusal to come to grips with real problems in concrete contexts. Considering the nature of the cold war and the insolubility of the problems it spawned, the formulation of American objectives in abstract terms usually did little harm and occasionally considerable good. But the issues of the future will not respond to either temporizing or evasion; if the United States is not to be left hopelessly behind events, Americans must develop notions of purpose that are adequate to the concrete conditions. *Peace* as an American purpose means little to Africans and little more to Americans; the creation of conditions that will maximize internal stability and international harmony among the new states of Africa is a purpose that has much the same meaning to Africans and Americans alike. In like manner all problems will demand increased specificity in the goals the United States is seeking.

The Vindication of Ends Over Means.

The translation of purpose into concrete terms will mean a reversal of the American preference for means as against ends. The means of foreign policy—the action programs of all sorts—will lose their status as fixed points in American policy and will instead be repeatedly evaluated in terms of their contribution to concrete purposes. Foreign policy, in other words, will again emphasize the "policy decision" and will downgrade the "program." Nor will the United States any longer be able to afford infatuations with particular techniques of action automatically applied to widely varying situations; neither foreign aid, military assistance, security pacts, nor General Assembly votes will have any particular preferability except as any of them advances an American purpose in a particular context. Only by making the ends (purposes) of policy paramount can rational choices be made among the several means that may be available.

The Threshold of Acceptability.

As the generalized concept of national purpose is translated into sets of concrete goals, there will be added something that has been strangely absent in much recent American action: the formulation of a minimum level of acceptability, defined as the least the United States will accept as a satisfactory outcome of a problem. Nothing more helpful to an effective policy in a dynamic environment could be suggested.

Any state, as it formulates its objectives, realizes that the infinite number of possibilities inherent in any international situation virtually guarantees that any of several outcomes are possible in the train of the action it may take. Although its policy-makers attempt to formulate these in order of likelihood, any unforeseen contingency may intervene to produce an unexpected result. Wise statesmanship allows for this and develops—independently of any other considerations—a notion of which outcomes would be minimally acceptable, which would be unacceptable, and which would represent positive accomplishment beyond the minimum. The only method for making such a determination in advance is the application of a concretized purpose to the situation under consideration in order to establish what we call the threshold of acceptability.

Much of American policy toward the Soviet has been marked by the absence of any such determination; the United States has acted as if the only choices open to it were total victory or total frustration. Neither in the de-emphasized cold war of the future nor in the increasing number of problems lacking cold-war relevance will the United States be able any longer to dispense with this guide to policy. With the pace of change rising to such a high level, for America to insist on complete satisfaction of its wishes or indefinite stalemate is suicidal. Too many issues clamor for resolution, and too many forces are at work for any such simple dichotomy to be valid. The United States must enter into any new situation armed not only with a clear picture of what it wants, but also knowing the least it will accept. Only by exploiting the range of outcomes between the minimum and the maximum can America succeed in affecting the outcome of events to its own advantage.

THE IMPROVEMENT OF ORGANIZATION

A second area where inexorable demands are being and will continue to be made on the United States is the improvement of its organization for foreign policy. Both in the formulation and in the execution of policy, evidence has accumulated that the American government's existing structure is not fully adequate to the tasks imposed upon it. We have alluded to many of the shortcomings in earlier chapters; in this section we will content ourselves with pointing out some of the more critical areas.

The Presidency.

The new kinds of decisions and actions the United States will be called upon to make will add to the already crushing burden borne by the President. He cannot escape from his awful responsibility—all executive acts will continue to be performed in his name—but he will need augmented assistance in bearing the load of decisions. The discovery of instruments and principles for the delegation of power that will free the President for the role that is appropriately his will be a task of high priority for later administrations.

One obvious necessity is for what we might call a "general manager" for foreign affairs: an intimate subordinate of the President with the power to act for him in implementing executive decisions and coordinating action. Whether Vice-President Nixon's 1960 suggestion of the Vice-President as such a "chief of staff" is accepted or whether one of the several proposals for the creation of a "super" Secretary of Foreign Affairs wins approval is not of major moment; what counts is the availability of this form of assistance to the President.

Other suggestions with considerable merit call for an expanded White House staff of foreign-policy specialists, improvements in the National Security Council system, and improved coordinating devices. Each is important to improving the President's capacity to act promptly, decisively, and effectively; each will, however, have to run the gauntlet of political and bureaucratic pressures before being accepted. Strengthening the Presidency will demand long and intensive effort, but the need permits of no relaxation.

The Role of the Military.

So long as the cold war imposed a clear and well-understood military component on American foreign policy, the central place of the military establishment in the policy process was not seriously challenged by spokesmen from civilian agencies. No one was disposed to query either the motives or the accuracy of men pledged to the defense of the United States as long as the danger of attack was deemed to be real. But the new environment of international affairs gives the military no such clear role; the denigration of military power as a tool of policy and the development of new nonforceful techniques of coercion in international politics raise serious questions about the future contributions of military departments and personnel to the foreign-policy process in the United States. A new role for the military must be found.

The issue is not one of the prospective disappearance of military influence on American foreign policy. The armed forces will naturally continue to have a major impact on American responses to the USSR, regardless of the level of tension at which Soviet-American relations may be conducted. Nor will the military's relative share of government expenditures decrease at a rate anything resembling the shift away from military concerns in world politics; this alone would ensure an extensive tenure of authority to spokesmen for the demands of national defense. The military will be with Americans indefinitely.

But we discovered in Chapter 16 that more and more important problems demanding American action will arise without any clear military dimension. It is with these that we are concerned in this discussion. The armed forces have won the right to participation in general foreign-policy decisions, and there is no little doubt that henceforth they will perform this function in a more complex situation than any with which they have had much experience.

If "security"—a goal to which all Americans subscribe—is no longer phrased only in military or quasi-military terms but instead encompasses a complex mixture of political, economic, and psychic connotations, how will the military react? Will it adapt to the new situation, will it retreat into pure professionalism and dismiss as "politics" all facets of the problem which do not fit its own technical and technological categories, or will it refuse to admit that conditions have changed and insist on fitting all the new problems into the familiar "military security policy" context?

No one can answer such questions with assurance. In large part the answers will depend upon the extent to which the military has learned its political lessons and how easily it adjusts to a changed role. The diminution in relevance of military ponderables in world affairs does not necessarily mean a corresponding reduction in the contribution of military personnel to the total of American foreign policy judgments. There are new opportunities for action by military representatives opening in the new world, opportunities that only uniformed professionals can exploit. Throughout the non-Western world, for example, military dictatorship of young and unstable states has become almost a standardized technique of rapid development and modernization. Via such existing instrumentalities as the many MAAG groups already resident in the non-Western world and such new forms of military representation and cooperation as may be developed, the armed forces of the United States have a unique channel directly into the inner circles of power in many non-Western states. No more orthodox diplomat would be able to move as freely and as authoritatively as these professionals in communicating with their colleagues in other societies. This would be a diplomatic task of first importance, peculiarly suited to their training, experience, and inclinations.

Our inability to forecast the future role of the military, however, cannot conceal the inevitability of change in its present one. If means must remain subservient to ends in American policy, and if the ends sought by the United States are to become less military in nature (and, as we suggested in the preceding chapter, less political as well), the military must in turn accept new roles, new status, and new relationships in the governmental mechanism.

Congress, like the President, will be forced to accept new responsibilities and new duties in foreign policy; any increase in international flexibility will be felt in the legislative process as well as in the executive branch. Congress and President alike must prepare themselves to act promptly and forcefully.

Without attempting the thankless task of spelling out possible organizational changes, we may suggest a few areas in which Congress must better equip itself for its foreign-policy mission. (1) Information: Congress must improve the amount and quality of the foreign-policy information it relies upon, using both its own resources and those of the executive establishment. (2) Legislative-executive relations: more harmonious and mutually helpful relations with the executive department are necessary, with a corresponding reduction in rivalry, bad feelings, and controversy between the two branches. (3) Public liaison: as concepts of purpose are clarified within the general public, Congress must accurately learn what people really think by some more reliable techniques than constituent mail, public opinion polls, press comments, and pressure group actvity. (4) Evaluation of action: Congress must establish more regular procedures for the prompt evaluation of the results of its own foreign-policy moves in the interest of being better able to make modifications as demanded by events. (5) Partisanship: without invoking the myth of "bipartisanship," Congress must develop the self-restraint to keep partisanship under adequate control as foreign-policy questions are considered.

Only by markedly improving its performance in these (and other) ways can Congress meet its challenges. Failure to do so would seriously inhibit the over-all impact the United States hopes to make.

Intelligence and Planning.

Our earlier prognosis of the nature of international relations places a high premium on an expansion of the intelligence and planning activities of the government. The greater number of relevant factors in any situation, the more rapid pace of events, and the fluidity of all international arrangements will all contribute to the absolute necessity of up-to-date, accurate, and complete information. A more thoroughgoing reliance on advance planning stems naturally from the clarification of national purpose we have postulated; the translation of purpose into action can be effectuated only if national aspirations are incorporated into a generalized set of plans.

The United States can no longer afford to be surprised in its foreign policy, nor will extemporization in an effort to sustain or restore the status quo be a sufficient justification of action. Much more intellectual and organizational effort must be devoted to the twin tasks of anticipating events and of responding to them in terms of a preconceived (if generalized) strategy. Perhaps no greater strain on traditional American patterns of political behavior can be imagined than this necessity of systematic analysis and advance planning, but none is more crucial to the success of American designs.

MATURITY OF ACTION

Underlying and giving increased emphasis to the specific requirements the United States must fulfill if it is to operate effectively in the world of the future is a more generalized imperative. We may phrase it as the development of a heightened maturity of international action. Only by acting with the level of purpose and courage that is implicit in the notion of *maturity* and by abandoning patterns of behavior that in an individual we could call adolescent can Americans face the troubled future with any confidence in their eventual vindication.

Maturity as a desirable emotional condition to which individuals attain is a much-discussed concept in contemporary American life; each critic, however, tends to incorporate in it such behavior characteristics as he himself finds commendable. Nothing approaching consensus as to its exact meaning can be discovered. We must, therefore, specify what we mean by the term. In this discussion, maturity of international political action demands two traits that ordinarily distinguish adults from juveniles, at least in American life: first, the capacity to make difficult decisions even though the outcome is unpredictable and could be unpleasant; second, the willingness to accept the consequences of one's own action without seeking to shift the onus of responsibility. Both these characteristics obviously bear upon the way the mass of Americans have behaved and will behave as they confront foreign-policy problems. A democratic foreign policy, to be defensible, must have optimum public performance in both areas.

We shall list and comment briefly upon a number of the components of what in the aggregate constitute maturity in our sense of the term. On none of them is the record of the United States an especially impressive one during the period since 1945; on each, marked improvement will be necessary before real progress can be made toward the achievement of American purposes. Nor are we suggesting that this list, in spite of its (perhaps illusory) specificity, is either all-inclusive or precise. It does, however, point out some directions in which American mass responses to international issues should evolve.

Self-confidence.

Although it would be impossible to assign any absolute priorities to the several points we shall make, we would not be far in error if we placed our major emphasis on the development (or rediscovery) of self-confidence among the American people. Volumes have been written about the crisis of confidence in contemporary American life and the blind search for some external source of *security* to which it has given rise. This wave of anxiety and self-doubt has had immediate and palpable foreign-policy consequences.

Americans generally doubt the validity and the worth of the purposes they purport to seek in foreign affairs. Taking refuge in the preference for techniques to which we have already referred, they either refuse to discuss purposes at all or else turn toward vague and quasi-Utopian formulations. Lacking confidence in their alleged goals, Americans seek to pursue a policy framed without reference to *a priori* postulations of ends.

This lack of confidence extends to the actual execution of foreign policy as well. Faced by evidence that they may have underestimated their difficulties, Americans tend to react by overestimating them. Unless the problem lends itself to easy solution, it frequently is classified as insoluble. Self-doubt permeates the American approach to the Soviet; only a people lacking self-confidence could fear the prospect of "competitive coexistence" as actually guaranteeing an inevitable Soviet victory.

On both counts Americans must muster the self-confidence worthy of the people of a great power before they can cut a truly impressive figure on the world stage. Goals must be chosen with confidence in their intrinsic worth as well as in their ultimate attainability; international encounters must be faced with trust in the capacity of the United States either to win through to victory or to endure a defeat.

The solution, as we all realize, is not to be found at all in world affairs or in the context of American foreign policy. The root of the difficulty is within American society. The failure of confidence in the American approach to the world only reflects a mass *malaise* that permeates American life. Excuses and explanations of this phenomenon are innumerable, but with issues of survival hanging in the balance the fine-spun theories of psychiatrists, social psychologists, and anthropologists do not provide any answers. The stark fact is that a successful American foreign policy requires that Americans find again within themselves the confidence in their own capacity that was once the envy of the world.

Persistence.

A second characteristic of mature behavior is what we might call persistence. Americans have shown a disconcerting tendency to react to problems in one almost convulsive effort. If it succeeds, the issue is forgotten; if it fails, the problem is written off as insoluble and little thought is invested in it thereafter except to justify inaction.

The United States could well learn a lesson here from the Soviet. The USSR, once it is firmly in command of its purposes, is unremitting in the effort it puts out in pursuit of an objective. Partial victories do not induce relaxation but instead serve as a base from which to launch the next move; defeats may cause a modification in tactics but do not dampen the ardor of the search. Communist pressure is constant, probing always for a favorable opportunity to advance; retreats are tactical and seldom represent abandonment of the original goal. In this regard, Soviet policy is a model for all states—not the least for the United States.

If a goal is worth striving for, it is worth long and persistent effort; if the goal, however, is considered to be of dubious worth, persistence is no great virtue. Here again we see the strategic part played by the formulation of goals in an effective foreign policy. Unless Americans can set their goals clearly and confidently, they will continue to lack the poise and determination to pursue them with tenacity.

The world of the future, however, will place a high premium on exactly this quality of persistence. Only by persistence can policies be constantly readjusted to meet rapidly changing conditions; only by persistence can satisfactory agreements be reached. Only by keeping purposes consistently in mind can the United States keep its balance among all the conflicting forces that buffet it.

Patience.

Closely related to persistence is patience. We have already considered the notorious impatience of the American people; results must follow swiftly upon the heels of any action taken by the United States if frustration and disillusionment are to be avoided. Such an attitude in foreign policy is always dangerous because of the unreasonable demands it makes of policy-makers.

Under contemporary and future conditions, the time span between action and result will be much less predictable than previously. On occasions it will be very short; often, however, a very long interval will elapse before any result emerges from an American venture, and when it appears it may not be what was hoped for in the first place. Even more galling to Americans, as the cold war continues to lose its grip on world affairs, will be the instances when no action at all is possible for the United States. All Americans can do in such a case is to wait as patiently as possible, avoiding the hasty reactions induced by frustration, until circumstances again permit effective moves.

Foreign policy, as we have suggested often in this book, is not a series of unrelated crises, each a struggle to win a victory or avoid a defeat. Instead it is an unending process of adjustment to external situations, a set of responses to a constant flow of stimuli. Total success in foreign policy is so unlikely that there is little use to plan on it; the most any people can realistically hope for is perceptible (if frequently jerky) progress toward the goals they set. Granting these apparently inescapable limits on what any state can accomplish, it would appear that a generous supply of patience is an indispensable requirement for Americans no less than for any people.

Sense of Proportion.

Of great assistance in the development of sufficient patience among Americans will be a sharpened sense of proportion: an increased sensitivity to the relative importance of the various goals they may be seeking. Under cold war conditions, American policy largely lost this ordering quality, and each issue assumed the same transcendent relevance. Defeat on any problem was interpreted as utter ignominy; victory, even on small points, was heralded as a vindication of the whole of American policy and as an augury of total future success. Any concession to Soviet demands was branded as "appeasement" and rejected categorically without any serious analysis of what the United States might obtain in return and a determination of the relative worth of the two sets of considerations.

Such a fragmentation of policy means that real negotiation is impossible, since bargaining cannot be unilateral. If the United States remains unwilling to sacrifice lesser objectives to gain greater ones, all remain equally out of reach. But even if the United States were to resolve to bargain realistically with all comers (including the USSR), no beginning could be made until a reordering of priorities was undertaken and concepts of greater and lesser centrality were applied to the many objectives of American action.

Once equipped with a reasonably clear formulation of what is critical and what is peripheral to American interest, however, the task of the policymaker and the negotiator will become immeasurably simpler. It will be possible to discover fairly quickly if accommodation of disagreements is possible and (if the finding is affirmative) to proceed to viable agreements by following the classic maxims of diplomacy. Unless such an ordering is made, however, true maneuver remains unattainable. The United States, on the threshold of an age in which maneuvering will again be a key to success, cannot afford to be deprived of this capability.

The Acceptance of Risk.

We have commented on the search for security in American life. In foreign affairs during the cold war era, it has resulted in a profound mass reluctance to assume the burden of risk inherent in any political venture. The pursuit of risk-free policies has led to the avoidance of encounter, an unwillingness to venture, and a growing immobility in the American posture.

As we have pointed out, once the cold war was stabilized it was possible for the United States at least to avoid increasing the load of risk it was carrying by maintaining the status quo vis-à-vis the Soviet Union. Today and in the future, however, the cold-war status quo has disappeared; the new world no longer permits the United States the luxury of framing policies upon the basis of minimum risk. Action is inescapable; more chances must be taken, for the stakes are higher. Political risk—the danger of miscalculation, of failure, of frustration—is the price that the United States and its fellow states must pay for the new opportunities that are opening. When nothing can be done, success or failure are equally unlikely; any increase in the possibility of success carries with it an equally augmented cargo of dangers.

Only with a generous supply of self-confidence, persistence, and patience, and with a highly developed sense of proportion, can these increased risks be borne by Americans. There is no automatic guarantee of success in the new world any more than there was in the old, no "security" in the sense of an infallible bulwark against the consequences of failure. But no people has the right to demand an unreasonably high level of performance from its government. The ubiquity of risk and the certainty of occasional defeat are characteristics of a flexible international order, and all states must accept them. To do so, and nonetheless to press forward on behalf of national purposes, is the mark of a mature people. To this standard Americans must attain.

INGREDIENTS OF AN EFFECTIVE POLICY

We now come to the crux of our discussion. We have analyzed the trends and forces that will shape the world in which American policy must be made, and we have considered the new behavior patterns that Americans and their government must adopt if the United States is not to be merely an impotent spectator of world events. There remains for us now only the task of fusing these two sets of considerations and producing our estimate of the ingredients of an effective foreign policy for the United States.

We will divide our discussion of what American foreign policy should be and—hopefully—will be, into five parts. In the first we shall list the general characteristics of American policy. In the second we shall examine the nature of the relations between the United States and the other great powers. In the third we shall generalize about the American reponse to the challenge of the non-Western world. In the fourth we shall consider the changing role of international organization in American policy. Finally, we shall examine a few special functional problems of policy. Out of our discussions will perhaps develop something of a synthesis.

General Characteristics

What kind of a foreign policy will be needed by the United States in the years ahead? Our first answer must be given in general terms. Above and beyond the discovery of solutions to specific problems, American foreign policy must consistently demonstrate a set of basic characteristics different from those marking the moves made by the United States during the 1950's. Here we shall attempt to list at least the more important feaures of such a different approach to international affairs.

Before examining our list in detail, however, we should anticipate at least two of the criticisms to which it might well be subject. In the first place, it is composed of abstractions and thus must always be susceptible to conflicting interpretations by friendly or hostile critics. Second, it is by no means peculiar to the situation of the United States, but instead represents the aspirations of every people as they frame and execute foreign policy. Neither of these points, however, need concern us unduly. Exactly what any of our preferred characteristics means in practice may be impossible to determine absolutely; what is more important, however, is that each is a legitimate goal at which to aim and a standard by which to evaluate performance. Nor is it particularly relevant that all states seek to demonstrate these same characteristics, except that it suggests the argument that the United States would indeed be well served to develop a policy that the other members of the international system would consider worthy of emulation.

Imagination.

The first necessary characteristic of American policy is imagination. For a nation that has dreamed great dreams and worked near-miracles in realizing them, recent American foreign policy has been far out of character. Much of the response of the United States has been all too predictable; far too little has involved the exploration of new channels, the exploitation of new opportunities, or the advocacy of new ideas. Strategy may indeed be, as the mathematicians tell us, inherently conservative rather than innovative; this is not synonymous, however, with the abandonment of creativity and the acceptance of the uninspired and the routine.

American policy should consciously seek to broaden its intellectual horizons. New approaches should be actively sought, old limitations should be consciously overstepped. The increasing complexity and fluidity of the international order should not be blindly denied or fled in fear, but should instead be enthusiastically welcomed as offering a broader stage and freer play for the national imagination. Other states, and especially the communist bloc, have already made their peace with the new world; the United States cannot dare to do any less.

The United States, in other words, should consciously seek out new, untried, and unexpected responses and, when a choice is open between such an imaginative approach and one that has been tested and found wanting, the decision should be in favor of novelty. Assumptions, objectives, and techniques alike should feel the impact of this heightened imaginativeness. At the very least, it will go far to restore movement to the United States; at best, it could contribute to the breakthrough in foreign policy that Americans have almost despaired of accomplishing under the conditions of the cold war.

Sensitivity.

Sensitivity, defined here as a deepened awareness of the points of view of other states, is also a critical aspect of an improved American policy. The United States has long been accused of an inability (or worse, a deliberate refusal) to appreciate any attitudes or points of view on world affairs other than its own. America, especially among the newer states of the non-Western world, is portrayed as arrogant, overbearing, and lacking in understanding; the wide acceptance of Soviet propaganda about American motives indicates the extent to which this impression has taken hold.

With the decline in the utility of the traditional techniques of coercion, the United States will be required increasingly to rely on the free consent of other states to support its policy. This will require a much greater willingness to accommodate American policies to the wishes of others. Such adaptability can be achieved only after the United States has learned better to sense the direction and the strength of the real motivations behind the policy moves of other peoples, and the empathy necessary to work such a modification in an exclusively nationalistic preoccupation is an inescapable requirement.

Even in situations of total opposition, a greater sensitivity will strengthen American hands. Awareness of the real motives, concerns, fears, and preoccupations of an adversary will spare American policy-makers the temptation to explain any disagreement to stupidity, evil intent, pernicious ideology, or flawed national character. It would also clarify the dimensions of possible dispute-settling accommodation much more quickly and easily.

Daring.

In like manner, the United States stands in dire need of greater daring in its policy. This is obviously related to our earlier discussion of the burden of risk; unless the American people are willing to bear greater risks, no policy-maker will venture far from the well-trodden and familiar path.

Why is daring so essential? Primarily because only by exploiting each situation to the full can maximum advantage be gained, and no less of a margin of success is adequate to the United States. No state can move forward in international affairs that confines itself to those courses of action the outcomes of which are fully predictable; no state can do any more than hold its own if it concentrates on neutralizing threats and ignores affirmative action. The United States must regularly launch policies with a sizeable element of unpredictability about them, and trust to its ability to capitalize on dynamic forces to maximize its success.

We are not recommending that American officials gamble recklessly with the nation's security or survival. Foolhardiness is not the appropriate antidote to an over-cautious policy. But the dichotomy between a safe policy and a dangerous one is false; there is always risk in any action at all, and in inaction as well. What we are arguing for here is a clearheaded acceptance of the burden of risk and a willingness to increase it if justified by the possible rewards. Some such daring enterprises may, of course, fail, and defeat will be no easier than ever to bear; the most a venturesome policy can hope for is an increasing margin of positive success that will outweigh the failures. Yet the alternative of increased caution and minimal risk does not offer even as attractive a prospect. The United States cannot evade the necessity of daring more to win more.

Restraint.

What we have been saying about daring should be taken in context with a corresponding emphasis on restraint. Again, we must be scrupulous not to over-interpret our term; restraint here does not mean a narrow conservatism of thought and action, but rather a wholesome understanding of the limitations on American freedom of action. The United States must develop a new version of "brinkmanship"; it must avoid contenting itself with less than the most the situation permits, but must also be alert not to attempt too much.

Verbalizations of policy would profit greatly by more restraint than has been common in recent history. The United States has often sought to compensate for inadequate action by excesses of words. Loose and reckless accusations, threats, justifications, or promises serve no policy pur-

Americans have nothing to gain by worsening the cold war. At worst, such an outcome could result in total nuclear conflict; at best, it would be little more than a digression from more important business.

If the Soviet indeed seeks to regularize its relations with the United States in certain policy areas (as seems to be a real possibility at some point in the future), it would be in the American interest to seize each opportunity and to exploit it vigorously. Indeed, the United States should go further and grasp the initiative in seeking settlements. The Soviet should be subjected to a barrage of proposals. These, be it noted, must not be phrased as propaganda embarrassments to Moscow, but should be at least within the Soviet's expected minimum range of acceptability as well as guaranteeing the interests the United States considers vital.

As part of the American effort to keep the cold war in perspective, it should make a steady effort to have as many specified areas of the world as possible declared out of bounds to the Soviet-American conflict. By gaining Russian agreement not to prosecute cold-war policies in certain regions (central Africa, for example), both states would gain in freedom of action and the over-all tension to which the world is subject would be appreciably decreased.

China.

There is a widespread suspicion that the major upsetting factor in world politics—at least from the point of view of the United States—during the next phase will be China. The development of an American policy toward China that includes the optimum proportions of caution and daring will be one of the critical tasks facing the United States.

A basic premise of any such effort will be that the possibility of direct American influence on Chinese behavior will remain slight, and that the orienting principle of the United States must be reliance on a set of supple responses to the various moves China might make. In this regard, we may accept as axiomatic the necessity of keeping China on notice that the United States will oppose any expansionist move with at least as great a vigor in Asia as in Europe, the Middle East, or Africa. Containment is probably more vital in Asia than anywhere else, at least as long as Communist China remains militant.

Beyond this essential but negative preliminary resolve, the United States should support any trace of restraint and reasonableness in China's policy. America should work to bring the Peiping regime more fully into the international order, to involve China is multilateral discussions and negotiations, and in general to dissipate both China's revolutionary fervor and the cloud of emotion that surrounds the "China problem" in American minds. Obviously no such policy is compatible with the long-standing

American commitment to non-recognition and non-admission of mainland China to the United Nations, and an early and thorough overhaul of this position is a matter of high priority for the United States.

Deliberately to bring China onto the world stage is admittedly a risky step; we should realize, however, that a China actively engaged in world affairs in company with the other states of the world would be susceptible to moderating pressures and influences, to which she is largely immune as a near-hermit. The increasing support among neutrals for Peiping's admission to the United Nations also raises the danger of eventual defeat for the United States on this issue, a possibility to be avoided if at all possible. What the United States requires with regard to China is primarily room for maneuver instead of the straitjacket of the 1950's; a more flexible policy could hardly be less productive than the former one, and might indeed be much more effective.

Great Britain.

Fewer problems are involved in the future of Anglo-American relations than in the future of American policy toward either the USSR or China. The high degree of coincidence in British and American interests and policies can be expected to continue; the partnership will retain its vigor. Complications may be expected, such as those that will arise from the prospective affiliation of Britain with the European Community, but the inevitable readjustments will not disrupt what has been a mutually profitable relationship. One possible use to which the United States might put the Anglo-American entente could be a reliance on Britain to make the initiatory and exploratory moves toward the Communist bloc (a practice already evident) when possible accommodation is under discussion.

India.

India feels that its distinctive approach to world affairs, rather than those of the United States or the Communists, is really the "wave of the future," and she has many supporters (both in the non-Western world and in the West itself) in this contention. The Indian emphasis on non-forceful and non-political approaches to world problems will obviously increase in power and influence; as it does, the United States must constantly recalculate the cost of retaining Indian sympathy and support. Great as it undoubtedly will be, it would be a brave American who could say confidently that it is too high. Granted the rise in importance of the non-western states of which India is the frequent spokesman, the United States will find itself more and more deeply involved in the questions that lie especially close to the heart of the Indian masses: disarmament, anticolonialism, development, and human rights. The real issue of American policy in this regard is whether

the United States can accede to these new demands gracefully and meaningfully or whether these emphases will be resisted as long as possible and
then accepted only grudgingly. There is little room for debate that the
former course would be the more profitable.

Europe.

What will be the American approach to the nascent political entity we
have called "Europe"? Here we dare not be overly specific, since the final
shape of integrated Europe has not yet been determined.

We may assume, however, that the new Europe will almost certainly be
a powerful world force for stability. This almost dictates a close American
relationship, perhaps even more intimate than that prevailing during the
cold war. Detailed political and military arrangements will, of course,
change; NATO as presently constituted will certainly be drastically modified. But new lines of association appropriate to the altered circumstances
will appear. A self-energizing Europe with an adequate power base of its
own will prove a far more effective partner of the United States than has
been the nationalistic mélange of the post-1945 period. The United States
must not allow the inevitable outbursts of "anti-Americanism" among
Europeans to divert it from the early establishment of the bases of this
firm relationship.

THE NON-WESTERN WORLD

The non-Western world is of critical importance to contemporary
and future international relations and to the foreign policy of the United
States. We have made many specific suggestions about the course American
action should take. All that remains to be done here is to characterize
broadly the policy emphases that must be built into American efforts to
deal with the new forces loose in the non-Western world.

Empathy.

The United States, in the first place, must call upon all its capacity for
empathy in dealing with the non-Western world. It must make a massive
effort not only to understand the concerns of these peoples but to identify
itself with them. These states simply do not accept the values of international life that are almost self-evident to Americans. They are, on the other
hand, quite explicit about what they want and not overly discriminating
about who gives it to them. Unless the United States is prepared to forego
any influence over two-thirds of the human race—as obviously it is not—
it must somehow persuade itself that the concerns of the non-Western world
are legitimate, worthy, and deserving of support.

Peaceful Orientation.

The non-Western states demand that the United States not only profess peaceful intentions, but that it also move concretely toward the achievement of peace. Any increase in American cold-war militancy produces strongly hostile reactions in the non-West; the affirmative response to each peaceful gesture the United States makes is equally clear. At least three major issues of American policy are viewed in this context as tests of the peaceful intent of the United States: disarmament, accommodation with the USSR, and alliance policy. American judgments can no longer analyze these and other problems of like import solely in the familiar power-politics categories, but must allow for the impact of non-Western opinion.

Economic Aid.

Economic and development assistance—with no political strings—is another of the minimum demands the non-Western states make of the United States. Considering the strength of the mass urge for development and the already demonstrated willingness of these states to ignore cold-war lines in seeking assistance, there seems no way for the United States to avoid reasonably large programs of economic aid for many years. Much of the strain on American emotions could be eliminated, however, if certain regions were ruled out of the cold war and all aid (from whatever national source) were funneled through the United Nations. There is some reason to believe that some such technique will eventually prove attractive to the USSR as well. We already know the non-Western states themselves would prefer it.

Status.

In the last analysis, the non-Western world looks for a set of status symbols of equality as its credentials of full membership in the international system. No real international stability is possible until these states have reached satisfaction in deference values. Here the United States has a real opportunity open before it.

If American policy can escape the twin dangers of patronizing on the one hand or fawning upon the non-Western states on the other, a viable basis for lasting understanding can be built. The approach of the United States must display dignity, sensitivity, and firmness; neither an obvious sense of guilt toward them nor a proclivity to pass irritating verdicts of unsophistication or lack of understanding of Communist wiles can do any more than further complicate relationships. Deference of the correct sort—if fitted into a carefully conceived and well-executed policy—is among the easiest forms of aid for the United States to give to the non-

Western world, yet none would be more certain of producing rapid and beneficial political consequences.

INTERNATIONAL ORGANIZATION

Not the least important of the characteristics of the new international environment is its increasing organization. A larger part than ever of the total foreign policy effort of the United States will be expended in evaluating these organizations as situational factors, in devising stratagems for use within the various bodies, and in participating in the several cooperative enterprises undertaken by international organizations.

Here we examine only three of the many facets of American policy toward (and within) international organization: first, the role of international organization as a conditioning factor in United States foreign policy; second, the place of the United Nations in the broad purview of American policy; third, the evolving issue of the United States vis-à-vis supranational organization.

International Organization as a Conditioning Factor.

The great increase in number and elaborateness of international organizations has created a markedly different environment for American policy makers. In the first place, the Wilsonian dream of a world public opinion capable of being focused on specific international issues has already been realized. This will increasingly serve both as a limiting factor on American policy and as a powerful ally when it is enlisted on the American side. Second, international organizations of all types constitute in the aggregate an impressive array of alternative techniques of action, frequently more productive of results under contemporary conditions than the classic unilateral approach; the range of American choice is broadened accordingly. Third, international organization has made multilateral contacts the most useful and normal vehicle of negotiation. "Conference diplomacy," with its unique advantages and its inevitable complexities, will increasingly become a routine political technique. The new organizations can thus be seen to have played a major part in the creation of the different environment of world politics which we have projected.

The United Nations and American Policy.

We can be fairly precise in forecasting the elements of American approaches to the United Nations, since the controlling trends have been operative already for some years.

In the first place, more and more of United States policy will be funneled through United Nations channels. Not only obviously political-diplomatic matters, but (and perhaps especially) the increasing family of so-called "non-political" issues as well will find their most propitious climate in the United Nations. Second, the increasing share of American attention demanded by United Nations matters will tend strongly toward the further minimization of the cold-war side of American policy; the inhospitability of the United Nations (particularly the General Assembly) to cold-war questions is already apparent. Third, operating in the United Nations and sharing in the construction of a very broad consensus will induce a more pronounced American preference for accommodation and honorable compromise as a preferred method of adjusting differences between states. Fourth, what remains of the influence of pure military power over world affairs will almost certainly come to rest in United Nations hands (as the only safe place for it to be). This will reinforce the first three factors mentioned and throw the United States even more directly into the United Nations arena as it searches for the most efficacious technique for the maximization of its interests.

We must not suppose that the new posture of the United States toward the United Nations will be greeted with total enthusiasm by all Americans. It is galling, so soon after the United States attained full international status, to face a future marked by serious limitations on action and the constant problem of adjusting to an unstable consensus. Yet whether or not the United States is happy about the prospect, there seems no escape; the United Nations may well become the most important single factor influencing American foreign policy.

Supranational Government.

We have said very little about the possibility of American entry into some supranational organization. It has never been a real issue before the United States. As international interdependence grows, however, and as the logic of some of the positions of the United States becomes more demanding, the question will be posed much more insistently.

It will probably present itself first in the context of the "Atlantic community": a merger (at least for certain economic, political, and possibly military purposes) of the states of western Europe with the United States and Canada. Brought to a new pitch after 1959 by the European moves toward a common market and the pressure on the United States to affiliate with it, the question can no longer be indefinitely evaded. Other possible federative enterprises, either regional or functional, that might involve the United States are of much less immediate impact.

What should the United States do? There is no virtue in supranational federation for its own sake; neither, however, is there any overriding significance (other than emotional) in the national state system. As Americans ponder the question in the future, their most reliable guide in particular choice situations can only be their basic national interest. In other words, if adherence to a supranational grouping is the most effective step open toward peace, order, and stability, then the step should be taken quickly and firmly. If, however, some other choice seems more promising, or even if the choice is not clear, membership should not be accepted. The irrevocable character of a transfer of sovereignty argues strongly in favor of making the move only in clear cases. But even so, the trends in world affairs all run in the direction of increasing the attractiveness of supranational organizations; the United States must remain alert to discover and act upon opportunities as they arise.

SOME SPECIAL FUNCTIONAL PROBLEMS

In bringing this study to a close, we should say a word about a few special problems of American policy that merit at least brief analysis apart from any larger analytical context. During the late 1950's and into the 1960's, a number of issues with a peculiar ambivalent twist found their way into American public discussion. These problems bore upon both the changing American self-image and the reality of American responses to problems in the real world. Since these questions go directly to the heart of the American foreign-policy problem, they provide a most appropriate final set of points for our examination.

The State of American Prestige.

The presidential campaign of 1960 was marked by wide and intensive discussion of the state of American "prestige." In spite of the heat which was generated on all sides, very few of the debaters attempted to define exactly what it was they were talking about. All the discussion really proved was that Americans were—as they have always been—very concerned about what others think of them.

The series of events triggered by the launching of Sputnik in 1957 made most Americans anxious about the "fall" of the United States from its place as "the world's leading power." The rise of the USSR in certain scientific and technical fields to the point where Premier Khrushchev could blatantly insist upon acceptance as a full status equal with the West was very disturbing; the willingness of much of the uncommitted world to accept the Russians on a plane of moral and status parity with the United States was accepted as evidence of something drastically wrong. American prestige—if it indeed meant universal acceptance of American primacy in all fields—undeniably fell between 1957 and 1960.

But it is by no means clear that this meaning of prestige is the most widely accepted one in contemporary world affairs, nor is it certain that any American "crash" program to "recapture leadership"—even if it seemed to succeed in regaining first place in space exploration, the range of missiles, and the like—would produce policy dividends. Most of the world does not agree with the United States that the total amount of prestige in the world is fixed, and that any increase in Russian (or Chinese, or Indian, or British) prestige means an equivalent diminution in American stature.

Prestige is meaningful only as a tool of policy; in world politics prestige does not accrue from an unrealistic pursuit of internalized images, but rather from the successful fulfillment of externalized expectations. The United States, in other words, could do far more to enhance its prestige in the world by playing to the full the role the world expects it to play than it could by an all-out competition with the Soviet in certain categories of "one-upmanship."

It is hard to escape the conclusion that most of the popular outcry about American prestige was more a reflection of mass uncertainty and insecurity in world affairs than a serious concern about objective weakness. "Prestige" tends to be confused with a meretricious and shoddy popularity; Americans fear they are becoming unpopular and yearn for the flattery and praise that would bolster their own shaken self-assurance. This *malaise* is curable only by firm commitment to positive goals, and not by seeking to win a series of cheap "victories" in a competition the world more and more dismisses as irrelevant.

Disarmament.

After more than a decade and a half of efforts at "disarmament," the United States has reaped no harvest beyond futility. The need for agreement is greater in the 1960's than ever before, but prospects for its achievement remain as dim as previously. Disarmament, if it is ever to amount to more than shear frustration, stands in need of a new attack.

The great stumbling block to even a minimal arms-reduction program— at least from the point of view of the United States—has been the Soviet refusal to accept a control system as a prior condition to any reduction in arms. Americans argue that unless a foolproof control system is established, any disarmament program would be open to extensive Soviet cheating and a consequent worsening in the military balance. Moscow, on the other hand, insists on "disarmament first, controls second."

To the United States, its own position seems unassailable: logical, cautious, and workable. Yet there has been no debate of one question that is implicit in the American argument: in what sense is an uncontrolled arms race to be preferred to a system of reduction and control of armaments, even one that allows for the possibility of cheating? If a positive answer to this question should be found, the entire disarmament effort should be immediately abandoned, since a "cheatproof" system is unattainable almost by definition. If no convincing answer is forthcoming, American discussion should shift forthwith to the determination of how great a risk of cheating the United States can assume in return for substantial reduction in armaments. Either alternative would result in a more realistic and dynamic policy than the United States has demonstrated in the past.

Haunting the discussion of disarmament in the United States are two broad considerations to which we have referred already: the increasing irrelevance of military power to the real purposes of American policy, and the insistence by the uncommitted states upon some early and effective action. The deadlock in American thinking, however, must be broken before the United States can make any change in its present immobility and indecision.

The American Image.

Our last point deals with the American image in the contemporary world. What can be done to improve the reception of the American image abroad; how can the United States better project itself?

We first state a truism: foreigners can never think better of the United States than do Americans themselves. American propaganda can never be believed abroad unless the American people accept it as a true reflection of their beliefs. The fumbling, inept, and contradictory statements of the United States government have been no more than revelations of the confusion to which Americans are and have been subject.

Before the United States can persuade others, it must first persuade itself. Before the audience for American propaganda can be made broader and more sympathetic, the United States must develop a purpose, a maturity, and a flexibility in keeping with its aspirations and its heritage. Let Americans, in a word, decide what they want and let them resolve to grapple with their problems with good sense, good will, and high devotion; the problem of projecting the appropriate image will then solve itself.

The world image of the United States is seriously blurred today. In the years to come the United States will need as sharp and well-focused an image as possible, both to guide itself and as a technique of communicating with other peoples. The discovery of its ingredients and the dedication to its principles is imperative of American foreign policy; it will be the real measure of the success or failure of the United States. No greater or fairer test of the survival value of American democracy could be devised.

Recommended Readings

Note: This reading list is highly selective. To include all the books of interest and relevance to a student of American foreign policy would require a list covering approximately as many pages as there are in this book. What follows here is a selection of titles whose inclusion is based on at least one of the following three criteria: unique relevance to the thesis of this study; major significance and lasting impact on the study and practice of American foreign policy; recent publication and promise of future importance. All the books in this list deal more or less directly with the theory and practice of American policy. Studies of other nations or problem areas are, with a few exceptions, not included.

Almond, Gabriel A., *The American People and Foreign Policy.* New York: Harcourt, Brace and Co., 1950. A leading book on the subject with a pronounced socio-psychological orientation.

American Friends Service Committee, *The United States and the Soviet Union.* New Haven: Yale University Press, 1949. The first clear call in the cold-war era for great-power reconciliation and the relaxation of tension.

———, *Steps to Peace.* No publisher, 1951. An elaboration of the general theme outlined in *The United States and the Soviet Union.*

Armstrong, H. F., ed., *The Foreign Affairs Reader.* New York: Harper & Bros., Inc., 1947. A collection of leading articles from *Foreign Affairs,* including "X," "The Sources of Soviet Conduct."

Bailey, Thomas A., *America Faces Russia.* Ithaca: Cornell University Press, 1950. A history of Russian-American relations, written in a sprightly style.

———, *A Diplomatic History of the American People.* 6th ed. New York: Appleton-Century-Crofts, Inc., 1958. A textbook written with dramatic sweep and a generous dash of humor, emphasizing public opinion and mass attitudes.

Barnes, Harry Elmer, ed., *Perpetual War for Perpetual Peace.* Caldwell, Idaho: Caxton, 1953. The most comprehensive "revisionist" attack on the Roosevelt-Truman foreign policy during and after World War II.

Barnett, Vincent, ed., *The Representation of the United States Abroad.* New York: The American Assembly of Columbia University, 1956. A discussion of problems of diplomatic, military, economic, and informational representation by experts, many of them practitioners themselves.

Barrett, Edward W., *Truth Is Our Weapon.* New York: Funk & Wagnalls, 1953. A pioneering study of American informational policy, urging the United States to have "a decent respect for the opinions of mankind."

Beloff, Max, *Foreign Policy and the Democratic Process.* Baltimore: Johns Hopkins University Press, 1955. An evaluation and criticism by a noted British historian of the manner in which democracies grapple with foreign policy.

Bemis, Samuel F., *A Diplomatic History of the United States,* 4th ed. New York: Henry Holt and Co., 1955. One of the standard histories, stressing the details of negotiation, the terms of treaties, and the calculations of American policy-makers.

Bingham, Jonathan B., *Shirt-sleeve Diplomacy: Point 4 in Action.* New York: John Day, 1954. An informal defense of Point 4 by the former administrator of the Technical Cooperation Administration, stressing the personal impact of technical assistance upon its recipients.

Bloomfield, Lincoln W., *The United Nations and U.S. Foreign Policy.* Boston: Little, Brown and Co., 1960. An analysis of the role of the United Nations in American policy, with particular emphasis upon the changing nature of the organization and the response of the United States.

Bowles, Chester, *Ideas, People and Peace.* New York: Harper & Bros., Inc., 1958. A plea for greater sensitivity and understanding in American policy, especially with regard to the non-Western world.

————, *The New Dimensions of Peace.* New York: Harper & Bros., Inc., 1955. The author's prescription for a more affirmative American foreign policy; the predecessor to *Ideas, People and Peace.*

Brookings Institution, *The Changing Environment of International Relations.* Washington: The Brookings Institution, 1956. Six lectures emphasizing aspects of the new international milieu: technology, new political forms, new states, etc.

————, *The Formulation and Administration of United States Foreign Policy.* Washington: U. S. Government Printing Office, 1960. The most complete evaluation of the current state of the foreign-policy process in the United States; of first importance.

————, *Major Problems of United States Foreign Policy.* Washington: The Brookings Institution, 6 vols., 1947–54. An annual series ending in 1954, with convenient summaries of events and a detailed analysis of major problems for each year.

Brown, William A., and Redvers Opie, *American Foreign Assistance.* Washington: The Brookings Institution, 1953. A study of American foreign assistance programs between 1940 and 1952, with emphasis on the postwar period.

Burnham, James, *The Struggle for the World.* New York: John Day, 1947. An influential exposition of the theory of the "total" cold war: the prize is the world, and American objectives must include the destruction of the Soviet and the utter obliteration of communism.

Byrnes, James F., *Speaking Frankly.* New York: Harper & Bros., Inc., 1947. The highly personal account of former Secretary of State Byrnes as he sought to bring the Soviet to agreement on a peace settlement.

Carroll, Holbert N., *The House of Representatives in Foreign Affairs.* Pittsburgh: University of Pittsburgh Press, 1958. A revealing examination of the extent to which the House has made a major role for itself in this area.

Cheever, Daniel, and H. Field Haviland, *American Foreign Policy and the Separation of Powers.* Cambridge: Harvard University Press, 1952. An analysis of legislative-executive conflict in the making and execution of American foreign policy.

Cohen, Bernard C., *The Political Process and Foreign Policy.* Princeton:

Princeton University Press, 1957. An analytical study of the "political process" as it operated in a case study, the making of the Japanese peace settlement; generally unsympathetic to elitist hypotheses.

Council on Foreign Relations, *The United States in World Affairs*. New York: Harper & Bros., Inc., 11 vols., 1947–59. An annual series, entirely narrative and historical; most useful for research involving events too recent to be in standard reference works.

Dahl, Robert, *Congress and Foreign Policy*. New York: Harcourt, Brace and Co., 1950. The author elaborates the reasons for the limited role that Congress and Congressmen play in American foreign policy and suggests some remedies.

Dennett, Raymond, and Joseph E. Johnson, eds., *Negotiating with the Russians*. Boston: World Peace Foundation, 1951. A series of studies by various Americans who have had the experience of negotiating with Soviet diplomats.

Dulles, John Foster, *War or Peace*. New York: The Macmillan Co., 1957. Reissued with new foreword. The former Secretary of State's personal analysis of the cold war, originally written some three years before he assumed office.

Elliott, William Y., *et al.*, *The Political Economy of American Foreign Policy*. New York: Henry Holt and Co., 1955. A rather technical overview of the economic aspects of American foreign policy by a group of experts.

Feis, Herbert, *The Road to Pearl Harbor*. Princeton: Princeton University Press, 1950. The most balanced of the postwar attempts to "explain" Pearl Harbor, avoiding the "devil" theory and distributing praise and blame more or less impartially.

Finletter, Thomas K., *Foreign Policy: The Next Phase, The 1960's*. New York: Frederick A. Praeger, 1960. The former Secretary of the Air Force makes a dramatic plea for an entirely new approach for the United States, much along the same lines as those of Chester Bowles.

Fosdick, Dorothy, *Common Sense and World Affairs*. New York: Harcourt, Brace and Co., 1955. An appeal by a former member of the Policy Planning Staff of the State Department for the application of "principles of common sense" to questions of foreign policy.

Furniss, Edgar S., Jr., ed., *American Military Policy*. New York: Rinehart and Company, Inc., 1957. A collection providing an over-view of the military component of American foreign policy.

Gibson, Hugh, *The Road to Foreign Policy*. Garden City: Doubleday, Doran and Co., 1944. An older book by a pioneer career diplomat, but still astonishingly up-to-date in its defense of the professional and its criticism of backseat driving from Washington.

Goldman, Eric F., *The Crucial Decade and After: America 1945–1960*. New York: Alfred A. Knopf, Inc., 1960. A vivid account of the first postwar decade and a half, valuable for the light it throws on public attitudes while American foreign policy was being formed.

Gross, Feliks, *Foreign Policy Analysis*. New York: Philosophical Library, 1954. An attempt at the development of a methodology for analyzing foreign policy as part of a "social process," emphasizing factors of power and ideological considerations.

Haines, C. Grove, ed., *The Threat of Soviet Imperialism*. Baltimore: Johns

Hopkins University Press, 1954. A symposium dealing with the phenomenon of Soviet expansionism, conveying little hope of an early shift in Soviet strategy.

Halle, Louis J., *Civilization and Foreign Policy*. New York: Harper & Bros., Inc., 1955. An analysis of foreign policy in the context of the social aspirations of the American people, emphasizing the roles of *force* and *consent* in the achievement of national ends.

Hero, Alfred O., *Americans in World Affairs*. Boston: World Peace Foundation, 1959. A summarization of research findings on citizen participation in world affairs, with some surprising and disturbing conclusions.

Hilsman, Roger, *Strategic Intelligence and National Decisions*. Glencoe, Ill.: The Free Press, 1956. An astute and detailed study of the role of strategic intelligence in reaching policy decisions.

Hughes, Emmet John, *America the Vincible*. Garden City: Doubleday & Co., 1959. A scathing criticism of American thought and action on world affairs, and a plea for an end to illusion.

Hull, Cordell, *The Memoirs of Cordell Hull*, 2 vols. New York: The Macmillan Co., 1948. An evocation of the New Deal foreign policy and the events leading up to American entry in World War II, by Franklin D. Roosevelt's Secretary of State.

Hunter, Floyd, *Top Leadership, U.S.A.* Chapel Hill: University of North Carolina Press, 1959. An examination of the interrelations among the "network" of top-level leaders in the United States.

Huntington, Samuel P., *The Soldier and the State*. Cambridge: Harvard University Press, 1957. A consistently provocative approach to a new theory of civil-military relations in the United States.

Jones, Joseph M., *The Fifteen Weeks*. New York: The Viking Press, 1955. An introspective study of the weeks in early 1947 when the Truman doctrine and the Marshall Plan were born.

Kaufmann, W. W., ed., *Military Power and National Security*. Princeton: Princeton University Press, 1956. One of the first and still one of the best symposia on American military policy, stressing limited war and rejecting "massive retaliation."

Kennan, George F., *American Diplomacy, 1900–1950*. Chicago: University of Chicago Press, 1951. Kennan's first book; all of his later positions are foreshadowed here.

————, *Realities of American Foreign Policy*. Princeton: Princeton University Press, 1955. An application of the Kennan approach to the immediate problems of the cold war.

————, *Russia, the Atom and the West*. New York: Harper & Bros., Inc., 1958. The controversial Reith Lectures in which Kennan argued for wholesale revisions in the American approach to the Soviet.

Kissinger, Henry A., *Nuclear Weapons and Foreign Policy*. New York: Harper & Bros., Inc., 1957. The famous evocation of the "limited-war" doctrine and of a foreign policy to accompany it.

Knorr, Klaus, ed., *NATO and American Security*. Princeton: Princeton University Press, 1959. A symposium evaluating the contemporary military and political significance of NATO to the United States.

————, *The War Potential of Nations*. Princeton: Princeton University Press, 1956. A re-evaluation of the notion of "war potential" in a nuclear era, concluding that it retains validity if defined accurately.

Langer, William L., and Everett Gleason, *The Challenge to Isolation; The Undeclared War*. New York: Harper & Bros., Inc., 1952, 1953. A detailed and generally pro-Roosevelt study of American diplomacy from 1937 to Pearl Harbor.

Lippmann, Walter, *The Cold War*. New York: Harper & Bros., Inc., 1947. A reply to George Kennan's "Sources of Soviet Conduct," challenging the containment thesis as destructive of intelligent diplomacy and urging a less rigid approach.

———, *The Public Philosophy*. Boston: Little, Brown and Co., 1955. A polemic, arguing that most of the troubles of contemporary political life stem from the runaway power of mass emotions and urging a return to a sense of "decency" and due respect for the superior abilities of experts.

Liska, George, *The New Statecraft*. Chicago: University of Chicago Press, 1960. An analysis of the place of foreign aid in the totality of American foreign policy, emphasizing its political character and purposes.

McCloy, John J., *The Challenge to American Foreign Policy*. Cambridge: Harvard University Press, 1953. A former U. S. High Commissioner to Germany makes a plea for affirmative responses to Soviet challenges.

Macmahon, Arthur W., *Administration in Foreign Affairs*. University, Ala.: University of Alabama Press, 1953. An influential analysis of the administrative aspects of foreign policy that throws considerable light on the substantive aspects.

Markel, Lester, *et al.*, *Public Opinion and Foreign Policy*. New York: Harper & Bros., 1949. A symposium directed mainly at evaluating the early postwar "public information" policy of the American government on foreign-policy matters; highly critical in many aspects.

Marshall, Charles B., *The Limits of Foreign Policy*. New York: Henry Holt and Company, Inc., 1954. A plea by a former State Department official for greater public awareness of the limits on the actual freedom of action of government officials dealing with foreign affairs.

Mikesell, Raymond F., *United States Economic Policy and International Relations*. New York: McGraw-Hill Book Co., Inc., 1952. A scholarly study of the foreign economic policy of the United States, stressing both historical development and the impact of recent situational changes.

Millis, Walter, *et al.*, *Arms and the State*. New York: Twentieth Century Fund, 1958. A thorough exploration of civil-military relations in the United States since the end of World War II.

Mills, C. Wright, *The Causes of World War III*. New York: Simon & Schuster, Inc., 1958. A heated condemnation of the "drift" in American policy that the author believes is leading the world to war; the book's formula for action has the virtue of novelty.

———, *The Power Elite*. New York: Oxford University Press, 1956. An angry book asserting that America is actually ruled by an interlocking "power elite" drawn from corporate, military, and political leadership.

Morgenthau, Hans J., *In Defense of the National Interest*. New York: Alfred A. Knopf, Inc., 1951. An earnest defense of the national interest as the preferred motivation for American foreign policy.

———, *The Purpose of American Politics*. New York: Alfred A. Knopf, Inc., 1960. A major revision of the author's ideas for American policy, arguing that the national state has outlived its usefulness and calling for a world authority to guarantee security.

Northrop, F. S. C., *European Union and United States Foreign Policy*. New York: The Macmillan Co., 1954. A study in "sociological jurisprudence," contending that the "living law" of Europe already augurs union and that the United States should seek to transform this moral consensus into positive union.

Osgood, Robert, *Ideals and Self-interest in America's Foreign Relations*. Chicago: University of Chicago Press, 1953. An argument that the main-springs of American policy since 1900 have been rooted in self-interest; the author derides morality and idealism as self-deceiving subterfuges.

Perkins, Dexter, *The American Approach to Foreign Policy*. Cambridge: Harvard University Press, 1952. A series of lectures that paint a portrait of American foreign policy as springing from the indigenous American culture.

Plischke, Elmer, *Conduct of American Diplomacy*. New York: D. Van Nostrand Company, Inc., 1950. A textbook study of the mechanisms by which American diplomatic representation takes place.

————, *Summit Diplomacy*. College Park: University of Maryland, College of Business and Public Administration, 1958. A history and analysis of the participation of the President in direct diplomatic efforts.

Pratt, Julius W., *A History of United States Foreign Policy*. Englewood Cliffs: Prentice-Hall, Inc., 1955. A textbook concentrating upon the history of policy rather than upon the details of negotiation.

Price, Don K., ed., *The Secretary of State*. Englewood Cliffs: Prentice-Hall, Inc., 1960. The background papers of the 17th American Assembly of Columbia University, containing a series of studies by scholars and practitioners.

Price, Harry Bayard, *The Marshall Plan and Its Meaning*. Ithaca: Cornell University Press, 1955. A retrospective analysis of the Marshall Plan in the context of the main stream of American policy.

Ransom, Harry Howe, *Central Intelligence and National Security*. Cambridge: Harvard University Press, 1958. A full-dress study of the "intelligence community" within the American government.

Riesman, David, Nathan Glazer, and Reuel Denny, *The Lonely Crowd*. New Haven: Yale University Press, 1950. A pioneering study of the changing American character, giving to the American language the by-now-familiar categories of "inner-directed" and "other-directed" men.

Reitzel, William A., Morton A. Kaplan, and Constance G. Coblentz, *United States Foreign Policy 1945–1955*. Washington: The Brookings Institution, 1956. A historical-topical study of ten years of American foreign policy, concluding with an array of open-ended questions about key issues.

Roberts, Henry L., *Russia and America: Dangers and Prospects*. New York: Harper & Bros., Inc., 1956. An attempt to analyze American-Soviet relations in the changing atmosphere of the cold war, with much objectivity but few recommendations for action.

Rostow, W. W., with Richard W. Hatch, *An American Policy in Asia*. New York: John Wiley & Sons, 1955. A project for a new American approach to Asia, emphasizing the danger of political and economic

erosion and minimizing the likelihood of a military attack on the West.
————, *The United States in the World Arena.* New York: Harper &
Bros., Inc., 1960. An ambitious "essay in recent history" that seeks to
find meaning in the course of American foreign policy since 1945.

Sapin, Burton M., and Richard C. Snyder, *The Role of the Military in
American Foreign Policy.* Garden City: Doubleday and Company, Inc.,
1954. An examination of the present and possible future part played by
military personnel, military concepts, and military objectives in American
foreign policy.

Spanier, John W., *American Foreign Policy Since World War II.* New
York: Frederick A. Praeger, 1960. A brief review of events and a serious
criticism of the American "liberal" position as being insufficiently aware
of the importance of military power in foreign policy.

Smith, Louis, *American Democracy and Military Power.* Chicago: University of Chicago Press, 1951. A historical study of the principle of civilian
supremacy over the military in the United States.

Spykman, Nicholas J., *America's Strategy in World Politics.* New York:
Harcourt, Brace and Co., 1942. An early and extremely influential
attempt to formulate a geopolitical strategy for the United States.

Staley, Eugene, *The Future of Underdeveloped Countries.* New York:
Harper & Bros., Inc., 1954. An early but sophisticated analysis of the
political implications for the United States of the process of economic
development.

Stanley, Timothy W., *American Defense and National Security.* Washington: Public Affairs Press, 1956. A historical sketch and evaluation of
the 1947–56 decade in national security policy, by an official of the
Department of Defense.

Stuart, Graham, *American Diplomatic and Consular Practice,* 2nd ed. New
York: Appleton-Century-Crofts, Inc., 1952. The standard manual on
the subject.

Tannenbaum, Frank, *The American Tradition in Foreign Policy.* Norman:
University of Oklahoma Press, 1955. An argument for the theory of the
"coordinate state" as the basis of American foreign policy and a rejection of *Realpolitik.*

Thompson, Kenneth W., *Political Realism and the Crisis of World Politics.*
Princeton: Princeton University Press, 1960. A refinement and application of the theories of political realism to American international concerns and an assault on all soft-minded idealists.

Toynbee, Arnold, *The World and the West.* New York: Oxford University
Press, 1953. The noted historian's speculations on the impact of the
West on the non-Western world.

Truman, Harry S., *Memoirs* (Vol. I: *Year of Decisions;* Vol. II: *Years of
Trial and Hope*). Garden City: Doubleday and Company, Inc., 1955,
1956. The former President's own recollections, full of detail and
personal insights.

Turner, Gordon, and Richard Challener, eds., *American Strategy in the
Nuclear Age.* New York: Frederick A. Praeger, 1960. A collection of
essays on the general subject of strategy, admittedly oriented toward a
defense of the "limited war" and "peripheral strategy" point of view.

Vandenburg, Arthur W., Jr., ed., *The Private Papers of Senator Vanden-*

burg. Boston: Houghton Mifflin Co., 1952. The role of the leading Republican advocate of bipartisanship during the early phases of the cold war.

Ward, Barbara, *The Interplay of East and West.* New York: W. W. Norton & Co., Inc., 1957. A plea for intercultural accommodation between East and West by the famous British commentator on world affairs.

Ways, Max, *Beyond Survival.* New York: Harper & Bros., Inc., 1959. A demand for a moral and religious base for American policy in order to point out positive purposes for the United States.

Welles, Sumner, and Donald McKay, eds. *The American Foreign Policy Library.* Cambridge: Harvard University Press. A valuable series for the general reader, each volume prepared by an expert; even the older titles are valuable for their points of view and their insights.

    Brinton, Crane, *The United States and Britain,* rev. ed., 1948.
    Brown, W. Norman, *The United States and India and Pakistan,* 1953.
    Cline, Howard F., *The United States and Mexico,* 1953.
    Dean, Vera M., *The United States and Russia,* 1947.
    Fairbank, John K., *The United States and China,* 1948.
    Hughes, J. J., *The United States and Italy,* 1953.
    McKay, Donald, *The United States and France,* 1951.
    Perkins, Dexter, *The United States and the Caribbean,* 1947.
    Rieschauer, Edwin O., *The United States and Japan,* 1950.
    Scott, F. D., *The United States and Scandinavia,* 1950.
    Speiser, E. A., *The United States and the Near East,* rev. ed., 1949.
    Thomas, L. V., and R. N. Frye, *The United States and Turkey and Iran,* 1951.
    Whitaker, Arthur P., *The United States and Argentina,* 1955.
    ———, *The United States and South America: the Northern Republics,* 1948.

Westerfield, Bradford W., *Foreign Policy and Party Politics.* New Haven: Yale University Press, 1955. A statistical and interpretative study of bipartisanship in foreign policy as expressed in Congressional votes on key issues.

Wolfers, Arnold, ed., *Alliance Policy in the Cold War.* Baltimore: Johns Hopkins University Press, 1959. A symposium covering various aspects of American alliance policy, generally stressing their military value and central place in American thinking.

Index

A

American Foreign Policy (*Cont.*)
  ambiguities, 265
  Anglo-American cooperation, nineteenth century, 101
  anti-colonialism and, 341
  arms limitation (See Also Disarmament), 375
  attitude, other powers, 112
  China, 105
  components of, 27
  containment (See Containment)
  content of, 26
  continental expansion, 97
  continuing issues:
    political, 319–376
      USSR relations, 320
  cost, 283
  decision making (See Decision making)
  defense of, 338
  democratic nature, 44
  disarmament (See Disarmament)
  economic issues, continuing, 376–402
  economic sanctions, 153
  effective:
    characteristics of, 476
    ingredients of, 475
  election issues and, 141
  ends versus means, 466
  Europe, nineteenth century, 103
  execution of, 85–95
    state department role, 86
  expanded frontier, 108
  Far East (See Far East)
  the Floridas, 98
  focus of, 297
  foreign aid (See Foreign aid)
  formative period, 97
  future:
    maturity of, 471
    patience, 473
    persistence, 472
    planning, 470
    requirements of, 463
    risk, acceptance of, 474
    self-confidence, 472
    sense of proportion, 474
  Gadsden Purchase, 99
  goals, 263
  good neighbor, 125
  great powers and, 112, 437
  great-power status, 107–112
  Hawaii, 106
  hemisphere hegemony, 146
  history, 96–136
  ideology (See Cold War, ideology)
  imperialism (See Imperialism)

American Foreign Policy (*Cont.*)
  inflexibility, 281
  ingredients:
    daring, 478
    generally, 476
    imagination, 476
    realism, 479
    restraint, 479
    sensitivity, 477
  international crisis and, 437
  isolationism (See Isolationism)
  Japan and, 106
  by law, 170
  legal nature, 153
  liberation formula, 284
  looking ahead, 432
  Louisiana Purchase, 98
  Manifest Destiny, 97
  method of, 151
  method of analysis, 26
  Mexican Cession, 99
  military aid (See Military aid)
  military issues (See Also Military issues), 71, 346–376
  military mission, 347
  Monroe Doctrine (See Monroe Doctrine)
  moral nature, 142
  mutual security context, 301
  negativism, end of, 465
  new components, 313
  new empire, 108
  new environment for, 435
  new power centers, 441
  new requirements, 464
  1956, change in, 345
  Open Door, 97, 110, 126
  Oregon, 98
  organization, improvement in, 467
  Pacific policy, 105–107
  partnership principle, 334
  party politics (See Also Political parties), 119
  pattern of, 259–287
    application, 277
    failures, 277
    modification, 287
    public and, 279
    successes, 277
  political issues, continuing, 319–376
  post-revolutionary, 103
  procedural base, 262
  protectionism (See Also Tariffs), 402
  psychological issues, 403
  public opinion (See Public Opinion)
  purposes of, classification, 464

American Foreign Policy (*Cont.*)
return of flexibility, 436
Samoa and, 106
sea-power, effect on, 102
sense of difference, 142
shortcomings, 281
small states and, 341
tariffs (See Tariffs)
Texas, 98
tradition of, 139–158
uniqueness, 142
United Nations (See Also United Nations), 336, 485
USSR (See USSR)
utopian nature, 144
world arena of, 180–206
World War I (See World War I)
World War II (See World War II)
Yellow Journalism and, 108
American heritage, inadequacies, 149
American image, 489
American Legion, 35, 37
American myth, 145
American policy making machinery, 4n
American public opinion (See Public opinion)
American revolution, 103
AMVETS, 37
"Anti-Americanism," 335
ANZUS:
American commitment, 358
Far Eastern security pacts, 303n
military policy, 90
obligation of, 360
Apartheid, 446
Appeasement, 129, 227, 280
Arab-Asian bloc, 440
Arab-Israeli quarrel, 278
Arabs (See Middle East)
Argentina, power of, 450
Armed forces (See Military)
Arms limitation (See Also Disarmament), 375
Armstrong, H. F., 102n, 216n, 266n, 308n
Aron, Raymond, 331n
Asia (See Also Far East):
communism and, 195
instability, 185
mood of, 192
non-political pressures, 186
power centers of, 443
revolution:
nature of, 186
roots of, 194
USSR approach, 408
Aspaturian, Vernon, 344n

Atlantic Charter, 132, 133, 135
Atlantic Community, 340
Atomic energy:
effect of, 197
EURATOM, 382
industrialization, 197
U.S. policy, 351
Atomic Energy Commission, 74
Atomic weapons, 198
"Attentive public," 33
Australia, ANZUS treaty, 303n
Australia-New Zealand-United States Security Treaty, 360
Austria:
annexation, 129
European Free Trade Association, 398
"Average citizen," 36, 47
Aviation (See Air-power)
Axis:
leadership in, 129
occupations, 192
states, 133
threats of, 126
Anti-colonialism:
impact on, 344
meaning, 344
new policy, 345
Azerbajan, 219

B

Backman, Jules, 240n
Baghdad Pact:
failure, 279
loss of name, 362
U.S. and, 313
Bailey, Thomas A., 97n, 99n, 106n, 130n, 132n
Balance of power (See Also Power politics):
Anglo-American cooperation, 324
open door in China, 97, 106, 126
"Balance of Terror," 200, 438
"Balanced force" argument, 354
Baldwin, Hanson W., 174n, 349n
Barnett, Vincent, 93n
Barrett, Edward W., 413n, 416n, 417, 420, 422n
Bartlett, Ruhl J., 97
Barzun, Jacques, 245n
Bass, R. H., 217n
Battle Act, 395
Beard, Charles A., 104, 128n, 141n
Belgium, 294, 388
Beloff, Max, 45n, 220n

Bemis, Samuel Flagg, 97n
Benelux states, European Economic Community, 398
Berelson, B., 43n
Berlin crisis, 298, 419
Bernstein, Marver H., 79n
Bessarabia, 208
Bidwell, Percy, 237n
"Big lie," 417
Bipartisanship, 39
Bipolarity:
  cold war, 296
  consolidation of, 304
  decline of, 307
  dynamics, 296
  effect of, 329, 436
  evolution of, 289
  highpoint of, 437
  interest in, 323
  trade and, 395
B.I.S., 424
Blocs, strains on, 440
Bloomfield, Lincoln, 213n
Bohlen, Charles, 79
Boorman, Howard L., 201n, 220n, 305n
Bosporus, 219
Boulding, Kenneth, 235n
Bouscaren, Anthony, 261n
Bowles, Chester, 167, 201n, 203n, 326n, 341n, 410n
Brazil, power of, 450
Bricker Amendment, 134
Brierly, J. L., 171n
Brines, Russell, 89n
Brinton, Crane, 102n
British Information Services, 424, 425
Brodie, Bernard, 174n 243n
Brown, Harrison, 196n, 236n
Brown, William A., 189n
Bruck, H. W., 24n, 47n
Bryan, William Jennings, 109
Buck, Philip W., 24n
Buell, Raymond Leslie, 121n
Bulganin, Premier, 308, 375
Bulgaria, 216
Bundy, H. H., 59n
Bureaucracy, and public, 55
Bureau of African Affairs, 67
Bureau of International Cultural Relations, 67n
Bureau of the Budget, 63, 75
Burgess, Ernest, 247n
Burma, 279, 443
Burnham, James, 261n, 286, 322n, 409n
Burns, James MacGregor, 84n
Buss, Claude, 308

Buy-American ruling, 392
Byrnes, James F., 209n, 224n, 228n

C

Cabinet departments, 74
Cairo Conference, 134
Campbell, John C., 80n, 291n, 298n, 428n
Camp David, 315
Canada, 294
Canning, Prime Minister, 101
Capabilities:
  state (See States, capabilities)
  United States (See United States, capabilities)
Caribbean:
  hegemony over, 109
  U.S. interest in, 114
Carr, E. H., 9n, 119
Carr, Robert K., 79n
Carroll, Holbert N., 78n
Casablanca Conference, 134
Castle, Eugene W., 389n
Castro:
  regime of, 177
  revolution, 438
Cavan, Ruth S., 247
CENTO (See Central Treaty Organization)
Central America, 450
Central Intelligence Agency, 63, 291
Central Treaty Organization:
  commitment, 358
  Eisenhower doctrine, 279
  Middle East, 279
  UN and, 278, 279
  U.S. and, 313, 362
Chain of policy, 7, 13
Chain reaction, 7
Challener, Frederick A., 71n, 355n
Chamberlain, John, 350n
Charge D'Affairs, 88
Cheever, Daniel, 77n, 84n, 214n, 336n
Chiang Kai-shek, 328, 426
Chief of Diplomatic Mission, 86
Childs, J. Rives, 67
China:
  admission to UN, 81
  American foreign policy and, 105
  civil war and USSR, 220
  cold war and, 289
  communist, 201
  Japan's war against, 129
  nationalist, propaganda by, 426
  open door, 97, 106, 110, 126
  as power, 443

China (*Cont.*)
 power vacuum, 297
 problems, 328
 threat of, 177
 treaty with, 363
 United States and, 326, 481
 USSR and, 277, 290
 White Paper, 278
China incident, 129
Churchill, Winston:
 Atlantic Charter, 132
 characterization of Russia, 274n
 Iron Curtain, 185
 Roosevelt, letter to, 227
 World War II conferences, 134
CIA, 63, 291
Citizen Genet, 87
Civil Aeronautics Board, 74
Civil War, American, 100
Clark, Reuben J., 125
Claude, Inis L., 172n, 213n
Cleveland, Harlan, 421n
Coblentz, Constance G., 14n, 330n, 335n,
 351n
"Coexistence," 169
 competitive, 311, 315
 evaluation of, 376
 USSR, as objective of, 406
Cold War, 200, 207
 American Military Mission, 349
 arms race and, 368
 battle of ideas in, 404
 Berlin crisis, 298
 bipolarity, 296
 China, 289
 crisis approach, 427
 decline of, 437
 disarmament (See Disarmament)
 ebb and flow, 288–315
 ECA, 292
 economic aid, 291
 end of, economic effect, 385
 Europe, 290
 European army, 303
 European defense community, 303
 European trends, 303
 Far East, 289, 299
 free world and, 264
 ideological battle, state of, 414
 ideological front, 404
 ideology:
  conflict of, 405
  disagreements on, 404
  as objective, 405
 India and, 296
 Indochina, 306

Cold War (*Cont.*)
 Indonesian Revolution, 296
 Korean war, 298
 Krushchev and, 310
 long view, 265
 Marshall Plan, 291
 MDAP, 292
 Middle East, 289, 295
 military aid, 291, 292
 Military Defense Assistance Program,
  293
 military planning, shift to, 301
 multilateralism, 392
 Mutual Security Act, 302
 mutual security context, 301
 neutral bloc, 302
 new, 282, 286, 307
 North Atlantic Treaty, 293
 oil politics, 295
 Palestine and, 295
 power vacuums, 297
 reasons for, 260
 reorganization, 290
 Rio Pact, 293
 Schuman plan, 302
 small states and, 341
 stalemate, 298
 standard of living and, 455
 Summit, 308, 315
 Truman Doctrine, 291
 two-power world of, 441
 United Nations and, 336
 United States:
  aid, 303
  ideological objectives, 407
  ideological techniques, 410
  leadership, 330
  motives, 229
  overseas defense commitments, 358
  softer approach, 331
  success in, 279
 USSR:
  ideological objectives, 406, 411
  ideological techniques, 409
  policy 1950–1954, 304
  soft approach, 310
  targets, 312
 verdict on, 411
 West Germany, 303
 Yugoslavia, 298
Commissions, Congressional, 85
Committees, Senate Foreign Relations, 82
Commonwealth nations, 341
Communism (See Also USSR), 261
 Afro-Asian, 195
 and change, 193

Communism (*Cont.*)
"coexistence," 169n
cold war (See Cold War)
and the discontented, 192
ideological aspects, 404
impact, 191
repelling, 349
rise of, 191
Soviet foreign policy and, 192
United States:
expectation, 262
rejection of, 269
"Communist Manifesto," 191
Communist propaganda, 213
"Compensation," pursuit of, 18
Conference diplomacy, 485
Congo:
crisis, 345, 438
tyranny of the weak, 439
U.N. act on, 338
USSR and, 445
Congress:
appropriations, 80
Commissions, 85
conflict with executive, 82
deliberateness, 83
foreign affairs powers, 60
foreign policy role, 76–84
function, 77
investigations, 85
investigations of, 80
lack of information, 83
legislative powers, 79
negativism, 81
negotiations, 81
political orientation, 82
powers, 78
President:
consulting with, 84
cooperation with, 84
liaison with, 84
public opinion and, 83
resolutions, 81
a role of, 470
Congress of Vienna, 104
Constitution, 60
foreign affairs powers, 60
Containment, 266–277
basic elements, 270
beginning of alliances, 293
cold war (See Cold War)
failure, 283
first steps, 289
indictment of, 283
phases of, 270, 274
popularity of, 279

Containment (*Cont.*)
restraint, need for, 273
vindication, 307
Continental expansion, 97
Cook, Thomas I., 46n
Corbett, P. E., 9n
Council of Economic Advisors, 63
Coyle, David Cushman, 385n, 386n
Crankshaw, Edward, 269n, 310n
Cuba:
attitude toward, 177
Castro revolution, 438
goading United States, 439
independence, 109
orientation of, 450
upheaval in, 447
Cultural Affairs Officer, 417
Czechoslovakia, 130, 213

D

Dahl, Robert, 77n
Dallin, David, 220n
Dardanelles, 219
Dean, Vera M., 204n
Deane, John A., 134n
Decision influencers, 32
interest groups, 34
mass media, 41
nonpolitical leadership elites, 42
political parties, 37
Decision makers, 6, 24
Decision making (See Also Public; Public Opinion; Policy):
decentralization of, 74
elites (See Elites)
executive branch, 59
conflict with Congress, 82
coordination, 74
framing, 58–95
government, 47
implementing, 58–95
leadership, executive, 59
legislation and, 79
military (See Also Military), 70–72
monopoly of, 47
professional attitude, 49
role of:
cabinet departments, 73
Congress, 76–84
non-cabinet agencies, 74
President (See President)
Treasury department, 73
"Defensive aggression," 268
Democracy, foreign policy in, 31–57
Democratic dilemma, 45

Popular preferences, 11
Population:
  explosion, 196, 454
  increase of, 454
  U.S., 235
Portugal:
  European Free Trade Association, 398
  NATO, 294
Potter, Pitman B., 308n
Power centers, new, 441
Power politics:
  distrust of, 148
  double standard, 143
  morality of, 148
  residue, 457
Pratt, Julius W., 97n, 98, 106n, 110n, 163n
President:
  advisory bodies to, 63
  assistants to, 62
  Congress:
    consulting, 84
    cooperation with, 84
    liaison with, 84
  delegation of powers, 61
  functions, 61
  his party, role of, 38
  inherent powers, 60
  personnel, staff of, 63
  powers, 60
  role of, 59–63, 467
President's Advisory Committee, 63
Pressure groups (See Also Interest Groups), 35, 44
Price, Don K., 64n
Price, Henry Bayard, 292n
Principles, defined, 14n
"Professionalism," 50
Propaganda:
  abstractions into specifics, 421
  accomplishment of, 414
  "big lie" and, 417
  British Information Services, 424
  communist, 213
  defined, 414
  English Speaking Union, 424
  foreign, 424
    lack of audience, 426
    successful, 425
    in United States, 423
  Iceland, 427
  International Information Administration, 94
  Israelian, 426
  Laos, 427
  liberation, 420

Propaganda (*Cont.*)
  Nationalist China, 426
  Paraguay, 427
  policy, relation to, 420
  program of, 94
  Spain, 427
  truth as, 417
  United States:
    content, 414
    expectations of, 420
    ideology, translating, 422
    Information Agency, 416
    media, 416
    message of, 417
    the people and, 423
    public, education of, 430
    purpose, 414
    relevance to foreign policy, 419
    shortcomings, 419, 421
    targets, 415
    unintentional, 421
    vehicles of, 416
  United States Information Agency, 95, 416
    cultural program, 418
    field organization, 417
    media, 416
    mission of, 418
  USIA (See Propaganda, United States Information Agency)
  USSR, 225
    rejection of, 424
  Voice of America, 95
  World Zionist Organization, 424
  Zionist Organization of America, 424
Protectionism (See Tariffs)
Psychological issues, 403
Public (See Also Public Opinion):
  and bureaucracy, 55
  as decision maker, 54
  denigration of the mass, 50
  as direction setter, 53
  education of, 430
  functioning of, 52
  kinds of, 33
  leadership, 56
  as limiting factor, 52
  opinion (See Public Opinion)
  responsibility, 56
  role of, 52
  State Department and, 69
  who speaks for, 34
  will of, 55
Public Affairs, division of, 95
Public Affairs Officer, 417
Public attitudes, mass media and, 41

Index ❖ *515*

Public interest, 46
Public Opinion (See Also Public):
  altruistic nature, 157
  characteristics, 154
  common sense nature, 157
  components of, 32
  debates and, 156
  defined, 32
  denigration of the mass, 50
  dichotomy preference, 156
  division of, 49
  effect on Congress, 83
  elites, 44
  emotionalism, 155
  enlightened, 56
  evaluation, preliminary, 158
  impatience of, 155
  invocation of, 152
  "several publics," 33
  strengths, 156
  uninformed nature, 154
  weaknesses, 154
  Yellow Journalism, 108
Public policy, foreign policy as, 4
Puleston, W. D., 347n

Q

Quarantine speech, 128
Quebec Conferences, 134
Quemoy, 363n

R

Racism, 445
Radford, Admiral Arthur B., 72n
Randall, Clarence, 401
Randall Commission's report, 401
Ranson, Harry Howe, 63n
Rauch, Basil, 128n
Raymond, Paul, 303n
Realism, need for, 275
Reciprocal Trade Agreement, 125, 400
Regionalism, 339
Reitzel, William A., 14n, 330n, 335n, 350n
Reparations, 124
Republican party, 39
Reshetar, Jr., John S., 20n
Resolution of Congress, 81
Resource utilization, 454
Revisionism, 165
  USSR, 207
"Revolution of Rising Expectations," 189
Rhee, Syngman, 438
Rich, S. Grover, 275n

Ridgeway, General, 243n, 353
Rieschauer, Edwin O., 328n
Riesman, David, 42n, 246n
Rio Pact, 293
Roberts, Henry L., 321n, 324n
Robinson, Kenneth, 344n
Rogers, J. G., 59n
Rogers, Will, 149
Rogers Act of 1924, 67
Romania, 216
Roosevelt, Eleanor, 296n
Roosevelt, F. D., 64, 211, 400
Roosevelt, Theodore, 114
Root-Takahira Agreement, 114
Rostow, W. W., 203n, 291n, 328n, 407n
Russell, Francis H., 55
Russia (See USSR)

S

SAC, 347, 355
SACEUR, 91
Salvadori, Massimo, 239n, 294n
Samoa, 106
San Francisco Conference, 136
Sapin, Burton M., 24, 47n, 62, 70n
Sargeant, Howland H., 93n
Satellitism, 215
Scandinavian states, European Free Trade
    Association, 398
Schlesinger, James R., 389
Schuman, Frederick L., 183n
Schuman plan, 303
Schwartz, Benjamin, 220n, 295n
Science race, 206
Scientists, United States, 249
SEATO (See Southeast Asia Treaty Or-
    ganization)
Secretary of Defense, 71, 72
Secretary of State (See Department of
    State)
Secretary's Public Committee on Person-
    nel, 68
Security Council:
  structure, 187
  use of, 337
  USSR, 213
  U-2 incident, 339n
Self-defense, 173
Senate:
  appointments, 78
  foreign policy powers, 78
  Foreign Relations Committee, 82
  treaty approval, 78
Seton-Watson, Hugh, 191n
Seward, Secretary of State, 104n

United States (*Cont.*)

non-western world (*Cont.*)
economic aid to, 484
empathy with, 483
status to, 484
OAS and, 358, 361
organization, need for, 171
Palestine and, 295
as a partner, 330
patience, 473
peace, cooperation for, 175
as peace loving, 168
persistence, 472
political strains, 246
political structure, 245
population, 235
President (See President)
prestige, state of, 487
propaganda (See Propaganda, United States)
public (See Also Public)
education of, 430
kinds of, 33
public debate in, 429
public opinion (See Public Opinion)
raw materials, 236
referee, role of, 314
regionalism and, 339
relationships:
allied, 329
theory of, 329
resentment against, 334
revisionism, 165
risk, acceptance of, 474
science race, 206
scientists, 249
SEATO (See Southeast Asia Treaty Organization)
self-confidence, 472
self-defense, 173, 174
sense of proportion, 474
small states and, 342
social structure, 245
Spain and, 363
stand-patism, 164
status quo in, 160, 162, 173
success of, 412
suitor, role of, 314
supranational government, entry in, 486
supranational organization and, 339
tactical theory, 243
tariffs (See Tariffs)
technical ability, 248
trade policy, 392
trade problems (See Trade Problems)

United States (*Cont.*)

understanding the, 418
unilateral action, 175
United Nations and, 338
attitude toward, 337
USSR:
accommodation, 274
agreement with, 322
approach to, 480
arms race with, 367
break with, 229
concessions to, 228
conflict, future of, 437
decision about, 267
fixation on, 295
imitation of, 282
new approaches to, 314
over-emphasis of, 280
patience and firmness, 230
policy implication, 323
power rivalry with, 261
realism, need for, 275
relations with, 211, 320
deterioration, 321
improvement, 321
threat of, 280
will to fight, 245
world government and, 340
world opinion and, 338
United States Chamber of Commerce, 37
United States Information Agency, 95, 416
Universal Postal Union, 214
USIA, 95, 416
USSR (See Also Communism):
action:
nature of, 268
roots of, 267
aggressive self-defense, 268
alliances, attitude toward, 208
anti-colonialism and, 345
arms control formula, 370
arms policy, 369
Asian revolution, approach to, 408
behavior trends, 210
bipolarity, 304
bombshell technique, 224
China and, 220, 277, 290, 328
coexistence, 229, 315
cold war (See Cold War)
compromise by, 223
Congo and, 445
consolidation of, 305
containment (See Containment)
defensive aggression, 268

V

Vandenburg, Senator, 40
Van Dyke, Vernon, 15
Vann Crabb, Cecil, 40n
Van Valkenburg, Samuel, 341n
Venezuelan boundary dispute, 102, 107
Versailles Treaty, 129
Vinson, John Chalmers, 121n
Voice of America, 95, 416, 420
Von Braun, Dr. Werner, 357
Von Vorys, Karl, 15n

W

Wake Island, 109
Wallace, Phyllis A., 384n
War:
  American view of, 149
  "balance of terror," 200
  big versus little, 349
  cold (See Cold War)
  decreasing danger, 438
  defensive, 169
  disappearing utility, 168
  function of, 150
  limited, 200, 348, 349
  military mission, prevention of war, 347
  new, 198
  peacetime, 150
  political, 174, 420
  prospects of, 461
  purpose of, 150
  psychological (See Also Propaganda), 94
  role of, 88
  total, 198, 348, 349
Warburg, James P., 218n, 378n
Ward, Barbara, 176n, 290n, 410n
War Debts, 123
War of 1812, 103
Warsaw, 130
Washington Conference, 121, 134
Washington's Farewell Address, 141
Watchful waiting, 455
Weapons supremacy, 71
Wei, Henry, 220n
Weinberg, Albert K., 145n
Welles, Sumner, 229n
Wertenbaker, Charles, 426n
Westerfield, H. Bradford, 38n, 40
Western Alliance, 309
Western European Union, 304
West Germany:
  aid from, 395

West Germany (*Cont.*)
  American aid, 388
  Cold War and, 303
  European Economic Community, 398
WEU, 304
Wheare, K. C., 247n
Whiting, Allen S., 226n
WHO, 214
Whyte, William A., 246n
Wiley, John, 328n
Williams, W. A., 106n
Willoughby, Charles A., 350n
Wilson, Charles E., 331, 350n, 354, 357
Wilson, Paul, 324n
Wilson, Woodrow, 115, 120
Wilsonian dream, 485
Wilsonianism, 115, 118
Wolfers, Arnold, 11n, 332n
World Bank, 391
World Disarmament Conference, 122
World Government, 340, 459, 486
World Health Organization, 214
World Meteorological Organization, 214
World opinion, 338
World politics:
  Africa and, 444
  flexibility, 307
  Khrushchevism, 310
  neutralism, 308
  new issues, 310
  new techniques, 204
    culture, 205
    economic assistance, 204
    internationalization, 205
    science, 205
    technical assistance, 205
  after 1945:
    Communism (See Communism)
    disappearance of power, 186
    economic discontent, 186
    economic stability, 189
    European dominance, end of, 184
    impact of technology, 195
    imperialism, 186
    "iron curtain," 185
    new forces in, 188
    new leaders, 183
    new warfare, 198
    political flux, 190
    political instability, 189
    redistribution, 182
    the small states, 184
    social discontent, 186
    trends, 200–206
      cold war, 200
      new rivalries, 201

Index ✤ *523*